THE
unofficial GUIDE®
ᵀᴼSan Francisco

7TH EDITION

THE *unofficial* GUIDE®

°TO San Francisco

7TH EDITION

RICHARD STERLING
revised by ELGY GILLESPIE

WILEY

Please note that prices fluctuate in the course of time and that travel information changes under the impact of many factors which influence the travel industry. We therefore suggest that you write or call ahead for confirmation when making your travel plans. Every effort has been made to ensure the accuracy of information throughout this book, and the contents of this publication are believed to be correct at the time of printing. Nevertheless, the publishers cannot accept responsibility for errors or omissions, for changes in details given in this guide, or for the consequences of any reliance on the information provided by the same. Assessments of attractions and so forth are based upon the author's own experience; therefore, descriptions given in this guide necessarily contain an element of subjective opinion, which may not reflect the publisher's opinion or dictate a reader's own experience on another occasion. Readers are invited to write the publisher with ideas, comments, and suggestions for future editions.

Published by:
John Wiley & Sons, Inc.
111 River Street
Hoboken, NJ 07030-5774

Produced by Menasha Ridge Press

Cover design by Michael J. Freeland

Interior design by Vertigo Design

For information on our other products and services or to obtain technical support, please contact our Customer Care Department within the United States at 877-762-2974, outside the United States at 317-572-3993, or by fax at 317-572-4002.

John Wiley & Sons, Inc., also publishes its books in a variety of electronic formats. Some content that appears in print may not be available in electronic formats.

ISBN 978-0-470-53326-0

Manufactured in the United States of America

5 4 3 2 1

CONTENTS

LIST *of* MAPS

ABOUT *the* AUTHOR

RICHARD STERLING IS THE AUTHOR OF AND CONTRIBUTOR to numerous cookbooks and guidebooks covering California, Latin America, and Asia. Richard is well known in the Bay Area for his varied and eclectic accomplishments.

Elgy Gillespie, who revised this edition, is an author of several guidebooks and cookbooks and has lived in San Francisco's Mission District since the Big One of 1989 with her roommates and cat. She teaches at a community college and also writes for several magazines and newspapers about history, the outdoors, food, and movies in California and elsewhere—often all of the above together. Thanks also go to Regina Comaich and Catherine Barry, who contributed to this edition.

THE
unofficial GUIDE®
ᵀᴼSan Francisco

7TH EDITION

The Bay Area

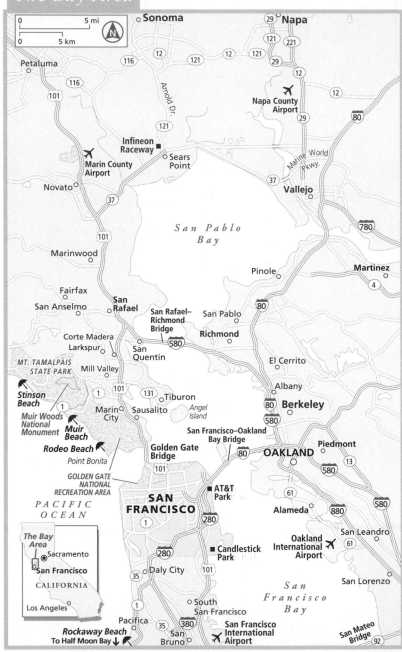

0   5 mi
0   5 km
N

Sonoma

Napa

Petaluma

29
121
221
116
12
121
12
121
29
101
116
Arnold Dr.
12

121

Napa County Airport
29
80

Infineon Raceway
Sears Point

Marin County Airport
Marine World Pkwy.

Novato
37
Vallejo
780

101

San Pablo Bay

Marinwood
Pinole
Martinez
4

Fairfax
80

San Anselmo
San Rafael
San Rafael–Richmond Bridge
San Pablo
Richmond

Corte Madera
Larkspur
San Quentin
580
El Cerrito

MT. TAMALPAIS STATE PARK
Mill Valley
Albany

Stinson Beach
1
101
131
Tiburon
80
Berkeley
580

Muir Woods National Monument
Muir Beach
Marin City
Sausalito
Angel Island

Rodeo Beach
Point Bonita

San Francisco–Oakland Bay Bridge
Piedmont

GOLDEN GATE NATIONAL RECREATION AREA
Golden Gate Bridge
101
80
OAKLAND
580
13

PACIFIC OCEAN

AT&T Park
61
Alameda
880
580

SAN FRANCISCO
1
280
Oakland International Airport
San Leandro
61

The Bay Area
Sacramento
280
Candlestick Park
101
35
Daly City
San Lorenzo

San Francisco Bay

San Francisco
CALIFORNIA
Los Angeles

Pacifica
Rockaway Beach
To Half Moon Bay ↓
1
35
380
South San Francisco
San Francisco International Airport
San Bruno
San Mateo Bridge
92

INTRODUCTION

The CITY by the BAY:
A Metropolitan Mecca

FACE WEST. Yes, west—toward that revered and endeared bay city we call San Francisco. Gold diggers armed with little more than a pan and a dream pointed their wagons west to brave the new frontier. Westbound beatniks hitched rides with pockets full of poems, prepared for philosophical face-offs. Hippies happily hitched, carrying all they could possibly want: a joint and a cause. Ivy League graduates hungry for opportunity headed west with an idea and a business plan—and made millions incidentally. East Coasters with a desire for "more" (and better weather) packed up and settled here. And visitors looking for active or relaxing vacations have found everything they are looking for in one city—San Francisco, the Mecca of the West.

You won't find a single bit of bad press on San Francisco (San Fran for short, *never* Frisco). Sure, the boom fizzled and the lights may go dim from time to time, but this Paris of the Pacific, Athens of the West, continues to leave the welcome mat out and the door unlocked for anyone desiring to experience its magical spirit and breadth of opportunity.

The city never fails to live up to expectations. If thick afternoon fog has put a damper on your day, sunny skies await across any bridge. Not used to the towering buildings of downtown? Less than 20 minutes away, across the Golden Gate, are fat-tire trails, blazed hiking trails, cycling paths, romantic hideaways, and some of the best views in the country. There are certain things you can always count on in San Francisco—civic and cultural pride, cool summers, foghorns, hilly streets, mountain vistas and ocean views, and sunny skies across both bridges (the Golden Gate and the Bay Bridge). You will put on and take off a sweater at least three times on any walk, so count on carrying one, as there are distinct pockets of climate in different areas of the city. Maybe that's why visitors come year after year: San Francisco is different, diverse, and easy to love. Even its parameters are easy: seven by seven miles, which includes 43 steep hills! A simple formula for a simply enchanting place.

In spite of the gentrification that swept many of San Francisco's neighborhoods during the late 1990s, there remains a strong mix of culture and cultural identity. The gateway to Asia, San Francisco supports a multicultural population of Chinese, Japanese, and Filipinos. And, lucky you, such cultural diversity brings an amazing assortment of culinary delights. For dim sum or the latest in Chinese herbal medicine, a stroll in Chinatown will cure any craving or cramp. Homemade ravioli is redolent through the streets of North Beach, the city's little Italy. For great Hispanic food, head on over to Cha Cha Cha's after perusing the vibrant art at the Mexican Museum. And what good is a city by a bay if it doesn't boast seafood? Alioto's and Scoma's at Fisherman's Wharf are musts for newbies. Adding to this cosmopolitan bouillabaisse is a gay population that may constitute as much as 25 percent of the city's total population. The neighborhoods of San Francisco overlap and interrelate, but they maintain distinct identities.

As a result of such strong cultural influences, the arts flourish here. The Mission District is a melting pot of public murals (more than 60 in an eight-block area). More organized venues exist as well: Fort Mason, where you can touch down artistically on three continents; museums showcasing Mexican, Italian American, and African American culture; and a world-class opera house, symphony, and ballet company. Contemporary-art lovers will enjoy the renaissance of SoMa, the Soho of San Francisco. The opening of the Museum of Modern Art and the Center for the Arts sparked a gallery boom South of Market (SoMa). Whether you like independent theater, poetry readings, or opera, it is all represented here. And no exploration of the city's arts would be complete without a perusal of Victorians. The houses line the steep hills of the city like trim on a wedding cake. A must do—to really take in the beauty of the homes, hills, and views that the city offers—is a drive down (and I mean down) Divisadero Street. This is just one of a bunch of vantage points that allow you, in one glance, to capture the beauty and enchantment of the city with your camera and your heart.

Europeans love San Francisco because it's the most European of American cities, and Hispanics gravitate to its Spanish-speaking community. San Francisco is home to one of the largest Chinese populations in the United States. Even tough-skinned and proud New Yorkers adore San Francisco, comparing it favorably with the Big Apple.

This book is equally designed for planning a solo getaway, a romantic escape, a visit to a friend or family member, or a family trip. It's for anyone who wants to see San Francisco's famous vistas, distinct neighborhoods, excellent museums, theater companies, and fabled nightlife; and it is also for business travelers who want to avoid its worst hassles. We show you the best times to visit San Francisco's best-known sights, how to get off the beaten path, and how to avoid the worst crowds and traffic. We suggest the best seasons to visit and offer detailed itineraries and touring strategies for seeing some spectacular destinations beyond the city limits.

In spite of the challenges it presents to first-time visitors, San Francisco never fails to charm. Like the joke says, San Francisco is everyone's favorite city—even people who have never been there. Locals love their city and most of them enjoy sharing its attractions. With their help, and armed with this book, you're ready to discover the incomparable City by the Bay.

ABOUT *this* GUIDE

HOW COME "UNOFFICIAL"?

JUST AS THE CITY OF SAN FRANCISCO INSPIRES unconventional ideas and promotes individuality, so does the goal of the "Unofficial" series. Most "official" guides to San Francisco tout the well-known sights, promote the local restaurants and hotels indiscriminately, and leave out the nitty-gritty. This one is different. We'll be up-front with you. There is more than Fisherman's Wharf, after all. Instead of nabbing you by the ankles in a tourist trap, we'll tell you if it's not worth the wait for the mediocre food served at a well-known restaurant. We'll complain loudly about overpriced hotel rooms that aren't convenient to downtown or the Moscone Convention Center, and we'll guide you away from the crowds and congestion for a break now and then. We'll direct you to little-known local joints and other unique experiences so you can earn bragging rights and satisfy your adrenaline craving.

We sent in a team of evaluators who toured downtown and its outlying neighborhoods and popular attractions, ate in the Bay Area's best and most unique restaurants, performed critical evaluations of the hotels, and visited San Francisco's best and most offbeat nightclubs. If a museum is boring or a major attraction is overrated, we say so—and, in the process, make your visit exactly that: *your* visit.

We got into the guidebook business because we were unhappy with the way travel guides make the reader work to get any usable information. Wouldn't it be nice, we thought, if we made guides that were easy to use?

OTHER GUIDEBOOKS

MOST GUIDEBOOKS ARE COMPILATIONS OF LISTS. This is true regardless of whether the information is presented in list form or artfully distributed through pages of prose. There is insufficient detail in a list, and with prose the presentation can be tedious and contain large helpings of nonessential or marginally useful information. Not enough wheat, so to speak, for nourishment in one instance, and too much chaff in the other. Either way, other guides provide little more than departure points from which readers initiate their own quests.

Sure, many guides are readable and well researched, but they tend to be difficult to use. To select a hotel, for example, a reader must study several pages of descriptions with only the names of the hotels in bold type breaking up the text. Because each description essentially deals with the same variables, it is difficult to recall what was said concerning a particular hotel. Readers generally have no alternative but to work through all the write-ups before beginning to narrow their choices. The presentation of restaurants, clubs, and attractions is similar except that even more reading is usually required. To use such a guide is to undertake an exhaustive research process that requires examining nearly as many options and possibilities as starting from scratch. Recommendations, if any, lack depth and conviction. By failing to narrow travelers' choices down to a thoughtfully considered, well-distilled, and manageable few, these guides compound rather than solve problems.

HOW *UNOFFICIAL GUIDES* ARE DIFFERENT

WHILE A LOT OF GUIDEBOOKS HAVE BEEN WRITTEN about San Francisco, very little has been evaluative. Most guides come close to regurgitating the hotels' and tourist offices' own promotional material. In preparing this work, however, nothing was taken for granted. Each museum, monument, art gallery, hotel, restaurant, shop, and attraction was visited by a team of trained observers who conducted detailed evaluations and rated each place according to formal criteria. Interviews were conducted to determine what tourists of all ages enjoyed most and least during their visits to San Francisco.

Readers care about the author's opinion. The author, after all, is supposed to know what he is talking about. This, coupled with the fact that the traveler wants quick answers (as opposed to endless alternatives), dictates that authors should be explicit, prescriptive, and, above all, direct. The *Unofficial Guide* tries to do just that. It spells out alternatives and recommends specific courses of action. It simplifies complicated destinations and attractions and allows the traveler to feel in control in the most unfamiliar environments. The objective of the *Unofficial Guide* is not to have the most information or all of the information; it aims to have the most accessible, useful information, unbiased by affiliation with any organization or industry.

An *Unofficial Guide* is a critical reference work that focuses on a travel destination that appears especially complex. Our authors and research team are completely independent from the attractions, restaurants, and hotels we describe. The *Unofficial Guide* to *San Francisco* is designed for everyone—couples, women, groups, or individuals traveling for fun, as well as for business travelers and convention-goers, especially those visiting the city for the first time. The guide is directed at value-conscious, consumer-oriented adults who seek a cost-effective, though not spartan, travel style.

In compiling this guide, we recognize that tourists' ages, backgrounds, and interests will strongly influence their taste in San Francisco's wide array of activities and attractions and will account for a preference of one over another. Our sole objective is to provide the reader with sufficient description, critical evaluation, and pertinent data to make knowledgeable decisions according to individual tastes.

SPECIAL FEATURES

The *Unofficial Guide* incorporates the following special features:

- Friendly introductions to San Francisco's array of fascinating neighborhoods.
- "Best of" listings giving our qualified opinion on things ranging from bagels to baguettes, five-star hotels to the best views of San Francisco and the Bay Area by night.
- Listings keyed to your interests, so you can pick and choose.
- Advice to sightseers on how to avoid crowds; advice to business travelers on how to avoid traffic and excessive cost.
- A hotel chart that helps narrow your choices fast, according to your needs.
- Shorter listings that include only those restaurants, nightclubs, and hotels we think are worth considering.
- A detailed index and table of contents to help you find things quickly.

HOW THIS GUIDE WAS RESEARCHED AND WRITTEN

WHILE OUR OBSERVERS ARE INDEPENDENT and impartial, they do not claim to have special expertise. Like you, they visited San Francisco as tourists or business travelers, noting their satisfaction or dissatisfaction.

The primary difference between the average tourist and the trained evaluator is the evaluator's skills in organization, preparation, and observation. The trained evaluator is responsible for much more than simply observing and cataloging. While the average tourist is engrossed when touring Alcatraz, for instance, the professional is rating the attraction in terms of pace, how quickly crowds move, the location of restrooms, and how well children can see through the cellhouse windows to the San Francisco skyline across the Bay. The evaluator also checks out other nearby attractions, alternative places to go if the line at a main attraction is too long, and the best local lunch options. Observer teams used detailed checklists to analyze hotel rooms, restaurants, nightclubs, and attractions. Finally, evaluator ratings and observations were integrated with tourist reactions and the opinions of patrons for a comprehensive profile of each feature and service.

HOW INFORMATION IS ORGANIZED: BY SUBJECT AND BY GEOGRAPHIC AREA

TO GIVE YOU FAST ACCESS TO INFORMATION about the best of San Francisco, we've organized material in several formats.

HOTELS Because most people visiting San Francisco stay in one hotel for the duration of their trip, we have summarized our coverage of hotels in charts, maps, ratings, and rankings that allow you to quickly focus your decision-making process. We do not go on for page after page describing lobbies and rooms that, in the final analysis, sound much the same. Instead we concentrate on the variables that differentiate one hotel from another: location, size, room quality, services, amenities, and cost.

RESTAURANTS We provide a lot of detail when it comes to restaurants. Because you will probably eat a dozen or more restaurant meals during your stay, and because not even you can predict what you might be in the mood for on Saturday night, we provide thorough profiles of the best restaurants in and around San Francisco.

ATTRACTIONS There are those of you who love taking in all the sights and attractions, and those of you who are offended at the thought of taking a cable car to Fisherman's Wharf or Coit Tower. OK, OK. We understand the needs of all our selective readers and, as such, have organized much of the city's sites into a handy time-saving chart divided by geographic area. Gonna be in the Marina for dinner? Well, see what's in the area and organize your day accordingly. Saves you time, money, and foot ache!

ENTERTAINMENT AND NIGHTLIFE Visitors frequently try several different clubs or nightspots during their stay. Because clubs and nightspots, like restaurants, are usually selected spontaneously after arriving in San Francisco, we believe detailed descriptions are warranted. The best nightspots and lounges in San Francisco are profiled by category under nightlife in the same section.

GEOGRAPHIC AREA Once you've decided where you're going, getting there becomes the issue. To help you do that, we have divided the San Francisco Bay Area into geographic areas.

Civic Center	North Beach	District
Union Square	SoMa/Mission District,	Tiburon/Sausalito
Financial District	including Noe Valley	Suburban Marin
Marina District	and Potrero Hill	Marin Headlands to
	Richmond/Sunset	Point Reyes

LETTERS, COMMENTS, AND QUESTIONS FROM READERS

DO YOU HAVE SOME ISSUES with our suggestion for the best place to find a scoop of ice cream or cup of joe to go, or did we overlook a well-known San Francisco institution? We want to hear from you! We expect to learn from our mistakes, as well as from the input of our readers, and to improve with each book and edition. Many of those who use the *Unofficial Guide* write to us asking questions, making comments, or sharing their own discoveries and lessons learned in San Francisco. We appreciate your input, both positive and critical, and encourage our readers to continue writing. Readers' comments and observations will be frequently incorporated into revised editions of the *Unofficial Guide* and will contribute immeasurably to its improvement.

How to Write to the Author

Richard Sterling and Elgy Gillespie
The Unofficial Guide to San Francisco
P.O. Box 43673
Birmingham, AL 35243
UnofficialGuides@menasharidge.com

When you write by mail, be sure to put your return address on your letter as well as on the envelope—sometimes envelopes and letters get separated. And remember, our work takes us out of the office for long periods of time, so please forgive us if our response is delayed.

Our warmest welcome to San Francisco, the City by the Bay.

San Francisco Neighborhoods

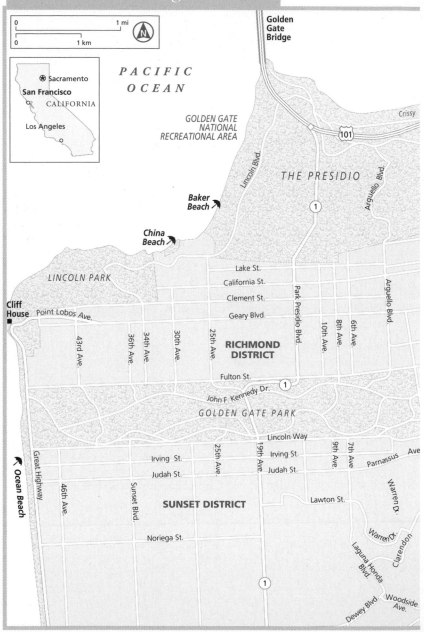

0   1 mi
0   1 km

⊛ Sacramento
San Francisco
CALIFORNIA
Los Angeles

PACIFIC OCEAN

Golden
Gate
Bridge

Crissy

GOLDEN GATE
NATIONAL
RECREATIONAL AREA

Lincoln Blvd.

THE PRESIDIO

Arguello Blvd.

101

Baker
Beach

China
Beach

LINCOLN PARK

Lake St.

California St.

Clement St.

Geary Blvd.

1

Cliff
House   Point Lobos Ave.

43rd Ave.

36th Ave.

34th Ave.

30th Ave.

25th Ave.

Park Presidio Blvd.

10th Ave.

8th Ave.

6th Ave.

Arguello Blvd.

**RICHMOND
DISTRICT**

Fulton St.

John F. Kennedy Dr.

1

GOLDEN GATE PARK

Lincoln Way

Ocean Beach

Great Highway

46th Ave.

Sunset Blvd.

Irving St.

Judah St.

25th Ave.

19th Ave.

Irving St.

Judah St.

9th Ave.

7th Ave

Parnassus   Ave

SUNSET DISTRICT

Lawton St.

Warren Dr.

Warren Dr.

Noriega St.

Laguna Honda Blvd.

Clarendon

1

Dewey Blvd.   Woodside
Ave.

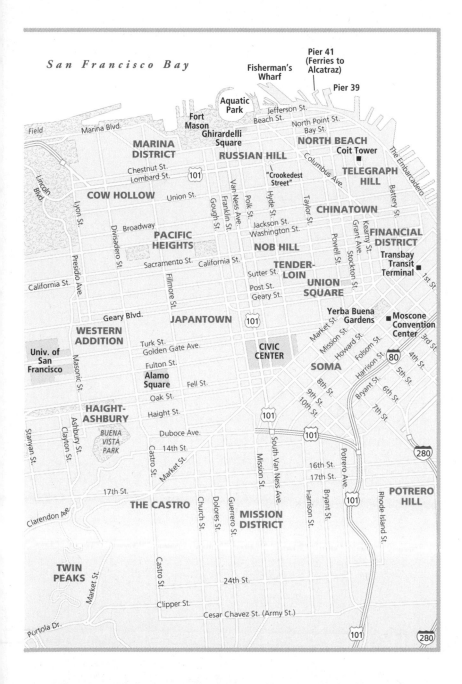

PART ONE

PLANNING
your VISIT

UNDERSTANDING *the* CITY:
A Brief History of San Francisco

AFTER NEW YORK CITY, San Francisco is the most densely populated city in the United States, with more than 809,000 people crowded on a 49-square-mile peninsula. Understanding why so many people choose to live here is easy: You really never need a down-filled coat or shorts or high heels–unless you happen to be a cross-dresser, of course, and the city serves as a backdrop to some of the most beautiful natural landscapes on the planet. The Golden Gate Bridge, red and towering above the misty fog that engulfs the city predictably every summer and on early mornings, is photographed widely. Make a turn down Marina Boulevard toward the bridge and you will certainly feel a sense of wonder and peace at the surreal beauty that is within the city and across the bridge. Mountains abound, scenic drives with hairy cliff-top drops are everywhere, palm trees and parks punctuate the city . . . it is one of the most beautiful and interesting cities you will ever experience.

THE ORIGINAL NATIVES

THE FIRST SPANISH SETTLERS ARRIVED over 200 years ago. But for thousands of years before that, the Bay Area was occupied by the Ohlone, and further afield by Miwok and other Native Americans who lived across California. They formed tribelets and survived mainly by hunting and fishing. Ohlone culture was oral, and they expressed the moment in songs and poetry. Records from Spanish soldiers, clergy, and others supply details, and we can read about their culture in songs such as "Dancing on the Rim of the World," thanks to contemporary historian-publishers. Marvel at the intricate Ohlone handiwork in recreated Ohlone settings such as Coyote Hills Visitors Center near Newark, at Berkeley's Bancroft Library, Golden

Gate Park's de Young Museum, and Sacramento's California State Indian Museum. One colonist, Juan Manuel de Ayala, characterized the Native Americans as "constant in their good friendship and gentle in their manners." But without any political or social organization beyond the tribal level, it did not take long after the first Spanish settlement for the local tribes to be wiped out, probably through epidemics brought by the settlers rather than outright genocide. You can visit a mass Native American grave at the cemetery of Mission Dolores, a mute testimony to their fate. Today, Native American–run casinos prosper, and though the lives of Bay Area Native Americans are in no way the lives they lived for centuries until the Spanish arrived, their welcoming and tolerant outlook somehow survives.

EARLY EXPLORERS

AS YOU DRINK IN THE VIEW from Fort Point or the visitor center at the southern end of the Golden Gate Bridge, it's hard to imagine that ships cruising up or down the California coast could miss such an impressive bay. But they did. Dozens of European explorers, including heavy hitters Juan Cabrillo, Sir Francis Drake, and Sebastián Vizcaíno sailed past for centuries, oblivious of the great harbor beyond. Why? The opening is cloaked in fog for much of the year; even on clear days, the East Bay hills rise behind the opening and disguise the entrance to the point of invisibility.

Sir Francis Drake may have come closest. In 1579, while on a mission from Queen Elizabeth I to "annoy" and pillage the Spanish provinces, he passed by the bay's entrance. Like so many other explorers, he never saw it. Instead he recorded "stynkinge fogges" in his log, and then anchored his small, storm-battered galleon, the *Golden Hind,* somewhere near latitude 38 just to the north, sending several landing parties ashore. He was met by a band of Miwoks who greeted him with a feathered headdress and food and drink. Drake claimed their land for Queen Elizabeth and named it Nova Albion (New England), before going on to plunder more Spanish ships. The tiny *Golden Hind* took almost three years to circle the globe. A commemorative plate known as Drake's Plate of Brasse "discovered" in 1936 was, however, exposed as a hoax in 2003—by the University of California–Berkeley's own Bancroft Library.

The next Europeans to cast their eyes on the Bay Area and the site of the future San Francisco were in a company of 60 Spanish soldiers, mule skinners, priests, and Native Americans led by Gaspar de Portolá. This small contingent was the advance party of 200 soldiers and clergy on an overland mission from Mexico in 1769 to secure lands north of the colony for Spain and convert the heathens. Somewhere around Half Moon Bay, south of San Francisco, Portolá sent out two scouting parties, one north up the coast and the other east into the mountains. Both groups returned with extraordinary descriptions of the Golden Gate—

the entrance from the Pacific into the safe waters of the harbor—and the huge bay. On November 4 the entire party gathered on an exposed ridge, overwhelmed by the incredible view. Father Juan Crespi, their priest, wrote that the bay "would contain not only all the Armadas of Our Catholic Monarch but all those of Europe."

FIRST SETTLEMENT

IT WAS ANOTHER SIX YEARS before the Spanish sent an expedition to explore the bay Portolá had discovered. In May 1775, Juan Manuel de Ayala became the first European to sail into San Francisco Bay, when he piloted the *San Carlos* through the Golden Gate. A year later Captain Juan Bautista de Anza came back with 200 soldiers and settlers to establish the Presidio of San Francisco overlooking the Golden Gate. He also established a mission three miles to the southeast along a creek he named Nuestra Señora de Dolores—"Our Lady of Sorrows"—from which comes the mission's name, Mission Dolores. (It's the oldest building in San Francisco.)

Four more missions were established in the Bay Area in the following years. Each was similar, with a church and cloistered residence surrounded by irrigated fields, vineyards, and ranch lands. A contingent of soldiers protected the missions, which were usually worked by Native Americans, and Native Americans attacked some, too. To resist fire, the ubiquitous red-tiled roof replaced the thatched roof. By the end of the 18th century, the Bay Area settlements' population remained less than 1,000. Northern California was still a remote outpost and held little appeal for foreign adventurers. While the garrison was strong enough to resist Native American attacks, it would have easily fallen to attacks from the sea, had there been any.

Small towns, called pueblos, were established to grow food for the missions and to attract settlers. The first, San Jose, was built in a broad, fertile valley south of Mission Santa Clara. Though the town was considered successful, fewer than 500 inhabitants lived there until well into the 1800s. Another small village, not sanctioned by Spanish authorities, emerged between Mission Dolores and the presidio around a deepwater landing spot southeast of Telegraph Hill. Called Yerba Buena, or "good herb" (after the sweet-smelling mint that grew wild on the nearby hills), it was little more than a collection of shanties and ramshackle jetties. Although not renamed San Francisco until the late 1840s, this was the beginning of the city.

MEXICAN INDEPENDENCE AND AMERICAN SETTLERS

IN THE 1820s, the Bay Area was still a remote backwater. The mission era ended with the independence of Mexico in 1821; in a few years the missions were secularized, and their lands were handed over to Californios—mostly former soldiers who had settled there after completing their service. The Mexican government hardly exercised any control over distant Yerba Buena and was more willing than the Spanish to let foreigners settle and remain.

In the early part of the decade, a number of Americans and Brits started to arrive in the Bay Area. Many were sailors who jumped ship—even in its toddler years, San Francisco attracted those souls seeking a better life!

Other settlers came, started businesses, and influenced the development of San Francisco into a major port. William Richardson, for example, arrived on a whaling ship in 1822 and stayed for the rest of his life. He married the daughter of the presidio commander, eventually owned most of southern Marin County, started a profitable shipping company, and ran the only ferry service across the treacherous bay waters.

While the locals were doing well by the 1840s, the Bay Area wasn't viewed as being rich in natural resources, and as a result it wasn't a major factor in international relations. In the 1830s the U.S. government decided to buy all of Mexico north of the Rio Grande, but nothing happened until June 1846, when the Mexican-American War broke out in Texas. U.S. naval forces quickly took over the West Coast—the fulfillment of the United States' "manifest destiny" to cover the continent from coast to coast—and captured San Francisco's presidio on July 9.

At about the same time, an interesting—although historically insignificant—event occurred north of San Francisco. An ambitious U.S. army captain, John C. Fremont, had been encouraging unhappy settlers to declare independence from Mexico and set him up as their leader. He assembled an unofficial force of about 60 sharpshooting

LOLALAND

SHE MAY HAVE BEEN A BAD DANCER—booed and hissed off stage most of her performing life—but she made history with her vicious temper, whip snapping, and bedroom antics. The infamous femme fatale of the Victorian age, Irish-born Lola Montez (real name Eliza Gilbert) stormed the gold rush in California for a fresh start—after many marriages and a decade of seducing kings and czars across Europe—to pursue her dream of becoming a respected performer and actress.

She moved into a house (now the chamber of commerce) in a boisterous mining town called Grass Valley, and performed at the old theater in neighboring Nevada City. Her act included Louis XVI cabinets, ormolu mirrors, priceless jewels from her ex-husbands, a pet bear, a swan bed, gold leaf, and one extra-large deep-red-top billiard table with dragons carved on its legs. With a bosom worth as much as nuggets of gold and her crazy delusions of capturing California from the United States and becoming the Queen of "Lolaland," she attracted governors, senators, and millionaires and eventually inspired the song "Whatever Lola Wants, Lola Gets!" before moving on to an appreciative Australia.

ex-soldiers, spread rumors that war with Mexico was imminent, and persuaded settlers to join him. The result was the Bear Flag Revolt. On June 14, 1846, a force descended on the abandoned presidio in Sonoma, took the retired commander captive, raised a makeshift flag over the plaza, and declared California independent. The flag, featuring a grizzly bear above the words *California Republic,* was eventually adopted as the California state flag.

But the republic was short-lived. Three weeks after the disgruntled settlers hoisted the flag, it was replaced by the Stars and Stripes. California was now U.S. territory. Ironically, on January 24, 1848, just nine days before the U.S. government took formal control at the signing of the Treaty of Guadalupe (which ended the war with Mexico and ceded California to the United States), sawmill owner John Sutter and carpenter James Marshall discovered gold in the Sierra Nevada foothills 100 miles east of San Francisco. It changed the face of the city—and California—forever.

SUTTER'S SAWMILL AND THE GLEAM OF GOLD!

IT ALL STARTED WITH A SAWMILL. Contractor James Marshall and a work crew were commissioned to construct a sawmill for John Sutter, a Swiss immigrant whose Sacramento Valley ranch had been granted to him by the Mexican governor of California. On January 24, 1848, along the American River near Sacramento, Marshall uncovered a few tiny gold nuggets. Sutter tried to keep the find under his cap, but word got out. Aided by a notice printed in *The Californian* in San Francisco, as well as by more discoveries of gold by General John Bidwell, the great human migration west began. More than a half-million pioneering spirits from around the world descended upon California in search of instant wealth. By the end of May the editor of *The Californian* announced the suspension of his newspaper because the entire staff had quit. "The whole country from San Francisco to Los Angeles and from the sea shore to the base of the Sierra Nevada," he wrote, "resounds with the sordid cry of gold! GOLD! GOLD!— while the field is left half-planted, the house half-built, and everything neglected but the manufacture of shovels and pickaxes." Before the year was over, more prospectors arrived from neighboring territories, Mexico, and South America.

At the time gold was discovered, the total population of the Bay Area was around 2,000, about a quarter of whom lived in tiny San Francisco (changed from Yerba Buena the year before). Within a year, 100,000 men, known collectively as forty-niners (now you'll have one correct answer to a sports trivia question—that's the origin of the modern-day football team's name), had arrived in California; it was one of the most madcap migrations in history. While many of the prospectors passed through San Francisco, few stayed long before moving on to the gold fields. About half made a three-month slog across the continent to get there. And once there, as reflected in an essay written by a gold-hopeful Mr. Chandler, they were "bound to stick awhile longer." The lure of fortune was irresistible. Others arrived by ship in San Francisco, which at that time consisted of a few shoddily constructed buildings, abandoned hulks in the harbor, and rats overrunning filthy streets; there was also a shortage of drinking water. But by the winter of 1850, the shantytown settlement began to evolve into a proper city. Former miners set up foundries and sawmills to supply prospectors, while traders arrived to cash in on miners' success, selling them clothing, food, drink, and entertainment.

Liquor was sold at 537 places in the newborn city—which was one barman for every 67 gold-rush hopefuls—along with brothels, gambling houses, and rooming houses. Where were they to spend their dollars and leisure if not in the saloons of the Barbary Coast?

The city where successful miners came to blow their hard-earned cash now boasted luxury hotels and burlesque theaters, some of which featured the semi-clad "spider dance" of Lola Montez—the famous femme fatale of the gold rush. Throughout the 1850s, immigrants continued to pour into San Francisco. While many headed on to the mines, enough stuck around to increase the city's population to about 35,000 by the end of 1853. More than half were foreigners, chiefly Mexicans, Germans, Chinese, and Italians. In 1848, two Chinese men and one Chinese woman had disembarked from a brig called the *Eagle,* having heard distant rumors of the gold rush back home in Canton. By 1852, there were 3,000 to 4,000 Chinese in the city. Soon, the Chinatown population was growing as fast as the city.

Early comers to the gold fields made instant fortunes by merely washing nuggets out of streams or scraping gold dust from easily accessible veins in the rock, but it was much more difficult for later arrivals. Reports of exuberant miners trading a shot glass full of gold dust for an equal amount of whiskey abounded—something like $1,000 a shot. The real necessities were buckets, shovels, dippers, and pans, and merchants charged outrageous prices for essentials: $50 for a dozen eggs, $100 for a shovel or pickax. Before long, those who supplied everyday items to prospectors were richer than the miners themselves. Levi Strauss, for instance, who was born in Bavaria, began a dry goods business in San Francisco, but he ended up converting his supply of canvas into durable pants with riveted seams. Women, too, were in short supply. Hundreds of prostitutes boarded ships in Mexico and South America, knowing their fares would be paid on arrival by captains selling them to the highest bidder.

THE GOLD BUST

FIVE YEARS AFTER THE DISCOVERY OF GOLD, the easy pickings were gone, and the freewheeling mining camps evolved into corporate operations. San Francisco swelled from a frontier outpost to a bustling city with growing industry, a branch of the U.S. Mint, and a few newspapers. But when revenues from the gold fields leveled out in the late 1850s, the speculative base that had made so many fortunes dried up. Building lots that had been advertised at premium rates couldn't be given away, banks went belly-up, and San Francisco declared bankruptcy, following years of political corruption. The freewheeling city descended into near anarchy, and mobs roamed the streets. By the summer of 1856, the Committee of Vigilance was the city's de facto government and hanged petty criminals in front of enthusiastic mobs. Soon, though, cooler heads prevailed, and the city was restored to legitimate governance. The rest of the 1850s was relatively uneventful.

BOOM . . .

BUT WHATEVER CHANCE SAN FRANCISCO HAD of becoming placid ended in 1859, when another torrent of riches flowed down the slopes of the Sierras. This time it was silver, not gold. The Comstock Lode, one of the most fantastic deposits ever discovered, was a solid vein of silver mixed with gold, ranging from 10 to more than 100 feet wide and stretching to more than two miles long. It would be an even bigger boom than the gold rush of a decade before.

Most of the silver, however, was buried several hundred feet underground, and mining it would be nothing like the freelance prospecting of the early gold rush. Many of San Francisco's great engineers, including George Hearst, Andrew Hallidie, and Adolf Sutro, put their talents to the formidable task. As the mines went deeper to get at the valuable ore, the mining companies needed larger infusions of capital, which they attracted by issuing shares dealt on the San Francisco Stock Exchange. Speculation was rampant, and the value of shares vacillated wildly, depending on daily rumors and forecasts. Fortunes were made and lost in a day's trading; cagier speculators made millions. By 1863, $40 million in silver had been wrenched from the tunnels around the boomtown of Virginia City, 105 miles from San Francisco, and 2,000 mining companies had traded shares on the city's mining exchange, further pumping up the city's economy.

. . . AND BUST

WHILE SAN FRANCISCO ENJOYED unsurpassed prosperity in the 1860s, another major development was taking place: the construction of a transcontinental railroad, completed in 1869 thanks to thousands of Chinese laborers at the western end and Irish navvies at the eastern. The human cost was horrific, mainly among the long-suffering Chinese. Although the trains opened up California, they also brought problems. The Southern Pacific ensnared San Francisco in its web, creating a monopoly over transportation in the Bay Area. Besides controlling long-distance railroads, the firm also owned the city's streetcar system, the network of ferryboats that crisscrossed the bay, and even the cable-car line that lifted rich San Franciscans up California Street to their Nob Hill palaces.

The coming of the railroad usurped San Francisco's role as the West Coast's primary supply point, and products began to flood in from the East well under prices that local industry could meet. At about the time the Comstock mines began to taper off, a depression set in. A series of droughts wiped out agricultural harvests, followed by the arrival of thousands of now-unwanted Chinese workers back from the railroads. As unemployment rose through the late 1870s, frustrated workers took out their aggression on the city's substantial Chinese population and helped push through the notorious Chinese Exclusion Act. At mass demonstrations, thousands rallied behind the slogan, "The Chinese Must Go!" For much of the late 19th century, San Francisco wrestled with problems of nativism, the need to build a varied, stable economy, and corruption in city politics.

A GOLDEN AGE

AT THE BEGINNING OF THE EARLY 20TH CENTURY, San Francisco was entering a golden age. The city now boasted a population of some 400,000 inhabitants—about 45 percent of the population of California (today it's about 2 percent). Political corruption was still a problem, but the economy was expanding—due in equal parts to the Spanish-American War and the Klondike gold rush in Alaska. Both events increased ship traffic in the port, where dockworkers were beginning to organize themselves into unions on an unprecedented scale.

THE GREAT EARTHQUAKE

CIVIC REFORM EFFORTS TO REVERSE MUNICIPAL abuses were well underway when one of San Francisco's most defining events occurred: the Great Earthquake of 1906. On April 18, the city was awakened by violent earth tremors. As much as 8.25 on the Richter scale, it was the worst earthquake to hit the United States before or since (more than ten times as strong as the 1989 quake). The earthquake lasted 48 seconds, yet destroyed hundreds of buildings, because the post-quake conflagration caused massive damage. Crucially, fire chief engineer Dennis Sullivan perished in an accidental fall during the earthquake on the first night, leaving the firefighting force in disarray. Ruptured natural gas mains exploded and chimneys toppled, starting fires across the city that destroyed 28,000 buildings. Looting was rampant, forcing the mayor to post a shoot-to-kill order. The fire raged for three days and all but leveled the entire area from the waterfront north to south of Market Street and west to Van Ness Avenue (where mansions were dynamited to form a firebreak). At least 500 people (most likely a vast underestimate) were killed in the immense disaster, and 100,000 were left homeless. The tenor Enrico Caruso, fresh from a triumph in *Carmen* at the Mission Opera House, flung open his Palace Hotel window to survey the scene and then flung on his coat to flee via the Oakland Ferry. Those who didn't flee the city made camp in what is now Golden Gate Park, where soldiers from the presidio set up a tent city for 20,000 displaced San Franciscans who claimed they preferred living in tents to abandoning their city. Today you can pay tribute to one of the allies of the fight against total devastation—one fire hydrant that saved the Mission District from burning to the ground. The heroic 1906 earthquake fire hydrant is on the corner of 20th and Church streets.

RECOVERY

RESTORATION OF THE RUINED CITY began almost immediately. Financial assistance flooded in from around the world, $8 million in a few weeks. Even the hated Southern Pacific railroad pitched in, freighting in supplies without charge, offering free passage out of the city, and putting heavy equipment and cranes to work on clearing up rubble.

Much of the reconstruction was completed by 1912, and an era of political reform and economic restructuring was ushered in when James "Sunny Jim" Rolph was elected mayor. The opening of the Panama Canal in 1914 made the long sea journey around Cape Horn obsolete, and the first transcontinental phone call later that year (from Alexander Graham Bell to his assistant in San Francisco) held great significance for the city. The rebuilding of city hall and completion of the civic center, as well as the opening of the Panama Pacific International Exhibition (which attracted 19 million visitors), were icing on the cake. The distant war in Europe had few repercussions in San Francisco beyond boosting the economy.

THE ROARING '20s AND THE DEPRESSION

PROHIBITION WAS VERY GOOD to San Francisco indeed. The modern-day speakeasy Bourbon & Branch at 501 Jones Street may be an all-new tribute, but in the 1920s, San Francisco was wetter than the entire Pacific Ocean: One speakeasy featured a trapdoor that hid a slide down to a basement bar below. After serving bootleg alcohol at a party in his suite at the St. Francis Hotel, actor and comedian Roscoe "Fatty" Arbuckle was arrested for the accidental death of Virginia Rappe, and his career was ruined despite former detective and *Maltese Falcon* author Dashiell Hammett's assertion that he had been framed.

Movie stars habitually came to San Francisco for impromptu fun in a looser city at speakeasies such as Izzy Gomez's, Monk Young's, Cafe Dan's, Hoffman Grill, and Hotel D'Oloron. The House of Shields and Café Du Nord survive from the Jazz Age. Clark Gable had a special private dining nook at Amelio's in North Beach (now Peña Pachamama).

Like most American cities, San Francisco roared through the 1920s after recovering from a steep drop in employment after World War I. Financiers and industrialists such as Emanuel Charles Christian Russ

GRILLED CHOPS AND GUMSHOES

IT'S HARD NOT TO TRIP OVER Samuel Dashiell Hammett's ghost in this town, to feel his lean, mean presence 90 years after he moved into San Francisco's Tenderloin. When the "slumming angel" of *Maltese Falcon* and Sam Spade fame was demobbed from the Great War with bad lungs, he returned to his assignment at Pinkerton's as a private investigator. He found a cheap room on Ellis Street and married a nurse, Jose Dolan, whom he'd fallen for in a hospital. He also supposedly began his daily diet of lamb chops, tomatoes, and a baked potato (Sam Spade's choice) at John's Grill at 63 Ellis Street. At Pinkerton's he was assigned the Roscoe "Fatty" Arbuckle rape and murder case to investigate and concluded that Fatty had been framed "by some of the corrupt local newspaper boys"—a likely reference to William Randolph Hearst, owner of the *San Francisco Examiner*. Poor Fatty was ruined by the power of the press, but Hammett went on to Hollywood. Check out Don Herron's Hammett walking tour from the main library; **donherron.com**.

After the stock market crash of 1929, San Francisco bore the full brunt of a recession that hit the city's port activities particularly hard. In 1934, one of the most severe strikes in its history broke out. On July 5—Bloody Thursday—police protecting strikebreakers from angry picketers fired into the crowd, wounding 30 and killing 2. The army was sent in to restore order; in retaliation, unions called a strike, and 125,000 workers put down their tools, halting San Francisco's economy for four days.

It was also an era that saw some of the city's finest monuments take form—for example, Coit Tower. In 1933, Alcatraz Island became the site of America's notorious federal prison. But most important, two great structures over San Francisco Bay, the Golden Gate Bridge and the San Francisco–Oakland Bay Bridge, were built. Before the bridges opened, the Bay Area was served by an impressive number of ferryboats; in 1935, their peak year, 100,000 commuters crossed San Francisco Bay by boat each day. Just five years later, most of the ferries were withdrawn from service, unable to compete with the new bridges. Today's ferries still ply the bay to Sausalito, Tiburon, Oakland, and Vallejo, among others, but in sparser numbers.

and Adam Grant erected high-rises, and the jazz clubs and speakeasies of the Barbary Coast District were in full swing. Now completely recovered from the 1906 quake, San Francisco was the West Coast's premier arts and culture center—a role that it passed to Los Angeles in the next decade. It was also a major banking center: First-generation immigrant A. P. Giannini, who saved his assets from the Great Quake in vegetable carts, founded Bank of America here. The B of A eventually became the largest bank in the world.

WORLD WAR II

FOLLOWING JAPAN'S ATTACK ON PEARL HARBOR and the advent of World War II, San Francisco became the main military port on the Pacific; more than 1.5 million servicemen were shipped to the South

Pacific from Fort Mason. New shipyards sprang up within months, the number of factories tripled, and the Bay Area was transformed into a massive war machine. The Kaiser Shipyards in Richmond, the largest shipbuilding facility in the United States, employed more than 100,000 workers on round-the-clock shifts. Owner Henry Kaiser founded the thriving health insurance company that bears his name for these same workers. Kaiser Permanente continues to thrive.

Men and women poured into the region from all over the country for jobs in the plants. Today, Hunters Point, one of the most economically distressed neighborhoods in San Francisco, and Marin City, one of its most affluent suburbs, are remnants of cities built to house the influx of workers who moved to the Bay Area during the war.

THE 1950s: EMERGENCE OF THE BEAT GENERATION

FOLLOWING THE WAR, THOUSANDS of GIs returning from the South Pacific passed through San Francisco, and many decided to stay. New neighborhoods such as the Sunset District, with massive tracts of look-alike housing, were formed, and huge highways were built. The postwar years brought prosperity but also created a backlash. As the middle class moved out of the inner city, many of their offspring moved back in. North Beach bars and cafes incubated a wellspring of iconoclastic, antiestablishment youth in what was to become the Greenwich Village of the West Coast. Leading this movement was writer Jack Kerouac, who, after the publication of the movement-defining book *On the Road*, was asked by reporters to define the term *beat*. He first heard the term a decade before his writing, from a rough-and-tumble 42nd Street hustler who used the term to describe a state of exalted exhaustion. The novel was a classic story that broke open conformist 1950s America. The Beat generation was news, and Kerouac had been officially dubbed its chief incarnation. Tired of conventional America, this tribe was on a quest for spiritual identity and vision, and many of them found clarity in San Francisco.

The Beat generation rebelled against the empty materialism of the 1950s; many lost themselves in orgies of jazz, drugs, and Buddhism. The new counterculture also fostered a highly personal, expressive blend of prose and poetry. City Lights Bookstore in North Beach became the focal point for the new literary movement, which included poets Lawrence Ferlinghetti (the shop's owner, whom you can still spot in between bookshelves—usually the poetry section) and the late Allen Ginsberg.

PSYCHEDELIC 1960s

BY THE EARLY 1960S the steam was gone from the Beat movement. Shortly thereafter, though, an offshoot of the antiestablishment trend surfaced—the hippies. Originally the term was a Beat putdown for the inexperienced, enthusiastic young people following in the footsteps of their countercultural elders. The first hippies appeared on college campuses around San Francisco.

There was a difference, though. Hippies were experimenting with a new hallucinogenic drug called LSD (better known by its street name, acid). Around 1965, hippies began moving into communes in low-rent Victorian houses in the Haight-Ashbury District, west of the city's center. It was the beginning of flower power and would culminate in 1967's "summer of love," when 100,000 young people converged on the area.

REVOLUTIONARY POLITICS

WHILE HIPPIES TUNED INTO PSYCHEDELIC music by bands such as Jefferson Airplane, Big Brother and the Holding Company, and the Grateful Dead, across the bay in Berkeley and Oakland, it was politics, not acid and acid rock, that topped the agenda. The free speech movement began at the UC–Berkeley campus in 1964 and laid the groundwork for passionate protests against the Vietnam War in the Bay Area and around the country later in the decade.

The most famous protest took place in Berkeley's People's Park, a plot of university-owned land that local activists took over as a community open space. On May 15, 1969, when police erected a fence around the park and barred entry, students rallied. An army of police under the command of Edwin Meese (later attorney general under President Ronald Reagan) teargassed demonstrators and stormed the park, accidentally killing one bystander and seriously injuring more than 100 others.

In response to the era's overt racism, the Black Panthers emerged in the impoverished flatlands of Oakland. Formed in 1966 by Bobby Seale, Huey Newton, and Eldridge Cleaver, the Panthers were a heavily armed but outnumbered band of activists who wanted self-determination for blacks. A nationwide organization sprung from the Oakland headquarters; 30 members across the country died in gun battles with police and the FBI.

MAKING HEADLINES: THE 1970s AND 1980s

STUDENT UNREST, ANTIWAR PROTESTS, and flower power spilled over into the early 1970s, though at a less-fevered pitch. One headline-grabbing event was the 1974 kidnapping of Patty Hearst, who was snatched from her Berkeley apartment by the Symbionese Liberation Army, a hardcore group of revolutionaries demanding free food for Oakland's poor in exchange for the rich heiress. Later on during her captivity, Hearst helped the SLA and was photographed wielding a submachine gun in the robbery of a San Francisco bank.

Compared to the 1960s, most of the decade was quiet. The Bay Area

THE NEW BAY BRIDGE

BADLY DAMAGED IN THE 1989 QUAKE that swallowed two cars and killed a motorist, the Bay Bridge is being replaced with a $6 billion new span that parallels and will eventually replace the 1936 $77 million original. After many delays and debates, 280,000 commuters who use the bridge will get the new one by 2013. A stilettolike silver tower will have suspension cables anchored into the bridge deck itself, Santiago Calatrava–style. Tolls have been upped to $4 to pay for it—but if the 20-year brainstorming makes the bridge as beautiful and quakeproof as they promise, so be it.

Rapid Transit (BART) finally opened, and the Golden Gate National Recreation Area was established to protect 75,000 acres of incredibly scenic open areas on both ends of the Golden Gate Bridge. In 1973, the Transamerica Pyramid was completed, receiving mixed reviews from San Francisco critics; today it's a beloved piece of the city's skyline.

New battle lines were being drawn. The city's homosexuals, inspired by the 1969 Stonewall Riots in New York City, began to organize, demanding equal status with heterosexuals. Just as important, gays and lesbians came out, refusing to hide their sexuality and giving rise to the gay liberation movement. When gay politician Harvey Milk was assassinated in 1978 along with Mayor George Moscone, the entire city was shaken. A riot ensued when Milk's killer, former Supervisor Dan White, was found guilty of manslaughter and not murder after using the infamous "Twinkie defense" and was paroled early from a derisory short five-year sentence.

In the 1980s, San Francisco's gay community retreated somewhat, hit by a staggering AIDS epidemic that toned down a notoriously promiscuous bathhouse scene. The gay community, in conjunction with city hall, continues to fight the disease while possible vaccines undergo trials.

During Mayor (now Senator) Diane Feinstein's term, San Francisco added millions of square feet of office towers to downtown's Financial District as some bemoaned the manhattanization of the city.

There were also setbacks. In October 1989, 100 million people watched on national television as a 7.1-magnitude earthquake shook San Francisco during the third game of the World Series between Bay Area rivals the San Francisco Giants and the Oakland A's; a freeway collapsed, power was out for three days, and 63 were killed. Two years later a horrific fire in the Oakland hills killed 26 people and destroyed 3,000 homes. In the early 1990s, most of the problems San Francisco faced were similar to those in other American cities: urban poverty, drug abuse, homelessness, and AIDS. An ongoing economic turndown in California was amplified by post–Cold War military cutbacks, which saw the closure of military bases in the Bay Area and the loss of 35,000 civilian jobs. But things were brewing about 30 miles south of San Francisco that would send the city into a mass of hysterics reminiscent of the flash and fortune during the gold-rush era.

THE DOT-COM BOOM: RIP

NOTHING DEFINES THE ECONOMIC and social climate in San Francisco in the mid-1990s more than a dot. The dot-com, as the Internet industry became known, redefined the global economy and sent investors running like dogs to a bone. In this case, the apparent billion-dollar bone would prove in the end to be bare for most investors and entrepreneurs alike.

The NASDAQ was at an all-time high, jobs were plentiful, and San Francisco more than any other city was riding high on the dot-com coattails, thanks to the technological revolution emerging from neighboring Silicon Valley. Industrial SoMa district became the hub of Internet companies, trendy bars, and elaborate bashes. Rents soared, neighborhoods became gentrified, and stock options landed in the laps of everyone from landlords to graduating nieces. It seemed that retiring at the ripe old age of 30 wasn't just a pipe dream, and a million dollars could be earned by anyone from the mail clerk to the janitor. Hopes were high, bank accounts overflowing, and Mercedes and BMW dealerships quite busy.

Then in April 2000, a crash sent heads spinning and doors slamming in the Internet industry. As hard as it tried, the dot-com empire couldn't keep out profit loss, market devaluation, and downsizing. Pioneering fortune seekers were left in the rubble, sharing casualty stories at pink-slip parties. Their inflated titles and salaries faced judgment day in the face of a more frugal post-dot-com market. Jobs were hard to come by, and as a result most returned from where they came, with their tails between their legs.

Today, the city is still recovering from the crash. The building boom that followed, exceeded only by that following the earthquake of 1906, has been drastically hit by the subprime mortgage slump. But without doubt, the skyline of the city has already changed dramatically. Most of the new construction took place in the SoMa district and near the Embarcadero, spreading to the South Park and new ballpark and beyond, toward Mission Bay and its new UCSF campus. Not only office buildings but also condos and apartments, live/work spaces, shopping centers, entertainment facilities, restaurants, clubs, and all things needed to support urban life continue to fill in a former hinterland despite the slump, and some tower blocks have vacancies. No one can say what the final result will be, but in its many self-reinventions, San Francisco has always satisfied.

WHEN TO GO:
The Sweater Season and the . . .
Well, Sweater (Wetter) Season

MAYBE YOU HAVEN'T HEARD, but San Francisco isn't very warm—and summer is its coolest time. So right now you are probably staring at your suitcase packed with tanks, shorts, and swimsuits, thinking, "What the heck do I pack?" The answer is simple. Pack the fleece, the hoodie, maybe even the turtleneck, *and* the tank. The City by the Bay is in fact just that—a city by a bay—and it is regularly swept by winds from the water that surrounds it on three sides. Yet it boasts one of the most stable climates in the world. Temperatures during the day rarely venture more than 5°F from the average 60°F. Temperatures at night rarely drop lower than 40°F, and snow is virtually unheard of. This weather, however, is impossible to predict. With sunny rays beaming through your window, you'll wake up anticipating a bright, warm day, and by the time you've showered and tied your shoes, the fog is thick enough to cut with a knife, and the temperature has turned chilly. We don't mean to sound like a nagging old grandmother, but dress in layers!

Now for the tank. Take a drive over any bridge—or take a ferry across the bay—and you'll feel a heat resurrection. The toes will start to uncurl and the hairs will flatten as all things simmer under the sun and heat that await in the East Bay, South Bay, and Marin County. Almost everywhere else in the Bay Area is warmer than San Francisco, especially in the summer, when Berkeley and Oakland bask in sunshine, and the wine country and surrounding valleys shrivel like prunes under intense heat.

THE DRY SEASON

SORRY-I'M-NOT-THAT-WARM San Francisco has two kinds of weather: wet and dry. The dry season starts in April and usually lasts through October (and sometimes into November). If the virtually dry months of July and August sound too good to be true, you're right. It is too good to be true. There's a catch—the city's fabled fog envelops the city mornings and evenings during much of the summer, hovering over the Golden Gate and obscuring the bridge. But the fog usually burns off by early afternoon—just in time for you to burn off that burrito by jogging, biking, or kayaking.

Summer is also the most crowded. If you're visiting in the summer, don't be like the rest of the shivering shorts-clad tourists at Fisherman's Wharf—bring the sweater! San Franciscans get tired of

unofficial **TIP**
A quick note: When dense afternoon fogs roll in during the summer months, the temperature can drop as much as 20° F in less than an hour.

Mark Twain's oft-quoted, "The coldest winter I ever saw was a summer in . . . "—you guessed it. The city can be decidedly unsummerlike in July and August, especially at waterside locales such as the wharf, Fort Point, the ocean beaches, and the Golden Gate Bridge.

THE WET SEASON

WINTER BRINGS MOST OF SAN FRANCISCO'S rainfall, usually starting sometime in November and continuing through March. Often the rain is quite torrential, especially in December and January. Yet daytime highs rarely plunge far below 60°F, and the lows hover in the mid-40s. Two days in a row without rain are rare on a winter trip to the city, but crowds are nonexistent and finding a convenient and reasonably priced hotel room is less of a hassle. And again, bring the sweaters.

THE SHOULDER SEASONS

IF YOU WANT TO ENJOY SAN FRANCISCO when the weather is on its best behavior, and if you want to avoid large crowds, you have two options: spring and fall. These are the favorite seasons of *Unofficial Guide* researchers. In May and June the hills are at their greenest and are covered with wildflowers. Yet rainfall is almost nil, and daytime highs average in the mid-60s. Crowds at major tourist attractions usually don't pick up until later in the summer, when families with children begin to arrive. September and October are San Francisco's warmest months. They're popular months with visitors, but they lack the big crowds that pack the city's attractions during the height of the summer season. Warm, cloudless days are the norm. As a bonus, it's grape-harvesting season in the wine country, making a one- or two-day excursion to Napa or Sonoma imperative.

unofficial **TIP**
September and October are the city's least foggy months (although many visitors don't seem to mind the fog).

AVOIDING CROWDS

IN GENERAL, POPULAR TOURIST SITES are busier on weekends, and Saturdays are busier than Sundays. The summer season by far is the busiest time of year at most attractions. If Alcatraz is on your itinerary (and if you're a first-time visitor to San Francisco, it should be), call in advance for tickets on a weekday, and hit attractions at Fisherman's Wharf on the same day. On summer weekends, the wharf is jammed with visitors.

Driving anywhere in the Bay Area during commute hours is an exercise in frustration. The major arteries and bridges are true chock points, and you should try to avoid them at busy times. If you're driving to the city on a weekday, avoid hitting town between 6 a.m. and 10 a.m. and between 3 p.m. and 6 or even 7 p.m. If you're driving in on a weekend, you're still not off the hook. Traffic in and around San Francisco on Saturday and Sunday afternoons sometimes exceeds weekday rush-hour intensity. The worst time of all is at the beginning and the end of a three-day weekend. One theory is that frisky San Franciscans like to head to playgrounds outside of the city. Evidence of this is seen as cars toting surfboards, snowboards, bikes, kayaks, and ropes venture across the bridges. Another theory is that the region around the city, the fifth largest in the country, registers a population of more than 7 million. On weekends, residents of San Jose, Berkeley, Oakland, and other towns nearby do what you would if you lived here—they drive to San Francisco. Try to arrive before noon on weekends and you'll miss the worst of the weekend crush.

HOW *to* GET MORE INFORMATION *before* YOU VISIT

FOR ADDITIONAL INFORMATION on entertainment, sightseeing, maps, shopping, dining, and lodging in San Francisco, call or write:

San Francisco Convention and Visitors Bureau
Hallidie Plaza, 900 Market Street
San Francisco, CA 94102-2804
☎ 415-391-2000
onlyinsanfrancisco.com

The Convention and Visitors Bureau's Visitor Information Center is in the Benjamin Swig Pavilion on the lower level of Hallidie Plaza at Market and Powell streets. It's easy to find, and the center's multilingual staff can help answer any questions you may have. Hours are 8:30 a.m. to 5 p.m. The center is closed Easter, Thanksgiving, Christmas, and New Year's Day.

Several great Web sites can help in your preparation. A few to check out include:

- **yelp.com** for the skinny on everything from restaurants and nightlife to hotels, and it delivers bad news as often as good.
- **sfstation.com** for up-to-the-minute events and insider information.
- **sfarts.org** will give you the scoop on everything indie, controversial, and artistic that's happening in all forms of art.
- **stchamber.com** offers run-of-the-mill tourist information from the chamber of commerce. It's handy for maps and mainstream attractions.
- **sfgate.com** is a branch of the *Chronicle* newspaper. Great place for current events and activities, as well as jobs (if the city inspires you enough to move!).
- **bayarea.citysearch.com** is the San Francisco leg of the popular "what to do and where to go" nationwide city guide.
- **sonoma.com** is your guide to everything wine in Sonoma County, including current info on Napa lodgings, dining, and tours.

GAYS *and* LESBIANS

IN SAN FRANCISCO, "the love that dare not speak its name" is expressed more loudly than in any other U.S., or indeed world, city. San Francisco boasts the largest gay and lesbian population of any city in America—with some reports estimating that 15 percent of its total population of 809,000 is gay—and rainbow flags fly over many a home. Hundreds of businesses and services are owned and operated by gays, who enjoy a high level of visibility, acceptance, and political clout in the community at large.

HISTORY

THE ROOTS OF THE CITY'S LARGE GAY population and its live-and-let-live ambience go back to the waning days of World War II, when the U.S. military began purging its ranks of homosexuals and suspected homosexuals, booting them out at the point of embarkation. This was often San Francisco, the major military stepping-off point. Many of the men, officially stigmatized, stayed in the Bay Area. Another migration occurred in the McCarthy era of the early 1950s, when the federal government dismissed thousands of homosexuals from their jobs. Persecution by the U.S. military and local police was common in the postwar years; in the early 1960s, gays began organizing for their civil rights.

unofficial **TIP**
"It's an odd thing, but anyone who disappears is said to be seen in San Francisco. It must be a delightful city and possess all the attractions of the next world!"
 –Oscar Wilde

By the 1970s, an estimated one in four San Francisco voters was gay, and homosexuals were an influential minority group. It didn't hurt that gays voted in larger numbers and contributed to political candidates who supported issues important to gays. As gays of the flower-power generation began moving in and restoring Victorian town houses, Castro Street (formerly an Irish American neighborhood going to seed) became a flourishing enclave and the embodiment of the gay drive for acceptance, all of which is familiar now from Sean Penn's stunning turn in *Milk*, the movie about the gay local politician.

In 1977, the Castro District elected Harvey Milk to the city board of supervisors. Milk, a gay activist who organized the district's merchants group, became the first openly gay city official elected in the United States. The drama of gay liberation heightened when former Supervisor Dan White, a former cop and firefighter and the city's most anti-gay politician, assassinated Milk and pro-gay Mayor George Moscone in city hall in 1978. Six months later, White was sentenced to only five years for the killings, and a mob marched on city hall, drawing worldwide attention and headlines. Paroled in 1985, White eventually committed suicide after failing to make a new life. Although San Francisco was notorious for its bar-and-bathhouse culture and its anonymous promiscuity, to say nothing of its cocaine and marijuana habits, its reputation toned down after AIDS struck in the early 1980s, causing more than 7,000 deaths in San Francisco in the '80s alone. Socially, the city's gay scene mellowed in the 1990s, although gay bars, gay pride parades, and street fairs still thrive.

The 1980s also saw a flowering of the city's lesbian culture that parallels the male upswing of the 1970s. Today, as in most American cities, the lesbian community is subtler and less visible than the gay scene, but it's just as powerful politically. Much smaller than the Castro, the main lesbian community is concentrated around 16th and Valencia streets or Bernal Heights in the Mission District, while larger lesbian communities are across the bay in Oakland and Berkeley.

In the late 1990s, the city's gays and lesbians escaped the moral backlash provoked by AIDS in other parts of the country, thanks to San Francisco's tolerance and the community's support of people with AIDS and their survivors. Gays have, by and large, melded into the mainstream. Gay life is less ghettoized, and gay bars and clubs are scattered all over town. For years the city has had gay and lesbian political leaders, police officers, bureaucrats, and judges. It can be argued that one of the major aims of the gay liberation movement has been met here—the acceptance of people regardless of whether they're gay or straight.

GAY VISITORS

WHAT DOES ALL THIS MEAN FOR GAY and lesbian visitors to the city? By and large, you needn't concern yourself with fitting in during a visit to San Francisco. Take, for example, getting a room. While many hotels are gay-owned and cater to a gay clientele, the Bay Area's level of tolerance just about guarantees that a visitor's sexual orientation—and the roommate's gender—isn't going to be an issue at any hotel in or around San Francisco.

BEFORE YOU GO

FOR INFORMATION on the city's gay scene, check out **timeout.com/ sanfrancisco/gay.** A good site for tours is **allsanfranciscotours.com.**

GAY AND LESBIAN PUBLICATIONS AND COMMUNITY BULLETIN BOARDS

NUMEROUS NEWSPAPERS AND MAGAZINES in San Francisco cater to the gay and lesbian community. The largest and best known are the *San Francisco Bay Times* (distributed every other Thursday; ☎ 415-626-0260; **sfbaytimes.com**) and the weekly *Bay Area Reporter* (distributed on Thursdays; ☎ 415-861-5019; **ebar.com**). Both are free and are distributed to bookstores, bars, and street vending boxes. The newspapers provide complete event calendars and resource listings for gays and lesbians.

Other publications include *Girlfriends* (a monthly magazine for lesbians; ☎ 905-619-6565; **girlfriendsmag.com**) and *Odyssey* (a gay nightclub and listing guide published every other Friday; ☎ 323-874-8788; **odysseymagazine.net**). The *Gay Guide* and *Betty and Pansy's Severe Queer Review* are more underground papers found at cafes throughout the Castro and the Mission. An excellent place to find these publications and others under one roof is the bookstore **A Different Light** (489 Castro Street; ☎ 415-431-0891).

The San Francisco gay and lesbian community has several information resources. One of the more popular is the **Women's Building** of the Bay Area in the Mission District (☎ 415-431-1180; **womensbuilding. org**). It's a clearinghouse for feminist and lesbian art, entertainment, and resource information; call from 9 a.m. to 5 p.m. weekdays.

CELEBRATE GAY TIMES: TOP GAY ATTRACTIONS

- **AIDS Memorial Chapel** and the **Keith Haring Altarpiece** in Grace Cathedral off of California Street, ☎ 415-749-6300.
- **Gay, Lesbian, and Transgender Pride Parade** (☎ 415-864-0831; **sfpride.org**) every June follows Market Street from the civic center to the Embarcadero. The parade is for the flamboyant, shy, family, couple . . . everybody wanting to express themselves for a day! Dykes on Bikes kicks off the celebration; $3 donation requested.
- **Castro Street Fair** in October is a scaled-down version of the Pride Parade. Costumes, shopping, and munching are all part of the festivities (☎ 415-841-1824; **castrostreetfair.org**).
- **A Different Light Bookshop** (489 Castro Street; ☎ 415-431-0891; **adlbooks.com**) stocks its shelves with mostly gay and lesbian literature by gay and lesbian authors.
- **Theatre Rhinoceros** (1360 Mission Street, Suite 200; ☎ 800-838-3006; **therhino.org**) is the place to come for gay performance art.
- **Bay to Breakers Race** (☎ 415-359-2800; **baytobreakers.com**) held in May is not just the largest footrace in the world, it's also the most fun you'll ever have on a Sunday afternoon! Come dressed up (although clothes are optional), bring the beer or margarita, and race your way from Fremont Street to Ocean Beach or walk if crowds are too heavy.
- **Cruisin' the Castro Tour** on Tuesdays through Saturdays (☎ 415-255-1821; **cruisinthecastro.com**) takes you on a walking tour to all the sights of the Castro, highlighting history along the way.

GAY NEIGHBORHOODS

THE TRADITIONAL NEIGHBORHOOD for gay men has been the now-gentrified Castro, now more typified by prepped-up, well-heeled yuppies than the disheveled leftists and ex-hippies that symbolized the early days of the gay liberation movement. SoMa, the city's emerging art-and-nightlife district, features a gay enclave around Folsom Street, site of the still-startling Folsom Street Fair and raunchiest gay bars; the look tends toward black leather and chains. Polk Street and the edges of the Tenderloin District is the tight-blue-jeans-and-pimps zone of young gay transients; it's not the safest part of town at 2 a.m. (or anytime—see below). An enclave of successful gay business executives resides in posh and proper Pacific Heights. Bernal ("maternal") Heights and Hayes Valley are San Francisco's newest lesbian- and gay-oriented neighborhoods. Just take a look inside Bernal's dyke bar **Wild Side West**—the oldest women's bar in the city with its dreamy back garden and tolerant attitude toward stray men.

A footnote: While San Francisco is hands-down the most tolerant city in the country, gay bashing is still alive occasionally. Avoid displays of affection in the Mission District, the largely Hispanic neighborhood where street gangs have attacked gay men. While the Polk Street area has a long gay history, it's now primarily a hustling scene with many bars and porn shops; it's a dangerous area, and more gay bashing is reported here than in any other part of the city.

A **CALENDAR** of **FESTIVALS** and **EVENTS**

SAN FRANCISCO HOSTS A VARIETY OF ANNUAL special events throughout the year, including films, jazz and blues festivals, craft fairs, art festivals, street fairs, and ethnic festivals. Exact dates are subject to change, so be sure to call the number indicated if you are interested in attending.

January

ANNUAL ZINFANDEL FESTIVAL Often called California's claret, zin has a worldwide following. This festival typically draws some 10,000 devotees of the noble grape. **zinfandel.org.**

 unofficial **TIP**
We've highlighted some not-to-be-missed events that are true showcases of the city's vibrant arts, funk, and soul (look for the ★).

MARTIN LUTHER KING JR.'S BIRTHDAY CELEBRATION A host of festivities highlights the city's commemoration of Dr. King's life. San Francisco Exploratorium. ☎ 415-561-0360; **exploratorium.edu.**

NOIR CITY San Francisco is one of the most popular cities for use as backdrop and location for the film noir genre. This festival, held at the Art Deco–era Castro Theatre, is dedicated to the style and philosophy of film noir. **noircity.com.**

SAN FRANCISCO INDEPENDENT FILM FESTIVAL Showcases the best of indie films from the Bay Area and beyond. Various locations. ☎ 415-820-3907; **sfindie.com.**

SEA LIONS' ANNUAL ARRIVAL AT PIER 39 Most years, spectators can see, hear, and enjoy hundreds of sea lions in close proximity. ☎ 415-981-1280; **pier39.com.**

GUERNEVILLE

ANOTHER PLACE YOU won't find any discrimination whatsoever is the town of **Guerneville,** just west of Healdsburg, where gays from 50 states come for wine tasting, hot tubs under redwoods, or just the chance to relax in a tolerant spot. Cute and incurably friendly, this small Russian River town off I-101 in the wine country can be described as "Mayberry meets the Village People." It's one of a cluster of tiny towns such as El Rio, Forestville, and Rio Nido that seem stuck in the 1950s. Guerneville hosts an annual gay festival, and the area has a thumping disco scene. At gay-friendly resorts such as Highlands, you'll have log fires in your cabin and a chance to strip to the buff and soak next to assorted hunks; just don't bring great-aunt Fanny. Or do—you never know; she'll probably love the place. ☎ 707-869-0333; **highlandsresort.com.**

February

CHINESE NEW YEAR CELEBRATION The city's largest festival with a parade from Market and Second streets to Columbus Avenue. ☎ 415-986-1370; **chineseparade.com.**

MACWORLD EXPO Where better to see the latest in chips, bytes, and megahertz than San Francisco! Moscone Center. ☎ 415-974-4000; **macworldexpo.com.**

PACIFIC ORCHID EXPOSITION The orchid expo typically displays up to 100,000 flowers, many of them award-winning specimens. Fort Mason Center. ☎ 415-665-2468; **orchidsanfrancisco.org.**

SAN FRANCISCO ARTS OF PACIFIC ASIA SHOW Exhibitors from around the world offer antiques and art from the Pacific Asia region. Fort Mason. ☎ 415-581-3500; **asianart.org.**

SAN FRANCISCO SPORTS AND BOAT SHOW Boats, fishing tackle, camping gear, and hunting equipment on display. Cow Palace. ☎ 415-931-2500; **sfboatshow.com.**

SAN FRANCISCO TRIBAL, FOLK, AND TEXTILE ARTS SHOW More than 80 folk and ethnic art dealers sell North American pottery, basketry, textiles, and jewelry. Fort Mason. ☎ 310-455-2886; **caskeylees.com.**

★ **TULIPMANIA** View more than 40,000 brilliantly colored tulips from around the world. Pier 39, Fisherman's Wharf. ☎ 415-981-1280; **pier39.com.**

March

ACROSS THE BAY 12K RACE The largest run ever to cross the Golden Gate Bridge. It ends with a bang, at the party at Fisherman's Wharf. Sausalito to Fisherman's Wharf. ☎ 415-759-2690; **rhodyco.com.**

BOUQUETS TO ART Lectures by horticultural experts, works by 100 floral designers, luncheons, and tea service. California Palace of the Legion of Honor. ☎ 415-750-3600; **famsf.org**.

JEWISH MUSIC FESTIVAL Jewish musicians from around the world congregate to perform a wide variety of Jewish musical styles at locations across the city. **jewishmusicfestival.org**.

MACY'S FLOWER SHOW For more than 60 years Macy's has bedecked itself with flowers and made the city more beautiful. Guest speakers and special in-store events make it even better. **macys.com**.

SAN FRANCISCO FLOWER AND GARDEN SHOW 27 gardens, 300 market booths, orchid show, and 75 free seminars. Cow Palace. ☎ 415-684-7278; **sfgardenshow.com**.

SAN FRANCISCO INTERNATIONAL ASIAN AMERICAN FILM FESTIVAL The biggest ever in North America dedicated to the exhibition of Asian American and Asian cinema. AMC Kabuki Theaters. ☎ 415-863-0814; **festival.asianamericanmedia.org**.

★ **ST. PATRICK'S DAY PARADE DOWNTOWN** The Irish have an annual march from Fifth and Market streets to the Embarcadero. ☎ 415-586-4826; **sfstpatricksdayparade.com**.

April

CHERRY BLOSSOM FESTIVAL Taiko drumming, martial arts, Japanese food. A parade from civic center to Japantown's Peace Plaza. Japantown. ☎ 415-563-2313; **nccbf.org**.

GOLDEN GATE PARK BAND For more than 100 years the Golden Gate Park Band has been offering performances in the park. Bring a picnic and the kids if ya got 'em. **golden-gate-park.com**

★ **SAN FRANCISCO INTERNATIONAL FILM FESTIVAL** (April through May) More than a hundred films and videos from around the world bring stars to the city, mostly to Sundance Kabuki in Japantown and the Castro Theatre. ☎ 415-561-5000; **sffs.org**.

May

★ **THE BAY TO BREAKERS FOOTRACE** Come sporting your birthday suit or whatever costume you can muster up and take part in the world's largest footrace. Clothes optional, beer mandatory. The Embarcadero to the Great Highway. ☎ 415-359-2800; **baytobreakers.com**

CARNAVAL San Francisco's version of Mardi Gras turns the Mission District into one of the best street parties and parades in the nation, with Aztec dancers and colorful floats. **carnavalsf.com**.

CINCO DE MAYO CELEBRATION Arts, crafts, and food, as well as a parade to celebrate Mexican independence. Mission District. ☎ 415-647-1533; **sfcincodemayo.com**.

SAN FRANCISCO DECORATOR SHOWCASE   Top Bay Area designers display the latest design innovations at luxurious San Francisco homes. Pacific Heights. ☎ 415-447-3115; **decoratorshowcase.org**.

June

FILLMORE STREET JAZZ FESTIVAL   Three days of food, drink, and hundreds of jazz musicians on Fillmore. **fillmorejazzfestival.com**.

★ **HAIGHT STREET FAIR**   Bring out the tie-dye and lava lamps—the Haight celebrates its roots with arts, crafts, and entertainment. Haight Street. ☎ 415-292-3293; **haightashburystreetfair.org**.

JUNETEENTH FESTIVAL   An annual outdoor event celebrating African American culture. Fillmore Street. ☎ 415-931-2729; **sfjuneteenth.org**.

★ **LESBIAN, GAY, BISEXUAL, TRANSGENDER PRIDE CELEBRATION FESTIVAL AND PARADE**   San Francisco's celebration of lesbian and gay pride. Castro District. ☎ 415-864-0831; **sfpride.org**.

NORTH BEACH FESTIVAL   San Francisco's oldest street fair offers arts, crafts, and live entertainment. Grant Avenue and Green Street. ☎ 415-989-2220; **sfnorthbeach.org**.

SAN FRANCISCO INTERNATIONAL LESBIAN AND GAY FILM FESTIVAL   The second-largest film festival in California showcases more than 100 films and videos from around the world. Castro Theatre and other locations. ☎ 415-703-8650; **frameline.org/festival**.

★ **UNION STREET ECO-URBAN FESTIVAL**   Arts and crafts made of recycled or sustainable materials, food, and music. Union Street. ☎ 800-310-6563; **unionstreetfestival.com**.

July

CABLE CAR BELL-RINGING COMPETITION   Where the cars come to belt out their favorite tune—operators clang out melodies on the cars' bells and compete for top bell-ringer. Fisherman's Wharf. ☎ 415-474-1887; **cablecarmuseum.org**.

FOURTH OF JULY CELEBRATION   It's that childhood favorite, fireworks! Entertainment, food, arts and crafts at Fisherman's Wharf and fireworks over Crissy Fields. ☎ 415-705-5500; **pier39.com**.

JEWISH FILM FESTIVAL   Films from American and international filmmakers showcase Jewish culture. Castro Theatre. ☎ 415-621-0556; **sfjff.org**.

SILENT FILM FESTIVAL   This is cinematic art as history and cultural treasure. At the Castro Theatre. **silentfilm.org**.

August

ACC CRAFT FAIR   The largest juried craft fair on the West Coast features necklaces, stoneware, silk scarves, and quilts. Fort Mason. ☎ 212-274-0634; **craftcouncil.org.**

AFRO SOLO ARTS FESTIVAL Festival commemorating the African American experience through solo performances. Yerba Buena Center for the Arts and other locations. ☎ 415-771-2376; **afrosolo.org.**

GOLDEN GATEWAY TO GEMS Minerals, crystals, and jewelry from all over the world. San Francisco County Fair Building in Golden Gate Park. ☎ 415-564-4230; **sfgms.org.**

NIHONMACHI STREET FAIR Lion dancers, taiko drummers, Japanese arts and crafts, music, food, and children's events. Japantown and Japan Center. ☎ 415-771-9861; **nihonmachistreetfair.org.**

NILES ANTIQUE FAIR AND FLEA MARKET One of the area's biggest annual flea markets brings the world to Niles in Fremont, also home to the Essanay Silent Film Museum and vintage-train rides. **niles.org.**

September

AUTUMN MOON FESTIVAL Multicultural entertainment, traditional lion and dragon dances, Chinese costumes, and children's activities. Grant Avenue between California and Pacific streets. ☎ 415-982-6306; **moonfestival.org.**

FOLSOM STREET FAIR A popular fair with the leather straps and chaps set, it sells kinky collectibles, entertainment, and food. For obvious reasons, it's for adults only! Folsom Street. ☎ 415-861-3247; **folsomstreetfair.com.**

GHIRARDELLI SQUARE CHOCOLATE FESTIVAL A chocolate lover's dream! Sample chocolate treats and more. Ghirardelli Square. ☎ 415-775-5500; **ghirardellisq.com.**

★ **SAN FRANCISCO BLUES FESTIVAL** The oldest blues festival in the country. Great Meadow, Fort Mason. ☎ 415-979-5588; **sfblues.com.**

SAN FRANCISCO FRINGE FESTIVAL Marathon of 260 performances by 50 theater companies in various venues. Downtown. ☎ 415-931-1094; **sffringe.org.**

SAN FRANCISCO SHAKESPEARE FESTIVAL All of Shakespeare's classics. Pack a picnic lunch and your *Cliffs Notes* and enjoy Saturdays and Sundays on several weekends throughout the summer; locals arrive by noon for a seat. Golden Gate Park. ☎ 415-558-0888; **sfshakes.org.**

SAUSALITO ART FESTIVAL A fine-arts festival with more than 20,000 original works of art from around the world. Sausalito. ☎ 415-332-3555; **sausalitoartfestival.org.**

October

FLEET WEEK Every year the U.S. Navy and Marines come to San

Francisco. There are shop tours, parties, and an eardrum-bursting air show by the Blue Angels. **fleetweek.us.**

HARDLY STRICTLY BLUEGRASS Always star-studded yet absolutely free, this epic hootenanny cornucopia takes over the western half of Golden Gate Park for the first weekend in October on six stages and somehow always snags the best weather of the year. Founder Warren Hellman offers a loaded weekend of live country bands, plus his own Wronglers, along with diva Emmylou Harris and big names such as Elvis Costello and the Chieftains. Bring something to sit on, sunscreen, and a sweater—and watch out for those spiked brownies! **strictlybluegrass.com.**

INTERNATIONAL VINTAGE POSTER FAIR The oldest and largest vintage poster fair in the world. Fort Mason Center. ☎ 800-856-8069; **poster fair.com.**

ITALIAN HERITAGE PARADE AND FESTIVAL A commemoration of the city's Italian heritage with a parade through North Beach. North Beach, Fisherman's Wharf. ☎ 415-703-9888; **sfcolumbusday.org/parade.**

SAN FRANCISCO JAZZ FESTIVAL Features local, national, and international jazz artists at locations throughout the city. ☎ 866-920-5299; **sfjazz.org.**

November–December

CHRISTMAS AT SEA Caroling, storytelling, hot cider, cookies, children's crafts, and Santa. Hyde Street Pier. ☎ 415-561-6662.

DIA DE LOS MUERTOS The day after Halloween offers a very hungover yet enjoyable walk to Garfield Park in the Mission District, where altars toast the departed in traditional Latino style. **dayofthedeadsf.org.**

GHIRARDELLI SQUARE ANNUAL TREE LIGHTING CEREMONY Deck the 35-foot Christmas tree with cheer and good tidings. Ghirardelli Square. ☎ 415-775-5500; **ghirardellisq.com.**

GUERNEVILLE HOLIDAY PARADE OF LIGHTS Cute and incurably friendly, this small Russian River town offers a pre-Christmas procession, embracing everyone from poodles to vintage cars and more. **russianriver.com.**

SAN FRANCISCO BALLET'S *NUTCRACKER* America's oldest ballet company, regarded as one of its finest, presented the first American *Nutcracker* right here in the same spot and ritually hosts Tchaikovsky's beloved family classic every December. War Memorial Opera House. ☎ 415-865-2000; **sfballet.org.**

SAN FRANCISCO INTERNATIONAL AUTO SHOW The latest and greatest in automobiles. Moscone Center. ☎ 415-331-4406; **sfautoshow.com.**

PART TWO

ACCOMMODATIONS

■ DECIDING WHERE *to* STAY

SAN FRANCISCO HOTELS GENERALLY OFFER GOOD VALUE, interesting Pacific urban architecture and decor, and remarkably diverse amenities. As a generalization, service at San Francisco hotels, if not quirky, is somewhat differently defined. At the bar your drinks may not come any faster than they would at home, and your room-service breakfast may arrive cold. But ask your bartender or food server, "What should I do next?" and you're in for a spirited and opinionated discourse on the city.

unofficial **TIP**
Nowadays you can check out dozens or even hundreds of independent reviews that give you the unvarnished truth on every hotel online at **tripadvisor.com, sanfrancisco. travelontheway.com,** or **yelp.com.** Dig in deep!

The idea that information is the most valuable service a hotel can offer is novel in most cities. In San Francisco, however, hotels that don't even have room service or a bar may publish their own guidebooks and pamphlets on attractions, or they may have 24-hour concierge service. With 32 percent of San Francisco guest rooms scoring four stars or higher, the quality of guest rooms is exceptionally high. Plus, guest rooms in the Bay Area are reasonably priced. On average, rooms here are less expensive than rooms in New York City, Washington, D.C., Chicago, and other comparable destinations. This combination of high-quality rooms and reasonable rates makes San Francisco attractive for both leisure and business travelers.

Hotels dot the San Francisco peninsula and Bay Area suburbs, so you need not be more than ten minutes from tourist attractions or businesses. As in most cities, guest-room rates are higher in more desirable areas. The steepest rates are generally found within walking distance of Union Square, and some of the best hotel bargains are located in less fashionable neighborhoods. Of these, many have excellent on-premises security and may be of particular interest to those who plan to tour by car.

A distinctive characteristic of San Francisco's hotel scene is an artful marriage of historic architecture with modern interior design. Some of the city's hotels are modern, but the vast majority are housed in older buildings. Historic hotel buildings include some of the world's oldest skyscrapers and quaint Victorian and Edwardian mansions.

Step inside the nicer San Francisco hotels, and you'll find some of the more inventive interior design you'll encounter in this country. Though palatial room size is not characteristic of San Francisco hotels, utilizing square footage wisely is. In both common areas and guest rooms, the *Unofficial Guide* hotel inspectors were impressed by how creatively form and function are blended. Several of San Francisco's nicest hotels have such ergonomically exact guest rooms that we were reminded of Tokyo. The comfortable integration of modern technology, such as microwaves and coffeemakers, is noteworthy in guest rooms that are sometimes smaller than 200 square feet.

In San Francisco, you are more likely to find a guest room suited to your individual needs than in destinations where hotel homogeneity rules. San Francisco hotels market and cater to diverse groups, and their amenities and ambience reflect this trend. While some properties target business or leisure travelers, others have more specific markets. These include opera fans at the **Inn at the Opera,** wine lovers at many Bay Area hotels, and spa junkies at others. Movie lovers will want to check out **Hotel Bijou,** which offers a small movie theater showing complimentary double features daily. The outwardly unassuming **Hotel des Arts** is also an art gallery in which most of the works are for sale.

Hotel decor runs the gamut of historical and modern styles. Classic opulence—signaled by airplane hangar–sized lobbies, chandeliers the size of canoes, and richly textured upholstery—can be found at hotels such as the **Fairmont** and the **Westin St. Francis.** There is also an emphasis on modern interior decorating. Using elements of Art Deco, Art Nouveau, and modern art, the finished interior in the modern design style contains whimsically curved lines, bold patterns, and metallic and bright colors.

A few hotel chains have recently produced some unique offerings in the San Francisco accommodation ring. The Joie de Vivre group specializes in buying fixer-uppers and has created some prized boutique hotels in California. Each one oozes its own distinct character. Most are small and intimate. Some contain excellent little restaurants, popular bars, or even dance clubs. The first of the group was the **Phoenix,** once a run-down Tenderloin dive surrounded by hookers and drug dealers. Now it's the premier rock-and-roll hotel, where the better touring bands stay. The **Best Western Americania Hotel** in SoMa, with its midcentury decor, offers light and bright surroundings, and for Japanese pop-culture inspiration during your stay, there's **Best Western Hotel Tomo!** in Japantown. All offer inexpensive rates in unique settings.

As hip boutique hotels become more appealing, there are more from which to choose, such as the Kimpton group's **Hotel Triton,** with suites designed by Jerry Garcia and Kathy Griffin. Triton offers special packages including an Eco Package that offers Muni passes and water bottles, bring-your-pet specials, and a Wellness Package with an in-room movie and bamboo wind chimes. The romantic **Hotel Monaco** is itself a French-inspired work of art, using lush textures and deep colors, including red, gold, and green, to create a glamorous look.

Living up to the playful, eccentric, and stylish reputation of San Francisco, the Personality Hotels group provides kitschy, hip and cool, or plain sophisticated right-in-the-center-of-the-action accommodations. Located in the heart of the theater district, **Hotel Diva,** with its black-and-cobalt color scheme and metal accents, offers packages such as Cougars with Personality (stay in the Cougar's Den and receive an animal-print thong and a road map to the city's hottest cougar bars!). They may be hip, but standards are high too: The whimsical **Hotel Vertigo,** named for its role in the Hitchcock classic, offers touches usually enjoyed only in more expensive hotels. Visit **jdvhotels.com, kimptonhotels.com,** and **personalityhotels.com** for more information.

A FEW OTHER NOTEWORTHY PROPERTIES

SAN FRANCISCO IS HOME TO A FEW NOTEWORTHY properties that we have not ranked and rated because their clientele is so narrowly defined. Those wishing to relive the "summer of love" may want to stay at the **Red Victorian Bed, Breakfast, and Art Center.** Owned and run by veteran flower child Sami Sunchild, the bed-and-breakfast is in the heart of the historic Haight-Ashbury neighborhood. Each of its 18 rooms is decorated with a different theme, ranging from the Summer of Love room and the Rainbow room to the Japanese Tea Garden room and the Butterfly room. Room rates at the Red Victorian Bed, Breakfast, and Art Center range from $89 to $229. For more information, call ☎ 415-864-1978 or visit **redvic.com.**

If you're looking for a bed-and-breakfast that touts itself as "home away from home," you might try the **Hayes Valley Inn,** located in the Civic Center area at Gough and Hayes streets. The opera and symphony are nearby, and neighboring eateries and bars sparkle. Rates range from $76 to $105, with all rooms having shared baths in the hall. Contact ☎ 800-930-7999 or visit **hayesvalleyinn.com** for information and reservations.

Most of the hotels and bed-and-breakfasts in the Castro District are places where everyone will feel comfortable, though they are particularly convenient for gay travelers wishing to explore shops and clubs in the Castro area.

Edward II Inn and Suites offers two of its guest rooms equipped with private entrances in a European-style inn and, like an increasing number of properties, has a strict nonsmoking policy. Call ☎ 415-922-3000 or visit **edwardii.com.**

By now you may be wondering, "Can't I just get a normal room in San Francisco?" The answer, of course, is yes. For conservative tastes, traditional hotel rooms are easy to find. But you will need to ask for what you want. In San Francisco, the difference between name-brand corporate hotels and freestanding, proprietary, or boutique hotels is not clearly delineated. The reason is that many of the corporate hotels in San Francisco occupy older buildings that once housed freestanding and family-owned hotels. Don't expect cookie-cutter guest rooms just because you're staying at your favorite name-brand hotel. If you prefer to stay in a rectangular room with the bathroom adjacent to the front door, two double beds, and a picture window opposite the front door, be sure to shop around.

unofficial **TIP**
If you are a smoker, be aware that most properties in San Francisco are nonsmoking. Be wise and call ahead or consult the hotel's Web site.

GETTING *a* GOOD DEAL *on a* ROOM

MONEY-SAVING TIPS

TO SAY THAT YOU RECEIVE GOOD VALUE for your lodging dollar in San Francisco doesn't mean that San Francisco is cheap. If you are looking for ways to save money beyond getting a discount on the price of a room, consider the following.

1. Stay in a less-than-fashionable neighborhood in less pristine surroundings or at a budget motel in the suburbs. One of the motels along the Lombard Street strip or in the Sunset District may be half the cost. The most expensive areas are Union Square and Nob Hill.

2. Seek a suite that includes a kitchen. Several hotels offer this option; suites can accommodate four or more people and help save on restaurant bills.

3. Stay at the worst room at a good hotel instead of the best one at a lesser hotel. Ask for the smallest room on the lowest floor with the worst view. The cost differential can be considerable, although the rest of the hotel services, amenities, and public rooms remain the same. You're getting the biggest bang for your buck.

4. If you eat like a local rather than a tourist, you will save money. Avoid room service and minibars. Bring food up from groceries, delis, or convenience stores. Or make like a resident and have a restaurant deliver (allowed at some hotels, frowned on at others—check first). Neighborhood restaurants, especially the ethnics, are good and reasonable.

5. Skip the in-house movies. Bring a book. Better yet, walk down the street to see dramatic stories and sights beyond fiction.

6. Try a bed-and-breakfast. They are plentiful in the Bay Area and range from accommodations in houseboats and Victorian mansions to Junior's room when he's away at college. For information and options, contact Bed & Breakfast California at **bedandbreakfast.com.**

7. You'll be agreeably surprised by competitive rates at smaller hotels. The Grant Plaza opposite the Chinatown gateway has an antique stained glass skylight and wins bang-for-your-buck awards, while the Cornell Hotel de France (☎ 800-232-9698; **cornellhotel.com**) has the venerable French Jeanne d'Arc bistro in its basement—and those are just two examples. Rooms are smaller but value compensates.

8. Fun affordable hostels abound for the rough and ready. Backpackers and students opt for the Adelaide Hostel off Union Square (☎ 877-359-1915; **adelaidehostel.com**), Green Tortoise in North Beach (☎ 800-867-8647; **greentortoisehostel.com**), or the newer Elements in the Mission (☎ 866-327-8407; **elementssf.com**). Check out the Green Tortoise's fun and funky buses to Las Vegas and national parks, too.

GETTING A DISCOUNTED RATE

BECAUSE SAN FRANCISCO IS POPULAR year-round, room rates tend not to fluctuate much. Even so, the market is highly competitive, and there are deals for the smart shopper. Check out deals through ads, agents, special events, weekend and convention deals, frequent-mileage clubs, automobile or other travel clubs, senior rates (some with age requirements as low as 50 years), military or government discounts, corporate or shareholder rates, packages, long-stay rates (usually at least five nights), and travel industry rates. Some hotels might even give lower rates if you are visiting because of bereavement or medical problems. You can also try some of the following.

Surf the Net

Check out the Internet and book with your airline ticket. Last-minute bargains are often available online. You can judge comparative value by seeing a listing of hotels—what they offer, where they are located, and what they charge.

Special Weekend Rates

Most hotels that cater to business, government, and convention travelers offer special weekend discount rates that range from 15 percent to 40 percent below normal weekday rates. Find out about weekend specials by calling individual hotels or consulting your travel agent.

Getting Corporate Rates

Many hotels offer discounted corporate rates (5 percent to 20 percent off rack rate). Usually you do not need to work for a large company or have a special relationship with the hotel to obtain these rates. Simply call the hotel of your choice and ask for their corporate rates. Many hotels will guarantee you the discounted rate on the phone when you make your reservation. Others may make the rate conditional on providing some sort of verification, for instance a company credit card or business card upon check-in. Generally the screening is not rigorous.

Preferred Rates

If you cannot book the hotel of your choice through a half-price program (see below), you or your travel agent may have to search for a smaller discount, often called a preferred rate. A preferred rate might be a discount available to travel agents to stimulate their booking activity or a discount initiated to attract a certain class of traveler. Most preferred rates are promoted through travel industry publications and are accessible only through an agent.

We recommend sounding out your travel agent about possible deals. Be aware, however, that the rates shown on agents' reservations systems are not always the lowest rates obtainable. Zero in on a couple of hotels that fill your needs in terms of location and quality. Again, there are certain specials that hotel reps will disclose only to agents. Travel agents also come in handy when the hotel you want is supposedly booked. A personal appeal from your agent to the hotel's director of sales and marketing will get you a room more than half the time.

Half-price Programs

Larger discounts on rooms (35 percent to 60 percent) in San Francisco or anywhere else are available through half-price hotel programs, often called travel clubs. Program operators contract with an individual hotel to provide rooms at deep discounts, usually 50 percent off, on a space available basis. Space available in practice means that you can reserve a room at the discounted rate whenever the hotel expects to be at less than 80 percent occupancy. A little calendar sleuthing to help you avoid special events and citywide conventions will increase your chances of choosing a time when these discounts are available.

Most half-price programs charge an annual membership fee or directory subscription rate of $25 to $125. Once you're enrolled, you'll receive a membership card and a directory listing participating hotels. You will notice immediately that there are many restrictions and exceptions. Some hotels, for instance, black out certain dates or times of year. Others may offer the discount only on certain days of the week or require you to stay a certain number of nights. Still others may offer a much smaller discount than 50 percent off the rack rate.

Programs specialize in domestic travel, international travel, or both. More established operators offer members between 1,000 and 4,000 hotels in the United States from which to choose. All of the programs have a heavy concentration of hotels in California and Florida, and most have a very limited selection of participating properties in New York or Boston. Offerings in other cities and regions of the United States vary considerably. The programs with the largest selections of San Francisco hotels are Encore, ITC-50, Great American Traveler, Quest, Privilege Card International, and Entertainment Publications. Each of these programs lists between 25 (Great American Traveler) and more than 60 (Encore) hotels in the greater San Francisco area.

Encore	☎ 800-444-9800; preferredtraveller.com
Entertainment Publications	☎ 800-445-4137; entertainment.com
Great American Traveler	☎ 800-548-2812
ITC-50	☎ 800-513-7000; itc50online.com
Privilege Card International	☎ 800-236-9732; privilegecard.com
Quest	☎ 800-742-3543; questprograms.com

One problem with half-price programs is that not all hotels offer a full 50 percent discount. Another slippery problem is the base rate against which the discount is applied. Some hotels figure the discount on an exaggerated rack rate that nobody would ever have to pay. A few participating hotels may deduct the discount from a supposed "superior" or "upgraded" room rate, even though the room you get is the hotel's standard accommodation. Though hard to pin down, the majority of participating properties base discounts on the rate published in the *Hotel & Travel Index* (a quarterly travel agents' reference) and work within the spirit of their agreement with the program operator. As a rule, if you travel several times a year, your room-rate savings will easily compensate you for program membership fees.

A noteworthy addendum: Deeply discounted rooms through half-price programs are not commissionable to travel agents. If you travel frequently, however, and use your agent often, he or she will probably do your legwork, lack of commission notwithstanding.

Wholesalers, Consolidators, and Reservation Services

If you do not want to join a program or buy a discount directory, you can take advantage of the services of a wholesaler or consolidator. Wholesalers and consolidators buy rooms or options on rooms (room blocks) from hotels at a low, negotiated rate. Then they resell the rooms at a profit through travel agents or tour operators, or directly to the public. Most wholesalers and consolidators have a provision for returning unsold rooms to participating hotels, but if they return rooms unsold, the hotel may not make as many rooms available to them the next time around. Thus wholesalers and consolidators often offer rooms at bargain rates, anywhere from 15 percent to 50 percent off rack, occasionally sacrificing their profit margins in the process, to avoid returning the rooms to the hotel unsold.

When wholesalers and consolidators deal directly with the public, they frequently represent themselves as reservation services. When you call, you can ask for a rate quote for a particular hotel or ask for their best available deal in the area you prefer. If there is a maximum amount you are willing to pay, say so. Chances are that the service will find something that will work for you, even if they have to shave a dollar or two off their own profit. A list of services that sell rooms in San Francisco follows.

Accommodations Express	☎ 800-444-7666; accommodationsexpress.com
Central Reservations Service	☎ 800-548-3311; crshotels.com
Hotel Locators	☎ 800-576-0003; hotellocators.com
Hotel Reservations Network	☎ 800-964-6835; hoteldiscounts.com
Quikbook	☎ 800-789-9887; quikbook.com
San Francisco Reservations	☎ 800-677-1570; hotelres.com

The discount available (if any) from a reservation service depends on whether the service functions as a consolidator or a wholesaler. Consolidators are strictly sales agents who do not own or control the room inventory they are trying to sell. Their discounts are determined by the hotels with rooms to fill and vary enormously, depending on how desperate the hotel is to unload the rooms. When you deal with a room reservation service that operates as a consolidator, you pay for your room as usual when you check out of the hotel.

Wholesalers have longstanding contracts with hotels; this allows the wholesaler to purchase rooms at an established deep discount. Some wholesalers hold purchase options on blocks of rooms, while others actually pay for rooms and own the inventory. Because a wholesaler controls the room inventory, it can offer whatever discount it pleases consistent with current demand. In practice, most wholesaler-reservation-service discounts fall in the 10 percent to 40 percent range. When you reserve a room with a reservation service that operates as a wholesaler, you must usually pay for your entire stay in advance with your credit card. The service then sends you a written confirmation and usually a voucher (indicating prepayment) for you to present at the hotel.

Our experience has been that the reservation services are more useful for finding rooms when availability is scarce than for obtaining deep discounts. When we called the hotels ourselves, we were often able to beat the reservation services' rates when rooms were generally available. When the city was booked, however, and we could not find a room by calling the hotels ourselves, the reservation services could almost always get us a room at a fair price.

HOW TO EVALUATE A TRAVEL PACKAGE

HUNDREDS OF SAN FRANCISCO package vacations are offered to the public each year. Packages should be a win-win proposition for both the buyer and the seller. The buyer has to make only one online booking or one phone call and deal with a single salesperson to set up the whole vacation—transportation, rental car, lodging, meals, attraction admissions, and even golf and tennis. The seller, likewise, has to deal with the buyer only once, eliminating the need for separate sales, confirmations, and billing. In addition to streamlining sales, processing, and administration, some packagers also buy airfares in bulk on contract like a broker playing the commodities market. Buying a large number of airfares in advance allows the packager to buy them at a significant savings from posted fares. The same practice is applied to hotel rooms. Because selling vacation packages is an efficient way of doing business, and because the packager can often buy individual package components (airfare, lodging, and the like) in bulk at a discount, savings in operating expenses realized by the seller are sometimes passed on to the buyer. This means that, in addition to convenience, the package is an exceptional value. In any event, that's the way it is supposed to work.

In practice, all too often the seller cashes in on discounts and passes none on to the buyer. In some instances, packages are loaded with extras that cost the packager next to nothing but inflate the retail price sky-high. As you would expect, the savings to be passed along to customers do not materialize.

When considering a package, you should choose one that includes features you are sure to use; whether you use all the features or not, you will most certainly pay for them. Second, if cost is of greater concern than convenience, make a few phone calls and see what the package would cost if you booked its individual components (airfare, rental car, lodging, and such) on your own. If the package price is less than the à la carte cost, the package is a good deal. If the costs are about the same, the package is probably worth buying just for the convenience.

If your package includes a choice of rental car or airport transfers (transportation to and from the airport), take the car if your hotel offers free (or at least affordable) parking. Take the transfers if you plan to spend your time in the area from Nob Hill and Union Square down to San Francisco Bay. If you want to run around town or go on excursions outside the city, take the car. And if you take the car, be sure to ask if the package includes free parking at your hotel.

Tour operators, of course, prefer to sell you a whole vacation package. When business is slow, however, they will often agree to sell you just the lodging component of the package, usually at a nicely discounted rate.

Hotel-Sponsored Packages

Hotels, like tour operators, frequently offer packages. Usually land only (that is, no airfare included), the hotel packages are sometimes exceptional deals. Promotion of hotel specials tends to be limited to the hotel's primary markets, which for most properties is California, Washington, Oregon, Arizona, Hawaii, Nevada, Texas, Illinois, and New York. If you live in other parts of the country, you can take advantage of the packages but probably will not see them advertised locally. An important point regarding hotel specials is that the hotel reservationists do not usually inform you of existing specials or offer them to you. In other words, you have to ask.

HELPING YOUR TRAVEL AGENT HELP YOU

When you call your travel agent, ask if he or she has been to San Francisco. If the answer is no, be prepared to give your travel agent some direction. Do not accept any recommendations at face value. Check out the location and rates of each suggested hotel, and make sure the hotel is suited to your itinerary.

Because some travel agents are unfamiliar with San Francisco, your agent may try to plug you into a tour operator's preset package. This essentially allows the travel agent to set up your whole trip with a single phone call and still collect an 8 percent to 10 percent commission. The problem with this scenario is that most agents will place 90 percent of their San Francisco business with only one or two wholesalers or tour operators. In other words, it's the line of least resistance for them and leaves you with very little choice.

Travel agents will often use wholesalers who run packages in conjunction with airlines, such as Delta Vacations or American Airlines' Fly-Away Vacations. Because of the wholesaler's exclusive relationship with the carrier, these trips are easy for travel agents to book. However, they will probably be more expensive than a package offered by a high-volume wholesaler who works with a number of airlines in a primary San Francisco market.

To help your travel agent get you the best possible deal, do the following:

1. Determine where you want to stay in San Francisco, and, if possible, choose a specific hotel. This can be accomplished by reviewing the hotel information in this guide and by calling hotels that interest you.
2. Check out the hotel deals and package vacations advertised online or in the Sunday travel sections of the *Los Angeles Times, San Francisco Chronicle,* or *Dallas Morning News* newspapers. See if you can find specials that fit your plans and include a hotel you like.
3. Call the hotels or tour operators whose ads you have collected. Ask any questions you have about their packages, but do not book your trip with them directly.

4. Tell your travel agent about the deals you find and ask if he or she can get you something better. The deals in the paper will serve as a benchmark against which to compare alternatives your agent proposes.

5. Choose from the options that you and your travel agent uncover. No matter which option you select, have your agent book it. Even if you go with one of the packages you found, it will probably be commissionable (at no additional cost to you) and will provide the agent some return on the time invested on your behalf. Also, as a travel professional, your agent should be able to verify the quality and integrity of the deal.

IF YOU MAKE YOUR OWN RESERVATION

AS YOU POKE AROUND TRYING TO FIND A GOOD DEAL, there are several inside tips to keep in mind. First, always call the specific hotel rather than the hotel chain's national, toll-free number. Quite often, the reservationists at the national number are unaware of local specials. Always ask about specials before you inquire about corporate rates. Do not be reluctant to bargain. If you are buying a hotel's weekend package, for example, and want to extend your stay into the following week, you can often obtain at least the corporate rate for the extra days. Do your bargaining, however, before you check in, preferably when you make your reservations. Use our list of hotel and motel national toll-free numbers to find the local numbers, or to investigate chain-wide promotions.

HOTELS AND MOTELS:
Rated and Ranked

WHAT'S IN A ROOM?

EXCEPT FOR CLEANLINESS, STATE OF REPAIR, and decor, most travelers do not pay much attention to hotel rooms. There is, of course, a discernible standard of quality and luxury that differentiates Motel 6 from Holiday Inn, Holiday Inn from Marriott, and so on. In general, however, hotel guests fail to appreciate the fact that some rooms are better engineered than others.

Contrary to what you might suppose, designing a hotel room is (or should be) more complex than picking a bedspread to match the carpet and drapes. Making the room usable to its occupants is an art, a planning discipline that combines form and function.

Decor and taste are important, certainly. No one wants to spend several days in a room that is dated, garish, or even ugly. But beyond the decor, several variables determine how livable a hotel room is. In San Francisco, for example, we have seen some beautifully appointed rooms that are simply not well designed for human habitation. The next time you stay in a hotel, pay attention to the details and design

Hotel and Motel Toll-free Numbers

Best Western   ☎ 800-528-1234 U.S. and Canada | ☎ 800-528-2222 TDD

Comfort Inn   ☎ 800-228-5150 U.S. and Canada | ☎ 800-228-3323 TDD

Courtyard by Marriott   ☎ 888-236-2427 U.S. | ☎ 800-228-7014 TDD

Days Inn   ☎ 800-325-2525 U.S. | ☎ 800-329-7155 TDD

Doubletree Hotels   ☎ 800-222-8733 U.S. and Canada |
☎ 800-451-4833 TDD

Econo Lodge   ☎ 877-424-6423 U.S. | ☎ 800-228-3323 TDD

Embassy Suites   ☎ 800-362-2779 U.S. and Canada | ☎ 800-528-9898 TDD

Hampton Inn   ☎ 800-426-7866 U.S. and Canada | ☎ 800-451-4833 TDD

Hilton   ☎ 800-445-8667 U.S. and Canada | ☎ 800-368-1133 TDD

Holiday Inn   ☎ 800-465-4329 U.S. and Canada | ☎ 800-238-5544 TDD

Howard Johnson   ☎ 800-654-2000 U.S. and Canada

Hyatt   ☎ 800-233-1234 U.S. and Canada | ☎ 800-228-9548 TDD

Marriott   ☎ 888-236-2427 U.S. and Canada | ☎ 800-228-7014 TDD

Quality Inn   ☎ 800-228-5151 U.S. and Canada | ☎ 800-228-3323 TDD

Radisson   ☎ 800-333-3333 U.S. and Canada | ☎ 800-906-2200 TDD

Ramada Inn   ☎ 800-272-6232 U.S. | ☎ 800-228-3232 TDD

Renaissance Hotels and Resorts   ☎ 800-468-3571 U.S. and Canada

Ritz-Carlton   ☎ 800-241-3333 U.S.

Sheraton   ☎ 800-325-3535 U.S. and Canada | ☎ 800-329-7155 TDD

Wyndham   ☎ 800-996-3426 U.S.

elements of your room. Even more than decor, these will make you feel comfortable and at home.

It takes the *Unofficial Guide* researchers quite a while to inspect a hotel room. Here are a few things we check and suggest you check too.

ROOM SIZE While some smaller rooms are cozy and well designed, a large and uncluttered room is generally preferable, especially for a stay of more than three days.

TEMPERATURE CONTROL, VENTILATION, AND ODOR The guest should be able to control the temperature of the room. The best system, because it's so quiet, is central heating and air-conditioning controlled by the room's own thermostat. The next best system is a room module heater and air-conditioner, preferably controlled by an automatic thermostat but usually by manually operated button controls.

The worst system is central heating and air without any sort of room thermostat or guest control.

The vast majority of hotel rooms have windows or balcony doors that have been permanently sealed. Though there are some legitimate safety and liability issues involved, we prefer windows and balcony doors that can be opened to admit fresh air. Hotel rooms should be odor free and smoke free, and they should not feel stuffy or damp.

ROOM SECURITY Better rooms have locks that require a plastic card instead of the traditional lock and key. Card-and-slot systems allow the hotel to change the combination or entry code of the lock with each new guest. A burglar who has somehow acquired a conventional room key can afford to wait until the situation is right before using the key to gain access. Not so with a card-and-slot system. Though larger hotels and hotel chains with lock-and-key systems usually rotate their locks once each year, they remain vulnerable to hotel thieves much of the time. Many smaller or independent properties rarely rotate their locks.

In addition to the entry lock system, the door should have a deadbolt and preferably a chain that can be locked from the inside as well. A chain by itself is not sufficient. Doors should also have a peephole. Windows and balcony doors should have secure locks.

SAFETY Every room should have a fire or smoke alarm, clear fire instructions, and preferably a sprinkler system. Bathtubs should have a nonskid surface, and shower stalls should have doors that open outward or slide side to side. Bathroom electrical outlets should be high on the wall and not too close to the sink. Balconies should have sturdy, high rails.

NOISE Most travelers have been kept awake by the television, partying, or amorous activities of people in the next room, or by traffic on the street outside. Better hotels are designed with noise control in mind. Wall and ceiling constructions are substantial, effectively screening routine noise. Carpets and drapes, in addition to being decorative, also absorb and muffle sounds. Mattresses mounted on stable platforms or sturdy bed frames do not squeak even when challenged by the most acrobatic lovers. Televisions are enclosed in cabinets and have volume governors so that they rarely disturb guests in adjacent rooms.

In better hotels, the air-conditioning and heating system is well maintained and operates without noise or vibration. Likewise, plumbing is quiet and positioned away from the sleeping area. Doors to the hall and adjoining rooms are thick and well fitted to better block out noise.

If you are easily disturbed by noise, ask for a room on a higher floor, off of main thoroughfares, and away from elevators and vending machines.

DARKNESS CONTROL Ever been in a hotel room where the curtains would not quite meet in the middle? Thick, lined curtains that close completely in the center and extend beyond the edges of the window or doorframe are required. In a well-planned room, the curtains, shades, or blinds should almost totally block light at any time of day.

LIGHTING Poor lighting is a common problem in American hotel rooms. The lighting is usually adequate for dressing, relaxing, or watching television, but not for reading or working. Lighting needs to be bright over tables and desks and beside couches and easy chairs. Since so many people read in bed, there should be a separate light for each person. A room with two queen beds should have individual lights for four people. Better bedside reading lights illuminate a small area, so if one person wants to sleep and another wants to read, the sleeper will not be bothered by the light. The worst situation by far is a single lamp on a table between beds. In each bed, only the person next to the lamp has sufficient light to read. This deficiency is often compounded by weak lightbulbs.

In addition, closet areas should be well lit, and there should be a switch near the door that turns on room lights when you enter. A desirable but seldom-seen feature is a bedside console that allows a guest to control all or most lights in the room from bed.

FURNISHINGS At a bare minimum, the bed(s) should be firm. Pillows should be made with non-allergenic fillers, and a blanket should be provided in addition to the sheets and a spread. Bedclothes should be laundered with fabric softener and changed daily. Better hotels usually provide extra blankets and pillows in the room or on request, and they sometimes place a second top sheet between the blanket and spread.

There should be a dresser large enough to hold clothes for two people during a five-day stay. A small table with two chairs, or a desk with a chair, should be provided. The room should be equipped with a luggage rack and a three-quarter- to full-length mirror.

The television should be cable-connected; ideally, it should have a volume governor and a remote control. It should be mounted on a swivel base and preferably enclosed in a cabinet. Local channels should be posted on the set, and a local TV program guide should be supplied. The telephone should be touch-tone and conveniently situated for bedside use, and it should have on or near it clear dialing instructions and a rate card. Local White and Yellow Pages should be provided. Better hotels install phones in the bathroom and equip room phones with long cords.

Well-designed hotel rooms usually have a plush armchair or a sleeper sofa for lounging and reading. Better headboards are padded for comfortable reading in bed, and there should be a nightstand or table on each side of the bed(s). Nice extras in any hotel room include a small refrigerator, a digital alarm clock, and a coffeemaker.

BATHROOM Two sinks are better than one, and you cannot have too much counter space. A sink outside the bath is a great convenience when one person bathes as another dresses. Better bathrooms have a tub and shower with a nonslip bottom. Tub and shower controls should be easy to operate. Adjustable showerheads are preferred. The bath needs to be well lit and should have an exhaust fan and a guest-controlled bathroom heater. Towels and washcloths should be large, soft, fluffy, and generously supplied. There should be an electrical outlet for each sink, conveniently and safely placed.

Complimentary shampoo, conditioner, and lotion are a plus, as are robes and bathmats. Better hotels supply tissues and extra toilet paper in the bathrooms. Luxurious baths feature a phone, a hair dryer, and sometimes a small television or even a Jacuzzi.

VENDING Complimentary ice and a drink machine should be located on each floor. Welcome additions include a snack machine and a sundries (combs, toothpaste) machine. The latter are seldom found in large hotels that have restaurants and shops.

ROOM RATINGS

TO DISTINGUISH PROPERTIES according to quality, tastefulness, state of repair, cleanliness, and size of standard rooms, we have grouped the hotels and motels into classifications denoted by stars. Star ratings in this guide apply to San Francisco–area properties only and do not necessarily correspond to ratings awarded by Mobil, AAA, or other travel critics. Because stars carry little weight when awarded in the absence of commonly recognized standards of comparison, we have linked our ratings to expected levels of quality established by specific American hotel corporations.

★★★★★	Superior	*Tasteful and luxurious by any standard*
★★★★	Extremely Nice	*What you would expect at a Hyatt Regency or Marriott*
★★★	Nice	*Holiday Inn or comparable quality*
★★	Adequate	*Clean, comfortable, and functional without frills— like a Motel 6*
★	Budget	*Spartan, not aesthetically pleasing, but clean*

Star ratings apply to room quality only and describe the property's standard accommodations. For most hotels and motels, a standard accommodation is a hotel room with either one king bed or two queen beds. In an all-suite property, the standard accommodation is either a one- or two-room suite. In addition to standard accommodations, many hotels offer luxury rooms and special suites that are not rated in this guide. Star ratings for rooms are assigned without regard to whether a property has restaurant(s), recreational facilities, entertainment, or other extras.

In addition to stars (which delineate broad categories), we also employ a numerical rating system. Our rating scale is 0 to 100, with 100 as the best possible rating. Numerical ratings are presented to show the difference we perceive between one property and another. For instance, rooms at the **Fairmont Hotel,** the **Hotel Monaco,** and the **Westin St. Francis** are all rated as four-and-a-half stars (4.5). In the supplemental numerical ratings, the Fairmont Hotel is rated a 95, the Hotel Monaco is rated a 94, and the Westin St. Francis is a 91. This means that within the four-and-a-half-star category, the Fairmont Hotel and Hotel Monaco are comparable, and both have slightly nicer rooms than the Westin St. Francis.

The location column identifies the greater San Francisco area where you will find a particular property.

HOW THE HOTELS COMPARE

COST ESTIMATES ARE BASED ON the hotel's published rack rates for standard rooms. Each "$" represents $50. Thus a cost symbol of "$$$" means that a room (or suite) at that hotel will cost about $150 a night.

Below is a hit parade of the nicest rooms in town. We've focused strictly on room quality and have excluded any consideration of location, services, recreation, or amenities. In some instances, a one- or two-room suite can be had for the same price or less than that of a hotel room.

If you use subsequent editions of this guide, you will notice that many of the ratings and rankings change. In addition to the inclusion of new properties, these changes also consider renovations or improved maintenance and housekeeping. A failure to properly maintain guest rooms or a lapse in housekeeping standards can affect the ratings negatively. Finally, before you begin to shop for a hotel, take a hard look at this letter we received from a couple in Hot Springs, Arkansas:

> We cancelled our room reservations to follow the advice in your book and reserved a hotel room highly ranked by the Unofficial Guide. We wanted inexpensive, but clean and cheerful. We got inexpensive, but [also] dirty, grim, and depressing. I really felt disappointed in your advice and the room. It was the pits. That was the one real piece of information I needed from your book! The room spoiled the holiday for me aside from our touring.

Needless to say, this letter was as unsettling to us as the bad room was to our reader. Our integrity as travel journalists, after all, is based on the quality of the information we give our readers. Even with the best of intentions and the most conscientious research, however, we cannot inspect every room in every hotel. What we do, in statistical terms, is take a sample. We check out several rooms selected at random

San Francisco Hotels by Neighborhood

NOB HILL
Fairmont Hotel
Huntington Hotel
Mark Hopkins Inter-
  Continental
Ritz-Carlton
Stanford Court
Renaissance Hotel

CIVIC CENTER
Best Western Hotel
  Tomo
Hotel Carlton
Hotel Kabuki
Hotel Majestic
Inn at the Opera
The Jackson Court
Phoenix Hotel
Queen Anne Hotel

UNION SQUARE
Andrews Hotel
Beresford Arms
Campton Place Hotel
Clift Hotel
Cornell Hotel de France
The Donatello
Fitzgerald Hotel
Galleria Park Hotel
Grand Hyatt San
  Francisco
Grant Plaza
Handlery Union Square
  Hotel
Hilton San Francisco
Hotel Abri
Hotel Adagio
Hotel Beresford
Hotel Bijou
Hotel des Arts
Hotel Diva

Hotel Frank
Hotel Monaco
Hotel Nikko
Hotel Rex
Hotel Triton
Hotel Union Square
Hotel Vertigo
Inn at Union Square
JW Marriott Union
  Square
Kensington Park Hotel
King George Hotel
Larkspur Hotel
Nob Hill Lambourne
Petite Auberge
Prescott Hotel
Renaissance Parc Fifty
  Five
San Francisco Marriott
  Union Square
Serrano Hotel
Sir Francis Drake Hotel
Villa Florence
Warwick Regis Hotel
Westin St. Francis
White Swan Inn

FINANCIAL DISTRICT
Hotel Vitale
Hyatt Regency
  San Francisco
Mandarin Oriental

MARINA DISTRICT
Buena Vista Motor Inn
Comfort Inn by the Bay
Cow Hollow Motor Inn
  and Suites
Days Inn Lombard
Edward II Inn
Hotel del Sol

Marina Motel
Motel Capri
Pacific Heights Inn
Super 8 Motel
Town House Motel
Travelodge by the Bay
Travelodge Golden Gate
Union Street Inn

NORTH BEACH
Hyatt Fisherman's Wharf
Marriott Fisherman's
  Wharf
Radisson Fisherman's
  Wharf
Sheraton at Fisherman's
  Wharf

SOMA/
MISSION DISTRICT
Best Western Americana
Best Western Carriage
  Inn
Four Seasons Hotel
Good Hotel
Harbor Court Hotel
Hotel Palomar
InterContinental San
  Francisco
San Francisco Marriott
Sheraton Palace Hotel
W Hotel San Francisco

RICHMOND/
SUNSET DISTRICT
Days Inn at the Beach
Hotel Drisco
Laurel Inn
Oceanview Motel
Seal Rock Inn
Stanyan Park Hotel

in each hotel and base our ratings and rankings on those rooms. The inspections are conducted anonymously and without the knowledge of the management. Although unusual, it is certainly possible that the rooms we randomly inspect are not representative of the majority of rooms at a particular hotel. Another possibility is that the rooms we inspect in a given hotel are representative, but that by bad luck a reader is assigned a room that is inferior. When we rechecked the hotel our reader disliked, we discovered that our rating was correctly representative, but that he and his wife had unfortunately been assigned to one of a small number of threadbare rooms scheduled for renovation.

The key to avoiding disappointment is to snoop around in advance. We recommend that you look on the hotel's Web site for a photo of a standard guest room before you book, or at least get a copy of the hotel's promotional brochure. Be forewarned, however, that some hotel chains use the same guest-room photo in their promotional literature for all hotels in the chain; a specific guest room may not resemble the brochure photo. When you or your travel agent call, ask how old the property is and when your guest room was last renovated. If you arrive and are assigned a room inferior to that which you had been led to expect, demand to be moved to another room.

Union Square and Nob Hill Accommodations

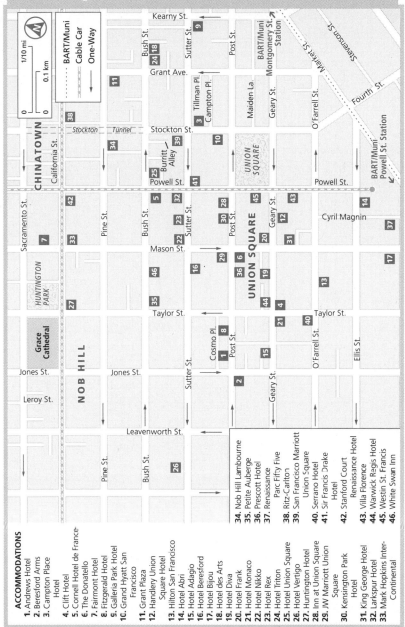

ACCOMMODATIONS
1. Andrews Hotel
2. Beresford Arms
3. Campton Place Hotel
4. Clift Hotel
5. Cornell Hotel de France
6. The Donatello
7. Fairmont Hotel
8. Fitzgerald Hotel
9. Galleria Park Hotel
10. Grand Hyatt San Francisco
11. Grant Plaza
12. Handlery Union Square Hotel
13. Hilton San Francisco
14. Hotel Abri
15. Hotel Adagio
16. Hotel Beresford
17. Hotel Bijou
18. Hotel des Arts
19. Hotel Diva
20. Hotel Frank
21. Hotel Monaco
22. Hotel Nikko
23. Hotel Rex
24. Hotel Triton
25. Hotel Union Square
26. Hotel Vertigo
27. Huntington Hotel
28. Inn at Union Square
29. JW Marriott Union Square
30. Kensington Park Hotel
31. King George Hotel
32. Larkspur Hotel
33. Mark Hopkins Inter-Continental
34. Nob Hill Lambourne
35. Petite Auberge
36. Prescott Hotel
37. Renaissance Parc Fifty Five
38. Ritz-Carlton
39. San Francisco Marriott Union Square
40. Serrano Hotel
41. Sir Francis Drake Hotel
42. Stanford Court Renaissance Hotel
43. Villa Florence
44. Warwick Regis Hotel
45. Westin St. Francis
46. White Swan Inn

Accommodations around Town

1. Best Western Americania
2. Best Western Carriage Inn
3. Best Western Hotel Tomo
4. Buena Vista Motor Inn
5. Comfort Inn by the Bay
6. Cow Hollow Motor Inn and Suites
7. Days Inn Lombard
8. Edward II Inn
9. Four Seasons Hotel
10. Good Hotel
11. Harbor Court Hotel
12. Hotel Carlton
13. Hotel del Sol
14. Hotel Drisco
15. Hotel Kabuki
16. Hotel Majestic
17. Hotel Palomar
18. Hotel Vitale
19. Hyatt Fisherman's Wharf
20. Hyatt Regency San Francisco
21. Inn at the Opera
22. InterContinental San Francisco
23. The Jackson Court
24. Laurel Inn
25. Mandarin Oriental
26. Marina Motel
27. Marriott Fisherman's Wharf
28. Motel Capri
29. Oceanview Motel
30. Pacific Heights Inn
31. The Phoenix Hotel
32. Queen Anne Hotel
33. Radisson Fisherman's Wharf
34. San Francisco Marriott
35. Seal Rock Inn
36. Sheraton at Fisherman's Wharf
37. Sheraton Palace Hotel
38. Stanyan Park Hotel
39. Super 8 Motel
40. Town House Motel
41. Travelodge by the Bay
42. Travelodge Golden Gate
43. Union Street Inn
44. W Hotel San Francisco

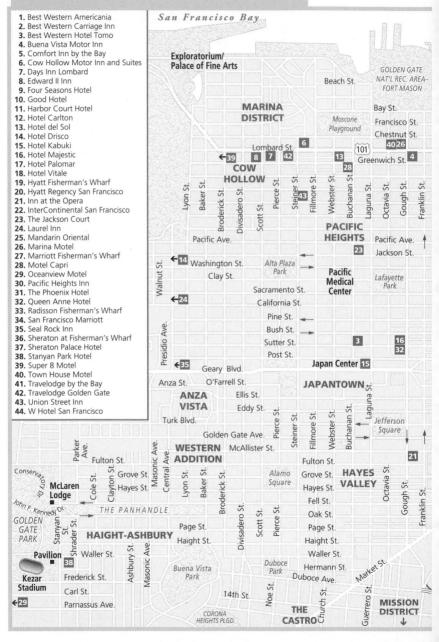

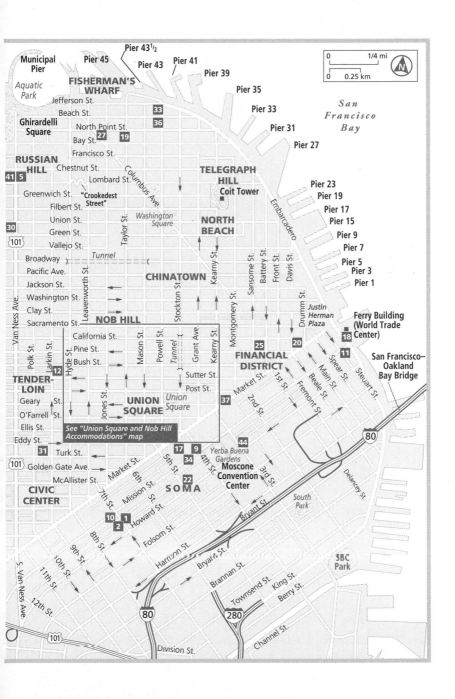

How the Hotels Compare in San Francisco

HOTEL	OVERALL RATING	QUALITY RATING	COST ($=$50)
Four Seasons Hotel	★★★★★	98	$$$$$$
Mandarin Oriental	★★★★★	98	$$$$$$$+
Campton Place Hotel	★★★★★	97	$$$$$$$+
Hotel Nikko	★★★★★	96	$$$$$+
Ritz-Carlton	★★★★★	96	$$$$$$$$
Fairmont Hotel	★★★★½	95	$$$$$$−
W Hotel San Francisco	★★★★½	95	$$$$$
Hotel Monaco	★★★★½	94	$$$$$−
Nob Hill Lambourne	★★★★½	92	$$$−
Prescott Hotel	★★★★½	92	$$$$$$+
Clift Hotel	★★★★½	91	$$$$$
Westin St. Francis	★★★★½	91	$$$$$$−
Hotel Carlton	★★★★½	90	$$$−
Hotel Diva	★★★★½	90	$$$$−
Hotel Vitale	★★★★½	90	$$$$$$−
Huntington Hotel	★★★★½	90	$$$$$+
Inn at the Opera	★★★★½	90	$$$+
InterContinental San Francisco	★★★★½	90	$$$$$
The Jackson Court	★★★★½	90	$$$$−
JW Marriott Union Square	★★★★½	90	$$$$$−
Stanford Court Renaissance Hotel	★★★★½	90	$$$+
White Swan Inn	★★★★½	90	$$$$$−
Hotel Majestic	★★★★	89	$$$−
Hotel Palomar	★★★★	89	$$$$$$−
Sheraton Palace Hotel	★★★★	89	$$$$$$
Hyatt Fisherman's Wharf	★★★★	88	$$$$$−
Hyatt Regency San Francisco	★★★★	88	$$$$+
Grand Hyatt San Francisco	★★★★	87	$$$$$+
The Donatello	★★★★	86	$$$$−
Hilton San Francisco	★★★★	86	$$$$$−
Hotel Triton	★★★★	86	$$$$−

HOTEL	OVERALL RATING	QUALITY RATING	COST ($=$50)
San Francisco Marriott	★★★★	86	$$$$+
Fitzgerald Hotel	★★★★	85	$$$−
Harbor Court Hotel	★★★★	85	$$$$+
Hotel Adagio	★★★★	85	$$$−
Hotel des Arts	★★★★	85	$$
Hotel Drisco	★★★★	85	$$$$
Hotel Rex	★★★★	85	$$$$$
Hotel Vertigo	★★★★	85	$$+
Renaissance Parc Fifty Five	★★★★	85	$$$$+
Galleria Park Hotel	★★★★	84	$$$+
Mark Hopkins InterContinental	★★★★	84	$$$$+
Kensington Park Hotel	★★★★	83	$$$$
Serrano Hotel	★★★★	83	$$$$−
Warwick Regis Hotel	★★★★	83	$$$$
Hotel Bijou	★★★½	82	$$+
Sheraton at Fisherman's Wharf	★★★½	82	$$$$−
Sir Francis Drake Hotel	★★★½	82	$$$$$
Union Street Inn	★★★½	82	$$$$$$$−
Andrews Hotel	★★★½	80	$$$
Hotel Abri	★★★½	80	$$$$
Hotel del Sol	★★★½	80	$$$−
Hotel Frank	★★★½	80	$$$$+
Hotel Union Square	★★★½	80	$$$−
Inn at Union Square	★★★½	80	$$$$$
Laurel Inn	★★★½	80	$$$+
Marriott Fisherman's Wharf	★★★½	80	$$$$$−
Queen Anne Hotel	★★★¼	80	$$$
Villa Florence	★★★½	80	$$$$$−
Best Western Hotel Tomo	★★★½	77	$$$−
Grant Plaza	★★★½	77	$$−
Hotel Kabuki	★★★½	76	$$$$−
San Francisco Marriott Union Square	★★★½	76	$$$$−

How the Hotels Compare in San Francisco (continued)

HOTEL	OVERALL RATING	QUALITY RATING	COST ($=$50)
Beresford Arms	★★★½	75	$$$$+
Best Western Americania	★★★½	75	$$$+
Best Western Carriage Inn	★★★½	75	$$+
Buena Vista Motor Inn	★★★½	75	$$+
Cornell Hotel de France	★★★½	75	$$$–
Good Hotel	★★★½	75	$$$–
Larkspur Hotel	★★★½	75	$$$$$
Petite Auberge	★★★½	75	$$$+
Seal Rock Inn	★★★½	75	$$+
Stanyan Park Hotel	★★★½	75	$$$
Edward II Inn	★★★	74	$$$
Handlery Union Square Hotel	★★★	72	$$$$–
Cow Hollow Motor Inn and Suites	★★★	70	$$$
Motel Capri	★★★	70	$$
Pacific Heights Inn	★★★	70	$$$
Radisson Fisherman's Wharf	★★★	70	$$$$+
King George Hotel	★★★	65	$$$–
Marina Motel	★★★	65	$$$
Days Inn at the Beach	★★½	64	$$$–
Super 8 Motel	★★½	62	$$$$–
Travelodge by the Bay	★★½	62	$$$–
Comfort Inn by the Bay	★★½	60	$$$+
Hotel Beresford	★★½	60	$$$$–
Phoenix Hotel	★★½	60	$$$
Town House Motel	★★½	60	$$$–
Travelodge Golden Gate	★★½	60	$$+
Days Inn Lombard	★★	55	$$–
Oceanview Motel	★★	55	$$+

How the Hotels Compare in Outside Areas

HOTEL	OVERALL RATING	QUALITY RATING	COST ($=$50)
MARIN COUNTY			
Mill Valley Inn	★★★★½	95	$$$$$−
Inn Above Tide	★★★★½	93	$$$$$$+
Casa Madrona	★★★★½	90	$$$$$
Embassy Suites Hotel	★★★★	83	$$+
Acqua Hotel	★★★½	80	$$$$−
BERKELEY			
Claremont Resort & Spa	★★★★½	92	$$$$$−
Doubletree Hotel Berkeley Marina	★★★½	80	$$$−
Hotel Durant	★★★½	75	$$$+
OAKLAND			
Oakland Airport Hilton	★★★½	80	$$$−
Waterfront Plaza Hotel	★★★½	80	$$$$−
La Quinta Inn Oakland Airport	★★★½	75	$$$
Oakland Marriott City Center	★★★	74	$$$−
SOUTH BAY			
Ritz-Carlton Half Moon Bay	★★★★★	97	$$$$$$$+
SAN FRANCISCO AIRPORT			
Hyatt Regency San Francisco Airport	★★★★	86	$$$
Embassy Suites SFO	★★★★	85	$$$
San Francisco Airport Marriott	★★★★	83	$$$+
Hilton San Francisco Airport	★★★½	82	$$$
Doubletree Hotel San Francisco Airport	★★★½	80	$$$−
Westin Hotel San Francisco Airport	★★★½	80	$$$−
Best Western Grosvenor Hotel	★★★	70	$$+
Travelodge San Francisco Airport North	★★★	70	$
Red Roof Inn San Francisco Airport	★★½	60	$$−

Hotels in the Wine Country

HOW THE HOTELS COMPARE

HOTEL	OVERALL RATING	QUALITY RATING	COST ($=$50)
Auberge du Soleil	★★★★★	99	$$$$$$$$$$$$$$+
Inn at Southbridge	★★★★½	92	$$$$$$$
Vintage Inn	★★★★½	91	$$$$$$$$$−
Napa Valley Lodge	★★★★½	90	$$$$$−
Sonoma Mission Inn and Spa	★★★★½	90	$$$$$$$+
Rancho Caymus	★★★★	87	$$$$+
Cedar Gables Inn	★★★★	85	$$$$$+
El Dorado Hotel	★★★★	85	$$$$
Silverado Country Club and Resort	★★★★	85	$$$$$$$
Sonoma Hotel	★★★★	85	$$$+
Harvest Inn	★★★★	84	$$$$$$$+
Napa Valley Marriott Hotel	★★★★	84	$$$$$$$−
Mount View Hotel	★★★½	81	$$$$$−
Best Western Sonoma Valley Inn	★★★½	80	$$$$
El Bonita Motel	★★★½	80	$$$+
Dr. Wilkinson's Hot Springs Resort	★★★½	75	$$$
El Pueblo Inn	★★★½	75	$$$$
Hotel St. Helena	★★★	74	$$$+
John Muir Inn	★★★	65	$$$+

THE TOP 10 BEST DEALS

HOTEL	OVERALL RATING	QUALITY RATING	COST ($=$50)
1. Sonoma Hotel	★★★★	85	$$$+
2. El Dorado Hotel	★★★★	85	$$$$
3. El Bonita Motel	★★★½	80	$$$+
4. Best Western Sonoma Valley Inn	★★★½	80	$$$$
5. Cedar Gables Inn	★★★★	85	$$$$$+
6. El Pueblo Inn	★★★½	75	$$$$
7. John Muir Inn	★★★	65	$$$+
8. Napa Valley Marriott Hotel	★★★★	84	$$$$$$$−
9. Dr. Wilkinson's Hot Springs Resort	★★★½	75	$$$
10. Vintage Inn	★★★★½	91	$$$$$$$$$−

The Top 30 Best Deals in San Francisco

HOTEL	OVERALL RATING	QUALITY RATING	COST ($=$50)
1. Hotel des Arts	★★★★	85	$$
2. Grant Plaza	★★★½	77	$$–
3. Hotel Carlton	★★★★½	90	$$$–
4. Nob Hill Lambourne	★★★★½	92	$$$–
5. Hotel Vertigo	★★★★	85	$$+
6. Hotel Majestic	★★★★	89	$$$–
7. Fitzgerald Hotel	★★★★	85	$$$–
8. Hotel Adagio	★★★★	85	$$$–
9. Inn at the Opera	★★★★½	90	$$$+
10. Stanford Court Renaissance Hotel	★★★★½	90	$$$+
11. Hotel Bijou	★★★½	82	$$+
12. Buena Vista Motor Inn	★★★½	75	$$+
13. Hotel Diva	★★★★½	90	$$$$–
14. Best Western Carriage Inn	★★★½	75	$$+
15. Hotel del Sol	★★★½	80	$$$–
16. Seal Rock Inn	★★★½	75	$$+
17. The Jackson Court	★★★★½	90	$$$$–
18. Motel Capri	★★★	70	$$
19. Best Western Hotel Tomo	★★★½	77	$$$–
20. Hotel Union Square	★★★½	80	$$$–
21. Good Hotel	★★★½	75	$$$–
22. Galleria Park Hotel	★★★★	84	$$$+
23. Queen Anne Hotel	★★★½	80	$$$
24. Hotel Triton	★★★★	86	$$$$–
25. The Donatello	★★★★	86	$$$$–
26. Andrews Hotel	★★★½	80	$$$
27. Cornell Hotel de France	★★★½	76	$$$
28. Hotel Nikko	★★★★★	96	$$$$$+
29. White Swan Inn	★★★★½	90	$$$$$–
30. Hotel Monaco	★★★★½	94	$$$$$–

Hotel Information Chart

Acqua Hotel ★★★½
555 Redwood Highway
Mill Valley, CA 94941
☎ 415-877-4684
TOLL-FREE 888-815-1593
acquahotel.com

QUALITY	80
COST	$$$$–
LOCATION	Marin County
DISCOUNTS	AAA, AARP, senior, gov't.
NO. OF ROOMS	49
ON-SITE DINING	–
ROOM SERVICE	–
BAR	–
PARKING PER DAY	Free
MEETING FACILITIES	•
EXTRA AMENITIES	Free breakfast, afternoon tea, evening wine, robes, minibar, Internet
BUSINESS AMENITIES	Dataport, 2-line phone, business center, voice mail, secretarial services
DECOR	Contemporary modern
POOL/SAUNA	–
EXERCISE FACILITIES	–

Andrews Hotel ★★★½
624 Post Street
San Francisco, CA 94109
☎ 415-563-6877
TOLL-FREE 800-926-3739
andrewshotel.com

QUALITY	80
COST	$$$
LOCATION	Union Square
DISCOUNTS	AAA, AARP, senior, gov't., military
NO. OF ROOMS	48
ON-SITE DINING	–
ROOM SERVICE	–
BAR	–
PARKING PER DAY	$28 valet
MEETING FACILITIES	–
EXTRA AMENITIES	Free breakfast, free wine, Wi-Fi, DVD players, free movies
BUSINESS AMENITIES	Dataport, 2-line phone, voice mail
DECOR	Queen Anne, Victorian
POOL/SAUNA	–
EXERCISE FACILITIES	–

Auberge du Soleil ★★★★★
180 Rutherford Hill Road
Rutherford, CA 94573
☎ 707-963-1211
TOLL-FREE 800-348-5406
aubergedusoleil.com

QUALITY	99
COST	$$$$$$$$$$$$$$+
LOCATION	Wine Country
DISCOUNTS	
NO. OF ROOMS	50
ON-SITE DINING	•
ROOM SERVICE	•
BAR	•
PARKING PER DAY	Free
MEETING FACILITIES	•
EXTRA AMENITIES	Safe, DVD player, fruit, massage, robes, slippers, minibar, coffeemaker, toaster, Wi-Fi
BUSINESS AMENITIES	Dataport, voice mail
DECOR	Mediterranean-inspired
POOL/SAUNA	Pool, steam room, spa, whirlpool
EXERCISE FACILITIES	Fitness center

Best Western Grosvenor Hotel ★★★
380 South Airport Boulevard
South San Francisco, CA 94080
☎ 650-873-3200
TOLL-FREE 800-722-7141
grosvenorsfo.com

QUALITY	70
COST	$$+
LOCATION	SF Int'l Airport
DISCOUNTS	AAA, AARP, gov't., senior
NO. OF ROOMS	207
ON-SITE DINING	•
ROOM SERVICE	•
BAR	•
PARKING PER DAY	$3
MEETING FACILITIES	•
EXTRA AMENITIES	Free breakfast, airport shuttle, coffeemaker, Wi-Fi
BUSINESS AMENITIES	Dataport, voice mail
DECOR	European
POOL/SAUNA	Pool, sauna, whirlpool
EXERCISE FACILITIES	Fitness room

Best Western Hotel Tomo ★★★½
1800 Sutter Street
San Francisco, CA 94115
☎ 415-921-4000
TOLL-FREE 800-468-3578
jdvhotels.com/tomo

QUALITY	77
COST	$$$–
LOCATION	Civic Center
DISCOUNTS	AAA, AARP
NO. OF ROOMS	125
ON-SITE DINING	•
ROOM SERVICE	•
BAR	•
PARKING PER DAY	limited, $20
MEETING FACILITIES	–
EXTRA AMENITIES	Breakfast, family friendly, Wi-Fi, flat-panel TV, coffee/tea maker, laundry and dry cleaning, safe, iPod docking station, robes
BUSINESS AMENITIES	Business stations with dataport, fax
DECOR	Japanese pop with anime and munga
POOL/SAUNA	–
EXERCISE FACILITIES	Fitness facility

Best Western Sonoma Valley Inn ★★★½
550 Second Street West
Sonoma, CA 95476
☎ 707-938-9200
TOLL-FREE 800-334-5784
sonomavalleyinn.com

QUALITY	80
COST	$$$$
LOCATION	Wine Country
DISCOUNTS	AAA, AARP
NO. OF ROOMS	73
ON-SITE DINING	–
ROOM SERVICE	–
BAR	–
PARKING PER DAY	Free
MEETING FACILITIES	•
EXTRA AMENITIES	Free breakfast, wine in room, pet friendly with daily fee, coffeemaker, fridge, some fireplaces, Wi-Fi
BUSINESS AMENITIES	Dataport
DECOR	Modern Californian
POOL/SAUNA	Pool, whirlpool
EXERCISE FACILITIES	Cardio-fitness center

Beresford Arms ★★★½
701 Post Street
San Francisco, CA 94109
☎ 415-673-2600
TOLL-FREE 800-533-6533
beresford.com

QUALITY	75
COST	$$$$+
LOCATION	Union Square
DISCOUNTS	AAA, AARP, gov't.
NO. OF ROOMS	95
ON-SITE DINING	–
ROOM SERVICE	–
BAR	•
PARKING PER DAY	$24
MEETING FACILITIES	–
EXTRA AMENITIES	Free breakfast, wet bar or kitchenette, p.m. tea and wine, Wi-Fi, whirlpool bath
BUSINESS AMENITIES	Dataport, 2-line phone, fax, copy
DECOR	Victorian charm
POOL/SAUNA	Whirlpool
EXERCISE FACILITIES	–

Best Western Americania ★★★½
121 Seventh Street
San Francisco, CA 94103
☎ 415-626-0200
TOLL-FREE 800-738-7477
somahotels.com

QUALITY	75
COST	$$$+
LOCATION	SoMa/Mission District
DISCOUNTS	AAA, AARP
NO. OF ROOMS	143
ON-SITE DINING	•
ROOM SERVICE	•
BAR	•
PARKING PER DAY	$26
MEETING FACILITIES	•
EXTRA AMENITIES	Breakfast, child and pet friendly, free Internet, cable TV and DVD, iPod docking station, coffeemaker, laundromat, free bikes on loan, free tour
BUSINESS AMENITIES	Dataport, 2-line phone, fax
DECOR	Midcentury style
POOL/SAUNA	outdoor heated pool
EXERCISE FACILITIES	Fitness center

Best Western Carriage Inn ★★★½
140 Seventh Street
San Francisco, CA 94103
☎ 415-552-8600
TOLL-FREE 800-738-7477
somahotels.com

QUALITY	75
COST	$$+
LOCATION	SoMa/Mission District
DISCOUNTS	AAA, AARP
NO. OF ROOMS	48
ON-SITE DINING	–
ROOM SERVICE	–
BAR	•
PARKING PER DAY	$26
MEETING FACILITIES	–
EXTRA AMENITIES	Breakfast, free Wi-Fi, flat-panel TV and DVD, iPod docking station, coffeemaker, safe, robes, refrigerator, dry cleaning, free tour
BUSINESS AMENITIES	Dataport, 2-line phone, fax
DECOR	Trad Americana with witty local touches and literary theme
POOL/SAUNA	Hot tub access and outdoor heated pool
EXERCISE FACILITIES	Fitness room across the street

Buena Vista Motor Inn ★★★½
1599 Lombard Street
San Francisco, CA 94123
☎ 415-923-9600
TOLL-FREE 800-835-4980
buenavistamotorinn.com

QUALITY	75
COST	$$+
LOCATION	Marina District
DISCOUNTS	AAA, AARP
NO. OF ROOMS	50
ON-SITE DINING	–
ROOM SERVICE	–
BAR	–
PARKING PER DAY	Free
MEETING FACILITIES	–
EXTRA AMENITIES	Rooftop sun deck, tea/coffeemaker, tours, breakfast
BUSINESS AMENITIES	Dataport, fax, copier
DECOR	Stylish pastel
POOL/SAUNA	–
EXERCISE FACILITIES	–

Campton Place Hotel ★★★★★
340 Stockton Street
San Francisco, CA 94108
☎ 415-781-5555
TOLL-FREE 800-235-4300
tajhotels.com/camptonplace

QUALITY	97
COST	$$$$$$$$+
LOCATION	Union Square
DISCOUNTS	AAA
NO. OF ROOMS	110
ON-SITE DINING	•
ROOM SERVICE	•
BAR	•
PARKING PER DAY	$45
MEETING FACILITIES	•
EXTRA AMENITIES	Fitness terrace, safe, minibar, Bose stereo, slippers
BUSINESS AMENITIES	Dataport, 2-line phone, fax
DECOR	European
POOL/SAUNA	–
EXERCISE FACILITIES	Basic gym

Casa Madrona ★★★★½
801 Bridgeway
Sausalito, CA 94965
☎ 415-332-0502
TOLL-FREE 800-288-0502
casamadrona.com

QUALITY	90
COST	$$$$$
LOCATION	Marin County
DISCOUNTS	–
NO. OF ROOMS	63
ON-SITE DINING	•
ROOM SERVICE	•
BAR	•
PARKING PER DAY	$25
MEETING FACILITIES	–
EXTRA AMENITIES	Free breakfast, p.m. wine and cheese, minibar, coffeemaker
BUSINESS AMENITIES	Dataport, voice mail
DECOR	Choose from classic original or new contemporary
POOL/SAUNA	Spa
EXERCISE FACILITIES	–

Hotel Information Chart *(continued)*

Cedar Gables Inn ★★★★
486 Coombs Street
Napa, CA 94559
☎ 707-224-7969
TOLL-FREE 800-309-7969
cedargablesinn.com

QUALITY	85
COST	$$$$$+
LOCATION	Wine Country
DISCOUNTS	AAA, AARP
NO. OF ROOMS	9
ON-SITE DINING	–
ROOM SERVICE	–
BAR	–
PARKING PER DAY	Free
MEETING FACILITIES	–
EXTRA AMENITIES	Breakfast, wine, hors d'oeuvres
BUSINESS AMENITIES	–
DECOR	English country manor
POOL/SAUNA	–
EXERCISE FACILITIES	–

Claremont Resort & Spa ★★★★½
41 Tunnel Road
Berkeley, CA 94705
☎ 510-843-3000
TOLL-FREE 800-551-7266
claremontresort.com

QUALITY	92
COST	$$$$$–
LOCATION	Berkeley
DISCOUNTS	AAA, AARP
NO. OF ROOMS	279
ON-SITE DINING	•
ROOM SERVICE	•
BAR	•
PARKING PER DAY	$22
MEETING FACILITIES	•
EXTRA AMENITIES	Full spa, tennis courts, robes, safe
BUSINESS AMENITIES	Double dataports, 2-line phone, voice mail
DECOR	Old World charm
POOL/SAUNA	Pool, sauna, whirlpool
EXERCISE FACILITIES	Fitness classes (yoga, Pilates, Tai Chi)

Clift Hotel ★★★★½
495 Geary Street
San Francisco, CA 94102
☎ 415-775-4700
TOLL-FREE 800-697-1791
clifthotel.com

QUALITY	91
COST	$$$$
LOCATION	Union Square
DISCOUNTS	AAA, corp.
NO. OF ROOMS	363
ON-SITE DINING	•
ROOM SERVICE	•
BAR	•
PARKING PER DAY	$45
MEETING FACILITIES	•
EXTRA AMENITIES	Babysitting, DVD, CD, video game library, board games, massage
BUSINESS AMENITIES	Dataport, fax, 2-line phone, voice mail, business center
DECOR	European
POOL/SAUNA	–
EXERCISE FACILITIES	Fitness room

Days Inn at the Beach ★★½
2600 Sloat Boulevard
San Francisco, CA 94116
☎ 415-665-9000
TOLL-FREE 800-329-7466
daysinn.com

QUALITY	64
COST	$$$–
LOCATION	Richmond/ Sunset District
DISCOUNTS	AAA, AARP, gov't.
NO. OF ROOMS	33
ON-SITE DINING	–
ROOM SERVICE	–
BAR	–
PARKING PER DAY	Free
MEETING FACILITIES	–
EXTRA AMENITIES	Free breakfast, microwave
BUSINESS AMENITIES	–
DECOR	Modern
POOL/SAUNA	–
EXERCISE FACILITIES	–

Days Inn Lombard ★★
2358 Lombard Street
San Francisco, CA 94123
☎ 415-922-2010
TOLL-FREE 800-329-7466
daysinn.com

QUALITY	55
COST	$$–
LOCATION	Marina District
DISCOUNTS	AAA, AARP, gov't.
NO. OF ROOMS	22
ON-SITE DINING	–
ROOM SERVICE	–
BAR	–
PARKING PER DAY	Free
MEETING FACILITIES	–
EXTRA AMENITIES	Free breakfast, tennis
BUSINESS AMENITIES	–
DECOR	Modern
POOL/SAUNA	–
EXERCISE FACILITIES	Tennis court

The Donatello ★★★★
501 Post Street
San Francisco, CA 94102
☎ 415-441-7100
TOLL-FREE 866-729-7182
shellhospitality.com

QUALITY	86
COST	$$$$–
LOCATION	Union Square
DISCOUNTS	AAA, AARP, gov't.
NO. OF ROOMS	94
ON-SITE DINING	•
ROOM SERVICE	•
BAR	•
PARKING PER DAY	$32
MEETING FACILITIES	–
EXTRA AMENITIES	Lounge music, spa services, sound-proofing, safe, tennis, microwave, safe, fridge, babysitting, newspaper
BUSINESS AMENITIES	Dataport, 2-line phone, voice mail
DECOR	European boutique
POOL/SAUNA	Sauna, whirlpool
EXERCISE FACILITIES	Fitness room

Comfort Inn by the Bay ★★½
2775 Van Ness Avenue
San Francisco, CA 94109
☎ 415-928-5000
TOLL-FREE 800-228-5150
choicehotels.com

QUALITY	60
COST	$$$+
LOCATION	Marina District
DISCOUNTS	AAA, AARP, military
NO. OF ROOMS	138
ON-SITE DINING	–
ROOM SERVICE	–
BAR	–
PARKING PER DAY	$26
MEETING FACILITIES	–
EXTRA AMENITIES	Breakfast, coffee-maker, newspaper, tennis courts, safe, tours
BUSINESS AMENITIES	Dataport, fax, copier, voice mail
DECOR	Modern
POOL/SAUNA	–
EXERCISE FACILITIES	Tennis court

Cornell Hotel de France ★★★½
715 Bush Street
San Francisco, CA 94108
☎ 415-421-3154
TOLL-FREE 800-232-9698
cornellhotel.com

QUALITY	75
COST	$$$–
LOCATION	Nob Hill
DISCOUNTS	AAA, AARP, special holiday packages
NO. OF ROOMS	50
ON-SITE DINING	•
ROOM SERVICE	•
BAR	•
PARKING PER DAY	Sutter-Stockton garage nearby; averages $26.30 daily
MEETING FACILITIES	–
EXTRA AMENITIES	Breakfast, cable TV, tours
BUSINESS AMENITIES	Dataport, desk, Internet, radio
DECOR	Authentic traditional French with antique armor
POOL/SAUNA	–
EXERCISE FACILITIES	Nearby

Cow Hollow Motor Inn and Suites ★★★
2190 Lombard Street
San Francisco, CA 94123
☎ 415-921-5800
cowhollowmotorinn.com

QUALITY	70
COST	$$$
LOCATION	Marina District
DISCOUNTS	AAA
NO. OF ROOMS	129
ON-SITE DINING	•
ROOM SERVICE	–
BAR	–
PARKING PER DAY	Free
MEETING FACILITIES	–
EXTRA AMENITIES	Coffeemaker, hair dryer, Wi-Fi
BUSINESS AMENITIES	–
DECOR	Modern
POOL/SAUNA	–
EXERCISE FACILITIES	–

Doubletree Hotel Berkeley Marina ★★★½
200 Marina Boulevard
Berkeley, CA 94710
☎ 510-548-7920
TOLL-FREE 800-222-TREE
doubletree.com

QUALITY	80
COST	$$$–
LOCATION	Berkeley
DISCOUNTS	AAA, AARP, gov't., military
NO. OF ROOMS	378
ON-SITE DINING	•
ROOM SERVICE	•
BAR	•
PARKING PER DAY	Free
MEETING FACILITIES	•
EXTRA AMENITIES	Marina, coffee-maker, newspaper, cookies, pet friendly, gift shop
BUSINESS AMENITIES	Dataport, 2-line phone, voice mail
DECOR	Contemporary
POOL/SAUNA	Pool, sauna, whirlpool
EXERCISE FACILITIES	Fitness center

Doubletree Hotel San Francisco Airport ★★★½
835 Airport Boulevard
Burlingame, CA 94010
☎ 415-344-5500
TOLL-FREE 800-222-TREE
doubletree.com

QUALITY	80
COST	$$$
LOCATION	SF Int'l Airport
DISCOUNTS	AAA, AARP, gov't., military
NO. OF ROOMS	395
ON-SITE DINING	•
ROOM SERVICE	•
BAR	•
PARKING PER DAY	$22
MEETING FACILITIES	•
EXTRA AMENITIES	Airport shuttle, pet friendly, gift shop, safe, free golf rental
BUSINESS AMENITIES	Dataport, notary public, fax, audiovisual, video conference
DECOR	European
POOL/SAUNA	–
EXERCISE FACILITIES	Fitness center

Dr. Wilkinson's Hot Springs Resort ★★★½
1507 Lincoln Avenue
Calistoga, CA 94515
☎ 707-942-4102
drwilkinson.com

QUALITY	75
COST	$$$
LOCATION	Wine Country
DISCOUNTS	–
NO. OF ROOMS	42
ON-SITE DINING	–
ROOM SERVICE	–
BAR	–
PARKING PER DAY	Free
MEETING FACILITIES	•
EXTRA AMENITIES	Spa, massage, wine tours, tea/coffee-maker, hot chocolate
BUSINESS AMENITIES	Dataport, voice mail
DECOR	Victorian, neo-Deco
POOL/SAUNA	Pool, whirlpool, steam room
EXERCISE FACILITIES	–

Hotel Information Chart (continued)

Edward II Inn ★★★
3155 Scott Street
San Francisco, CA 94123
☎ 415-922-3000
TOLL-FREE 800-473-2846
edwardii.com

QUALITY	74
COST	$$$
LOCATION	Marina District
DISCOUNTS	AAA
NO. OF ROOMS	30
ON-SITE DINING	•
ROOM SERVICE	•
BAR	•
PARKING PER DAY	$12
MEETING FACILITIES	–
EXTRA AMENITIES	Free breakfast, robes, newspaper, coffee, tea, hot chocolate, manicure, pedicure, p.m. refreshments at the pub, gift shop
BUSINESS AMENITIES	Fax
DECOR	English country
POOL/SAUNA	Spa nearby
EXERCISE FACILITIES	Fitness room, meditation room

El Bonita Motel ★★★½
195 Main Street
St. Helena, CA 94574
☎ 707-963-3216
TOLL-FREE 800-541-3284
elbonita.com

QUALITY	80
COST	$$$+
LOCATION	Wine Country
DISCOUNTS	AAA, AARP
NO. OF ROOMS	40
ON-SITE DINING	–
ROOM SERVICE	–
BAR	–
PARKING PER DAY	Free
MEETING FACILITIES	–
EXTRA AMENITIES	Free breakfast, coffeemaker, fridge, microwave, pet friendly
BUSINESS AMENITIES	Business center
DECOR	1950s
POOL/SAUNA	Whirlpool, pool, sauna
EXERCISE FACILITIES	–

El Dorado Hotel ★★★★
405 First Street West
Sonoma, CA 95476
☎ 707-996-3220
TOLL-FREE 800-289-3031
eldoradosonoma.com

QUALITY	85
COST	$$$$
LOCATION	Wine Country
DISCOUNTS	–
NO. OF ROOMS	27
ON-SITE DINING	•
ROOM SERVICE	–
BAR	•
PARKING PER DAY	Free
MEETING FACILITIES	–
EXTRA AMENITIES	Free breakfast, coffee, tea, DVD/CD player, fridge, newspaper
BUSINESS AMENITIES	Dataport, voice mail, fax, copier
DECOR	Old World
POOL/SAUNA	Pool
EXERCISE FACILITIES	–

Fairmont Hotel ★★★★½
950 Mason Street
San Francisco, CA 94108
☎ 415-772-5000
TOLL-FREE 800-678-8946
fairmont.com

QUALITY	95
COST	$$$$$–
LOCATION	Nob Hill
DISCOUNTS	AAA, AARP, gov't.
NO. OF ROOMS	591
ON-SITE DINING	•
ROOM SERVICE	–
BAR	•
PARKING PER DAY	$50
MEETING FACILITIES	•
EXTRA AMENITIES	Massage, safe, robes, fridge, salon, spa
BUSINESS AMENITIES	Dataport, 2-line phone, fax, business center, audiovisual, video conference, voice mail
DECOR	Grand hotel
POOL/SAUNA	Sauna, whirlpool
EXERCISE FACILITIES	Health center and spa

Fitzgerald Hotel ★★★★
620 Post Street
San Francisco, CA 94109
☎ 415-775-8100
TOLL-FREE 800-334-6835
fitzgeraldhotel.com

QUALITY	85
COST	$$$–
LOCATION	Union Square
DISCOUNTS	AAA, AARP, gov't.
NO. OF ROOMS	46
ON-SITE DINING	–
ROOM SERVICE	–
BAR	•
PARKING PER DAY	$25–$30
MEETING FACILITIES	–
EXTRA AMENITIES	Free breakfast, fridge, microwave, coffeemaker
BUSINESS AMENITIES	Dataport, 2-line phone
DECOR	European
POOL/SAUNA	Privileges
EXERCISE FACILITIES	Privileges

Four Seasons Hotel ★★★★★
757 Market Street
San Francisco, CA 94103
☎ 415-633-3000
TOLL-FREE 800-332-3442
fourseasons.com

QUALITY	98
COST	$$$$$$$
LOCATION	SoMa/Mission District
DISCOUNTS	–
NO. OF ROOMS	277
ON-SITE DINING	•
ROOM SERVICE	•
BAR	•
PARKING PER DAY	$50
MEETING FACILITIES	•
EXTRA AMENITIES	Technology center, in-room dining, free breakfast, gift shop
BUSINESS AMENITIES	24-hour facilities, fax, delivery, computer center, multiline phone, audiovisual equipment
DECOR	Contemporary
POOL/SAUNA	Pool
EXERCISE FACILITIES	Health club, basketball, golf course

El Pueblo Inn ★★★½
896 West Napa Street
Sonoma, CA 95476
☎ 707-996-3651
TOLL-FREE 800-900-8844
elpuebloinn.com

QUALITY	75
COST	$$$$
LOCATION	Wine Country
DISCOUNTS	AAA, AARP
NO. OF ROOMS	53
ON-SITE DINING	–
ROOM SERVICE	–
BAR	–
PARKING PER DAY	Free
MEETING FACILITIES	•
EXTRA AMENITIES	Coffeemaker, biscotti, tea, hot chocolate, fridge, massage
BUSINESS AMENITIES	Dataport, voice mail
DECOR	Early California
POOL/SAUNA	Pool, whirlpool
EXERCISE FACILITIES	–

Embassy Suites Hotel ★★★★
101 McInnis Parkway
San Rafael, CA 94903
☎ 415-499-9222
TOLL-FREE 800-EMBASSY
embassymarin.com

QUALITY	83
COST	$$+
LOCATION	Marin County
DISCOUNTS	AAA, AARP, gov't.
NO. OF ROOMS	235
ON-SITE DINING	•
ROOM SERVICE	•
BAR	•
PARKING PER DAY	Free
MEETING FACILITIES	•
EXTRA AMENITIES	Free breakfast, p.m. reception, salon, gift shop, ATM, safe, newsstand, multilingual staff, fridge, microwave, coffeemaker
BUSINESS AMENITIES	Dataport, 2-line phone, fax, business center, audiovisual, video conference
DECOR	Contemporary
POOL/SAUNA	Pool, whirlpool
EXERCISE FACILITIES	Fitness room, walking/jogging track

Embassy Suites SFO ★★★★
150 Anza Boulevard
Burlingame, CA 94010
☎ 650-342-4600
TOLL-FREE 800-EMBASSY
embassysuites.com

QUALITY	85
COST	$$$
LOCATION	SF Int'l Airport
DISCOUNTS	AAA, AARP, gov't., military
NO. OF ROOMS	340
ON-SITE DINING	•
ROOM SERVICE	•
BAR	•
PARKING PER DAY	Free
MEETING FACILITIES	•
EXTRA AMENITIES	Free breakfast, p.m. reception, microwave, ATM, fridge, coffeemaker, safe, pet friendly, newsstand
BUSINESS AMENITIES	Dataport, 2-line phone, fax, business center, audiovisual, video conference
DECOR	Atrium hotel
POOL/SAUNA	Pool, sauna, steam room
EXERCISE FACILITIES	Fitness center

Galleria Park Hotel ★★★★
191 Sutter Street
San Francisco, CA 94104
☎ 415-781-3060
TOLL-FREE 866-756-3036
jdvhotels.com/galleria_park

QUALITY	84
COST	$$$+
LOCATION	Union Square
DISCOUNTS	AAA, AARP, gov't.
NO. OF ROOMS	177
ON-SITE DINING	•
ROOM SERVICE	•
BAR	•
PARKING PER DAY	$35
MEETING FACILITIES	•
EXTRA AMENITIES	Rooftop track, park, safe, pet friendly
BUSINESS AMENITIES	Dataport, 2-line phone, 24-hour business center
DECOR	1940s glamour
POOL/SAUNA	–
EXERCISE FACILITIES	Fitness studio

Good Hotel ★★★½
112 Seventh Street
San Francisco, CA 94103
☎ 415-413-4720
thegoodhotel.com

QUALITY	75
COST	$$$–
LOCATION	SoMa/Mission District
DISCOUNTS	AAA, AARP
NO. OF ROOMS	117
ON-SITE DINING	•
ROOM SERVICE	•
BAR	•
PARKING PER DAY	$20
MEETING FACILITIES	–
EXTRA AMENITIES	Breakfast, pet friendly, Wi-Fi, flat-panel TV, coffee/tea maker, iPod docking station, free bikes on loan
BUSINESS AMENITIES	Business stations with dataport, fax
DECOR	Hip, ecofriendly design
POOL/SAUNA	Outdoor heated pool access across street
EXERCISE FACILITIES	–

Grand Hyatt San Francisco ★★★★
345 Stockton Street
San Francisco, CA 94108
☎ 415-398-1234
TOLL-FREE 800-233-1234
hyatt.com

QUALITY	87
COST	$$$$$+
LOCATION	Union Square
DISCOUNTS	AAA, senior, gov't.
NO. OF ROOMS	685
ON-SITE DINING	•
ROOM SERVICE	•
BAR	•
PARKING PER DAY	$49
MEETING FACILITIES	•
EXTRA AMENITIES	Babysitting, pillow-top mattresses, coffeemaker, minibar, wine reception, safe
BUSINESS AMENITIES	Dataport, 2-line phone
DECOR	European with Oriental accents
POOL/SAUNA	–
EXERCISE FACILITIES	Fitness center

Hotel Information Chart (continued)

Grant Plaza ★★★½
465 Grant Avenue
San Francisco, CA 94108
☎ 415-434-3883
TOLL-FREE 800-472-6899
grantplaza.com

QUALITY	77
COST	$$–
LOCATION	Union Square
DISCOUNTS	AAA, AARP, gov't.
NO. OF ROOMS	72
ON-SITE DINING	–
ROOM SERVICE	–
BAR	–
PARKING PER DAY	$22
MEETING FACILITIES	–
EXTRA AMENITIES	•
BUSINESS AMENITIES	Dataport, voice mail
DECOR	Contemporary
POOL/SAUNA	–
EXERCISE FACILITIES	Privileges (fee)

Handlery Union Square Hotel ★★★
351 Geary Street
San Francisco, CA 94102
☎ 415-781-7800
TOLL-FREE 800-843-4343
handlery.com

QUALITY	72
COST	$$$$–
LOCATION	Union Square
DISCOUNTS	AAA, AARP
NO. OF ROOMS	284
ON-SITE DINING	•
ROOM SERVICE	•
BAR	•
PARKING PER DAY	$40
MEETING FACILITIES	•
EXTRA AMENITIES	barber shop, babysitting, video games, newspaper
BUSINESS AMENITIES	Dataport, modem, multi-line phone
DECOR	Traditional European
POOL/SAUNA	Pool, sauna
EXERCISE FACILITIES	Privileges (fee)

Harbor Court Hotel ★★★★
165 Steuart Street
San Francisco, CA 94105
☎ 415-882-1300
TOLL-FREE 800-346-0555
harborcourthotel.com

QUALITY	85
COST	$$$$+
LOCATION	SoMa/Mission District
DISCOUNTS	AAA, AARP, gov't., military
NO. OF ROOMS	131
ON-SITE DINING	•
ROOM SERVICE	•
BAR	•
PARKING PER DAY	$30 hybrid, $40
MEETING FACILITIES	•
EXTRA AMENITIES	Wine reception, Wi-Fi, newspaper
BUSINESS AMENITIES	Dataport, 2-line phone
DECOR	1907 landmark building
POOL/SAUNA	Privileges
EXERCISE FACILITIES	Privileges

Hotel Abri ★★★½
127 Ellis Street
San Francisco, CA 94102
☎ 415-392-8800
TOLL-FREE 866-823-4669
larkspurhotels.com

QUALITY	80
COST	$$$$
LOCATION	Union Square
DISCOUNTS	AAA, AARP, gov't., senior
NO. OF ROOMS	91
ON-SITE DINING	•
ROOM SERVICE	•
BAR	•
PARKING PER DAY	$45
MEETING FACILITIES	•
EXTRA AMENITIES	Breakfast, p.m. wine, pet friendly, in-room spa services
BUSINESS AMENITIES	Dataport, fax, 2-line phone, voice mail
DECOR	Contemporary modern
POOL/SAUNA	Privileges (fee)
EXERCISE FACILITIES	Privileges (fee)

Hotel Adagio ★★★★
550 Geary Street
San Francisco, CA 94102
☎ 415-775-5000
TOLL-FREE 800-228-8830
jdvhotels.com/adagio

QUALITY	85
COST	$$$–
LOCATION	Union Square
DISCOUNTS	AAA, AARP, gov't., senior
NO. OF ROOMS	171
ON-SITE DINING	•
ROOM SERVICE	•
BAR	•
PARKING PER DAY	$39
MEETING FACILITIES	•
EXTRA AMENITIES	Internet, in-room dining
BUSINESS AMENITIES	Dataport, 2-line phone, business center, voice mail, secretarial services
DECOR	Spanish Colonial
POOL/SAUNA	–
EXERCISE FACILITIES	Fitness center

Hotel Beresford ★★½
635 Sutter Street
San Francisco, CA 94102
☎ 415-673-9900
TOLL-FREE 800-533-6533
beresford.com

QUALITY	60
COST	$$$$–
LOCATION	Union Square
DISCOUNTS	AAA, AARP, gov't., senior
NO. OF ROOMS	114
ON-SITE DINING	•
ROOM SERVICE	–
BAR	•
PARKING PER DAY	$25–$40 valet
MEETING FACILITIES	–
EXTRA AMENITIES	Free breakfast, satellite TV
BUSINESS AMENITIES	Dataport, copier, fax
DECOR	Victorian
POOL/SAUNA	–
EXERCISE FACILITIES	None

Harvest Inn ★★★★
1 Main Street
St. Helena, CA 94574
☎ 707-963-9463
TOLL-FREE 800-950-8466
harvestinn.com

QUALITY	84
COST	$$$$$$$+
LOCATION	Wine Country
DISCOUNTS	AAA
NO. OF ROOMS	74
ON-SITE DINING	•
ROOM SERVICE	–
BAR	•
PARKING PER DAY	Free
MEETING FACILITIES	•
EXTRA AMENITIES	Free breakfast, DVD, voice mail, in-room spa treatments
BUSINESS AMENITIES	Dataport, 2-line phone
DECOR	English Tudor
POOL/SAUNA	Pool, whirlpool
EXERCISE FACILITIES	–

Hilton San Francisco ★★★★
333 O'Farrell Street
San Francisco, CA 94102
☎ 415-771-1400
TOLL-FREE 800-hiltons
hilton.com

QUALITY	86
COST	$$$$$–
LOCATION	Union Square
DISCOUNTS	AAA, AARP, gov't.
NO. OF ROOMS	1,908
ON-SITE DINING	•
ROOM SERVICE	•
BAR	•
PARKING PER DAY	$51
MEETING FACILITIES	•
EXTRA AMENITIES	Gift shop, babysitting, pet friendly
BUSINESS AMENITIES	Dataport, 2-line phone
DECOR	Modern
POOL/SAUNA	Pool, sauna, whirlpool
EXERCISE FACILITIES	Fitness room

Hilton San Francisco Airport ★★★½
600 Airport Boulevard
Burlingame, CA 94010
☎ 650-340-8500
TOLL-FREE 800-774-1500
hilton.com

QUALITY	82
COST	$$$
LOCATION	SF Int'l Airport
DISCOUNTS	AAA, AARP, gov't., military
NO. OF ROOMS	404
ON-SITE DINING	•
ROOM SERVICE	–
BAR	•
PARKING PER DAY	$18 self, $25 valet
MEETING FACILITIES	•
EXTRA AMENITIES	Coffeemaker, ATM, pet friendly, multi-lingual staff, safety deposit boxes
BUSINESS AMENITIES	Dataport, 2-line phone, 24-hour business center, voice mail
DECOR	Traditional
POOL/SAUNA	Pool, sauna, whirlpool
EXERCISE FACILITIES	Fitness room, jogging path

Hotel Bijou ★★★½
111 Mason Street
San Francisco, CA 94102
☎ 415-771-1200
TOLL-FREE 800-771-1022
jdvhotels.com/bijou

QUALITY	82
COST	$$+
LOCATION	Union Square
DISCOUNTS	AAA, AARP, gov't., senior
NO. OF ROOMS	65
ON-SITE DINING	–
ROOM SERVICE	–
BAR	–
PARKING PER DAY	$30
MEETING FACILITIES	•
EXTRA AMENITIES	Breakfast, theater film tours casting calls
BUSINESS AMENITIES	Dataport, 2-line phone, voice mail
DECOR	San Francisco cinema
POOL/SAUNA	–
EXERCISE FACILITIES	–

Hotel Carlton ★★★★½
1075 Sutter Street
San Francisco, CA 94109
☎ 415-673-0242
TOLL-FREE 800-922-7586
jdvhotels.com/carlton

QUALITY	90
COST	$$$–
LOCATION	Civic Center
DISCOUNTS	AAA, AARP
NO. OF ROOMS	161
ON-SITE DINING	•
ROOM SERVICE	•
BAR	–
PARKING PER DAY	$30 valet
MEETING FACILITIES	•
EXTRA AMENITIES	Pet friendly
BUSINESS AMENITIES	Dataport
DECOR	Early San Francisco estate
POOL/SAUNA	–
EXERCISE FACILITIES	–

Hotel del Sol ★★★½
3100 Webster Street
San Francisco, CA 94123
☎ 415-921-5520
TOLL-FREE 877-433-5765
jdvhotels.com/del_sol

QUALITY	80
COST	$$$–
LOCATION	Marina District
DISCOUNTS	–
NO. OF ROOMS	57
ON-SITE DINING	–
ROOM SERVICE	–
BAR	–
PARKING PER DAY	Free
MEETING FACILITIES	•
EXTRA AMENITIES	Breakfast, VCR and DVD, tours, cookies, safe
BUSINESS AMENITIES	Dataport, 2-line phone, voice mail
DECOR	European
POOL/SAUNA	Pool
EXERCISE FACILITIES	–

Hotel Information Chart (continued)

Hotel des Arts ★★★★
447 Bush Street
San Francisco, CA 94108
☎ 415-956-3232
TOLL-FREE 800-956-4322
sfhoteldesarts.com

QUALITY	85
COST	$$
LOCATION	Union Square
DISCOUNTS	Special rates by Facebook, e-mail, fax, phone
NO. OF ROOMS	57
ON-SITE DINING	–
ROOM SERVICE	•
BAR	•
PARKING PER DAY	Sutter-Stockton garage nearby, averages $12 an hour, $40 daily
MEETING FACILITIES	–
EXTRA AMENITIES	Breakfast, Wi-Fi, satellite TV, tours
BUSINESS AMENITIES	Dataport, 2-line phone, voice mail
DECOR	Original artwork, special painted rooms
POOL/SAUNA	–
EXERCISE FACILITIES	–

Hotel Diva ★★★★½
440 Geary Street
San Francisco, CA 94102
☎ 415-885-0200
TOLL-FREE 800-553-1900
hoteldiva.com

QUALITY	90
COST	$$$$–
LOCATION	Union Square
DISCOUNTS	–
NO. OF ROOMS	1,102
ON-SITE DINING	–
ROOM SERVICE	–
BAR	–
PARKING PER DAY	$35
MEETING FACILITIES	•
EXTRA AMENITIES	CD player, iPod docks
BUSINESS AMENITIES	Dataport, voice mail, 24-hour business center
DECOR	Contemporary
POOL/SAUNA	–
EXERCISE FACILITIES	Fitness room

Hotel Drisco ★★★★
2901 Pacific Avenue
San Francisco, CA 94115
☎ 415-346-2880
TOLL-FREE 800-634-7277
jdvhotels.com/drisco

QUALITY	85
COST	$$$$
LOCATION	Richmond/ Sunset District
DISCOUNTS	Internet specials
NO. OF ROOMS	48
ON-SITE DINING	–
ROOM SERVICE	Limited
BAR	–
PARKING PER DAY	Street parking only
MEETING FACILITIES	–
EXTRA AMENITIES	Breakfast, robes, slippers, minibar, p.m. wine, tours, newspaper, coffee/ tea, DVD
BUSINESS AMENITIES	Dataport, 2-line phone, speaker phone, voice mail, business center
DECOR	Traditional
POOL/SAUNA	–
EXERCISE FACILITIES	Fitness room and YMCA privileges

Hotel Majestic ★★★★
1500 Sutter Street
San Francisco, CA 94109
☎ 415-441-1100
TOLL-FREE 800-869-8966
thehotelmajestic.com

QUALITY	89
COST	$$$–
LOCATION	Civic Center
DISCOUNTS	AAA, AARP, gov't.
NO. OF ROOMS	57
ON-SITE DINING	•
ROOM SERVICE	•
BAR	•
PARKING PER DAY	$25
MEETING FACILITIES	•
EXTRA AMENITIES	In-room dining, free breakfast
BUSINESS AMENITIES	Dataport, 2-line phone
DECOR	Victorian boutique
POOL/SAUNA	–
EXERCISE FACILITIES	–

Hotel Monaco ★★★★½
501 Geary Street
San Francisco, CA 94102
☎ 415-292-0100
TOLL-FREE 866-622-5284
monaco-sf.com

QUALITY	94
COST	$$$$$–
LOCATION	Union Square
DISCOUNTS	AAA, AARP, gov't., senior
NO. OF ROOMS	201
ON-SITE DINING	•
ROOM SERVICE	•
BAR	•
PARKING PER DAY	$49
MEETING FACILITIES	•
EXTRA AMENITIES	Massage, wine, pet friendly, Aveda bath products, newspaper, safe
BUSINESS AMENITIES	Dataport, 2-line phone, voice mail
DECOR	Beaux arts, modern eclectic
POOL/SAUNA	Whirlpool, steam room, sauna
EXERCISE FACILITIES	Fitness center

Hotel Nikko ★★★★★
222 Mason Street
San Francisco, CA 94102
☎ 415-394-1111
TOLL-FREE 800-NIKKO-US
hotelnikkosf.com

QUALITY	96
COST	$$$$$+
LOCATION	Union Square
DISCOUNTS	AAA, gov't., senior
NO. OF ROOMS	533
ON-SITE DINING	•
ROOM SERVICE	–
BAR	•
PARKING PER DAY	$45 valet
MEETING FACILITIES	•
EXTRA AMENITIES	Hair salon, art gallery, Starbucks
BUSINESS AMENITIES	Dataport, 2-line phone, voice mail, business center, overhead transparencies, color copiers, binding, faxing, packing, shipping
DECOR	Modern
POOL/SAUNA	Pool, whirlpool, sauna
EXERCISE FACILITIES	Health club

Hotel Durant ★★★½
2600 Durant Avenue
Berkeley, CA 94704
☎ 510-845-8981
TOLL-FREE 800-2-DURANT
jdvhotels.com/durant

QUALITY	75
COST	$$$+
LOCATION	Berkeley
DISCOUNTS	AAA, AARP, gov't.
NO. OF ROOMS	144
ON-SITE DINING	•
ROOM SERVICE	Limited
BAR	•
PARKING PER DAY	$12–$25 valet
MEETING FACILITIES	•
EXTRA AMENITIES	iPod docks, safe, newspaper, pet friendly
BUSINESS AMENITIES	Dataport, voice mail, business center, postal service
DECOR	Old Europe
POOL/SAUNA	–
EXERCISE FACILITIES	–

Hotel Frank ★★★½
386 Geary Street
San Francisco, CA 94102
☎ 415-986-2000
TOLL-FREE 800-553-1900
hotelfranksf.com

QUALITY	80
COST	$$$$+
LOCATION	Union Square
DISCOUNTS	AAA, AARP
NO. OF ROOMS	153
ON-SITE DINING	•
ROOM SERVICE	•
BAR	•
PARKING PER DAY	$35 valet
MEETING FACILITIES	•
EXTRA AMENITIES	Safe, newspaper, tours, pet friendly
BUSINESS AMENITIES	Dataport, 2-line phone, voice mail
DECOR	Contemporary
POOL/SAUNA	–
EXERCISE FACILITIES	Privileges

Hotel Kabuki ★★★½
1625 Post Street
San Francisco, CA 94115
☎ 415-922-3200
TOLL-FREE 800-533-4567
jdvhotels.com

QUALITY	76
COST	$$$$–
LOCATION	Civic Center
DISCOUNTS	AAA, AARP, gov't.
NO. OF ROOMS	218
ON-SITE DINING	•
ROOM SERVICE	•
BAR	•
PARKING PER DAY	$35 valet
MEETING FACILITIES	•
EXTRA AMENITIES	Japanese rooms available, in-room massage, fridge, robes, newspaper
BUSINESS AMENITIES	Dataport, voice mail, 2-line phone, business center
DECOR	Japanese style
POOL/SAUNA	Dry saunas in some suites
EXERCISE FACILITIES	Fitness room

Hotel Palomar ★★★★
12 Fourth Street
San Francisco, CA 94103
☎ 415-348-1111
TOLL-FREE 866-373-4941
hotelpalomarsf.com

QUALITY	89
COST	$$$$$–
LOCATION	SoMa/Mission District
DISCOUNTS	AAA, AARP, corp., gov't., military
NO. OF ROOMS	198
ON-SITE DINING	•
ROOM SERVICE	•
BAR	•
PARKING PER DAY	$45
MEETING FACILITIES	•
EXTRA AMENITIES	Pet friendly, newspaper, L'Occitane bath products, in-room spa treatments, safe
BUSINESS AMENITIES	Dataport, fax, 2-line phone
DECOR	Modern neoclassical with exotic touches
POOL/SAUNA	Whirlpool in some rooms
EXERCISE FACILITIES	Fitness room

Hotel Rex ★★★★
562 Sutter Street
San Francisco, CA 94102
☎ 415-433-4434
TOLL-FREE 800-433-4434
jdvhotels.com/rex

QUALITY	85
COST	$$$$$
LOCATION	Union Square
DISCOUNTS	AAA, AARP, gov't.
NO. OF ROOMS	94
ON-SITE DINING	•
ROOM SERVICE	•
BAR	•
PARKING PER DAY	$35
MEETING FACILITIES	•
EXTRA AMENITIES	Newspaper, p.m. wine
BUSINESS AMENITIES	Dataport, 2-line phone, voice mail
DECOR	1920s–1940s literary salon
POOL/SAUNA	–
EXERCISE FACILITIES	Privileges (fee) across street

Hotel St. Helena ★★★
1309 Main Street
St. Helena, CA 94574
☎ 707-963-4388
TOLL-FREE 888-478-4355
hotelsthelena.net

QUALITY	74
COST	$$$+
LOCATION	Wine Country
DISCOUNTS	Mid-week
NO. OF ROOMS	18
ON-SITE DINING	–
ROOM SERVICE	–
BAR	–
PARKING PER DAY	Free
MEETING FACILITIES	–
EXTRA AMENITIES	Free breakfast, p.m. wine
BUSINESS AMENITIES	–
DECOR	Victorian
POOL/SAUNA	–
EXERCISE FACILITIES	–

Hotel Information Chart (continued)

Hotel Triton ★★★★	
342 Grant Avenue	
San Francisco, CA 94108	
☎ 415-394-0500	
TOLL-FREE 800-800-1299	
hoteltriton.com	
QUALITY	86
COST	$$$$–
LOCATION	Union Square
DISCOUNTS	AAA, AARP, gov't.
NO. OF ROOMS	140
ON-SITE DINING	–
ROOM SERVICE	–
BAR	–
PARKING PER DAY	$42
MEETING FACILITIES	•
EXTRA AMENITIES	Tarot card reader, yoga, p.m. wine, art gallery, DJ on Fridays, massages, pet friendly
BUSINESS AMENITIES	Dataport, business center
DECOR	Ultramodern
POOL/SAUNA	–
EXERCISE FACILITIES	Fitness room

Hotel Union Square ★★★½	
114 Powell Street	
San Francisco, CA 94102	
☎ 415-397-3000	
TOLL-FREE 800-553-1900	
hotelunionsquare.com	
QUALITY	80
COST	$$$–
LOCATION	Union Square
DISCOUNTS	Corp., gov't., military
NO. OF ROOMS	131
ON-SITE DINING	–
ROOM SERVICE	–
BAR	–
PARKING PER DAY	$30
MEETING FACILITIES	•
EXTRA AMENITIES	Breakfast, boutique, Nintendo
BUSINESS AMENITIES	Dataport, voice mail, 24-hour business center
DECOR	Traditional European
POOL/SAUNA	Privileges
EXERCISE FACILITIES	Privileges

Hotel Vertigo ★★★★	
940 Sutter Street	
San Francisco, CA 94109	
☎ 415-885-6800	
TOLL-FREE 800-553-1900	
hotelvertigosf.com	
QUALITY	85
COST	$$+
LOCATION	Union Square
DISCOUNTS	AAA, AARP, gov't., corp.
NO. OF ROOMS	102
ON-SITE DINING	–
ROOM SERVICE	–
BAR	–
PARKING PER DAY	Valet $35 plus tax or public garage
MEETING FACILITIES	–
EXTRA AMENITIES	Pet friendly, big TVs
BUSINESS AMENITIES	Dataport, voice mail
DECOR	Contemporary with character
POOL/SAUNA	–
EXERCISE FACILITIES	Privileges

Hyatt Regency San Francisco ★★★★	
5 Embarcadero Center	
San Francisco, CA 94111	
☎ 415-788-1234	
TOLL-FREE 800-233-1234	
hyatt.com	
QUALITY	88
COST	$$$$+
LOCATION	Financial District
DISCOUNTS	AAA, gov't., senior
NO. OF ROOMS	802
ON-SITE DINING	•
ROOM SERVICE	•
BAR	•
PARKING PER DAY	$32 self, $50 valet
MEETING FACILITIES	•
EXTRA AMENITIES	Safe, newspaper, coffeemaker, mini-bar, on-call doctor
BUSINESS AMENITIES	Dataport, 2-line phone, voice mail, speaker phone
DECOR	Modern atrium high-rise
POOL/SAUNA	Privileges
EXERCISE FACILITIES	Privileges and fitness room

Hyatt Regency San Francisco Airport ★★★★	
1333 Bayshore Highway	
Burlingame, CA 94010	
☎ 415-347-1234	
TOLL-FREE 800-233-1234	
hyatt.com	
QUALITY	86
COST	$$$
LOCATION	SF Int'l Airport
DISCOUNTS	AAA, AARP, gov't., senior
NO. OF ROOMS	789
ON-SITE DINING	•
ROOM SERVICE	•
BAR	•
PARKING PER DAY	$18 self, $25 valet
MEETING FACILITIES	•
EXTRA AMENITIES	Newspaper, coffeemaker
BUSINESS AMENITIES	Dataport, 2-line phone, business center
DECOR	Modern
POOL/SAUNA	Pool, whirlpool
EXERCISE FACILITIES	Fitness room

Inn Above Tide ★★★★½	
30 El Portal	
Sausalito, CA 94965	
☎ 415-332-9535	
TOLL-FREE 800-893-8433	
innabovetide.com	
QUALITY	93
COST	$$$$$$+
LOCATION	Marin County
DISCOUNTS	–
NO. OF ROOMS	29
ON-SITE DINING	–
ROOM SERVICE	–
BAR	•
PARKING PER DAY	$18
MEETING FACILITIES	–
EXTRA AMENITIES	Breakfast, wine and cheese, newspaper, in-room dining, robes, slippers
BUSINESS AMENITIES	Dataport, 2-line phone, Internet, 24-hour fax and copy service
DECOR	Nautical
POOL/SAUNA	Spa services
EXERCISE FACILITIES	–

Hotel Vitale ★★★★½
8 Mission Street
San Francisco, CA 94105
☎ 415-278-3700
TOLL-FREE 888-890-8688
jdvhotels.com/vitale

QUALITY	90
COST	$$$$$–
LOCATION	Financial District
DISCOUNTS	–
NO. OF ROOMS	199
ON-SITE DINING	•
ROOM SERVICE	•
BAR	•
PARKING PER DAY	$45
MEETING FACILITIES	–
EXTRA AMENITIES	Newspaper, slippers, robes, safe, spa
BUSINESS AMENITIES	Dataport, voice mail, business center
DECOR	Modern
POOL/SAUNA	Whirlpool
EXERCISE FACILITIES	Fitness room

Huntington Hotel ★★★★½
1075 California Street
San Francisco, CA 94108
☎ 415-474-5400
TOLL-FREE 800-227-4683
huntingtonhotel.com

QUALITY	90
COST	$$$$$+
LOCATION	Nob Hill
DISCOUNTS	Gov't.
NO. OF ROOMS	135
ON-SITE DINING	•
ROOM SERVICE	•
BAR	•
PARKING PER DAY	$40
MEETING FACILITIES	•
EXTRA AMENITIES	Limo service, sherry, safe, newpaper, Nob Hill Spa
BUSINESS AMENITIES	Dataport, 2-line phone, voice mail, business center
DECOR	European
POOL/SAUNA	Pool, Jacuzzi, sauna
EXERCISE FACILITIES	Spa and fitness center

Hyatt Fisherman's Wharf ★★★★
555 North Point Street
San Francisco, CA 94133
☎ 415-563-1234
TOLL-FREE 800-233-1234
hyatt.com

QUALITY	88
COST	$$$$$–
LOCATION	North Beach
DISCOUNTS	AAA, gov't., senior
NO. OF ROOMS	313
ON-SITE DINING	•
ROOM SERVICE	•
BAR	•
PARKING PER DAY	$6 an hour, $45 daily
MEETING FACILITIES	•
EXTRA AMENITIES	Breakfast, newspaper, pillow-top mattresses, safe
BUSINESS AMENITIES	Dataport, 2-line phone, voice mail
DECOR	Wharf, Victorian
POOL/SAUNA	Pool, whirlpool
EXERCISE FACILITIES	Fitness center

Inn at Southbridge ★★★★½
1020 Main Street
St. Helena, CA 94574
☎ 707-967-9400
TOLL-FREE 800-520-6800
innatsouthbridge.com

QUALITY	92
COST	$$$$$$$
LOCATION	Wine Country
DISCOUNTS	AARP
NO. OF ROOMS	21
ON-SITE DINING	–
ROOM SERVICE	•
BAR	•
PARKING PER DAY	Free
MEETING FACILITIES	•
EXTRA AMENITIES	Full spa, wine bar, breakfast, safe, minifridge
BUSINESS AMENITIES	Dataport, 2-line phone
DECOR	European
POOL/SAUNA	Access
EXERCISE FACILITIES	Privileges (fee)

Inn at the Opera ★★★★½
333 Fulton Street
San Francisco, CA 94102
☎ 415-863-8400
TOLL-FREE 800-590-0157
shellhospitality.com

QUALITY	90
COST	$$$+
LOCATION	Civic Center
DISCOUNTS	AAA, gov't., corp.
NO. OF ROOMS	48
ON-SITE DINING	•
ROOM SERVICE	Dinner
BAR	•
PARKING PER DAY	$30
MEETING FACILITIES	–
EXTRA AMENITIES	Breakfast, newspaper, robes, cookies
BUSINESS AMENITIES	Dataport, 2-line phone, business center
DECOR	Classic European
POOL/SAUNA	–
EXERCISE FACILITIES	–

Inn at Union Square ★★★½
440 Post Street
San Francisco, CA 94102
☎ 415-397-3510
TOLL-FREE 800-288-4346
unionsquare.com

QUALITY	80
COST	$$$$$
LOCATION	Union Square
DISCOUNTS	Senior
NO. OF ROOMS	30
ON-SITE DINING	–
ROOM SERVICE	–
BAR	–
PARKING PER DAY	Free self, $38–$45 valet
MEETING FACILITIES	•
EXTRA AMENITIES	Breakfast, p.m. wine and appetizers, robes
BUSINESS AMENITIES	Dataport, 2-line phone, voice mail
DECOR	Boutique
POOL/SAUNA	Privileges
EXERCISE FACILITIES	Privileges

Hotel Information Chart (continued)

InterContinental
San Francisco ★★★★½
888 Howard Street
San Francisco, CA 94103
☎ 415-626-6500
TOLL-FREE 866-781-2364
intercontinentalsanfrancisco.com

QUALITY	90
COST	$$$$$
LOCATION	SoMa/Mission District
DISCOUNTS	AARP
NO. OF ROOMS	550
ON-SITE DINING	•
ROOM SERVICE	•
BAR	•
PARKING PER DAY	$61 valet
MEETING FACILITIES	•
EXTRA AMENITIES	Breakfast, wine and appetizers, pet friendly, gift shop
BUSINESS AMENITIES	Dataport, 2-line phone, voice mail
DECOR	Modern luxurious
POOL/SAUNA	Pool and spa
EXERCISE FACILITIES	Fitness center

The Jackson Court ★★★★½
2198 Jackson Street
San Francisco, CA 94115
☎ 415-929-7670
jacksoncourt.com

QUALITY	90
COST	$$$$–
LOCATION	Civic Center
DISCOUNTS	–
NO. OF ROOMS	10
ON-SITE DINING	–
ROOM SERVICE	–
BAR	–
PARKING PER DAY	$22
MEETING FACILITIES	–
EXTRA AMENITIES	Breakfast, tea and cookies, tours, newspaper, game room, dry cleaning
BUSINESS AMENITIES	–
DECOR	Contemporary
POOL/SAUNA	–
EXERCISE FACILITIES	–

John Muir Inn ★★★
1998 Trower Avenue
Napa, CA 94558
☎ 707-257-7220
TOLL-FREE 800-522-8999
johnmuirnapa.com

QUALITY	65
COST	$$$+
LOCATION	Wine Country
DISCOUNTS	AAA, AARP, gov't., senior
NO. OF ROOMS	60
ON-SITE DINING	–
ROOM SERVICE	–
BAR	–
PARKING PER DAY	Free
MEETING FACILITIES	•
EXTRA AMENITIES	Breakfast
BUSINESS AMENITIES	Dataport
DECOR	Traditional
POOL/SAUNA	Pool, whirlpool
EXERCISE FACILITIES	–

La Quinta Inn Oakland
Airport ★★★½
8465 Enterprise Way
Oakland, CA 94621
☎ 510-632-8900
TOLL-FREE 866-725-1661
lq.com

QUALITY	75
COST	$$$
LOCATION	Oakland Int'l Airport
DISCOUNTS	AAA, AARP, gov't., senior
NO. OF ROOMS	152
ON-SITE DINING	–
ROOM SERVICE	–
BAR	–
PARKING PER DAY	Free, Park & Fly pkg. $129/week
MEETING FACILITIES	•
EXTRA AMENITIES	Breakfast, airport shuttle, coffeemaker, pet friendly
BUSINESS AMENITIES	–
DECOR	Modern
POOL/SAUNA	Pool
EXERCISE FACILITIES	Privileges

Larkspur Hotel ★★★½
524 Sutter Street
San Francisco, CA 94102
☎ 415-421-2865
TOLL-FREE 866-823-4669
larkspurhotelunionsquare.com

QUALITY	75
COST	$$$$$
LOCATION	Union Square
DISCOUNTS	AAA, AARP
NO. OF ROOMS	114
ON-SITE DINING	–
ROOM SERVICE	–
BAR	–
PARKING PER DAY	$27 self, $40 valet
MEETING FACILITIES	•
EXTRA AMENITIES	Free breakfast, wine/tea hour, coffeemaker, pet friendly, newspaper
BUSINESS AMENITIES	Dataport, 2-line phone, voice mail
DECOR	European boutique
POOL/SAUNA	Privileges
EXERCISE FACILITIES	Privileges

Laurel Inn ★★★½
444 Presidio Avenue
San Francisco, CA 94115
☎ 415-567-8467
TOLL-FREE 800-552-8735
jdvhotels.com/laurel_inn

QUALITY	80
COST	$$$+
LOCATION	Richmond/ Sunset District
DISCOUNTS	AAA, AARP, gov't., senior, military, corp.
NO. OF ROOMS	49
ON-SITE DINING	–
ROOM SERVICE	–
BAR	–
PARKING PER DAY	Free
MEETING FACILITIES	–
EXTRA AMENITIES	Breakfast, kitchenettes, DVD, pet friendly
BUSINESS AMENITIES	Dataport, voice mail, 2-line phone
DECOR	Modern
POOL/SAUNA	–
EXERCISE FACILITIES	Privileges

JW Marriott Union Square ★★★★½
500 Post Street
San Francisco, CA 94102
☎ 415-771-8600
TOLL-FREE 800-533-6465
marriott.com

QUALITY	90
COST	$$$$$–
LOCATION	Union Square
DISCOUNTS	AAA, AARP, gov't.
NO. OF ROOMS	338
ON-SITE DINING	•
ROOM SERVICE	•
BAR	•
PARKING PER DAY	$52
MEETING FACILITIES	•
EXTRA AMENITIES	Limo service, pillow preference, safe, newspaper, luxury locker storage space
BUSINESS AMENITIES	Dataport, fax, business center
DECOR	Modern
POOL/SAUNA	–
EXERCISE FACILITIES	Fitness room

Kensington Park Hotel ★★★★
450 Post Street
San Francisco, CA 94102
☎ 415-788-6400
TOLL-FREE 800-553-1900
kensingtonparkhotel.com

QUALITY	83
COST	$$$$
LOCATION	Union Square
DISCOUNTS	AAA, AARP, gov't.
NO. OF ROOMS	90
ON-SITE DINING	•
ROOM SERVICE	–
BAR	•
PARKING PER DAY	$35
MEETING FACILITIES	•
EXTRA AMENITIES	Pet friendly, p.m. sherry and tea
BUSINESS AMENITIES	Dataport, business center
DECOR	Queen Anne
POOL/SAUNA	Privileges
EXERCISE FACILITIES	Access

King George Hotel ★★★
334 Mason Street
San Francisco, CA 94102
☎ 415-781-5050
TOLL-FREE 800-288-6005
kinggeorge.com

QUALITY	65
COST	$$$–
LOCATION	Union Square
DISCOUNTS	AAA, AARP, gov't.
NO. OF ROOMS	153
ON-SITE DINING	•
ROOM SERVICE	•
BAR	•
PARKING PER DAY	$30 self, $42 valet
MEETING FACILITIES	•
EXTRA AMENITIES	Apples, newspaper, safe
BUSINESS AMENITIES	Dataport, voice mail, 24-hour business center
DECOR	English boutique
POOL/SAUNA	Privileges
EXERCISE FACILITIES	Privileges

Mandarin Oriental ★★★★★
222 Sansome Street
San Francisco, CA 94104
☎ 415-276-9888
TOLL-FREE 800-622-0404
mandarinoriental.com/sanfrancisco

QUALITY	98
COST	$$$$$$$$+
LOCATION	Financial District
DISCOUNTS	Govt.
NO. OF ROOMS	158
ON-SITE DINING	•
ROOM SERVICE	•
BAR	•
PARKING PER DAY	$50
MEETING FACILITIES	•
EXTRA AMENITIES	Nintendo, safe, pet friendly, newspaper, robes, tea, cookies, binoculars
BUSINESS AMENITIES	Dataport, voice mail, 2-line phone, fax, copying
DECOR	Modern
POOL/SAUNA	–
EXERCISE FACILITIES	Fitness room

Marina Motel ★★★
2576 Lombard Street
San Francisco, CA 94123
☎ 415-921-9406
TOLL-FREE 800-346-6118
marinamotel.com

QUALITY	65
COST	$$$
LOCATION	Marina District
DISCOUNTS	–
NO. OF ROOMS	39
ON-SITE DINING	–
ROOM SERVICE	–
BAR	–
PARKING PER DAY	Free
MEETING FACILITIES	–
EXTRA AMENITIES	Kitchenettes, breakfast coupons
BUSINESS AMENITIES	–
DECOR	Historic 1930s
POOL/SAUNA	–
EXERCISE FACILITIES	–

Mark Hopkins InterContinental ★★★★
1 Nob Hill
San Francisco, CA 94108
☎ 415-392-3434
TOLL-FREE 800-327-0200
ichotelsgroup.com

QUALITY	84
COST	$$$$+
LOCATION	Nob Hill
DISCOUNTS	AAA, AARP, gov't., military
NO. OF ROOMS	422
ON-SITE DINING	•
ROOM SERVICE	•
BAR	•
PARKING PER DAY	$51
MEETING FACILITIES	•
EXTRA AMENITIES	Lounge music, car rental, robes, newspaper, safe
BUSINESS AMENITIES	Dataport, 2-line phone, voice mail, business center
DECOR	Grand hotel
POOL/SAUNA	–
EXERCISE FACILITIES	Fitness center

Hotel Information Chart (continued)

Marriott Fisherman's Wharf ★★★½
1250 Columbus Avenue
San Francisco, CA 94133
☎ 415-775-7555
TOLL-FREE 800-228-9290
marriott.com

QUALITY	80
COST	$$$$–
LOCATION	North Beach
DISCOUNTS	AAA, AARP, gov't., military, senior
NO. OF ROOMS	285
ON-SITE DINING	•
ROOM SERVICE	–
BAR	•
PARKING PER DAY	$13 an hour, $45 daily
MEETING FACILITIES	•
EXTRA AMENITIES	Minibar, pet friendly, newspaper
BUSINESS AMENITIES	Dataport, 2-line phone, voice mail
DECOR	Modern
POOL/SAUNA	Sauna, whirlpool
EXERCISE FACILITIES	Fitness room

Mill Valley Inn ★★★★½
165 Throckmorton Avenue
Mill Valley, CA 94941
☎ 415-389-6608
TOLL-FREE 800-595-2100
millvalleyinn.com

QUALITY	95
COST	$$$$$–
LOCATION	Marin County
DISCOUNTS	–
NO. OF ROOMS	25
ON-SITE DINING	–
ROOM SERVICE	–
BAR	–
PARKING PER DAY	Free
MEETING FACILITIES	•
EXTRA AMENITIES	Breakfast, robes, newspaper, p.m. wine
BUSINESS AMENITIES	Dataport, voice mail, fax
DECOR	European traditional
POOL/SAUNA	–
EXERCISE FACILITIES	Access

Motel Capri ★★★
2015 Greenwich Street
San Francisco, CA 94123
☎ 415-346-4667
TOLL-FREE 800-975-2905
sfmotelcapri.com

QUALITY	70
COST	$$
LOCATION	Marina District
DISCOUNTS	AAA, gov't.
NO. OF ROOMS	46
ON-SITE DINING	–
ROOM SERVICE	–
BAR	–
PARKING PER DAY	Free
MEETING FACILITIES	–
EXTRA AMENITIES	Coffee, tea, hot chocolate
BUSINESS AMENITIES	–
DECOR	Modern
POOL/SAUNA	–
EXERCISE FACILITIES	–

Nob Hill Lambourne ★★★★½
725 Pine Street
San Francisco, CA 94108
☎ 415-433-2287
TOLL-FREE 800-274-8466
nobhilllambourne.com

QUALITY	92
COST	$$$–
LOCATION	Union Square
DISCOUNTS	AAA, AARP
NO. OF ROOMS	20
ON-SITE DINING	–
ROOM SERVICE	–
BAR	–
PARKING PER DAY	$36
MEETING FACILITIES	•
EXTRA AMENITIES	Breakfast, wine, kitchenette, robes, TV
BUSINESS AMENITIES	Dataport, fax, 2-line phone, voice mail
DECOR	Business and wellness boutique
POOL/SAUNA	–
EXERCISE FACILITIES	Wellness center

Oakland Airport Hilton ★★★½
1 Hegenberger Road
Oakland, CA 94621
☎ 510-635-5000
TOLL-FREE 800-HILTONS
hilton.com

QUALITY	80
COST	$$$–
LOCATION	Oakland Int'l Airport
DISCOUNTS	AAA, AARP, gov't., military
NO. OF ROOMS	363
ON-SITE DINING	•
ROOM SERVICE	•
BAR	•
PARKING PER DAY	$10
MEETING FACILITIES	•
EXTRA AMENITIES	Airport shuttle, pet friendly, newspaper, robes
BUSINESS AMENITIES	Dataport, 2-line phone, voice mail, printer, copier, fax, notary public, audio-visual equipment
DECOR	Modern
POOL/SAUNA	Pool
EXERCISE FACILITIES	Fitness room

Oakland Marriott City Center ★★★
1001 Broadway
Oakland, CA 94607
☎ 510-451-4000
TOLL-FREE 800-228-9290
marriott.com

QUALITY	74
COST	$$$–
LOCATION	Oakland
DISCOUNTS	AAA, AARP, gov't., military, senior
NO. OF ROOMS	484
ON-SITE DINING	•
ROOM SERVICE	•
BAR	•
PARKING PER DAY	$20 self, $26 valet
MEETING FACILITIES	•
EXTRA AMENITIES	Massage service, newspaper
BUSINESS AMENITIES	Dataport, 2-line phone, voice mail, 24-hour business center, audiovisual equipment
DECOR	Modern
POOL/SAUNA	Pool
EXERCISE FACILITIES	Fitness room

Mount View Hotel ★★★½
1457 Lincoln Avenue
Calistoga, CA 94515
☎ 707-942-6877
TOLL-FREE 800-816-6877
mountviewhotel.com

QUALITY	81
COST	$$$$$–
LOCATION	Wine Country
DISCOUNTS	AAA
NO. OF ROOMS	32
ON-SITE DINING	•
ROOM SERVICE	–
BAR	•
PARKING PER DAY	Free
MEETING FACILITIES	–
EXTRA AMENITIES	Breakfast, full spa, DVD players, Aveda bath products, robes
BUSINESS AMENITIES	Dataport, fax, voice mail
DECOR	California spa
POOL/SAUNA	Whirlpool, spa, sauna
EXERCISE FACILITIES	

Napa Valley Lodge ★★★★½
2230 Madison Street
Yountville, CA 94599
☎ 707-944-2468
TOLL-FREE 800-368-2468
woodsidehotels.com

QUALITY	90
COST	$$$$$–
LOCATION	Wine Country
DISCOUNTS	AAA, AARP
NO. OF ROOMS	55
ON-SITE DINING	–
ROOM SERVICE	–
BAR	–
PARKING PER DAY	Free
MEETING FACILITIES	•
EXTRA AMENITIES	Free Champagne, breakfast, wine tasting
BUSINESS AMENITIES	Dataport
DECOR	California
POOL/SAUNA	Pool, sauna, whirlpool
EXERCISE FACILITIES	Fitness room

Napa Valley Marriott Hotel ★★★★
3425 Solano Avenue
Napa, CA 94558
☎ 707-253-7433
TOLL-FREE 800-228-9290
napavalleymarriott.com

QUALITY	84
COST	$$$$$$$–
LOCATION	Wine Country
DISCOUNTS	AAA, AARP, gov't., senior
NO. OF ROOMS	274
ON-SITE DINING	•
ROOM SERVICE	•
BAR	•
PARKING PER DAY	Free
MEETING FACILITIES	•
EXTRA AMENITIES	Basketball and tennis courts, salon
BUSINESS AMENITIES	Dataport
DECOR	Modern
POOL/SAUNA	Pool, whirlpool, spa
EXERCISE FACILITIES	Fitness room

Oceanview Motel ★★
4340 Judah Street
San Francisco, CA 94122
☎ 415-661-2300
oceanviewmotelsf.com

QUALITY	55
COST	$$+
LOCATION	Richmond/ Sunset District
DISCOUNTS	AAA, AARP
NO. OF ROOMS	55
ON-SITE DINING	–
ROOM SERVICE	•
BAR	–
PARKING PER DAY	Free
MEETING FACILITIES	–
EXTRA AMENITIES	Breakfast, newspaper, some kitchenettes
BUSINESS AMENITIES	–
DECOR	Local motel-style
POOL/SAUNA	–
EXERCISE FACILITIES	Walks on Ocean Beach or Golden Gate Park

Pacific Heights Inn ★★★
1555 Union Street
San Francisco, CA 94123
☎ 415-776-3310
TOLL-FREE 800-523-1801
pacificheightsinn.com

QUALITY	70
COST	$$$
LOCATION	Marina District
DISCOUNTS	AAA, AARP, gov't.
NO. OF ROOMS	40
ON-SITE DINING	–
ROOM SERVICE	–
BAR	–
PARKING PER DAY	Free
MEETING FACILITIES	–
EXTRA AMENITIES	Breakfast, newspaper, some kitchenettes
BUSINESS AMENITIES	–
DECOR	Modern
POOL/SAUNA	Whirlpool in some rooms
EXERCISE FACILITIES	–

Petite Auberge ★★★½
863 Bush Street
San Francisco, CA 94108
☎ 415-928-6000
TOLL-FREE 888-824-0386
jdvhotels.com/petite_auberge

QUALITY	75
COST	$$$+
LOCATION	Union Square
DISCOUNTS	–
NO. OF ROOMS	26
ON-SITE DINING	–
ROOM SERVICE	–
BAR	–
PARKING PER DAY	$32
MEETING FACILITIES	–
EXTRA AMENITIES	Breakfast, p.m. wine and hors d'oeuvres, tours
BUSINESS AMENITIES	Dataport, voice mail
DECOR	French Country inn
POOL/SAUNA	–
EXERCISE FACILITIES	–

Hotel Information Chart *(continued)*

Phoenix Hotel ★★½
601 Eddy Street
San Francisco, CA 94109
☎ 415-776-1380
TOLL-FREE 800-248-9466
jdvhotels.com/phoenix

QUALITY	60
COST	$$$
LOCATION	Civic Center
DISCOUNTS	AAA, gov't.
NO. OF ROOMS	44
ON-SITE DINING	•
ROOM SERVICE	–
BAR	•
PARKING PER DAY	Free
MEETING FACILITIES	–
EXTRA AMENITIES	Breakfast
BUSINESS AMENITIES	Dataport, voice mail
DECOR	Tropical bungalow
POOL/SAUNA	Pool
EXERCISE FACILITIES	Access

Prescott Hotel ★★★★½
545 Post Street
San Francisco, CA 94102
☎ 415-563-0303
TOLL-FREE 866-271-3632
prescotthotel.com

QUALITY	92
COST	$$$$$$+
LOCATION	Union Square
DISCOUNTS	AAA, AARP, gov't., military
NO. OF ROOMS	164
ON-SITE DINING	•
ROOM SERVICE	•
BAR	•
PARKING PER DAY	$45 valet
MEETING FACILITIES	–
EXTRA AMENITIES	Newspaper, p.m. wine, safety deposit boxes, pet friendly
BUSINESS AMENITIES	Dataport, fax, 2-line phone
DECOR	Early California
POOL/SAUNA	–
EXERCISE FACILITIES	Fitness room

Queen Anne Hotel ★★★½
1590 Sutter Street
San Francisco, CA 94109
☎ 415-441-2828
TOLL-FREE 800-227-3970
queenanne.com

QUALITY	80
COST	$$$
LOCATION	Civic Center
DISCOUNTS	AAA, AARP, gov't.
NO. OF ROOMS	48
ON-SITE DINING	–
ROOM SERVICE	Limited
BAR	–
PARKING PER DAY	$24 self, $34 valet
MEETING FACILITIES	•
EXTRA AMENITIES	Free breakfast, p.m. tea and sherry
BUSINESS AMENITIES	Dataport, voice mail
DECOR	Victorian
POOL/SAUNA	Privileges
EXERCISE FACILITIES	Privileges

Renaissance Parc Fifty Five ★★★★
55 Cyril Magnin Market
San Francisco, CA 94102
☎ 415-392-8000
TOLL-FREE 800-650-7272
parc55hotel.com

QUALITY	85
COST	$$$$+
LOCATION	Union Square
DISCOUNTS	AAA, AARP, gov't.
NO. OF ROOMS	1,025
ON-SITE DINING	•
ROOM SERVICE	•
BAR	•
PARKING PER DAY	$45
MEETING FACILITIES	•
EXTRA AMENITIES	Video games, bay windows, newspaper, fridge, safety deposit boxes
BUSINESS AMENITIES	Dataport, 2-line phone, business center
DECOR	Modern
POOL/SAUNA	Sauna
EXERCISE FACILITIES	Health club

Ritz-Carlton ★★★★★
600 Stockton Street
San Francisco, CA 94108
☎ 415-296-7465
TOLL-FREE 800-241-3333
ritzcarlton.com

QUALITY	96
COST	$$$$$$$$
LOCATION	Nob Hill
DISCOUNTS	–
NO. OF ROOMS	336
ON-SITE DINING	•
ROOM SERVICE	•
BAR	•
PARKING PER DAY	$72
MEETING FACILITIES	•
EXTRA AMENITIES	Massage service, robes, slippers
BUSINESS AMENITIES	Dataport, 2-line phone, voice mail
DECOR	Traditional
POOL/SAUNA	Pool, sauna, whirlpool
EXERCISE FACILITIES	Fitness room

Ritz-Carlton Half Moon Bay ★★★★★
1 Miramontes Point Road
Half Moon Bay, CA 94019
☎ 650-712-7000
TOLL-FREE 800-241-3333
ritzcarlton.com

QUALITY	97
COST	$$$$$$$+
LOCATION	South Bay
DISCOUNTS	–
NO. OF ROOMS	261
ON-SITE DINING	•
ROOM SERVICE	•
BAR	•
PARKING PER DAY	$45
MEETING FACILITIES	•
EXTRA AMENITIES	Golf, spa, shuttle, robes, fridge, safe
BUSINESS AMENITIES	Dataport, 2-line phone, voice mail
DECOR	Traditional
POOL/SAUNA	Whirlpool, sauna, steam room, spa
EXERCISE FACILITIES	Fitness room, yoga studio

Radisson Fisherman's Wharf ★★★
250 Beach Street
San Francisco, CA 94133
☎ 415-392-6700
TOLL-FREE 800-390-7046
radisson.com

QUALITY	70
COST	$$$$+
LOCATION	North Beach
DISCOUNTS	AAA, AARP, gov't.
NO. OF ROOMS	355
ON-SITE DINING	–
ROOM SERVICE	–
BAR	–
PARKING PER DAY	$37
MEETING FACILITIES	•
EXTRA AMENITIES	Bay views, in-room safe
BUSINESS AMENITIES	Dataport, voice mail, 2-line phone
DECOR	Contemporary
POOL/SAUNA	Pool
EXERCISE FACILITIES	Fitness room

Rancho Caymus ★★★★
1140 Rutherford Road
Rutherford, CA 94573
☎ 707-963-1777
TOLL-FREE 800-845-1777
ranchocaymus.com

QUALITY	87
COST	$$$$+
LOCATION	Wine Country
DISCOUNTS	AAA, AARP
NO. OF ROOMS	26
ON-SITE DINING	•
ROOM SERVICE	–
BAR	•
PARKING PER DAY	Free
MEETING FACILITIES	–
EXTRA AMENITIES	Breakfast, fridge, robes
BUSINESS AMENITIES	–
DECOR	California mission
POOL/SAUNA	–
EXERCISE FACILITIES	–

Red Roof Inn San Francisco Airport ★★½
777 Airport Boulevard
Burlingame, CA 94010
☎ 415-342-7772
TOLL-FREE 800-RED-ROOF
redroof.com

QUALITY	60
COST	$$–
LOCATION	SF Int'l Airport
DISCOUNTS	AAA, senior
NO. OF ROOMS	200
ON-SITE DINING	•
ROOM SERVICE	–
BAR	–
PARKING PER DAY	Free
MEETING FACILITIES	–
EXTRA AMENITIES	Free shuttle; park, stay, and fly; pet friendly
BUSINESS AMENITIES	Dataport, fax, copier
DECOR	Modern
POOL/SAUNA	Pool
EXERCISE FACILITIES	Privileges

San Francisco Airport Marriott ★★★★
1800 Old Bayshore Highway
Burlingame, CA 94010
☎ 650-692-9100
TOLL-FREE 800-228-9290
marriott.com

QUALITY	83
COST	$$$+
LOCATION	SF Int'l Airport
DISCOUNTS	AAA, AARP, gov't., military, senior
NO. OF ROOMS	706
ON-SITE DINING	•
ROOM SERVICE	–
BAR	•
PARKING PER DAY	$18 self, $25 valet
MEETING FACILITIES	•
EXTRA AMENITIES	Video games, running path, pet friendly
BUSINESS AMENITIES	Dataport, 2-line phone, voice mail
DECOR	Traditional
POOL/SAUNA	Pool, sauna, whirlpool
EXERCISE FACILITIES	Fitness room

San Francisco Marriott ★★★★
55 Fourth Street
San Francisco, CA 94103
☎ 415-896-1600
TOLL-FREE 800-228-9290
sfmarriott.com

QUALITY	86
COST	$$$$+
LOCATION	SoMa/Mission District
DISCOUNTS	AAA, AARP, gov't., military, senior
NO. OF ROOMS	1,498
ON-SITE DINING	•
ROOM SERVICE	•
BAR	•
PARKING PER DAY	$13 an hour, $56 daily
MEETING FACILITIES	•
EXTRA AMENITIES	Newspaper, shoe shine, rental cars, safety deposit boxes
BUSINESS AMENITIES	Dataport, 2-line phone, business center, voice mail, audiovisual equipment, notary public
DECOR	Modern
POOL/SAUNA	Pool, sauna, whirlpool
EXERCISE FACILITIES	Fitness room

San Francisco Marriott Union Square ★★★½
480 Sutter Street
San Francisco, CA 94108
☎ 415-398-8900
TOLL-FREE 866-912-0973
marriott.com

QUALITY	76
COST	$$$$–
LOCATION	Union Square
DISCOUNTS	AAA, AARP, gov't., military
NO. OF ROOMS	404
ON-SITE DINING	•
ROOM SERVICE	•
BAR	•
PARKING PER DAY	$11 an hour, $53 daily
MEETING FACILITIES	•
EXTRA AMENITIES	Newsstand, CD player, pet friendly, safe, multilingual staff
BUSINESS AMENITIES	Dataport, 2-line phone, voice mail
DECOR	Modern
POOL/SAUNA	–
EXERCISE FACILITIES	Fitness center

Hotel Information Chart (continued)

Seal Rock Inn ★★★½
545 Point Lobos Avenue
San Francisco, CA 94121
☎ 415-752-8000
TOLL-FREE 888-732-5762
sealrockinn.com

QUALITY	75
COST	$$+
LOCATION	Richmond/ Sunset District
DISCOUNTS	–
NO. OF ROOMS	27
ON-SITE DINING	•
ROOM SERVICE	–
BAR	–
PARKING PER DAY	Free
MEETING FACILITIES	–
EXTRA AMENITIES	Kitchenettes, fireplace, fridge
BUSINESS AMENITIES	Dataport, 2-line phone
DECOR	Modern
POOL/SAUNA	Pool
EXERCISE FACILITIES	Ping pong, badminton

Serrano Hotel ★★★★
405 Taylor Street
San Francisco, CA 94102
☎ 415-885-2500
TOLL-FREE 866-289-6561
serranohotel.com

QUALITY	83
COST	$$$$–
LOCATION	Union Square
DISCOUNTS	AAA, corp., gov't., military, senior
NO. OF ROOMS	236
ON-SITE DINING	•
ROOM SERVICE	•
BAR	•
PARKING PER DAY	$42
MEETING FACILITIES	•
EXTRA AMENITIES	Pet friendly, p.m. wine, video games, Internet
BUSINESS AMENITIES	Dataport, fax, 2-line phone, voice mail, audiovisual, business center
DECOR	Eclectic Californian
POOL/SAUNA	Sauna
EXERCISE FACILITIES	Fitness room

Sheraton at Fisherman's Wharf ★★★½
2500 Mason Street
San Francisco, CA 94133
☎ 415-362-5500
TOLL-FREE 800-325-3535
sheratonatthewharf.com

QUALITY	82
COST	$$$$–
LOCATION	North Beach
DISCOUNTS	AAA, gov't.
NO. OF ROOMS	529
ON-SITE DINING	•
ROOM SERVICE	•
BAR	•
PARKING PER DAY	$43
MEETING FACILITIES	•
EXTRA AMENITIES	Video games, tea/coffeemakers, car rental, newspaper, safety deposit boxes
BUSINESS AMENITIES	Dataport, 24-hour business center and currency exchange, voice mail, 2-line phone
DECOR	Modern
POOL/SAUNA	Pool
EXERCISE FACILITIES	Fitness room

Sonoma Hotel ★★★★
110 West Spain Street
Sonoma, CA 95476
☎ 707-996-2996
TOLL-FREE 800-468-6016
sonomahotel.com

QUALITY	85
COST	$$$+
LOCATION	Wine Country
DISCOUNTS	Group
NO. OF ROOMS	16
ON-SITE DINING	•
ROOM SERVICE	–
BAR	•
PARKING PER DAY	Free
MEETING FACILITIES	–
EXTRA AMENITIES	Breakfast, wine tasting, handmade soaps
BUSINESS AMENITIES	Dataport
DECOR	French Provencal
POOL/SAUNA	–
EXERCISE FACILITIES	–

Sonoma Mission Inn and Spa ★★★★½
100 Boyes Boulevard
Boyes Hot Springs, CA 95476
☎ 707-938-9000
TOLL-FREE 800-862-4945
fairmont.com/sonoma

QUALITY	90
COST	$$$$$$$+
LOCATION	Wine Country
DISCOUNTS	–
NO. OF ROOMS	226
ON-SITE DINING	•
ROOM SERVICE	•
BAR	•
PARKING PER DAY	$25 valet, free self-parking for hybrids
MEETING FACILITIES	•
EXTRA AMENITIES	Full spa, massage, golf course, babysitting, robes, safe
BUSINESS AMENITIES	Dataport, voice mail, 24-hour business center
DECOR	Variety
POOL/SAUNA	Pool, sauna, steam room
EXERCISE FACILITIES	Fitness room, golf, yoga, Pilates, aquatic classes

Stanford Court Renaissance Hotel ★★★★½
905 California Street
San Francisco, CA 94108
☎ 415-989-3500
TOLL-FREE 800-468-3571
marriott.com

QUALITY	90
COST	$$$+
LOCATION	Nob Hill
DISCOUNTS	AAA, AARP, gov't., military, senior
NO. OF ROOMS	393
ON-SITE DINING	•
ROOM SERVICE	–
BAR	•
PARKING PER DAY	$8 an hour, $52 valet
MEETING FACILITIES	•
EXTRA AMENITIES	Pet friendly, robes, video games
BUSINESS AMENITIES	Dataport, 2-line phone, business center
DECOR	Contemporary urban
POOL/SAUNA	–
EXERCISE FACILITIES	Fitness room

Sheraton Palace Hotel ★★★★
2 New Montgomery Street
San Francisco, CA 94105
☎ 415-512-1111
TOLL-FREE 800-325-3535
sfpalace.com

QUALITY	89
COST	$$$$$$
LOCATION	SoMa/Mission District
DISCOUNTS	AAA, gov't.
NO. OF ROOMS	553
ON-SITE DINING	•
ROOM SERVICE	–
BAR	•
PARKING PER DAY	$42
MEETING FACILITIES	•
EXTRA AMENITIES	Massage, safe, robes, fridge, pet friendly
BUSINESS AMENITIES	Dataport, 2-line phone, voice mail
DECOR	Grand hotel
POOL/SAUNA	Pool, sauna, whirlpool
EXERCISE FACILITIES	Fitness room

Silverado Country Club and Resort ★★★★
1600 Atlas Peak Road
Napa, CA 94558
☎ 707-257-0200
TOLL-FREE 800-532-0500
silveradoresort.com

QUALITY	85
COST	$$$$$$
LOCATION	Wine Country
DISCOUNTS	AAA, AARP
NO. OF ROOMS	281
ON-SITE DINING	•
ROOM SERVICE	–
BAR	•
PARKING PER DAY	Free
MEETING FACILITIES	•
EXTRA AMENITIES	Golf course, spa, tennis, massage
BUSINESS AMENITIES	Dataport, 2-line phone, audiovisual equipment
DECOR	Contemporary
POOL/SAUNA	Pool, sauna, whirlpool
EXERCISE FACILITIES	Fitness room, yoga and aquatic classes, golf, tennis

Sir Francis Drake Hotel ★★★½
450 Powell Street
San Francisco, CA 94102
☎ 415-392-7755
TOLL-FREE 800-795-7129
sirfrancisdrake.com

QUALITY	82
COST	$$$$
LOCATION	Union Square
DISCOUNTS	AAA, AARP, gov't., senior
NO. OF ROOMS	416
ON-SITE DINING	•
ROOM SERVICE	•
BAR	•
PARKING PER DAY	$47 valet
MEETING FACILITIES	•
EXTRA AMENITIES	Pet friendly, minibar, fridge, safety deposit boxes
BUSINESS AMENITIES	2-line phone, voice mail, business center
DECOR	California Colonial
POOL/SAUNA	In-room spa
EXERCISE FACILITIES	Fitness room

Stanyan Park Hotel ★★★½
750 Stanyon Street
San Francisco, CA 94117
☎ 415-751-1000
stanyanpark.com

QUALITY	75
COST	$$$
LOCATION	Richmond/ Sunset District
DISCOUNTS	AAA
NO. OF ROOMS	36
ON-SITE DINING	•
ROOM SERVICE	–
BAR	–
PARKING PER DAY	$15-$20 across street
MEETING FACILITIES	–
EXTRA AMENITIES	Breakfast, p.m. tea and coffee
BUSINESS AMENITIES	Dataport, voice mail
DECOR	Victorian
POOL/SAUNA	–
EXERCISE FACILITIES	–

Super 8 Motel ★★½
2440 Lombard Street
San Francisco, CA 94123
☎ 415-922-0244
TOLL-FREE 800-800-8000
super8.com

QUALITY	62
COST	$$$$–
LOCATION	Marina District
DISCOUNTS	AAA, AARP, gov't., senior
NO. OF ROOMS	32
ON-SITE DINING	–
ROOM SERVICE	–
BAR	–
PARKING PER DAY	Free
MEETING FACILITIES	–
EXTRA AMENITIES	Microwave, fridge, Jacuzzi, DVD player and remote, breakfast
BUSINESS AMENITIES	–
DECOR	Modern
POOL/SAUNA	–
EXERCISE FACILITIES	Privileges

Town House Motel ★★½
1650 Lombard Street
San Francisco, CA 94123
☎ 415-885-5163
TOLL-FREE 800-255-1516
sftownhousemotel.com

QUALITY	60
COST	$$$–
LOCATION	Marina District
DISCOUNTS	AARP, gov't.
NO. OF ROOMS	23
ON-SITE DINING	–
ROOM SERVICE	–
BAR	–
PARKING PER DAY	Free
MEETING FACILITIES	–
EXTRA AMENITIES	Breakfast, fridge
BUSINESS AMENITIES	–
DECOR	Modern
POOL/SAUNA	–
EXERCISE FACILITIES	–

Hotel Information Chart (continued)

Travelodge by the Bay ★★½
1450 Lombard Street
San Francisco, CA 94123
☎ 415-673-0691
TOLL-FREE 800-578-7878
travelodgebythebay.com

QUALITY	62
COST	$$$–
LOCATION	Marina District
DISCOUNTS	AAA, AARP, gov't., senior
NO. OF ROOMS	72
ON-SITE DINING	•
ROOM SERVICE	–
BAR	•
PARKING PER DAY	$14
MEETING FACILITIES	–
EXTRA AMENITIES	Breakfast, coffeemaker, newspaper, safe, pet friendly
BUSINESS AMENITIES	Dataport, fax
DECOR	Modern
POOL/SAUNA	–
EXERCISE FACILITIES	Nearby

Travelodge Golden Gate ★★½
2230 Lombard Street
San Francisco, CA 94123
☎ 415-922-3900
TOLL-FREE 800-578-7878
travelodge.com

QUALITY	60
COST	$$+
LOCATION	Marina District
DISCOUNTS	AAA, AARP, gov't., senior
NO. OF ROOMS	29
ON-SITE DINING	–
ROOM SERVICE	–
BAR	–
PARKING PER DAY	Free
MEETING FACILITIES	–
EXTRA AMENITIES	Newspaper, safe, coffeemaker, tours
BUSINESS AMENITIES	Dataport, fax
DECOR	Modern
POOL/SAUNA	–
EXERCISE FACILITIES	Nearby

Travelodge San Francisco Airport North ★★★
326 South Airport Boulevard
San Francisco, CA 94080
☎ 650-583-9600
TOLL-FREE 800-578-7878
travelodge.com

QUALITY	70
COST	$
LOCATION	SF Int'l Airport
DISCOUNTS	AAA, AARP, gov't., senior
NO. OF ROOMS	199
ON-SITE DINING	•
ROOM SERVICE	–
BAR	–
PARKING PER DAY	Free
MEETING FACILITIES	•
EXTRA AMENITIES	Coffee, safe, fridge, microwave, sofa bed, ATM
BUSINESS AMENITIES	Dataport, voice mail, fax
DECOR	Modern tropical
POOL/SAUNA	Pool
EXERCISE FACILITIES	–

W Hotel San Francisco ★★★★½
181 Third Street
San Francisco, CA 94103
☎ 415-777-5300
TOLL-FREE 877-WHOTELS
whotel.com

QUALITY	95
COST	$$$$$
LOCATION	SoMa/Mission District
DISCOUNTS	AAA, gov't., senior
NO. OF ROOMS	410
ON-SITE DINING	•
ROOM SERVICE	•
BAR	•
PARKING PER DAY	$35 hybrid, $45 valet
MEETING FACILITIES	•
EXTRA AMENITIES	Stereo, videos, newspaper, robes, safe, minibar, coffeemaker, DVD players, pet friendly
BUSINESS AMENITIES	Dataport, fax, 2-line phone
DECOR	Ultramodern
POOL/SAUNA	Pool, steam, whirlpool
EXERCISE FACILITIES	Fitness room, yoga

Warwick Regis Hotel ★★★★
490 Geary Street
San Francisco, CA 94102
☎ 415-928-7900
TOLL-FREE 800-203-3232
warwicksf.com

QUALITY	83
COST	$$$$
LOCATION	Union Square
DISCOUNTS	AAA, AARP, gov't.
NO. OF ROOMS	74
ON-SITE DINING	•
ROOM SERVICE	•
BAR	•
PARKING PER DAY	$35
MEETING FACILITIES	•
EXTRA AMENITIES	Safe, robes, video games, umbrellas
BUSINESS AMENITIES	Dataport, 2-line phone, voice mail
DECOR	European boutique
POOL/SAUNA	Privileges
EXERCISE FACILITIES	Privileges (fee)

Waterfront Plaza Hotel ★★★½
10 Washington Street
Oakland, CA 94607
☎ 510-836-3800
TOLL-FREE 800-729-3638
waterfrontplaza.com

QUALITY	80
COST	$$$$–
LOCATION	Oakland
DISCOUNTS	AAA, AARP
NO. OF ROOMS	145
ON-SITE DINING	•
ROOM SERVICE	–
BAR	–
PARKING PER DAY	$12 day use, $20 overnight
MEETING FACILITIES	•
EXTRA AMENITIES	Ferry to San Francisco, video games, safe, minibar, coffee/tea maker
BUSINESS AMENITIES	Dataport, voice mail
DECOR	Nautical
POOL/SAUNA	Pool, sauna
EXERCISE FACILITIES	Fitness room

Union Street Inn ★★★½
2229 Union Street
San Francisco, CA 94123
☎ 415-346-0424
unionstreetinn.com

QUALITY	82
COST	$$$$$$$–
LOCATION	Marina District
DISCOUNTS	–
NO. OF ROOMS	6
ON-SITE DINING	–
ROOM SERVICE	–
BAR	–
PARKING PER DAY	$15
MEETING FACILITIES	–
EXTRA AMENITIES	Full breakfast, p.m. wine
BUSINESS AMENITIES	–
DECOR	Victorian
POOL/SAUNA	–
EXERCISE FACILITIES	–

Villa Florence ★★★½
225 Powell Street
San Francisco, CA 94102
☎ 415-397-7700
TOLL-FREE 800-553-4411
villaflorence.com

QUALITY	80
COST	$$$$$–
LOCATION	Union Square
DISCOUNTS	AAA, AARP, gov't., senior
NO. OF ROOMS	183
ON-SITE DINING	•
ROOM SERVICE	–
BAR	•
PARKING PER DAY	$40
MEETING FACILITIES	–
EXTRA AMENITIES	Nintendo, p.m. wine, newspaper, pet friendly, in-room spa services
BUSINESS AMENITIES	Dataport, voice mail, copier, fax, printer
DECOR	Italian Renaissance
POOL/SAUNA	–
EXERCISE FACILITIES	Fitness center

Vintage Inn ★★★★½
6541 Washington Street
Yountville, CA 94599
☎ 707-944-1112
TOLL-FREE 800-351-1133
vintageinn.com

QUALITY	91
COST	$$$$$$$$$–
LOCATION	Wine Country
DISCOUNTS	AAA, AARP
NO. OF ROOMS	80
ON-SITE DINING	–
ROOM SERVICE	–
BAR	•
PARKING PER DAY	Free
MEETING FACILITIES	•
EXTRA AMENITIES	Wine, spa, free breakfast
BUSINESS AMENITIES	Dataport, 2-line phone, business center, audiovisual equipment
DECOR	California
POOL/SAUNA	Pool, sauna, whirlpool
EXERCISE FACILITIES	Cycling, tennis, golf

Westin Hotel San Francisco Airport ★★★½
1 Old Bayshore Highway
Milbrae, CA 94030
☎ 650-692-3500
TOLL-FREE 800-228-3000
starwoodhotels.com

QUALITY	80
COST	$$$–
LOCATION	SF Int'l Airport
DISCOUNTS	AAA, senior, gov't.
NO. OF ROOMS	396
ON-SITE DINING	•
ROOM SERVICE	•
BAR	•
PARKING PER DAY	$18 self, $26 valet
MEETING FACILITIES	•
EXTRA AMENITIES	Airport shuttle, soundproof rooms, coffee/tea maker, safe, refreshment center
BUSINESS AMENITIES	Dataport, business center, voice mail, 2-line phone
DECOR	Modern
POOL/SAUNA	Pool, whirlpool
EXERCISE FACILITIES	Fitness room

Westin St. Francis ★★★★½
335 Powell Street
San Francisco, CA 94102
☎ 415-397-7000
TOLL-FREE 800-937-8461
westinstfrancis.com

QUALITY	91
COST	$$$$$–
LOCATION	Union Square
DISCOUNTS	AAA, AARP, gov't.
NO. OF ROOMS	1,195
ON-SITE DINING	•
ROOM SERVICE	•
BAR	•
PARKING PER DAY	$49
MEETING FACILITIES	•
EXTRA AMENITIES	Tours, in-room massages, safe, minibar
BUSINESS AMENITIES	Dataport, wireless phone, audiovisual equipment
DECOR	Grand hotel
POOL/SAUNA	Spa
EXERCISE FACILITIES	Fee

White Swan Inn ★★★★½
845 Bush Street
San Francisco, CA 94108
☎ 415-775-1755
TOLL-FREE 800-999-9570
jdvhotels.com/white_swan_inn

QUALITY	90
COST	$$$$$–
LOCATION	Union Square
DISCOUNTS	–
NO. OF ROOMS	26
ON-SITE DINING	–
ROOM SERVICE	–
BAR	–
PARKING PER DAY	$32
MEETING FACILITIES	•
EXTRA AMENITIES	Breakfast, tea and cookies, fireplace, wet bar, robes, coffeemaker, newspaper, p.m. wine and hors d'oeuvres, chocolates
BUSINESS AMENITIES	Dataport, voice mail, computer station, audiovisual equipment
DECOR	English garden inn
POOL/SAUNA	Privileges
EXERCISE FACILITIES	Fitness room

PART THREE

VISITING
on BUSINESS

NOT ALL VISITORS *are* HEADED *for* FISHERMAN'S WHARF

WHILE SOME PEOPLE MAKE IT THEIR BUSINESS to vacation in San Francisco, others have no choice. Whether those lucky few who are being forced to visit this wonderful city know it or not, San Francisco is a business traveler's dream. The city is compact enough to allow you to make deals in the afternoon, catch some of the city's natural wonders as the sun is setting, and go to dinner by evening.

In case you haven't noticed, Silicon Valley, about 50 miles south of San Francisco, is a global center for high-technology business and manufacturing. Headquarters of major corporations make their home here: Chevron, Hewlett-Packard, Intel, Apple Computer, Sun Microsystems, Wells Fargo, Seagate Technology, and Gap.

The city is also a major center for higher education and biotechnology. It's the home of San Francisco State University, the University of San Francisco, Hastings College of Law (California State University), the University of California Medical Center, the San Francisco Art Institute, and other public and private colleges. Across the bay is the University of California, Berkeley, one of the world's great research institutions. As a result, San Francisco hosts many visiting academics, college administrators, and students and their families.

In many ways, the problems facing business visitors on their first trip to San Francisco don't differ much from the problems of folks in town intent on seeing its best-known tourist attractions and breathtaking scenery. Business visitors need to stay in a convenient hotel, avoid the worst of the city's traffic, get around in an unfamiliar city, and know the locations of San Francisco's best restaurants. For the most part, though, business visitors aren't nearly as flexible about the timing of their visit as folks who pick San Francisco as a vacation destination.

While we advise that the best times to visit are the shoulder seasons between winter and summer, the necessities of business may dictate that a foggy August or a rainy January is when you pull into town. No matter the time of year, you should certainly find the time to squeeze a morning or afternoon out of your busy schedule and spend a few hours exploring.

THE MOSCONE CENTER

SAN FRANCISCO IS HOME TO ONE MAJOR CONVENTION CENTER, the 1.6-million-square-foot Moscone Center (747 Howard Street, San Francisco, CA 94103; ☎ 415-974-4000; **moscone.com**). The facility is actually three convention venues (Moscone North, Moscone West, and Moscone South) on adjacent 11-acre blocks bounded by Mission, Folsom, Third, and Fourth streets near the heart of downtown. Named for San Francisco Mayor George R. Moscone (murdered in 1978 along with Supervisor Harvey Milk), this modern, $420 million convention center is located in the booming SoMa District (South of Market) four blocks south of Union Square.

Within walking distance are 20,000 hotel rooms, the city's main shopping district, and the Powell Street cable cars to Chinatown, Nob Hill, Fisherman's Wharf, and San Francisco's best restaurants. Next door is the San Francisco Museum of Modern Art (SFMOMA), and across the street is Yerba Buena Gardens, with a park, theaters, cafes, ice-skating and bowling, art located throughout, and The Rooftop children's area. Nearby is Metreon, a shopping center with four stories and 350,000 square feet offering 15 movie theaters, an IMAX theater, and six restaurants. The huge and fairly new Westfield San Francisco Centre (865 Market Street; ☎ 415-512-6776; **westfield.com**) with Bloomingdale's and boutiques beckons shoppers, while its restaurants beckon diners budgeting dollars with the ever-popular food concourse, where everything from tasty and low-priced Korean barbecue to European pastries and Vietnamese sandwiches are on tap. Without a doubt, Westfield Centre is one of the best places for business visitors to kill time or to meet a client on a rainy day—and there's a good movie theater and bookstore upstairs.

New museums are storming SoMa's Yerba Buena arts district. Already home to the San Francisco Museum of Modern Art (with its new impressive bequest of de Koonings and Twomblys from Gap founders Don and Doris Fisher), the Museum of Craft and Folk Art, the California Historical Society, the Cartoon Art Museum, and several art galleries, SoMa is welcoming several new San Francisco museums—the Mexican Museum (☎ 415-202-9700; **mexican museum.org**), the Museum of the African Diaspora (685 Mission Street; ☎ 415-358-7200; **moadsf.org**), and the Contemporary Jewish Museum (736 Mission Street; ☎ 415-655-7800; **thecjm.org**).

The American Bookbinders Museum (2736 16th Street; ☎ 415-671-2233; **bookbindersmuseum.com**), open weekdays by appointment, is just a few blocks away.

The Layout

Moscone South offers 260,560 square feet of primary exhibit area in a column-free space that can be divided into three halls. (The distinctive arches that make the hall column-free also reduce usable floor space by about 40 feet.) Forty-one flexible meeting rooms provide more than 60,000 square feet of meeting space. The lobby-level, 42,675-square-foot Esplanade Ballroom accommodates more than 5,000 delegates and is surrounded by terraced patios.

Across the street and connected to Moscone South by an underground concourse and a pedestrian sky bridge is the smaller Moscone North, which opened in 1992 and contains 181,440 square feet of exhibit space in two halls and up to 53,410 square feet of flexible meeting space in 17 rooms. The lobby provides a striking entrance to the exhibit level; delegates descend on escalators and stairs illuminated by skylights.

The freestanding Moscone West, a 300,000-square-foot, three-story convention hall that opened in 2003, is on the corner of Fourth and Howard streets, just a few steps away from Moscone North and South. Designed to snag smaller conventions when the big shows at its sister facilities are setting up and breaking down, Moscone West provides nearly 100,000 square feet of dedicated function space per floor. Using the latest technology such as its second-floor "air curtains"—suspended panels that allow the floor to be configured into meeting rooms—Moscone West is designed to handle a wide range of meetings and shows. The entrance to Moscone West's nine underground loading docks is on Howard Street.

The buildings are modern, bright, and airy, featuring extensive use of skylights and large expanses of glass that admit ample light to the mostly underground site. Outside, landscaped walkways, gardens, patios, sculptures, and a walk-through fountain enliven the setting. The meeting rooms on the mezzanine level in Moscone South have windows that overlook the main hall, while the second- and third-floor lobbies in Moscone West provide good views of the city.

All major exhibit areas and most meeting rooms are on one underground level linked by the underground concourse; additional meeting rooms are located on Moscone South's mezzanine level. Twenty completely enclosed

unofficial **TIP**
A note to exhibitors: All installation and dismantling of exhibits and all handling of materials require union labor, including signs and carpet laying. But union labor isn't required for the unpacking and placement of exhibitors' merchandise in the booth, or if the display is installed by one person in less than 30 minutes without the use of tools.

loading docks are located on the same level as the main halls, providing direct drive-in access to Moscone North and South.

Services

Two business centers, one each in the lower lobbies of Moscone North and Moscone South, provide access to photocopying and fax services, transparencies, overnight mail, UPS, office supplies, and cellular phone rental. The centers are open during event hours, and major credit cards are accepted for purchases and services.

Nursing services are on site during events at first-aid stations in Moscone North, Moscone South, and the esplanade level. A gift shop in the Moscone South lower lobby sells souvenirs. Hungry? Each convention group works with the Moscone Center to set up food service, so food availability differs with each convention. However, the neighborhood is full of places to eat, ranging from fast food and cafes to gourmet fare. The closest places to grab a quick bite to eat are the two cafes located in Yerba Buena Gardens (Mission at Third Street; ☎ 415-978-2787) and the Museum of Modern Art cafe (151 Third Street; ☎ 415-357-4000), which offers sandwiches, salads, and wine (closed Wednesdays).

Parking and Public Transportation

The Moscone Center has no on-site parking. But 5,000 parking spaces can be found within walking distance in garages and parking lots and even on the street. Still, dealing with a car in this dense city scene is a hassle. With so many hotels, restaurants, museums, art galleries, and public transportation within walking distance of the convention center, why bother with a car?

unofficial **TIP**
Because the convention sponsor brings big business to San Francisco, it usually can negotiate volume discounts on hotels substantially below rack rate. Some conventions and trade shows have more bargaining clout and negotiating skill than others, and your convention sponsor may not be one of them.

Consider using San Francisco's public transportation systems instead. Powell Street Station, only two blocks from the convention center, provides access to BART (Bay Area Rapid Transit) and Muni Metro (streetcars); adjacent are the Powell Street cable-car lines to Nob Hill and Fisherman's Wharf (although the wait in line to board a cable car can be lengthy during peak tourist seasons, unless you hike up to the next stop).

Muni Metro will get you to the Financial District and the city's outlying neighborhoods, while BART can whisk you beyond the city to Oakland and Berkeley. Muni buses and cable cars will get you just about everywhere else. Plus, there are cabs.

Lodging within Walking Distance of the Moscone Center

A couple of major hotels are within an easy stroll of the Moscone Center: The San Francisco Marriott (55 Fourth Street; ☎ 415-896-

Executive Amusement

CLIMBING THE LADDER If you are feeling stuck at the mid-management level, consider climbing to new heights at one of the world's largest indoor climbing gyms, Mission Cliffs (2295 Harrison Street; ☎ 415-550-0515; **touchstoneclimbing.com/mc.html**).

PRESIDENTIAL PUTTING GREENS Lincoln Park (34th Avenue and Clement Street; ☎ 415-221-9911) has one of the most amazing panoramic vistas of downtown San Francisco anywhere. And it's close to home!

BEST TOUR TEMPTATION Feeling trapped by the confines of corporate America? Head to Alcatraz—not just the run-of-the-mill tour but the Alcatraz Night Tour. It's amazing what is revealed when the lights go out in The Rock. A chilling extra: During the cell-lock demonstration, hear the famous lockdown clunk in the dark—the noise made by slamming cell doors shut for the night, recorded for many movies and unmistakable. Book well ahead at ☎ 415-981-ROCK or **alcatrazcruises. com**, and prepare to part with $33.

BETTER THAN A PUNCHING BAG Feeling the urge to stalk and shoot after a rather stressful day of meetings? Instead head to Pacific Rod and Gun Club (520 Muir Drive; ☎ 415-586-8349; **prgc.net**). You know the cue, "pull," and BAM!—shoot that skeet!

MA AND PA CAR RENTAL If you are tired of dealing with big rental-car agencies that simply ask for a corporate number, head to City Rent-A-Car (1433 Bush Street; ☎ 866-359-1331; **cityrentacar.com**). You get small-town service by the two brothers who own it, and the rates are cheaper than those of the big guns.

1600; **marriott.com**) offers 1,500 rooms; the Palace Hotel (2 New Montgomery Street; ☎ 415-512-1111; **sfpalace.com**) has 550 rooms; The Westin San Francisco (50 Third Street; ☎ 415-974-6400; **westinsf. com**) has 667 rooms; and the Galleria Park Hotel (1921 Sutter Street; ☎ 415-781-3060; **jdvhotels.com**) offers 177 rooms.

Convention Rates: How They Work and How to Do Better

If you're attending a major convention or trade show, the meeting's sponsoring organization has probably negotiated convention rates with a number of hotels. Under this arrangement, hotels agree to block a certain number of rooms at an agreed-upon price for conventioneers. In the case of a small meeting, only one hotel may be involved, but citywide conventions may involve almost all downtown and airport hotels.

Once a convention or trade show sponsor completes negotiations with participating hotels, it sends its attendees a housing list that includes all the hotels serving the convention, along with the

unofficial TIP
Check the Moscone
Center's Web site at
moscone.com for a
complete and up-to-date
list of 2010 and 2011
conventions and trade
shows scheduled beyond. It
can help you plan your trip
for less busy times.

special convention rate for each. Using the
strategies covered in the previous section,
you then can compare these convention rates
with the rack rates.

If the negotiated convention rate doesn't
sound like a good deal, try to reserve a room
using a half-price club, a consolidator, or
a tour operator. Remember, however, that
many of the deep discounts are available
only when the hotel expects to be at less
than 80 percent occupancy, a rarity when a
big convention is in town.

Strategies for Beating Convention Rates

- Reserve early. Most big conventions and trade shows announce meeting sites one to three years in advance. Get your reservation booked as far in advance as possible using a half-price club. If you book well ahead of the time the convention sponsor sends out the housing list, chances are good that the hotel will accept your discounted reservation.
- Compare your convention's housing list with the list of hotels presented in this guide. You may be able to find a suitable hotel not on the housing list.
- Use a local reservations agency or consolidator. This is also a good strategy if you need to make reservations at the last minute. Local reservations agencies and consolidators almost always control some rooms, even in the midst of a huge convention or trade show.

The Moscone Center can have a considerable impact on the city
when, say, 65,000 exhibitors and trade-show attendees come into town
and snatch up almost every hotel room in San Francisco. Luckily,
though, the large conventions and trade shows register no discernible
effect on the availability of restaurant tables or traffic congestion; it's
just hotel rooms that get scarce.

PART FOUR

ARRIVING *and* GETTING ORIENTED

COMING *into the* CITY

BY CAR

SAN FRANCISCO IS LOCATED ON THE TIP of a peninsula linked to the mainland by two bridges. As a result, visitors arriving by car enter the city by one of three routes: from the south on US 101, from the east on I-80 (via the San Francisco–Oakland Bay Bridge), or from the north on US 101 (on the Golden Gate Bridge).

US 101 and a parallel highway, I-280, link the city to the rest of the peninsula to the south, including Palo Alto, Santa Clara, and San Jose, located at the southern end of San Francisco Bay. US 101 is also the coastal highway that continues farther south to Gilroy, Salinas, San Luis Obispo, Santa Barbara, and Los Angeles, 400 miles away. A more scenic—and significantly slower—option that hugs the coast is California Route 1, which leads directly to Santa Cruz, Carmel, Big Sur, and Morro Bay.

Travelers coming from the east on I-80 (which goes through Sacramento, Reno, Salt Lake City, Omaha, Chicago, and other points east before reaching New York City) pass through Oakland before crossing San Francisco Bay on the Bay Bridge and entering downtown San Francisco. It's also the route for people coming to the Bay Area on I-5, the north-south interstate through California's Central Valley (and the fastest driving route from Los Angeles).

Drivers coming through Oakland are confronted with a maze of interstate highways that link to form a kind of beltway around San Francisco. In addition to the San Francisco–Oakland Bay Bridge, two more bridges to the south—Highways 92 and 84—connect the San Francisco peninsula south of the city to the East Bay.

I-580 crosses San Pablo Bay north of San Francisco, where the San Rafael Bridge connects the East Bay city of Richmond with San Rafael in Marin.

US 101 to the north crosses the Golden Gate Bridge, linking San Francisco to Marin County and the rest of Northern California, including San Rafael, Petaluma, Healdsburg, and Eureka. California Route 1 is the slow and scenic option; the two-lane road follows the coast north and south—and spectacularly!

BY PLANE

MOST DOMESTIC AND FOREIGN VISITORS who fly to San Francisco land at the San Francisco International Airport, 14 miles south of downtown directly on US 101. It's the fifth-busiest airport in the United States, and it's undergoing a major expansion. Luckily, many domestic fliers have a choice: Oakland International Airport, a smaller, more distant facility, is worth considering, especially if you can get a direct flight from your hometown. Oakland International is located five miles south of downtown Oakland, across San Francisco Bay (about 24 miles from downtown San Francisco).

San Francisco International Airport (SFO)

Seventy-four percent of visitors arrive by air, most of them through the San Francisco International Airport (SFO); **flysfo.com**. A $2.4-billion construction project—including a state-of-the-art international terminal, the airport rail-transit AirTrain, a BART (Bay Area Rapid Transit) station, and elevated roadways—has readied the airport for a projected volume of more than 50 million annual passengers, although the 2009 recession canceled flights and routes and shrank the numbers. The centerpiece of the program is the 2-million-square-foot international terminal that was completed in the spring of 2000.

THE LAYOUT SFO handles an average of 109,000 passengers a day on 71 passenger airlines. It's shaped somewhat like a ship's wheel with the spokes radiating out. There are four terminals, numbers 1, 2, 3, and the International Terminal. The terminals surround a parking garage and are linked by indoor corridors featuring various changing art exhibits (nice if you've got time to kill) and the AirTrain, an automated light-rail system that connects the terminals, parking garages, rental-car station, and BART station. Each terminal features shops, restaurants, and newsstands, and the International Terminal has a small shopping mall with an excellent Sephora outlet, a Museum of Modern Art boutique, bookshops, fine restaurants, and snack stands at food courts. Five airport information booths, open from 8 a.m. to midnight, are located in the baggage-claim areas; multilingual agents can provide information on ground transportation, Bay Area lodging, and cultural events.

ARRIVING From your gate, follow the signs down to the baggage area on the lower level. After getting your luggage, step outside to the center island to catch a door-to-door or hotel shuttle van, or a cab or limo. Short-term parking is across the street. To reach the central parking garage or the BART station (the cheapest way to San Francisco, but best if you don't have much luggage), follow signs down another level to the AirTrain where you change for the automated light rail line). The Blue Line goes to the rental-car facility, while the Red Line links the terminals and parking garages.

AIRPORT SECURITY Airport security at SFO is pretty much the same as you'll find at any international airport. The list of permitted and prohibited items is now too long and impossibly specific to include in a guidebook. Some common-sense suggestions and required procedures are listed below. For a complete list, see the Transportation Security Administration (TSA) Web site at **tsa.gov/travelers/airtravel.**

unofficial **TIP**
If you've got time to kill, give **the free AirTrain** and BART a spin; the views are interesting. The AirTrain whisks you to BART, where an $8.10 fare takes you to the city's downtown and a few dollars more takes you beyond to the East Bay. All trains go north to the city center. For Oakland, Berkeley, and beyond, check destinations on the train cars using the on-site BART map.

- Carry-on and checked luggage will be screened.
- Arrive two hours prior to departure for domestic flights and three hours prior to departure for international flights to be on the safe side.
- Unattended vehicles left in front of the terminal will be ticketed and towed.
- Government-issued identification is required. You will be asked to show your ID at several points in the pre-flight/boarding process.
- Only passengers with airline tickets are allowed beyond screening checkpoints.
- Passengers must remove coats, jackets, blazers, but not shoes unless specifically instructed to do so.
- Electronic devices are subject to screening at checkpoints.
- Laptops and video cams must be removed from their cases.
- Passengers are limited to one carry-on bag plus one personal carry-on item.
- Knives of any length must be placed in checked baggage.
- Cutting and puncturing instruments and athletic equipment that can be used as a weapon must be placed in checked baggage.

For the latest information on security procedures at SFO, visit its Web site at **flysfo.com.**

Getting Downtown

DRIVING If you're renting a car, take the AirTrain Blue Line to the central rental-car facility. After picking up your car keys, get explicit directions to US 101, which goes to downtown San Francisco.

To reach Market Street near Union Square (the main downtown hotel district), take US 101 to I-280 north using the left three lanes; then take the Sixth Street exit. Market Street is about six blocks west from the end of the exit; across Market Street, Sixth Street

unofficial **TIP**
It's a good idea to call ahead to your hotel for turn-by-turn driving directions. The Third Street exit, for instance, may not be the same Third Street that takes you to the ballpark downtown and can mislead you disastrously.

becomes Taylor Street, a one-way street heading north toward Fisherman's Wharf. It's about a 25-minute drive to downtown from the airport (longer during rush hour).

CABS AND SHUTTLES Cabs are available outside the baggage area near the yellow column at all terminals. Typical fares to downtown San Francisco are about $29–$44; up to five riders can split the cost. Door-to-door shared van service to downtown San Francisco, available outside the doors of the arrival level on the center island, is priced at around $14–$17 per person ($7–$14 for children). The vans leave every 15 to 20 minutes between 6 a.m. and 11 p.m. and every 30 minutes during late-night hours.

Major shuttle services include **Bay Shuttle** (☎ 415-564-3400) and **Supershuttle** (☎ 415-558-8500; **supershuttle.com**), which allows you to make back-to-the-airport reservations on their Web site. You can also reserve by phone a return trip with any of the shuttle services. For more information, contact one of the van services or the SFO ground transportation hotline (call ☎ 511 within the San Francisco Bay Area, ☎ 510-817-1717 outside the San Francisco Bay Area, or visit **511.org**).

PUBLIC TRANSPORTATION The easiest way into the city is via BART, whose trains run right up to the International Terminal. For only $8.10 one-way, travelers are now whisked to downtown San Francisco

Shuttle Savvy: Tips for a Smooth Ride

1. Generally shuttles to and from both SFO and Oakland are similar in service and price—you can expect to pay around $35–$45 per person from Oakland and about $17 from SFO.

2. The trip downtown from SFO generally takes about 30 minutes, although traffic can sometimes make it up to an hour. Oakland is farther away and the Bay Bridge traffic can be relentless; expect about an hour commute into downtown.

3. If there are two or more in your party, it might be cheaper and quicker to split the cost of a taxi (no waiting). Be sure to check with the shuttle for departure times. Often, the shuttle waits for a few flights to land to fill up before heading out. So if you are first, be prepared to wait. There seems to be a rule, however, that the ground transportation center enforces that states shuttles must leave within ten minutes of its first customer.

4. If there are numerous people in the shuttle, check to see where on the drop-off list you fit. If you are last to be dropped off, you're in for a torturously long trip.

inside a half hour. To reach the BART station, follow signs to Air-Train, the airport's light rail system. When you arrive at the station, be ready to fumble with the automated ticket machine. Luggage is permitted on the trains in two open-space areas on each car (small luggage will fit under the seats). The trains run every 15 minutes during regular business hours and every 20 minutes in the evenings and on weekends. Hours of operation are 4 a.m. to midnight weekdays, 6 a.m. to midnight on Saturdays, and 8 a.m. to midnight on Sundays.

Oakland International Airport (OAK)

Smaller is sometimes better at Oakland International Airport (**fly oakland.com**), across the bay from San Francisco and five miles south of downtown Oakland. With only two terminals on one level, Oakland is a lot less confusing to weary travelers.

THE LAYOUT Terminal 1 handles all domestic and international airlines, with the exception of Southwest Airlines, which claims all of Terminal 2. From your gate, follow signs to the baggage area near the entrance and to the right. Ground transportation is outside the door, including shuttle vans to downtown San Francisco (to the left of Terminal 1 under the covered walkway). Most rental-car agencies are across the street; no need to take a shuttle bus to a remote lot.

unofficial **TIP**
While Oakland is the obvious airport choice if your destination is in the East Bay area, it's also a hassle-free alternative for San Francisco–bound travelers —at least, the ones who can book a direct flight from their hometowns.

Getting Downtown

DRIVING To reach downtown San Francisco from Oakland International, exit the airport and take Hegenberger Road to I-880 north. Follow signs for I-80, which takes you across the double-decker San Francisco–Oakland Bay Bridge ($4 toll for westbound). The first two exits after the bridge take you downtown. It's about a 30-minute drive (longer during rush hour).

CABS AND SHUTTLES Cabs are usually outside the baggage areas between Terminals 1 and 2; fare to downtown San Francisco is about $50. Door-to-door shuttle services to downtown (about $35 to $45) include **City Express** (☎ 888-874-8885 or 510-638-8830), **Air Transit Shuttle** (☎ 510-568-3434), and **Citywide Shuttle Service** (☎ 510-336-0090).

PUBLIC TRANSPORTATION Shuttle service via AirBART to the BART Oakland Coliseum station is $3 one way (50 cents for children under age 11, disabled passengers, and seniors). Ticket machines for Air-BART are in Terminals 1 and 2. To purchase a BART ticket at the station, you'll need $1, $5, $10, or $20 bills for the ticket machines, or a debit or credit card. (Note that the machines will not dispense more than $4.95 in change for any one transaction.) The ride should

unofficial **TIP**
Shuttles to the car parks, car rentals, and AirBART shuttle bus service to and from the Oakland-Coliseum BART station are located just outside the terminals. Fares are paid on board with exact change only or with a $1 or $3 BART ticket (available for purchase at the Coliseum station). Bus drivers do not make change and lack humor about this: No exceptions. Don't miss your plane for want of a quarter!

take about 15 minutes. Once you arrive at the Coliseum station, take a BART train to one of four downtown San Francisco stations on Market Street ($3.35 one-way). For BART info, call ☎ 510-465-2278 or visit **bart.gov.**

BY TRAIN

AMTRAK'S STAFFED TICKET OFFICE, waiting room, and baggage check is located in the Ferry Building at the foot of Market Street. Motor coaches transport passengers to the Amtrak station in Emeryville, near Oakland, and to three other downtown San Francisco points: Pier 39 in Fisherman's Wharf, the Hyatt Regency in the Financial District, and Macy's near Union Square.

The motor-coach trip from Emeryville takes about ten minutes (traffic permitting); your luggage is checked through to your final stop downtown (or, for departing passengers, to your train). Cities with daily round-trip service to San Francisco are Los Angeles and San Diego (five trips a day), Sacramento (four trips a day), Seattle and Portland (one trip a day), and Chicago (one trip a day). For exact schedule and fare information, check **amtrak.com** or call ☎ 800-USA-RAIL.

WHERE TO FIND TOURIST INFORMATION IN SAN FRANCISCO

IF YOU'RE SHORT ON MAPS or need more information on sightseeing, restaurants, hotels, shopping, or things to do in San Francisco and the Bay Area, there are several places to stop and pick up maps and brochures.

- Berkeley Convention and Visitor Bureau, 2015 Center Street, Berkeley, CA 94704; ☎ 800-847-4823 or 510-549-7040; **visitberkeley.com.**
- San Francisco Convention and Visitors Bureau, Hallidie Plaza at Powell and Market streets (lower level); ☎ 415-283-0177; **onlyinsan francisco.com.** Weekdays 9 a.m. through 5 p.m.; weekends 9 a.m. to 3 p.m.; closed Easter, Thanksgiving, Christmas, and New Year's days.
- Marin County Convention and Visitors Bureau, 1013 Larkspur Landing Circle, Larkspur; ☎ 415-925-2060; **visitmarin.org.** Weekdays 9 a.m. to 5 p.m.; closed Thanksgiving, Christmas, and New Year's days.
- Napa Valley Conference and Visitors Bureau, 1310 Napa Town Center; ☎ 707-226-7459; **napavalley.com.** Daily 9 a.m. to 5 p.m.; closed Thanksgiving, Christmas, and New Year's days.

- Sonoma Valley Visitors Bureau, 453 First Street East;
  ☎ 707-996-1090; **sonomavalley.com.** Daily 9 a.m. to 5 p.m.

A **GEOGRAPHIC OVERVIEW** of **SAN FRANCISCO** and the **BAY AREA**

SAN FRANCISCO IS ONLY THE FOURTH LARGEST Californian city, but with more than 809,000 residents, it is the second most densely populated major city in the country after New York. On the West Coast of the United States about halfway between the northern and southern ends of California, the city occupies the tip of a hilly peninsula jutting into San Francisco Bay and overlooking the Pacific Ocean. San Francisco is the epicenter of a larger metropolitan area with a total population of about 7 million, making the Bay Area the sixth-largest urban area in the United States.

California, the most populous and third largest state in the Union (with the largest economy of any U.S. state), is bordered to the east by Arizona and Nevada. To the north is Oregon and the Pacific Northwest; to the south is the international border with Mexico. Along California's nearly 800-mile coastline, which forms the western edge of the state, is the Pacific Ocean. The largest city in California is Los Angeles, 400 miles to the south; the state capital is Sacramento, about 90 miles northeast of San Francisco.

THE BIG ONE!

WE'VE ALL HEARD STORIES AS KIDS that "the Big One" is going to rock California and forever knock it off our map, sending the state to find restful solitude in the Pacific Ocean. And the culprit of such a sinking fate? The San Andreas Fault, of course. The San Andreas Fault, the active frontier between the Pacific and North American tectonic plates, runs vertically through California. And like a nose on a dangerous face, San Francisco is smack dab in the center, which allows the fault to create violent tremors and devastating earthquakes as it readjusts itself in the earth below. She is temperamental, as evidenced by the quakes of 1906 and 1989, as well as the impending granddaddy of them all predicted for sometime in the future.

Seismologists are unable to predict when tremors or earthquakes will occur or how severe they'll be. The actual shifting of the plates

unofficial **TIP**
For more detailed information on what to do in the event of a tremor while you're in San Francisco, check the local phone directory, which has pages full of detailed advice.

doesn't cause the damage; instead, the resulting collapses, fires, and landslides can kill hundreds. That's why the standard advice is to take cover below a sturdy piece of furniture. Since the 1989 quake, many San Francisco buildings have been strengthened to withstand tremors, and shelters (such as the one at the Moscone Convention Center) are stocked as emergency relief sites. In addition, most hotels have their own evacuation procedures.

YOU OUGHTA BE IN PICTURES!

VISITORS LOVE SAN FRANCISCO, in large part because of its breathtaking beauty and sense of care and compassion of its inhabitants. It is an easy place to live in, visit, navigate, and fall in love with. If you are not convinced at first glimpse of the Golden Gate Bridge, just look beyond at the Marin Headlands, the carpet of mountains that in the spring become covered with flowers and chaparral. Year-round, the Headlands harbor secret playgrounds for adrenaline junkies of all ages. Farther away from the Headlands is Mount Tamalpais, or Mount Tam as it is affectionately called. Hike, bike, drive . . . you name it, and the mountain will provide it. It also has one of the best views of the city and the surrounding bay area—on a clear day you can see across to the Sierra Nevada range. If you survive the hike or winding drive to the top, you can head south to Stinson Beach or toward Muir Woods, where you can drive your car through one of the giant redwoods that tower in the forest. Both ends of the Golden Gate Bridge are anchored in the Golden Gate National Recreation Area, more than 75,000 acres of parkland managed by the National Park Service; it's a recreational playground to San Franciscans.

North of the Marin Headlands is Point Reyes National Seashore, a windswept peninsula on the Pacific Coast covered with woodlands, prairies, and marshes. A geologic "island" cut off from the mainland by the San Andreas Fault, Point Reyes was "discovered" and claimed for Queen Elizabeth I by Sir Francis Drake in 1579. Today it is a carefully preserved sanctuary for more than 350 species of birds and a paradise for botanists and nature lovers, who, with a little luck, can spot elk, lynx, coyotes, and falcons. Winter visitors can watch migrating whales at an overlook near the 1870 Point Reyes Lighthouse.

Closer to home within the bay (one of the greatest natural harbors in the world) is Angel Island, only reachable by ferry from Tiburon, Oakland, and San Francisco. No motorized vehicles are allowed in this state park, which is chock-full of trails for hiking or biking, as well as recently pioneered Segway rentals, barbecued oysters, and the new museum of immigration! Throughout the island are picnic tables and campsites and beaches where you can splash, and there are now renovated ruins of the military garrison known as the Ellis Island of the West, a quarantine station for Asian immigrants until November 1940. And nearby Alcatraz is becoming a place that you don't want to escape—it's now making a comeback as a nature and wildlife habitat.

Heaven exists south, also. Just follow the number "1"—Route 1 South, that is. Its narrow road winds along the crashing waves of the Pacific Ocean. You'll be so close to the edge and the water that you may even feel the salty spray from below. It's a high like no other. Along the way are fishing villages and tiny towns such as Half Moon Bay, Pescadero, or Davenport, and the occasional surfing, windsurfing, hang gliding, or even nude beach. The Santa Cruz Mountains, running down the spine of the San Francisco peninsula, provide a dramatic backdrop to crashing ocean waves and offer fantastic views of the ocean and bay along Skyline Boulevard, which follows the mountain ridges.

SAN FRANCISCO NEIGHBORHOODS

HILLS OR NO HILLS, the first developers of the city decided on a grid system. It was a convenient way to organize neighborhoods and streets, but they did not have to consider the stick-shift vehicle back then! Daniel Burnham's City Beautiful plan to organize streets around gentler contours with winding streets and fewer severe inclines was abandoned overnight when the 1906 Big One meant rebuilding as fast as humanly possible. San Francisco's hills, more than anything else, thrill visitors with astounding vistas. Surrounded by the shimmering waters of the bay and the Pacific Ocean, the city's land mass is packed on and around nearly four dozen hills—steep markers that delineate San Francisco's shifting moods and economic prosperity—the higher you get, the higher the real estate. The Financial District is the granddaddy of commercial square footage, while the rest of the city remains charming in its residential—almost suburban—nature. "It's a city you can actually live in," is the catch phrase most use when explaining the benefits of this urban bliss.

Armed with a good map, comfortable walking shoes, and ankle weights (if you are so inclined) to take advantage of the quad workout while pounding the hills, you'll find that the best way to absorb the city's aura is to walk. You can hit most of downtown San Francisco's major sights and neighborhoods in a day. The city is compact, and thanks to that grid layout, well organized. It's easy to foot the city, and the bus maps are free and easy to read.

Chinatown

North along Grant Avenue and through the flamboyant, green-and-ocher imperial Dragon Gate is bustling Chinatown, a dense warren of restaurants and tacky tourist shops that's the second-largest Chinese community outside of Asia and definitely the oldest in North America (Manhattan's is bigger but not as dense). Since gold-rush days, 24-square-block Chinatown has served as the hub for San Francisco's

Chinese population, who now make up one third of the population in the area. Old Chinatown is a city within a city, crowded with retail outlets and sidewalk displays jammed with silk, porcelain, teak furniture, handmade jewelry, and the usual tourist gewgaws (the farther you walk up Grant Avenue, the cheaper the postcards get). Walk a little farther to Chinatown's open-air markets, glitzy emporiums, and herbalists' shops filled with exotic herbs and spices. Stockton Street is the main Chinese food-shopping district, crowded with displays of unfamiliar fruits (you have to try the infamous Durian fruit—"smells like hell but tastes like heaven") and fish stores with tanks of live eels, fish, frogs, and turtles waiting to be killed on the spot for customers. Residents from other areas heavily populated by people of Chinese descent, such as the Richmond district, the Sunset, and Visitacion Valley, still flock here to shop on weekends; the new Central Subway will make Stockton Street even busier.

If you have only one experience in Chinatown, make it dim sum. The delicious tidbits, generally served for brunch, are a local institution. Most dim sum houses open at 10 a.m. and close by mid- or late afternoon. Typically, servers circle the restaurant's dining room, pushing carts stacked with covered bamboo or stainless-steel containers filled with steamed or fried dumplings, shrimp balls, spring rolls, steamed buns, and Chinese pastries. Just point to what looks appealing; the waiters usually don't speak much English and ordering is done by gestures. It's cheap, too—you have to order an awful lot of food to spend more than $15 to $20 a person. The undisputed oldest dim sum institution in Chinatown is the Hang Ah Tea Room on Pagoda Place, off Sacramento and Stockton streets with its photos of beauty queens from the 1950s and quaint clippings. Keeping in tune with 24-hour breakfasts, it is open until 9 p.m. Dim sum at dusk? Why not!

unofficial **TIP**
For a feel of the real, non-touristy Chinatown, duck away from touristy Grant Avenue into the side alleys (such as Waverly Street, which parallels Grant Avenue between Clay and Washington streets), where you'll see daily Chinatown life and stores that sell lychee wine, interesting tea and herbal remedies, Chinese newspapers, dried lotus, shark fins, and powdered horns and antlers (reputed to restore male virility).

While New Asia, Gold Mountain, and Lotus Garden get the biggest turnovers and tables, we like the Great Eastern and even the rustic yet retro Seasons at the Four Seasons.

Ross Alley, which runs above Grant Avenue between Washington and Jackson streets, houses small garment shops, laundries, florists, and one-chair barber shops. At the Golden Gate Fortune Cookie Company at 56 Ross Alley, visitors can watch local wives and aunties fold bits of wisdom into that oh-so-familiar shape, said to have been invented here. At the edge of Chinatown, the Imperial Tea Court (1411 Powell Street) is the place for your inner tea snob to flourish. Late January or February is the Chinese New Year's fest and parade. Slithering giant snakes and dragons, lanterns, and floats march down Grant Avenue in celebration. For an abbreviated version of the Chinese New Year celebrations, the lion dance—performed during other festivals such as the Autumn Moon Festival too—snaps, crackles, and pops its way down Grant Avenue.

Civic Center and the Tenderloin

Eight blocks west of Union Square on Geary Boulevard is Van Ness Avenue, a broad north-south boulevard and the main thoroughfare of the Civic Center District, acclaimed by critics as one of the finest collections of Beaux Arts buildings in the country. **City Hall,** rebuilt in 1915 after the 1906 earthquake and modeled on the national Capitol—but taller—is widely considered one of the most beautiful public buildings in America; on a historical note, it's also the building in which Dan White shot Mayor George Moscone and Supervisor Harvey Milk in 1978.

Across the plaza from City Hall two blocks away is the contemporary **San Francisco Main Public Library** (1996), a modern interpretation of the classic Beaux Arts style with a circular interior atrium, cute Mint Café, bookstore, and international center. On the top floor are art exhibits and a well-tended historical section. You can do worse than hang out here on a rainy day.

Next door, the stately former public library is now the home of the **Asian Art Museum,** with the largest collection of Asian art in the West. The south end of the plaza contains the **Civic Auditorium** (built in 1913 and associated with impresario Bill Graham), and on the north side is the **State Office Building** (1926). Also in the neighborhood are a few other distinguished buildings, including the **Veterans Auditorium Building** (1932), the splendid 1932 **Opera House,** and the glittering **Louise M. Davies Symphony Hall.** Surrounding the area is a diverse collection of restaurants, antiques shops, and galleries. Sidling up alongside the grandeur of the Civic Center is the seedy and misunderstood Tenderloin District. But it's a small patch of hope and despair with some nefarious goings-on—and very good, cheap food as well, be it Pakistani or Turkish or Vietnamese. Dropouts and homeless wander the streets and sleep on them because this is the home of the 85 percent of the city's homeless agencies and churches that minister free food, such as the Glide Memorial Church. Just-arrived poor yet eager immigrants establish small businesses, restaurants, and shops here. They gain their American-ness and a grubstake, and then get out.

These streets are worth a film-noirish wander in daytime—try the free **City Guides Tenderloin** walking tour with Peter Fields (**sfcityguides. org**) or **Don Herron's Dashiell Hammett** tour for $10 (**donherron.com**). Check the mural on the east wall of the building at 895 O'Farrell Street, and the one at 434 Ellis Street. Have authentic Turkish food at **A La Turca** (869 Geary Street; **alaturcasf.com**) or the delicious and

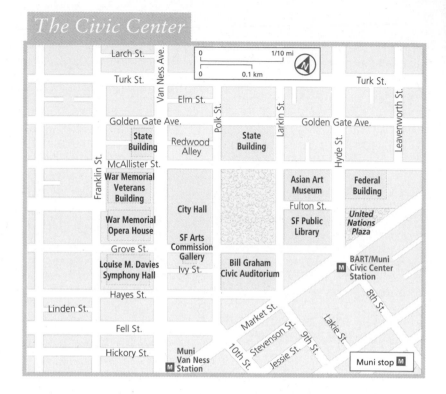

The Civic Center

cheap Vietnamese vegetarian food at **Golden Era Vegetarian Restaurant** (572 O'Farrell Street; **goldeneravegetarian.com**). Try a stellar Reuben sandwich and house-made soup at **Morty's Delicatessen** (280 Golden Gate Avenue at Hyde Street; **mortysdeli.com**), the asparagus and shrimp roll at **Golden House** (366 Golden Gate Avenue at Larkin Street; ☎ 415-775-3577), or the arresting seven-course beef and clay pot dishes at **Pagolac** at 655 Larkin Street (☎ 415-776-3234). Don't forget the *banh mi* at **Saigon Sandwich,** one block south at 560 Larkin Street (☎ 415-474-5698).

Nob Hill/Russian Hill

In a city renowned for its hills, Nob Hill heads the list. As California novelist and journalist Joan Didion wrote, Nob Hill is "the symbolic nexus of all old California money and power." Its mansions, exclusive hotels, and posh restaurants tower over the rest of the city. While early San Franciscans of wealth preferred lower sections of town, the installation of cable cars in the 1870s turned Nob Hill into a valuable piece of real estate. The generally accepted borders of Nob Hill are Bush Street and Pacific Avenue, and Stockton and Larkin streets.

Gaze at the exteriors of exclusive clubs (such as the **Pacific Union Club** at 1000 California Street), and stop at a hotel bar, such as the **Big 4,** named for the wealthy railroad barons who built their mansions here, in the **Huntington Hotel.** Its bar menu includes a very popular grilled cheese sandwich accompanied by a cup of creamy tomato soup for dipping. Then bask in the aura of privilege and luxury that distinguishes this most famous of San Francisco locales.

You won't find a better hotel bar than one of the grandes dames of Nob Hill—the **Inter-Continental Mark Hopkins San Francisco,** a 380-room hotel at California and Mason streets; a dedicated elevator whisks you up to great views at the **Top of the Mark** lounge, which dates from 1939 and is a charming place to watch the setting sun. More Nob Hill treasures include **Huntington Park,** a flowered square where visitors can see nannies pushing trendy baby joggers and walking well-groomed poodles.

Russian Hill, on the next hill over, is a land of swanky apartments and gorgeous houses, all bristling with bay windows, some of which were in Hitchcock's tense thriller *Vertigo,* set in the city and starring Jimmy Stewart and Kim Novak. Little galleries, such as the **Diego Rivera** (800 Chestnut Street) dot the landscape, as do unique little neighborhood restaurants that only the locals seem to know about. The original **Swenson's Ice Creamery** is at 1999 Hyde Street; the view from Ina Coolbrith Park is worth the trudge up the hill. Then you can descend via "the crookedest street in the world" (**Lombard Street,** with eight turns in one block at its eastern end). Russian Hill, within walking distance of Union Square, is bordered by Broadway and Chestnut, Taylor, and Larkin streets.

Union Square

Perhaps the nearest thing to a city center in San Francisco is the refurbished Union Square, its liveliest urban space. A few acres of concrete and greenery surrounded by huge department stores, swank hotels, and expensive shops, its adjacent streets are jammed with cars and tour buses, upscale shoppers, befuddled tourists, street musicians, beggars and street people bumming quarters, and businesspeople late for

unofficial **TIP**
Nob Hill offers fantastic views from the top of the "nob" (slang from the Hindu word *nawab*), which is 376 feet above sea level. Your best bet is to wander the great, gray eminence atop Nob Hill on California Street, **Grace Cathedral,** which was influenced by the architecture of Notre Dame and is the third-largest Episcopal cathedral in the nation. Among its splendors are two laby-rinths (one inside and one outside) and gilded bronze doors that are replicas of those created by Lorenzo Ghiberti for the Baptistry in Florence. The doors' ten rectangular reliefs depict scenes from the Old Testament. They stand at the top of the steps to the cathedral's east entrance.

unofficial **TIP**
Russian Hill, named for a graveyard (long since removed) for Russian seamen, is also where Armistead Maupin's fictional crew in *Tales of the City* made their home.

appointments. It's all here, from the sleazy to the sublime.

In addition to giving credit cards a workout at Neiman Marcus, Saks Fifth Avenue, or Macy's with their high- and low-end eateries (Neiman Marcus has the poshest on its tiered fourth-floor balcony, and Macy's top-floor Cheesecake Factory is busiest), you can catch a cable car on Powell Street for a ride up Nob Hill or board a motorized trolley for a city tour. Maiden Lane, an elegant, tree-lined alley that was once lined with brothels—the name is satirical—extends two blocks east of Union Square from Stockton to Kearny streets and boasts the Frank Lloyd Wright–designed **Circle Gallery** among exclusive shops and restaurants. Union Square is also the focal point for the city's main hotel district, so for a lot of visitors it's the obvious place to start a walking tour.

*un*official **TIP**
Local tip for catching a Powell-Mason cable car minus a wait: Walk uphill a block or so and then you can jump straight on.

Union Square is also San Francisco's primary theater district. **The American Conservatory Theater** (ACT) at the Geary Theater (415 Geary Boulevard) offers both classic and contemporary works (and a penchant for Molière) in a restored landmark theater that reopened in 1996. The city's premier African American theater company calls the **Lorraine Hansberry Theater** (620 Sutter Street) home, while the **Curran Theatre** (445 Geary Boulevard) and the **Marine's Memorial** (609 Sutter Street) present Broadway musicals from New York. Pick up half-price tickets at the TIX kiosk (on the square) for performances that day; cash only.

The Financial District

Frequently called the Wall Street of the West, the Financial District lies northeast of Union Square in an area bordered by Embarcadero and Market, Third, Kearny, and Washington streets. Among the towering skyscrapers are several corporate headquarters and the Pacific Stock Exchange building—with its Art Deco interior complete with **Diego Rivera** mural (now the swanky City Club at Sansome and Pine; City Guide tours allow you a peek: **sfcityguides.org**)—with lots of elaborate corporate architecture, including the city's tallest landmark, the Transamerica Pyramid, next to a miniature redwood grove.

Brokers, bankers, and insurance agents pursue wealth during the week on several acres of landfill on and around Montgomery Street; unlike most cities' financial areas, the Financial District pretty much empties on evenings and weekends, but still offers some nightlife thanks to its restaurants. What motivates these financial movers and shakers can be studied at the **Wells Fargo History Museum** (420 Montgomery Street), which offers insight into the city's rich history.

The Marina District and Pacific Heights

So what if the Marina District is snubbed by many anti-yuppies as the mecca for all things moneyed? And so what if it is built on an earthquake-vulnerable landfill? Filled with Mediterranean-style houses painted in lollipop colors, the Marina District is one of the most beautiful districts in the city, which is why most of its inhabitants are young 20- and 30-something professionals or families. Prices are high, and some would argue that so are the egos. With the Presidio to the west and Fort Mason to the east, the Marina is also one of the city's greenest neighborhoods. Yacht clubs, kite fliers, and joggers make the district feel somewhat like a resort. Ironically, the Marina, built to celebrate the rebirth of the city after the 1906 quake, was the city's worst casualty in the 1989 disaster. Tremors tore through the unstable landfill on which the district is built, and many homes collapsed into smoldering ruins. Rebuilding occurred almost immediately, though, and many of the shimmering new homes are just that—new houses built after the last major earthquake. Nor was the disaster enough to bring rents down; the Marina continues to attract a very well-heeled and smart set.

The Marina's main commercial drag is Chestnut Street, an urban thoroughfare with a swinging-singles reputation; the local Safeway has been dubbed "the Body Shop" for the inordinate amount of cruising that goes on there. A long stretch of turf at Marina Green is popular with the fit, the Lycra-clad, and Frisbee-catching dogs.

unofficial **TIP**
Fort Mason and Municipal Pier are great spots to escape the congestion of nearby Fisherman's Wharf.

A bit east of the Marina is **Fort Mason,** located on the other side of **Aquatic Park** and the 1,800-foot curving **Municipal Pier.** Millions of GIs shipped out to the South Pacific in World War II from Fort Mason, but today it's a public park. Some locals call it Fort Culture— here you'll find in old, shedlike buildings a variety of nonprofit arts organizations, museums, and galleries.

Although mainly a daytime destination, Fort Mason attracts crowds at night for performances of its acclaimed **Magic Theatre,** haunt of playwright Sam Shepard and still one of the oldest and most respected theater companies on the West Coast despite fierce cutbacks. At night, the fort's pretty bluff is one of the most romantic spots in the city. Fort Mason is also the start of the Golden Gate Promenade, a three-and-a-half-mile paved walkway along San Francisco Bay that ends at **Fort Point National Historical Site,** directly under the Golden Gate Bridge. Also here is **Crissy Field,** a former biplane-era landing field. It's now a 100-acre park with both green grass and beach sand, great for barbecues and picnics, as well as watching kites flying, people hang gliding, or seals at play just offshore. What's more, it's one of the best places to observe and appreciate, even contemplate, that stunning, massive Art

Deco masterpiece known as the Golden Gate Bridge, fog permitting. On bright days the sun plays on the geometric and crenellated surfaces of the bridge so that, like a fine painting, the picture is ever-changing with the light. Bring a bottle of wine to enjoy with the view.

At the westernmost edge of the Marina is its most notable landmark, the **Palace of Fine Arts** (at Baker and Beach streets). An interpretation of a classical ruin complete with manicured lawns, ponds, and ducks, it's all that's left of the 1915 Panama Pacific Exhibition. Next door is the **Exploratorium,** a unique science museum with more than 700 hands-on science exhibits for kids and teens, including the ever-popular pitch-dark Tactile Dome.

When a cable-car line opened in the Pacific Heights District in 1878, this neighborhood south of Fort Mason and west of Van Ness Avenue quickly evolved into an enclave for San Francisco's nouveaux riches. Attempting to outdo the wooden castles on Nob Hill with mansions featuring Gothic arches, Byzantine domes, and stained-glass windows, the denizens of Pacific Heights created monuments to the bonanza era of the late 19th century. But the opulence and magnificence was short-lived. The earthquake of 1906 reduced the exquisite homes to shambles and the district never fully recovered. Much of the area was rebuilt with luxury apartment houses, but many original "painted ladies" or Victorian houses remain.

Today, Pacific Heights, along with the adjacent Cow Hollow and Presidio Heights districts, are home to more college graduates, professionals, and high-income families than any other city district. A fine collection of Victorian houses on Union Street has evolved into a premiere shopping area with more than 300 boutiques, restaurants, antique shops, and coffeehouses.

Fisherman's Wharf

Although visitors are hard-pressed to find vestiges of its once-busy shipbuilding, fishing, and industrial might, Fisherman's Wharf was once an active crab-fishing port. Then, about 40 years ago, the area was transformed into a tourist circus, and that's what it remains today. Here your tourist dollar is pursued with a vengeance at T-shirt shops, fast-food joints, stalls selling sweatshirts and baseball caps, and piers transformed into souvenir complexes, overpriced restaurants, and places to take a cruise on the bay.

In spite of the lamentable statistic that more than 10 million visitors a year come to Fisherman's Wharf, it's tempting to say that unless you've got restless children in tow, stay away. While by and large that's good advice, kids will disagree strongly, and there remain good reasons to come, aside from the view.

Probably the best is **Alcatraz,** 12 minutes away by ferry in San Francisco Bay; it's one of the best places to go in San Francisco and

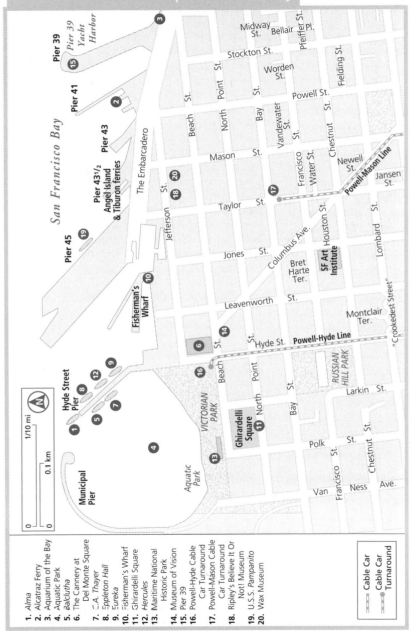

Fisherman's Wharf and Vicinity

shouldn't be missed. The ferry leaves from Pier 41; advance reservations are essential. Other worthwhile activities at the wharf include taking a cruise on the bay, renting a bike or a Segway, taking Mr. Toad's Bus Tour, or strolling down the **Golden Gate Promenade,** a three-and-a-half-mile paved path by the bay leading to the bridge of the same name. Last but not least, walk out on Pier 41 and wave at the collection of barking sea lions just offshore.

unofficial **TIP**

A fun way to see Ocean Beach, Golden Gate Park, the Palace of Fine Arts, Angel Island, or Fisherman's Wharf is on a Segway. These self-balancing, upright electric scooters each come with a helmet and a lesson, and since they don't go faster than 12 miles an hour, you won't be in any danger! Tours start at $30 for an hour (☎ 415-716-9910; **segwaysfbay.com**). You can even tour Fisherman's Wharf and North Beach by night on a Segway, starting at $70; **electrictour company.com**.

For those restless kids, a cluster of pricey attractions should do the trick. **Aquarium of the Bay** is a commercial aquarium where visitors walk through a submerged transparent tunnel and view Pacific Coast marine creatures. Along Jefferson Street are two rainy-day places: the **Wax Museum** and **Ripley's Believe It or Not.** Things get better at the **Hyde Street Pier,** where the National Park Service has berthed a collection of real 19th-century ships open to the public. Another block west is the **Maritime Museum,** a gorgeous Art Deco building full of nautical treasures.

The wharf also has two refurbished shopping complexes. **The Cannery,** a former fruit-packing factory on Jefferson Street at Leavenworth Street, has three levels of shops and restaurants. **Ghirardelli Square** at 900 North Point Street (at the western end of Fisherman's Wharf) is a boutique mall that's come a long way since its days as a chocolate factory. Its handsome redbrick facade and red neon sign are San Francisco landmarks.

While there you can get a tasty snack at **Kara's Cupcakes.** These are cupcakes raised to the level of ambrosia. See **ghirardellisq.com** and **karascupcakes.com** for more information.

North Beach

The Italians moved the Irish out in the late 19th century, causing quite a fury. In the 1950s, the beatniks stomped the area, causing everyone to complain. And now that the neighborhood is becoming increasingly Chinese thanks to its Chinatown borders, the Italians are ready to fling fettuccine. But despite such changing of the guard over the decades, North Beach remains one of the city's most interesting districts—thanks to the diverse cultural invasions. It was once San Francisco's original waterfront, and years later, landfill extended the waterfront farther north. One of the city's oldest neighborhoods, North Beach still has the well-worn feel of a pair of old, comfortable shoes. Often known as Little Italy, it is a great place for lingering and malingering in cafes and bars, casual shopping and browsing, and exploring side streets on foot. To get a feel for the neighborhood's melting-pot ethnic mix, stop by **Washington Square,** where you'll see elderly Italians playing bocce ball and Chinese gracefully slicing through the air in the early morning doing their Tai Chi routines.

unofficial **TIP**
The best possible view of the whole of North Beach is from the roof level of the parking garage at the corner of Vallejo and Powell streets. And it's easy parking!

Kick off the shoes, lay in the park, and gaze up at the spires of the Church of St. Peter and Paul.

Get up early one morning and head to Molinari's Deli, which opened in 1896; leave the swinging salamis and pick up fresh-baked focaccia at Liguria Bakery on the northeast corner of Washington Square; or head for Mario's Bohemian Cigar Store Café on the southwest tip for a brunch of eggplant sandwiches and espresso con Vov (566 Columbus Avenue; ☎ 415-362-0536). When the caffeine kicks in, consider walking up **Telegraph Hill** to **Coit Tower** for a great vista of San Francisco (see below).

Broadway separates North Beach from Chinatown. It's here you'll find the remnants of the city's high-end strip joints, as well as fine restaurants with live music like Enrico's (see profile in Dining).

THE MARRIAGE OF JOLTIN' JOE DIMAGGIO TO MARILYN MONROE

On January 14, 1954 at City Hall, 39-year-old Yankee slugger Joe DiMaggio married 27-year-old Marilyn Monroe. Both divorcees from youthful marriages, America's two most famous celebrities sneaked in to Judge Charles Perry's chambers to say their vows.

Monroe was wearing a dark brown suit with fur at the neck. The couple ducked a mob of photographers and fans to jump into DiMaggio's blue Cadillac and drove to the Church of St. Peter and Paul in Washington Square to take wedding photographs at the church steps before heading to Paso Robles for their honeymoon.

A loyal San Franciscan, DiMaggio grew up in a strict Sicilian Catholic family in North Beach where his father fished crabs on the wharf. By age 18 he'd signed for the San Francisco Seals; not long after that, he was slugging for the Yankees as Joltin' Joe DiMaggio.

But DiMaggio's Sicilian values lost out to Monroe's sewn-on dresses and Hollywood career in the end. The marriage lasted just nine months, and DiMaggio moved to New York, leaving behind his family. But **Joe DiMaggio's Italian Chophouse** in the North Beach is full of Joe DiMaggio and Marilyn Monroe memorabilia (601 Union Street at Columbus Avenue; ☎ 415-421-5633, **joedimaggiosrestaurant.com**).

Columbus Avenue runs right through the heart of the neighborhood. Most of it is lined with trees and cafes with sidewalk seating under heat lamps, and just walking along it is a recipe for good times. Atmospheric cafes and Italian pastry shops line either side. Bimbo's 365 Club (**bimbos365club.com**) at 1025 Columbus Avenue is a fabled music venue (in this instance, *bimbo* is Italian for "little boy"). Vesuvio (**vesuvio.com**) at 255 Columbus and Specs at 12 William Saroyan Place are hallowed bar haunts with a Beat past.

Tosca Café (242 Columbus Avenue, between Broadway and Pacific) is the place for White Nuns and opera music (see more in Nightlife). For a taste of North Beach's literary and beatnik past, stop in **City Lights Bookstore** at Columbus Avenue and Broadway, ground zero for the Beat generation; the small alley that runs down the side of the shop is now called Jack Kerouac Street after the most famous of the Beat writers. Shopping is great on Grant Street. Vallejo Street offers such famed little places as Caffe Trieste (at number 601) with its coffee and conviviality.

Telegraph Hill

Bordering North Beach is Telegraph Hill, praised for its views of the bay, vine-covered lanes, quaint cottages, pastel clapboard homes, and lousy parking. Once the home of struggling writers and artists, and before that an immigrant slum known as Little Chile during Barbary Coast days, Telegraph Hill is now occupied by a wealthier class of people. At the top is **Coit Tower,** named for Lillie Hitchcock Coit, who bequeathed the funds to build this popular tourist landmark. This is where muralist Diego Rivera inspired a Works Progress Administration project of 25 local painters to paint interior city scenes. Despite local rumors, the tower was not meant to imitate a fireman's nozzle, although it's true that Lillie Coit loved firefighters. It's been getting a makeover lately, which is a bit of a shame—it was already fine. Getting there, though, can be a chore. Many of the houses dangle precipitously over the steep inclines, and the sidewalks turn to steps as you near the top. An easier option is to take the No. 39 bus to the tower and then walk down the **Greenwich Steps,** a brick staircase lined with ivy and roses that descends steeply to Montgomery Street and Levi's Plaza, home of the original blue jeans factory with its authentic miners' copper-riveted denims. Near the base of the steps is an all-glass-brick Art Deco apartment house used in the Humphrey Bogart noir thriller *Dark Passage*.

The Castro District

One of the most fascinating, social, and educational gay-oriented parts of the city is the Castro District. The lesbian and gay community that makes its home in the Castro has contributed significantly to every aspect of the city's life, from economics and the arts to politics. (It's said that no San Francisco politician can win citywide election without the backing of the gay community.) Some say that the Castro is still the wildest neighborhood in town, and others say that it's merely a shadow of its former self. It's a good guess that much of the Castro's energy and unabashed hedonism has been channeled into AIDS support groups, care for the sick, and city politics. In the 1970s, the gay community transformed the neighborhood into a fashionable, upscale enclave of restaurants, bars, and restored homes. Formerly an Irish enclave, these days it's a lot tamer. You'll have to try very hard to feel out of place!

Probably the best way to explore the Castro is by taking a walking tour. One of the best we have found is Cruisin' the Castro Tour, which meets Tuesday through Saturday mornings at 10 a.m. at the Rainbow Flag at the corner of Castro and Market streets above the Castro Muni subway station (☎ 415-255-1821; **cruisinthecastro.com**). On this tour you will learn about gay history in the district from 1849 to present. The tour includes America's only "Pink Triangle Park"; Harvey Milk's residence and camera shop; the legendary Castro Theatre, which specializes in foreign, repertory, and art films; the Human Rights Campaign Action Center; unique shops; and lunch at the delicious Firewood Café. If you get hungry, you must visit a few Castro institutions such as gay landmark **Cafe Flore** at 2298 Market Street (**cafeflore.com**). For sensational sounds try **Café du Nord,** old-school funky rather than gay and ridiculously atmospheric, at 2170 Market Street (**cafedunord.com**).

The Mission District

For culture vultures craving salsa or an authentic taqueria, the Mission is the place to come. This mostly Latino neighborhood is hip, happening, and historical, made up of Mexican, Central American and, increasingly, a wave of New Bohemia residents. Named for Mission Dolores, San Francisco's oldest building (3321 16th Street) and the sixth in a chain of Spanish settlements that stretched for 650 miles, the district is no longer one of the cheaper districts to live in because its Bohemian appeal has inevitably been followed by the hipness factor.

Positioned just south of downtown, the Mission is blanketed in sun and warmth most of the summer while the rest of the city suffocates in the rolling afternoon fog. The district is large and is serviced by two BART stations, one at each end. The 16th Street station can be a dodgy spot late at night, so be careful if walking alone.

The Mission is an international hodge-podge, with large numbers of South Americans,

unofficial **TIP**
Corona Heights is the rocky pink outcrop just to the north of the Castro on the way up to Buena Vista Park. It's treacherously stony, but many a visitor has reached the top and testified to new joys. Nearby is the charming children's Randall Museum of nature exhibits.

Samoans, Vietnamese, Koreans, and Native Americans moving in; it's considered San Francisco's most diverse neighborhood. Mission and Valencia streets are a carnival of used clothing stores, ethnic groceries, leading edge restaurants, dive bars and swanky clubs, taquerias and creperies, street people of all descriptions, storefront Pentecostal churches, voodoo shops, pawnbrokers with musical instruments of all kinds, and even banks. Foreign Cinema Restaurant (2534 Mission) gives you dinner and a movie while Ramblas Tapas Bar (557 Valencia) and Andalu (3198 16th Street at Guerrero) set a tapas table. For drinking, Radio Habana Social Club at 1109 Valencia, El Rio at 3158 Mission, Argus Lounge at 3187 Mission Street, and the Liberties at 998 Guerrero each bills itself as a local dive. Go upscale at Martuni's (see Nightlife), downscale for beers and bratwursts at Zeitgeist (199 Valencia), Medjool for rooftop eating and dancing (2522 Mission), or combine dinner with the best Latin drag show at Esta Noche (3079 16th Street).

Mission Street is also a good place to start a tour of the Mission's 200-odd murals, painted as a result of a City Hall scheme to channel the energy of the district's poor youth; the biggest concentration is along 24th Street between Mission Street and South Van Ness Avenue. Ask a passerby to point you to Balmy Alley. More Latino culture is on display at the **Mission Cultural Center** (2868 Mission Street), where visitors can enjoy temporary art exhibits, theatrical productions, and poetry readings.

Noe Valley

One of the hipper neighborhoods bordering the Mission is Noe (Noee) Valley. This was *the* place to live in the 1990s, but those hipsters have settled down now. A walk up Valencia Street to 24th Street will take you to the heart of this beloved and sunny neighborhood. It is the land of organic produce, smoothies, fashionista haunts, New Age music, and paint-it-yourself pottery stores. Trendy cafes and bookstores and funky jewelry boutiques are everywhere, and it seems that many Missionaries-made-good have migrated here for its quaint village feel. Chocolate Covered (4069 24th Street) offers everything chocolate, while the well-stocked and affordable Phoenix Books has moved across 24th Street to number 3957. Get crepes at Savor (3913 24th Street), lunch in the minute backyard at oh-so-French Le Zinc (4063 24th Street), or down patty melts and spinach pies for ever so much less at always-cheerful Joe's 24th Street Café (3853 24th Street).

The next hill over is the Bernal Heights neighborhood with its large lesbian population and a slew of fair eateries along Cortland Avenue; the Wild Side West Saloon (242 Cortland Avenue) is their popular hangout but welcomes all people of good will. Also noticeable are the new moms and dads or moms and moms, and babies that crawl, stroll, and toddle the streets of Noe and Bernal. Both are safer and quieter than the lower-down Mission and were once cheaper to rent. No more! **Dolores Park** is nearby and is one of the best features of Noe-Castro, with views of downtown that will inspire you, free symphony concerts, and mime troupe performances in summer, when the Hunky Jesus contest is another hit. But it can be iffy by night when sundry drug dealers infest it.

Potrero Hill

Tucked away from the hustle and bustle of city life, Potrero Hill is probably San Francisco's most photogenic enclave. Quiet streets, whimsical houses that seem right out of the movie *Edward Scissorhands*, and unobstructed views of downtown from every vantage point make it one of the most livable of neighborhoods. Everything has a homegrown feel to it—you won't find a Barnes and Noble or Starbucks here. Its recent revitalization in art, theater, healing arts, and loft and warehouse spaces makes Potrero worth a visit. Vista Point (405 Florida Street) and Southern Exposure (401 Alabama Street) are two typical neighborhood galleries. Aperto is one of the leaders of Cal-Italian gastronomy on 18th Street, while Klein's supplies deli delights named after famous women, and the Bottom of the Hill is the watering hole. This is a neighborhood to come to for calm. And for those in the know, the crookedest street doesn't reside on Lombard but at Vermont and 20th streets. The end of Vermont Street packs more thrilling twists and turns into its eight switchbacks than Lombard.

South of Market (SoMa)

Over the last 15 years or so, this dreary area of old factory spaces has been spruced up into galleries, a convention center, trendy restaurants, museums, gay bars, and nightclubs. SoMa was becoming the West Coast version of New York's SoHo fast when the big downturn hit. The **San Francisco Museum of Modern Art** (151 Third Street) is housed in a $62 million structure that some critics say is more beautiful than any of the art inside.

Whether you are purveying Picasso or pump-up-the-music VIP clubs, SoMa is where property prices have been soaring. The district can be divided roughly into four regions: the increasingly developed area around the art museums, including the Moscone Convention Center and the Metreon entertainment center; the nightclub region around 11th and Folsom streets, where crowds line up outside Slim's and the DNA Lounge nightly; the blocks between Third and Fourth streets where you'll find the new Yerba Buena Center; and the still underdeveloped dock areas of Mission Rock and China Basin, although they are next to the leafy and trendy little South Park and earmarked for more live/work lofts. Artists, dancers, and musicians once liked SoMa for the low rents and for spaces they could convert into so-called live/work lofts. These are now fashionably high-priced.

By day, SoMa remains an oddly colorless and semi-industrial neighborhood of warehouses and factory outlets. That's no surprise, considering that the area has always been home to industry. Several foundries were located in SoMa in the 1850s, along with rows of prefabricated housing imported from the East, making the neighborhood San Francisco's first industrial population. But in the late 1990s, the city's denizens, including artists, trendsetters, and hipsters of all kinds, descended on a formerly gray landscape lit up by the neon facades of bars and clubs.

If you've already hit the Top of the Mark (see Nob Hill, above), you can continue your high-altitude buzz at the Saul Steinberg–esque **San Francisco Marriott Hotel** and its 39th-floor bar, the **View Lounge.** Located near Fourth and Market streets south of Union Square near the edge of SoMa, the bar features concentric parabolic windows that slope backward to form a kind of half dome, creating the illusion that you're floating over the city in the nose of a helicopter. Drink prices surpass the bar's altitude, but absorbing the view is an experience worth the price. On your way out, pay tribute to the sole surviving martini glass forever enshrined in the bar—it stood the test of the 1989 earthquake that rocked the hotel's walls on opening night!

The Presidio, Fort Point, and the Golden Gate Bridge

After hundreds of years of sporadic military occupation by Spain, Mexico, and the United States, this northwestern tip of the San Francisco peninsula was handed over to the National Park Service in 1994. Now the former Army base is in the slow process of evolving into a national park. Blissfully free of developed attractions, the **Presidio** offers miles of eucalyptus-scented roadways, trails, ancient gun fortifications, and incredible views from its sandy bluffs. Almost 30 of its 1,500 acres are part of the **San Francisco National Military Cemetery.** A digital arts center, built by George Lucas of *Star Wars* fame, also covers a portion of the Presidio's grounds.

The Presidio's main entrance is on Lombard Street, west of Pacific Heights and the Marina District. Small military buildings remain scattered across the former Army post. The Presidio's dramatic location (and maybe the most impressive view in the city) is **Fort Point,** the ruins of an old brick fortress overlooking the impossibly scenic Golden Gate, with breathtaking vistas that include the San Francisco skyline on one side and the Marin Headlands across the strait.

Overhead at Fort Point, traffic roars on the **Golden Gate Bridge,** probably the most famous bridge in the world. Formerly thought unbridgeable, the mile-wide Golden Gate between the tip of the San Francisco peninsula

unofficial **TIP**
Visitors should consider both driving and walking across the bridge; the drive is thrilling as you pass under the huge towers, and the half-hour walk allows the bridge's enormous size and spectacular views to sink in.

and Marin County was finally spanned in 1937, and until 1959 it ranked as the world's longest suspension bridge (4,200 feet). A sobering note: About 30 to 40 people a year commit suicide by jumping off the bridge to the water 260 feet below. The total reached more than 1,300 by 2009, prompting a grim documentary and an outcry for more guardrails. A steel net under the bridge to prevent deaths is in the works.

There's a viewing area off the northbound lanes of US 101, with parking and access to trails and the bridge's walkways. (There's no need to cross the bridge by car to return to US 101 southbound.) If you drive across to Marin County, a $6 toll for cars is collected at the southern end of the bridge.

The Beaches, Lands End, the Palace of the Legion of Honor, and Cliff House

South of the Golden Gate Bridge along the Pacific coastline are some of the city's finest beaches. Former military installations hidden among trees and behind sand dunes provide protection from the wind for picnickers. The sandy shoreline of **Baker Beach** faces the entrance of Golden Gate, a scenic backdrop for hiking, fishing, and sunbathing; swimming in these treacherous waters, alas, is dangerous. Behind Baker Beach, **Battery Chamberlain** points a 95,000-pound cannon ominously to sea.

We never tire of telling folks about the 1.5-mile coastal trail around **Lands End,** a shoreline noted for the romantic and curious Sutro ruins and its abundance of birds, trees, scenic vistas, the sound of the ocean, the smell of pine and cypress, and coastal scenery. At low tide, the wrecks of ships that fell victim to the treacherous water are visible. You can also follow the route of an abandoned 19th-century railroad that once led to Cliff House, but stay on the main trail because the cliffs are steep and dangerous. Visitors can also explore defense batteries at **West Fort Miley.**

At the south end of Lands End is the **Palace of the Legion of Honor,** a white-pillared twin of the famous Legion d'Honneur in Paris. Most say that it's the city's best art museum, but there's no argument about its spectacularly scenic setting overlooking the Pacific Ocean and attractive cafe. With Rodin's *Thinker* in the courtyard, this art museum makes an indelible impression.

Cliff House, a mainstay of San Francisco tourism for more than a century, still attracts plenty of visitors, sometimes by the busload. Just offshore from the restaurant and gift shop are **Seal Rocks,** home base for sea lions and marine birds. Next door are the ruins of the once-elaborate **Sutro Baths,** a 19th-century swimming emporium that could hold 24,000 people in its heyday; it burned to the ground in the 1960s. Come just before sunset for cocktails and a view of Seal Rocks and the setting sun from the restaurant; it's a San Francisco tradition.

unofficial TIP
A bit farther south, **China Beach** provides an intimate atmosphere on a small beach nestled on a steep shoreline—perfect for family outings and picnics. It's also San Francisco's safest swimming beach (although not as popular as the more accessible Baker Beach).

Cliff House also marks the northern terminus of **Ocean Beach,** a four-mile stretch of sand and crashing surf that's always windy and wavy. You won't find much in the way of frills or stunning scenery, but the beach is a great place for jogging, walking, and people-watching. Don't go in the water, though. The ocean is always dangerous, even when it looks calm. By night it lights up with campfires and spontaneous parties.

Farther down the coast are two more notable San Francisco locales. The **San Francisco Zoo** (at Great Highway and Sloat Boulevard) is Northern California's largest animal emporium and features animals in grassy enclosures behind moats, not pacing in cages. (Since the December 2007 tiger incident, the big-cat enclosures have reopened with raised walls, electrified wires, and new glass barriers.) Next is Fort Funston, with easy hiking trails, great views of the ocean, and hang gliders overhead. Locals call this place Fort Fun.

Golden Gate Park

In a city awash in greenery, Golden Gate Park is San Francisco's biggest open space; in fact, it's the largest man-made urban park in the world. The park dazzles visitors with a nearly endless succession of sandy beaches, urban vistas, rolling coastal hills, and the wide expanse of the Pacific Ocean. Exploration of the 1,040-acre park, which stretches from Haight-Ashbury in the east for 52 blocks to the Pacific coast in the west, could take days. Ideally, the best way to discover Golden Gate Park is to wander aimlessly. That, unfortunately, isn't an option for most visitors. The park slopes gently from east to west and is roughly divided into two parts. The easternmost part contains all the main attractions— art and science museums, horticultural gardens, bandstands, and the Japanese Tea Garden. The western end is less developed, contains more open space and trails, and has a less-sculpted look. It's also where you'll find a herd of buffalo and a Dutch windmill.

Golden Gate Park's major attraction is the **de Young Memorial Museum,** a gallery of mostly American art (see Attractions).

Across the Music Concourse is the **California Academy of Sciences** (**calacademy.org**), a state-of-the-art destination for families that includes a planetarium and an aquarium; kids love the place. Since its grand reopening in October 2008, it has introduced NightLife, a night-in-the-museum-evoking disco and nightclub with cocktails and live music. Its green living roof, fascinating rain forest, lower-floor mangrove swamp, coral reef, and reptile pool with an ancient, crowd-favorite albino alligator continue to entice and educate. But the planetarium is its biggest draw; head to it first to line up for passes.

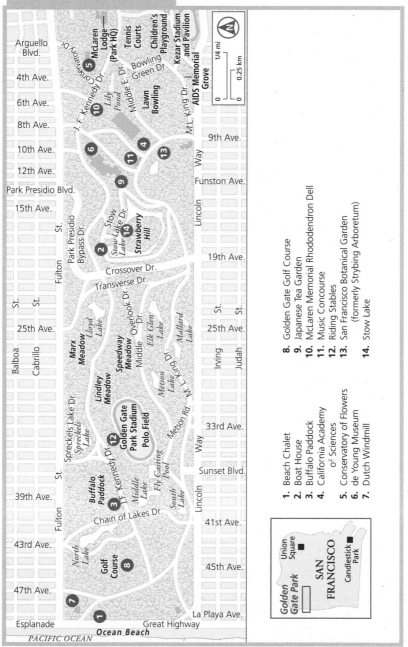

Golden Gate Park

8. Golden Gate Golf Course
9. Japanese Tea Garden
10. McLaren Memorial Rhododendron Dell
11. Music Concourse
12. Riding Stables
13. San Francisco Botanical Garden
    (formerly Strybing Arboretum)
14. Stow Lake

1. Beach Chalet
2. Boat House
3. Buffalo Paddock
4. California Academy
   of Sciences
5. Conservatory of Flowers
6. de Young Museum
7. Dutch Windmill

Its cafe is fun and cheap with pastas and fries; the Moss Room restaurant is very impressive and not cheap; neither is museum admission, which begins at $25 for adults. But for that you get planetarium shows every hour on the half hour, coral reef dives at 11:30 a.m. and 2:30 p.m., penguin feedings at 10:30 a.m. and 3:30 p.m., and everyone's favorite, the albino alligator at 1 p.m.

The **Japanese Tea Garden** shows how trees, landscape, rocks, and an added pagoda can make a work of art; you also get tea and cookies served by kimono-clad waitresses. The **San Francisco Botanical Garden** is 70 gorgeous acres of lawns and trees illustrating the diversity of plant life that thrives in San Francisco's Mediterranean-style climate, and it hosts regular bird-watching tours.

The **Conservatory of Flowers** is a curvaceous white wedding cake of hothouse glass. With its tropical vines and shrubs, special shows of carnivorous plants and butterflies, and giant water lilies, it's also hugely in demand for photo ops.

While most people head to the western end of the park to do nothing whatsoever, **Stow Lake** can also feed the urge to loaf. Boats of all types—including the non-rowing kind—are available for rent by the hour, as are bicycles and in-line skates. You'll also find restrooms, drinking water, and a snack bar.

A herd of buffalo roams inside the **Bison Paddock** off JFK Drive at 38th Avenue. You can get close to the shaggy (and once nearly extinct) beasts at their feeding area near the western end. At the edge of the park near the ocean are a tulip garden and a Dutch windmill (a can't-be-missed landmark).

Haight-Ashbury

Hippies and the Haight. You can't have one without the other. The Haight was once the free-love zone, and although the era of free love, sex, drugs, and the Grateful Dead has found restful solitude in the hearts of its followers and present-day wannabes, the Haight remains true to its tie-dye roots. Just take a stroll and you'll see for yourself—from Mama's Tattoo Parlor, leather and vintage shops, to the flowers and candles left at 710 Ashbury Street, the one-time home of the Grateful Dead. The biggest flashback of the year occurs during the **Haight Street Fair** in June—a must-see for all! Today the Haight is a lovely, somewhat calmer neighborhood divided into the upper and, down the hill, the lower sections. Upper Haight was where it all happened in the 1960s. Now, though there is still a faint aroma of the 1960s, you can shop at the Gap or sip a microbrew at the **Magnolia** (1398 Haight). You can still shop at **Bound Together** (1369 Haight) for radical fringe books, and then get a martini at the **Aub Zam Zam** with its great jukebox (1633 Haight), or hie down to the **Alembic** (1725 Haight) for froufrou cocktails.

Haight-Ashbury and the Castro

Down in the lower Haight they shrug off the notoriety of the upper, content to be left alone by throngs of tourists. There they can enjoy shopping for old 45 rpm records at **Rooky's** and "stuff for your place" at **Mickey's Monkey** (218 Pierce Street). Then they can go to the Pork Store Café (1451 Haight) for legendary diner food, to **Rosamunde** for a zillion grilled dogs (545 Haight), or **Memphis Minnie's** for barbecue (576 Haight, and another favorite). Vegetarians and vegans go to **Axum Cafe** for Ethiopian fare and really good deals (698 Haight).

The relatively small Haight-Ashbury zone contains eight parks and green spaces, including **Alamo Square** at Hayes and Steiner streets. There you can see the famous "painted ladies," the row of beautiful Victorian homes on the east side of the square.

Japantown

Bounded by Geary Boulevard and California, Octavia, and Fillmore streets, nowadays Japantown is called home by only about 4 percent of San Francisco's Japanese-American residents. Most, though, return regularly for shopping and social and religious activities. The construction of Japan Center in 1968 was the inspiration for a community renewal effort, with residents and merchants pitching in to beautify the surrounding blocks. Japan Center has three interlinked buildings, including the Miyako with its less visited but fascinating restaurants such as Takara and the occasional sushi bar. The block-long Buchanan Mall, landscaped with flowering trees and fountains, marks the center's northern entrance.

unofficial **TIP**
For a taste of ethnicity, visit Japantown on weekends, especially in spring and summer, when many Japanese cultural events—from tea ceremonies to martial arts demonstrations and musical performances— take place.

Full of restaurants and stores, **Japan Center** is also the home of many noodle and sushi choices and Hello Kitty–style souvenir shops, plus **Sundance Kabuki Cinemas,** Robert Redford's eight-screen, ultramodern movie complex serving gourmet fare, wine, and cocktails with the latest films. The Sundance Kitchen bistro is next door, and the complex is one of the venues for the annual San Francisco International Film Festival. The other highlight at the Japan Center is the **Kabuki Springs & Spa,** genuine Japanese baths that offer shiatsu massage, steam baths, and other luxuriating facilities; some days are men or women only, so check ahead.

Compared to Chinatown, Japantown appears well tended and new. But it's experiencing something of a revival, and exploring its many nooks will yield various places of interest from the **Buddhist Church of San Francisco** (Pine and Octavia streets), a sumptuous temple filled with what are claimed to be relics of Buddha, to the ethnic markets, bakeries, tea shops, and antique stores.

A couple of blocks south is **The Cathedral of Saint Mary of the Assumption** (where Geary Boulevard meets Gough Street), the city's ultrawhite giant Roman Catholic cathedral (1971), sometimes known as "the Washing Machine." Walk inside and gaze at the cathedral's 190-foot dome, mighty organ, and stained-glass windows.

Twin Peaks

Ah yes, the Jekyll and Hyde temperament of Twin Peaks! It is at once the granddaddy of inspiration points and one of San Francisco's most distinctive landmarks and, at the same time, the foggiest, most mist-filled part of town. You love it for the views but hate it for the behind-a-waterfall, bring-the-raincoat, and need-some-Prozac kinda weather. Why is the district called Twin Peaks? There are two hills that make up the area, and Spanish explorers first called them "breasts of the Indian girl," but prudish Americans settled on the less-descriptive Twin Peaks. The peak slopes contain curving roads that feature some of the most expensive homes in San Francisco, a testament to the theory that the better the view, the higher the price of real estate. And what a view! The 360-degree overlook on a clear evening is magical. A little lower down is Tank Hill, with almost no visitors and another showstopping view.

Luckily, Twin Peaks is one of a few hills in the city spared from development, making a walk, bike ride, or drive to the top doable. It's between the Clayton-17th Street intersection of Upper Cole Valley and the Portola stretch of Diamond Heights, making it an especially interesting transurban hike combined with Glen Canyon Park and Sutro Heights.

unofficial **TIP**
Fillmore Street—with its fashionable boutiques, bakeries, and bistros—runs north. The world-famous **Yoshi's Jazz Club (yoshis. com)** with its superb sushi bar sits near unpredictable **Rasselas (rasselasjazzclub. com)** with its revolving fare; **The Fillmore (thefillmore.com)**, a fabled music venue of 1960s fame; and John L. Hooker's blues-tooting **Boom Boom Room (boomboomblues. com)** on the Geary-Fillmore corners.

Richmond and the Sunset

Don't let the name fool you. The Sunset is not very sunny. Due to the heavy fog that blankets the area through most of the year, much of the Sunset District has developed a distinctly quiet and residential character. The vast size of the district, however, has fostered the development of some quirky architecture and several varied and vibrant neighborhoods. The west end of the Sunset (abutting the Pacific Ocean) bears a closer resemblance to a beach town than a suburb; surfers and nature lovers brave the cool sea spray to combine the convenience of city living with a raw outdoor lifestyle. The San Francisco Zoo borders the Sunset to the south, as does the Stonestown Galleria, a large mall complex. Along the northeastern border, the Upper Haight meets the Sunset to produce a quieter and more upscale neighborhood with a 1960s-influenced mindset, including the requisite cafes and poetry readings.

Irving is the main drag for new Sunset foodie discoveries, mainly Asian and capped by the popular Thanh Long with the An family's Green Dragon cocktail, Vietnamese roast crab, and legendary garlic noodle recipes. Many more fine neighborhood restaurants are also scattered across the Richmond district north of

unofficial **TIP**
Both the Golden Gate and Bay bridges are visible here, as is all of downtown and its surrounding districts. A hot date spot for sure!

the park, particularly along Clement Street and Geary Boulevard. Aziza serves outstanding Moroccan fare, and westwards on the Great Highway, the Beach Chalet is an open secret (see them all in Dining).

ACROSS TWO BRIDGES: THE BAY AREA AND NEARBY CITIES

THE EAST BAY, AS YOU WILL HEAR IT REFERRED TO, consists of Berkeley and Oakland and is connected to San Francisco via the double-decker, recently reinforced Bay Bridge, which had suffered in the 1989 quake. The red pillars of the Golden Gate Bridge connect the city to points north, including Marin County, Sausalito, Tiburon, Marin City, and Mill Valley. North of these points on US 101 above Marin County are small towns Petaluma and Santa Rosa (57 miles away) leading to the Russian River with its wineries and beyond, and, slightly to the east, the Wine Country valleys Napa and Sonoma (about 60 miles away). About 125 miles north along the rugged coastline is Mendocino, a small picturesque seaside resort that was once a logging village, then became a haven for artists in the 1950s, and is now a lot pricier. The Oregon state line is almost 400 miles to the north past the remote, lovely, and unspoilt Lost Coast.

The Sierra Nevada Mountains and the Nevada state line are about 200 miles east of the city. Yosemite National Park, southeast of San Francisco in the Sierra Nevada range, is 184 miles away. Fifty miles south along the peninsula (below the southern end of San Francisco Bay) are San Jose and Silicon Valley. South along the coast are the cities of Santa Cruz (80 miles), Monterey (115 miles), Santa Barbara (320 miles), Los Angeles (400 miles), and San Diego (550 miles).

THE MAJOR HIGHWAYS

SAN FRANCISCO'S MAJOR HIGHWAY, US 101, links Seattle and San Diego along the Pacific Coast. The freeway threads its way through the city on Van Ness Avenue after crossing the Golden Gate Bridge at the northwestern tip of the city and continues south along the peninsula to San Jose and beyond.

I-80 crosses the San Francisco–Oakland Bay Bridge and continues northeasterly to Sacramento. I-80 also intersects with I-580 and I-880 in Oakland. I-580 (the Eastshore Freeway) heads north toward Richmond and then swings west across San Pablo Bay to San Rafael and US 101, north of San Francisco. To the south, I-880 follows the eastern shore of San Francisco Bay south toward San Jose, while I-580 swings east toward Stockton and an intersection with I-5, the inland interstate link that runs from Vancouver to San Diego.

Below San Francisco, I-280 begins south of the city and parallels US 101 toward Redwood City, Stanford, and Sunnyvale; its northern end is one of the most beautiful stretches of interstate highway in the country. US 101 (here called the Bayshore Freeway) follows the western shore of San Francisco Bay on a more direct route to the cities of Palo Alto, Santa Clara, and San Jose.

The Layout

Someone back in the day had the idea to lay the city out on a grid. A nice concept when considering flat terrain like New York City, but when you are negotiating steep Divisadero, Lombard, or Filbert streets, you'll be sweating bricks and cursing the wise guy! Admittedly the city is easy to navigate as a result of this checkerboard pattern. The city's 42 hills, like stones beneath a checked tablecloth, divide the city into areas that are the foundation for distinctive neighborhoods. If you know the cross street when searching for an address, the task is fairly simple. The major east-west axis is Geary Boulevard, which runs from downtown to the Pacific Ocean. The major north-south streets are Van Ness Avenue, Divisadero Street, and Park Presidio Boulevard.

The exception is Market Street, which cuts diagonally across the city from the Embarcadero to the Castro. Most of San Francisco's streets are very long, with numbers typically ranging from 1 to 4000. Street numbers get higher going from east to west and from south to north. Distances are measured in blocks, with numbers rising by 100 from block to block. It would be simpler to find your way along Market Street if the numbers were in sync with the intersecting numerical streets, but they're not.

South of Market Street the streets are numbered beginning with First Street and continuing through 30th Street. Do not confuse these streets with the numbered avenues that begin three miles west of downtown and run from Second Avenue to 48th Avenue at the ocean.

Throughout the northwest sector of the city (downtown to Fisherman's Wharf) and in the cookie-cutter neighborhood of Sunset, streets are one-way, with the exceptions of Columbus Avenue, Market Street, and Van Ness Avenue. When traffic on a street goes only one way, the traffic in the two streets on either side of it move in the opposite direction.

MAJOR ARTERIES AND STREETS

MARKET STREET IS SAN FRANCISCO'S MAIN DRAG. Many of the city's buses and streetcars follow this route from the outlying suburbs past the Castro and Mission districts, Civic Center, SoMa, and Union Square to the downtown Financial District. Underground subways operated by BART and light-rail trains operated by Muni Metro load and disgorge passengers at seven underground stations located along Market Street.

The tall office buildings clustered downtown are at the northeast end of Market Street; one block beyond lie the Embarcadero and the bay. The building with the tall tower at the end of the street is the Ferry Building, one of a few major structures to survive the 1906 earthquake and fire and now a ritzy refurbished food and produce market with top-class eateries such as The Slanted Door. The Embarcadero curves along San Francisco Bay from south of the Bay Bridge to the northeast perimeter of the city and ends at Fisherman's Wharf, San Francisco's famous cluster of piers and tourist attractions. The elevated freeway used to continue along the bay west of the wharf but was almost completely removed after the 1989 earthquake, much to the relief of many San Franciscans, who can now enjoy unimpeded views of the bay. Beyond Fisherman's Wharf are Aquatic Park, Fort Mason, the Presidio, and Golden Gate National Recreation Area, all linked by the Golden Gate Promenade, a three-and-a-half-mile pedestrian walkway.

From the eastern perimeter of Fort Mason, Van Ness Avenue runs due south back to Market Street; it's also US 101 south of the Golden Gate Bridge. The rough triangle formed by these three major thoroughfares—Market Street to the southeast, the Embarcadero and the waterfront to the north, and Van Ness Avenue to the west—contains most of the city's major tourist attractions and neighborhoods of interest to visitors.

OTHER MAJOR STREETS

A FEW OTHER MAJOR THOROUGHFARES that visitors are bound to encounter include Mission Street, which parallels Market Street to the south in SoMa; it's also the main street in the Mission District south of downtown. Montgomery Street in the Financial District links to Columbus Avenue in North Beach, while Bay, Jefferson, and Beach streets are major east-west arteries in and around Fisherman's Wharf.

Grant Avenue is Chinatown's touristy main street, while Powell Street runs north-south from Market Street to the bay past Union Square; it's also a major cable-car route, as the street climbs Nob Hill. Lincoln Boulevard is the major road through the Presidio, a former Army base at the northwest corner of the city that's now part of Golden Gate National Recreation Area.

Geary Boulevard, California Street, and Broadway are major east-west streets downtown; Geary goes the distance to the Pacific Ocean, where it merges with Point Lobos Avenue just before reaching Cliff House, a major tourist landmark. Visitors following signs for US 101 on Van Ness Avenue to reach the Golden Gate Bridge will make a left onto Lombard Street, and then zoom past the Palace of Fine Arts as they approach the famous span.

At the southern end of Market Street (just past Twin Peaks), the name changes to Portola Drive and skirts the happy little neighborhood of West Portal with more fine eateries and a mini movie theater; turn right on Sloat Boulevard to reach the San Francisco Zoo and Ocean Beach. There you'll find the Great Highway, which parallels the ocean and eventually combines with part of Highway 1. Highway 1 crosses the Presidio and Golden Gate Park to join 19th Avenue, and then runs straight into I-280 at Junipero Serra Boulevard before splitting for Pacifica and the coast.

Turn right on Great Highway and head north to reach the western end of Golden Gate Park (look for the windmill). The park's main drag is John F. Kennedy Drive, a portion of which is closed to traffic on Saturdays April through September. The entire drive is closed year-round on Sundays. At the eastern end of Golden Gate Park are Fell and Oak streets, which head east to Van Ness Avenue and Market Street.

THINGS *the* NATIVES *Already* KNOW

TIPPING

EVERYBODY NEEDS A REFRESHER COURSE on tipping protocol. To start, tipping is not a question. Do tip; it's as simple as that. You'll find service to be outstanding at restaurants, hotels, and even in taxis. Here are some guidelines for those sticky moments when you are left wondering if the hotel or restaurant staff is spitting in your food or naming their firstborn after you.

PORTERS AND SKYCAPS $2 a bag.

CAB DRIVERS A lot depends on service and courtesy. If the fare is less than $8, give the driver the change and $1. Example: If the fare is $4.50, give the cabbie fifty cents and a buck for tip. If the fare is more than $8, give the driver the change and $2. If you ask the cabbie to take you only a block or two, the fare will be small, but your tip should be large ($2 to $3) to make up for his or her wait in line and to partially compensate him or her for missing a better-paying fare. Add an extra dollar to your tip if the driver handles a lot of luggage.

> *un*official **TIP**
> You'll find the cab drivers in San Francisco the most amusing and interesting of most major cities. Strike up a conversation and learn what makes them tick!

PARKING VALETS $2 is correct if the valet is courteous and demonstrates some hustle. $1 will do if the service is just OK. Pay only when you check your car out, not when you leave it.

BELLMEN AND DOORMEN When a bellman greets you at your car with a rolling luggage cart and handles all of your bags, $5 is about right. The more luggage you carry yourself, of course, the less you should tip. Add another $1 or $2 if the bellman opens your room. For calling a taxi, tip the doorman $1 to $2.

WAITERS Whether in a coffee shop, an upscale eatery, or room service from the hotel kitchen, the standard gratuity range is 15 percent to 20 percent of the tab, before sales tax. At a buffet or brunch where you serve yourself, leave a dollar or two for the person who brings your drinks. Some restaurants, however, are adopting the European custom of automatically adding a 15 percent gratuity to the bill, so check before leaving a cash tip.

COCKTAIL WAITERS AND BARTENDERS Here you tip by the round. For two people, $1 a round; for more than two people, $2 a round. For a large group, use your judgment: Is everyone drinking beer, or is the order long and complicated? Tip accordingly.

HOTEL MAIDS When you check out, leave $1 to $3 per day for each day of your stay, provided service was good.

HOW TO LOOK AND SOUND LIKE A NATIVE

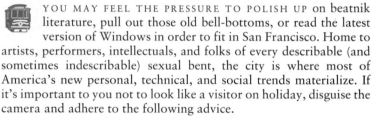
YOU MAY FEEL THE PRESSURE TO POLISH UP on beatnik literature, pull out those old bell-bottoms, or read the latest version of Windows in order to fit in San Francisco. Home to artists, performers, intellectuals, and folks of every describable (and sometimes indescribable) sexual bent, the city is where most of America's new personal, technical, and social trends materialize. If it's important to you not to look like a visitor on holiday, disguise the camera and adhere to the following advice.

1. If you do the Fishermen's Wharf thing, don't wear shorts and a T-shirt; freezing, underdressed tourists huddling for warmth at the wharf is an enduring San Francisco cliché.

2. Don't call cable cars "trolleys."

3. Don't pronounce Ghirardelli with a soft *g;* the square's name is pronounced "GEAR-ar-delly."

4. People will tell you to never utter the two-syllable *Frisco* as though it passes for the 11th Commandment around here. They add that they are not responsible for what could happen should you get caught saying this. But there are signs that this is changing little by little, and calling it The City, as the *San Francisco Chronicle* insists, is not mandatory either. In other words, call it whatever you like!

5. Carry a sweater when it's 75° outside, because chances are the temperature will drop.

6. Rice-A-Roni originated on Madison Avenue. Nobody here eats it.

LOCAL PUBLICATIONS

SAN FRANCISCO HAS ONE OF THE OLDEST daily newspapers in the country, the *San Francisco Chronicle*, **sfgate.com,** published in the morning. The Sunday edition "pink section," so called because—

hold onto your hats—it's pink, is the Bay Area's bible of arts, leisure, entertainment, and all other social goings-on. The Thursday *96 Hours* supplement holds all the happenings and listings, as well as tips on cheap eats.

Free weekly tabloid papers include the *San Francisco Bay Guardian*, **sfbg.com**, and the *SF Weekly*, **sfweekly.com**. Both offer coverage on everything from art to politics and generally provide more detailed information on local nightlife and entertainment than the dailies. *Where San Francisco* is a free monthly magazine for tourists, offering information on shopping, dining, and entertainment, as well as maps and listings of things to do while in town; look for a copy in your hotel room. *Bay City Guide*, **baycityguide.com**, found in many museums and shops, is a free monthly magazine; it provides maps and listings of things to do for visitors.

San Francisco Magazine, **sanfran.com**, is the city's leading glossy magazine, and it focuses on dining, the arts, entertainment, and ten-best lists. A city magazine in direct competition with *San Francisco Magazine* is *7 x 7*, **7x7.com**—named for the city's square area. It aims to provide more in-depth, investigative pieces as opposed to the cookie-cutter top-ten lists and such that *San Francisco Magazine* produces. *San Francisco Arts Monthly*, **sfarts. org**, is a tabloid listing the city's visual and performing arts calendars. *Street Sheet*, sold by homeless and formerly homeless people on the city's streets for a buck, provides a street-level view of homelessness and helps the homeless earn money. The *Bay Area Reporter*, **ebar.com**, distributed free on Thursdays, covers the gay community, including in-depth news, information, and a weekly calendar of goings-on for gays and lesbians.

LIVE FROM SAN FRANCISCO

ASIDE FROM THE BABBLE OF FORMAT ROCK, easy listening, and country music stations, San Francisco is home to radio stations that really stand out for high-quality broadcasting. Tune in to what hip San Franciscans listen to.

SAN FRANCISCO'S HIGH-QUALITY RADIO STATIONS		
FORMAT	FREQUENCY	STATION
Jazz	91.1 FM	KCSM
NPR	88.5 FM	KQED
Talk, classical, community affairs	94.1 FM	KPFA
Classical	102.1 FM	KDFC
Rock	104.5 FM	KFOG
Alternative rock	105.3 FM	KITS

A good Saturday-morning outing is to NPR's taping of *West Coast Live* radio show, hosted by Sedge Thomson at Fort Mason. For $15 to $18 you can be part of the audience of fascinating interviews with musicians, authors, poets, comics, and so on. Bring your best sound effects because the audience is usually called upon to create some together. (Contact at ☎ 415-664-9500 or **wcl.org.**)

ACCESS FOR THE DISABLED

STEEP HILLS ASIDE, TRAVELERS WITH MOBILITY PROBLEMS are likely to find San Francisco more in tune with their needs than other U.S. cities; it's considered one of the most barrier-free towns around. Nearly all buildings and public transportation are equipped for easy access. In compliance with the Americans with Disabilities Act, direction signs, toilets, and entrances are adapted for blind and disabled visitors. Many theaters (both movie and stage) offer special audio equipment for hearing-impaired people.

Parking spaces reserved for people with disabled permits are marked by a blue-and-white sign and a blue curb; a wheelchair outline is painted on the pavement. With your permit, you can park without paying; in other words, you are golden. To get a temporary permit, disabled persons pay a $6 fee and present a state-of-origin permit or plaque with photo I.D. at the Department of Motor Vehicles (1377 Fell Street; ☎ 415-557-1170; **dmv.ca.gov**). There's a service window reserved for the disabled, and you can download and fill out the correct form and apply by mail too.

Most street corners downtown have dropped curbs and most city buses have wheelchair lifts. Major museums throughout the Bay Area are fitted with wheelchair ramps, and many hotels offer special accommodations and services for wheelchair-bound visitors.

All Muni Metro and BART stations are wheelchair accessible. Wheelchair-boarding platforms are located at many stops, including some islands on Market Street. In addition, Muni operates more than 30 accessible bus lines. For a complete listing of transit lines, including a chart indicating which lines offer disabled access, pick up a copy of the *Official San Francisco Street and Transit Map,* available at most newsstands for $3. Call ☎ 415-923-6336 (touch-tone only) to get recorded schedule information. For more information on disabled access to public transportation or a *Muni Access Guide,* write to the Accessible Services Program, 949 Presidio, San Francisco, CA 94115, call ☎ 415-673-6864 or 415-923-6366 (TDD), or visit **sfmuni.com/rider.**

The Paratransit Taxi Service provides discount taxi service to qualified disabled persons unable to use fixed Muni lines; to get a certificate, call the San Francisco Paratransit Broker at ☎ 415-351-7000.

Golden Gate Transit, which operates buses between the city and Marin County, publishes a handbook on accessible equipment and procedures; to get a copy of *Welcome Aboard,* call ☎ 415-923-2000 or 415-257-4554 (TDD).

TIME ZONE

SAN FRANCISCO IS IN THE PACIFIC TIME ZONE, which puts it three hours behind New York, two hours behind Chicago, one hour behind the Rocky Mountains, and eight hours behind Greenwich Mean Time.

PHONES

THE SAN FRANCISCO AREA IS SERVED BY THREE AREA CODES: **415** inside the city and Marin County, **510** in Alameda and Contra Costa counties in the East Bay (including Oakland and Berkeley), and **650** to the south in San Mateo County and around San Francisco International Airport. Calls from pay phones range from 50 cents (depending on which carrier owns the pay phone); if you talk for more than three minutes, additional payments may be requested. To call outside the 415 area code, dial 1 plus the appropriate area code and the seven-digit number. Because of the universal use of cell phones, working public phones are not as easy to find as they were once. Buying a $30 cell phone and new SIM card for your phone will probably be easier!

LIQUOR, TAXES, AND SMOKING

LIQUOR AND GROCERY STORES and some drugstores sell packaged alcohol from 6 a.m. to 2 a.m. daily. Most restaurants, bars, and nightclubs are licensed to serve a full line of alcoholic beverages during these hours, although some have permits to sell beer and wine only. The legal drinking age is 21.

A 9.5 percent sales tax is added to purchases in San Francisco unless the purchase is of food not yet prepared. If your purchases are shipped to a destination outside of California, they're exempt from the sales tax. A 9.5 percent tax is added to restaurant bills, and most hotels tack on a 14 percent room tax to the bill.

Before you light up, think twice. San Francisco has stiff antismoking laws, making it illegal to light up in offices, public buildings, banks, lobbies, stores, sports arenas, stadiums, public transportation, and theaters. This extends into bars and restaurants. The no-smoking-in-bars law gets cheers and jeers. Nonsmokers, you won't come home smelling like the Marlboro man, but you may find yourself solo at the bar while your compadres escape to the front for a drag every 15 minutes.

HOW *to* AVOID CRIME *and* KEEP SAFE *in* PUBLIC PLACES

CRIME IN SAN FRANCISCO

SAN FRANCISCO, LIKE ANY LARGE CITY, has its share of violent crime, drug abuse, and poverty. But the good news for visitors is that by and large the city is safe. San Francisco ranks low among U.S. cities for serious crime.

Downtown San Francisco, where tourists and business visitors spend most of their time, is unusually safe for a large city. "One good thing is that we've got a very lively downtown with lots of different things going on at all hours of the day. It's never completely dead," notes Dewayne Tully, a police-service aide with the San Francisco Police Department. "Even the Financial District, an area usually dead at night in most cities, has lots of clubs and restaurants." Because of crowds and 24-hour foot, horse, motorcycle, and car patrols by San Francisco's finest, few visitors to San Francisco are victims of street crime.

EXERCISING CAUTION: SOME HOT SPOTS

CERTAIN NEIGHBORHOODS REQUIRE DIFFERENT behaviors. The Tenderloin area on the downtown side of the Civic Center is a rather seedy part of town if not exactly dangerous. Interesting culturally, this area houses most of the city's diminishing minority populations and has been written about fully by author William Vollmann in *Whores for Gloria*. Along with Bayview to the southeast, it has resisted the gentrification that has swept most of the city's neighborhoods. But after dark the Tenderloin gets sketchier. There are usually hookers and dealers hanging around. If you come from other big cities, like New York, Miami, or Chicago, it will be nothing you aren't used to. Just take a few precautions. Girls should brace themselves for come-ons. Put money in your bras, and leave sparkling carats in the jewelry boxes at home. Checking over your shoulder constantly will only bring attention to your wary wanderings. Be cautious but look confident and secure, and you should be fine. South of downtown, Market Street also gets seedy and

unofficial **TIP**
Men can carry two wallets. Carry an inexpensive wallet in your hip pocket with about $20 in cash and some expired credit cards. This is the one you hand over if you're accosted. Your real credit cards and the bulk of whatever cash you have should be in a money clip or a second wallet hidden elsewhere on your person. Women can carry a fake wallet in their purse and keep the real one in a pocket or money belt.

is a haven for vagrants from about Fifth Street west to Gough Street. If you head out to any of these areas at night, simply take a taxi to your destination. If you have to walk a few blocks, you will most likely be fine. Some of San Francisco's hottest neighborhoods for nightlife, including Mission, SoMa, and Haight-Ashbury, also require some extra caution at night.

If you are the victim of a crime or witness one, you can get immediate police, fire, or medical assistance by dialing 911 from any pay phone without inserting money. For nonemergency help (for instance, to report a car break-in), dial the San Francisco Police Department at ☎ 415-553-0123. For more information on personal safety in San Francisco, call San Francisco SAFE, Inc. (SAFE stands for Safety Awareness for Everyone) at ☎ 415-673-SAFE; **sfsafe.org.**

THE DOS AND DON'TS

1. Have a plan: Random violence and street crime are facts of life in any large city. Be cautious and alert, and plan ahead. When you're out and about, know your route and have your agenda somewhat outlined; that way you appear to know what you are doing and where you are going.
2. Confirm your route or transportation with your hotel.
3. Leave all valuables in a safe deposit box in your hotel or at home.
4. Leave identification on your children indicating a phone number or hotel where you are staying in case they become lost or separated from you.
5. Write down all traveler's check numbers and leave them at home or at the hotel.
6. Girls, the bra is still a viable option for money! Guys, a money belt below the pants is a convenient way to carry wallet and money.
7. At night—women, keep your purses tucked under your arm; if you're wearing a coat, put it on over your shoulder-bag strap. If you're wearing rings, turn the setting palm-in.
8. Be discreet: Don't wave money around.

IF YOU'RE APPROACHED OR ACCOSTED

IN PUBLIC TRANSPORT Transportation in the city is quite organized and generally safe. It becomes questionable late at night when riders are few. If you find yourself riding the bus or train at night, it is best to take a seat close to the conductor or bus driver. These people have a phone and can summon help in the event of trouble.

IN CABS At night, it's best to go to one of the hotel stands or phone for a cab. If you suspect foul play on the cab driver's part, check the driver's certificate, which by law must be posted on the dashboard. Address the cabbie by his last name or mention the number of his cab. This alerts the driver to the fact that you are going to remember him and/or his cab. Not only will this contribute to your safety, it will keep your cabbie from trying to run up the fare. Generally, though, the cabs in the city are safe and the drivers can be quite interesting to talk with!

If you need to catch a cab at the train stations, bus terminals, or airports, always use the taxi queue. Taxis in the official queue are properly licensed and regulated. Never accept an offer for a cab or limo made by a stranger in the terminal or baggage claim. At best, you may be significantly overcharged for the ride. At worst, you may be abducted.

SELF-DEFENSE

IN A SITUATION WHERE IT IS IMPOSSIBLE to run, you'll need to be prepared to defend yourself. Most police insist that a gun or knife is not much use to the average person. More often than not, they say, the weapon will be turned against the victim. The best self-defense device for the average person is Mace or pepper spray. Not only is it legal in most states, but it's also nonlethal and easy to use, though truthfully you probably won't need it.

CARJACKINGS AND HIGHWAY ROBBERY

"KEEP ALERT WHEN YOU'RE DRIVING IN TRAFFIC," one police official warns. "Keep your doors locked, with the windows rolled up and the air-conditioning or heat on. In traffic, leave enough space in front of you so that you can make a U-turn and aren't blocked in. That way, if someone approaches your car and starts beating on your windshield, you can drive off." Store your purse or briefcase under your knees when you are driving, not on the seat beside you.

Also be aware of other drivers bumping you from the rear or driving alongside you and gesturing that something is wrong with your car. In either case, do not stop or get out of your car. Continue until you reach a very public and well-lit place where you can check things out and, if necessary, get help.

RIPOFFS AND SCAMS

A LIVELY STREET SCENE IS AN INCUBATOR for ripoffs and scams. Although pickpockets, scam artists, and tricksters work throughout San Francisco, they are particularly thick in Union Square, along the Embarcadero and Fisherman's Wharf, and at BART stations. While some scams are relatively harmless, others can be both costly and dangerous.

Pickpockets work in teams, sometimes using children. One person creates a diversion, such as dropping coins, spilling ice cream on you, or trying to sell you something, and a second person deftly picks your pocket. In most cases your stolen wallet is almost instantaneously passed to a third team member walking by. Even if you realize immediately that your wallet has been lifted, the pickpocket will have unburdened the evidence.

Because pickpockets come in all sizes and shapes, be especially wary of any encounter with a stranger. Anyone from a man in a nice suit asking directions or a six-year-old wobbling toward you on in-line skates could be creating a diversion for a pickpocket. The primary tip-off to a con or scam is someone approaching you. If you ask help of somebody in a store or restaurant, you are doing the approaching and the chances of being the victim of a scam are quite small. When a stranger approaches you, however, regardless of the reason, beware.

Most travelers carry a lot more cash, credit cards, and other stuff in their wallet than they need. If you plan to walk in San Francisco or anywhere else, transfer exactly what you think you will need to a very small, low-profile wallet or pouch. When the *Unofficial Guide* authors are on the street, they carry one American Express card, one VISA card, and a minimum amount of cash. Think about it. You do not need your gas credit cards if you're walking, and you don't need all those hometown department store credit cards if you're away from home.

Don't carry your wallet and valuables in a fanny pack. Thieves and pickpockets can easily snip the belt and disappear into the crowd with the pack before you realize what's happened. As far as pockets are concerned, front pockets are safer than back pockets or coat pockets, though pickpockets (with a little extra effort) can get at front pockets, too. The safest place to carry valuables is under your arm in a holster-style shoulder pouch. Lightweight, comfortable, and especially accessible when worn under a coat or vest, shoulder pouches are available from catalogs and most good travel stores. Incidentally, avoid pouches that are worn on your chest and suspended by a cord around your neck. Like the fanny pack, they can be easily cut off or removed by pickpockets.

THE HOMELESS

IF YOU'RE NOT FROM A BIG CITY or haven't visited one in a while, you're in for a shock when you come to San Francisco, where there is a large homeless population. This is a tolerant city with a big heart, and many agencies help care for this multifaceted and intractable issue that has broken the stride of successive over-optimistic mayors.

Most homeless would love not to be homeless and crave recognition, work, and kindness. Their loneliness is heartbreaking, as is their great love for pets. The homeless are more evident in some areas than others, but you're likely to bump into them just about anywhere. Take a drive down Van Ness Avenue and you will see one perched at almost every street corner with the most amusing signs. "No lies. It's for beer," reads one. They definitely are most creative in their approach.

Most are harmless and are simply looking for a little help here and there. Don't be afraid of them, and if you feel the urge to give, keep a little pocket change handy. If you are approached for money and don't want to or can't give anything, the best method is to say, "Sorry, I don't have anything." A simple acknowledgment goes a long way and they most likely will part your company with a "Have a nice day," or "God bless you." There is a notion, perhaps valid in some instances, that money given to a homeless person generally goes toward the purchase of alcohol or drugs. If this bothers you, carry granola bars for distribution or buy some inexpensive gift coupons that can be redeemed at a McDonald's or other fast-food restaurant for coffee or a sandwich.

Those moved to get more involved in the nationwide problem of homelessness can send inquiries—or a check—to the National Coalition for the Homeless, 1612 K Street, NW, Suite 1004, Washington, DC 20006; **nationalhomeless.org.**

PART FIVE

GETTING AROUND

◼ DRIVING *your* CAR

YOU'LL HAVE A LOVE/HATE RELATIONSHIP with driving in San Francisco. In one sense, the city's best sites and scenery are most easily explored in a car (mix one convertible and a sunny day for an unforgettable experience). From Route 1 along the Pacific Coast, across the Golden Gate Bridge to the Headlands or Mount Tamalpais, or through rolling vineyards of Napa or Sonoma, the Bay Area offers the best of scenic drives. And the hills . . . Filbert between Hyde and Leavenworth, Hill Street at 22nd, or Divisadero from Broadway to the Marina . . . white-knuckled and gasping, you'll plunge over the edge maniacally laughing, yodeling, screaming . . . whatever inspires you! Stick-shift novices need not apply; stick to automatic. The city is compact enough to get in a good bit of sights on your own time, too.

Here's where the tricky part comes in. Finding parking—legal parking that is (many innovative parking-blazers have initiated rather creative solutions to the crunch)—is frustrating. And to add insult to injury, traffic is a nightmare. There are even Web sites devoted to the highway horror (for example **sfbaytraffic.info**), or you can call ☎ 511 for up-to-date info on bridges and freeways. Downtown, near the financial center, is usually crowded throughout the day, but during peak rush hours of about 8 a.m. to 10 a.m. and 4:30 p.m. to 6:30 p.m., you'll feel about as slow-moving and cramped as the Tin Man without a lube job. Most of the traffic frustration comes when crossing either of the two main bridges. The same goes for North Beach, Chinatown, and Telegraph Hill, areas infamous for traffic congestion and scarce parking.

unofficial TIP
Keep your car in your hotel's garage, and use it only for excursions beyond the city or in the evenings after rush hour.

RENTAL CARS

ALL THE MAJOR CAR-RENTAL AGENCIES operate in the city and have desks at the airports. Take your pick from the national agencies of Alamo, Avis, Budget, Dollar, Hertz, National, and Thrifty. There are also some cheaper homegrown places to rent a car, such as City Rent-A-Car (☎ 415-861-1312, **cityrentacar.com**), Fox Rent-A-Car (☎ 800-225-4369, **foxrentacar. com**), or Specialty Car Rental (☎ 800-400-8412, **specialtyrentals.com**), for your chance at that convertible or dream BMW 323i.

unofficial **TIP**
Before heading out of the city by car, call California Road Conditions for information. They can inform you of any mudslides, construction, or hazardous weather. Call ☎ 800-427-ROAD (7623) if calling from within California or ☎ 916-445-ROAD (7623) if calling from outside California. Or tune in to 88.5 FM for its regular traffic reports.

All car-rental agencies usually require a minimum age of 25, and fares range depending on class of car, length of rental, where and when you pick up and drop off, and mileage plans. Usually you can find good deals online (**expedia.com** or **travelocity.com**). If you are an uninsured driver, you may want to buy an insurance plan for the duration of your rental. The city is notorious for fender benders and nicks and scrapes on vehicles, so protect yourself—purchase the insurance. Keep in mind that some credit cards offer protection as well. Inquire with the credit card company, or if you do have car insurance, call to verify your plan.

TIME OF DAY

unofficial **TIP**
Weekday rush hours are from 6 a.m. to 10 a.m. and from 3 p.m. to 7 p.m.

IN BETWEEN SAN FRANCISCO'S WEEKDAY rush hours, traffic is congested but usually flows—at least beyond downtown and Fisherman's Wharf.

Weekends, on the other hand, can be just as bad as weekday rush hours—and often worse. While traffic on Saturday and Sunday mornings is usually light, it picks up around noon and doesn't let up until well into the evening. Remember, about 7 million people live in the Bay Area, and on weekends many of them jump in their cars and head to San Francisco or to surrounding playgrounds across either bridge.

A PRAYER BEFORE PARKING

PARKING IS ONE OF THE MAIN REASONS *not* to explore San Francisco by car. In some areas you will drive around blocks for more than an hour before finding a vacant spot. Often, the meter is timed to allow only a half hour of parking (not a lot of time to go sightseeing or attend a business meeting), or if it's a nonmetered street, you have only two hours without a color-coded neighborhood permit. Rules, rules, rules. Traffic cops and meter maids on their mini-mobiles uphold those rules diligently, and the meters, unless posted otherwise, are in effect Monday through Saturday, usually from 8 a.m. to 6 p.m. (Meter rates: downtown, $3.50 for one hour; Fisherman's Wharf, $3 for one hour; rest of the city, $2 for one hour.)

Colored curbs in San Francisco indicate reserved parking zones. Red means no stopping or parking; yellow indicates a half-hour loading limit for vehicles with commercial plates; yellow and black means a half-hour loading limit for trucks with commercial plates; green, yellow, and black indicates a taxi zone; and blue is for vehicles marked with a California-issued disabled placard or plate. Green is a ten-minute parking zone for all vehicles, and white is a five-minute limit for all vehicles. A couple of feet either side of a fire hydrant is strictly forbidden too.

San Francisco cops don't take parking regulations lightly, and any improperly used spot can become a tow-away zone. The number one source of citations in the city is failing to recognize street cleaning, which requires one side of the street to be vacated on particular days, usually during morning hours. Be aware of street-cleaning signs and stay out of parking lanes opened up for rush-hour traffic. Many residential neighborhoods have permit parking, and a parking ticket can cost you more than $50, plus $100 for towing and additional charges for storage. Parking in a bus zone or wheelchair-access space can set you back $250, while parking in a space marked handicapped or blocking access to a wheelchair ramp costs $275. If you get towed, go to the nearest district police department for a release and then pick up your car at the towing company, or call Auto Return at the Hall of Justice (☎ 415-621-8605), and give them your license plate number to see if it's at their compound around the corner on 7th Street at Folsom.

With meters, color-coded permits and curbs, and the task of parallel parking—and, let's face it, some of you haven't done it since driver's ed—you may wonder how to survive your trip without parking citations taking up half your scrapbook. You can opt for one of many city parking garages. They cost anywhere from $20 to $30 a day. Or take advantage of the city's convenient and reliable public transportation, or our favorite, foot it. Not for naught do we call this the walking city.

When you're parking on San Francisco's steep hills, there is only one way to rest easy: Curb your wheels. Turn the front tires away from the curb when your car is facing uphill, so that if the brake fails, the car rolls back into the curb. If facing downhill, turn your wheels toward the curb so that the car can roll forward into the curb, effectively using it as a block. Because even the best brakes can fail, curbing your wheels is the law in San Francisco (and you'll see plenty of street signs to remind you).

unofficial **TIP**
Check with your hotel to see if you can get a reduced rate at a nearby garage.

THE "YOU DIDN'T KNOW TO ASK" Q & A:

- *Should I park in the middle turning lane when I see others doing it?* What you'll see sometimes in and around the Mission and SoMa, especially on busy weekend evenings, is that middle turning lanes become a row of parked cars. Do *not* follow the leader here—the city will dispatch tow trucks faster than you can say, "Hold the anchovies."

- *What time in the morning should I move my car if it's parked in a two-hour permit zone?* Usually the permit zones are enforced from 8 a.m. to 6 p.m. If you have left your car overnight, you have until 10 a.m. (two hours past 8 a.m.).

- *How do the traffic cops know that my car has exceeded the meter or permit limit?* Remember kindergarten? Chalk! They chalk tires and check back to see if the car has or hasn't moved. One way around this is to check for chalk marks on your tires. If there are none, you might be good for another two hours. Or simply roll your car back and forth to get rid of it.

- *Which areas are easiest for parking?* The Marina is fairly easy but *do not* even come an inch over someone's driveway. They are sticklers about that sort of thing. Bernal Heights, Potrero Hill, and parts of Noe Valley are all pretty stress-free. What constitutes stress-free, you might ask? Less than a 15-minute search.

- *Where should I worry about theft or vandalism?* The Mission, Chinatown, Financial, and Tenderloin districts are hot spots for broken windows, car break-ins, and keying. Never leave laptops or smartphones where they are visible from the window. These days, they are the only things worth stealing, so store them in the trunk.

- *Why do I sometimes see cars parked on the sidewalks outside a house or apartment building?* There is something fun about pulling up the curb onto the sidewalk and parking your vehicle! The thrill of trespassing is sweet indeed. There is a level of understanding between parking officials and residents. Usually it is tolerated during late hours (after midnight). But be ready for an early morning wake-up call to move it before anybody complains, or worse, you get busted!

PUBLIC TRANSPORTATION

SAN FRANCISCO MUNICIPAL RAILWAY (**sfmta.com**), commonly called Muni, is a citywide transportation system that consists of all cable cars, streetcars (called Muni Metro), conventional buses, and electric buses. All fares are $2 for adults and 75 cents for seniors, disabled passengers (with a valid Regional Transit Connection Discount Card), and children ages 5 to 17; children age 4 and under ride free. Cable-car fare is $5 per person (kids age 4 and under ride free). One-dollar bills are accepted on most buses, but the drivers don't give change. If you need a transfer, ask for one when you board; it's free and valid for two hours and a maximum of two rides in any direction.

Many San Franciscans feel a fierce devotion to the system; some affectionately call it "Joe Muni." No wonder; it's a European-style transportation system that gets people around the city cheaply and efficiently. You're never more than a couple of blocks from a bus stop or train station. Not that it's without some drawbacks—buses can be jam-packed, especially at rush hour and on weekends, and occasionally you may have to wait for a bus while fully loaded buses pass you by. Yet despite its problems, riding Muni is interesting. You can learn more about the city from the friendly bus drivers and helpful passengers than from any guidebook.

unofficial **TIP**
Muni passports allow unlimited use of the entire public transportation system and provide discounts at many city attractions and tours.

PASSPORT TO SAVINGS

MUNI PASSPORTS ALLOW UNLIMITED USE of all buses, cable cars, and Muni Metro streetcars in San Francisco. It's a great money-saving deal that makes it even easier and more convenient to use San Francisco's public transportation. In addition, Muni passports provide discounts at dozens of city attractions, including museums, theaters, and bay tours.

Muni passports come in three versions: one-day ($13), three-day ($20), and seven-day ($26). Pocket-sized and easy to use, the passports are available at the airport, Montgomery Station, SFMTA Customer Service (11 South Van Ness Avenue, ☎ 415-701-3000, where you can also swap defective passes), and kiosks at Powell and Market streets, Hyde and Beach streets, and Bay and Taylor streets. Be sure to pick up a copy of the *Official San Francisco Street and Transit Map* for $3. To use a passport, scratch off the dates of the day (or days) you're using the pass, and simply show it to the driver, who will wave you aboard.

unofficial **TIP**
Two kinds of passes save fuss and money. The monthly $70 Fast Pass is available at citywide markets and outlets, as well as the kiosk at the Embarcadero station, is valid for 30 days, and is the only pass for BART (within San Francisco only), buses, streetcars, and even cable cars. For East Bay jaunts, you'll need an extra top-up. The Muni passport supplies every bus, street, or cable car but not BART.

BUSES

YOU'LL NEVER SEE A CLEANER, QUIETER, more pollutant-free (thanks to some of the electric buses), or friendlier bus service in any other city, or have a more entertaining ride. Some routes are more flamboyant than others: the 14 to Persia or "Orient Express" number 30. Some glass shelters hold maps with digital messages announcing approaching bus times. Bus service in San Francisco reaches into all parts of the city and beyond. Along Market Street, some buses stop at the curb while others stop at islands in the street.

When you board, stuff two dollar bills into the driver's meter, and ask for a transfer right away if you need it, or flash your Muni passport. The next bus driver rips off a transfer ticket, and it is usually good for two hours, but you can keep on using it with luck! It's one of those little treasures of public transportation. If you're not sure about where to get off, ask the driver to let you know when you're near your destination. Drivers are usually considerate and glad to help. The buses get very crowded at times. Fellow passengers are invariably cordial and helpful, and you'll be pleased when "back door please" is yelled out in your favor, or "wait" as the driver pulls away too soon. Rush hour is obviously busy, but also consider the after-school rush between 2 p.m. and 3 p.m. Kids talking Britney, boys, and basketball snap their gum and fling their backpacks as they load onto the buses on their way home.

Most bus lines operate from 6 a.m. to midnight, after which there is an infrequent night owl service; it's sometimes eventful if not really dangerous, but if you find drunks and displays of public eccentricity alarming, take a cab at those late hours. Popular tourist bus routes include numbers 5 and 71, which go to Golden Gate Park; numbers 41 and 45, which go up and down ritzy Union Street; and number 30 or the so-called "Orient Express," which runs past Union Square, Chinatown, Ghirardelli Square, North Beach, and the Marina. If you need help figuring out which bus or buses to take to reach a specific destination, call Muni at ☎ 415-673-MUNI (6864), or visit **sfmuni. com**. The large maps have all routes marked, making it easy to plan your path and see where different routes intersect.

MUNI METRO STREETCARS

MUNI STREETCARS OPERATE UNDERGROUND downtown and on the streets in the outer neighborhoods. At four underground stations along Market Street downtown, Muni shares quarters with BART, the Bay Area's commuter train system. Orange, yellow, and white illuminated signs mark the station entrances; when you get inside the terminal, look for the separate Muni entrance.

Pay or show your Muni passport and go down to the platform. To go west, choose the outbound side of the platform; to go east, choose the downtown side. Electronic signs with the name of the next train begin to flash as it approaches. The doors open automatically; stand aside to let arriving passengers depart before you step aboard. To open the doors and exit at your stop, push on the low bar next to the door.

unofficial **TIP**
Call 511 or check **511**.org whenever you have a city transport question.

Five of Muni Metro's seven streetcar lines are designated J, K, L, M, and N, and these share tracks downtown beneath Market Street but diverge below the Civic Center into the outer neighborhoods. The J line goes to

Mission Dolores; the K, L, and M lines go to Castro Street; and the N line parallels Golden Gate Park. The newest T line travels past Third Street to the AT&T ballpark and Embarcadero from the southeastern suburbs. The sleek trains run about every 15 minutes and more frequently during rush hours. Service is offered daily from 5 a.m. to 12:30 a.m., Saturday from 6 a.m. to 12:30 a.m., and Sunday from 8 a.m. to 12:20 a.m.

An addition to the streetcar system (and its eighth route) is the F-Market line running on beautiful vintage cars from turn-of-the-century Milan and green and cream–colored, 1930s-era streetcars that run along Market Street from downtown to the Castro District and back. They include Tennessee William's Streetcar Named Desire from New Orleans, now suitably adapted for disabled use. These historic cars are charming, and they're a hassle-free alternative to crowded buses and underground terminals.

BART

BART (**bart.gov**), an ACRONYM FOR BAY AREA RAPID TRANSIT, is a 103-mile system of high-speed trains that connects San Francisco with the East Bay cities of Berkeley, Oakland, Richmond, Concord, Fremont, and Warm Springs (scheduled for completion in 2013), and to the south, with San Francisco International Airport and Millbrae.

Four stations are located underground along Market Street (these also provide access to Muni Metro streetcars). Fares vary depending on distance; tickets are dispensed from self-service machines in the station lobbies. The trains run every 10 to 20 minutes on weekdays from 4 a.m. to midnight, on Saturday from 6 a.m. to midnight, and on Sunday from 8 a.m. to midnight.

BART is mostly used by commuters from the East Bay and is not a very useful means of traveling in the city for visitors. The stop in Berkeley, however, is close enough to the campus and other sites of interest. One other exception is the BART extension to San Francisco International Airport.

CABLE CARS

AFTER THE RED CROWN OF THE GOLDEN GATE BRIDGE atop fluffy clouds, cable cars are probably San Francisco's most famous symbol. And they are the nation's only mobile historical monuments. Ride one just to say you've personally experienced its ringing bells on Powell Street. Cynical natives will snub their noses at such a thing—it's as if they are being asked to eat a bowl full of Rice-A-Roni. But get them alone and they'll swear by it, especially the

unofficial **TIP**
Funding has been provided for work on a Central Subway arm of the T-line to Chinatown. And the final BART stops to San Jose to circumnavigate the bay aren't far behind. We voted for a two-hour super-train to downtown Los Angeles too—so let's see how long it takes!

California Street line, the one that tourists tend to miss. It's a fun thing to bring the kids to do—and anybody can appreciate the Willy Wonka–esque Cable Car Museum on Mason Street (☎ 415-474-1887; **cablecarmuseum.org**); there you can stand at an observation platform and watch the cable wind around the giant wheels. The cars, pulled by cables buried underneath the streets, operate on three lines from 6:30 a.m. to 12:30 a.m. daily at about 15-minute intervals.

Andrew Hallidie's first San Francisco cable car made its maiden voyage in 1873 after the Scotsman reportedly saw a horse being dragged down Jackson Street under its heavy load. This story may just be local color, for the Scots engineer had a cable-gripping patent to peddle. By 1906, just before the earthquake, the system hit its peak, with 600 cars on a 110-mile route. But the system was heavily damaged by the quake and fire, and many lines weren't rebuilt.

unofficial **TIP**
Beat the interminable wait at the Powell Street Turnaround by following tracks uphill to the Union Square corner nearest Saks Fifth Avenue and jump on there.

Electric trolleys took over some routes, and the number of cable cars dwindled over the years. In the 1950s and '60s there was talk of scrapping the system entirely, but once it was declared a historical monument it had to be saved. In 1984, the city spent more than $60 million on a two-year renovation of the system, including new track and cable vaults, renovation of the Cable Car Barn, and restoration of the cars, which were given a new coat of shiny maroon, blue, and gold paint, as well as new brakes, seats, and wheels. Today there are 40 cable cars in all, with 27 in use at peak times. An average of 8 million people travel on the 9 miles of tracks each year—more than 21,500 people a day.

Three Lines

There are three cable-car lines in San Francisco. The most popular route for tourists is the Powell-Hyde line, which starts at the Powell and Market streets turntable south of Union Square. The line skirts Union Square, climbs Nob Hill (with good views of Chinatown), goes past the Cable Car Barn, crosses Lombard Street, and descends to Hyde Street to the turntable near Aquatic Park and Fisherman's Wharf. The Powell-Mason line starts at the same place, but after the Cable Car Barn, it passes by North Beach and ends at Bay Street. For the best views on either line, try to face east.

The California line runs from California and Market streets to Van Ness Avenue, passing through the Financial District and Chinatown; it's used more by commuters than tourists (a tourist attraction in itself). At Nob Hill the Powell lines cross over the California line, so passengers can transfer between lines (but they have to pay again). At the end of all lines, all passengers must get off.

For each of the three lines, the return journey follows the outward route, so riders can catch different views from the other side of the car. If you'd rather sit than stand, try boarding at the end of the line. During peak tourist seasons and on weekends, lines are long to board the cars at the turntables where the cars get turned around, and boarding at cable-car stops along the routes can be impossible as the cars rumble by, full of smiling, camera-toting tourists.

Safety Tips

Fun as the cable cars are to ride, it's important to keep safety in mind when you're on one. If it's not crowded, you can choose to sit or stand inside, sit outside on a bench, or stand at the end of the car. Adventurous types and some cable-car purists prefer hanging on to a pole while standing on a side running board. But wherever you decide to ride, hang on tight.

Try not to get in the way of the gripman, who operates the grip lever that holds and releases the cable pulling the car; he needs a lot of room. A yellow stripe on the floor marks an off-limits area, and passengers should stay out of it. Be extra cautious while the car is moving. Passing other cable cars is exciting because they pass so close, but be careful not to lean out too far. And be careful getting on and off. Often cable cars stop in the middle of busy intersections; you don't want to step in front of a moving car or truck.

FERRIES

IN THE DAYS BEFORE THE GOLDEN GATE AND BAY BRIDGES were built, Bay Area commuters relied on hundreds of ferries to transport them to and from the northern counties and the East Bay. Although no longer a necessity, ferries continue to operate in smaller numbers, transporting suburban commuters who prefer a tension-free boat ride across the bay to the headache of rush-hour traffic. The ferries are also favorite ways for local residents and visitors to enjoy San Francisco's scenery. On weekends, many suburban families leave their cars at home and take the ferries for fun and relaxation.

One person's commute can be another's excursion. Although the ferries don't offer the narrated audio tours of the commercial sight-seeing cruises offered at Fisherman's Wharf, they're less expensive. Food and full bar service is offered on board, but the modern ferries only transport foot traffic and bicycles, not cars.

The Ferry Building at the foot of Market Street is the terminus for ferries to Sausalito and Larkspur. For prices and schedules, call Golden Gate Transit at ☎ 415-923-2000, or visit **goldengateferry. org/schedules.** Private ferry service to Sausalito, Tiburon, and Angel Island operates from Pier 41 at Fisherman's Wharf. For more information, call the Blue & Gold Fleet at ☎ 415-705-8200, or visit

blueandgoldfleet.com, or contact Angel Island–Tiburon Ferry at ☎ 415-435-2131 or **angelislandferry.com.**

TAXIS

UNLIKE NEW YORK AND CHICAGO, cabs in San Francisco tend to be expensive and scarce. However, if you're in the center of town, no ride will be longer than about three miles. You can usually hail a moving taxi downtown, but in general it's better to call and make arrangements for pickup, if you're not actually on the street at the time. The dispatch will call your number to alert you of the taxi's arrival. Another option is to head toward a cabstand at a major hotel, but the wait can be long during rush hour and in bad weather.

San Francisco taxis have rooftop signs that are illuminated when the cab is empty. Rates are $3.10 for the first 0.2 miles and increase 45 cents each additional fifth of a mile (this is subject to change, especially due to the fluctuating price of oil). Major cab companies include Veteran's Cab, ☎ 415-552-1300; Yellow Cab, ☎ 415-626-2345; DeSoto Cab, ☎ 415-970-1300; and Luxor Cab, ☎ 415-282-4141.

WALKING

FORGET THE GYM. You have a leg press on almost every street in San Francisco. Pump your quads as you tread the hills—some so steep that stairs have been cut to make the trek easier, and your spirit will be fed dessert as the brightly colored Victorians and backdrop of blue ocean surprise at every corner. It's a walker's nirvana. What separates this city from others is its compact size and well-laid streets. Major tourist areas are within a half hour or less of one another. Another nice feature to footing the city is the surprising number of green spaces still firmly rooted within the city. Duck under a tree or sit in one of the many parks for a picnic as you glare at the glass-covered skyscrapers of downtown.

unofficial **TIP**
Be aware that the traffic lights don't have delayed timing. As soon as one side turns red, the other instantly turns green.

You don't have to ask the Scarecrow for directions here—most street intersections are marked with green-and-white signs bearing the name of the cross street; this can get confusing along Market Street, where street names are different on each side of the thoroughfare. Street names are also frequently imprinted in the pavement at corners. Often, electronic walk signs indicate when it's safe (and legal) to cross the street.

A Walk for Any Mood

Even if walks have never been a highlight for you, you will find inspiration in San Francisco to lace up and put feet to the path. One of the most active and exhilarating walks is Golden Gate Promenade's three-and-a-half-mile path. Along its trail are joggers, and views of Alcatraz

To Cross or Not to Cross?

San Francisco ranks among the top in pedestrian fatality rates in the country, though in recent years this rate has been coming down. But be constantly aware that both jaywalking pedestrians with the pro-pedestrian city ordinance on their side and "California sliders," or red-light runners, are a bit of a plague here, especially on wide-open arteries such as Howard Street or 19th Avenue. Whether walking or driving, be sure you've got the green light, and look both ways to be sure no one is screaming down the road in your direction. Another thing to be aware of when crossing the street or aggressively pursuing a yellow light in a car: The traffic lights in San Francisco, unlike pedestrian-heavy cities like New York or D.C., don't have delayed timing. As soon as one side turns red, the other instantly turns green.

and those warm-blooded souls braving the frigid Pacific as they wind-surf or kite-surf. All along the way are pit stops—Aquatic Park, Fort Mason, Marina Green, and the newly renovated Crissy Field. For a more romantic stroll, the Presidio is one of the most valuable green spaces in the city. And the fact that there is a spot called Lover's Lane should be indicative enough. The whole trail takes only about 15 minutes. Another killer spot within the Presidio is Inspiration Point, which looks out toward the Palace of Fine Arts and the Golden Gate. A mandatory walk that would fit in nicely if you are already strolling The Golden Gate Promenade is to walk across the Golden Gate Bridge. You'll be humming Tony Bennett's classic in no time! If you are a foodie and love to walk, stop, eat, walk, stop, eat, then a stroll down Union Street or Chestnut in the Marina or almost any street in the Mission will satisfy your craving. Bernal Heights is one neighborhood being resurrected with community gardens and green spaces and an all-out funky vibe. A walk down Cortland Avenue, the main drag here, takes you to Good Prospect Community Garden, and further along on Eugenia Street, you climb hidden stairways past bizarre and brightly colored Victorians and bungalows to Bernal Community Gardens. The cherry on top of this walk is the short hike to the bald top of Bernal Hill, which offers views of Mount Diablo and the Golden Gate. It's really one of the best vantage points to watch the foggy fingers move in and choke the bridge and surrounding neighborhoods. There are great walks even for bargain shoppers. The secondhand stores on Upper Fillmore Street are chock-full of great deals on hot brand-name items; try the immaculately groomed Goodwill (☎ 415-354-8570; **sfgoodwill. org**) opposite Sundance Kabuki Cinema.

Top Ten Urban Hikes

- Enjoy a leisurely 1.5-mile coastal trail from the Sutro Baths to SeaCliff, and walk back around the Palace of the Legion of Honor in Lincoln Park.

- From Aquatic Park to Fort Point is a 2-mile waterfront stroll with an amble around the Civil War–era Fort Point and across the Golden Gate Bridge and back, with Vista Point, too.

- The Presidio is almost all walks, but check out the Log Cabin, the decommissioned Army barracks, the old Spanish buildings, and more.

- The 5-mile circumnavigation of Angel Island–sure, you could rent a bike, but these views require a slower pace, and there are places to swim, too.

- From Glen Canyon Park over Twin Peaks to Sutro Heights is an almost unbroken 5-mile hike to the Panhandle and Golden Gate Park, and you can forge ahead to Lands End too: **weekendsherpa.com** is a great site to check.

- Take a full moon or sunset hike to the top of Corona Heights via the Randall Museum grounds to see if the rumored magic hits you!

- Bernal Heights is well loved for its stairway walks, interesting views, and friendly dog walkers.

- John McLaren Park offers bird-watching and the Jerry Garcia Amphitheater, and is surprisingly underappreciated.

- San Bruno Mountain is also astonishingly unknown and wild . . .

- As is Mount Davidson, famous for the last scenes of the movie *Dirty Harry!*

- Last but not least, walk, don't run Bay to Breakers (**baytobreakers .com**). You notice far more than you would running, and it's full of oddball and entertaining sights.

PART SIX

SIGHTSEEING, TOURS, *and* ATTRACTIONS

TOURING SAN FRANCISCO

THE BEAUTY OF TOURING SAN FRANCISCO is that Grandma can feel right at home sitting on a bench near Dolores Park in the Mission while the college grad can sit on the grass in the same park and feel a compatible vibe. It's a friendly city for anybody who wants to experience its spectrum of offerings. The Marina District, devastated by the 1989 earthquake, is thriving with new and rebuilt Mediterranean-style houses in lollipop colors. The waterfront is reawakening, the Presidio is transforming into a national park, and major projects such as the Yerba Buena Gardens are changing the face of the city.

unofficial **TIP**
"San Francisco is 49 square miles surrounded by reality."
—Paul Kantner, Jefferson Airplane

Half the fun of discovering this town is wandering around and stumbling on great views, interesting shops, and a location used in a favorite movie. And if you do get lost, you can't go too far because the city is surrounded by water on three sides. Here are some hints for first-time visitors.

TAKING AN ORIENTATION TOUR

VISITORS TO SAN FRANCISCO CAN'T HELP but notice the regular procession of open-air tour buses—"motorized cable cars" is probably a more accurate term—that prowl Union Square, Fisherman's Wharf, North Beach, and major tourist spots. **Gray Line** features two-and-a-half-hour tours with a tour guide; passengers board at Union Square or Pier 39 in Fisherman's Wharf.

The guides also suggest good places to eat and drop tidbits of interesting and often funny San Francisco trivia. On the on/off tour, visitors can get off and reboard at Pier 39, the Palace of Fine Arts, Fort Point, the Golden Gate Bridge, the Presidio, and Union Square, so you can get off at any scheduled stop to tour, eat, shop, or explore. If it rains, tours may be canceled or an enclosed vehicle may be substituted.

The cost for the tour is $14 for adults; $8 for children ages 5 to 11; and $12 for seniors age 60 and over. Departures begin at 10 a.m. daily and continue about every 45 minutes until 4 p.m.; during the winter, the tours depart hourly. Passengers can pay an additional $19 and go on a bay cruise departing from Fisherman's Wharf. Tickets for the tours can be purchased at booths in Union Square or at Pier 39 in Fisherman's Wharf. For more information, call ☎ 888-428-6937, or visit **sanfranciscosightseeing.com.**

SPECIALIZED TOURS

GRAY LINE OFFERS SEVERAL GENERAL-INTEREST TOURS around the city and special tours to destinations beyond San Francisco. A four-hour deluxe city tour via motor coach takes visitors to the city's major attractions, including the Civic Center, Mission Dolores, Twin Peaks, Golden Gate Park, and Cliff House. Reservations are required for the tour, which departs daily at 9:15 a.m., 11:15 a.m., and 2:15 p.m. The price is $41 for adults and $39 for seniors age 60 and over.

Gray Line offers tours to Muir Woods and Sausalito daily; the three-and-a-half-hour tours leave at 9:15 a.m. and 11:15 a.m. The cost is $44 for adults, $20 for children ages 5 to 11, and $42 for seniors age 60 and over. Gray Line also offers day tours to Yosemite, the wine country, and Monterey, as well as airplane and helicopter tours. Coach tours from San Francisco include pick-up and drop-off at your hotel. For more information or reservations, call ☎ 888-428-6937 or ☎ 415-558-9400, or visit **sanfranciscosightseeing.com.**

Tower Tours leads a deluxe city tour to Chinatown, North Beach, Telegraph Hill and Coit Tower, the Marina District, the Presidio, Cliff House and Seal Rocks, and Golden Gate Park. Scheduled stops on the tour (which uses minibuses with large windows, not motor coaches) are Vista Point at the Golden Gate Bridge, Cliff House above Seal Rocks, the Japanese Tea Garden in Golden Gate Park (small admission fee not included), and Twin Peaks (weather permitting).

Three-and-a-half-hour tours depart daily at 9 a.m., 11 a.m., and 2 p.m.; $47 for adults, $26 for children ages 5 to 11. Tower Tours also offers day trips to Muir Woods and Sausalito, Yosemite, Alcatraz, and Monterey and Carmel.

All tours include pick-up and return to your hotel; meals aren't included. Call ☎ 888-657-4520 or visit **towertours.net**.

BAY CRUISES

VISITORS CAN ENJOY SPECTACULAR VIEWS of the city skyline, the Golden Gate and Bay bridges, and Alcatraz Island on narrated cruises around San Francisco Bay. **Red & White Fleet** offers a Golden Gate Bridge cruise that passes Fort Mason, the Presidio, and Fort Point before going under the famous bridge. The hour-long cruises depart from Pier 43 in Fisherman's Wharf every 45 minutes, 10 a.m.– 6 p.m. in the summer and 10 a.m.–4:45 p.m. in the winter. The price is $22 for adults, $18 for seniors and children ages 12 to 17, and $16 for children ages 5 to 11. For more information, call ☎ 415-673-2900 or visit **redandwhite.com.**

Blue & Gold Fleet offers one-hour cruises in San Francisco Bay departing from Pier 39 in Fisherman's Wharf every day except Christmas. The boats leave every half hour 10 a.m.–6:45 p.m. spring through fall, and every 45 minutes 10 a.m.–4 p.m. in the winter. The price is $24 for adults, $20 for seniors and children ages 12 to 17, and $16 for children ages 5 to 11. Blue & Gold also offers ferry service to Sausalito and Tiburon from Pier 41, a Muir Woods tour, and a Napa-Sonoma wine-country tour. For more information, call ☎ 415-773-1188; to make advance reservations, call ☎ 415-705-5555 or visit **blueandgoldfleet.com**.

The **Angel Island–Tiburon Ferry** operates daily in summer and on weekends in winter. Round-trip fares are $13.50 for adults and $11.50 for children ages 6 to12. A $1 fee is charged for bicycles. If you are a scuba diver, they can also arrange for you and yours to dive with the sharks off the Farallon Islands. For schedule information and directions, call ☎ 415-435-2131, or visit **angelislandferry.com**.

AIR TOURS

FOR 50 YEARS **San Francisco Seaplane Tours** has whisked visitors aloft from the waters of the San Francisco Bay on flights over the city and its famous landmarks. Thirty-minute sightseeing rides from Pier 39 in Fisherman's Wharf leave daily at 10:30 a.m., noon, 1:30 p.m., 3 p.m., and 4:30 p.m.; the price is $149 for adults and $119 for children (minimum of two passengers). Champagne sunset tours leave 30 minutes before sundown; the ride lasts 35 to 40 minutes and costs $195 per person. Reservations are recommended for all tours and required for the sunset tour; call ☎ 415-332-4843 or visit **seaplane.com**.

San Francisco Helicopter Tours and Charters offers jet helicopter flights daily from San Francisco International Airport, about a half hour south of downtown. Thirty-minute flights are $160 for adults and $120 for children. Hotel pick-up and return is included in the price; the maximum number of passengers is between four and six.

For more information and reservations (required), call ☎ 800-400-2404 or visit **sfhelicoptertours.com.**

WALKING TOURS

CITY GUIDES WALKING TOURS, presented by the San Francisco Friends of the Library, conducts around 40 different neighborhood history walks each month. The one- to two-hour tours are led by volunteers daily year-round, rain or shine. And here's the good part: The guided walks are free. An expanded schedule, offered in May and October, provides different walks, with more than 125 free tours available. Walking tours are offered of San Francisco's most famous (and, in some cases, infamous) districts, as well as hidden neighborhoods most tourists miss. A Tenderloin prostitution tour, anyone? The Wild West and Wyatt Earp in the Inner Richmond? Check out Peter Fields and his specialties: sinners and whores of yesteryear in Sin City.

unofficial **TIP**
San Francisco is best seen up close, and the best way to do that is on a walking tour.

No reservations are required; just meet at the place and time designated in the current tour schedule. Wear comfortable shoes (although tours are not strenuous unless so listed) and look for the City Guide, who should be wearing a badge. For a recorded schedule of walks, call ☎ 415-557-4266 or visit **sfcityguides.org.** You can pick up a schedule at the San Francisco Convention and Visitors Bureau, Hallidie Plaza at Powell and Market streets, or at any city library.

Victorian Home Walk takes visitors on tours of the city's famed Victorian houses, with an emphasis on exploring neighborhoods off the beaten tourist path. Tours depart daily at 11 a.m. from the lobby of the Westin St. Francis Hotel at 335 Powell Street; rates are $25 a person (no credit cards accepted). The walk lasts about two-and-a-half hours, and transportation is included. Cost: $20. For more information or to make reservations (required), call ☎ 415-252-9485 or visit **victorianwalk.com.**

Feel like a native on **Helen's Walk Tour,** a three-and-a-half-hour exploration of Union Square, Chinatown, and North Beach offered Monday through Thursday. The walk begins at 9 a.m. "under the clock" in the lobby of the Westin St. Francis Hotel on Union Square. The cost is $40 for three people per person or $100 total for just two; family and group rates are available. For more information and to make reservations (required), call ☎ 888-808-6505 or 510-524-4544 or visit **helenswalktour.com.**

unofficial **TIP**
"Leaving San Francisco is like saying goodbye to an old sweetheart. You want to linger as long as possible." *—Walter Cronkite*

Relive the 1960s on the two-hour **Haight-Ashbury Flower Power** walking tour. Learn about the Summer of Love and the Diggers and see shrines to the late Jerry Garcia (of the Grateful Dead). The tours depart at 9:30 a.m.

on Tuesdays and Saturdays at the corner of Stanyan and Waller streets in the Haight; the cost is $20 per person. Reservations are required; call ahead at ☎ 415-863-1621; **haight ashburytour.com**.

For free, in-depth walking tours of Golden Gate Park, call Friends of Recreation & Parks at ☎ 415-263-0991 or visit **frp.org**. A variety of guided walks are offered

unofficial **TIP**
"When you get tired of walking around in San Francisco, you can always lean against it."
—Anonymous

throughout the week, including tours of the Japanese Tea Garden and Stern Grove.

Cruisin' the Castro is an award-winning tour with an emphasis on the neighborhood's history; sights include Harvey Milk's camera shop and the AIDS-quilt museum. The walk—offered Monday and Tuesday and Thursday through Saturday—starts at 10 a.m. and lasts three hours; lunch is included. The cost is $35 per person. For reservations, call ☎ 415-550-8110 or visit **cruisinthecastro.com**.

All About Chinatown takes visitors on a behind-the-scenes walk of this colorful neighborhood, covering its history, culture, and traditions. Tours leave daily at 10 a.m. from Old St. Mary's Cathedral, 660 California Street at Grant Avenue. The three-hour walk finishes with a dim sum lunch (two hours without lunch). The cost is $45 a person with lunch, $30 without lunch; children ages 6 to 17, $35 with lunch, $20 without; under age 6 is free. For more information and reservations (required), call ☎ 415-982-8839 or visit **allabout chinatown.com**.

TOURING ON YOUR OWN: OUR FAVORITE ITINERARIES

IF YOUR TIME IS LIMITED and you want to experience the best of San Francisco in a day or two, here are some suggested itineraries. The schedules assume you're staying at a downtown hotel, have already eaten breakfast, and are ready to go around 9 a.m. If you've got two days, make reservations for a morning ferry ride to Alcatraz Island and for *Beach Blanket Babylon* (Wednesday through Sunday evenings at Club Fugazi in North Beach) before you hit town.

Day One

1. Walk to Union Square or Fisherman's Wharf and tour San Francisco's major sights on one of the open-air, motorized cable car services; Gray Line offers unlimited reboarding privileges for the day. You can also pay an additional $17 for a one-hour narrated cruise of San Francisco Bay.

2. At Fisherman's Wharf, skip touristy Pier 39 unless you want a quick pick-me-up at the storied Eagle Cafe (☎ 415-433-3689; **thetinfish. net**) or an appletini and crab sandwich at Crab House (☎ 415-434-2722; **crabhouse.com**), and walk west to the Hyde Street Pier, where you can explore real 19th-century ships; or walk another block or two to

the National Maritime Museum, which is free and chock-full of nautical goodies. Or, if it's a nice day, take a bay cruise.

3. Alternately for lunch, try the clam chowder served in a bowl of sour-dough bread at Boudin Bakery in Fisherman's Wharf; it's fast and cheap (about $6).

4. On the cable car tour, stop at the Golden Gate Bridge. Don't just gaze at the scenery from the overlook near the visitor center; walk onto the bridge for even better views. Take a jacket (it gets very windy).

5. Back at Union Square after your circuit on the cable car, walk up Grant Avenue to Chinatown; to get the real flavor of this exotic neighbor-hood, walk a block west to Stockton Street, which is less touristy.

6. Continue walking north through Chinatown to Columbus Avenue; now you're in North Beach. Settle in at a nice sidewalk cafe for a latte and primo people-watching; then browse at City Lights Bookstore, a North Beach landmark.

7. For a spectacular view of San Francisco, hike up Telegraph Hill to Coit Tower; if your legs and feet aren't up for the steep walk, take the No. 39 bus (board near Washington Square). After savoring the view (best around sunset), walk down the Greenwich Steps, a brick staircase lined with ivy and roses that descends steeply to Montgomery Street. Near the base of the steps is a glass-brick, Art Deco apartment house used in the Humphrey Bogart film *Dark Passage.*

8. Have dinner at Enrico's (504 Broadway; ☎ 415-982-6223; **enricossf. com**), an Italian-inspired California restaurant. This jazz supper club with live music and dancing is popular with locals as well as tourists.

Day Two

1. Get to Fisherman's Wharf for a morning ferry ride to Alcatraz. Allow at least two hours to explore the prison ruins and island.

2. Have lunch at Greens (in Building A at Fort Mason), with a full view of the Golden Gate Bridge and the Marin Headlands. It's an outstanding vegetarian restaurant (not just sprouts and tofu) in a former enclosed pier with polished wood floors and a serene atmosphere. Call ahead for reservations: ☎ 415-771-6222.

3. Take a stroll along the Marina Green where kite fliers, happy joggers, and prancing dogs converge. You can continue toward Crissy Field (closer to the Golden Gate Bridge) or turn on Broderick or Divisadero, and then explore the Marina District and its beautiful waterside houses. If you've got time, stroll the parklike grounds of the Palace of Fine Arts. Right off of the Marina Green is a simple snack stand that serves hot chili, hot dogs, veggie sandwiches, ice cream, and other hunger-curbing snacks. It's convenient if you want to picnic near the Palace of Fine Arts.

4. Take the cable car from the Beach and Hyde streets turnaround (Powell-Mason line) or the turnaround near Taylor and Bay streets

(Powell-Hyde line); both head toward Union Square as they pass through Nob Hill. If it's a nice day, hop off and explore Nob Hill and Russian Hill. At sunset, order cocktails at the Top of the Mark lounge in the Mark Hopkins InterContinental at California and Mason streets.

5. Have dinner at John's Grill (63 Ellis Street near Union Square; ☎ 415-986-3274; **johnsgrill.com**), where you can pay homage to Dashiell Hammett and Sam Spade while enjoying 1930s dining at its best with chops, baked potatoes, and tomatoes (reportedly Hammett's favorite), and a Bloody Brigid (as in O'Shaughnessy) cocktail.

6. Enjoy an evening of zany entertainment at *Beach Blanket Babylon* (at Club Fugazi in North Beach), San Francisco's long-running musical revue famous for its excellent singers, enormous hats, and stunning costumes; advance reservations are required.

If You've Got More Time

If you're spending more than two days in town or if this is not your first visit, consider some of these options.

1. Drive or take a bus up Van Ness Avenue to Union Street and Pacific Heights, where you'll find some of the best examples of San Francisco's famed Victorian houses. The Union Street shops are a very upscale retail experience indeed, with more than 300 boutiques, restaurants, antique shops, and coffeehouses.

2. Visit the California Palace of the Legion of Honor, a world-class European art museum in Lincoln Park with a spectacular view of the Pacific and the Marin Headlands. It's also a location used in Hitchcock's classic thriller *Vertigo*. Drive or take the No. 38 bus from Union Square.

3. Spend at least half a day in Golden Gate Park. The Japanese Tea Garden is a work of art; families should head to the California Academy of Sciences. Other options include renting a bike or rowboat.

4. Go to Sausalito or Tiburon for lunch and an afternoon. You can drive, but taking the ferry from Fisherman's Wharf is a better way to reach these two upscale, bayside communities across from San Francisco.

5. Serious shoppers will want to exercise their credit cards around Union Square, where they'll find the city's major department stores and many high-end specialty shops. Discount shoppers should head to SoMa, which is loaded with warehouse retail spaces. On-the-edge fashion victims and vintage-clothes browsers should head to Haight-Ashbury.

6. If you've got a car, make the trip across the Golden Gate Bridge to Muir Woods (giant redwoods) and Mount Tamalpais (a lovely view of San Francisco Bay and the Pacific). You can do both in half a day.

7. Drive up Twin Peaks for its stunning view of the city (from its highest location). *Hint:* Go at night (and take a jacket or sweater).

8. The San Francisco Museum of Modern Art is the city's newest art emporium, and even if you're not a big fan of modern art, the building alone is worth the price of admission. It's a knockout.

9. Don't miss Fort Point. While the Civil War–era brick fortress isn't much to get excited about, the view, framed by the Golden Gate Bridge, is. It's got our vote as the most scenic spot in the city, and it's where Jimmy Stewart pulls Kim Novak out of the water in Hitchcock's *Vertigo*.

10. Take a drive along the city's western edge south of the Golden Gate Bridge, and you'll see yet another reason why San Franciscans love it here. The views of the Pacific and the coast are spectacular. Explore Seal Rocks, Cliff House, Ocean Beach, or Fort Funston.

THE GALLOPING GOURMET TOUR

THERE ARE TWO THINGS EVERYONE RAVES about in San Francisco —the weather and the food. Here's an agenda for you foodies out there who want to take in the diverse flavor of the city. A word on planning: Definitely make a reservation for dinner. Eating is the main event for most on weekends and even weekdays for top restaurants. It's just the way—so call ahead.

Day 1

BREAKFAST We're going to start this day's gastronomic adventures in Berkeley. As the T-shirt boasts, you get "friendly service and good food" at one of the most loved breakfast joints in the Bay Area, **Bette's Oceanview Diner** (1807 Fourth Street, Berkeley; ☎ 510-644-3230; **bettesdiner.com**). You'll come for the pancakes, as most people do, and want to endure the never-ending lines for the fat omelets. Or are you a scrapple fan? They've got that, too! The lines are extraordinarily long with people coming from all over, so be sure to get there early if you want to be seated in a timely manner. If you get there late, don't fret. Stroll along Fourth Street shops and you'll hear your name yelled over the loudspeaker.

LUNCH While you are in Berkeley, after shopping or taking in the hippies on Telegraph near campus, a must-stop is **Vik's Distributors Inc.** (726 Allston Way, Berkeley; ☎ 510-644-4412). International cuisine in San Francisco is fantastic, evidenced by the publicity their sushi and Chinese food get. But Vik's is probably one of the best Indian food restaurants anywhere! Don't expect frills here. It resembles a warehouse with folding chairs and tables, and you have to order at the counter and wait for your name to be announced when it is ready. What makes this place stand out from the rest is the freshness and hard-to-find Indian dishes you may never have tried before.

unofficial **TIP**
At Vik's, order from the *chaat*—the snack bar. Portions are small, so you can sample more of the menu (a billboard on the wall).

DINNER After eating such a heavy Indian meal, we're going to take it down a notch and direct you to **Millennium Restaurant** (580 Geary

Street; ☎ 415-345-3900; **millenniumrestaurant.com**) for the most creative and innovative vegetarian meals. It's probably the one place where vegans equal the omnivores. You'll be amazed at the many different uses for tofu. This restaurant is in constant competition with another top vegetarian haunt—Greens. But the atmosphere (and the food) here is truly elegant. On Sundays closest to a full moon, they dish a splurge-worthy Aphrodisiac Dinner menu, complete with the key to a room in the hotel upstairs.

Full-fledged vegans have another option at Café Gratitude on 2400 Harrison Street (☎ 415-830-3014; or 1730 Shattuck; ☎ 510-725-4418; **cafegratitude.com**), where raw-food dining is utterly delicious.

AFTER-DINNER CAFE So you had a long day touring Berkeley, survived the Bay Bridge traffic getting back into the city, settled your insides with Millennium's plantain torte, and now what? Head to North Beach to the popular Beat generation watering hole, Caffe Trieste (609 Vallejo Street; ☎ 415-392-6739) for the best coffee in town. Its imported Italian coffee is sold by the cup or by the bean. Snacks like pizza and sandwiches are available, and on Saturday afternoons, musicians and opera singers take over the existential vibe and perform.

Or you'll scream for **Mitchell's Ice Cream** (688 San Jose Avenue in the Outer Mission; ☎ 415-648-2300), arguably the best ice cream in town, as evidenced by the lines of people waiting for their number to be called in this Mission District favorite. The range of unique flavors—Chicago Cheesecake, Avocado, and Halo-Halo (a popular East Asian–style mélange) to name a few—are true representations of the diverse cultural population and dining experiences in San Francisco. Unexplainably delicious.

SUBDUED LATE NIGHT Unlike New York, San Francisco isn't open all night. It's hard to find a place open at midnight to grab a bite to eat— not just a bite but a big slab of hearty meat if you are up for it! One neighborhood late-night favorite is **Brazen Head** (see Dining) in Cow Hollow. It's open until 2 a.m., and the atmosphere is mellow, publike but with a down-home, cozy feeling.

Failing that, **Yuet Lee** in Chinatown (1300 Stockton Street at Broadway; ☎ 415-982-6020) remains open until 3 a.m. on Fridays and Saturdays and midnight the rest of the week (try the salt-and-pepper prawns), and pizza-lovers and hipster-haven **Beretta** (1199 Valencia Street; ☎ 415-695-1199; **berettasf.com**) is also open until the wee hours, or 1 a.m. at least.

PIANO BAR LATE NIGHT If you are just coming from a showing of *Beach Blanket Babylon,* then **Lefty O'Doul's** at Union Square (333 Geary Boulevard; ☎ 415-982-8900; **leftyodouls.biz**) is in order. The music is mirthful, though the singers are often off-key, and the steam table is one of the most popular in town. It's pure comfort food, so don't eat too much if you're going dancing afterward, and you can join in the baseball game–watching.

Did we mention **Martuni's** (4 Valencia Street; ☎ 415-241-0205; **martunis.ypguides.net**)? If you like the Great American Songbook, you've never really heard it done with true panache until you've seen transvestite torch singers like Veronica Klaus belt out songs around the huge grand, with a fancy cocktail in hand as you sing along.

Day 2

 BREAKFAST For more than 90 years, **Sears Fine Foods Restaurant** in the heart of Union Square (439 Powell Street; ☎ 415-986-0700; **searsfinefood.com**) has been flipping more than 16 varieties of pancakes, some no bigger than a silver dollar, for locals and tourists alike who have made this a city landmark. Lines form on weekends at this eatery, resembling an old-style diner from the 1940s, so be sure to get an early jump on the day. If flapjacks aren't your thing, then try their hard-to-beat corned beef with hash, or varieties of eggs and omelets. Don't bring ultra-sophisticated gourmet types here—they won't get it.

BRUNCH If you do get a late start to your day, you may want to consider participating in a citywide tradition—Sunday brunch. Fresh flowers at each table, thoughtful place settings, and the open kitchen attract locals to **Ella's Restaurant** (500 Presidio Avenue; ☎ 415-441-5669), which is attentive to every detail, right down to the lemon-and-ginger oatmeal pancakes. Menus change weekly, but expect eclectic lunches and creative soups. The restaurant also serves dinner, but it is an obligatory brunch destination on weekends. It's a bit far out to the west, but worth the trip. Closer to downtown is The Garden Court (see Dining).

> *unofficial* **TIP**
> "A mad city, inhabited for the most part by perfectly insane people whose women are of remarkable beauty."
> —*Rudyard Kipling*

DINNER There are two things you can't leave the city without trying—sushi and burritos. We've got your bases covered. Decide on what you crave first. You can't go wrong with most of the sushi restaurants in town, but **Ebisu Sushi** in the Sunset District (1283 Ninth Avenue; ☎ 415-566-1770; **ebisusushi.com**) is voted as one of the best. The sushi chefs at this lively place will become your closest friends after one sitting of their spicy tuna rolls. The fish is the freshest, and rolls are very creative. It's also along the main strip in the Sunset District, so an after-meal stroll to see other restaurants or stores is possible.

Or if the idea of raw fish isn't to your liking, **La Taqueria** (2889 Mission Street; ☎ 415-285-7117) will roll you the best burrito in town. It's a rather rundown place in the Mission, but looks are deceiving.

It's fresh, cheap, and filling. There are tons of Mexican taco stands in this part of town, so keep an eye out for the bright red electric sign.

THE ADRENALINE TOUR

YOU'LL NEVER FIND A PLACE so chock-full of outdoor activity as San Francisco. Its never-break-a-sweat weather and bay breezes, not to mention mountains and proximity to national parks and the ocean, make it a prime destination for outdoor enthusiasts.

Day 1: Close to Home

TO START YOUR DAY Pick up a smoothie with a wheat-grass booster at Jamba Juice (800 Chestnut at Pierce streets) and take an early morning misty walk along the Marina Green. You have two choices—you can walk along the water toward the bridge and then over the bridge toward the **Marin Headlands,** or you can drive across the bridge. Either way, hiking the Headlands is a must-do while in San Francisco. It's so close to the city, offers dramatic views, and it's a great way to get the heart rate and spirit escalated. Any hiker of any ability can do the Headlands. You can begin shortly after exiting the Golden Gate Bridge at the Bay Area Ridge Trail, also known as the Coastal Trail. The trail can get narrow and steep, but the effort is worthwhile. The trail loops around, and about midway don't forget to look back—you will see clear across the famous Golden Gate out to sea, and if it's a clear day, you can see the jagged silhouette of the Farallon Islands 22 miles away. You can get trail maps and more information on the Headlands by stopping at the visitor center, which is to the right off the exit ramp onto Alexander Avenue. Turn left on Bunker Road and you'll see signs. A trek in the Headlands is completely self-led and vast—great for couples and power hikers. Their Web site is **nps.gov/goga/marin-headlands.htm.**

If you want something a bit more confined and subdued, particularly if you have children with you, give **Angel Island** your morning attention. Ferries leave from Fisherman's Wharf every half hour or so and deposit you at the car-free island in the middle of the bay. You will be dropped at Perimeter Trailhead, which takes you around the island along well-groomed, wide trails passing shops for bicycle rentals, tram tours, kayak rentals, and the Cove Café. For more information, call ☎ 415-435-1915.

A BREATHER . . . Return from your hike and deposit yourself along the beach at Crissy Field near the Marina District for a mug of java or hot chocolate at the Warming Hut. You can sit outside and watch the kite fliers and the wind or kite surfers in the water circle the pillars of the Golden Gate Bridge. Bring a drink and a snack. If it's time to try a Segway, there's **San Francisco Segway Tours** (rear parking lot, 757 Beach Street, ☎ 415-474-3130; **electrictourcompany.com**), or lazier still, **Mr. Toad's**

Tours, a cute and colorful minibus (2699 Mason Street, ☎ 877-467-8623; **mrtoadstours.com**).

OR NOT... If you haven't had enough, you can rent a bike at **Blazing Saddles** (1095 Columbus Avenue; ☎ 415-202-8888; **blazingsaddles .com**). The obligatory bike route for those who want the best scenery and burn for their body is taking the Great Highway bike path. The path leads you right into Fort Funston and Lake Merced—which takes you into late afternoon.

A GREAT FINISH **Lake Merced** off the Great Highway to Skyline Boulevard offers you the chance to jog, in-line skate, bike, or hike. If you've never tried it (and the wind is right), the lake offers windsurfing lessons, including all equipment. You can pick up a bite to eat and rehydrate yourself with a thick malt beer or the pure H2O at the Boat House. On the drive or pedal back toward the city, you can watch the sunset and decompress at **Fort Funston** off of the Great Highway. Pick a perch—benches conveniently offered—and watch the hang gliders soar weightlessly off a cliff and over the crashing waves below.

Day 2: Farther Afield

TO START THE DAY What in-line skating was in the 1990s, mountain biking is today. And **Mount Tamalpais,** or Mount Tam for those in the know, is supposedly the place where it originated. Many bike trails crisscross the mountain (across the Golden Gate from San Francisco proper), and most lead to the popular **Old Railroad Grade.** Which section to take depends on how far you want to go. You could choose to start your fat-tire tryst from quaint Mill Valley off West Blithedale Avenue, or you could drive up Summit Avenue if you are feeling less ambitious. If you need bike rentals, you can get them before taking off at Blazing Saddles (1095 Columbus Avenue; ☎ 415-202-8888).

A BREATHER... There is no better place on that side of the bridge to take lunch or brunch than **Sam's Anchor Cafe** (27 Main Street; ☎ 415-435-4527; **samscafe.com**) in Tiburon. It is one of the most popular brunch places in the city because of its relaxed seaside mood and excellent views. Grab a cold one.

OR NOT... Close to Tiburon is the savvy town of Sausalito. Here you will find **Sea Trek Ocean Kayaking Center,** an all-inclusive rental service. They offer classes, guided trips, and kayaks for newbies and pros alike. Their prices are reasonable and service is top notch. You'll slice through the water starting out at Sausalito's Schoonmaker Point Marina, and there's a good chance of meeting face to face with seals, pelicans, and even the occasional whale in Richardson Bay. Best of all is the Full Moon kayaking trip along the Sausalito waterfront. For more information, call ☎ 415-488-1000, or check out **seatrek.com**. The currents in the bay are very strong, and with the occasional huge cargo ship coming through the Golden Gate from an overseas journey, you can expect to battle waves. You will sweat! Just remain calm and stick close to your party or a guide if that makes you more comfortable. Life jackets are provided. You'll be too exhausted for anything else, so spend the evening at a movie or soaking in a hot bath!

Or, if rumors of great white sharks lurking 22 miles away at the Farallon Islands deter you from sticking an inch of your toe in the bay (although according to locals, sharks *never* enter the bay), we have another plan. Instead of heading to Sausalito from Mount Tam, continue your adrenaline journey along Highway 1 down toward **Stinson Beach,** where the lowest tides uncover genuine hot springs that you can try out, and cabins with stoves are for rent at Steep Ravine Cabins (801 Panoramic Highway, Mill Valley; ☎ 415-388-2070; **parks.ca.gov/?page_id=471;** reservations recommended; closed in October). On the way you'll pass tourist mecca Muir Woods and the ever popular Pelican Inn (10 Pacific Way, Muir Beach; **pelicaninn. com**). The drive is winding, twisting, and at some points nail-biting, but the heights of the pavement will prepare you for the heights of the cliff face that you can scale just south of Stinson Beach at **Red Rock Beach,** also known by locals as Mickey's. You'll climb your way up a cliff overlooking the Pacific below. The route is pretty challenging, and only those who are seasoned climbers should attempt it. For more information, call ☎ 415-388-2070.

SAN FRANCISCO *for* CHILDREN

FITTING ANY VACATION AND TOUR around diaper changes, feeding times, and cranky kids is about as challenging as getting a tan during San Francisco summers. So what do you do? San Francisco offers plenty of fun-filled places and things to do that will satisfy the most curious— and fidgety—kids. But the beauty is that you will love it, too.

The *Unofficial Guide* rating system for attractions includes an "appeal to different age groups" category with a range of appeal from one star (1), don't bother, to five stars (5), not to be missed. Before we get you started on specific attractions that will keep you and the little ones occupied, here are some tips to smooth over any sticky situations that may arise, and prevent further gray hairs.

There is a reason that the mats came out at noon during kindergarten. And there is a reason that parents are droopy-eyed at 6 a.m. while their kids are bright-eyed and bushy-tailed. Kids are morning people— and it seems that energy fades around mid-afternoon. Try to plan the bulk of activities in the early morning, when their attention is easily harnessed. There are plenty of mellow activities to plan after lunch— like sitting in a park, watching the boats in the bay. . . . If you have

unofficial **TIP**
Any parent-survival manual will tell you this, but it is our responsibility to remind you, too: Pack a bag of goodies for the kids. Their favorite coloring book with some crayons, action figures, a portable radio, Teddy Grahams, diced peaches . . . whatever it will take to make things less traumatic for you, them, and those around you. Buses can take longer than expected, and lines can be frustratingly long even for the grown-ups.

babies with you, make sure that you are allowed to bring them in to certain "grown-up" places.

SOME SUGGESTIONS

SAN FRANCISCO HAS MORE FOR KIDS to enjoy than museums, a zoo, and vistas of the bay. A cable-car ride never fails to delight—let's face it, even a ride on BART could be a fun experience for kids. The icing on the cake is a stop at the **Cable Car Museum** (☎ 415-474-1887) near Chinatown (it's free). And while you are near **Chinatown,** take a stroll. All the trinkets and barking toys that the shops have on display will amuse—and thankfully, if ripping that fuzzy eraser from the hand causes a tantrum, almost everything here is cheap!

Another kid pleaser raved about by native parents is the **Basic Brown Bear** (The Cannery, 2801 Leavenworth Street; ☎ 415-409-2806; **basic brownbear.com**). Kids can select a teddy bear from among dozens of styles and then stuff it themselves. Tours of the factory are offered daily from 10 a.m. to 5 p.m.

A PARK FOR EVERY SUE, SAM, AND SPOT

SO THE EXPLORATORIUM sent the kids spinning in orbit. What to do with all that energy? A great cool-down option for you, and a place for them to release their energy in a vast open space, is to visit one of the many parks found within the city. **Golden Gate Park** is your best option. It is huge and has the **Children's Playground,** with a carousel that's fun for toddlers. You can also rent a boat on Stow Lake; bicycles, in-line skates, and roller skates are also available for rent. Call ☎ 415-752-0347 for boat rentals, ☎ 415-668-6699 for bike rentals.

Bay Area Discovery Museum (Fort Baker, 557 McReynolds Road, Sausalito; ☎ 415-339-3900; **baykidsmuseum.org**), just on the other side of Golden Gate Bridge, is an old Army base transformed into a playpen for the shorter set with activities and interactive fun stuff galore. Check out our free museum day chart—theirs is the first Wednesday of every month.

On the Wharf at Pier 45 is Musee Mecanique (☎ 415-346-2000; **museemecaniquesf.com**), a funfair of Victorian amusements from the old Playland at the Beach arcade; Laffing Sal and Susie the Can-Can Dancer still enchant.

Finally, and this is a surefire winner, if they love the sea lions that leave their "arfs" in San Francisco along Pier 39, they will really go for the Headlands Marine Mammal Center at the end of a winding cliff-top road on the other side of the Golden Gate Bridge. How to make fish shakes, how seals grow from pups, where they hang out—it's all part of the great educational material here, and you can visit with the recovering seals as they convalesce here too: 2000 Bunker Road, Fort Cronkhite, Sausalito; ☎ 415-289-7325; **marinemammalcenter.org.**

Another bizarre kid-pleasing attraction in Golden Gate Park is the **Buffalo Paddock** at the western end. You won't be able to get close enough to pet them, but it is an oddly amusing sight to see buffalo roaming in the prairie of a city park. Near the paddock is **Spreckels Lake,** where remote-control boats cruise up and down. It's fun to sit and watch the miniboats go by. **The Presidio** is second runner-up. It's big, green, has a children's playground, a pretty cheap and uncrowded bowling alley, and cannons to climb on, and there is even a Burger King. There is plenty of free parking here, too. Near the Presidio is the Marina Green, a strip of green that runs along the bay by the Marina. It is kite-flying heaven—and a great place for a picnic.

unofficial **TIP**
Great city places to walk include the **Golden Gate Promenade** (a three-and-a-half-mile paved walkway that starts near Fisherman's Wharf and follows the bay shore west to the bridge of the same name) and Ocean Beach, a four-mile stretch of sand beginning just south of Cliff House.

While you are in the Marina, be sure to visit the **wave organ**—a funky creation of granite pipes nestled at different depths within the breaking water. The "organ" creates different tones when the waves hit the pipes. Expect sounds of orchestral proportions at high tide.

If you happen to catch a hot, sunny day in the city, head to **China Beach,** one of the most kid-friendly beaches in our view. It's located in the posh Sea Cliff neighborhood, and the beach is small enough to keep your eye on the kids as they run free. The facilities here are spotless, and the surf is calm, thanks to the protective cliffs and coves that surround the beach. Along the Great Highway 1, right after the San Francisco Zoo, is **Fort Funston.** It is one of the only places to watch hang gliders 1-2-3-jump off a cliff right next to your bench and soar above the crashing Pacific Ocean.

Most kids might also enjoy taking a bay cruise and seeing San Francisco from the water. And don't forget another place popular with both children and adults: **Lombard Street,** "the crookedest street in the world," so steep that the road has to zigzag to make the descent (between Hyde and Leavenworth streets).

RAINY-DAY BLUES

KIDS CLIMBING THE HOTEL WALLS? Let them work it off at **Mission Cliffs,** the world's largest indoor climbing gym (2295 Harrison Street at 19th Street; ☎ 415-550-0515; **mission-cliffs.com**).

Another option is a movie. The **AMC Loews Metreon** is a 15-screen theater complex, plus one IMAX theater, that's sure to be playing something in 3-D that the kids will enjoy. **Metreon Center** (101 Fourth

Street at Mission Street; ☎ 415-369-6000) features eight restaurants and shopping, just three blocks south of Union Square. Also check out the brand-new **Walt Disney Family Museum** in the Presidio (☎ 415-345-6800; **waltdisney.org;** book ahead online; entry is pre-timed). Shopping excursions could include a stop at Westfield San Francisco Centre.

KID-FRIENDLY MENUS

IF YOU ARE TIRED OF MAKING STOPS at the golden arches or Pizza Hut, several options will please your palate as well as satisfy the picky taste of your little ones. **The Garden Terrace** in the Downtown Marriott has kids in mind for sure. They offer a half-price kids' buffet, and drinks are served with a straw straight from the crookedest street in San Fran. The menu was also designed by kids. Other dining spots children enjoy include the **Hard Rock Café,** featuring great burgers, rock memorabilia, and yet another deafening sound level (Pier 39; ☎ 415-956-2013); and **Mel's Drive-In,** straight out of *American Graffiti* and as American as it gets, with greasy fries, frothy milk shakes, and Patsy Cline crooning on the tabletop jukeboxes (2165 Lombard Street; ☎ 415-921-3039; or 3355 Geary Boulevard; ☎ 415-387-2244). **Johnny Rockets** is open late and has burgers, fries, and shakes (short walk from the Marina Green, at 2201 Chestnut Street; ☎ 415-931-6258) and is right next to **Mrs. Field's Cookies** (☎ 415-441-1978). **Barney's Hamburgers** (3344 Steiner Street; ☎ 415-563-0307 or 4138 24th Street; ☎ 415-282-7770) has a wide selection of beef burgers but also could be the kids' first introduction to alternative patties, such as tofu or garden burgers.

unofficial **TIP**
It's a safe hunch that kids won't enjoy anything more than a splurge-worthy trip to Benihana in Japantown, where the chefs' flashing knife skills furnish extra thrills (1737 Post Street, second floor of the Japan Center; ☎ 415-563-4844; benihana.com). That said, there is no better place to have your first sushi experience than San Francisco. Give it a go— if anything, it will be fun to see the kids' faces when you tell them it is raw fish. You'll have choices in Japantown, so let them pick!

PRO SPORTS AND OTHER AMUSEMENTS

DEPENDING ON THE SEASON AND TICKET AVAILABILITY, take the gang to a 49ers, Giants, Golden State Warriors, Oakland As, or Oakland Raiders game. Tickets to a baseball game at the **AT&T Park** in China Basin can be had for less than $15 for a seat in the bleachers, and the ballpark has the infamous soda bottle slide—*whooooosh!*— and other things beloved by kids from hot dogs to garlic fries.

Across the bay in the Oakland Hills, a trip to **Chabot Space & Science Museum** in Joaquin Miller Park—with its hands-on activities and telescope lens-grinding sessions—is another smash hit. Chabot occasionally throws full moon–guided walks for kids to watch the planets out here in the inky-black unpolluted skies (10000 Skyline Boulevard, Oakland; ☎ 510-336-7300; **chabotspace.org**).

They will enjoy sailing on **Lake Merritt** and particularly **Children's Fairyland** on the north shore of Lake Merritt; it's one of the most imaginative children's parks in the country (☎ 510-452-2259; **fairyland.org**). Admission is $7 (only adults accompanied by a child or children accompanied by an adult are admitted). Something to combine with a scenic drive down Route 1 along the Pacific Coast is a stop at **Monterey Bay Aquarium** (886 Cannery Row, Monterey; ☎ 831-648-4888). The neon jellyfish tank and the walk-through tour of the Monterey Bay that starts underwater make this one of the best aquariums in the country.

A little less ambitious than roller coasters and glow-in-the-dark fish is the age-old backup plan—bowling. On the beautiful Presidio, try the **Presidio Bowl** (93 Presidio Boulevard; ☎ 415-561-2695).

HELPFUL TIPS *for* TOURISTS

SAVE 50 PERCENT WHEN YOU VISIT San Francisco's most popular museums and attractions with a **CityPass.** Participating attractions are the California Academy of Sciences, California Palace of the Legion of Honor, Exploratorium, Steinhart Aquarium, San Francisco Bay Cruise, and the San Francisco Museum of Modern Art. Passes cost $59 for adults and $39 for children ages 5 to 17. Children age 4 and under pay the regular reduced fare at each attraction. Ticket books are sold at participating attractions and are good for nine days beginning with the first day you use them. Don't remove the individual tickets from the booklet; just present the CityPass at each attraction, the clerk at the site removes the ticket, and you walk in. Also included is a seven-day Muni Passport valid for unlimited rides on cable cars, light rail, and buses (☎ 888-330-5008; **citypass.com/city/sanfrancisco.html**).

WHEN ADMISSION IS FREE

MANY SAN FRANCISCO MUSEUMS usually open their doors for free one day a month. If you'd like to save a few bucks during your visit, use the following list when planning your itinerary. However, check the Web site before you go, as free and closed days may change.

Free Museum Days

FREE FIRST SUNDAYS

Asian Art Museum

200 Larkin Street (between Fulton and McAllister streets), Civic Center, across from City Hall; ☎ 415-581-3500; **asianart.org**

San Francisco Maritime National Historical Park

499 Jefferson Street (at Hyde Street); ☎ 415-447-5000; **nps.gov/safr**

FREE FIRST TUESDAYS

Cartoon Art Museum

655 Mission Street (between Second and Third streets); ☎ 415-227-8666; **cartoonart.org** • *First Tuesday of month is Pay What You Wish Day.*

de Young Museum

Golden Gate Park, 50 Hagiwara Tea Garden Drive, Golden Gate Park; ☎ 415-750-3600; **famsf.org/deyoung** • *$2 discount on admission with Muni pass/transfer.*

Legion of Honor

Lincoln Park, 34th Avenue at Clement Street; ☎ 415-750-3600; **famsf.org/legion** • *$2 discount on regular admission with Muni pass/transfer.*

Museum of Craft and Folk Art

51 Yerba Buena Lane; ☎ 415-227-4888; **mocfa.org**

San Francisco Museum of Modern Art (SF MOMA)

151 Third Street (between Mission and Howard streets); ☎ 415-357-4000; **sfmoma.org** • *Half-price admission on Thursdays from 6–8:45 p.m.*

Yerba Buena Center for the Arts Galleries

701 Mission Street; ☎ 415-978-2700; **ybca.org**

FREE FIRST WEDNESDAYS

Bay Area Discovery Museum

For children age 8 and under. Fort Baker, 557 McReynolds Road, Sausalito; ☎ 415-339-3900; **baykidsmuseum.org** • *From 9 a.m. to 4 p.m.; groups not eligible.*

Exploratorium at the Palace of Fine Arts

3601 Lyon Street; ☎ 415-561-0360; **exploratorium.edu**

FREE FIRST THURSDAYS

Berkeley Art Museum & Pacific Film Archive

2626 Bancroft Way/2621 Durant Avenue (between College and Telegraph streets), Berkeley; ☎ 510-642-0808; **bampfa.berkeley.edu**

Burlingame Museum of PEZ Memorabilia

214 California Drive, Burlingame; ☎ 650-347-2301; **burlingamepezmuseum.com**

ALWAYS FREE

Cable Car Museum

1201 Mason Street; ☎ 415-474-1887; **cablecarmuseum.org**

Chinese Culture Center Gallery

750 Kearny Street, Third Floor; ☎ 415-986-1822; **c-c-c.org**

Museo Italo Americano

Fort Mason Center, Building C, 99 Marina Boulevard; ☎ 415-673-2200; **museoitaloamericano.org**

San Francisco Fire Department Museum

655 Presidio Avenue (at Pine Street); ☎ 415-563-4630, or after hours ☎ 415-558-3546; **guardiansofthecity.org**

Wells Fargo History Museum

420 Montgomery Street (at California Street); ☎ 415-396-2619; **wellsfargohistory.com**

FREE EAST AND SOUTH BAY MUSEUMS

Cantor Arts Center

328 Lomita Drive (at Museum Way), Stanford; ☎ 650-723-4177; **museum.stanford.edu**

Marin History Museum

1125 B Street, San Rafael; ☎ 415-454-8538; **marinhistory.org**

Phoebe A. Hearst Museum of Anthropology

103 Kroeber Hall (at Bancroft Way and College Avenue), Berkeley; ☎ 510-642-3682; **hearstmuseum.berkeley.edu**

Takara Sake Museum

708 Addison Street, Berkeley; ☎ 510-540-8250; **takarasake.com/company/ museum.htm** • *One-room museum with free sake tasting.*

FREE GUIDED WALKS

San Francisco Botanical Garden

Ninth Avenue at Lincoln Way; ☎ 415-661-1316; **sfbotanicalgardensociety.org** • *At 1:30 p.m. daily*

San Francisco City Guides

☎ 415-557-4266; **sfcityguides.org** • *Walking tours to various locations.*

In addition, a few other worthy attractions around town are always free:

- Berkeley Rose Garden
- Fort Point National Historic Site
- Golden Gate Bridge for pedestrians and bicyclists
- Golden Gate Park Band concerts (Sundays, 1 p.m., April–October)
- Musee Mecanique at Pier 45
- Museum of Money of the American West
- Randall Museum for children
- San Francisco Shakespeare Festival (September)
- Stern Grove Festival (Stern Grove, Sloat Boulevard at 19th Avenue, Sundays, 2 p.m., June–August)

GET A VIRTUAL FRIEND

THE BEST WAY TO EXPLORE SAN FRANCISCO and find the stuff most tourists never see is to talk to a local, right? Now you can, sort of: Joie de Vivre Hospitality, a chain of boutique hotels in the Bay Area, provides "virtual friends" on its Web site (**jdvhotels.com/californiaLocals Talk**). "Locals" will describe a perfect day in the city. Ranging from Donald, "a hip San Francisco doctor with an appetite for eclectic restaurants" to Teri, "a helicopter pilot who loves baseball, dinner with friends, and flying under the Golden Gate Bridge," these real San Franciscans offer insider advice for visitors. You can even take a test on the Web site that matches you to two of the personalities most similar to yours. The Web site also provides many pages of insider info (click "Things to Do"), including favorite restaurants, visual arts, romantic hideouts and peaceful retreats, hidden places, great walking tours, and more. And it's all free.

unofficial **TIP**
"San Francisco is a golden handcuff with the key thrown away."
—John Steinbeck

BREATHTAKING VIEWS

WE ARE ALL DRAWN TO THE VIEW—a glimpse of something larger, majestic, something that can breathe new life in us or suck it out if it so chooses. Breathtaking. Whether it's nature at its most expansive, or the sparkling twilight of a sky filled with stars, or a cityscape bright with energy—everyone requests a view. You don't have to know the manager of the Fairmont Hotel to get compelling views in San Francisco. Simply take a stroll and use our list of some of the best views in the city as your guide.

1. **Fort Point.** Ideally, you should be blindfolded and brought to this Civil War–era fortress. You should remove the blind as you face the Marin Headlands across the Golden Gate. Overhead is the massive Golden Gate Bridge, perhaps the most beautiful suspension bridge in the world.

2. Although it's better at night, the view from **Twin Peaks** is a stupendous, 360-degree view of San Francisco whenever the weather is clear.

3. The best view of the city's skyline is from **Treasure Island.** To get there, take the Treasure Island exit from the Bay Bridge and drive to the parking area just outside the naval station.

4. For the best view of the waterfront, hike up **Telegraph Hill** to **Coit Tower.** Don't drive; parking is scarce. Either walk or take the 39 bus.

5. Drive across the **Golden Gate Bridge,** get off in Sausalito, and follow signs to Mount Tamalpais, where you can drive to the 2,800-foot summit (well, almost) for a heart-stopping view of San Francisco Bay, the city, the Golden Gate and Bay bridges, and the Pacific Ocean.

6. For a view of the bay that's almost as good as the one from Mount Tam, go to Berkeley, through the University of California–Berkeley campus, and find Grizzly Peak Boulevard. Then drive up the winding

road to the **Lawrence Hall of Science.** Park in the lot and enjoy the vista from the plaza of the Children's Science Museum.

7. The view from the **Golden Gate Bridge** is best at sunset, when the slanting sun casts shadowy patterns on the lofty bridge towers and on the sea below—and the tour buses have left for the day. The pedestrian walkway is open until 9 p.m.

8. For an even better view of **Seal Rocks** than the one you get at Cliff House, walk up to Sutro Heights Park, which overlooks the Pacific from a lofty vantage point. Park in the lot just north of Cliff House (on the other side of the Great Highway).

9. Drive across the Golden Gate Bridge to **Vista Point,** which offers superb views of the bridge and the San Francisco skyline. It's beautiful on a sunny day, but it might be even better when the fog rolls over the hills or at night when the city glimmers beyond the Golden Gate. **The Headlands** offer postcard-perfect views of the city and the approaching fog just knocking at the gate.

10. The neighborhood of Potrero Hill, at 19th and Texas streets, makes the city skyline appear like a pop-up book. Honorable mention goes to **Dolores Park.**

SECRET STAIRCASES

SCATTERED THROUGHOUT SAN FRANCISCO'S MANY HILLS are pocket parks, restful benches, and many stairways—about 350 of them, mostly in residential neighborhoods and often adorned with flowers planted by neighbors. The stairways are used by residents to allow direct vertical access from one street to another; because most streets wind around the hills, people frequently use staircases as shortcuts.

A walk centered around an exploration of the city's staircases is cheaper than a fitness center and frequently offers views that rival what you'll find on the Golden Gate Bridge. Put on your walking shoes, grab your camera, and explore some of the city's oldest, most scenic hidden attractions—its stairways. For a comprehensive guide to the city's stairways, pick up a copy of *Stairway Walks in San Francisco,* 6th edition, by Adah Bakalinsky, available in bookstores or directly from the Wilderness Press (☎ 510-558-1666), or on **amazon. com**. Here's a sampling of some of San Francisco's best stairways.

1. The carefully landscaped stairs found near the famous Lombard Street (between Hyde and Leavenworth streets).

2. At **Broadway** and **Lyon Street,** more than ten flights of majestic stone steps surrounded by well-kept greenery and regal views of the Palace of Fine Arts, the bay, and the Marin Headlands.

3. The **Greenwich Street Steps** at the base of Coit Tower on Telegraph Hill; more than three separate flights of stairs that climb through tall trees and past hillside gardens and stunning views (see Part 10, Exercise and Recreation, for more specifics).

4. The **Fort Mason/Aquatic Park Steps** overlooking Alcatraz; the small clearing at the top features tranquility and picnic tables.

5. **Pemberton Stairway** in the Twin Peaks neighborhood, newly renovated with terra-cotta concrete stairs and just-planted gardens.

6. **Filbert Street Steps,** between Sansome Street and Telegraph Hill, a 377-step climb through verdant flower gardens and charming 19th-century cottages.

7. **Moraga Street Steps** off 16th Avenue in the Sunset District.

SAN FRANCISCO *on* FILM

SOME OF YOU MAY REMEMBER THAT SCENE in the classic *It Came from Beneath the Sea* circa 1955, in which a giant octopus attacks the Golden Gate Bridge and tears it in half. If you don't, it's a sure rental before you set out seeing the sights of the city. If you are a movie junkie and love to relive favorite scenes, then San Francisco is just the fix. Before renting any flicks, pick up a copy of *The San Francisco Movie Map*, sold at the California Historical Society gift shop and other locations around town. Then grab a copy of Alfred Hitchcock's *Vertigo* to get in the mood!

Vertigo (1958) Alfred Hitchcock loved San Francisco, and he shows the town at its best in this film starring James Stewart and Kim Novak. Locations in the movie include Mission Dolores, the California Palace of the Legion of Honor (the movie's scenes were filmed in Gallery 6), the Palace of Fine Arts, and Fort Point (where Stewart dives into San Francisco Bay to save Novak). He also filmed the Mission at San Juan Bautista south of San Jose, at Muir Woods in Marin, and at Pebble Beach near Monterey.

Some other notable movies that feature San Francisco include:

- **Milk** (2008) is Gus Van Sant's account of the life and tragic death of Supervisor Harvey Milk, played in a towering performance by Sean Penn.
- **The Bridge** (2006) is director Eric Steel's documentary about a handful of people who jumped to their deaths off the Golden Gate Bridge.
- **Sweet November** (2000), starring Keanu Reeves and Charlize Theron, was a flop at the box office, but it showcased the best of San Francisco as the couple pranced around Potrero Hill and Noe Valley.
- **The Rock** (1996), starring Sean Connery, Nicolas Cage, and Ed Harris, was another Alcatraz action adventure.
- **Interview with the Vampire** (1994) The devilish leader of the vampires played by Tom Cruise offers Christian Slater "the choice" in a nighttime drive across the Golden Gate Bridge.
- **The Joy Luck Club** (1993), noted for its realistic depiction of Chinese Americans, was made in Chinatown.

- **Basic Instinct** (1992) You know the scene—that crossing-the-legs-with-no-panties shot that made the movie famous. The entire movie was filmed in San Francisco, evidenced by the car-chase scenes through town.
- **Hammett** (1982), German director Wim Wenders' tribute to the gumshoe immortalized by Dashiell Hammett, contains great glimpses of Chinatown, but it sank like a stone at the box office, thanks to a hatchet in the editing room and a repetitious if haunting score.
- **Escape from Alcatraz** (1979), a true story starring Clint Eastwood as the leader of a trio of escapees who actually made it off the Rock.
- **What's Up, Doc?** (1972), a screwball comedy starring Barbra Streisand and Ryan O'Neal, was filmed at the San Francisco Hilton (33 O'Farrell Street), called Hotel Bristol in the film. While we are on hotels: The lobby of the Fairmont Hotel on Nob Hill was featured in that 1980s television series *Hotel*.
- **Dirty Harry** (1971), another never-fail spellbinder said to be based on real police characters, and the first of Clint Eastwood's big hits. You'll see everything from North Beach to Mount Davidson and the Forest Hill Muni tunnel.
- **Bullitt** (1968), a rattling good thriller starring Steve McQueen, Robert Vaughn, and Jacqueline Bisset, and stuffed with car chases galore and routes that are geographically farfetched.
- **Birdman of Alcatraz** (1962) with Burt Lancaster as Robert Stroud, the convict turned ornithologist.
- **Dark Passage** (1947) is an early Humphrey Bogart and Lauren Bacall classic noir with a preposterous plot involving plastic surgery on Bogey plus black-and-white shots of the Golden Gate Bridge and more.

Many other movies were made near or around the city, from classics such as *The Birds* and *Shadow of a Doubt* (Bodega Bay and Santa Rosa) from Alfred Hitchcock to Clint Eastwood's *Play Misty for Me* (Carmel) and even Werner Herzog documentaries *Little Dieter Needs to Fly* and *My Best Fiend Klaus Kinski* (West Marin). The stylish noir *The Maltese Falcon* (1941) made Dashiell Hammett famous."

Mack Sennett made *Mabel and Fatty Viewing the World's Fair at San Francisco* (1915), and Charlie Chaplin made *The Tramp* and 13 other silent movies in East Bay's Niles in 1915 for Essanay Studios. Mary Pickford, a silent movie star, had her studios at nearby Pleasanton.

The WINE COUNTRY

AFTER A FEW DAYS OF TOURING HECTIC SAN FRANCISCO, what could be better than relaxing in a setting of pastoral splendor only an hour from Union Square? Quaint country inns and designer restaurants with massive wine lists are abundant in the wine country and pamper the visitors who flock to these valleys, defined by low oak-and-chaparral-covered ridges.

For most folks, the visual grandeur is secondary to the lure of the fruit of the land. The wines produced in the Napa, Russian River, and Sonoma valleys rival the best vintages of France—and everybody wants to see where the magic is made. Wineries are everywhere in the two neighboring valleys, located north of San Francisco and inland of the Pacific Coast. They are so numerous that it's easy to think this is the winemaking capital of California. In fact, only about 5 percent of the state's total production comes from the region. But far and away the best wines produced in the country come from here. The reason is the region's Mediterranean climate: Hot, dry summers and cool, wet winters result in stressed-out grapevines that produce small, thick-skinned fruit. Because most of a wine's flavor and character comes from the skin rather than the pulp, the grapes that grow in these valleys result in premium vintages that impress wine snobs around the world.

unofficial **TIP**
"I have seen purer liquors, better cigars, finer tobacco, truer guns and pistols, larger dirk and Bowie knives, and prettier courtesans here in San Francisco than in any other place I have ever visited, and it is my unbiased opinion that California can and does furnish the best bad things that are obtainable in America."
—Hinton R. Helper, in *The Land of Gold; Reality Versus Fiction,* 1855

Wine has been made in the valleys since the 18th century, when clerics in Spanish missions planted vineyards to produce black grapes for sacramental wines. After centuries of ups and downs, the wine business began booming in the 1960s. Wine has evolved into an increasingly popular national drink, and the valleys have recovered from the last slump caused by Prohibition, when many vineyards were converted into orchards.

Today's renaissance is extraordinary; acreage has expanded exponentially and big business has moved in, most notably Coca-Cola and Nestlé. Even the French, formerly aloof, have formed partnerships with local growers. Napa Valley boasts more than 250 (mostly small) wineries, while Sonoma Valley has scores of them, as does the Russian River Valley. Winemaking in California is now a multibillion-dollar business, and millions of folks tour the wine country each year.

WHICH VALLEY?

DAY-TRIPPERS ON A SELF-GUIDED DAY TOUR of the wine country are faced with a choice: glamorous **Napa,** rural **Russian River,** or sleepy **Sonoma**? Alas, touring all three valleys in one day just isn't practical. Napa, the easternmost valley, is by far the best known of the two. It stretches for 35 miles from the town of Napa north to the resort town of Calistoga. In the long, narrow valley, grape arbors alternate with wild grasses, and the rich bottomland gives way to forested slopes of the surrounding ridges. Once past the congested and unexciting town of Napa, the beautiful valley looks as much like southern France as northern California.

Yet Napa is fashionable beyond belief and attracts millionaires the way a magnet draws iron filings. The valley also seems to draw more than its fair share of pinch-faced connoisseurs who mutter in mangled French as they swirl and sniff premium vintages in the tasting rooms of the wineries. Thankfully, the wine snobs are vastly outnumbered. Napa Valley has been discovered, and hordes of tourists have made it one of California's most popular attractions.

Sonoma Valley, on the other hand, has fewer wineries. Most are relatively small, still family-run, and tucked away on side roads. There's also notably less pretension in the wine-tasting rooms. In addition, Sonoma has more to offer than wineries, including a Spanish mission and the former estate of Jack London, one of America's greatest writers. And it has such a laid-back character that locals like to call it "Slow-noma."

The Russian River Valley is the new kid on the block. Country lanes and two-lane blacktops meander through redwood and pine forests that follow the lazy Russian River from Healdsburg to River's End. Most wineries are family- or independently owned. Classic roadhouses offer steaks and chops. Taverns have beer and wine lists of equal length. The main town of Healdsburg is a 19th-century gem. People say that the Russian River Valley is what Napa used to be. Get it while you can.

TOURING STRATEGIES

VISITING THE WINE COUNTRY shouldn't be about following a strict itinerary and seeing how much you can do in one day. It's quite the opposite, a joie-de-vivre kind of thing: a celebration of the good things in life, such as wonderful scenery, great food, and good friends.

PLANNING

ALTHOUGH SEVERAL TOUR COMPANIES in San Francisco provide bus tours to the wine country, we think the best way to enjoy a visit is to rent a car. Plan on visiting one or two wineries that produce wines you enjoy at home; then leave some time for a spontaneous stop at one or two other wineries, a picnic in a park, a museum visit, or shopping in one of the many towns.

Don't plan on visiting more than two or three wineries in a day. Otherwise the day becomes a blur of wine-tasting rooms that run together in your memory and your palate—not to mention the problem of too much alcohol consumption. One advantage of a two-day wine-country tour is that you can trade off driving; that way, there's always someone who can taste the wine and someone who can drive.

Many folks pack a picnic lunch, visit a winery, buy a bottle of wine, and enjoy an outdoor meal in a picnic area provided at many

The Wine Country

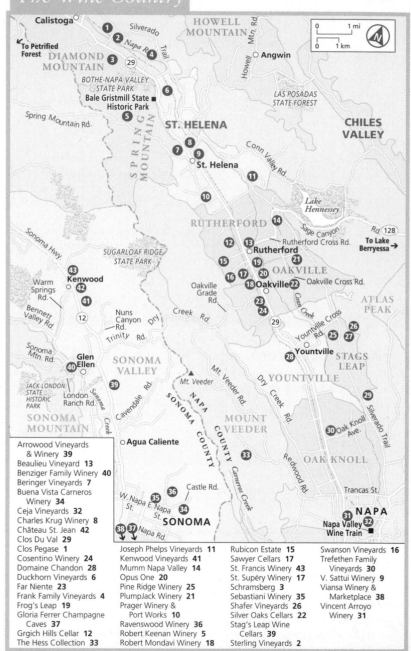

Arrowood Vineyards
& Winery **39**
Beaulieu Vineyard **13**
Benziger Family Winery **40**
Beringer Vineyards **7**
Buena Vista Carneros
Winery **34**
Ceja Vineyards **32**
Charles Krug Winery **8**
Château St. Jean **42**
Clos Du Val **29**
Clos Pegase **1**
Cosentino Winery **24**
Domaine Chandon **28**
Duckhorn Vineyards **6**
Far Niente **23**
Frank Family Vineyards **4**
Frog's Leap **19**
Gloria Ferrer Champagne
Caves **37**
Grgich Hills Cellar **12**
The Hess Collection **33**

Joseph Phelps Vineyards **11**
Kenwood Vineyards **41**
Mumm Napa Valley **14**
Opus One **20**
Pine Ridge Winery **25**
PlumpJack Winery **21**
Prager Winery &
Port Works **10**
Ravenswood Winery **36**
Robert Keenan Winery **5**
Robert Mondavi Winery **18**

Rubicon Estate **15**
Sawyer Cellars **17**
St. Francis Winery **43**
St. Supéry Winery **17**
Schramsberg **3**
Sebastiani Winery **35**
Shafer Vineyards **26**
Silver Oaks Cellars **22**
Stag's Leap Wine
Cellars **39**
Sterling Vineyards **2**

Swanson Vineyards **16**
Trefethen Family
Vineyards **30**
V. Sattui Winery **9**
Viansa Winery &
Marketplace **38**
Vincent Arroyo
Winery **31**

wineries. You can buy sandwiches or fixings at local delicatessens and groceries; don't forget to bring a corkscrew. Keep in mind that the whole point of visiting the wine country is to relax.

WINERY TOURS

WITH ABOUT 400 WINERIES TO CHOOSE FROM, picking a few to visit can be tough. You can just wander around and stop in wineries on a whim, but it pays to be selective. Visit a winery that makes a wine you like or, if you need some help, consult the list on pages 179, 183, and 188.

Virtually all of the wineries are open to the public from about 10 a.m. to 4 p.m. daily (and an hour to two later in the summer). Most have tasting rooms and maybe a picnic area outside. While many firms offer free wine tastings, increasingly some wineries (especially in Napa) are charging a few dollars for the opportunity to sample the fruits of their vineyards.

Larger winemakers, for example Mondavi in Napa, Korbel Champagne Cellars in the Russian River Valley, and Sebastiani in Sonoma, offer guided tours of the premises (some for a small fee). Visitors tour in groups of about 30; the tours last a half hour or so, ending with a visit to a tasting room. Smaller wineries, by and large, require reservations at least a day in advance (even earlier in the summer and fall) for a tour with a smaller group that may last two hours.

unofficial **TIP**
If at all possible, don't visit the wine country on a weekend; the best time to visit is early in the week. Plan on leaving San Francisco at 9 a.m. to get past the worst of morning rush-hour traffic and into the wine country by midmorning. Be sure to eat a good breakfast before leaving; you'll appreciate it later in the morning when you've sampled your first glass or two of wine.

WINE TASTING: TO SWIRL OR TO SNIFF? The ancient Greeks had it wrong: The nectar of the gods isn't sweet ambrosia; it's wine. Yet deciding which wine is the best can be like trying to determine the one true religion. A trip to the wine country can be the start of a lifetime enjoyment of the fermented grape as you begin an education on how to savor this mysterious beverage.

Keep in mind that there are two types of California wines: varietals, made primarily from a particular kind of grape, such as cabernet sauvignon or zinfandel, and the lower-quality generics, wines blended from several different grapes and often named for a European wine region such as Burgundy.

To learn more about wines, you need to taste them. First, the look or appearance is important. Wine should be clear and brilliant, not cloudy. Consider the smell, or "nose" of the vintage, which includes the aroma or scent of the grapes themselves, and the "bouquet," the smell from fermentation and aging. Finally, consider the taste. Let the wine wash around your mouth for a moment and determine if it's sweet or dry, light-bodied (watery) or full-bodied (like milk), rough or mellow. But mainly, enjoy. Chat it up with the winery employees

*un*official **TIP**
If you do plan to visit the wine country in the fall, try to go during the week, not on weekends, to avoid the worst of the tourist crush. It's also a good idea to make lodging and dinner reservations weeks in advance.

behind the counter and you'll gain more insight (and maybe they'll pour some reserve vintages for your tasting enjoyment).

WHEN TO GO

THE BEST TIME TO VISIT THE WINE COUNTRY is in the fall, when the harvest occurs and the air is redolent with the aroma of fermenting wine. Depending on the weather, this can be anytime in September or October. Yet there are drawbacks to visiting at harvest time: traffic clogging the major roads in both valleys and a decrease in attention from winery employees, who are justifiably consumed with getting the grapes in.

Spring and summer are also prime times for visiting the wine country. And it shows—CA 29 in Napa Valley is often backed up on weekends. (You'll encounter a bit less traffic in Sonoma on spring and summer weekends.) Summer in the wine country can be quite hot and dry, so be sure to pack a sun hat and try to get an early start.

PURCHASING WINE AT A WINERY

QUESTION: CAN YOU GET GREAT DEALS on wine sold at wineries? The answer, by and large, is no. The sales rooms in the wineries aren't there to compete with retail liquor outlets in your hometown. As a result, the prices are pretty much what you would pay at home, give or take a couple of bucks a bottle. Of course, the selection is usually a lot better, and you'll also find special vintages available only at the winery.

Wine is also sold by the case at the wineries. Depending on the state you live in, you can have your purchase shipped home (you pay the shipping cost). States that allow shipments from the wineries are California, Colorado, Idaho, Illinois, Iowa, Maine, Minnesota, Missouri, Nebraska, Nevada, New Mexico, North Dakota, Oregon, Washington, Washington, D.C., West Virginia, Wisconsin, and

*un*official **TIP**
Winter, the rainy season, is a good time to visit; although the landscape isn't as colorful, there's a stark beauty to the valleys and mountains and a more laid-back atmosphere in the wineries. And the crowds are minimal.

Wyoming. If you don't live in one of these states, you're not completely out of luck. Make your purchase and ship it home yourself (tax laws limit shipments by wineries to the states listed above). The cost is about $40 a case, and the folks at the winery can suggest where to take your purchase and have it shipped.

GETTING THERE

THE WINE COUNTRY SPREADS NORTH from the top of San Francisco Bay in three parallel valleys, Napa, Russian River, and Sonoma. To get there by car, cross the Golden Gate Bridge on US 101 to CA 37 east. Then take CA 121 east; next, turn left onto CA 12 for Sonoma Valley or drive a few miles more and turn left onto CA 29, Napa Valley's main drag. For the Russian River Valley, it's just 101 all the way to Healdsburg. In nonrush-hour traffic, it's about an hour's drive from downtown San Francisco to each of the valleys.

NAPA VALLEY

THE HEART OF AMERICA'S WINE CULTURE is found in Napa Valley, a region with roots going back to the mid-19th century. The valley is defined by two rough-hewn mountain ranges, and vestiges of its tumultuous geologic past still bubble to the surface of the earth at hot springs in Calistoga and at (the other) Old Faithful Geyser.

Napa Valley is anchored in the south by the town of the same name, and visitors on a one-day outing should pass it by. Continue up CA 29 toward the villages of Yountville, Oakville, and Rutherford, where things start to get more interesting (and scenic). Saint Helena, the next town, is considered the heart of Napa's wine-growing region, while Calistoga, a resort town for more than 100 years, is its northern anchor.

unofficial **TIP**
You can make a drive in the valley more interesting by heading south from Calistoga on the more scenic Silverado Trail, which creates a circuit instead of an out-and-back excursion. While not nearly as commercial, this pleasant two-lane highway passes plenty of wineries. The crossroads between the two parallel roads are also scenic and worth exploring.

NAPA VALLEY DINING AND LODGING

WHETHER YOU ARE PLANNING A MARRIAGE PROPOSAL, a solo retreat, or a gathering of friends, there are top-rated dining and lodging options in all areas of the wine country. Be advised that many, perhaps most, lodging places in the valley require a two-night minimum, especially on weekends and in high season. Here are a few we recommend:

Napa Dining

- **Cuvée** (1650 Soscol Avenue, Napa; ☎ 707-224-2330; cuveenapa.com).
  Cuvée is located downtown next to River Terrace Inn. Try the potato-encrusted salmon and tuna tartare on the riverside terrace.
- **Jonesy's Famous Steak House** (2044 Airport Road, off Highway 29;
  ☎ 707-255-2003; jonesyssteakhouse.net).
  The locals will tell you to come out to the airport, where, for more than 60 years, a hand-cut filet mignon or sirloin for two next to a fine sunset strikes many as the pinnacle of affordable pleasure.

- **Oxbow Public Market** (610 and 644 First Street; ☎ 707-226-6529; oxbowpublicmarket.com).
  Near the river, Oxbow Public Market is a fun foodie hangout of high quality with Hog Island Oyster Co., Taylor's Automatic Refresher, Pica Pica Maize Kitchen with anything Venezuelan, Folio and other wine bars, Kara's Cupcakes, Tillerman Tea, Ritual Coffee Roasters, and so on.

Napa Lodging

- **The Napa Inn Bed and Breakfast** (1137 Warren Street; ☎ 707-257-1444; about $225–$285 per night).
  Candlelight breakfasts and fireplaces make this a very romantic spot.
- **River Terrace Inn** (1600 Soscol Avenue; ☎ 866-NAPA-FUN; riverterraceinn.com; from $129 per night).
  Well-appointed downtown inn with river views and top class restaurant.
- **White House Inn and Spa** (443 Brown Street; ☎ 707-254-9301; napawhitehouseinn.com; about $225–$425 per night).
  Sophisticated 19th-century mansion with modern amenities.

Yountville Dining

- **Brix Restaurant** (7377 Saint Helena Highway; ☎ 707-944-2749).
  Watch the renowned chef in the exhibition kitchen that is the centerpiece of the beautifully decorated space. The menu is cutting-edge.
- **The French Laundry** (6640 Washington Street; ☎ 707-944-2380; frenchlaundry.com).
  Redolent of roses and pure culinary artistry atop the plate. Book ahead.

Yountville Lodging

- **Bordeaux House** (6600 Washington Street; ☎ 707-944-2855; about $120–$230 per night).
  Centrally located B&B. Perfect for those who like to stroll around.

Saint Helena Dining

- **Martini House** (1245 Spring Street; ☎ 707-963-2233).
  The service, food, and wine are all world-class, and the decor is stunningly gorgeous. And yet it never intimidates.
- **Wine Spectator Greystone Restaurant** (2555 Main Street; ☎ 707-967-1010).
  Their "today's temptations," a selection of the chef's daily creations, is a big table pleaser. Fresh herbs from the garden accompany French dishes.

Saint Helena Lodging

- **Harvest Inn** (One Main Street; ☎ 707-963-9463; about $270–$550 per night).
  Private terraces look out onto eight acres of beautiful landscape and vineyards. One of the most serene places in the valley.

Calistoga Dining

- **Brannan's Grill** (1374 Lincoln Avenue; ☎ 707-942-2233; brannansgrill.com).
The fare here is "seasonal new American." The Liberty duck is a signature dish, as is the triple cream cheeseburger.
- **Calistoga Inn** (1250 Lincoln Avenue; ☎ 707-942-4104; calistogainn.com).
One of the happiest dining rooms in the valley, specializing in comfort food. When you've had it with the high-toned eating common in Napa, come here for meat and potatoes perfectly rendered.

Calistoga Lodging

- **Safari West Wildlife Preserve and Tent Camp** (3115 Porter Creek Road; ☎ 707-579-2551; safariwest.com; about $170–$295 per night).
African animals in this luxury safari tent camp create a unique experience.
- **Silver Rose Resort Winery** (351 Rosedale Road; ☎ 800-995-9381; silverrose.com; about $165–$305 per night).
A romantic hideaway nestled among vineyards with its own winery and spa. Go to the daily barrel tasting in the winery.

NAPA VALLEY WINERIES

WITH SOMETHING LIKE 240 WINERIES in Napa Valley (most of which are open to the public), part of the fun is touring on your own without a rigid itinerary; both of the valley's two major routes (CA 29 and, to the east, the Silverado Trail) pass dozens of estates.

- **Robert Mondavi Winery** (on CA 29, Oakville; ☎ 888-766-6328; robertmondaviwinery.com).
This is wine central for the Napa wine industry. The winery was founded in 1966, when there were only about six wineries in the valley with national distribution. Today Mondavi offers one of the best tours in the valley, and its Spanish mission–style architecture is a knockout. A retail area sells wines, T-shirts, and books. There is a tasting room where reserve wine is sold by the glass. Tours are offered on the hour.
- **Frog's Leap** (8815 Conn Creek Road; ☎ 707-963-4704; frogsleap.com).
In Rutherford, Frog's Leap was once a deserted "ghost winery." Today it sits beside 40 acres of organically grown merlot and sauvignon blanc vines. Built in 1884, the winery features a big red barn with period photos dotting the interior. Winery tours are by reservation only.
- **Ceja Vineyards in Carneros, Napa** (☎ 877-633-3954; cejavineyards.com).
Ceja is an inspiring story, not least because Amelia Ceja Moran's father-in-law, Pablo, originally came to Napa from Michoacán, Mexico, to work as a *bracero*, or immigrant grape picker. Now daughter Amelia is the first female Mexican-American president of a winery, and their 113 acres of prime Napa Valley vines produce award-winning nonmalolactic

chardonnays and fruit-driven pinots that stand out in the award lists. Tastings are held at 1248 First Street, Napa, Sunday–Friday, noon–6 p.m. and Saturday, noon–5 p.m.

- **Sterling Vineyards** (1111 Dunaweal Lane; ☎ 707-942-3300; **sterlingvineyards.com**).
  At the top of the valley in Calistoga, Sterling was built with tourists in mind. An aerial tram leads to a white cluster of Mediterranean monastic stucco buildings that rise from a bluff south of town. The 300-foot knoll features a visitor center, tasting room, self-guided winery tour, gift shop, and retail room.

- **Vincent Arroyo Winery** (just north of Calistoga off CA 29 at 2361 Glenwood Avenue; ☎ 707-942-6995; **vincentarroyo.com**).
  For a low-key, off-the-beaten-path, and virtually noncommercial winery experience, stop by Vincent Arroyo Winery. Joy, the resident canine, has a wine named after her—and the petite sirah is superb. Call for directions.

NAPA VALLEY ATTRACTIONS

- **Bale Grist Mill State Historic Park** (north of Saint Helena on CA 29; ☎ 707-963-2236).
  This is a flour mill operation that predates California statehood. Built in 1846 and restored to operating condition, the mill features a 36-foot wooden waterwheel and large millstones. On weekends, a miller grinds grain, and visitors can see baking demonstrations. You can also purchase flour from the mill.

- **kids** **Old Faithful Geyser** (☎ 707-942-6463; **oldfaithfulgeyser.com**).
  Outside of Calistoga (not to be confused with a similar geothermal phenomena at Yellowstone National Park in Wyoming), Old Faithful offers a spectacular show by nature as 350°F water shoots 60 feet in the air for three or four minutes. The cycle repeats about every 45 minutes, and kids love it. The setting is breathtakingly scenic, with Mount Saint Helena and the craggy Palisades Mountains in the background. The cost is a pricey $10 for adults, $7 for seniors, and $3 for children ages 6 to 12 (free for ages 5 and under); and no, you can't see this natural performance from the parking lot—tall bamboo blocks the view.

- **Petrified Forest** (☎ 707-942-6667; **petrifiedforest.org**).
  West of Calistoga, the Petrified Forest offers a pleasant walk in the woods past 3.5-million-year-old fallen giants—fossilized redwoods, some of them eight feet in diameter. Alas, they're not upright and some of the specimens were buried and now lie in pits. It's a pleasant and scenic place to walk off that second (or third, or fourth) glass of wine. Admission is $8 adults, $6 seniors and children ages 12 to 17, $3 children ages 3 to 11.

OUTDOOR FUN IN NAPA VALLEY

NAPA VALLEY IS FAMOUS FOR BICYCLING, with gentle hills, wide shoulders on the main roads, low traffic on the side roads, and great scenery. **Saint Helena Cyclery** (1156 Main Street, St. Helena; ☎ 707-963-7736) rents bikes, and the town is a good, centrally located starting point to enjoy a ride. The hourly rate is $10 for high-quality hybrid (city) bikes; included are a lock, water bottle, rear rack, and bag to carry your picnic supplies. The daily rate is $35. The shop also provides maps and tour information. No reservations are accepted; the shop is open daily.

Getaway Adventures (1117 Lincoln Avenue; ☎ 800-499-2453; **getawayadventures.com**) in Calistoga has been leading bicycling, hiking, kayaking, and other outdoor tours since 1992. Offering both bike rentals and van-supported, single-day and multiday trips in the wine country, Getaway specializes in what owner Randy Johnson calls a "stop and smell the zinfandel pace."

Try horseback riding in Napa Valley. **Napa Valley Trail Rides** (☎ 707-996-8566 or **napasonoma trailrides.com**) provides horses and guides April through October at Skyline Wilderness Park. Rates start at $90 for a two-hour ride. There's an additional $5 park entrance fee.

Beyond Calistoga is the wild and winding road up Mount Helena to **Robert Louis Stevenson State Park** (☎707-942-4575; **parks.ca.gov/?page_id=472**). This is where the sickly Scots writer honeymooned with the scandalous divorcee Fanny Osbourne in a deteriorating bunkhouse, and his experiences here were written about in *Silverado Squatters* with reference to early settler winemaking. The bunkhouse is gone, but you can hike to their trysting spot at the top of Highway 29 seven miles north of Calistoga, and visit the small **Silverado Museum** at the local library (☎ 707-963-3757; **silveradomuseum.org**).

unofficial **TIP**
Randy Johnson, owner of **Getaway Adventures,** advises bicycle enthusiasts who want to explore the fabled back roads of Napa and nearby Sonoma to ship their bikes to the wine country. "I don't recommend bringing it on the plane because it's liable to get lost. Most shops will reassemble your bike for little or no cost. If you're in the wine country for more than a few days and cycling is your main focus, there's no way you'll duplicate the experience on a rental bike."

HEALTH SPAS IN NAPA VALLEY

FOR FOLKS WHO PREFER THEIR ENTERTAINMENT closer to the ground, Calistoga is home to about a dozen health spas featuring hot mineral springs, heated pools, mud baths, steam baths, and massages. At **Calistoga Spa Hot Springs** (1006 Washington Street; ☎ 707-942-6269; **calistogaspa.com**) guests can steep in four different mineral pools (starting at $25) or indulge in a volcanic-ash mud bath with steam rinse ($58). The spa also has 57 rooms, ranging from $127 to $185 a night.

Dr. Wilkinson's Hot Springs Resort (1507 Lincoln Avenue, Calistoga; ☎ 707-942-4102; **drwilkinson.com**) offers a full range of soothing treatments, including mud baths, mineral whirlpool baths, blanket wraps, therapeutic massage, facials, acupressure face-lifts, and salt glow scrubs. The Works, a two-hour spa treatment, is $129; facials start at $99. The resort is open daily, and appointments are recommended.

NAPA VALLEY WINE TRAIN

ENJOY A RELAXING GOURMET DINING EXCURSION on one of several restored 1915 Pullman railroad cars that run between Napa and Saint Helena year-round. The **Napa Valley Wine Train** (☎ 800-427-4124 or 707-253-2111; **winetrain.com**) offers a three-hour, 36-mile excursion through Napa Valley. You won't stop at any wineries, but you can enjoy classic European cuisine with California overtones prepared on board. There are two seatings for lunch and dinner; passengers spend half the trip in a dining car and half in a lounge car.

The train ride plus a three- or four-course lunch or dinner is $119–184 a person and includes a glass of wine (more for paired wines); train fare and tips are included. A trip without a meal in the Silverado Deli Car, where there's an à la carte menu, costs $47.50. Reservations are required.

unofficial **TIP**
In the spring, summer, or fall, remember that traffic along CA 29 is relentless. Make it a point to request sleeping quarters that face the vineyards, not the highway.

AMERICAN SAFARI CRUISES

TAKE A TRIP UP THE NAPA AND PETALUMA rivers, slip beneath the Golden Gate Bridge, nose around the north bay shore, all in dreamy comfort with a glass of merlot in hand. Boarding in San Francisco, American Safari operates multiday/night cruises through the northern bay and the wine country. During the day onboard guides lead informative tours to wineries, galleries, and historical sites. At night passengers cruise and dine and, if you like, party! The bar and kitchen are open as long as you are awake. You can go on the day tours, or stay on board and soak in the hot tub, watch movies in the lounge, or just veg out. Call ☎ 888-862-8881 or visit **amsafari.com**.

VISITOR INFORMATION

YOU CAN GET MORE INFORMATION on wineries, accommodations, dining, and attractions by contacting the **Napa Valley Conference and Visitors Bureau** (1310 Napa Town Center, Napa; ☎ 707-226-7459; **napavalley.org**). Other visitor contacts in Napa Valley include the **Calistoga Chamber of Commerce** (1458 Lincoln Avenue, Calistoga: ☎ 707-942-6333; 9 a.m.–5 p.m., Monday–Friday; **calistogafun.com**) and the **St. Helena Chamber of Commerce** (1010

Main Street, Suite A, Saint Helena; ☎ 800-799-6456 or 707-963-4456; **sthelena.com**).

For help finding a room, especially in the harvest season when this can be challenging, try these free reservation services: **Napa Valley Reservations Unlimited** (☎ 800-251-6272; **napavalleyreservations. com**) and **Wine Country Concierge** (☎ 888-946-3289 or 707-252-4472; 9 a.m.–5:30 p.m., Monday–Friday; **winetrip.com**). Both keep a list of available rooms at bed-and-breakfasts and other lodging.

▌ SONOMA VALLEY

WHILE NAPA VALLEY IS UPSCALE AND ELEGANT, its next-door neighbor, Sonoma Valley, is overalls and corduroy. Unlike the eye-catching architecture in the wineries of Napa, the wineries here tend to be understated converted barns. Smaller producers whose families have grown grapes for generations still make wine in rustic buildings that are often beautiful in their simplicity.

Sonoma Valley is home to Northern California's earliest wine-making, with stunning old vineyards planted on rolling hills. The Spanish-era town of Sonoma is the cultural hub for Sonoma Valley, one of four major wine regions found in Sonoma County (the others are Alexander Valley, Russian River Valley, and Dry Creek Valley). A charming eight-acre plaza green in Sonoma built by General Mariano Guadalupe Vallejo in 1834 is a rural oasis surrounded by the area's best shops and restaurants.

Crescent-shaped Sonoma Valley curves between oak-covered mountain ranges and, most folks say, beats its neighbor hands-down on looks. The valley presents a crisscross pattern of vineyards; unlike the nearly endless procession of megawineries lining the highway at Napa, most wineries are tucked away on winding back roads.

SONOMA VALLEY WINERIES

ABOUT A HALF-DOZEN WINERIES are located a mile east of Sonoma Plaza, down East Napa Street. You could combine a visit to a few of these wineries with a tour of the Sonoma Mission, lunch on the plaza, and a side trip to an attraction outside of town.

Wineries outside town are located on small back roads, so get a map from the tourist office on the plaza; also, keep your eyes peeled for signposts leading to the vineyards (it's easy to miss a turn).

- **Sebastiani Winery** (☎ 707-933-3200; **sebastiani.com**).
  For sheer convenience, Sebastiani can't be beat. Free shuttle buses whisk visitors from Sonoma Plaza to the stone winery about a mile away. Professional guides lead tours throughout the day, and visitors learn about winemaking, see a large collection of hand-carved casks, and view a display of antique winemaking equipment.

- **Buena Vista Carneros Winery** (☎ 800-678-8504;
  buenavistacarneros.com).
  Not as convenient to reach but a must-see is this winery east of
  Sonoma. Set among towering trees and fountains, this is the birthplace
  of California's premium wine industry. Prior to its founding in 1857,
  California wine was made with lesser grapes, such as the black mission.
  BV is also the first winery to grow the zinfandel grape. It's also drop-
  dead gorgeous, with huge stone buildings, a mezzanine art gallery, and
  historical exhibits. History tours are given at 11 a.m. and 2 p.m. daily
  ($15 per person); free self-guided tours are available 10 a.m. to 5 p.m.;
  there's also a beautiful, terraced picnic area.

- **Ravenswood Winery** (☎ 888-669-4629; **ravenswood-wine.com**).
  Ravenswood, also east of Sonoma, is a small winery in a gorgeous
  hillside setting. Best known for its hearty zinfandels and its anti–wine
  snob attitude, the winery offers reservation-only tours led by knowledgeable and enthusiastic employees. Winery tours start daily at
  10:30 a.m. ($15 per person).

- **Benziger Family Winery** (☎ 707-935-4046 or 888-490-2739;
  benziger.com).
  Head up CA 12 a few miles to reach this winery in Glen Ellen. The winery specializes in premium estate and Sonoma County wines; they're
  also well known for their labels designed by famous artists. Guided
  tram tours ($15 per person) and self-guided tours are offered daily.

SONOMA VALLEY ATTRACTIONS

THE TOWN OF SONOMA is the site of the last and the northernmost
of the 21 missions established by Spain and Mexico, called El Camino
Real ("the king's highway"). Popularly called **Sonoma Mission,** El
Camino Real was founded in 1823 and features a stark, white facade
and, inside, a small museum. Across the street is the **Sonoma Barracks,**
built with Native American labor in the 1830s to house Mexican
troops. It's a two-story adobe structure with sweeping balconies and
a museum dedicated to California history.

Next door, the **Toscano Hotel** is furnished as it was in the 19th
century, with wood-burning stoves, brocade armchairs, and gambling
tables. These and other antique buildings around Sonoma Plaza are
part of **Sonoma State Historic Park** (☎ 707-938-1519; **napanet.net/
~sshpa**). The admission is $2 for adults and $1 for children and gets
you into all of the historic buildings. In the oak-studded plaza across
the street is a monument to the Bear Flag Revolt, located on the spot
where California was declared an independent republic in 1846 (and
remained so for 25 days).

Another excellent pit stop before heading to sights farther in
Sonoma is the **Sonoma Cheese Factory** (2 Spain Street on Sonoma
Plaza, Sonoma; ☎ 707-996-1000; **sonomajack.com**). You can choose

to picnic here on the cute benches that are scattered nearby, or simply browse inside and watch them slap, drain, and drag clumps of Jack and Cheddar through cheesecloth. There are plenty of samples on hand for you to try.

If Napa Valley is Robert Louis Stevenson country, then Sonoma belongs to Jack London. A world adventurer and the most famous American writer of his time (he died in 1916 at age 40), London bought a 1,400-acre ranch a few miles northwest of Glen Ellen; today it's **Jack London State Historic Park** (☎ 707-938-5216). Attractions include a museum with memorabilia, a reconstruction of London's office, and exhibits on the fascinating life of the author of *The Call of the Wild*. There's also a continuously running video of a film made about the writer just days before his death; silent, grainy, and shaky, the short home movie is haunting.

Almost as spooky are the ruins of London's mansion, **Wolf House** (☎ 707-938-5216; **parks.ca.gov**), which mysteriously burned to the ground in 1913 before the author could move in. It's a half-mile stroll through gorgeous woods to the stone ruins; you can also detour to visit the writer's simple grave. For fans of American literature, the park is a real find. Admission is $6 a car.

OUTDOOR FUN IN SONOMA VALLEY

SONOMA VALLEY IS 7 MILES WIDE and 17 miles long, and with its rolling hills, 13,000 acres of vineyards, and forested mountains on either side, the valley offers much to do outdoors. **Goodtime Touring Company** (18503 Sonoma Highway, Sonoma; ☎ 888-525-0453; **goodtimetouring.com**) rents bikes for exploring the valley's miles of paved, low-traffic back roads. Rentals are $25 a day, including a helmet, lock, cable, maps, and road service and repair during regular business hours. The shop also offers lunch rides, including food, for $125 a person (reservations required three days in advance).

The **Sonoma Cattle Company** (☎ 707-996-8566; **napasonomatrailrides.com**) offers trail rides at Skyline Wilderness Park. The guided tours last for approximately two hours in the Skyline Wilderness. Reservations are required, and rates start at $90 per person.

SHOPPING IN SONOMA VALLEY

THE CENTRAL PLAZA IN THE OLD SPANISH TOWN of Sonoma is where you'll find the best shops, including gourmet stores, boutiques, a designer lingerie shop, antique stores, and a brass shop. The **Mercado,** a small shopping center just east of the plaza, houses several stores with unusual items. **Baksheesh** (423 First Street West; ☎ 707-939-2847) features handmade gifts crafted by Third World artisans. **Milagros** (414 First Street East; ☎ 707-935-8566) sells Mexican folk art, home furnishings, masks, and wood carvings.

DINING IN SONOMA VALLEY

AS IT IS THROUGHOUT THE WINE COUNTRY, dining is serious business in Sonoma Valley. Dinner reservations should be made at least two weeks in advance in summer and fall. Top-rated dining establishments include:

- **Carneros Bistro & Wine Bar** (1325 Broadway, Sonoma; ☎ 707-931-2042; **thelodgeatsonoma.com**). Up-and-coming chef Janine Falva takes a liquid nitrogen torch to ice cream and makes a wonderful Dr Pepper–braised pork belly.
- **Doce Lunas** (8910 Sonoma Highway, Kenwood; ☎ 707-833-4000). Entrees include lamb shank with garlic and rosemary, osso bucco, and pork spareribs. Try the sticky toffee pudding for dessert.
- **Saddles Steakhouse** (29 East MacArthur Street, Sonoma; ☎ 707-933-3191). Boots and saddles are the main features of the decor. The crispy red cornmeal onion rings are a mighty fine prelude to a steak or prime rib.
- **Saffron** (13648 Arnold Drive, Glen Ellen; ☎ 707-938-4844). Chef-owner Christopher Dever, a grad of California Culinary Academy, changes menus frequently, and features local produce, seafood, and a touch of saffron.

Top-rated Accommodations in Sonoma Valley

- **The Fairmont Sonoma Mission Inn** (18140 Sonoma Highway, Boyes Hot Springs; ☎ 800-257-7544; **sonomamissioninn.com**). Rates are $329 to $700. This resort and spa in Sonoma County has a superb bar and restaurant.
- **MacArthur Place** (29 East MacArthur Street, Sonoma; ☎ 707-938-2929; **macarthurplace.com**). Rates are $299 to $475. This historic inn and spa on what was a sprawling ranch is now a getaway villa with a spa and restaurant.
- **Sonoma Creek Inn** (239 Boyes Boulevard, Boyes Hot Springs; ☎ 888-712-1289; **sonomacreekinn.com**). Rates are $79 to $169. This charming little place was designed to recall the days of the Great American Road Trip via roads such as Route 66.

VISITOR INFORMATION

FOR MORE INFORMATION ON SONOMA VALLEY, contact the **Sonoma County Tourism Program** (420 Aviation Boulevard, Suite 106; ☎ 707-565-5384; **sonomacounty.com**); ask for a free visitors guide. Maps and brochures are available at the small visitor center on the east side of Sonoma Plaza. For help locating a room, especially in the busy summer and fall, contact **Wine Country Concierge** (☎ 888-946-3289 or 707-252-4472; **winetrip.com**), which has a list of available rooms at bed-and-breakfasts and other lodging.

A Two-day Excursion in the Wine Country

AFTER TOURING NAPA VALLEY, head to Calistoga, where your room at one of the hot-springs resorts awaits you—say, Dr. Wilkinson's Hot Springs or Calistoga Spa Hot Springs (see "Health Spas in Napa Valley" on page 181). Rooms range from basic motel-style and cheap (think Janet Leigh in *Psycho*) to Victorian and expensive (including **Hideaway Cottages;** ☎ 707-942-4108), all with kitchens and some with living rooms. Take a mud bath in a composition of volcanic ash, imported peat, and naturally boiling mineral hot-springs water. Folks have been coming to Calistoga for about 150 years to experience this; now it's your turn. For about 90 minutes, you will simmer at a temperature of about 104°F, and your body will love you for it. A full treatment costs about $75.

The next day, drive to Sonoma Valley. Get there either by heading south through Napa Valley on the Silverado Trail to CA 121 and west to CA 12, or by taking a back road. If you go the back-road route, you can spend the second day of your wine-country visit driving south through the valley. When you get to the southern end of Sonoma Valley at the end of the day, you're less than an hour from San Francisco.

RUSSIAN RIVER VALLEY

NAPA VALLEY HAS GONE OFF THE MAP for some people due to crowds and costs. Sonoma is thought by some to be headed in Napa's direction. But the Russian River Valley (RRV) beckons those who want more wide-open spaces, cozy family-run tasting rooms, unpretentious hostelries, and what might just be the most beautiful scenery in the northern half of the state. And whereas Napa might be snooty, and Sonoma might be in siesta mode, RRV is always ready to party down. The old town square in Healdsburg is host to festivals year-round, as well as a bustling farmer's market and craft fairs. Down river at Guerneville you'll find party central for greater Sonoma County, as well as the annual Jazz festival. And if that isn't enough you can attend the annual blues fest. And did we mention the wine? And the dining?

> ✳ *unofficial* **TIP**
> The ideal way for visitors to tour the wine country is to spend a night. That way you can visit Napa and Sonoma valleys, share the driving (you'll need a car), split wine-imbibing chores with a friend, and have a more relaxed trip.

RUSSIAN RIVER VALLEY WINERIES

FROM HEALDSBURG you can head west along Westside Road or on Old Redwood Highway and visit wineries all the way to the mouth of the Russian River. Or you can head east on Route 128 through the

Alexander Valley, which will take you eventually to the Napa Valley. In spring the drive alone is worth it.

- **White Oak Vineyards and Winery** (7505 Highway 128, about six miles east of Healdsburg; ☎ 707-433-8429; **whiteoakwines.com**).
A cheery fire burns near the rich wood bar, complete with a brass rail for that frontier feel. The wines are of a generally lighter style than many Californians. They are very food friendly.

- **Rosenblum Tasting Room** (250 Center Street, Healdsburg; ☎ 707-431-1169; **rosenblumcellars.com**).
Rosenblum's winery is in, of all places, Healdsburg! They buy grapes from all over the state, truck them to Healdsburg, and there they make their best-selling zinfandel. But the tasting room in Alameda just off the town square is not to be missed. Rosenblum makes a great range of wines, in many styles. You can get a wine education here, what with the variety and the very helpful and knowledgeable staff.

- **Davis Bynum Winery** (8075 Westside Road, Healdsburg; ☎ 800-826-1073; **davisbynum.com**).
You'll have to watch closely for this one as you tool along the tree-lined road. But it's well worth the effort. It's a relatively small affair, but one with some of the most charming grounds and architecture. The picnic area is the best place ever for alfresco dining, and in summer the winery offers catered lunches there.

- **Korbel Champagne Cellars** (13250 River Road, Guerneville; ☎ 707-824-7000).
Possibly the largest and best laid out wine operation in the valley. If you're a fan of bubbly, you should definitely make a pilgrimage here.

DAY TRIPS *in and around the* BAY AREA

IF YOU'VE GOT THE TIME or if your visit to San Francisco is a repeat trip, consider exploring outside the city. Northern California is spectacularly scenic, and a trip to the area really isn't complete unless you take at least one day to venture beyond town limits.

From Marin County, Point Reyes, and the wine country to the north; to the East Bay cities of Oakland and Berkeley; to the villages, mountains, and coastal scenery to the south, there's plenty to see and do. A trip beyond hectic San Francisco can be a welcome respite from the heavy traffic and round-the-clock activity in the city's livelier neighborhoods. Here are a few suggestions for day trips beyond the city's limits.

MARIN COUNTY

Sausalito and Tiburon

For folks on a tight schedule or without a car, these two bayside villages across from San Francisco are destinations well worth visiting. And with ferry service available from Fisherman's Wharf, it's a short trip that combines a refreshing boat ride with spectacular scenery. Neither destination requires a full day.

SAUSALITO Once a gritty little fishing village full of bars and bordellos, Sausalito today is decidedly more upscale. Think French Riviera, not Barbary Coast. With approximately 7,500 residents (not all of them cash-flush yuppies), the town still manages to hang on to a faintly bohemian air, although most of its attractions are upscale boutiques and restaurants. The main drag is Bridgeway, where sleek, Lycra-clad bicyclists, in-line skaters, and joggers flash by along the waterfront.

Caledonia Street, one block inland, has a wider selection of cafes and shops. Half a mile north of town, the tourist onslaught is less evident and visitors can see the town's well-known ad-hoc community of houseboats and barges. But most folks come just to shop or hang out in a bar or waterfront restaurant. And that's not a bad idea: The views of the bay and the San Francisco skyline are great.

The **Blue & Gold Fleet** provides ferry service to Sausalito, a 30-minute boat ride from Pier 41 in Fisherman's Wharf. One-way tickets are $11 for adults and $6.75 for children ages 5 to 11. For departure times and information, call ☎ 415-773-1188, or visit **blueandgoldfleet.com.**

Golden Gate Ferries depart from the Ferry Building at the foot of Market Street. One-way tickets are $7.85 for adults, $3.90 for seniors and the physically disabled, and $3.90 for children ages 6 to 18. For schedules, call ☎ 415-923-2000, or visit **goldengateferry.org.** If you're driving, take US 101 north across the Golden Gate Bridge; then take the first right, the Alexander Avenue exit. Alexander becomes Bridgeway in Sausalito.

TIBURON Less touristy but more upscale is the best way to describe Tiburon, which is frequently compared to a New England fishing village. (Maybe so, if the New Englanders are wealthy and commute to high-rise offices by

---

unofficial TIP

If you have a room in San Francisco and you're heading to the wine country, don't check out; the hassle of repeatedly packing and unpacking is too time consuming. Reserve a room at a hot-springs resort in Calistoga at the north end of the valley, pack the minimum, and get out of town. It's definitely hedonistic— and expensive—and totally in character with this vacation within a vacation.

unofficial TIP

For a local feel, try the **The No Name Bar** (757 Bridgeway; ☎ 415-332-1392), a no-frills Sausalito institution. It's smoky, small, and funky, with great Irish coffee and decent martinis. But don't try to order any froufrou drinks here. The regulars have been known to heckle those who do.

ferry every day.) Visitors can soak up this heady ambience in pricey waterfront restaurants and bars, then stroll the gorgeous promenade. Tiburon is also the most convenient stepping-off point to nearby Angel Island, where you can hike or bike on 12 miles of trails in the state park. A good lunch or dinner destination in Tiburon is **Guaymas** (5 Main Street; ☎ 415-435-6300), with authentic Mexican cuisine and a panoramic view of San Francisco and the bay.

Ferry service to Tiburon is provided by the **Blue & Gold Fleet** from Pier 41 in Fisherman's Wharf; one-way tickets are $11 for adults and $6.75 for children. For departure times and information, call ☎ 415-773-1188 or visit **blueandgoldfleet.com**. By car, take US 101 north across the Golden Gate Bridge to the Tiburon/CA 131 Exit, then follow Tiburon Boulevard all the way to downtown. It's about a 40-minute drive from San Francisco.

Angel Island

Over the years Angel Island has been a prison, a notorious quarantine station for immigrants, a missile base, and a favorite site for duels. Today the largest island in San Francisco Bay is a state park; it's a terrific destination for a picnic, stroll, hike, or mountain-bike ride, or simply a place to get away from traffic, phones, and television.

unofficial **TIP**
Tram tours and bike and kayak rentals are closed from late November to mid-March.

It's even possible to camp here. Angel Island, located across Raccoon Strait from Tiburon, is accessible only by ferry. Visitors arrive at a small marina abutting a huge lawn area equipped with picnic tables, benches, barbecue pits, and restrooms. There's also a small store, cafe, gift shop, and mountain bike rental concession. Tram tours highlight the island's history. You can also rent a stable, two-person sea kayak and see the island from the water. There are 12 miles of trails on the wooded island, and cyclists and hikers can explore the recently restored and doleful barracks of the former immigration center (called the Ellis Island of the West) with walls inscribed with sad Chinese poems.

Blue & Gold Fleet ferries to Angel Island depart from Pier 41 in Fisherman's Wharf daily in the summer and on weekends in the winter. One way is $9 for adults, $5.75 for children ages 6 to 12; free for children age 5 and under. For departure times and information, call ☎ 415-773-1188. The **Angel Island–Tiburon Ferry** operates daily in summer and on weekends in winter. Round-trip fares are $13.50 for adults, $11.50 for children ages 6 to 12, $3.50 for children ages 3 to 5, and children under age 2 are free. A $1 fee is charged for bicycles. For a schedule and directions, call ☎ 415-435-2131, or visit **angelislandferry.com.**

unofficial **TIP**
To save money, rent a bike in San Francisco and bring it on the ferry.

Marin Headlands

Aside from offering the postcard views of San Francisco, the **Headlands,** as they are affectionately called, is *the* playground for San Franciscans. You can park for free and within ten minutes of leaving your hotel or home, you can put boot to the dirt on tons of hiking trails. Or if you prefer fat-tire skirmishes, there are also plenty of mountain-biking opportunities—you would expect nothing less from the place that is said to be the origination of mountain biking as we know it. The Headlands, largely undeveloped terrain, are dominated by 2,800-foot Mount Tamalpais. The coastline here is more rugged than on the San Francisco side of the bridge, and it's a Mecca for nature lovers. Visitors are treated to great views of the city, ocean, and bay; hiking trails and rugged beaches; and the concrete remains of old forts and gun emplacements standing guard over the Golden Gate (no shots were ever fired in anger).

While physically close to San Francisco, the Headlands seem a world apart. Windswept ridges, protected valleys, and beaches offer the best of nature, but they're less than an hour's drive from the hectic city. The hillsides near the Golden Gate provide magnificent views of the entrance of the bay. The Marin Headlands Visitor Center (☎ 415-331-1540) is open daily from 9:30 a.m. to 4:30 p.m. and offers detailed information on enjoying the rugged countryside.

The Headlands, part of Golden Gate National Recreation Area, have abundant wildlife—deer, hawks, and seabirds are common, and bobcats and whales are sometimes sighted. Fog is heaviest in the summer in areas closer to the Golden Gate, and ocean swimming is always dangerous.

unofficial **TIP**
Always use caution when walking on the rocky coastline, where unwary hikers can be swept away by large waves or trapped by the incoming tide.

Major attractions include the Point Bonita Lighthouse (open spring through fall on weekends), Muir and Stinson beaches, Muir Woods, Mount Tamalpais, and Olema Valley. Hikers, cyclists, and equestrians can pick up detailed trail maps and information at the visitor center. And don't forget to bring your lunch: There are few places to eat in the Headlands.

To reach the Marin Headlands and the visitor center, drive north on US 101 across the Golden Gate Bridge, take the first exit (Alexander Avenue), bear left, and follow the road up the hill. Go through the one-way tunnel (there's a traffic light), which puts you on Bunker Road and leads to the visitor center, Rodeo Beach, and the Point Bonita Lighthouse.

unofficial **TIP**
Rugged and steep trails crisscross the Headlands; remember to bring drinking water and stay off the cliffs, which are prone to landslides and covered with poison oak.

Marin County

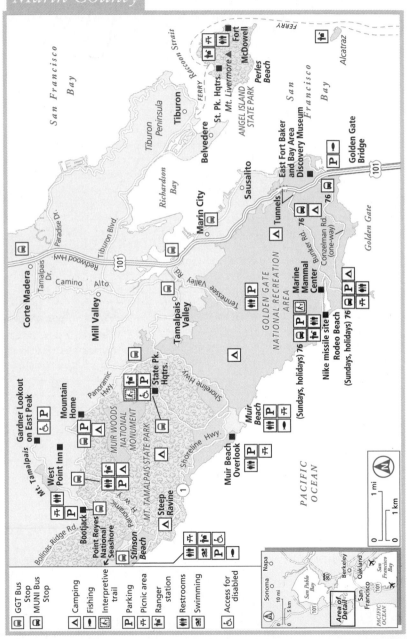

THE EAST BAY

ACROSS THE BAY BRIDGE FROM SAN FRANCISCO, two cities offer startling contrasts to the chic town on the peninsula. Oakland is a gritty, blue-collar city that earns its livelihood with shipping and transportation to and from the Port of Oakland, dominated by huge cranes. The city spreads north toward Berkeley, a college town that's home to a campus of the University of California and a fascinating cross-section of aging hippies and radicals, hustling young Republicans, students, and Nobel Prize laureates. Gertrude Stein and Jack London both grew up in the city at about the same time, albeit at different ends of the social spectrum.

unofficial TIP
A good lunch option on Telegraph Avenue is **Cafe Mattina** (2442 Telegraph Avenue, Berkeley; ☎ 510-849-4592; **cafemattina.com**), a crowded sandwich, salad, and soup place that serves great sandwiches on homemade bread.

Oakland

Located just over the Bay Bridge, or via BART, Oakland is the workhorse of the Bay Area, with one of the busiest ports on the West Coast. Yet in spite of its blue-collar reputation and Ms. Stein's oft-quoted withering reference to her hometown ("There is no there there"), Oakland has a few tricks up its sleeve that make the town worth a visit. Not the least of its attributes is the weather, often mild and sunny, while San Francisco is draped in chilly fog.

Leading the list is the **Oakland Museum of California** (1000 Oak Street at Tenth Street; ☎ 510-238-2200; **museumca.org;** open Wednesday, Saturday, and Sunday, 11 a.m.–5 p.m.; Thursday–Friday, 11 a.m.–8 p.m.). In May 2010, the museum—which focuses on the history, natural sciences, and culture of California—reopened. The museum also possesses a superb collection of the works of Californian photographers such as Ansel Adams and Dorothea Lange. Other things to do in Oakland include riding a genuine Italian gondola on downtown **Lake Merritt,** taking the kids to **Children's Fairyland** (on the north shore of Lake Merritt), or ogling the restored Art Deco interior of the **Oakland Paramount Theatre** (2025 Broadway; ☎ 510-893-2300; **paramounttheatre. com**). Tours of the beautiful theater are offered on the first and third Saturdays of the month (excluding holidays), starting at 10 a.m. and lasting two hours. The cost is $5 a person; no reservations are necessary. Children must be 10 years of age and accompanied by an adult.

Jack London Square is Oakland's version of Fisherman's Wharf and shamelessly plays up the city's connection with the writer, who grew up along the city's waterfront. The complex of boutiques and eateries is just about as tacky as its cousin across the bay—and about as far from "the call of the wild" as you can get. However, Jack

London's favorite watering hole is still pouring whiskey and gin and the famous local "steam beer." Find it at the south end of the square, **Heinholds First and Last Chance Saloon,** ☎ 510-839-6761. Some better eating options include **Bay Wolf** (3853 Piedmont Avenue; ☎ 510-655-6004), the city's most venerable and revered restaurant, serving Mediterranean-inspired California cuisine; and **Oliveto** (5655 College Avenue; ☎ 510-547-5356), owned by an alumnus of the famous Chez Panisse, serving the rustic fare of northern Italy.

To reach Oakland's Jack London Square by car, take the Bay Bridge to I-880 to Broadway, turn south, and go to the end. You'll find ample parking in the underground garage. On BART, get off at the 12th Street station and walk south along Broadway about a half mile (or grab the No. 51A bus to the foot of Broadway). To get to Lake Merritt, cross the Bay Bridge and follow signs to downtown Oakland and exit at Grand Avenue South. To get to the Oakland Museum, take I-580 to I-980 and exit at Jackson Street. Via BART, get off at the Lake Merritt station, a block south of the museum.

Berkeley

Probably more than any other town in the country, Berkeley conjures up images of the rebellious 1960s, when students of the University of California, Berkeley, led the protests against the Vietnam War. At times, virtual full-scale battles were fought almost daily between protestors and cops, both on campus and in the streets of the surrounding town (most notably in People's Park, off of Telegraph Avenue).

These days, things are more sedate in this college town, although admirers and detractors still refer to it as "Berzerkley" and the "People's Republic of Berkeley." While student angst is down, the progressive impulse lingers and is best experienced on **Telegraph Avenue,** south of the campus. On the four blocks or so closest to the university, it's a regular street fair filled with vendors selling handmade jewelry, tie-dyed T-shirts, and bumper stickers promoting leftist causes and lifestyles. The sidewalks on both sides of Telegraph Avenue are usually jammed with students, tourists, bearded academics, homeless people, and gray-haired hippies. Coffeehouses, restaurants, art and crafts boutiques, head shops, and excellent used-book-and-record stores line the street; order a latte and enjoy the endless procession of interesting people who throng the street most afternoons and evenings.

The selection of restaurants is truly intimidating in Berkeley; every ethnic cuisine in the world, it seems, is represented. The only thing you won't find is a steak house. And you'll find only three fast-food restaurants in the whole city.

The 31,000-student **University of California** campus is noted for its academic excellence and its 15 Nobel Prize winners. Several museums on campus are worth exploring, including the **Berkeley Art Museum** and, for kids, the **Lawrence Hall of Science** with an incredible view (easiest to reach if you've got a car).

To reach Berkeley, about ten miles northeast of San Francisco, take the Bay Bridge, follow I-80 east to the University Avenue exit, and follow the wide street until you hit the campus. To get to Telegraph Avenue, turn right on Oxford and drive three blocks to Durant. Turn left and drive three blocks and make a right onto Telegraph.

Parking close to campus is notoriously difficult, so try to arrive early on weekends and get a space in one of the many private parking lots located just off campus. Try **Center Street Garage** (2025 Center Street; ☎ 510-843-1788) or the **Allston Parking Facility** (2061 Allston Way; ☎ 510-981-9443). Another option is **BART,** which has a Berkeley station one block from the campus.

POINT REYES NATIONAL SEASHORE

THIS 85,000-ACRE PARK OF SANDY BEACH and scrubland is on a geologic "island" located about an hour's drive north of San Francisco. Windswept and ruggedly beautiful, Point Reyes is a wildlife paradise. Shorebirds, seabirds, invertebrates, and marine mammals thrive on this peninsula, which juts into the cold waters of the Pacific just west of the San Andreas Fault.

unofficial **TIP**
When visiting Point Reyes, wear hiking boots and be prepared for changes in the weather.

In 1579, English explorer Sir Francis Drake is said to have anchored his ship, the *Golden Hind,* in Drakes Bay, on the southern coast of the peninsula. There's evidence he careened his ship to make repairs and stayed about five weeks before sailing westward across the Pacific on his round-the-world voyage of discovery. Nearly 200 years passed before settlers arrived. After the United States' conquest of California, the land was broken into dozens of dairy ranches, and beef and dairy cattle have roamed the brushy flatlands of Point Reyes ever since.

Touring Suggestions

The best place to begin a visit is the **Bear Valley Visitor Center** with its extensive collection of exhibits, specimens, and artifacts. The center is open from 9 a.m. to 5 p.m. on weekdays and 8 a.m. to 5 p.m. on weekends and holidays. You can pick up maps and tide tables and get advice from a ranger on places to hike, picnic, and view wildlife. Ranger-led tours are also offered on a varying schedule, and several hiking trails are accessible from the visitor center. For more information, call ☎ 415-464-5100, or visit **nps.gov/pore.**

From December through March, **gray whales** make their 10,000-mile migration between the Bering Sea and Baja California, swimming past Point Reyes. The best spot to view the whales is from **Point Reyes Lighthouse,** which has limited parking. Because of the popularity of whale watching on weekends, the park provides shuttles to the

unofficial **TIP**
A better bet for whale watching on Point Reyes is to come early on a week-day to avoid the crowds. Dress warmly—it's usually cold and windy—and bring binoculars and a camera with a telephoto lens.

lighthouse from Bear Valley.

Nearly 500 tule elk roam Point Reyes (reintroduced following an absence of more than 100 years). The **Tule Elk Preserve** is at the northern tip of the park, and you're apt to spot some elk on a walk down the moderately difficult **Tomales Point Trail.** Other good places to view wildlife include **Fivebrooks Pond** (waterfowl), the wetlands of Limantour (ducks), and the promontory overlooking Chimney Rock (sea lions, harbor seals, and seabirds).

A Car Tour

Point Reyes is worth a full day or more of exploration. But if your time is limited, you can get a good sampling of what Point Reyes has to offer in about half a day—mostly through the windows of your car. From the visitor center, continue on Bear Valley Road to Sir Francis Drake Boulevard, pass through the village of Inverness, and follow signs for the Point Reyes Lighthouse. For a spectacular view of the entire peninsula, turn right on Mount Vision Road, a steep and twisty paved lane that rises to almost 1,300 feet before it dead-ends.

Return to Sir Francis Drake Boulevard and turn left to continue toward the lighthouse. On the right are two beaches ripe for exploration (but not swimming; the waters are cold and dangerous) before you reach the **Lighthouse Visitor Center.** The lighthouse offers a spectacularly scenic view of the ocean and the tip of the peninsula; it's just under a half-mile walk from the parking area, followed by a 300-step descent down the cliff to the lighthouse. The visitor center is open Thursday through Monday, 10 a.m. to 4:30 p.m. (call ☎ 415-669-1534 or visit **ptreyeslight.com/lthouse.html**).

After you visit the lighthouse, backtrack by car to the turn to **Chimney Rock** (a good place to view wildlife) or continue driving to the mainland. To reach the elk reserve, turn left about two miles past Mount Vision Road, and then turn left on Pierce Point Road and drive to **Pierce Point Ranch,** a renovated dairy ranch with a self-guided trail through the historic complex. Then hike down the **Tomales Point Trail,** and you may spot some elk.

Food, Lodging, and Directions

You'll find restaurants, cafes, delicatessens, general stores, and bakeries in the nearby villages of Olema, Point Reyes Station, Inverness, and Marshall; a cafe is located at Drakes Beach inside the park at the Kenneth C. Patrick Visitor Center (☎ 415-669-1250). Inns and bed-and-breakfasts are also nearby. **Point Reyes Lodging** (call ☎ 800-539-1872 or visit **ptreyes.com**) specializes in booking cottages and small inns in the Point Reyes area.

To reach Point Reyes from San Francisco, cross the Golden Gate Bridge and stay on US 101 north. Exit at Sir Francis Drake Boulevard and head west; it's about a 20-mile drive (much of it through congested Marin County, although the scenery improves dramatically around Taylor State Park) to CA 1 at Olema. From here it's about a one-minute drive to the Bear Valley Visitor Center. A longer and more scenic route is CA 1, reached from US 101 in Sausalito.

unofficial **TIP**
If you want to make a weekend of your visit to Point Reyes, consider camping. Backcountry camping is limited to four areas maintained by the park service: Coast, Sky, Glenn, and Wildcat camps.

SOUTH OF SAN FRANCISCO

CA 1 IS A SPECTACULARLY SCENIC ROAD that stretches south of San Francisco to Carmel, winding past cliffs and coves, pocket beaches, lighthouses, and historic towns and villages. Visitors to San Francisco can enjoy driving along the coast for about 75 miles to Santa Cruz. From there, turn inland and north to return along the crest of the Santa Cruz Mountains for scenery from a higher perspective.

A Scenic Car Tour

For a full day of scenic car touring, get started around 9 a.m. and head to the Great Highway (south of Cliff House and at the western end of Golden Gate Park) and drive south. Bring picnic supplies or grab a bite in one of the many towns along the way. You'll have time to get out and enjoy many of the attractions, but don't linger too long if you want to get back before evening. And don't forget to bring a state highway map in case of detours or to devise your own circuit route).

The coastline of the San Francisco peninsula south of the city is largely undeveloped. Bluffs protect the many nudist beaches from prying eyes and make excellent launching points for hang gliders, as you can see at Fort Funston. Skyline Boulevard follows the coast past Daly City, a community of ticky-tacky housing that's probably the ugliest thing most folks will see on a visit to San Francisco.

But things improve after you reach CA 1. San Pedro Beach marks the end of San Francisco's suburban sprawl and is a popular surfing beach. Continually eroding cliffs offer great scenery from the road but don't handle the presence of the highway well, and the road is washed away regularly in winter storms. Gray Whale Cove State Beach is clothing-optional and, in spite of its name, isn't an especially good place for whale watching.

Half Moon Bay and a Scenic Side Trip

Main Street in Half Moon Bay features a shopping area with gift shops, bookstores, a saddlery, jewelry stores, bars, restaurants, and art galleries. There's also a full-size grocery store that sells sandwiches and picnic supplies. For a view of the town's eponymous bay, go to **Half Moon Bay State Beach** (Kelly Avenue from CA 1; ☎ 650-726-8819). Parking is $2 to $4.

For a contrast to the surf, continue south on CA 1 and turn right onto Higgins-Purisima Creek Road. The narrow paved road winds and climbs for eight miles through ranch country before returning to CA 1. Turn left to continue south. **Pigeon Point Lighthouse** (☎ 650-879-2120; **parksca.gov**) is in a spectacular coastal setting, and free guided half-hour historical tours of the lighthouse grounds are available from 10 a.m. to 4 p.m., Friday through Sunday, except on rainy days. Children under age 8 must be chaperoned by an adult; reservations are requested.

Elephant Seals

For sightings of some unusual wildlife, stop at **Año Nuevo State Reserve** just south of Pigeon Point. Huge northern elephant seals come ashore from early December through March to give birth and mate. Bull seals often engage in battles for breeding access to the females.

Popular guided walks to view the wildlife activity are offered by trained naturalists from December 15 through March 31. Advance reservations are recommended for the two-hour, three-mile (round-trip) hike. The cost is $7 per person, plus $10 for parking. Call ☎ 800-444-7275 between 8 a.m. and 5 p.m. to reserve a spot; for additional information, call ☎ 650-879-2025. Juvenile seals are present year-round, and you can walk the trail unescorted to see them; in the winter, when 300 to 400 adults appear, visitors must be on guided tours.

Just north of Santa Cruz is **Wilder Ranch State Park,** a cultural preserve with adobe farm buildings from the Spanish Mission era and buildings from the late 19th century. Docent-led tours are offered on weekends; there are also 28 miles of trails for hiking.

Mountain Scenery and Giant Redwoods

Grab something to eat in Santa Cruz, but on a one-day outing there isn't enough time to explore this resort city, famous for its boardwalk and roller coaster. It's a good turnaround point; you can head back to San Francisco through the mountains. Follow signs to CA 9 north, a scenic road that twists and turns through mountains, forests, and the towns of Felton and Boulder Creek, where you turn left onto CA 236.

At **Big Basin Redwoods State Park** you don't need to get out of the car to be overwhelmed by the huge trees. This forest of giant redwoods is more impressive than the stand at Muir Woods in Marin. But get out of the car anyway to explore the park headquarters and a small museum. Then continue toward San Francisco, 67 miles away. CA 236 gets narrow and twisty before returning to CA 9; turn left to continue north.

Next, turn left on CA 35 (Skyline Drive) for more incredible scenery; views are of the Pacific on the left and San Francisco Bay on the right.

Do You Know the Way to San Jose?

TOP THREE DAYS OUT FOR BIG AND BIGGER KIDS

San Jose has to be terrific for some things, yes? It is. **Raging Waters** (Off Highways 101 or 280 not far past the city, 2333 South White Road, San Jose; ☎ 408-238-9900; **rwsplash.com**) takes the top thrills award for the young and restless—and plain hot: lots of ways to get soaked at high speed.

What child can resist a full-scale replica of a mummy's tomb and at least two real mummies? Not this one. **The Rosicrucian Egyptian Museum and Planetarium** (1664 Park Avenue, San Jose; ☎ 408-947-3636; **egyptian museum.org**) is an enchantingly odd re-creation of the Temple of Amon at Karnak, buried in the suburbs of San Jose an hour south of San Francisco down US 101. Their Junior Archaeologist program features "the most fun graduation ceremony this side of the Nile!" and their planetarium traces the history of telescopes and even dabbles in Stephen Hawking quotes and Mithraic mysteries.

While San Jose's **Tech Museum of Innovation** (201 South Market Street, San Jose; ☎ 408-294-8324; **thetech.org**) lacks the Exploratorium's cachet and isn't next to the Golden Gate Bridge either, it *does* have a bigger dome: an IMAX dome, plus the Wall of Musical Buttons and Musical Seats exhibits, a building full of inventions, and then some. The huge Hackworth IMAX Dome Theater replays *Under the Sea* and *Star Trek* a couple of times a day.

Runner up is the **Hiller Aviation Museum** (601 Skyway Road, San Carlos at the airport; ☎ 650-654-0200; hiller.org)—a fascinating collection of vintage and futuristic aircraft.

There are pricier attractions near San Jose, but these three knock the socks right off all the others. For a nearer day trip with the shorter set, try Pacifica down Highway 1, a sweet seaside spot en route to Half Moon Bay, with a multitude of child attractions from Frontierland Park nestling in the hills off Linda Mar Boulevard, to a terrific bowling alley, Sea Bowl on Coast Highway.

There are plenty of overlooks where you can stop and enjoy the vistas. Next, take CA 92/35 (a right turn) and then turn left onto CA 35, which leads to I-80, a 20-mile stretch of some of the most scenic interstate highway in the country—and, in a few minutes, San Francisco.

Beyond the **BAY AREA**

MANY OUTSTANDING DESTINATIONS are too far from San Francisco for a day trip but close enough to consider for an overnight trek. Leading the list is **Yosemite National Park** (☎ 209-372-0200; **nps.gov/ yose**), a wilderness of evergreen forests, alpine meadows, and sheer walls of granite. Spectacular Yosemite Valley features soaring cliffs, plunging waterfalls, gigantic trees, and rugged canyons. The park is about 200 miles from San Francisco, or about a five-hour drive. World-famous Yosemite attracts about 4 million visitors a year. Peak tourist season is June to August, and crowds diminish in the fall. Advance lodging reservations are essential year-round.

Lake Tahoe (Lake Tahoe Visitors Authority, ☎ 800-288-2463 or 530-544-5050; **bluelaketahoe.com**), about 200 miles from the city, is rated one of the most beautiful bodies of water in the world. It lies in an alpine bowl on the border between Nevada and California and is surrounded by forested peaks. Tahoe features resorts, gambling, hiking trails, lakeside cabins, historic architecture, and special events such as golf tournaments.

South of the city down the Pacific coast is **Monterey Bay,** with Santa Cruz at its northern end and Monterey at its southern end. The first capital of California, Monterey was established by the Spanish in 1770; many Spanish, Mexican, and early American buildings still stand. South of Monterey is **Carmel-by-the-Sea,** a pretty hillside town founded as an artists' colony in the early 20th century. The **Monterey Peninsula** (Monterey Peninsula Visitors and Convention Bureau, ☎ 831-649-1770) is about a two-hour drive from San Francisco.

North of San Francisco along the rugged coastline is **Mendocino** (Discover Mendocino County, ☎ 866-466-3636; **gomendo.com**), a small picturesque town that was once a logging village. In the 1950s it became a haven for artists and was so well restored that the town was declared a historic monument. Inland from town are forests of giant redwood trees. The town itself is tucked away on a rocky promontory above the Pacific and retains the charm of its logging days. Mendocino is about 125 miles from San Francisco; a leisurely drive up the spectacular coast can take as long as ten hours one-way.

 # ATTRACTION PROFILES

FISHERMAN'S WHARF AND BEYOND

LET'S FACE IT. THERE ARE JUST SOME PLACES that you need to see when you visit San Francisco. You'll want to show off those obligatory shots of you in the "I escaped Alcatraz" T-shirt, or standing next to the barking sea lions at Pier 39 near Fisherman's Wharf. But the beauty of this city is that the untourist track is just as interesting and colors a vivid picture of San Francisco's creative, innovative, and quaint spirit. The streets of San Francisco offer even the cheapskate a brisk walk up a hill and a lovely view of the bridge.

This book provides you with a comprehensive guide to San Francisco's top attractions, including some "coulda left San Fran without it" sights. We give you enough information so that you can choose the places you want to see, and we've organized attractions by neighborhood so you can plan your visit logically, without spending valuable time crisscrossing the city.

unofficial **TIP**
"San Francisco has only one drawback—'tis hard to leave."
—Rudyard Kipling

A TIME-SAVING CHART

BECAUSE OF THE WIDE RANGE OF ATTRACTIONS in and around San Francisco—from a hall filled with sculptures by Rodin at the Legion of Honor, to historic ships that you can explore at Hyde Street Pier in Fisherman's Wharf—we've provided a chart on page 206 to help you prioritize your touring. In it, you'll find the location, authors' rating from one star (skip it) to five stars (not to be missed), and a brief description of the attraction. Each attraction is individually profiled below.

 Alcatraz Island ★★★★★

APPEAL BY AGE	PRESCHOOL ★★★	GRADE SCHOOL ★★★★★	TEENS ★★★★★
YOUNG ADULTS ★★★★★		OVER 30 ★★★★★	SENIORS ★★★★★

In San Francisco Bay, North Beach; to get there, take the Alcatraz Cruise from Pier 33 (in Fisherman's Wharf, near Powell); ☎ 415-981-7625 or 415-561-4900; alcatrazcruises.com or nps.gov/alcatraz

Type of attraction The island in San Francisco Bay is best known for its maximum-security, minimum-privilege federal penitentiary, with a cell-house tour, trails, museum exhibits, wildflowers, wildlife, and spectacular views of the San Francisco skyline. Audio and guided tours. **Admission** $26 for adults and children over age 12, $24.50 for seniors, and $16 for children ages 5–11. Family rate for two adults and two children is $79. Night tour is $33 for adults, $32 for children ages 12–17, $30.50 for seniors, and $19.50 for children ages 5–11. **Hours** Cruises leave about every half hour throughout the day, beginning at 9 a.m. and ending at 1:55 p.m., except for the night tour. Closed on Thanksgiving, Christmas, and New Year's Day. Special evening tours are also available. **When to go** Try to make the first cruise of the day; it's less crowded, and the weather is generally better and less windy. **Special comments** Weather in the middle of San Francisco Bay is unpredictable; shorts and T-shirts are not a good idea. You have to hike steep grades to get to the cell house; wear sturdy shoes. There's no food service on the island, but you can buy a snack on the ferry. Restrooms, telephones, drinking water, and soft-drink vending machines are available on the island. **Authors' rating** A San Francisco and U.S. landmark that shouldn't be missed; the audio tour of the cell house is outstanding. ★★★★★. **How much**

continued on page 204

Attractions around Town

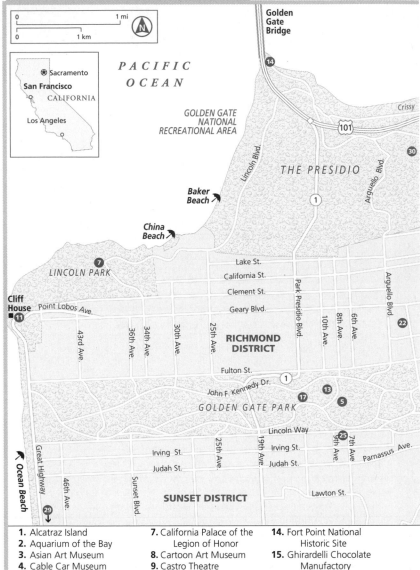

0 ——— 1 mi
0 ——— 1 km

N

Sacramento
San Francisco
CALIFORNIA
Los Angeles

*PACIFIC
OCEAN*

**Golden
Gate
Bridge**

14

*GOLDEN GATE
NATIONAL
RECREATIONAL AREA*

Crissy

101

THE PRESIDIO

Lincoln Blvd.

Arguello Blvd.

30

*Baker
Beach* ↗

1

*China
Beach* ↗

Lake St.

LINCOLN PARK

California St.

Clement St.

Park Presidio Blvd.

Arguello Blvd.

7

**Cliff
House**   Point Lobos Ave.

Geary Blvd.

25th Ave.

43rd Ave.
36th Ave.
34th Ave.
30th Ave.

10th Ave.
8th Ave.
6th Ave.

22

11

**RICHMOND
DISTRICT**

Fulton St.

John F. Kennedy Dr.

1

17   13

5

GOLDEN GATE PARK

Lincoln Way

25

Great Highway

Irving St.

25th Ave.

19th Ave.

Irving St.
Judah St.

9th Ave
7th Ave

Parnassus Ave.

Judah St.

Ocean Beach ↗

46th Ave.

Sunset Blvd.

SUNSET DISTRICT

Lawton St.

29

1. Alcatraz Island
2. Aquarium of the Bay
3. Asian Art Museum
4. Cable Car Museum
5. California Academy of
   Sciences
6. California Historical
   Society

7. California Palace of the
   Legion of Honor
8. Cartoon Art Museum
9. Castro Theatre
10. City Lights Bookstore
11. Cliff House
12. Coit Tower
13. de Young Museum

14. Fort Point National
    Historic Site
15. Ghirardelli Chocolate
    Manufactory
16. Haas-Lilienthal House
17. Japanese Tea Garden
18. Mission Dolores
19. Museum of Craft and Folk Art

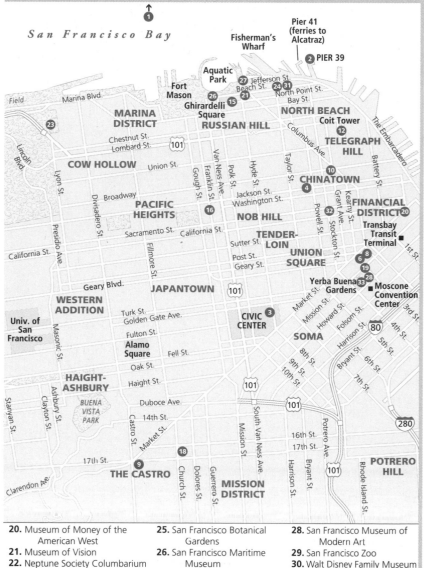

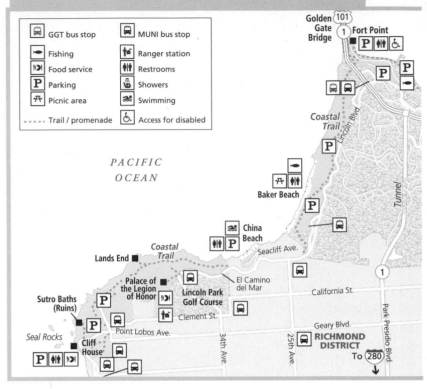

Golden Gate National Recreation Area

continued from page 201

time to allow At least 2 hours; bring a lunch and you can easily spend half a day on the Rock. You can catch any returning ferry back to Fisherman's Wharf; a schedule is posted at the dock.

DESCRIPTION AND COMMENTS One of San Francisco's most popular destinations, Alcatraz Island offers a close-up look at a federal prison long off-limits to the public, and it has captured almost everyone's imagination. Virtually no one is disappointed.

The island is best known for its sinister reputation. It was called the Rock, Hell-catraz, and Uncle Sam's Devil Island by the hardened criminals who lived there during its federal penitentiary years (1934–1963). Most of the 1,545 men who did time were deemed to be escape risks and troublemakers. Only a handful were truly notorious; the list includes Al "Scarface" Capone, Doc Barker, Alvin "Creepy" Karpis, George "Machine Gun" Kelly, and Robert Stroud, the Birdman of

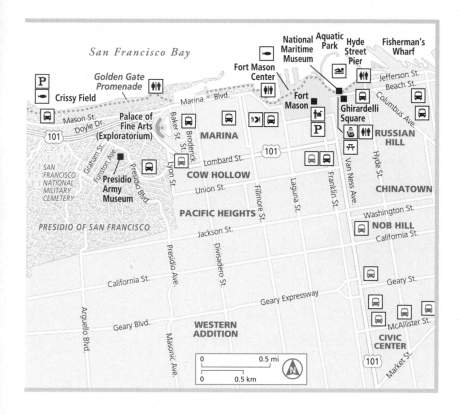

Alcatraz (who actually conducted his famous bird studies as a prisoner in another federal pen, Leavenworth).

On the cell-house tour you'll see why a sentence to Alcatraz was rated hard time by prisoners. The cells are tiny (inmates were confined 23 hours a day), and extreme precautions were taken to control the prisoners, prevent escapes, and quell riots. In the dining room, considered potentially the most dangerous place in the prison, tear-gas canisters are visible in the ceiling. Some cells are also furnished as they were when Alcatraz was a working prison, with cots, personal items (such as packets of cigarette tobacco, brushes, and books), and a few pictures.

In stark contrast to the deteriorating prison, Alcatraz (Spanish for "pelican") is a place of natural beauty. On trails around the island, visitors can see flowers such as fuchsias, geraniums, jade trees, agave, and periwinkles, as well as outstanding views of San Francisco and Oakland. Tide pools teem with marine life, including crabs and sea stars.

TOURING TIPS Make advance reservations; Alcatraz is very popular. During peak summer and holiday periods, ferry rides to the island are booked

San Francisco Attractions

NAME	TYPE	AUTHOR'S RATING
CHINATOWN		
Cable Car Museum	History and real machinery	★★½
CIVIC CENTER		
Asian Art Museum	Largest collection in West	★★½
Haas-Lilienthal House	Handsome Victorian-era mansion	★★★
FINANCIAL DISTRICT		
Museum of Money of the American West	History of the West	★★
Wells Fargo History Museum	Pony Express and more	★★½
MARINA DISTRICT		
Ghirardelli Chocolate Manufactory and Soda Fountain	Demonstrates how chocolate is made	★★★
Mexican Museum	Temporary exhibits until relocation	N/A
Museum of Craft and Folk Art	Small gallery	N/A
Palace of Fine Arts/ Exploratorium	Classical rotunda, science museum	★★★½
San Francisco Maritime Museum	Seafaring exhibits	★★★½
San Francisco Maritime National Historical Park–Hyde Street Pier	19th-century ships that visitors can board	★★★★
NORTH BEACH		
Alcatraz Island	Island prison/pelican destination	★★★★★
Aquarium of the Bay	Commercial aquarium	★★
City Lights Bookstore	Iconic Beat bookstore	★★★★
Coit Tower	View from Telegraph Hill plus fine WPA murals	★★★★½
Museum of Vision	Museum of all things eyes	★★
Ripley's Believe It or Not! Museum	Museum of the odd and unusual	★
Wax Museum at Fisherman's Wharf	250 wax figures	★
SOMA/MISSION DISTRICT		
California Historical Society	History exhibits	★★
Cartoon Art Museum	Gallery of cartoons	★★★★
Castro Theatre	Landmark repertory screen	★★★★½
Mission Dolores	Oldest city church plus museum and cemetery	★★★
San Francisco Museum of Modern Art	Huge modern art gallery	★★★★★

AUTHOR'S NAME	TYPE	RATING
SOMA/MISSION DISTRICT (CONTINUED)		
Yerba Buena Gardens/ Center for the Arts	Art complex and gardens plus ice rink, carousel	★★★
RICHMOND/SUNSET DISTRICT		
California Academy of Sciences	Planetarium, aquarium, rainforest, roof garden	★★★★★
California Palace of the Legion of Honor	Museum of ancient and European art in park	★★★★
Cliff House	Oceanside tourist landmark	★★★★
de Young Museum	San Francisco's oldest fine arts gallery	★★★★½
Fort Point National Historic Site	Civil War–era fort, great views	★★★★★
Japanese Tea Garden	Pagoda garden in park	★★★★
Neptune Society Columbarium	Cemetery in copper-domed memorial	★★★
San Francisco Botanical Garden	70 acres of gardens	★★★
San Francisco Zoo	Largest zoo in northern California	★★★
Walt Disney Family Museum	A museum for Mickey's creator	★★
MARIN HEADLANDS TO POINT REYES		
Marine Mammal Center	Rehabilitation and education center	★★★★
Mount Tamalpais–East Peak	Panoramic hike with railcar	★★★½
Muir Woods National Monument	Grove of coastal redwoods	★★★★
BERKELEY		
Berkeley Art Museum and Pacific Film Archive	Eclectic art on UC–Berkeley campus	★★★
Berkeley Rose Garden	Landmark with terraced gardens	★★★
Lawrence Hall of Science	Hands-on children's science museum	★
Phoebe A. Hearst Museum of Anthropology	Native American artifacts	★½
OAKLAND		
Niles Essanay Silent Film Museum	A former silent movie studios	★★★★
Oakland Museum of California	Museum of state's ecology	★★★½

as much as a week in advance. The down side to advance reservations is that no refunds are given if the weather is lousy. But Alcatraz in bad weather is better than no Alcatraz at all.

After disembarking and listening to a park ranger's introductory remarks, go inside for the 13-minute video presentation that gives a good overview of the island's history (including the takeover by Native Americans that began on November 20, 1969, and lasted 19 months). Make note of the schedule of outdoor ranger walks offered daily that discuss the island's military history, famous inmates, escapes, natural history, and the Native American occupation. Try to catch the first ferry of the day (strongly recommended). Take the audio cell-house tour while it's not too crowded; after the video ends, walk up to the cell house for the 35-minute audio tour narrated by guards and inmates. Their recounting of daily life is vivid, blunt, and often scary. After the tour, go on a ranger-led tour or hike some of the trails to discover the natural beauty and abundant wildlife (hawks, ravens, geese, finches, and hummingbirds) on this evolving ecological preserve.

OTHER THINGS TO DO NEARBY UnderWater World, the San Francisco Maritime Museum, and historic ships at Hyde Pier are nearby. Take ferries to Angel Island and Tiburon or a cruise on San Francisco Bay. Or rent a bike and ride the Golden Gate Promenade to the famous bridge with the same name; it's three-and-a-half miles one way.

kids Aquarium of the Bay ★★

APPEAL BY AGE	PRESCHOOL ★★★★	GRADE SCHOOL ★★★★★	TEENS ★★★★
YOUNG ADULTS ★★★★		OVER 30 ★★★	SENIORS ★★★

Pier 39, San Francisco 94133; in Fisherman's Wharf, North Beach;
☎ **415-623-5300; aquariumofthebay.com**

Type of attraction An aquarium where visitors are transported on a moving walkway through a clear tunnel to view thousands of marine animals. A self-guided audio tour. **Admission** $15.95 for adults, $8 for seniors age 65 and over and children ages 3–11. Free for kids age 2 and younger. Family rate for two adults and either one or two children is $39.95. **Hours** Monday–Thursday, 10 a.m.–6 p.m.; Friday–Sunday, 10 a.m.–7 p.m.; summer hours, 9 a.m.–8 p.m. Closed on Christmas Day. **When to go** Anytime. **Special comments** Don't refuse the audio-tour gizmo handed out before the tour begins—it will make a lot more sense. Not for claustrophobics or folks who get sweaty hands in highway tunnels. **Author's rating** While it's great to see a shark or ray glide overhead, this is a small attraction—and too expensive. ★★. **How much time to allow** 40 minutes to 1 hour.

DESCRIPTION AND COMMENTS Aquarium of the Bay offers a different take on the massive fish emporiums that are sprouting like mushrooms across America's urban landscape. Instead of walking past windows and peering into large tanks, you'll find yourself transported on a moving walkway through tanks in clear tunnels where you look at fish and other marine creatures on both sides and overhead. Sharks pass directly over you—only inches away. The emphasis is on the marine life of northern California; the audio tour provides a commentary as you're transported through the aquarium, which also has a "touch tank" for the kids.

TOURING TIPS On weekends and holidays, the line for the audio tour contraption and the elevator can get long. But once under way, the line moves briskly. If a tour bus pulls in front of you and disgorges 40 tourists, go window-shopping on Pier 39 to kill some time until the line goes down (it won't take long).

OTHER THINGS TO DO NEARBY Walk on Pier 41 (where the Alcatraz ferry departs) and wave at the barking sea lions that congregate just offshore. If you bought tickets in advance, take the ferry to Alcatraz. Or visit the San Francisco Maritime Museum and the Museum of the City of San Francisco (in the Cannery).

Asian Art Museum ★★½

APPEAL BY AGE	PRESCHOOL ★	GRADE SCHOOL ★★	TEENS ★★
YOUNG ADULTS ★★★	OVER 30 ★★★		SENIORS ★★★½

200 Larkin Street, Civic Center Plaza, San Francisco 94102 (in the former main library, across from City Hall); ☎ 415-581-3500; asianart.org

Type of attraction One of the largest museums in the Western world devoted exclusively to Asian art. A self-guided tour. **Admission** $12 for adults, $8 for seniors, and $7 for college students with ID and children ages 13–17; children age 12 and under free; $5 after 5 p.m. on Thursday; free to everyone on the first Sunday of the month. **Hours** Tuesday–Sunday, 10 a.m.–5 p.m.; until 9 p.m. on Thursday; closed on Monday. **When to go** Anytime. **Special comments** Go on Thursday nights when admission is $5 after 5 p.m. and check out the latest special exhibition, or browse through 2,500 treasures in the galleries with performances, demonstrations, and special lectures showcasing the art and culture from all corners of Asia. **Author's rating** Fabulous and exotic art—but a little cold. ★★½. **How much time to allow** 2 hours.

DESCRIPTION AND COMMENTS The Asian Art Museum's collection is built around art donated by industrialist Avery Brundage. Today its holdings include nearly 2,500 art objects spanning 6,000 years of history and representing more than 40 Asian countries.

There are 29,000 square feet of gallery space enhanced with state-of-the-art displays and programs. The museum's three floors include exhibits of furniture, jade, scrolls, ceramics, tapestries, Buddhist temple bells, jewelry, folding screens, books and manuscripts, armor, swords, knives, and baskets. The first floor features temporary exhibition space and an excellent cafe.

TOURING TIPS Take the escalator to the third floor to a series of small exhibit rooms that start with Indian art, progress to art from the Persian world, and finish with West Asian art. On the second floor, walk across the enclosed bridge for spectacular Samsung Hall. Free docent-led tours are offered at 11 a.m. and 1 p.m. daily; a Highlights of China tour at 11:30 a.m. daily; and architectural tours of the building at noon and 2:30 p.m. daily (with an additional tour at 6 p.m. on Thursday).

OTHER THINGS TO DO NEARBY Across the plaza is City Hall with a spectacular rotunda. Take the elevator to the fourth floor for the best view.

Berkeley Art Museum/Pacific Film Archive ★★★

APPEAL BY AGE	PRESCHOOL ★	GRADE SCHOOL ★★	TEENS ★★★
YOUNG ADULTS ★★★		OVER 30 ★★★	SENIORS ★★★

2626 Bancroft Way, Berkeley 94720 (on the University of California at Berkeley campus); ☎ 510-642-0808; bampfa.berkeley.edu

Type of attraction One of the largest university art museums in the world. A self-guided tour. **Admission** $9.50 for adults; $6.50 for seniors and children ages 13–17, non–UC Berkeley students, and disabled persons; free for Berkeley students and children age 12 and under. Free to everyone on the first Thursday of the month. **Hours** Wednesday, Friday–Sunday, 11 a.m.–5 p.m.; Thursday, 11 a.m.–7 p.m. Closed Monday, Tuesday, and major holidays. **When to go** Anytime. **Special comments** The museum's seven galleries are linked by carpeted ramps and stairs, and an elevator is available. **Author's rating** It's not on par with the Legion of Honor or the de Young Museum across the bay, but it's still a major collection in a visually striking building. ★★★. **How much time to allow** 1–2 hours.

DESCRIPTION AND COMMENTS In seven linked, spiraling galleries, the Berkeley Art Museum displays its collections of Asian art, Western art from the Renaissance to the present, and the work of 20th-century painter Hans Hoffmann. The other four galleries are devoted to exhibitions that change about four times a year.

TOURING TIPS Parking in Berkeley is notoriously bad; arrive as early as possible to find a space in one of the public lots near the campus. A better bet from San Francisco is BART; the Berkeley station is located at Center and Shattuck streets, and it's a short walk east to the campus. The museum store offers a wide range of books and periodicals. Café Muse features better-than-average museum dining.

OTHER THINGS TO DO NEARBY The Hearst Museum of Anthropology is across Bancroft Way on the ground floor of Kroeber Hall. Museum of Paleontology houses one of the largest and oldest collections of fossils in North America. It's free and open Monday–Friday, noon–4 p.m., and it's located in the Valley Life Sciences Building on campus. The Lawrence Hall of Science, a hands-on science museum, has a spectacular view of the Bay Area. Drive or take a University Hill Service Shuttle to get there.

Berkeley Rose Garden ★★★

APPEAL BY AGE	PRESCHOOL ★★	GRADE SCHOOL ★★	TEENS ★★★
YOUNG ADULTS ★★★		OVER 30 ★★★	SENIORS ★★

At Euclid and Eunice streets, in Berkeley; ci.berkeley.ca.us

Type of attraction A 3.6-acre Berkeley landmark with terraces of roses. **Admission** Free. **Hours** From dawn to dusk. **When to go** Late spring and early summer are the best times to catch the roses in full bloom. **Author's rating** ★★★. **How much time to allow** A half hour would be sufficient, but stay longer if you are looking for a quiet place to relax.

DESCRIPTION AND COMMENTS A terraced amphitheater redolent with the smell of roses. The garden was built between 1933 and 1937 and has been maintained by a volunteer group, the Friends of the Berkeley Garden. It is no wonder that it's a popular wedding place—it is truly an inspiration and romantic stop.

TOURING TIPS Come when the sun is setting. The views of the city skyline and the sparkling bay are breathtaking. Park your car along the side of the street and get out and walk. There is no formal place to park.

OTHER THINGS TO DO NEARBY Visit the Essig Museum of Entomology on the Berkeley campus, room 211 of Wellman Hall, ☎ 510-643-0804.

Cable Car Museum ★★½

APPEAL BY AGE	PRESCHOOL ★★½	GRADE SCHOOL ★★★	TEENS ★★
YOUNG ADULTS ★★½		OVER 30 ★★½	SENIORS ★★★

1201 Mason Street (at Washington Street), San Francisco 94108 (Nob Hill); ☎ 415-474-1887; cablecarmuseum.org

Type of attraction A building housing the machinery that moves the city's famed cable cars; museum features photographs, old cable cars, signposts, mechanical devices, and a video explaining the system. A self-guided tour. **Admission** Free. **Hours** April–September, daily, 10 a.m.–6 p.m.; rest of the year, daily, 10 a.m.–5 p.m. Closed on major holidays. **When to go** Anytime. **Special comments** Go up to the mezzanine viewing area or down to an enclosed area where you can see inside the system. **Author's rating** It's fun to watch the machinery that pulls San Francisco's famed cable cars, and the price is right. ★★½. **How much time to allow** 30 minutes to 1 hour.

DESCRIPTION AND COMMENTS When you try to envision what makes San Francisco's cable cars go, think horizontal elevator. Here you can see the machinery that moves the cables pulling the cars on the four lines of the only cable-car operation in the world. You'll also see an old cable car, 19th-century photos, some of the machinery that grips and releases the cable running under the streets, and a video. It's noisy and smells like a factory. A must for railroad buffs and most children.

TOURING TIPS If you're frustrated in your attempts to board the jam-packed cable cars, at least stop in to satisfy your curiosity about how it works.

OTHER THINGS TO DO NEARBY Chinatown is only two blocks away. Three blocks south at California and Mason streets is the Mark Hopkins Inter-Continental Hotel, famous for its Top of the Mark lounge.

California Academy of Sciences   ★★★★★

| APPEAL BY AGE   PRESCHOOL ★★★★★   GRADE SCHOOL ★★★★★   TEENS ★★★★★ |
| YOUNG ADULTS ★★★★   OVER 30 ★★★★   SENIORS ★★★★ |

55 Music Concourse Drive, Golden Gate Park, San Francisco 94118;
☎ **415-379-8000; calacademy.org.**

Type of attraction A natural history museum, aquarium, and planetarium. A self-guided tour. **Admission** $25 for adults; $20 for seniors, students, and children ages 12–17; $15 for children ages 4–11. Free the third Wednesday of the month. **Hours** Monday–Saturday, 9:30 a.m.–5 p.m.; Sunday, 11 a.m.–5 p.m. Closed Thanksgiving and Christmas. **When to go** To avoid boisterous school groups on school days, go in the afternoon. Penguins are fed at 10:30 a.m. and 3:30 p.m.; a coral reef dive is at 11:30 a.m. and 2:30 p.m. **Special comments** Tickets to the planetarium are first-come, first-served, and limited seating is available. It's popular, so get tickets early. **Author's rating** Kids go nuts over this place. The aquarium and rain forest are their favorites. ★★★★★. **How much time to allow** 2 hours.

DESCRIPTION AND COMMENTS Since its grand reopening in October 2008, the California Academy of Sciences has introduced NightLife, a night-in-the-museum-evoking disco and nightclub with cocktails and live music. The West's oldest scientific institution (founded in 1853) continues to entice and educate visitors with its green living roof, its fascinating rain forest, lower-floor mangrove swamp, coral reef, and reptile pool with an ancient, crowd-favorite albino alligator. Its cafe is fun and cheap; the Moss Room restaurant is fancy and not cheap.

TOURING TIPS The planetarium is its biggest draw, so head to it first to line up for passes. At the Philippine Coral Reef, listen to a diver explain how the reef works. At the Discovery Tidepool, kids can actually touch some of the creatures, and the rain forest even has birds and butterflies flying around.

OTHER THINGS TO DO NEARBY The Japanese Tea Garden is across the Music Concourse. Behind the natural history museum is Shakespeare Garden, an oasis of quiet that could prove beneficial to adults after a hectic tour of the California Academy of Sciences. Gardeners—and just about everyone else—will enjoy the San Francisco Botanical Garden, 70 acres of plants and gardens just past the Japanese Tea Garden. If it's a nice day, drive or walk to Stow Lake and rent a rowboat ($13 an hour) or a bike (starting at $5 an hour). You'll find a snack bar at Stow Lake.

California Historical Society ★★

APPEAL BY AGE	PRESCHOOL ★	GRADE SCHOOL ★	TEENS ★★
YOUNG ADULTS ★★		OVER 30 ★★	SENIORS ★★★

678 Mission Street, San Francisco 94105; in SoMa near Third Street; ☎ 415-357-1848; californiahistoricalsociety.org.

Type of attraction A gallery displaying temporary exhibitions from the society's collection of paintings, watercolors, drawings, lithographs, photographs, and artifacts. A self-guided tour. **Admission** $3 for adults, $1 for seniors and students, free for children age 6 and under with an adult. **Hours** Wednesday–Saturday, noon–4:30 p.m. Closed Saturday–Tuesday and major holidays. **When to go** Anytime. **Special comments** The gallery is all on one level. **Author's rating** The airy central gallery is beautiful, but its small size relegates this museum to the fill-in category. ★★. **How much time to allow** 1 hour.

DESCRIPTION AND COMMENTS Founded in 1871, the California Historical Society moved to this location in 1995. Items from the society's vast collection rotate about four times a year, so what you see on your visit won't be what we saw on ours. But it's a very attractive gallery and worth a stop, especially for first-time visitors to California looking for insight into the state's fascinating history.

TOURING TIPS Don't miss the storefront bookstore, which features books about the people, places, and events of California.

OTHER THINGS TO DO NEARBY Yerba Buena Gardens is a block away, and just beyond that is the San Francisco Museum of Modern Art.

California Palace of the Legion of Honor ★★★★

APPEAL BY AGE	PRESCHOOL ★★	GRADE SCHOOL ★★★	TEENS ★★★
YOUNG ADULTS ★★★★	°	OVER 30 ★★★★	SENIORS ★★★★

In the northwest corner of San Francisco at 34th Avenue and Clement Street, in Lincoln Park; ☎ 415-863-3330 (recorded information); ☎ 415-750-3600 (main switchboard); legionofhonor.org

Type of attraction A museum of ancient and European art housed in a reproduction of an 18th-century French palace; a spectacularly scenic setting. Guided tours available. **Admission** $10 for adults, $7 for seniors, $6 for children ages 12–17; children age 11 and under, free. A $2 discount is given to holders of Muni bus transfers; free to all the first Tuesday of the month. **Hours** Tuesday–Sunday, 9:30 a.m.–5:15 p.m. Closed Monday and Thanksgiving, Christmas, and New Year's Day. **When to go** Anytime. **Special comments** Admission to the Legion of Honor also gives you free, same-day admission to the de Young Museum in Golden Gate Park. **Author's rating** Rather highbrow in tone, but the building and much of the art and physical location are spectacular. ★★★★. **How much time to allow** 2 hours.

DESCRIPTION AND COMMENTS Built in the 1920s and dedicated to the thousands of California servicemen who died in France in World War I, the Legion of Honor is visually stunning. Visitors enter through a magnificent courtyard dominated by an original cast of Auguste Rodin's *The Thinker*. The building is in an eye-popping location overlooking the Golden Gate Bridge and the Marin Headlands; its design was inspired by the Palais de la Legion d'Honneur in Paris, built in 1786. If it all looks vaguely familiar, that's because you've watched *Vertigo* too many times on late-night TV; it's where Kim Novak went to gaze upon the portrait of Carlotta (a movie prop you won't find in the museum).

Inside is an impressive collection of ancient and European art, as well as extensive collections of furniture, silver, and ceramics, covering 4,000 years. Heavy hitters include Rodin, Monet, Manet, Degas, Reynolds, Rubens, Rembrandt, Van Gogh, Dalí, Picasso, Renoir, and Seurat.

TOURING TIPS Most of the art is on the main level, and ancient art and ceramics are on the lower-level terrace. Probably the most popular galleries are the two dedicated to Rodin; these stunning rooms are just past the central rotunda on the main level. Galleries 1 through 9 (to the left as you face the entrance) feature medieval, Renaissance, and 18th-century art; galleries 11 through 19 (to the right) contain art from the 18th through the early 20th centuries. Gallery 10 is the main Auguste Rodin gallery. Special exhibits are held in Rosekrans Court, housed under a glass structure that floods the galleries with natural light.

Parking is abundant around the museum. For public transportation, from Union Square, take the No. 38 bus to 33rd and Clement streets; transfer to the No. 18 bus (and save $2 on admission) or walk uphill to the museum.

OTHER THINGS TO DO NEARBY Cliff House, a mile or so south on the coast, provides fantastic views of the Pacific, Marin coast, and Seal Rocks—home base for sea lions, a variety of marine birds, migratory whales, and frolicking dolphins. Bring binoculars. There are two restaurants here: the casual Bistro and the upscale Sutro's, both complete with spectacular views. To the north are Fort Point and the Golden Gate Bridge; to the south are Ocean Beach (the water is cold and dangerous) and Golden Gate Park.

Cartoon Art Museum ★★★★

APPEAL BY AGE	PRESCHOOL ★★	GRADE SCHOOL ★★★	TEENS ★★★
YOUNG ADULTS ★★★	OVER 30 ★★★★		SENIORS ★★★

655 Mission Street, between New Montgomery and Third Street in SoMa; ☎ 415-CARTOON or 415-227-8666; cartoonart.org

Type of attraction The only museum west of the Mississippi dedicated to the preservation, collection, and exhibition of original cartoon art. A self-guided tour. Admission $6 adults, $4 students and seniors, $2 children ages 6–12. First

Tuesday of the month is "pay what you wish" day. **Hours** Tuesday–Sunday, 11 a.m.–5 p.m.; closed Mondays and all major holidays. **When to go** Anytime. **Special comments** While there's lots here to delight children, cartoons of an explicitly adult nature are placed in rooms restricted to visitors age 18 and older. Cartoons are displayed at adult eye level. Call ahead to make sure the museum isn't closed due to installation of a new exhibit. **Author's rating** How can you resist a cartoon art museum? ★★★★. **How much time to allow** 1–2 hours.

DESCRIPTION AND COMMENTS From at least the turn of the 20th century, the Bay Area has been home to a healthy population of professional cartoonists. Well-known cartoonists spotlighted in this small museum over the years include Scott Adams (*Dilbert*), Bill Griffith (*Zippy the Pinhead*), Morrie Turner (*Wee Pals*), Phil Frank (*Farley*), and Paul Mavrides (*The Fabulous Furry Freak Brothers*). Many of the cartoons hail from San Francisco's underground "comix" movement of the late 1960s and early 1970s. Needless to say, most of the art is satirical, scathingly funny, and often risqué. Wonderful, in other words.

TOURING TIPS The new space is larger than the previous space, so exhibits have been expanded. There are more than three major shows a year.

OTHER THINGS TO DO NEARBY Yerba Buena Gardens and Center for the Arts is a block down Mission Street, and the Museum of Modern Art is on Third Street on the other side of Yerba Buena Gardens. The California Historical Society has a small gallery at 678 Mission Street.

Castro Theatre ★★★★½

APPEAL BY AGE	PRESCHOOL ★	GRADE SCHOOL ★	TEENS ★
YOUNG ADULTS ★★	OVER 30 ★★★★	SENIORS ★★★★	

429 Castro Street, San Francisco 94144; in the Mission District; ☎ 415-621-6120 is the information line with a recording of current movies; to reach the box office directly call 415-621-6350; thecastrotheatre.com

Type of attraction A city landmark that stands as an icon to one of the world's most prominent gay neighborhoods. **Admission** Movie tickets unless otherwise noted are $10 for adults. Matinee tickets and tickets for senior citizens and children under age 12 are $7.50. *Note:* cash only payments. **Hours** The box office opens an hour before the first movie of the day and only sells tickets for the current day. **When to go** Anytime. **Special comments** The theater is easily spotted; just look for the massive marquee on Castro Street—easily becoming as recognizable as the Transamerica Building. **Author's rating** From classic movies like *Funny Girl* to its interesting architecture, it's a nice way to either see the inside of a neighborhood icon or step in for a night at the movies. ★★★★½. **How much time to allow** Movies usually run about 2 hours.

DESCRIPTION AND COMMENTS This historic landmark on Castro Street can't make up its mind whether its motif is Roman, Asian, Arabic, or that

Miami-style Art Deco. After a major renovation, the theater still boasts an interior and exterior that remain true to its 1920s and 1930s heyday and the vision of designer Timothy Pflueger (the same guy who gave the city the Paramount Theater in Oakland, the former I. Magnin building on Union Square, 450 Sutter, and the Pacific Telephone Building on New Montgomery).

The ceiling and light fixtures are elaborate, as is most of the interior. Be sure to get to the theater early to take in the splendor of this classic space. The small theater feels a bit like an opera house, with the help of the huge Wurlitzer organ that begins each movie. It rises out of the theater pit just before show time, leading the audience in a series of classic show tunes followed by "San Francisco."

TOURING TIPS The hooting and hollering and sing-alongs of the audience bring down the house! Loads of fun, especially if they are showing such campy classics as *My Fair Lady* or *Return of the Body Snatchers*.

 ## City Lights Bookstore ★★★★

APPEAL BY AGE	PRESCHOOL —	GRADE SCHOOL —	TEENS —
YOUNG ADULTS ★★	OVER 30 ★★★		SENIORS ★★★★

261 Columbus Avenue (off Broadway in North Beach), San Francisco 94133; ☎ 415-362-8193; citylights.com

Type of attraction A Beat bookstore made famous by its Beat inhabitants such as Jack Kerouac, Allen Ginsberg, and owner/artist Lawrence Ferlinghetti. **Admission** Free (all new poetry welcome!). **Hours** Daily, 10 a.m.–midnight. **When to go** Anytime. **Special comments** If you see a gray-haired and bearded man standing in the aisles, chances are it is the Beat owner and poet laureate himself—Lawrence Ferlinghetti. **Author's rating** You'll feel a sudden surge of creative energy just by reading the titles of the new releases from independent literary forces. The Beat Generation held such a spell over the city, and this bookstore is one of the few landmarks left. A definite stop. ★★★★. **How much time to allow** Anywhere from a few minutes to purchase a postcard to all day, browsing the poetry and literature stacked on the wooden shelves.

DESCRIPTION AND COMMENTS Founded in 1953 by poet Lawrence Ferlinghetti and Peter D. Martin, City Lights is one of the few truly great independent bookstores or alternative literary scenes in the United States. Famed the world over for unique "finds" and rare first editions, it is made even more famous by the icons of a generation—those beatniks—who nurtured their creative restlessness here.

TOURING TIPS Often the bookstore hosts readings and book signings. Contact them directly for a schedule of guest authors and poets.

OTHER THINGS TO DO NEARBY Stop by Vesuvio Café across the street, the famous bar and literary hangout that was once the favorite watering hole of Jack Kerouac. Coit Tower is also in North Beach. Pick up a good read and head to the top!

kids **Cliff House** ★★★★

APPEAL BY AGE PRESCHOOL ★★★★ GRADE SCHOOL ★★★★ TEENS ★★★★
YOUNG ADULTS ★★★★   OVER 30 ★★★★   SENIORS ★★★★

1090 Point Lobos Avenue (at the Great Highway), San Francisco 94121; Cliff House Restaurant ☎ 415-386-3330; Visitor Center ☎ 415-556-8642; cliffhouse.com

Type of attraction A San Francisco oceanside tourist landmark with a spectacular view, restaurants, and a gift shop. Self-guided tour. **Admission** Free. **Hours** Restaurants: Sutro's: 11:30 a.m.–3:30 p.m. for lunch, 5 p.m.–9:30 p.m. for dinner. A Champagne buffet is served on Sunday in the Terrace Room from 10 a.m.–3:45 p.m. Bistro, 9 a.m.–3:30 p.m. for breakfast and lunch, 4:15 p.m.–9 p.m. for dinner, and until 10 p.m. on Friday and Saturday. **When to go** When the coast isn't socked in by fog. Cocktails at sunset in the restaurants are a San Francisco tradition. **Special comments** Lots of stairs if you opt to explore Sutro Heights Park and the ruins of Sutro Baths. **Author's rating** Best place in town to watch the sunset, superb restaurants, San Francisco history, and if that isn't enough, the seals have returned to the rocks. ★★★★. **How much time to allow** 30 minutes to 1 hour (longer if you dine).

DESCRIPTION AND COMMENTS A San Francisco tourist landmark for more than 100 years, the newly renovated Cliff House still packs them in—often by the busload. The attraction? Dining with a magnificent view of the Pacific, and Seal Rocks in the foreground just offshore. A special Sunday Champagne buffet is offered in the Terrace Room. Next door are the concrete ruins of Sutro Baths, a three-acre swimming emporium that once rented 20,000 bathing suits and 40,000 towels a day. You can also visit The Giant Camera, a huge walk-in camera obscura. It provides the viewer with an image of Seal Rocks magnified onto a huge parabolic screen.

TOURING TIPS Across the Great Highway and just up the hill is Sutro Heights Park, where you walk up a short, steep path to a great view overlooking Cliff House, Seal Rocks, the ruins of Sutro Baths and the Pacific.

OTHER THINGS TO DO NEARBY Drive a few miles south to Fort Funston and watch hang gliders calmly jump off cliffs and swoop and soar along the shore. Or you can take a walk along Ocean Beach, which starts just below Cliff House.

Coit Tower ★★★★½

APPEAL BY AGE PRESCHOOL ★★★ GRADE SCHOOL ★★★ TEENS ★★★
YOUNG ADULTS ★★★   OVER 30 ★★★   SENIORS ★★★

At the top of Telegraph Hill Boulevard, near North Beach in San Francisco; sftravel.com/coit-tower-san-francisco.html

Type of attraction A landmark tower with an observation deck atop Telegraph Hill. A self-guided tour. **Admission** The elevator ride to the top is $4.50 per person. Admission to the murals and the ground-floor gift shop is free. The Diego Rivera–inspired murals on the second floor are available only on tour at 11 a.m. on Saturday or by special arrangement. **Hours** Daily, 10 a.m.–5 p.m. **When to go** Anytime. **Special comments** The elevator doesn't go all the way to the top; you must negotiate a set of steep, winding stairs to the observation deck. Small children will need a lift to see the outstanding 360-degree view. Skip it in lousy weather. **Author's rating** A great view, and beautiful WPA murals. ★★★★½. **How much time to allow** 30 minutes to 1 hour.

DESCRIPTION AND COMMENTS Built as a monument to San Francisco's volunteer firefighters with funds left by renowned eccentric Lillie Hitchcock Coit, this landmark provides a breathtaking view of the city, San Francisco Bay, the Oakland and Golden Gate bridges—the works. Some say the tower is shaped to resemble a fire-hose nozzle, but others disagree. There's no doubt about Ms. Coit's dedication to firefighters. Early in the gold rush, she is said to have deserted a wedding party and chased after her favorite fire engine. Lillie died in 1929 at age 86, leaving the city $125,000 to "expend in an appropriate manner . . . to the beauty of San Francisco." Coit Tower is the result. In the lobby of the tower base are 19 WPA-era murals depicting labor-union workers.

TOURING TIPS Don't drive; the parking lot at the base of Coit Tower is small, and the wait for a space can be long. Walk the steep hill or take the No. 39 Coit bus at Washington Square Park (board at Columbus Avenue and Union Street), which will take you up Telegraph Hill.

OTHER THINGS TO DO NEARBY Walk down steep Telegraph Hill to Washington Square and North Beach, the city's Bohemian district of bars, Italian restaurants, coffee houses, and City Lights Bookstore, the former hangout of Jack Kerouac, Allen Ginsberg, and other Beatnik greats.

de Young Museum ★★★★½

APPEAL BY AGE	PRESCHOOL, GRADE SCHOOL ★★★	TEENS ★★★
YOUNG ADULTS ★★★	OVER 30 ★★★★	SENIORS ★★★★★

Golden Gate Park, 50 Hagiwara Tea Garden Drive, San Francisco 94118; ☎ 415-750-3600; famsf.org/deyoung

Type of attraction San Francisco's oldest art museum features American paintings, decorative arts, and sculpture from the 17th century to the present; native arts from the Americas, Oceania, and Africa; and textiles from numerous areas and periods. **Admission** $10 for adults, $7 for seniors age 65 and older, $6 for youth ages 13–17, $6 for college students with ID, free for children age 12 and under. **Admission** Tickets to the de Young can be used on the same day for the Legion of Honor Museum. The first Tuesday of each month is free. Muni riders with a Fast Pass or transfers receive a $2 discount. **Hours** Tuesday–Sunday, 9:30 a.m.–5:15 p.m. Tower closes at 4:30 p.m. **When to go** Anytime. **Special comments** On Sundays John F. Kennedy Drive in Golden Gate Park is closed; walk, ride a bike, or take public transportation to the museum. The Concourse underground parking garage is accessible from the north via Tenth Avenue. **Author's rating** ★★★★½. **How much time to allow** 2 hours.

DESCRIPTION AND COMMENTS Designed by Herzog and de Meuron, the new de Young has been a controversial building since its re-opening in 2005. With a soaring tower in the middle of an asymmetrical structure, perforated copper cladding, and wide windows that draw in the surrounding gardens, the design has encouraged impassioned discussion from its inception. The museum includes a basement gallery for special exhibits, two floors of permanent exhibits, and a 144-foot tower with one of the best views of the city from the observation deck. Audio tours are available as well as ongoing docent-led tours of permanent and special exhibitions. Private tours can be arranged for ten or more by calling ☎ 415-750-3638. More information about both the de Young and the Legion of Honor museums can be found at **thinker.org.**

TOURING TIPS Visiting the museum during the week is a much quieter experience; the weekends are often busy. Parking can be difficult on Sundays since John F. Kennedy Drive is closed to vehicle traffic. Try and pick up a docent-led tour, which can bring new insight into the collections; then kick back at its lovely cafe.

OTHER THINGS TO DO NEARBY Next door to the museum is the Japanese Tea Garden, where in the spring you can stroll through flowering cherry trees, and all year-round have tea and cookies in the Tea House and climb over charming moon bridges. Walk across Martin Luther King Jr. Drive and turn right to reach the north entrance of the beautifully restored San Francisco Botanical Garden at Strybing Arboretum, surrounded by 70 acres of gardens and tranquility. If visiting during the week, a leisurely tour of Golden Gate Park is a good choice.

NIGHTS AT THE MUSEUMS

EVERY THURSDAY, California Academy of Sciences opens its doors to adults from 6 p.m. to 10 p.m. Tottering in their Manolos and cocktail dresses, the coolest of the young and restless come here to chat up the albino alligator. Explore the museum while partaking in world-class music, talks, and activities. Your $12 ticket gives you free entry to regularly scheduled events, such as the planetarium shows and tropical rain forest walkway. Maybe it was that Ben Stiller movie about the animals coming to life after dark, but suddenly museum evenings are all the rage around here. The Contemporary Jewish Museum has Oy Vey Thursdays for young professionals during the summer into fall, and the Asian Art Museum occasionally has MATCHA events on Thursday evenings for just $10, with drinks, DJs, and performances, in addition to the gallery tours and latest exhibition. The de Young has live music and an open bar on Friday nights from mid-January to November for regular admission price. Whatever's gotten in to the museums seems to be working—these days they're packed and people-pleasing!

Fort Point National Historic Site   ★★★★★

APPEAL BY AGE   PRESCHOOL ★★★   GRADE SCHOOL ★★★★   TEENS ★★★
YOUNG ADULTS ★★★★   OVER 30 ★★★★★   SENIORS ★★★★★

**In the Presidio at the end of Marine Drive (at the southern end of the
Golden Gate Bridge), San Francisco; ☎ 415-556-1693; nps.gov/fopo**

Type of attraction A Civil War–era brick coastal fortification beneath Golden
Gate Bridge; superb vistas of San Francisco's key topographical features. Guided
and self-guided tours. **Admission** Free; donation requested. **Hours** Friday–
Sunday, 10 a.m.–5 p.m. Closed Thanksgiving, Christmas, and New Year's Day.
When to go In July and August come before noon if you're driving; the small
parking lot fills fast. A better option in these busy months (or whenever the
weather is nice) is to bike or walk along the Golden Gate Promenade to the fort
and its dramatic setting. **Special comments** Lots of steep, narrow stairs, tricky
footing, and a scarcity of handrails in the fort. Portable restrooms are located
outside the entrance of the fort, and flush toilets are near the wharf on Marine
Drive. Bring a jacket or sweater; Fort Point can be very windy and cool. **Author's
rating** Come just for the view. Put this on your must-see list. ★★★★★. **How
much time to allow** 1 hour; longer for a guided tour and a demonstration.

DESCRIPTION AND COMMENTS   This fort, built between 1853 and 1861 by the
U.S. Army Corps of Engineers, was designed to prevent the entrance of
a foreign fleet into San Francisco Bay. The setting—the Golden Gate
Bridge overhead, the San Francisco skyline to the east, the rugged Marin
Headlands across the strait, and the Pacific Ocean stretching to the
horizon—is breathtaking.

   History buffs will enjoy exploring the fort, which symbolizes the commercial and strategic military importance of San Francisco. But most
visitors will simply want to hoof it to the fourth (and highest) level for
an even better view of the dramatic panorama (with Golden Gate Bridge
traffic pounding overhead). The interior of the fort is bare bones, but
some of the rooms on upper levels contain photo exhibits about its past.
Film buffs will recognize the spot where James Stewart fished Kim Novak
out of San Francisco Bay in Alfred Hitchcock's classic thriller, *Vertigo*. A
final note: the fort's impressive muzzle-loading cannons (rendered obsolete by rifled cannons during the Civil War0) were never fired in anger.

TOURING TIPS   Go to the gift shop on the ground level for a free 17-minute
video introduction to the fort. You can sign up here for a free guided
tour, pick up a self-guided tour booklet, and see a schedule of demonstrations (such as gun-loading by costumed personnel). You can also rent
a 40-minute audio tour of the fort ($2.50 for adults, $1 for children). Be
sure to walk around the sea wall to the chain-link fence for a full view of
the Pacific Ocean. You may also see die-hard surfers and swimmers in
wetsuits negotiating the surf and ships passing under the bridge.

OTHER THINGS TO DO NEARBY The Presidio, a former U.S. Army base that's now part of Golden Gate National Recreation Area, is filled with old buildings, a museum, a military cemetery, a golf course, trails, and stands of eucalyptus trees planted with military precision.

Drive south along the Pacific for more great views, magnificent private residences, the California Palace of the Legion of Honor, Cliff House, and Ocean Beach.

kids Ghirardelli Chocolate Manufactory and Soda Fountain ★★★

APPEAL BY AGE	PRESCHOOL ★★★	GRADE SCHOOL ★★★★	TEENS ★★★★★
YOUNG ADULTS ★★★★★		OVER 30 ★★★★	SENIORS ★★★

Ghirardelli Square Clock Tower, 900 North Point Street, San Francisco 94109; near the Marina District; ☎ 415-474-3938; ghirardelli.com

Type of attraction Come and see how the chocolate is made. An excellent excursion for the little ones. Self-guided tour. Admission Free. Hours Weekdays, 9 a.m.–11:30 a.m.; weekends, 9 a.m.–midnight. When to go Anytime; great for dessert. Special comments Start at the soda fountain. Author's rating It's probably going to be a major hit with the kids. But who outgrows chocolate? ★★★. How much time to allow 1 hour or more, depending on cravings!

DESCRIPTION AND COMMENTS It's the garden of delectable chocolates, from truffles to their world-famous hot fudge sundaes and the ever-popular Alcatraz Rock (rocky road ice cream in a shell of hard chocolate). It's interactive tasting while you see the machinery that pumps out delicious treats.

TOURING TIPS If you want to avoid crowds, come on a weekday, preferably in the morning. That's when the goodies are fresh anyway.

OTHER THINGS TO DO NEARBY Of course, Fisherman's Wharf is a hop, skip, and a jump away, and Pier 39 is close also.

Haas-Lilienthal House ★★★

APPEAL BY AGE	PRESCHOOL ★	GRADE SCHOOL ★★	TEENS ★★
YOUNG ADULTS ★★		OVER 30 ★★★	SENIORS ★★★

2007 Franklin Street, San Francisco 94109; near Washington Street in Pacific Heights; ☎ 415-441-3000; sfheritage.org

Type of attraction The only fully furnished Victorian house in San Francisco open to the public. A guided tour. Admission $8 per person; $5 for seniors and children under age 12. Hours Wednesday, noon–3 p.m.; Sunday, 11 a.m.–4 p.m. When to go Anytime. Special comments Two flights of stairs on the tour. Author's rating A fascinating glimpse into the life of an upper-middle-class San Francisco family of the late 19th century. ★★★. How much time to allow 1 hour.

DESCRIPTION AND COMMENTS This exquisite 1886 high Victorian mansion has been maintained in nearly original condition since the last descendant of the builders to live in the house died in 1972. The hour-long, docent-led tour reveals a wealth of details on the house (one of a very few to survive the 1906 earthquake and fire) and the life of a rich (but not fabulously so) Jewish merchant family. The distinctive Queen Anne, third-floor tower is strictly decorative; the windows are nine feet above the floor.

Inside, the formal front parlor was used for receiving important guests, and the family parlor behind it was used for guests lower on the social scale. More fascinating details include the small dining room off the main dining room used by children and servants; what appears to be a window at the back is in fact a jib door that slides up and may have been built so that coffins could be passed in and out of the house when a family member died.

unofficial **TIP**
"What I like best about San Francisco is San Francisco."
—Frank Lloyd Wright, Architect

TOURING TIPS Don't walk up the stairs to the main entrance; you'll get to do this later. Instead, walk to the right (as you face the house) and down the sidewalk to the tour entrance.

OTHER THINGS TO DO NEARBY Two other Victorian houses are worth a look, but you can't go in: the Edward Coleman House at Franklin and California streets; and the Bransten House at 1735 Franklin Street. Stroll the neighborhood, and lunch on either Union or Chestnut streets.

Japanese Tea Garden ★★★★

APPEAL BY AGE	PRESCHOOL ★★	GRADE SCHOOL ★★	TEENS ★★
YOUNG ADULTS ★★★★	OVER 30 ★★★★		SENIORS ★★★★

In Golden Gate Park; ☎ 415-752-4227; jgarden.org/gardens.asp?ID=268

Type of attraction A stroll-style garden with a harmonious blend of architecture, landscape, bridges, footpaths, shrines, and gates; tea house serves tea, soft drinks, juices, and cookies. **Admission** $3.50 per person; children age 5 and under, free. Free tours are offered Wednesday and Sunday at 1 p.m. (inside the main gate). Scheduled events have a separate admission charge. **Hours** Daily, 8:30 a.m.–6:30 p.m. Open every day of the year. **When to go** In nice weather. In April, the cherry trees are in bloom. **Special comments** Some mild uphills and uneven footing. **Author's rating** Beautiful and fascinating. ★★★★. **How much time to allow** 1–2 hours.

DESCRIPTION AND COMMENTS In Japan, a garden is considered one of the highest art forms, and after a visit to the Japanese Tea Garden, you'll understand why. On winding paths visitors encounter carp pools, a pagoda, a bronze Buddha, dwarf trees, flowers, cherry trees, footbridges, and a Zen garden. Even when it's packed with hordes of visitors, this artfully designed garden imparts a sense of tranquility.

The garden was part of the Japanese Village exhibit of the California Midwinter International Exposition of 1894, which was held in what is now the Music Concourse in Golden Gate Park. It was built by Japanese artisans, and in the decades after the exposition closed, the garden was expanded from one acre to five acres. In that limited amount of space, the garden expresses the essence of nature by the use of specially selected plants and stones arranged in harmony with the landscape.

TOURING TIPS Come in nice weather and take your time. The atmosphere in the garden is extremely soothing—a perfect stop on a harried touring schedule. Tea service by a kimono-clad waitress in the Tea House is reasonable. The fortune cookies were originally introduced here in 1914. (Ironically, they're called Chinese fortune cookies now.) Stop in the gift shop to see a wide array of Japanese gifts and toys, including kites and fans.

OTHER THINGS TO DO NEARBY The Asian Art Museum, where you can find more Japanese art, is next door. Across Martin Luther King Jr. Drive is the San Francisco Botanical Garden, offering 70 acres of gardens. If it's a nice day, drive or walk to Stow Lake and rent a rowboat ($13 an hour) or a paddleboat ($17 an hour), with a $1 deposit; Stow Lake Boat Rentals (☎ 415-752-0347).

Lawrence Hall of Science ★

APPEAL BY AGE	PRESCHOOL ★★★★★	GRADE SCHOOL ★★★★★	TEENS ★★★
YOUNG ADULTS ★★	OVER 30 ★★		SENIORS ★★

Centennial Drive, Berkeley 94720 (below Grizzly Peak Boulevard, overlooking the University of California at Berkeley campus); ☎ 510-642-5132 for 24-hour information; lhs.berkeley.edu or lawrencehallofscience.org

Type of attraction A hands-on science museum for youngsters. A self-guided tour. **Admission** $12 for adults; $9 for seniors, students, and children ages 5–18; $6 for children ages 3–4. Planetarium shows on Saturday and Sunday at 1 p.m., 2 p.m., and 3 p.m. are $4. Children under age 6 are not admitted to the planetarium except to programs for kids ages 4–8. **Hours** Daily, 10 a.m.–5 p.m.; closed on major holidays. **When to go** When the weather is clear, this is the place to see Jupiter's moons. **Special comments** Parking is very tight on this hilltop setting, so try to arrive early. Visitors must pay $1.50 for the first hour, $1 per hour after, or $7 for a full day. Or take BART to the downtown Berkeley station and catch the local shuttle at Center Street and Shattuck Avenue. Then transfer to the Hill Service Shuttle at the Hearst Mining Circle on campus; ☎ 510-642-5132. **Author's rating** A great view of the bay but otherwise strictly for youngsters. ★. **How much time to allow** At least half a day for kids; you'll have to drag them away.

DESCRIPTION AND COMMENTS Named after Ernest O. Lawrence, Berkeley's best-known Nobel Prize laureates, this hands-on science museum enthralls tots through grade-schoolers. It's hard to list a sampling of the many activities available, but they include a gravity wall, earthquake exhibits, play areas, and math and chemistry exhibits (where kids play scientific sleuths and use real chemical and forensic tests to solve a whodunit). Hour-long planetarium shows suitable for children age 8 and up are offered on weekend and holiday afternoons; children under age 6 aren't admitted except for "Flying High" at 1 p.m., which is suitable for children age 4 and up.

TOURING TIPS Outside, youngsters can clamber on Pheena—a 50-foot, 3,000-pound replica of a fin whale—and a 60-foot long, scientifically accurate model of a double-helix DNA molecule. Adults can keep one eye on the kids and the other on the drop-dead view. A cafeteria on the lower level offers school lunch–style fare and a panoramic view, while the museum store sells books, games, puzzles, and science-oriented gift items.

OTHER THINGS TO DO NEARBY The university's botanical garden is located below the Lawrence Hall of Science and above the campus stadium. The Museum of Paleontology and Berkeley Art Museum are also on campus.

Marine Mammal Center ★★★★

APPEAL BY AGE	PRESCHOOL ★★★★	GRADE SCHOOL ★★★★	TEENS ★★★★
YOUNG ADULTS ★★★★		OVER 30 ★★★	SENIORS ★★★

Fort Cronkite near Rodeo Lagoon in the Marin Headlands;
☎ **415-289-7325; marinemammalcenter.org**

Type of attraction A rehabilitation and education center that nurtures orphaned or injured sea lions, seals, and any other marine mammal. **Admission** Free, but donations welcome. **Hours** Daily, 10 a.m.–4 p.m. except Thanksgiving, Christmas, and New Year's days. **When to go** The best time to visit depends on the season. Winter is usually inactive—they don't get many mammals in at that time. Spring, however, is pupping season when young pups are abundant in the waters—thus making the center busy. Winter and spring, there are more northern elephant seals and harbor seals. The summer and fall months see more California sea lions. Call the center to check on the number of "residents" they have that particular day. **Special comments** The organization receives funding from grants and loans. Although it's free to get in, donations would be a nice gesture. **Author's rating** When people have you going in circles (especially after Fisherman's Wharf), this is a nice escape. You truly get an understanding of the marine life in and around the bay. ★★★★. **How much time to allow** 1–2 hours.

DESCRIPTION AND COMMENTS This hospital in the headlands is one of the main organizations devoted to the welfare of the seals and sea lion population off of the Bay Area. Every year they get orphaned or injured pups and adult seals or sea lions. Volunteers are on hand at the center to answer any questions about patients at the center or about marine life in the bay in general, including whales. You can see the pups get bottle-fed, and read about the successful release of past patients.

TOURING TIPS Call to check on patients' availability. The health of the animals is their first priority, so sometimes the biologists keep many of the animals out of public viewing. Be respectful of the animals!

OTHER THINGS TO DO NEARBY The Headlands offer much in the way of outdoor recreation or scenic drives. Since you probably would drive to the center, consider driving to Mount Tamalpais for amazing views, or down along CA 1 to Stinson Beach, for vertigo-inducing cliffside roads, and R&R.

Mexican Museum

Fort Mason Center, Building D, Marina Boulevard and Buchanan Street, San Francisco, CA 94123; ☎ 415-202-9700; mexicanmuseum.org

Special comments At press time, the gallery was closed for relocation to Mission Street between Third and Fourth streets. It does conduct a regular Diego Rivera mural tour. Exhibits are almost always being held in various venues around town. See Web site for details.

Mission Dolores ★★★

APPEAL BY AGE	PRESCHOOL ★	GRADE SCHOOL ★★	TEENS ★★
YOUNG ADULTS ★★	OVER 30 ★★★		SENIORS ★★★

3321 16th Street in the Mission District, San Francisco 94114; ☎ 415-621-8203; missiondolores.org

Type of attraction San Francisco's oldest building (1791) and the 6th of 21 missions built by Franciscan priests along El Camino Real, the Spanish road linking the missions from Mexico to Sonoma. Self-guided and audio tours. Admission $5 for adults and teenagers, $4 for children ages 5–12. Hours Summer, daily, 9 a.m.–4:30 p.m.; other times of year, 9 a.m.–4 p.m. Closes at noon on Good Friday and at 2 p.m. on Easter. Closed Thanksgiving and Christmas. When to go Try to go when it's not raining; the cemetery, probably the most interesting part, is out in the open. Special comments Restrooms are near the cemetery entrance. Author's rating Surprisingly small, but worth visiting for an authentic taste of San Francisco's Spanish heritage. ★★★. How much time to allow 30 minutes–1 hour.

DESCRIPTION AND COMMENTS With adobe walls four feet thick and the original redwood logs supporting the roof, Mission Dolores has survived four major earthquakes and is the only one of the original missions along the El Camino Real (the Royal Way) that has not been rebuilt. Mass is still celebrated in the building, which is 114 feet long and 22 feet wide. The repainted ceiling depicts original Ohlone Indian designs done with vegetable dyes. The decorative altar came from Mexico in 1796, as did the two side altars (in 1810).

Outside the mission, a diorama shows how it appeared in 1791. Peek inside the basilica, completed in 1918, to view beautiful stained-glass windows. The small museum displays artifacts such as lithographs of the California missions and a revolving tabernacle from the Philippines. You can also see the adobe walls, which were formed and sun-dried nearby. The highlight (for us anyway) is the cemetery—really a lush garden with headstones. Most of the markers are dated in the years following the California gold rush and many of the family names are Irish.

TOURING TIPS Film buffs won't find the headstone of Carlotta Valdes in the mission's cemetery. It was a prop in Alfred Hitchcock's *Vertigo*, part of which was filmed here.

OTHER THINGS TO DO NEARBY Walk a couple of blocks down 16th Street for a selection of ethnic restaurants. Dolores Street, with an aisle of palm trees up and down the center, is fun and funky. The Mission District is full of the good and the bad—homeless people, taquerias, a thriving alternative scene, organic cafes, hash houses . . . you name it and the Mission's got it. Both 16th Street and Mission Street show off the Mission District's diverse flavors, including offbeat bookstores, Asian restaurants, and interesting shops. Good Vibrations (603 Valencia Street; ☎ 415-522-5460) features everything you wanted to know about sex, and then some. The Mission Cultural Center at 2868 Mission Street (Tuesday–Saturday, 10 a.m.–4 p.m.; ☎ 415-821-1155) has a large second-floor gallery with changing art exhibitions, usually with a Hispanic flavor; it's free.

Mount Tamalpais—East Peak ★★★½

| APPEAL BY AGE | PRESCHOOL ★★ | GRADE SCHOOL ★★★ | TEENS ★★★ |
| YOUNG ADULTS ★★★ | | OVER 30 ★★★ | SENIORS ★★ |

Mount Tamalpais State Park, 12 miles north of the Golden Gate Bridge in Marin County; exit US 101 at Sausalito and follow signs to the park; ☎ 415-388-2070; parks.ca.gov/?page_id=471

Type of attraction A half-mile hike to the summit of Mount Tamalpais and a stunning view of San Francisco, the bay, the Golden Gate Bridge, and the Pacific Ocean, along with a tiny new museum (**mttam.net**) of the old "crookedest railroad in the West." The railroad is long gone, but Fred Runner's campaign has salvaged a gravity car and other memories. **Admission** Free. **Parking** in the lot below the summit is $6 per car; $5 for seniors. **Hours** Daily, sunrise–sunset. **When to go** In clear weather. **Special comments** Locals call it "Mount Tam." Wear sturdy shoes if you opt for the steep hike to the summit. **Author's rating** May be the best view of San Francisco. ★★★½. **How much time to allow** 1 hour.

DESCRIPTION AND COMMENTS The incredible vistas you see on the drive up to the top of Tamalpais are a trip in themselves. *Warning:* Anyone afraid of heights and falling off narrow, cliff-clinging curved roads with a thousand-foot drop should either pass on the drive up or go blindfolded. Until 1930, tourists rode the Mount Tamalpais and Muir Woods Railway to the top, where a tavern and dance pavilion were located near the present parking lot. From the summit, the view is spectacular—including 3,890-foot Mount Diablo to the east and, on a clear day, the snow-capped Sierras 140 miles to the east. Any soaring birds you see are probably turkey vultures. If you're not up for the half-mile, 220-foot-elevation-gain hike to the summit, you can opt for a self-guided tour around the peak or just enjoy the view from the overlook near the restrooms.

TOURING TIPS Unless you're wearing hiking boots and are used to narrow foot trails, don't take the plank trail to the summit. Although it looks easy, it quickly gets very steep, with treacherous footing. Instead, take the Verna Dunshee Trail, a self-guided tour just over a half-mile long that goes counterclockwise around the peak; pick up a brochure in the gift shop. The trail starts to the right of the restrooms. A snack bar, phones, and drinking water are available near the parking lot.

OTHER THINGS TO DO NEARBY Muir Woods National Monument is a grove of majestic coastal redwoods, the tallest trees in the world. Stinson Beach, located beneath steep hills rising to Mount Tam, offers vistas of the sea and hills, while Muir Beach, farther south down Route 1, has a semicircular cove where you can relax and enjoy the scenery. To the north, Point Reyes National Seashore provides more stunning scenery, hiking trails, miles of undisturbed beaches, and, December through April, whale watching.

 ## Muir Woods National Monument ★★★★

APPEAL BY AGE	PRESCHOOL ★★★	GRADE SCHOOL ★★★★	TEENS ★★★★
YOUNG ADULTS ★★★★		OVER 30 ★★★★	SENIORS ★★★★

12 miles north of the Golden Gate Bridge in Marin County. Exit US 101 at Sausalito and follow the signs; ☎ 415-388-2595; nps.gov/muwo

Type of attraction A grove of majestic coastal redwoods, the tallest trees in the world. A self-guided tour. **Admission** $5 per person for visitors age 17 and up. **Hours** Daily, 8 a.m.–7 p.m.; visitor center is open daily, 9 a.m.–4:30 p.m. **When to go** When it's not raining. To avoid crowds, arrive before 10 a.m. or after 4 p.m. **Special comments** Roads leading to the park are steep and winding; vehicles more than 35 feet long are prohibited. No picnicking is allowed in Muir Woods. **Author's rating** Go ahead and hug a tree—if you are the Jolly Green Giant! These huge trees are truly awesome. ★★★★. **How much time to allow** 30 minutes to 1 hour to stroll the paved loops in Redwood Canyon; avid hikers can spend several hours or the entire day hiking unpaved trails leading to Mount Tamalpais State Park.

DESCRIPTION AND COMMENTS No trip to northern California would be complete without a glimpse of these world-famous giant redwood trees, which are much like the trees that covered much of the Northern Hemisphere 140 million years ago. Today, redwoods are only found in a narrow, 500-mile discontinuous strip of Pacific coast from southern

Oregon to below Monterey, California. The huge specimens in the Cathedral and Bohemian groves are the largest redwoods in Muir Woods. The tallest is 252 feet; the thickest is 14 feet across. The oldest is at least 1,000 years old, but most of the mature trees here are 500 to 800 years old. The towering trees, the fallen giants, and the canyon ferns impart awe and tranquility—even when the paved paths are clogged with visitors.

TOURING TIPS Take the time and the modest effort to walk the paved path to Cathedral Grove; you'll encounter fewer people, and there are more fallen trees. Try walking the paths in a figure 8 by crossing footbridges over Redwood Creek. Avoid visiting on weekends and holidays; parking is usually a real hassle. The best time to come is early or late in the day; you'll encounter fewer people, and there's a better chance of seeing wildlife. The park's 560 acres include six miles of walking trails; except for the mostly level and paved main trail, the footpaths are unpaved. Wear sturdy hiking boots and a jacket. If you plan to venture beyond the main trail, bring rain gear. A gift shop, snack bar, restrooms, drinking water, and telephones are located near the main entrance.

OTHER THINGS TO DO NEARBY Don't miss the Nike missile site, built as a defense against Russian invasion during the Cold War, at Fort Cronkhite. Dedicated volunteers and the National Park Service restored site SF-88, now a museum open Wednesday through Friday, 12:30 p.m.–2:30 p.m. For directions, visit **nps.gov/goga.** On a scenic drive through Marin County, stop at Stinson Beach (where you can relax and enjoy the coastal scenery) and take the white-knuckle curves along Route 1, which follows the Pacific coast. Drive north to Point Reyes National Seashore to enjoy windswept terrain, miles of undisturbed beaches, hiking trails, and whale watching (December through April). There are plenty of places to eat and drink in Mill Valley and Sausalito.

Museum of Craft and Folk Art

51 Yerba Buena Lane (at Mission between Third and Fourth), San Francisco 94103; ☎ 415-227-4888; mocfa.org

Type of attraction Temporary exhibitions of contemporary crafts, American folk art, and traditional ethnic art. A self-guided tour. **Admission** $5, $4 seniors, free for children under age 18. **Hours** Tuesday–Friday, 11 a.m.–6 p.m.; Saturday and Sunday, 11 a.m.–5 p.m. **When to go** Anytime. **Special comments** Formerly in Fort Mason, the museum is now housed in a new SoMa building. **Author's rating** The museum only features temporary shows, so it's not possible to give it a rating. **How much time to allow** 30 minutes to an hour.

DESCRIPTION AND COMMENTS It isn't just about basket weaving and throwing pots. Exhibits are both American and international. At press time, an exhibit featuring textile designs from Mali was on display.

TOURING TIPS Be careful of red-light runners in this area.

OTHER THINGS TO DO NEARBY It's not far from SFMOMA, so if you've had your fill of fine art, this will make for a welcome break.

Museum of Money of the American West ★★

| APPEAL BY AGE | PRESCHOOL ★ | GRADE SCHOOL ★★ | TEENS ★★ |
| YOUNG ADULTS ★★ | | OVER 30 ★★ | SENIORS ★★ |

Basement of the Union Bank of California, 400 California Street, San Francisco 94111; in the Financial District; ☎ 415-765-3434

Type of attraction A small museum highlighting the gold rush, gold mining, and the development of money in California's history. A self-guided tour. **Admission** Free. **Hours** Monday–Friday, 9 a.m.–4 p.m. Closed weekends and bank holidays. **When to go** Anytime. **Special comments** One set of stairs to climb and descend; restrooms are next to the museum entrance. **Author's rating** An interesting but narrow slice of California history that's worth a peek. ★★. **How much time to allow** 30 minutes.

DESCRIPTION AND COMMENTS California history and gold are the focus of this one-room museum in the basement of the huge Union Bank of California building. On display are gold nuggets, coins, old banknotes, diagrams of the Comstock mines (the source of the fortune that founded this bank and many civic projects in San Francisco), a set of dueling pistols, and plenty of 19th-century photos of the gold-rush era that put California on the map.

TOURING TIPS Check out the huge vault at the bottom of the stairs outside the entrance to the museum. You can't miss the stunning bank lobby in this colonnaded building, which was completed in 1908.

OTHER THINGS TO DO NEARBY The Wells Fargo History Museum is around the corner on Montgomery Street. Although its 27th-floor observation deck is now closed, the Transamerica Pyramid on Montgomery Street has a lobby observatory that lets you control cameras on the roof for TV-monitor views of the city; not nearly as exciting as seeing it with your own eyes, but it's free. Transamerica Redwood Park is next to the distinctive landmark; its fountains, greenery, and whimsical sculptures make for a nice place for a brown-bag lunch.

Museum of Vision ★★

| APPEAL BY AGE | PRESCHOOL ★★★ | GRADE SCHOOL ★★★★ | TEENS ★★★ |
| YOUNG ADULTS ★★★ | | OVER 30 ★★★ | SENIORS ★★★ |

655 Beach Street, third floor (at Columbus Avenue), near Fisherman's Wharf; ☎ 415-561-8502; museumofvision.org

Type of attraction A zany, offbeat stop after hitting the more conventional museums. It's a showcase of all things eyes. **Admission** Free. **Hours** Monday–Friday, 9 a.m.–5 p.m., by appointment only. **When to go** Anytime. Fun close to Halloween. **Special comments** Some of the preserved eyes may make you want to take lunch a bit late. But the kids will certainly get a kick out of it. **Author's rating** A small but interesting stop if you are so inclined to watch what watches! ★★. **How much time to allow** 1 hour.

DESCRIPTION AND COMMENTS On display are diseased eyeballs that have found rest in a jar of formaldehyde, as well as glass eyes, old surgical instruments, and rare books. It's a historical medical museum, so lectures are often given.

TOURING TIPS Information tours can be given if you choose not to self-guide.

OTHER THINGS TO DO NEARBY Fisherman's Wharf is around the corner.

Neptune Society Columbarium   ★★★

APPEAL BY AGE	PRESCHOOL ★	GRADE SCHOOL ★	TEENS ★★
YOUNG ADULTS ★★	OVER 30 ★★★		SENIORS ★★★

1 Loraine Court, off Anza and Stanyan streets; ☎ 415-771-0717; neptune-society.com

Type of attraction A cemetery of sorts—a beautiful copper-domed neoclassical work of Victorian architecture that serves as a repository for the ashes of some of San Francisco's famed and upper crust. **Admission** Free. **Hours** Weekdays, 10 a.m.–4 p.m.; weekends, 10 a.m.–2 p.m. **When to go** Anytime—especially when the tourists are flocking to other well-known sites in the city. **Special comments** Beautiful gardens to stroll through. **Author's rating** The architecture and the gardens are excellent; it's also a non-touristy and unique place. ★★★. **How much time to allow** 1 hour.

DESCRIPTION AND COMMENTS In the early 20th century, cemeteries were banned from San Francisco, so those wealthy few who were laid to rest in Odd Fellows' Cemetery in the Richmond had to be placed indoors. Thus the Columbarium. Those unlucky souls who didn't have the money to "move on up" still remain below. The Columbarium houses the ashes, tombstones, and interesting family memorabilia of the deceased. Most of them are wealthy aristocrats who made their stamp on the city. Among them are the remains of the Folgers of coffee fame, the Magnins, Kaisers, Eddys, Shattucks, Hayeses, and Brannans. You'll see fancy urns of alabaster, copper, and some more offbeat ones as well.

TOURING TIPS The caretaker leads guided tours. His stories are worth a visit!

OTHER THINGS TO DO NEARBY Golden Gate Park is nearby.

Niles Essanay Silent Film Museum   ★★★★

APPEAL BY AGE	PRESCHOOL ★★	GRADE SCHOOL ★★★	TEENS ★★★
YOUNG ADULTS ★★★	OVER 30 ★★★★		SENIORS ★★★★★

37417 Niles Boulevard in Fremont, 94536; ☎ 510-494-1411; nilesfilmmuseum.org.

Type of attraction A museum of silent film. **Admission** Contributions accepted for tours; special events and movie nights are extra. **Hours** Saturday–Sunday, noon–4 p.m. **When to go** Check out the weekend evening programs and special tours. **Special comments** Not just for passionate film buffs! Schoolchildren also enjoy it. **Author's rating** ★★★★. **How much time to allow** 1 hour, or 2 hours on movie nights.

DESCRIPTION AND COMMENTS   In 1915, Charlie Chaplin came to this out-of-the-way tiny East Bay community to make movies, including *The Tramp*. In one year, Chaplin made 14 movies for Essanay, though some were filmed in Oakland, San Francisco, Chicago, and Los Angeles. Niles is where Essanay Studios churned out silent movies from 1912 to 1916.

TOURING TIPS   For their piano-accompanied Saturday night film programs of Chaplin, Laurel, Hardy, and other silent greats, check the Web site.

OTHER THINGS TO DO NEARBY   A tiny excursion train goes around Niles Canyon to Sunol on Sundays. It can be combined with a visit to Ardenwood Historic Farm and a Niles walking tour.

Oakland Museum of California   ★★★½

APPEAL BY AGE	PRESCHOOL ★★★	GRADE SCHOOL ★★★★	TEENS ★★★
YOUNG ADULTS ★★★	OVER 30 ★★★★		SENIORS ★★★★

1000 Oak Street at 10th Street, Oakland 94607. The museum is one block from the Lake Merritt BART station. If you're driving from San Francisco, cross the Oakland Bridge and get on I-880 south; exit at Jackson Street. The museum parking garage has entrances on Oak Street and 12th Street; ☎ 510-238-2200; museumca.org.

Type of attraction A museum showcasing California's history, natural sciences, and culture. A self-guided tour. **Admission** As it just reopened in May 2010, check **museumca.org** for pricing. **Hours** Wednesday, Saturday, and Sunday, 11 a.m.–5 p.m.; Thursday–Friday, 11 a.m.–8 p.m. Closed Monday, Tuesday, July 4, Thanksgiving, Christmas, and New Year's Day. **When to go** Anytime. **Special comments** Free tours are available. Check with the information desk at the entrance of each gallery. **Author's rating** Everyone should find something to like in this large, attractive, and diversified museum. ★★★½. **How much time to allow** Depending on your interests in things Californian, anywhere from two hours to half a day.

DESCRIPTION AND COMMENTS   The Oakland Museum of California is actually three museums in one. The first level, which is closed until 2012 for renovation, houses the Natural Sciences Gallery. Level two focuses on history, culture, and technology from pre-Colonial days through the present. In the exhibits focusing on modern life, you'll find displays and artifacts that touch on Hollywood, the Beat movement, surfboards, political movements, labor strife, and most of the things we associate with the frenetic, hedonistic California lifestyle; a confusing jumble, but fascinating. Level three has 4,500 square feet of new art gallery space highlighting California artists and art ranging from sculpture and textiles to huge landscapes.

TOURING TIPS Plan to linger on the second level's exhibits on history, technology, and culture. California's multicultural past is on display in all its diversity, with stories of Native American weavers and hunters, Spanish missionaries, vaqueros, gold miners, railroad builders, factory workers, union organizers, and immigrants—virtually everyone who sought the California dream. Outside—integrated with the graceful, three-tiered building erected in 1969 and renovated and expanded in 2009–2010—are seven-and-a-half acres of gardens that give the museum the look of an old, overgrown villa. Flowers and fragrant plants line the walkways and the terraced central courtyard.

OTHER THINGS TO DO NEARBY The historic Paramount Theatre (at 21st Street and Broadway) is a spectacular example of Art Deco architecture; the old movie palace has been converted to a general entertainment complex. Oakland's waterfront Jack London Square is the city's version of Fisherman's Wharf—and just as contrived. At Lake Merritt, a beautiful outdoor wildlife sanctuary, you can rent a boat, take a lakeside stroll, and view wildlife. Kids will enjoy Children's Fairyland on the north side of the lake. Fairy tales come alive at old Geppetto's workshop and other settings from children's stories. A short walk up Tenth Street to Webster Street will bring you to Chinatown and a number of Asian restaurants.

kids Palace of Fine Arts/Exploratorium ★★★★

APPEAL BY AGE	PRESCHOOL ★★★★	GRADE SCHOOL ★★★★★	TEENS ★★★★
YOUNG ADULTS ★★★★		OVER 30 ★★★★	SENIORS ★★★

3601 Lyon Street, San Francisco 94123; in the Marina District just off US 101 near the Golden Gate Bridge; Exploratorium: ☎ 415-561-0360 (recorded information), ☎ 415-561-0399 (recorded directions), or ☎ 415-563-7337 (further information); exploratorium.edu

Type of attraction A landmark classical Roman rotunda originally built for the Panama-Pacific Exposition of 1915 and a hands-on science museum for children and adults. A self-guided tour. **Admission** Palace of Fine Arts and grounds, free. Exploratorium, $14 for adults; $11 for seniors, students, people with disabilities, and children ages 13–17; and $9 for children ages 4–12. Free to all on the first Wednesday of the month. The Tactile Dome is $17 per person and includes admission to the museum; advance reservations are required. **Hours** Palace: always open. Exploratorium: Tuesday–Sunday, 10 a.m.–5 p.m. Closed Mondays, except holidays. **When to go** Palace of Fine Arts: in nice weather, although the fake ruins are lovely in a light rain; just make sure you bring an umbrella. Exploratorium: avoid weekday mornings during the school year, when school field trips are scheduled. Weekends and holidays are almost always busy, but lines at exhibits are rare. **Special comments** The Palace of Fine Arts is outdoors; dress accordingly. Ample free parking is available for both attractions. **Author's rating** A restored re-creation of a Roman ruin and a hands-on science museum are an odd coupling, but both succeed. ★★★★. **How much time to allow** 2–4 hours for the Exploratorium; 30 minutes for the Palace of Fine Arts, although it's a scenic and peaceful setting that will tempt most visitors to linger.

DESCRIPTION AND COMMENTS Originally built in 1915 and restored in the late 1960s, the Palace of Fine Arts is a colossal fake Roman ruin with beautifully manicured greenery, an artificial lake, and waterfowl. The gorgeous setting is a great place to stroll, eat a picnic lunch, or take a break from a hectic touring schedule. The palace was so popular that after the 1915 Panama-Pacific Exhibition (which drew more than 18 million visitors), it was retained and later completely rebuilt (after decaying into real ruins). It's a San Francisco landmark and a favorite stop for tour buses.

Inside the adjacent exhibition shed is the Exploratorium, a hands-on science museum with more than 600 exhibits dedicated to the principle that one learns by doing. Exhibits range from a protein production line (where you chain together metal "molecules" to form DNA in a kind of jigsaw puzzle) to gyroscopes, a pendulum, AIDS exhibits, optical illusions, and a video-enhanced bobsled run—not to be missed for the 6- to 12-year-old set. Another major attraction is the Tactile Dome, a geodesic dome that visitors explore in the dark—crawling, climbing, sliding, and exploring different textures in 13 chambers. Advance reservations are required for the Tactile Dome, and an extra fee is charged; call ☎ 415-561-0362 weekdays between 10 a.m.–4 p.m. Not recommended for people in casts, women in the last trimester of pregnancy, or the claustrophobic.

TOURING TIPS Neither attraction lends itself to strategic touring. The palace, with its towering, curved colonnades and rotunda, is stunningly gorgeous—and otherwise empty (a great place for a brown-bag lunch). The Exploratorium is best approached with an open mind.

OTHER THINGS TO DO NEARBY The residences of the nearby Marina District reflect the Mediterranean-revival architecture popular in the 1920s, with pastel town houses on curving streets. Head toward Chestnut Street to find neighborhood restaurants and shops. The Presidio, a former army base now managed by the National Park Service, has hiking and biking trails and hundreds of historical buildings. On the shores of San Francisco Bay, Marina Green is often full of kite fliers, sunbathers, joggers, and yachters. The Golden Gate Promenade, a three-and-a-half-mile path stretching between Fisherman's Wharf and the Golden Gate Bridge, offers fine views, and you're near the halfway point.

Phoebe A. Hearst Museum of Anthropology ★½

APPEAL BY AGE	PRESCHOOL ★★	GRADE SCHOOL ★★	TEENS ★★
YOUNG ADULTS ★★	OVER 30 ★★		SENIORS ★★

University of California at Berkeley, 103 Kroeber Hall, Berkeley 94720 (Bancroft Way at College Avenue on the University of California at Berkeley campus); ☎ 510-643-7648; hearstmuseum.berkeley.edu

Type of attraction A small museum highlighting California cultural anthropology, ethnography, and archaeology. A self-guided tour. Admission General admission is free. Tours are $5 for adults, $2 children age 12 and under. Tours must be booked two weeks in advance. **Hours** Wednesday–Saturday, 10 a.m.–4:30 p.m.; Sunday, noon to 4 p.m. Closed Monday, Tuesday, and major holidays. **When to go** Anytime. **Special comments** The gift shop offers a good selection of handmade crafts. **Author's rating** Ho-hum. Unless you have a strong interest in anthropology, think of this small gallery of static exhibits as a fill-in spot. ★½. **How much time to allow** 30 minutes.

DESCRIPTION AND COMMENTS In this one-room gallery you'll find tools and implements of California's Native Americans, including food-preparation utensils, baskets, brushes, trays, paddles, bowls, fishing gear, and hunting tools such as slings, traps, and bows and arrows.

TOURING TIPS The most interesting display is a very small exhibit about Ishi, the last Yahi Indian of northern California who lived and worked in the museum from 1911 until his death in 1916.

OTHER THINGS TO DO NEARBY The Berkeley Art Museum is across the street. Fossil hunters will like the Museum of Paleontology, housing one of the largest and oldest collections of fossils in North America. It's open Monday through Friday, noon to 4 p.m.; it's located in the Valley Life Sciences Building on campus and admission is free. Youngsters will love the Lawrence Hall of Science, a hands-on science museum with a spectacular view of the Bay Area. Drive or take a university Hill Service Shuttle to get there. Telegraph Avenue features a lively street scene with an incredibly diverse selection of restaurants, gift shops, street vendors, street musicians, street people, and gray-haired hippies.

Ripley's Believe It or Not! Museum ★

APPEAL BY AGE	PRESCHOOL ★★★		GRADE SCHOOL ★★★★	TEENS ★★★★
YOUNG ADULTS ★★		OVER 30 ★★		SENIORS ★

175 Jefferson Street (at Taylor), San Francisco 94133; across from Fisherman's Wharf; ☎ 415-771-6188; ripleysf.com

Type of attraction 250 exhibits of the odd and unusual based on the comic strip by Robert Ripley, "the modern Marco Polo." A self-guided tour. **Admission** $13 for adults and older children, $8 for seniors and children ages 5–12. **Hours** Sunday–Thursday, 10 a.m.–10 p.m.; Friday and Saturday, 10 a.m.–midnight. **When to go** Anytime. **Special comments** Anyone nervous about earthquakes should skip the simulated event. **Author's rating** Silliness aimed at 11-year-old boys and not much on hand that has anything to do with San Francisco. ★. **How much time to allow** 1 hour.

DESCRIPTION AND COMMENTS Here's where you come to gawk at displays of human oddities such as Unicorn Man (with a 13-inch spike growing out of the back of his head), the world's tallest man, and grainy films of restless natives chowing down on baked crocodile. For minor titillation, a few sexy teasers are thrown in, such as the optical illusion of the naked lady on the beach who's not there when you walk back for a better look.

While the overwhelming majority of exhibits have nothing to do with San Francisco (and are repeated at other Ripley museums from Australia to Key West), there are a couple of exceptions: the scale model of a cable car made of matches and a simulated earthquake, along with pictures of the 1989 event. Neither is worth the price of admission.

TOURING TIPS Only come in lousy weather and in the company of adolescents. Better yet, send the youngsters in while you check out better options around Fisherman's Wharf.

OTHER THINGS TO DO NEARBY The San Francisco Maritime Museum is close, as is Aquarium of the Bay, a fish emporium that gives visitors a different perspective. A good and relatively cheap lunch alternative is the clam chowder in a bowl of sourdough bread, served across the street at Boudin Bakery.

San Francisco Botanical Garden ★★★

APPEAL BY AGE	PRESCHOOL ★★★	GRADE SCHOOL ★★	TEENS ★★
YOUNG ADULTS ★★★	OVER 30 ★★★		SENIORS ★★★★

Ninth Avenue at Lincoln Way, Golden Gate Park, San Francisco 94122; ☎ 415-661-1316; sfbotanicalgarden.org

Type of attraction A botanical garden featuring more than 7,500 plant species on 70 acres. Guided and self-guided tours. **Admission** Free. **Hours** Monday–Thursday, 8 a.m.–4:30 p.m.; Saturday, Sunday, and holidays, 10 a.m.–5 p.m. **When to go** When it's not raining or extremely windy. The California Native Garden is spectacular from early March to late April. **Special comments** Formerly known as Strybing Arboretum. Free docent tours are offered daily at 1:30 p.m.; no tours on major holidays. No bicycles, roller skates, skateboards, Frisbees, active sports, barbecues, or pets are allowed in the park. **Author's rating** Blissfully peaceful and beautiful; a chance to further appreciate San Francisco's Mediterranean climate. ★★★. **How much time to allow** 1–2 hours.

DESCRIPTION AND COMMENTS Manicured grounds, paved paths, benches, ponds, and towering trees that absorb most of the nearby traffic sounds are the hallmarks of this world-class botanical garden in Golden Gate Park, which opened in 1940. San Francisco's unusual climate allows an astounding range of plant life to flourish in the 22 gardens, grouped in three major collections—Mediterranean, mild-temperate, and montane tropic (cloud forest) climates—plus a meadow and specialty gardens.

TOURING TIPS The garden has a north entrance near the Japanese Tea Garden and a main entrance on Martin Luther King Jr. Drive near Lincoln Boulevard. Unless you have a specific interest in, say, the plant life found in New World cloud forests, just wander around in a clockwise or counterclockwise direction, and eventually you'll see everything. The bookstore offers botany and horticulture books, cards, gift items, and maps. Hard-core gardeners may want to check out the Helen Crocker Russell Library of Horticulture, the largest of its kind in

California; it's open daily (except major holidays), 10 a.m. to 4 p.m. The store and library are located near the main entrance.

OTHER THINGS TO DO NEARBY The Japanese Tea Garden is close to the north entrance of the garden. The California Academy of Sciences across the Music Concourse is very popular. Hungry? You'll find a snack bar at Stow Lake.

San Francisco Maritime Museum ★★★½

APPEAL BY AGE	PRESCHOOL ★★★	GRADE SCHOOL ★★★	TEENS ★★★
YOUNG ADULTS ★★★	OVER 30 ★★★		SENIORS ★★★★

900 Beach Street, San Francisco 94109; a few blocks west of Fisherman's Wharf; ☎ 415-556-3002; nps.gov/safr

Type of attraction Maritime art, ship figureheads, intricate models, and thematic exhibits echoing San Francisco's maritime past. A self-guided tour. **Admission** Free. Hyde Street Pier, $5 adults, free for kids under age 16. Free on first Sunday of each month. **Hours** Daily, 10 a.m.–5 p.m. **When to go** Anytime. **Special comments** One set of stairs; restrooms, drinking water, and telephones are available. **Author's rating** After exploring real ships at Hyde Street Pier, this museum is icing on the cake for folks fascinated by San Francisco's colorful seafaring past; an excellent, nontouristy destination at Fisherman's Wharf. ★★★½. **How much time to allow** 1–2 hours.

DESCRIPTION AND COMMENTS Located in a gorgeous Art Deco building at the foot of Polk Street, this small museum is jam-packed with an amazing array of maritime artifacts. While the exhibits are heavy on exquisitely detailed ship models (including the battleship U.S.S. *California* and a German five-masted schooner), also on hand are scrimshaw, carved nautilus shells, a ship's medicine box, a seagoing doll once owned by a sea captain's daughter (from the days when skippers took their families on long voyages), an exploding harpoon used to hunt whales, 19th-century photographs, and some small boats (not models). Not to be missed if you're fascinated by ships, nautical lore, and seafaring.

TOURING TIPS A great destination on a rainy day. If it's not foggy, the view of San Francisco Bay from the second-floor balcony is terrific. If looking at all those models makes you yearn for the real thing, walk a few blocks east to the Hyde Street Pier, where you can board and explore ships built in the 19th century.

OTHER THINGS TO DO NEARBY Aquatic Park features plenty of greenery and seating, a sandy shoreline, and great views. The Golden Gate Promenade is a scenic, usually windy, three-and-a-half-mile path to the bridge of the same name; walk or rent a bike, pack a lunch, and have a picnic at a quiet spot along the way. Aquatic Park surrounds the Hyde Street cable-car turnaround; if the line's not too long, hop on board. Ghirardelli Square and the Cannery are both only a credit card's throw away. Walk a few blocks east to Fisherman's Wharf and the heart of the tourist hubbub, where you can rent a bike, buy a T-shirt, eat clam chowder out of a bowl made of sourdough bread (at Boudin's Bakery), take a ferry to Alcatraz (with advance reservations), or walk across the bottom of a giant fish tank (at Aquarium of the Bay).

kids San Francisco Maritime National Historical Park—Hyde Street Pier ★★★★

APPEAL BY AGE	PRESCHOOL ★★★★	GRADE SCHOOL ★★★	TEENS ★★★
YOUNG ADULTS ★★★½		OVER 30 ★★★★	SENIORS ★★★½

At the foot of Hyde Street in San Francisco near Fisherman's Wharf; ☎ 415-556-0859 for tickets and info; nps.gov/safr

Type of attraction A collection of real 19th-century ships that visitors can board. Self-guided and guided tours. **Admission** $5. **Hours** Daily, 9:30 a.m.–5:30 p.m. **When to go** When the weather is good. Wind or rain can make for potentially perilous conditions on ship decks—and because the pier juts into San Francisco Bay, it can get cold. **Author's rating** Step aboard one of these great old ships and enter the long-gone world of Cape Horn passages and coastal runs under sail. Fabulous. ★★★★. **How much time to allow** 1 hour to half a day, depending on your interest.

DESCRIPTION AND COMMENTS   While you stroll the decks and explore the passageways in these ships, it's easy to make a mental trip back in time. On the C. A. Thayer, a three-masted schooner that once carried lumber and fished for cod in the Bering Sea, you can peer inside the captain's cabin and, below deck, watch a video of the ship's final voyage in 1950, narrated by her last skipper. This is nirvana for anyone who has fantasized about a sea voyage under sail.

Other ships to explore include the Eureka, a side-wheel ferry built in 1890 and the world's largest passenger ferry in her day. The Alma is the last San Francisco Bay scow schooner still afloat, and the Balclutha is a square-rigged Cape Horn sailing vessel launched in 1886 in Scotland. Around the corner on Pier 45, you can take an audio tour of the U.S.S. Pampanito, a restored World War II long-range submarine.

There are more ships to explore, and exhibits featuring boatbuilding and tools, old photographs, and detailed displays. You may also see riggers working high aloft on the masts of ships and shipwrights using traditional skills and tools. For newcomers to San Francisco, it's a pleasant surprise to discover this fascinating, high-quality national park plunked down in the dross of touristy Fisherman's Wharf.

TOURING TIPS   A guided tour of each ship is offered daily, based on ranger availability; stop by or call the day before for a schedule. Your ticket is good for five days.

OTHER THINGS TO DO NEARBY   More naval history and lore is on display in the Art Deco building housing the San Francisco Maritime Museum (at the foot of Polk Street). Aquatic Park is the perfect place for a breather after the stresses of exploring Fisherman's Wharf. You can also follow the Golden Gate Promenade past the museum all the way to the Golden Gate Bridge.

San Francisco Museum of Modern Art   ★★★★★

| APPEAL BY AGE | PRESCHOOL ★ | GRADE SCHOOL ★★ | TEENS ★★★ |
| YOUNG ADULTS ★★★ | OVER 30 ★★★★ | | SENIORS ★★★★★ |

151 Third Street, San Francisco 94103; south of Market Street below Union Square, between Mission and Howard streets (adjacent to Yerba Buena Gardens and across from Moscone Convention Center); ☎ 415-357-4000; sfmoma.org

Type of attraction Modern and contemporary art from the museum's permanent collection of 15,000 works and temporary shows. Self-guided and guided tours. **Admission** $15 for adults, $9 for seniors and students, free for children age 12 and under (with an adult); half-price admission on Thursday, 6–9 p.m.; free on the first Tuesday of the month. **Hours** Friday–Tuesday, 11 a.m.–5:45 p.m.; Thursday, 11 a.m.–8:45 p.m. From Memorial Day to Labor Day, the museum opens at 10 a.m. Closed Wednesday and July 4, Thanksgiving, Christmas, and New Year's Day. **When to go** Anytime. **Special comments** Free 45-minute gallery tours are offered daily, starting at 11:30 a.m. and about every hour thereafter. **Author's rating** World-class modern art in a magnificent gallery that's a work of art itself. ★★★★★. **How much time to allow** 2 hours to get the gist of the place, but art buffs should figure on half a day, easily.

DESCRIPTION AND COMMENTS This modern-art emporium is just what you'd expect in San Francisco, an international center of the avant garde. Physically stunning and fairly new, the museum is designed to let the Bay Area's fabled light flood the four gallery levels. Blond hardwood on a springy dance-floor base makes it easy on the feet. A central skylight bathes the piazza-inspired atrium in natural light; from above, you can watch other gallery visitors walk across a white metal bridge that spans the four levels below. Simply breathtaking.

TOURING TIPS Take a free 45-minute tour; the first is offered at 11:30 a.m. and skips around to various galleries, whetting your appetite and revealing the museum's layout. It usually starts on level two, where the permanent collection features works by Henri Matisse, one of the first modern artists to use color as an expression of emotion. In other rooms you'll see works by masters such as Pablo Picasso and Georges Braque. After viewing the art on level two, take the elevator to level five, which features changing exhibits from artists of the 1990s. Bring an open mind and be ready to have some fun. You'll find more outrageous art, such as large-scale contemporary works, on level four (walk across the white bridge and down the stairs) and a small photo gallery on level three. A rooftop garden is the latest addition.

The museum shop on the ground level is huge and has a great selection of postcards (none, alas, of the Golden Gate Bridge or Chinatown), among other things. Caffe Museo (☎ 415-357-4500) opens an hour before the museum and offers a good selection of reasonably priced items.

OTHER THINGS TO DO NEARBY Yerba Buena Gardens, with an art gallery and attractive grounds, is across the street. Market Street, with a wide selection of restaurants, is a block and a half away. The Cartoon Art Museum is nearby on Mission Street.

kids San Francisco Zoo ★★★

APPEAL BY AGE	PRESCHOOL ★★★★★	GRADE SCHOOL ★★★★★	TEENS ★★★★
YOUNG ADULTS ★★★★		OVER 30 ★★★	SENIORS ★★★

Sloat Boulevard at 47th Street; in southwest San Francisco near Great Highway and the Pacific Coast (a vehicles-only entrance is on the Great Highway); ☎ 415-753-7080; sfzoo.org

Type of attraction At 66 acres and growing, the largest zoo in northern California. A self-guided tour. **Admission** For nonresidents of San Francisco: $15 adults, $12 seniors, $9 children ages 4–14, free for children age 3 and under. For residents of San Francisco: $12 adults, $7.50 seniors, $5.50 children ages 4–14, free for children age 3 and under. Free on the first Wednesday of the month. **Hours** Daily, 10 a.m.–5 p.m. The Children's Zoo is open Monday–Friday, 11 a.m.–4 p.m.; Saturday and Sunday (and daily in the summer), 10:30 a.m.–4:30 p.m. **When to go** In nice weather. Also, animals are more active early in the day and late in the afternoon. **Special comments** Most animals are in unenclosed exhibits that are open to the elements; bring an umbrella if rain is expected. **Author's rating** An older zoo that's nice but not spectacular. Most animals are in natural habitats behind moats. ★★★. **How much time to allow** 2 hours to half a day.

DESCRIPTION AND COMMENTS This venerable animal park opened in 1929. Millions of dollars have been spent on innovative exhibits such as the Primate Discovery Center. Unlike most older zoos, the majority of the 1,000-plus animals are housed in naturalistic enclosures behind moats, and visitors can see the exotic wildlife hanging from trees, roaming through fields, and frequently snoozing in high grass. The fences and moats were recently updated to improve safety.

The zoo's major exhibits include Gorilla World, one of the largest naturalistic gorilla habitats in the world; visitors can get close-up views of the huge primates from strategically placed viewing areas. This is also one of only a handful of zoos in the United States with koalas. Penguin Island features a colony of more than 50 Magellanic penguins frolicking in a 200-foot pool (black tie required). Another recent addition is the Feline Conservation Center, a 20,000-square-foot sanctuary where rare and endangered cats such as snow, black, and Persian leopards are bred and studied; and the lemur forest, where you can watch 20 or so of these endangered primates leaping away. At the Children's Zoo, young-sters can pet and feed barnyard animals such as goats, sheep, chickens, donkeys, and even a llama. Be careful, though: if this South American cousin of the camel starts to smile, he may be about to spit.

TOURING TIPS The Little Puffer Steam Train (an actual steam locomotive built in 1904 and brought to the zoo in 1923) has been reintroduced to the public. Boarding is located across from the polar bears, adjacent to the Zoo Terrace Café. The locomotive takes passengers along a one-third mile route past the blackbuck, sea lions, bears, and lower lake. Each ride lasts about six minutes and is $2. Children under age 3 ride free.

The Leaping Lemur is the best lunch spot. The cafe provides indoor seating for visitors to escape the ocean breezes and fog that come from being so close to the ocean.

The Lion House does feedings at 2 p.m., and the penguins are fed at 3 p.m. except Thursday, when they chow at 2:30 p.m. Summers at the zoo allow the opportunity to sit in on the Meet the Keeper talks. Please call ahead to get the updated seasonal schedule.

OTHER THINGS TO DO NEARBY Breathe salt air and feel sand between your toes at nearby Ocean Beach, four miles long and always windy and wavy. But don't plan on a frolic in the surf; the water is always dangerous, even when it looks calm. To the south is Fort Funston ("Fort Fun" to the natives), where you'll find easy hiking trails, great views of the ocean and the seaside terrain, and hang gliders taking advantage of the area's high winds. Across from the entrance to the San Francisco Zoo is the Carousel Diner, a hot-dog stand out of the 1950s.

Walt Disney Family Museum ★★

APPEAL BY AGE	PRESCHOOL ★★	GRADE SCHOOL ★★	TEENS ★★★
YOUNG ADULTS ★★★	OVER 30 ★★★★	SENIORS ★★★★	

104 Montgomery Street in the Presidio; ☎ 415-345-6800; waltdisney.org

Type of attraction A museum of the Disney family and 20th-century animation history. **Admission** $20 for adults, $15 for seniors (age 65 and older) and students, $12.50 for children ages 6–17. Free for children under age 6 and members. **Hours** Wednesday–Monday, 10 a.m.–6 p.m. Closed New Year's Day, July 4, Thanksgiving, and Christmas. **When to go** Online time-booking guarantees it's never overcrowded. **Special comments** Older folks who grew up on *Fantasia* and *Old Yeller* are the folks who will get the most out of this. **Author's rating** Top marks! (As long as you can remember *Fantasia*.) ★★. **How much time to allow** 2–3 hours.

DESCRIPTION AND COMMENTS An entire wall of Uncle Walt's Oscars, including the specially made Oscar for *Snow White and the Seven Dwarfs,* greets you upon entering this excitingly designed museum, a veritable dreamboat of nostalgia for anybody who grew up on *Old Yeller, Snow White,* and

Fantasia, in other words anyone from ages 45 to 65 and up. Yes, it's an entire museum devoted to the creator of Mickey and Minnie Mouse and Pinocchio, right here in the historic buildings of the Presidio, idyllically situated next door to the Golden Gate Bridge and George Lucas' Industrial Light & Magic complex (*Star Wars*)! Be warned: It's a museum about the Disney family itself (no mention of cryonics) and his animation influences. Very small children will not be engrossed, though the earliest days of Disney's laugh-o-grams are enterprisingly shown across screens. Interactive and audio games reveal Disney's influence on animated film in America. As Uncle Walt's voice whispers memories in your ears, earliest photos reveal that the Disneys came from Kilkenny, Ireland, and were as Irish as they were American. His boyhood on a Missouri farm, wartime ambulance service, 1923 arrival in Hollywood, early animation triumphs, and beyond are all covered. A cafe and movie theater cap it all, and finding the place (it's on the Parade Ground at the Main Post) is the only hard part, since park signage is scarce. Parking is free and online booking staggers visitors in order not to overcrowd the exhibits. If this is the Disney family's way of clearing out the attic, we're not complaining.

TOURING TIPS In order to avoid overcrowding and permit relaxed viewing, tickets are exclusively time-booked online. Surprising innovations, such as a giant Disneyland model as Walt had imagined it, show off the handsome bones of this old landmark building, with its views of the Golden Gate—the best exhibit. Take time to drive or walk around the Presidio: It's a very lovely park with terrific views and a nice hike along the Baker Beach stretch.

OTHER THINGS TO DO NEARBY The Presidio has many historic buildings, from the Colonial-era Main Post buildings to the Log Cabin. At Baker Beach you can see the Golden Gate and fish. At Fort Point, you can view the site that has become a Civil War reenactment stage and revisit the *Vertigo* location too.

Wax Museum at Fisherman's Wharf ★

APPEAL BY AGE	PRESCHOOL ★★★	GRADE SCHOOL ★★★★	TEENS ★★★½
YOUNG ADULTS ★★		OVER 30 ★★	SENIORS ★★

Fisherman's Wharf (145 Jefferson Street, San Francisco 94133);
☎ **800-439-4305; waxmuseum.com**

Type of attraction Nearly 250 wax figures, ranging from the historical (Elizabeth Taylor as Cleopatra) to Hollywood (uh, Elizabeth Taylor as Cleopatra). A self-guided tour. **Admission** $14 for adults, $10 for seniors and children ages 12–17, $7 for children ages 6–11. On our visit, $3 off coupons were available in giveaway tourist guidebooks and on the museum's Web site. **Hours** Monday–Friday, 10 a.m.–9 p.m.; Saturday and Sunday, 9 a.m.–9 p.m. Open every day of the year. **When to go** Anytime. **Special comments** Located in the strip shopping center with all the tacky T-shirt shops and overpriced gift shops that face Fisherman's

Wharf. **Author's rating** This has nothing to do with San Francisco. ★. **How much time to allow** 1 hour.

DESCRIPTION AND COMMENTS Recently reopened after a multimillion dollar renovation, your reviewer's hopes ran high that the Wax Museum would emphasize San Francisco's rich visual history–the gold rush, the Earthquake and Great Fire, Dashiell Hammett gumshoeing in the 1920s and 1930s, the Beat Era, Haight-Ashbury and the Summer of Love, the dot-com boom and bust, the Quake of 1989. Yet what we get is just another cheesy tourist attraction that could be plopped down on any rundown boardwalk in any ocean resort in America–and with nary a reference to the City by the Bay. Inside the emphasis is on Hollywood (*Titanic,* Robin Williams, and an uncomfortable-looking Woody Allen), the historical (FDR, Winston Churchill, George W. Bush, John Major, but no Gordon Brown), the religious (these attractions always feature the Last Supper), and the gruesome (Boris Karloff as Frankenstein and lots of implements of torture). You've been warned.

TOURING TIPS Don't go. But if you're tugged inside by an insistent adolescent, don't miss a chance to shove the little monster into the electric chair, which administers a (visual) jolt. Kids love it.

OTHER THINGS TO DO NEARBY Fisherman's Wharf isn't all crummy, overpriced tourist rip-offs. The San Francisco Maritime National Historical Park–Hyde Street Pier and the San Francisco Maritime Museum are both worthwhile touring options. Visit Alcatraz (which may require advance reservations) or take a boat tour of San Francisco Bay. Or rent a bike and ride the Golden Gate Promenade on a windy, three-and-a-half mile stretch along the bay to Fort Point and the Golden Gate Bridge.

Wells Fargo History Museum ★★½

APPEAL BY AGE	PRESCHOOL ★★★	GRADE SCHOOL ★★★	TEENS ★★★
YOUNG ADULTS ★★	OVER 30 ★★		SENIORS ★★

**420 Montgomery Street (Financial District), San Francisco 94163;
☎ 415-396-2619; wellsfargohistory.com/museums**

Type of attraction A museum displaying artifacts and memorabilia of the American West and Wells Fargo, the banking and express firm founded in San Francisco in 1852. A self-guided tour. **Admission** Free. **Hours** Monday–Friday, 9 a.m.–5 p.m. Closed weekends and bank holidays. **When to go** Anytime. **Special comments** One set of stairs up to the mezzanine. **Author's rating** This small, attractive museum is chock-full of authentic items that make the Old West come alive; ★★½. **How much time to allow** 30 minutes to 1 hour.

DESCRIPTION AND COMMENTS A real, century-old stagecoach is the main attraction of this museum run by the Wells Fargo Bank, a firm famous for operating the Pony Express and a stagecoach empire throughout the western United States in the late 19th century. Other displays include mining tools, an incredibly complicated harness worn by the horses that pulled the stagecoaches, gold, money, treasure boxes, old postal envelopes, and photographs of the 1906 San Francisco earthquake and fire.

TOURING TIPS Don't miss the mezzanine level, where you can climb inside a stagecoach compartment and listen to a taped presentation. The real thing, on the main level below, is strictly hands-off.

OTHER THINGS TO DO NEARBY To stay with the Old West and gold-rush themes, have lunch at nearby Tadich Grill, established in 1849.

Yerba Buena Gardens/Center for the Arts ★★★

APPEAL BY AGE	PRESCHOOL ★★	GRADE SCHOOL ★★	TEENS ★★
YOUNG ADULTS ★★		OVER 30 ★★	SENIORS ★★★

701 Mission Street, San Francisco 94103; at Third Street south of Union Square in the SoMa District; ☎ 415-978-2700 (administration); ☎ 415-978-ARTS (ticket office); yerbabuenagardens.com or ybca.org

Type of attraction A cultural complex of grass and art, an art gallery, a theater, a memorial to Martin Luther King Jr., cafes, ice skating, and bowling. A self-guided tour. **Admission** Gallery: $6 for adults, $3 for students and seniors. Free for center members. Gardens are free. **Hours** Gallery and theater hours are Tuesday, Wednesday, Friday, Saturday, and Sunday, noon–5 p.m.; first Thursday of the month, noon–8 p.m. Gardens are open daily, sunrise–10 p.m. **When to go** Anytime for the art gallery; in nice weather for the outdoor gardens. **Special comments** A nice side trip—and a place to relax. **Author's rating** Of more interest to San Franciscans than to most visitors, who must take potluck on Yerba Buena's constantly changing schedule of exhibitions, shows, concerts, lectures, films, and videos. ★★★. **How much time to allow** 1 hour for the gallery and as long as you care to linger in the 5.5-acre gardens.

DESCRIPTION AND COMMENTS Yerba Buena is a nonprofit arts complex in the up-and-coming SoMa neighborhood. It features two buildings (a two-level art gallery and a theater) and a park with an outdoor stage, two cafes, the Butterfly Garden, a redwood grove, sculptures, a waterfall, and a memorial to Dr. Martin Luther King Jr. The small gallery features temporary art exhibits that change about every two-and-a-half months; on our visit there was a display of modern and avant-garde paintings and multimedia art—very San Francisco and a lot of fun.

TOURING TIPS Stop in the gallery and pick up a current copy of the *Center for the Arts* newsletter, which gives a complete description of events at Yerba Buena. If the exhibit looks interesting, tour the gallery. Don't miss the Martin Luther King Jr. Memorial and its 22-foot-high, 50 foot-wide waterfall. Free (with admission) walk-in gallery tours are offered on the second Saturday of the month at 1 p.m.

OTHER THINGS TO DO NEARBY The San Francisco Museum of Modern Art is across Third Street, and the Cartoon Art Museum is also nearby on Mission Street.

PART SEVEN

DINING *and* RESTAURANTS

THE VOLUPTUOUS PLEASURES of San Francisco's table still ring with the echoes of the Barbary Coast. People have been writing of memorable dining here since Mark Twain sojourned in the city and wrote of its charms in the 1860s. More than ever, people in San Francisco consider restaurants and the culinary arts one of the most important topics of discussion. And the chefs and their patrons concern themselves with both the end result and the entire process—from the origin and freshness of the ingredients, to the utensils with which they are prepared, to diners' and servers' states of mind. There's a personal quality to gastronomy in the city. Chefs adapt the lessons learned in European kitchens to the dictates of locally grown foodstuffs and further incorporate the diverse cultural influences of the region.

Perhaps unique to the city is the possibility of genuinely friendly service. The best San Francisco restaurants are not stuffy or formal and will not treat you with condescension. Most are happy to hear about unsatisfactory service or a dish that was improperly prepared. Unlike New York, San Francisco has few of the imposing, intimidating, ghastly expensive Taj Mahals whose raison d'être has been obscured by interests other than the table. And as for Los Angeles . . . well, San Francisco eats L.A.'s lunch!

This is the capital of the three-star restaurant. Diners want the best in food and service and the best in price. And they want no snooty waiters. Even the four- and five-star restaurants are short on pretense and long on service. The common person is king here; he (or she) just happens to have a discriminating palate.

Whence came this egalitarian attitude? The Old West—with its frontier meritocracy, lusty democracy, and demand for good vittles—is newest here. You still find the legacies of Spanish missionaries and ranchers, Chinese railroad workers, Italian vintners, and nouveau riche gold miners seeking to mirror European splendor. Mix in Japanese, Vietnamese, and Russian immigration. Add the organic and sustainable agriculture movement, local growers' experimentation with artisan crops such as Japanese persimmons, kiwis, habanero peppers, and heirloom varieties of fruits and vegetables; and the blossoming of boutique wineries, cheese makers, and game farms. Put these with a skepticism of high-falutin' New York ways, and you have the makings of the culinary revolution that began in the 1970s. Creative chefs are drawn to the area because of the year-round availability of superior produce and the relative sophistication of native palates and tastes, along with diners' senses of humor and commitment to a casual brand of elegance.

There's a restaurant to suit any occasion, appetite, or budget. There's also likely to be a very good, even great, place to dine within walking distance of anywhere you might be. San Francisco is known, after all, as the "walking city." A brisk walk through the cool tang of a San Francisco fog is one of the best appetizers the city has to offer. And it's free.

TOURIST PLACES

In the restaurant profiles that make up this section, you may notice that a few well-known or highly visible restaurants are missing. This is not an oversight. The following restaurants may come to your attention, but in our opinion they're not as worthwhile as other comparable options.

- **Boudin Bakery** *American* 160 Jefferson Street; ☎ 415-351-5561; **boudinbakery.com**
- **Empress of China** *Pan Chinese* 838 Grant Avenue; ☎ 415-434-1345; **empressofchinasf.com**
- **Lori's Diner** *Fabulous '50s diner* 500 Sutter Street, ☎ 415-981-1950; 149 Powell Street, ☎ 415-677-9999; 336 Mason Street, ☎ 415-392-8646; **lorisdiner.com**
- **Scoma's** *Seafood* Pier 47, Fisherman's Wharf; ☎ 415-771-4383; 588 Bridgeway, Sausalito; ☎ 415-332-9551
- **Sinbad's** *Seafood* Pier 2, Embarcadero Street; ☎ 415-781-2555

The RESTAURANTS

HITTING HOT SPOTS

CLIFF HOUSE (1090 Point Lobos Avenue; ☎ 415-386-3330; **cliffhouse. com**) This is still the ancient institution where San Franciscans whisk visitors for showy Mai Tais and sunsets, trading sunset views of Sutro Baths ruins and Seal Rocks for what used to be so-so food. Lately, though, the Cliff House has enjoyed a menu upgrade; try the Terrace Room for divine Sunday brunches, clubby Zinc Bar, and Sutro's or Bistro for lunch and dinner. A lavish Champagne brunch menu boasts eggs Benedict variations that blend sublimely with bubbly. Dungeness crab cakes sing. The Cliff House is still old-timey and remains a nostalgic favorite for surfer- and seal-watching.

ESPETUS CHURRASCARIA (1686 Market Street near Hayes Valley; ☎ 415-552-8792; **espetus.com**) White linen, warm wood, plus floor-to-ceiling iron girders and windows opening onto Market Street help you savor the slow-roasting skills of southern Brazil's grill-happy gauchos. Waiters rush a dozen large skewers of different meats to your table in dizzying, all-you-can-eat waves: sirloin, filet mignon, linguiça sausages, ribs, tenderloin, chicken hearts (a chewy, juicy specialty), or lamb chops. Knock it all back with *caipirinha* cocktails or jammy Malbecs.

FORBES ISLAND (Sea Lion Harbor, H dock, between Piers 39 and 41; ☎ 415-951-4900; **forbesisland.com**) Giant kitsch is what people think when they learn about the Bay Area's only floating island-restaurant—Lord, how cynical! A big Jules Verne fan, Forbes Kiddoo dreamed of his own Captain Nemo–style marine home and began his man-made island in the '70s. In 1999, Kiddoo moved Forbes Island and opened it as a restaurant. By then, it was 50 by 100 feet, with palms, a waterfall, Tahitian dining room, lighthouse, underwater dining room, bar, fireplace, wine cellar, and staterooms. Diners phone the island from H Dock under venerable Eagle Café to catch the tiki-boat shuttle. Start with calamari salad. Flatiron steak wears a mustard-cognac crème sauce; rack of lamb is herb-baked.

HAVANA (1518 Park Street, Alameda; ☎ 510-521-0130; **havana restaurant.net**) This so-called Cuban bar-bistro is a people-pleaser. A glass-fronted façade and shiny metal-and-aqua bar with vivid blowups of Buena Vista singers evoke either old Havana or a South Florida diner—you choose. An obliging barman serves customized mojitos. Soak up ceviche or garlic fries with guava-chipotle sauce or chimichurri aïoli. Halibut in plantain crust with tomatillo-avocado salsa, sea bass with corn cakes, chicken adobo, and chimichurri skirt steak is followed by flan for dessert.

URBAN TAVERN (333 O'Farrell Street, Union Square; ☎ 415-923-4400; **urbantavernsf.com**) A rollicking scene near the door gives way to emptier spots at the rear for quiet dining. The menu: localvore Californian from Berkshire pork chops with baked butter beans in a cast-iron skillet to summer vegetable stew with polenta and Parmesan. Bursting with freshness, chopped salad is not to be missed.

OUR FAVORITE SAN FRANCISCO RESTAURANTS

WE HAVE DEVELOPED DETAILED PROFILES for the best and most interesting restaurants (in our opinion) in town. Each profile features an easily scanned heading that allows you, in just a second, to check out the restaurant's name, cuisine, star rating, cost, quality rating, and value rating.

CUISINE This is actually less straightforward than it sounds. A couple of years ago, for example, "pan-Asian" restaurants were generally serving what was then generally described as "fusion" food—Asian ingredients with European techniques or vice versa. Since then, there has been a pan-Asian explosion in the area, but nearly all specialize in what would be street food back home: noodles, skewers, dumplings, and soups. Once-general categories have become subdivided—French into bistro fare and even Provencal; "new continental" into regional American and "eclectic"—while others have broadened and fused: Middle Eastern and Provencal into Mediterranean, Spanish and South American into Nuevo Latino, and so on. In these cases, we have generally used the broader terms (such as "French") but sometimes added a parenthetical phrase to give a clearer idea of the fare. Again, though, experimentation and "fusion" is growing more common, so don't hold us, or the chefs, to a strict style.

OVERALL RATING The overall rating encompasses the entire dining experience, including style, service, and ambience, in addition to the taste, presentation, and quality of the food. Five stars is the highest rating possible and connotes the best of everything. Four-star restaurants are exceptional and three-star restaurants are well above average. Two-star restaurants are good. One star is used to indicate an average restaurant that demonstrates an unusual capability in some area of specialization—for example, an otherwise unmemorable place that has great barbecue chicken.

COST The expense description provides a comparative sense of how much a complete meal will cost. A complete meal for our purposes consists of an entree with vegetable or side dish and choice of soup or salad. Appetizers, desserts, drinks, and tips are excluded.

Inexpensive	$14 and less per person
Moderate	$15–$25 per person
Expensive	$26–$40 per person
Very Expensive	More than $40 per person

A NOTE ON MENUS AND PRICES The better restaurants in The City and around the bay change their menus at least seasonally. Others change it monthly, weekly, or even daily. Or with what's available at the market, or with the chef's whim. Anything we tell you is on the menu today might not be there tomorrow. And, of course, prices will fluctuate with the menu changes—but not a lot, and they go down as well as up. Just don't be surprised if things aren't quite the same when you get there.

QUALITY RATING The food quality is rated on a scale of ★ to ★★★★★, with ★★★★★ being the best rating attainable. It is based expressly on the taste, freshness of ingredients, preparation, presentation, and creativity of food served. There is no consideration of price.

If you are a person who wants the best food available, and cost is not an issue, you need look no further than the quality ratings.

VALUE RATING If, on the other hand, you are looking for both quality and value, then you should check the value rating. The value ratings are defined as follows:

★★★★★	Exceptional value, a real bargain
★★★★	Good value
★★★	Fair value, you get exactly what you pay for
★★	Somewhat overpriced
★	Significantly overpriced

PAYMENT We've listed the type of payment accepted at each restaurant using the following code: AE equals American Express (Optima), CB equals Carte Blanche, D equals Discover, DC equals Diners Club, MC equals MasterCard, and V equals VISA.

WHO'S INCLUDED Restaurants in San Francisco open and close at an alarming rate. So, for the most part, we have tried to confine our list to establishments with a proven track record over a fairly long period of time. The exceptions here are the newer offspring of the demigods of the culinary world. These places are destined to last, at least until our next update. Newer or changed establishments that demonstrate staying power and consistency will be profiled in subsequent editions. Also, the list is highly selective. Noninclusion of a particular place does not necessarily indicate that the restaurant is not good, but only that it was not ranked among the best in its genre. Detailed profiles of individual restaurants follow in alphabetical order at the end of this chapter.

unofficial **TIP**
Home: Norman Rockwell–style mac and cheese, cornbread with honey butter, fried chicken with mashed potatoes and slaw, and pot roast with horseradish. This place is homey to the point of unsophistication, with plain old-fashioned bang for a buck. Banana bread pudding glories in bourbon. For more information, visit Home at 2100 Market Street; ☎ 415-503-0333; **home-sf.com.**

MORE RECOMMENDATIONS
The Best Bagels

- **Marin Bagel Company** 1560 Fourth Street, San Rafael; ☎ 415-457-0127
- **Noah's Bagels** 170 Bon Air Center, Greenbrae; ☎ 415-925-9971; noahs.com

The Best Beer Lists

- **Duke of Edinburgh** 10801 North Wolfe Road, Cupertino; ☎ 408-446-3853; theduke.com
- **The Mayflower Pub** 1533 Fourth Street, San Rafael; ☎ 415-456-1011; themayflowerpub.com

- **The Pelican Inn** 10 Pacific Way, Muir Beach; ☎ 415-383-6000; pelicaninn.com
- **Tommy's Joynt** 1101 Geary Boulevard, San Francisco; ☎ 415-775-4216; tommysjoynt.com

The Best Burgers

- **Bubba's** 566 San Anselmo Avenue, San Anselmo; ☎ 415-459-6862; bubbas-diner.net
- **Flipper's** 482 Hayes Street, San Francisco; ☎ 415-552-8880
- **Kirk's** 2388 South Bascom Avenue, Campbell; ☎ 408-371-3565; kirks-steakburgers.com
- **Louie's Bar & Grill** 55 Stevenson Street, San Francisco; ☎ 415-543-3540
- **Perry's** 1944 Union Street, San Francisco; ☎ 415-922-9022; **perryssf.com**
- **Rockridge Cafe** 5492 College Avenue, Oakland; ☎ 510-653-1567; rockridgecafe.com

The Best Bang for Your Buck

- **Park Chow** 1240 Ninth Avenue at Lincoln Way; ☎ 415-665-9912
- **Pho Phu Quoc (PPQ)** 1816 Irving Street at 19th Avenue; ☎ 415-661-8869; **ppqsf.com**
- **Sapporo-Ya** 1581 Webster Street (in Japan Center); ☎ 415-563-7400

unofficial **TIP**
Unless you grew up on Mars, you'll have heard of Chez Panisse (1517 Shattuck Avenue, Berkeley; ☎ 510-548-5525; chezpanisse.com) housed for four decades in a period Craftsman bungalow in Berkeley's gourmet ghetto. Its founder Alice Waters is the most influential of Californian foodies since Julia Child, espousing local, sustainable, and organic food. The upstairs cafe offers a relatively inexpensive prix fixe, and it is a calm and casual spot to enjoy hearty rustic Italian-influenced pastas or chicken baked under a brick, which were on a recent menu.

The Best Business Dining

- **Chez Panisse** 1517 Shattuck Avenue, Berkeley; ☎ 510-548-5525; **chezpanisse.com**
- **The Duck Club** 100 El Camino Real, Menlo Park; ☎ 650-330-2790; **stanfordparkhotel.com**
- **Spenger's Fresh Fish Grotto** 1919 Fourth Street, Berkeley; ☎ 510-845-7771; **spengers.com**
- **Tadich Grill** 240 California Street, San Francisco; ☎ 415-391-1849; **tadichgrill.com**

The Best Desserts

- **Campton Place Restaurant** 340 Stockton Street, San Francisco; ☎ 415-781-5555; **camptonplacesf.com**
- **Masa's Restaurant** 648 Bush Street, San Francisco; ☎ 415-989-7154; **masasrestaurant.com**

The Best Martinis

- **Buckeye Roadhouse** 15 Shoreline Highway, Mill Valley; ☎ 415-331-2600; **buckeyeroadhouse.com**

- **House of Prime Rib** 1906 Van Ness Avenue; ☎ 415-885-4605; **houseofprimerib.net**
- **No Name Bar** 757 Bridgeway, Sausalito; ☎ 415-332-1392

The Best Oyster Bars

- **Lulu** 816 Folsom Street, San Francisco; ☎ 415-495-5775; **restaurantlulu.com**
- **Swan Oyster Depot** 1517 Polk Street, San Francisco; ☎ 415-673-1101

The Best Pizza

- **Benissimo Ristorante & Bar** 18 Tamalpais Drive, Corte Madera; ☎ 415-927-2316; **benissimos.com**
- **Frankie, Johnnie & Luigi Too** 939 West El Camino Real, Mountain View; ☎ 650-967-5384; **fjlmountainview.com**
- **Milano Restaurant** 1 Blackfield Drive, Belvedere Tiburon; ☎ 415-388-9100; **milanotiburon.com**
- **Mulberry Street Pizzeria** 101 Smith Ranch Road, San Rafael; ☎ 415-472-7272; **mulberry-street-pizzeria.com**
- **Salute Ristorante** 706 Third Street, San Rafael; ☎ 415-453-7596

The Best Seafood

- **The Fish Market** 3150 El Camino Real, Palo Alto; ☎ 650-493-9188; **thefishmarket.com**
- **Rooney's Cafe and Grill** 38 Main Street, Tiburon; ☎ 415-435-1911
- **Sam's Anchor Cafe** 27 Main Street, Tiburon; ☎ 415-435-4527; **samscafe.com**
- **Spenger's Fresh Fish Grotto** 1919 Fourth Street, Berkeley; ☎ 510-845-7771; **spengers.com**
- **Tadich Grill** 240 California Street, San Francisco; ☎ 415-391-1849; **tadichgrill.com**

*un*official **TIP**
All-you-can-eat pizza on Sundays makes **Local Kitchen and Wine Merchant** (330 First Street; ☎ 415-777-4200; **sf-local. com**) a family pit stop of choice in sophisticated SoMa. Generally chef Ola Fendert's approach works better for grown-ups because of its dazzling modernist decor—a huge steel door leads to a sprawling counter and a high island-table, plus a dedicated wine bar with fabled wine flights. The service can be oddly erratic, sometimes wonderful and sometimes missing. Verdict: unpredictable, yet often interesting, and definitely a good evening spot for a slurp and a swirl of wine!

The Best Sunday Brunches

- **Buckeye Roadhouse** 15 Shoreline Highway, Mill Valley; ☎ 415-331-2600; **buckeyeroadhouse.com**
- **The Palace Hotel Garden Court** 2 New Montgomery Street, San Francisco; ☎ 415-546-5089; **sfpalacerestaurants.com/gardencourt**
- **Station House Cafe** 11180 Highway 1, Point Reyes Station; ☎ 415-663-1515; **stationhousecafe.com**

Lunch with a View

SAN FRANCISCO IS BLESSED with many places offering a bird's-eye view at lunchtime. We're not talking top-floor restaurants with big picture windows, though. This is about rooftop gardens scattered throughout the city, where you can take your deli takeout or other sack lunch (some of these rooftops even serve lunch) and get up and above it all for an hour of serenity among flowering plants and ferns and such. Just punch the top button on the elevator and be transported to the most relaxing lunch in town.

- **San Francisco Art Institute Café** 800 Chestnut Street between Jones and Leavenworth streets; ☎ 415-749-4567; **sfai.edu.** A short walk from Fisherman's Wharf or from North Beach where you can walk up Chestnut Street from Columbus Avenue.

- **Crocker Galleria Roof Terrace** 50 Post Street, enter from Post or Sutter streets. Also accessible to hotel guests of the Galleria Park Hotel at 191 Sutter Street.

- **Wells Fargo Roof Garden** One Montgomery at Market and Post streets. Monday to Friday, 10 a.m.–6 p.m.

- **First and Mission streets** 100 First Street at Mission; ☎ 415-243-8803.

- **343 Sansome Street** between California and Sacramento streets, 15th floor. Monday to Friday, 7 a.m. to 5:30 p.m.

- **Embarcadero Center and Maritime Plaza** Approach from Sansome Street, between Sacramento and Clay streets. Cross Sansome Street and ascend a stone staircase by an arched pergola and a playing fountain. On your right is the Old Federal Reserve Building and on your left the Hyatt Regency Hotel. The staircase leads to Embarcadero Center's Promenade Level. Ahead is the cinema and beyond that the black metal grid of the Maritime Plaza Building. Follow the walkway left through the Embarcadero Center Building 2.

- **Fairmont Hotel** 950 Mason Street at California Street, or the entrance on California Street. Take the elevator to the rooftop garden.

- **Yerba Buena Gardens** Mission and Fourth streets.

The Best Wee Hours Service

- **Marin Joe's Restaurant** 1585 Casa Buena Drive, Corte Madera; ☎ 415-924-2081; **marinjoesrestaurant.com**
- **Max's Opera Cafe** 601 Van Ness Avenue, San Francisco; ☎ 415-771-7300; **maxsworld.com**
- **Sam Wo** 813 Washington Street, San Francisco; ☎ 415-982-0596
- **Yuet Lee** 1300 Stockton Street, San Francisco; ☎ 415-982-6020

The Best Quiet Dining

- **Chez Panisse** 1517 Shattuck Avenue, Berkeley; ☎ 510-548-5525; **chezpanisse.com**
- **Digs Bistro** 1453 Dwight Way, Berkeley; ☎ 510-548-2322; **digsbistro.com**
- **Fleur de Lys** 777 Sutter Street, San Francisco; ☎ 415-673-7779; **fleurdelyssf.com**
- **Florio** 1915 Fillmore Street, San Francisco; ☎ 415-775-4300; **floriosf.com**
- **Masa's Restaurant** 648 Bush Street, San Francisco; ☎ 415-989-7154; **masasrestaurant.com**

RESTAURANT PROFILES

Ana Mandara ★★★★

MODERN VIETNAMESE	MOD/EXP	QUALITY ★★★★½	VALUE ★★★★

891 Beach Street, San Francisco, Marina District; ☎ 415-771-6800; anamandara.com

Reservations Recommended. **When to go** Anytime. **Entree range** $18–$32. **Payment** All major credit cards. **Service rating** ★★★★. **Friendliness rating** ★★★★. **Parking** Valet or 1½ hours free at Ghirardelli Square. **Bar** Full service. **Wine selection** Excellent. **Dress** Casually elegant. **Disabled access** Yes. **Customers** Locals, tourists, and celebs. **Hours** Monday–Thursday, 11:30 a.m.–2 p.m. and 5:30 p.m.–9:30 p.m.; Friday, 11:30 a.m.–2 p.m. and 5:30 p.m.–10:30 p.m.; Saturday, 5:30 p.m.–10:30 p.m.; Sunday, 5:30 p.m.–9:30 p.m.

SETTING AND ATMOSPHERE Exotic and inviting. Ana Mandara means "beautiful refuge," and it is. It's a luxury just to step inside the expansive main dining room filled with Asian art and antiques, fountains, a grand staircase, and theatrical lighting, the latter befitting a restaurant owned by actor Don Johnson. The brick building is historic, once serving as the old generator room for the Ghirardelli chocolate factory. So designers had to work with the cavernous space, adding smaller nooks on a floor-level faux balcony trimmed with bamboo window shades that look out over the main dining room. The brass-railed staircase leads up to the second-floor Cham Bar. Palm trees and full-grown ficus reach up to the ceiling. With all this grandeur, the feel is surprisingly comfortable. Black-and-white family photos grace one wall, relatives of Executive Chef Khai Duong. And several of his family members work in the restaurant, providing gracious service and sage menu suggestions.

HOUSE SPECIALTIES Classic Vietnamese dishes with a French touch. Chef Duong grew up in Vietnam and received his formal training at Le Cordon Bleu, resulting in delightful taste combinations: seared foie gras with truffle oil and fresh mango; or grilled rack of lamb with a

continued on page 256

The Best San Francisco Restaurants

TYPE AND NAME	OVERALL RATING	COST	QUALITY RATING	VALUE RATING
AFGHAN				
Helmand Palace	★★★	Inexp	★★★★	★★★★★
AMERICAN				
Five	★★★★	Mod	★★★★★	★★★★½
Boulevard	★★★★½	Exp	★★★★	★★★★½
Beach Chalet	★★★½	Mod	★★★★	★★★★
House of Prime Rib	★★★½	Exp	★★★★	★★★★
Tadich Grill	★★★	Mod	★★★★	★★★★★
Fog City Diner	★★★	Mod	★★★★	★★★★
Tommy's Joynt	★★	Inexp	★★★½	★★★★★
Luna Park Kitchen and Cocktails	★★	Mod	★★★½	★★★★
The Buena Vista	★	Inexp	★★★½	★★★
CALIFORNIAN				
Jardinière	★★★★★	Exp	★★★★★	★★★★½
Kuleto's	★★★½	Mod	★★★★	★★★★
Digs Bistro	★★★½	Mod	★★★	★★★★
Oola	★★★½	Mod	★★★	★★★★
Enrico's	★★★	Mod	★★★★	★★★★
West Bay Café	★★★	Mod	★★★★	★★★★
First Crush	★★★	Mod	★★★½	★★★★
CHINESE				
Tommy Toy's	★★★½	Mod	★★★★	★★★★½
Shanghai 1930	★★★	Mod	★★★	★★★★
Yank Sing	★★★	Inexp	★★★½	★★★★
Yuet Lee	★★½	Inexp/Mod	★★★½	★★★★★
CHINO-LATINO				
Asia de Cuba	★★★★	Exp	★★★★½	★★★★★
CONTEMPORARY ASIAN				
Ponzu	★★★★½	Mod/Exp	★★★★	★★★★
CONTINENTAL				
The Brazen Head Restaurant & Public House	★★★	Mod	★★★½	★★★★★
CRÊPERIE				
Ti Couz	★★	Inexp	★★	★★★

TYPE AND NAME	OVERALL RATING	COST	QUALITY RATING	VALUE RATING
DELI/BARBECUE				
Max's Opera Café	★½	Mod	★★★	★★★★
DIVE				
Red's Java House	★	Inexp	★★★	★★★★★
ECLECTIC				
Momi Toby's Revolution Café	★★	Inexp	★★★½	★★★
FRENCH				
Campton Place Restaurant	★★★★★	Exp	★★★★★	★★★★★
Masa's	★★★★★	Exp	★★★★★	★★★★★
La Toque	★★★★½	Exp	★★★★★	★★★★½
Fleur de Lys	★★★★	Exp	★★★★★	★★★★
Fringale	★★★★	Mod	★★★★½	★★★★★
Lulu	★★★½	Mod	★★★★	★★★★
South Park Café	★★★	Mod	★★★★	★★★★★
Café de la Presse	★★★	Mod	★★★★	★★★★
Chapeau!	★★★	Exp	★★★½	★★★
Chez Papa Resto	★★★	Mod	★★★	★★★½
Plouf	★★	Mod	★★★	★★★
FRENCH/VIETNAMESE				
Le Colonial	★★★½	Exp	★★★★	★★★
GREEK				
Kokkari Estiatorio	★★★½	Exp	★★★★½	★★★★
HOFBRAU				
Lefty O'Doul's	★★	Inexp	★★½	★★★★
ITALIAN				
Palio d'Asti	★★★★	Exp	★★★★★	★★★★★
Oliveto	★★★★	Exp	★★★★	★★★★
SPQR	★★★★	Mod	★★★★	★★★★
Trattoria Pinocchio	★★★½	Mod	★★★★½	★★★★★
Scala's Bistro	★★★½	Exp	★★★★	★★★★
Il Fornaio	★★★½	Mod	★★½	★★★★
Zuni Café and Grill	★★★★	Mod	★★★★	★★★★
Café Pescatore	★★★	Mod	★★★½	★★★★
Cafe Tiramisu	★★★	Mod	★★★	★★★

The Best San Francisco Restaurants (continued)

TYPE AND NAME	OVERALL RATING	COST	QUALITY RATING	VALUE RATING
ITALIAN (CONTINUED)				
Calzone's	★★	Mod	★★½	★★★
The Stinking Rose	★★	Mod	★★½	★★★
MEDITERRANEAN				
Farallon	★★★★★	Exp	★★★★★	★★★★★
Baywolf	★★★★½	Exp	★★★★½	★★★★½
Grand Café	★★★½	Exp	★★★★½	★★★★
MOROCCAN				
Aziza	★★★½	Mod	★★★	★★★★
NEW AMERICAN				
The Garden Court	★★★★	Exp	★★★★½	★★★★
Town's End Restaurant and Bakery	★★★	Mod	★★★★	★★★★
Clement Street Bar and Grill	★★★	Mod	★★★½	★★★
The Cosmopolitan Restaurant	★★★	Mod/Exp	★★★	★★★★
Paragon	★★	Mod	★★★½	★★★
PAN-ASIAN				
Bambuddha Lounge	★★★	Mod	★★★½	★★★★½
SEAFOOD				
McCormick & Kuleto's	★★★	Mod	★★★	★★★
Spenger's Fresh Fish Grotto	★★★	Mod/Exp	★★★	★★★★
Swan Oyster Depot	★★	Inexp	★★★½	★★★★★
SINGAPOREAN				
Straits Restaurant	★★★★	Mod	★★★★½	★★★★★

continued from page 253

Vietnamese cinnamon star-anise rub and a spicy tamarind sauce. The entree portions are quite large to encourage sharing, but you may not want to. The traditional clay pot fish is a favorite, with a spicy caramelized sauce over seared bass on a bed of snappy snow peas. You must have some starters and sides. The garlic noodles are yummy. The tender steamed dumplings with shrimp and chicken are a nice balance to the crispy lobster ravioli with mango and coconut sauce.

TYPE AND NAME	OVERALL RATING	COST	QUALITY RATING	VALUE RATING
SOUTHEAST ASIAN				
E&O Trading Company	★★★	Exp	★★★★	★★★★
SPANISH				
Zarzuela	★★★	Mod	★★★★	★★★★★
B44	★★★	Mod	★★★★	★★★★
Thirsty Bear Brewing Company	★★★	Mod	★★★½	★★★★
STEAK HOUSE				
Harris' Steakhouse	★★★★½	Exp	★★★★★	★★★★½
Izzy's Steak and Chop House	★★★	Mod	★★★★	★★★★★
John's Grill	★★★	Mod	★★★½	★★★★★
Ruth's Chris Steak House	★★½	Exp	★★★½	★★★★
THAI				
Dusit	★★½	Inexp	★★★½	★★★★
VEGETARIAN				
Greens	★★★★	Mod	★★★★	★★★★
Millennium	★★★½	Mod	★★★★½	★★★★
VIETNAMESE				
Ana Mandara	★★★★	Mod/Exp	★★★★½	★★★★
Le Cheval	★★★★	Mod	★★★★	★★★★
Thanh Long	★★★	Inexp/Mod	★★★★	★★★★
WEST COAST BASQUE				
Piperade's	★★★	Mod	★★★★	★★★★

OTHER RECOMMENDATIONS Have a cocktail before dinner from the inventive bartenders in the Cham Bar. One recent creation is the Fukien Mist, a sweet sensation of lychee-fruit liqueur with gin, a hint of lemon juice, and some grenadine to give it a rosy tone. It will give you a rosy tone, as well. To finish off the meal, try the mango spring rolls or the banana boat dessert, a twist on the classic fried banana, but a little lighter in a delicious, thick caramel sauce with candied walnuts.

SUMMARY AND COMMENTS Atmosphere is everything here—glamour and grace. There is live jazz in the Cham Bar Thursday, Friday, and Saturday

continued on page 261

Dining around Town

1. Ana Mandara
2. Aziza
3. Bambuddha Lounge
4. Beach Chalet
5. Boulevard
6. The Brazen Head
7. The Buena Vista
8. Cafe Pescatore
9. Calzone's
10. Chapeau!
11. Chez Papa Resto
12. Clement Street Bar and Grill
13. The Cosmopolitan Restaurant
14. Dusit
15. Enrico's
16. Fog City Diner
17. Fringale
18. Greens
19. Harris' Steakhouse
20. Helmand Palace
21. House of Prime Rib
22. Il Fornaio
23. Izzy's Steak and Chop House
24. Jardinière
25. Lulu
26. Luna Park Kitchen and Cocktails
27. Max's Opera Café
28. McCormick & Kuleto's
29. Millennium
30. Momi Toby's Revolution Café
31. Oola
32. Paragon
33. Piperade's
34. Red's Java House
35. Ruth's Chris Steak House
36. Shanghai 1930
37. South Park Café
38. SPQR
39. The Stinking Rose
40. Straits Restaurant
41. Swan Oyster Depot
42. Thanh Long
43. Thirsty Bear Brewing Co.
44. Ti Couz
45. Tommy's Joynt
46. Town's End Restaurant and Bakery
47. Trattoria Pinocchio
48. Yuet Lee
49. Zarzuela
50. Zuni Café and Grill

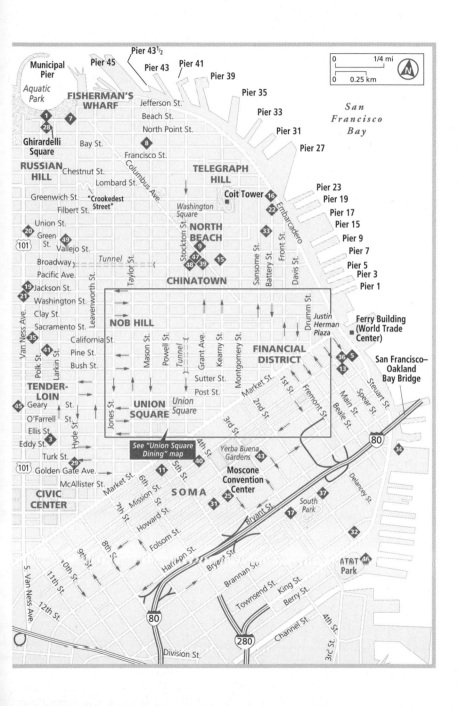

Pier 43½
Pier 45
Pier 43
Pier 41
Pier 39
Pier 35
Pier 33
Pier 31
Pier 27

Municipal Pier
Aquatic Park
FISHERMAN'S WHARF
Jefferson St.
Beach St.
North Point St.
Bay St.
Francisco St.
Ghirardelli Square

San Francisco Bay

0   1/4 mi
0   0.25 km

RUSSIAN HILL
Chestnut St.
Lombard St.
Greenwich St.
Filbert St.
Union St.
Green St.
Vallejo St.
Broadway
Pacific Ave.
Jackson St.
Washington St.
Clay St.
Sacramento St.

Columbus Ave.
"Crookedest Street"
Washington Square
Tunnel

TELEGRAPH HILL
Coit Tower

NORTH BEACH

Pier 23
Pier 19
Pier 17
Pier 15
Pier 9
Pier 7
Pier 5
Pier 3
Pier 1

Embarcadero

Stockton St.
Sansome St.
Battery St.
Front St.
Davis St.

CHINATOWN

NOB HILL
Leavenworth St.
Taylor St.
Mason St.
Powell St.
Tunnel
Grant Ave.
Kearny St.
Montgomery St.
California St.
Pine St.
Bush St.
Sutter St.
Post St.

Drumm St.
Justin Herman Plaza
FINANCIAL DISTRICT
Market St.
1st St.
Fremont St.

Ferry Building (World Trade Center)

San Francisco–Oakland Bay Bridge

Van Ness Ave.
Polk St.
Larkin St.

TENDER-LOIN
Geary St.
O'Farrell St.
Ellis St
Eddy St.
Turk St.
Golden Gate Ave.
McAllister St.

UNION SQUARE
Union Square
Jones St.
Hyde St.
4th St.
5th St.

See "Union Square Dining" map

CIVIC CENTER

Market St.
6th St.
7th St.
8th St.
9th St.
10th St.
11th St.
12th St.
S. Van Ness Ave.

Mission St.
Howard St.
Folsom St.
Harrison St.

SOMA

Yerba Buena Gardens
Moscone Convention Center
South Park

Bryant St.
Brannan St.
Townsend St.
King St.
Berry St.
Channel St.
3rd St.
4th St.

Stewart St.
Spear St.
Main St.
Beale St.
2nd St.
3rd St.

Delancey St.

AT&T Park

Division St.

Union Square Dining

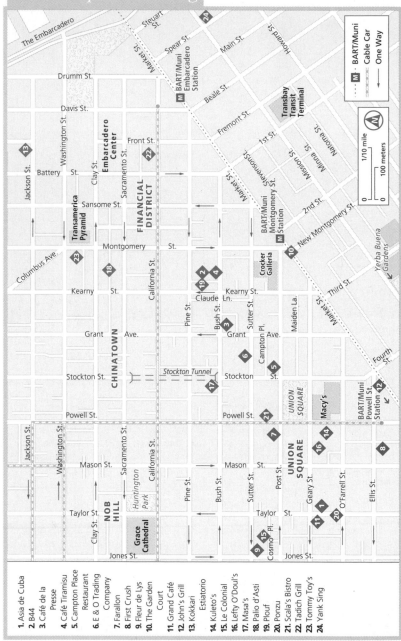

continued from page 257

nights. They take out the tables and chairs in the main dining room and turn it into a dance floor, catering to a well-dressed, mature crowd in their 30s and 40s. Though on touristy Fisherman's Wharf, lots of locals come to this refuge for special occasions—at least half a dozen weddings are held here every year. And the tourists who do make the find go back home and tell everyone about it.

Asia de Cuba ★★★★

CHINO-LATINO	EXPENSIVE	QUALITY ★★★★½	VALUE ★★★★★

Clift Hotel, 495 Geary Street, Union Square; ☎ 415-929-2300; clifthotel.com

Reservations Recommended. **When to go** All day and night. **Entree range** $22–$56. **Payment** All major credit cards. **Service rating** ★★★★. **Friendliness rating** ★★★. **Parking** Valet. **Bar** Full service. **Wine selection** Excellent. **Dress** Casually elegant. **Disabled access** Yes. **Customers** Local swells and wide-eyed tourists. **Hours** Sunday–Wednesday, 7 a.m.–2:30 p.m., and 5:30–10:30 p.m.; Thursday–Saturday, 7 a.m.–2:30 p.m. and 5:30 p.m.–12:30 a.m.

SETTING AND ATMOSPHERE Something San Francisco does best: In-your-face elegance backed up by unimpeachable quality and imbued with frontier egalitarianism. You can come here in a tux or sleek strapless gown; you can come here in a sweater or sport coat. It's dark and velvety and trimmed in redwood and held up by huge columns. Plush booths occupy the corners, tables are lined up by the walls, and a T-shaped bar in the center of the room is good for eating or just drinking.

HOUSE SPECIALTIES The cuisine is based on the Chino-Latino cookery of Chinese restaurants in pre-Castro Havana. Many Chinese emigrated to Miami, where they continued to prepare dishes that were recognizably of the Chinese school, yet doused with strictly local ingredients and cooking practices that give the finished product a unique and delicious character. Appetizers include tunapica, a spicy tartare with currants, almonds, and soy-lime vinaigrette; oxtail spring rolls; lobster pot stickers; and crab cakes with shiitake mushrooms. Signature entrees include coriander-encrusted flatiron steak with bonito mash; Chino-Latino Peking duck; and Hunan whole crispy fish.

OTHER RECOMMENDATIONS Entrees are meant to be shared family-style. But the side dishes are just as interesting and could be made into meals. Try stir-fried coconut rice, plantain fried rice, or black-bean croquettes.

SUMMARY AND COMMENTS You might start with a drink in the adjacent Redwood Room bar, a must-have-a-drink place for tourists and locals alike. At any rate, come here hungry and in no hurry. This is a superb place for lingering and malingering.

Aziza   ★★★½

| MOROCCAN | MODERATE | QUALITY ★★★ | VALUE ★★★★ |

5800 Geary Boulevard, Richmond District; ☎ 415-752-2222; aziza-sf.com

Reservations Recommended. **When to go** Dinner. **Entree range** $16–$23. **Payment** All major credit cards. **Service rating** ★★★★. **Friendliness rating** ★★★★. **Parking** Valet ($10), street. **Bar** Full service. **Wine selection** Good. **Dress** Business, casual. **Disabled access** Yes. **Customers** Locals from all over town. **Hours** Wednesday–Monday, 5:30–10 p.m.; closed Tuesday.

SETTING AND ATMOSPHERE   San Francisco has intriguing restaurants throughout its many neighborhoods, and Aziza, located in the Richmond, is one of them. Exquisite Moroccan food prepared with local organic produce and free-range meat, game, and poultry from local farms and ranches awaits those who leave the well-trampled gourmet path. The traditional Bedouin-tent style of most Moroccan restaurants has been replaced with intimate booths and elegant hand-carved tables. Spanish tiles cover bits and pieces of the walls, and brightly decorated arches give the three-room restaurant a mysterious, intimate air. Color is used lavishly throughout the rooms—watermelon, deep blues, tangerine, and saffron add to the dining excitement. A small cavelike bar seeped in dark-blue plaster and dimly lit by Moorish lanterns is popular for its specialty drinks.

HOUSE SPECIALTIES   Moroccan food with a light touch and delicate flavor. For starters, try a vegan soup of organic green lentils, lemony tomato broth, and cilantro-oil drizzle or medjool-date-and-sesame-crusted goat cheese with za'atar croutons. Entrees: Chicken b'steeya baked phyllo-dough pie with braised saffron chicken, spiced almonds, powdered sugar, cinnamon, and saffron; grilled rosemary lamb with steamed saffron couscous; black cod clay pot baked in Spanish saffron sauce with parsleyed little farm potatoes and green olives; Moroccan spiced prawn tagine on a bed of fresh herbed vegetable ragout.

OTHER RECOMMENDATIONS   For a full tour of the flavors and textures presented in the menu, try the $62 tasting menu. A culinary bang for the buck! Don't forget to sample the pastries by Melissa Chou.

SUMMARY AND COMMENTS   A trip to "the outback" of San Francisco is well rewarded at Aziza. Its superb cooking style, combining traditional and modern influences, will quickly change diners' perceptions of Moroccan cuisine as heavy and overcooked. The friendly and knowledgeable wait-staff rounds off a marvelous dining experience.

B44   ★★★

| SPANISH CATALONIAN | MODERATE | QU6ALITY ★★★★ | VALUE ★★★★ |

44 Belden Place, Financial District; ☎ 415-986-6287; b44sf.com

Reservations Recommended. **When to go** Anytime. **Entree range** $18–$24. **Payment** AE, MC, V. **Service rating** ★★★. **Friendliness rating** ★★★★. **Parking** Street. **Bar** Full service. **Wine selection** Excellent. **Dress** Casual. **Disabled access** Yes. **Customers** Local Bohemians and Europeans. **Hours** Monday–Thursday, 11:30 a.m.–11 p.m.; Friday, 11:30 a.m.–10:30 p.m.; Saturday, 5 p.m.–10:30 p.m.; Sunday, 4 p.m.–9 p.m.

SETTING AND ATMOSPHERE If it weren't for the fog, you might think you were in Barcelona. Most of the staff are Spanish; the food and wine are Iberian; the television in the restroom plays videos of Spanish scenes. Only the weather and the well-made martinis at the full-service bar proclaim that you're in The City.

HOUSE SPECIALTIES Arroz negra is a signature dish of Catalonia and of this restaurant. It's like paella, a rice casserole, but flavored and dyed with the ink of squids. Now don't turn the page! This stuff is music in your mouth, a common dish in Spain, and you should try it. If that doesn't float your boat, try lamb chops in a sauce based on aged sherry vinegar, roasted monkfish with clams and fingerling potatoes, or the dish of grilled veggies known as *escalivada.* Yum!

OTHER RECOMMENDATIONS Creamy Spanish desserts such as *crema catalana,* and lovely things made with chocolate.

SUMMARY AND COMMENTS Chef Daniel Olivella has spent his adult life pleasing the crowd, both as a chef and as a jazz musician. His current gig is bringing the genuine Spanish article to San Francisco. No cloying sangria; no bland, overcooked paella; and no fake Spanish ham. Nothing but the real thing. Included on the wine list is a good selection of sherry and manzanilla.

Bambuddha Lounge   ★★★

PAN-ASIAN	MODERATE	QUALITY ★★★½	VALUE ★★★★½

601 Eddy Street, Phoenix Hotel, near SoMa; ☎ 415-885-5088; bambuddhalounge.com

Reservations Accepted. **When to go** Late. **Entree range** $13–$18. **Payment** All major credit cards. **Service rating** ★★★★. **Friendliness rating** ★★★★. **Parking** Street, lot for motel guests. **Bar** Full service. **Wine selection** Excellent. **Dress** Business. **Disabled access** Good. **Customers** Locals, tourists. **Hours** Monday–Thursday, 6–10 p.m.; Friday and Saturday, 6–10:30 p.m.

SETTING AND ATMOSPHERE Located in the famous Phoenix Hotel, known as the city's "rock 'n' roll" hotel for its wild decor and attraction of traveling rock musicians. This restaurant is ultramodern and uberhip yet welcomes a very broad-based clientele. Hanging lamps cast a low red-gold light, and polished black reflecting walls amplify the effect. The fireplace crackles cheerily as the well-dressed crowd table-hops and schmoozes, keeping up a house-party atmosphere. On Friday and Saturday, the adjoining lounge teems with party-minded people as the DJ spins.

HOUSE SPECIALTIES Pan-Asian is something purists tend to run away from, and not without cause. But here it works, partly because most dishes are skillfully seasoned, rarely venturing into the land of bland. So why not sally forth into caramelized day-boat scallops; or ginger braised short ribs with shiitake mushrooms, baby turnips, and dark soy–star anise sauce. If you just have to have chicken, try the ginger-soy barbecued spring chicken with baby carrots, pea shoots, and spicy peanut sauce. And for a big piece of meat, choose the hoisin pork tenderloin with grilled five-spice pears and sweet black vinegar reduction.

OTHER RECOMMENDATIONS Drunken noodles with chiles, onions, oyster sauce, and Thai basil; or coconut-milk jasmine rice. A very thoughtful wine list with some fine German whites, which tend to go especially well with spicy fare.

SUMMARY AND COMMENTS Because so many musicians on tour stay in the motel, they often end up in the Bambuddha before or after their gigs. Though dinner service here ends at 10:30 p.m. on weekends, it still can turn into an all-night party. If you dine here with a party of up to four, call ahead and request the table next to the fireplace.

Baywolf ★★★★½

MEDITERRANEAN	EXPENSIVE	QUALITY ★★★★½	VALUE ★★★★½

3853 Piedmont Avenue, Oakland; ☎ 510-655-6004; baywolf.com

Reservations Recommended. **When to go** Anytime. **Entree range** $8–$28. **Payment** All major credit cards. **Service rating** ★★★. **Friendliness rating** ★★★. **Parking** Street. **Bar** Beer, wine. **Wine selection** Very good. **Dress** Casual. **Disabled access** Yes. **Customers** Locals, accidental tourists. **Hours** Tuesday–Friday, 11:30 a.m.–2 p.m.; Tuesday–Sunday, 5:30 p.m. until close.

SETTING AND ATMOSPHERE This handsome old converted house offers a collection of small, cozy dining areas decorated to feel like a French farmhouse, with all its welcoming warmth. Here is some of the most intimate dining in town. The place is fronted by a large veranda where the regulars like to dine alfresco. In contrast to the sedate interior, the atmosphere outside is more festive.

HOUSE SPECIALTIES The menu changes every month, or sometimes with availability or the chef's inspiration. Fortnightly offerings usually feature some particular region of the Mediterranean: Spain, Greece, Italy, South of France, and so on. On occasion, the menu will migrate to New Orleans or the American Southwest, maybe even to North Africa, but it always returns to its roots in the Middle Sea. Past offerings have included braised lamb shanks with polenta; chicken tagine with spiced couscous, lemon, olives, and artichokes; pan-seared petrale sole with lemon mashed potatoes and roasted Venetian broccoli; a richly flavored grilled duck with chutney; and horseradish mashed potatoes good enough to make a meal of.

OTHER RECOMMENDATIONS Seasonal produce is a real specialty here. Whatever is available in the farmers market is what to look for. They do especially wonderful things with tomatoes. And anything incorporating an artisanal cheese is worth trying.

SUMMARY AND COMMENTS Call ahead to ask for parking advice. There is plenty to be had, but you have to know where to find it. In its 30-plus years of operation, Baywolf has earned a loyal clientele of demanding people. Many local businesspeople come here for lunch almost every day. The owners began life in academia and literature, but their devotion to the culinary art led them to follow the path to Baywolf. If you arrive without reservations and the place is full, just take a walk up or down Piedmont Avenue. You'll find plenty of good alternatives.

Beach Chalet   ★★★½

AMERICAN BISTRO AND BREWPUB   MODERATE   QUALITY ★★★★   VALUE ★★★★

1000 Great Highway, Richmond/Sunset District; ☎ 415-386-8439; beachchalet.com

Reservations Recommended. **When to go** Sundown. **Entree range** $11–$29. **Payment** AE, D, MC, V. **Service rating** ★★★. **Friendliness rating** ★★★. **Parking** Free lot. **Bar** Full service. **Wine selection** Fair. **Dress** Casual. **Disabled access** Yes. **Customers** Locals and tourists in the know. **Hours** Monday–Thursday, 9 a.m–10 p.m.; Friday, 9 a.m.–11 p.m.; Saturday, 8 a.m.–11 p.m.; Sunday, 8 a.m.–10 p.m.

SETTING AND ATMOSPHERE Built in 1925 as a teahouse, the large, historic building sits hard by Ocean Beach at the western end of Golden Gate Park. In the 1930s, WPA artists executed a series of murals depicting life in The City, and their artwork is the first thing you'll see upon entering the ground floor. Upstairs it's big, boisterous, and beery—a bubble and hubbub as people enjoy the food, drink, each other, and the stunning view of the Pacific Ocean at sunset. The owners also have a second restaurant, on the park side as opposed to the beach side, called the Park Chalet. It's a rambling space that is both spacious and gracious, dominated by an impressive fireplace. Park Chalet is a bit dressier than Beach Chalet and specializes in small plates, though the house beers are still on the list.

HOUSE SPECIALTIES For breakfast, try eggs Benedict or buttermilk pancakes. For lunch you'll see soup, salad, sandwiches, and entrees such as seafood linguine, fish and chips, and roast chicken. Dinner features fish, New York steak, Texas-style barbecue baby-back ribs, grilled vegetables, and pasta. A children's menu is available for less than $6. In the adjacent Park Chalet, the truffled chicken and four-cheese macaroni is tasty, the snap peas are perfectly seasoned with sesame and spice, and the garlic fries are a perfect munch with a cold beer.

OTHER RECOMMENDATIONS The beers and ales. Several house brews from light to stout. You can also tour the brewery if you ask. There is also a decent, though short, wine list featuring California vintages, as well as a full bar.

There is live music on Tuesday and Friday nights, as well as Saturday and Sunday afternoons in the summer. Happy hour is Monday–Friday, 3 p.m.–6 p.m. with $4 22-ounce beers and $5 appetizers. Downstairs in the Park Chalet are $2 pints on Mondays, 5 p.m.–9 p.m., and Taco Tuesdays are 4 p.m.–9:30 p.m. with $2.50 tacos, two-for-one margaritas, $3 pints, and live music. Buy $3 pints and $5 appetizers Wednesday–Friday, 3 p.m.–6 p.m. Get there early for seating.

SUMMARY AND COMMENTS There are cozy corners for couples, plenty of space for families, and areas that can be screened off for private parties. This is a good place for a business lunch or dinner. The staff is well versed in the house beers and able to offer sound advice on matching them with food. Occasional live music makes this a good place to spend the whole evening. Call ahead.

Boulevard ★★★★½

AMERICAN/FRENCH	EXPENSIVE	QUALITY ★★★★★	VALUE ★★★★½

1 Mission Street, SoMa; ☎ 415-543-6084; boulevardrestaurant.com

Reservations Recommended. **When to go** Anytime. **Entree range** Lunch, $16–$21; dinner, $29–$40. **Payment** AE, CB, D, DC, MC, V. **Service rating** ★★★. **Friendliness rating** ★★★. **Parking** Valet, metered street. **Bar** Full service, fresh-squeezed juices. **Wine selection** Extensive. **Dress** Fashionable, business. **Disabled access** Adequate (elevator to restrooms). **Customers** Businesspeople and well-heeled young clientele, tourists, and families. **Hours** Monday–Thursday, 11:30 a.m.–2 p.m. and 5:30 p.m.–10 p.m.; Friday, 11:30 a.m.–2 p.m. and 5:30 p.m.–10:30 p.m.; Saturday, 5:30 p.m.–10:30 p.m.; Sunday, 5:30 p.m.–10 p.m.

SETTING AND ATMOSPHERE Dramatic, dark, Belle Epoque interior. Velvet curtains, artisan ironwork, and art nouveau light fixtures of hand-blown glass recall the French style of the Audiffred Building in which the restaurant is housed. Originally a saloon and boardinghouse for sailors and dockworkers, it was spared destruction by the post-quake fire of 1906 because the clever management pledged the house's entire beer and wine supply to the firemen who protected the structure.

HOUSE SPECIALTIES Chef Nancy Oakes takes great care in searching out the best ingredients for seasonal appetizers such as heirloom tomato salad, as well as perennial favorites such as Dungeness crab cakes, and roasted and slow-braised pork rib eye. Entrees include several seafood options and a variety of meats. The main dishes always have innovative flavorings from vegetables and spices, but are not laden with sauce. The dessert menu changes seasonally and often features fruit and chocolate treats. Be sure to try the caramel-bottom vanilla brûlée when available.

OTHER RECOMMENDATIONS The wine list is impressive and the waitstaff well informed, so don't hesitate to try a suggested glass to pair with your dish. You won't feel rushed here, so consider enjoying a drink from the excellent bar as you peruse the ample menu, and don't forget to save room for the fresh desserts, especially house sorbets and ice creams.

SUMMARY AND COMMENTS The experience of eating in this bustling restaurant is surprisingly relaxed. You can gaze out of large windows onto the Embarcadero and the Bay Bridge. The open kitchen also gives an entertaining view of the cooks working the grill and wood-fired oven. The feel here is at once cosmopolitan and comfortable as the crew goes about their work with professionalism and friendliness.

The Brazen Head Restaurant & Public House ★★★

CONTINENTAL	MODERATE	QUALITY ★★★½	VALUE ★★★★★

3166 Buchanan Street at Greenwich Avenue, Marina District;
☎ **415-921-7600; brazenheadsf.com**

Reservations Not accepted. **When to go** Before 8 p.m. and after 10 p.m. **Entree range** $16–$31. **Payment** No credit cards; ATM nearby; accepts cash only. **Service rating** ★★. **Friendliness rating** ★★★. **Parking** Street. **Bar** Full service. **Wine selection** Good. **Dress** Casual. **Disabled access** None. **Customers** Locals, other restaurant workers, writers. **Hours** Daily, 5 p.m.–1 a.m.; bar open 4 p.m.–2 a.m.

SETTING AND ATMOSPHERE Except for the lack of trophy animal heads, this place has the look and feel of a rich, cozy, European hunting lodge. All is deep and dark, with polished hardwood and brass trim. Antique etchings and photographs cover the walls. A loyal patronage returns regularly, and one sometimes gets the feeling of being in the television bar Cheers. No credit cards or checks are accepted, but there is an ATM next to the restrooms.

HOUSE SPECIALTIES Meat! (And fish.) As befits the hunting lodge atmosphere, grills and roasts of lamb, beef, and pork. Also veal piccata, sautéed prawns, chicken, burgers, and a daily pasta dish. All entrees include vegetable of the day and mashed potatoes or rice.

OTHER RECOMMENDATIONS A good selection of salads and appetizers, such as crab cakes and oysters; mixed greens and Caesar salads.

SUMMARY AND COMMENTS One of the great perennials in the restaurant firmament of the city. Situated on a street corner not far from the Golden Gate Bridge. The cheery lights of this place beckon through the San Francisco fog like a warm cabin in a cold wood. There is often a wait for a table, but you can join the locals and regulars at the bar for a convivial drink.

The Buena Vista ★

AMERICAN DINER	INEXPENSIVE	QUALITY ★★★½	VALUE ★★★

2765 Hyde Street (at Beach), Marina District; ☎ **415-474-5044;**
thebuenavista.com

Reservations Not accepted. **When to go** Anytime. **Entree range** $9–$16. **Payment** All major credit cards. **Service rating** ★. **Friendliness rating** ★★. **Parking** Lot and metered street. **Bar** Full service. **Wine selection** Limited. **Dress** Sporty. **Disabled access** None. **Customers** Tourists. **Hours** Monday–Friday, 9 a.m.–9:30 p.m.; Saturday–Sunday, 8 a.m.–9:30 p.m.; bar open until 2 a.m. nightly.

SETTING AND ATMOSPHERE   The Buena Vista is more than 100 years old and is situated across the street from The Cannery and the Hyde and Powell cable car turnaround. Communal tables of chunky brown wood and yellowing walls don't deter hordes of tourists who enjoy lively rounds of drinking at the bar and the excellent views of Alcatraz Island, the Golden Gate Bridge, and the Bay.

HOUSE SPECIALTIES   Tourists flock to The Buena Vista not only to visit one of the oldest restaurants in San Francisco, but also to experience "the best Irish coffee in the world." According to the restaurant's lore, the boozy beverage was perfected by one-time owner Jack Koeppler and travel writer Stanton Delaplane in 1952 (there's a barman at Shannon Airport in Ireland with a different version!). But the Irish coffee is indeed delicious and takes the edge off sore feet and cold fingers of tourists who have spent the day hiking through the fog.

OTHER RECOMMENDATIONS   Souvenirs are on the menu here, and The Buena Vista gift shop sells everything from ornaments to fleece vests emblazoned with the restaurant's logo. The food is standard pub fare with offerings like cheddar burgers and club sandwiches and nightly specials such as corned beef and cabbage. Chicken tenders and grilled cheese are available on the children's menu. Breakfast is served all day long. At day's end, The Buena Vista is the ideal place for a nightcap, and since it is open late, you can go there after the theater or even after a night of clubbing; but keep in mind the kitchen closes at 9:30 p.m.

SUMMARY AND COMMENTS   The Buena Vista seems to bask in the memory of its own good old days, but the bustling crowds of today are convivial. A trip to San Francisco is truly complete after a historic Irish coffee here.

Café de la Presse   ★★★

FRENCH/BASQUE   MODERATE   QUALITY ★★★★   VALUE ★★★★

352 Grant Avenue, Union Square; ☎ 415-398-2680;
cafedelapresse.com

Reservations Accepted. **When to go** Anytime. **Entree range** $9–$36. **Payment** AE, D, DC, MC, V. **Service rating** ★★★. **Friendliness rating** ★★★. **Parking** Street. **Bar** Full service. **Wine selection** Excellent. **Dress** Business casual. **Disabled access** Yes. **Customers** Local suits and downtown tourists. **Hours** Monday–Thursday, 7:30 a.m.–10 a.m., 11:30 a.m.–2:30 p.m., and 5:30–9:30 p.m.; Friday, 7:30 a.m.–10 a.m., 11:30 a.m.–2:30 p.m., and 5:30–10 p.m.; Saturday and Sunday, 8 a.m.– p.m., (brunch: 11:30 a.m.–4 p.m.), 11:30 a.m.–2 p.m., and 5:30–10 p.m.

SETTING AND ATMOSPHERE   It looks like it was designed and built in Paris and then shipped entire to San Francisco. It's a quiet haven popular with stockbroker types, and you can often tell how the market is doing just by their composure. The wall of windows gives you a good view of the street and all its passersby. Dark wood is warm and comforting, and the framed mirrors gracing the walls give it just a bit of whimsy.

HOUSE SPECIALTIES Croque monsieur (ham and cheese) or burger and fries are good for brunch; duck confit or the grilled rib eye is great for dinner. House-made charcuterie is good anytime. Anything from the sea is good, and people travel across town for onion soup gratinée.

OTHER RECOMMENDATIONS The pot de crème is outstanding.

SUMMARY AND COMMENTS The staff is knowledgeable about both food and wine, and you can rely on their advice. Be advised that not only is the food delicious, but the portions are large and on the heavy side. If you don't want to carry away a doggie bag, you might consider sharing a single entree. Next to the dining room is a reading room with more than 200 foreign magazines and newspapers.

Café Pescatore ★★★

ITALIAN/SEAFOOD	MODERATE	QUALITY ★★★½	VALUE ★★★★

2455 Mason Street, North Beach; ☎ 415-561-1111; cafepescatore.com

Reservations Accepted. **When to go** Sundown. **Entree range** $13–$25. **Payment** All major credit cards. **Service rating** ★★★. **Friendliness rating** ★★★. **Parking** Street. **Bar** Full service. **Wine selection** Good. **Dress** Casual. **Disabled access** Yes. **Customers** Tourists and neighborhood regulars. **Hours** Monday–Friday, 7–10:30 a.m. and 11:30 a.m.–10 p.m.; Saturday and Sunday, 7 a.m.–10 p.m. (brunch: 10 a.m.–2 p.m.).

SETTING AND ATMOSPHERE A lot of places in the Fisherman's Wharf area appeal to the casual tourist who might not give due consideration to dining. But Pescatore is not among them. Step in and you can tell immediately that the feel is old San Francisco. Creamy walls, wood trim, tile floors, and molding at the ceiling, as well as a full bar in the center of the room all speak "The City" in unambiguous terms. Call it wharf bistro decor with old-timey photographs, models of boats hanging from the ceiling, and all warmly lit. It's a comfort station in the fog.

HOUSE SPECIALTIES All the usual suspects in an old fisherman's eatery. Start with classic clam chowder or roasted tomato soup. Salads and antipasti, even pizza and bruschetta. Move on to linguine alla Raffaele, crab-stuffed ravioli, or oven-roasted sea bass.

OTHER RECOMMENDATIONS Cioppino is The City's signature dish, and purists say that it can only be made with the local Dungeness crab. But here they violate the rule and make it year-round from Alaskan king crab.

SUMMARY AND COMMENTS This is also a good place to drink—not to party and dance and get wild and loud—but to drink calmly, coolly, leisurely, as you gaze out the large picture windows. So it is fitting that the house offers a wide range of wines, liquors, and cordials. Enjoy a grappa, a single-malt scotch, or even a special espresso drink as you watch the local folk negotiate the gathering fog through the windows.

Cafe Tiramisu ★★★

ITALIAN	MODERATE	QUALITY ★★★	VALUE ★★★

28 Belden Place, Financial District; ☎ 415-421-7044; cafetiramisu.com

Reservations Recommended, especially for outdoor seating. **When to go** Lunch or dinner. **Entree range** $15–$38. **Payment** All major credit cards. **Service rating** ★★★. **Friendliness rating** ★★½. **Parking** Street. **Bar** Full service. **Wine selection** Vast. **Dress** Casual. **Disabled access** Yes. **Customers** Repeat locals, businesspeople, tourists. **Hours** Monday–Friday, 11:30 a.m.–10 p.m.; Saturday, 4:30–10 p.m.; closed Sunday.

SETTING AND ATMOSPHERE A mini trip to Europe, before you even get to the restaurant. This one-time alley became a dining destination in the early 1990s, and now beneath the mammoth Bank of America building bright umbrellas shade outdoor tables and jostle each other. Strings of white lights dangle above for an ever-starry sky. On the brief, block-long Belden Place, between Bush and Pine in the city's financial district, Cafe Tiramisu is clustered with several other fine restaurants, most with European flair—Cafe Bastille, Plouf, B44, Belden Taverna, Brindisi—all with hosts on the sidewalk wooing passersby with tempting menus. Tables nudge each other, and so do diners' knees. Next door is Sam's Grill with its old-timey cubicles, one of the oldest restaurants in the city, in business since 1867 and here since 1946, and half a block uphill down another alley, Café Claude flies the French flag too.

Outside Tiramisu, the warm hum of chatter blends with the clinking of plates, as energetic waiters nearly sprint from kitchen to table at this always-busy spot. Guests come in a variety of ages, and attire is anything from jeans and casual shirts to sport coats and even a tie here and there.

HOUSE SPECIALTIES The menu keeps close to Mother Italia with such elegant pasta dishes as linguine with clams and mushrooms, or the ravioli with braised lamb shank and truffle sauce. Venture into the seafood and meat dishes too by trying the Loch Duarte grilled salmon with roasted eggplant ravioli and fresh tomato concassé; the braised beef short ribs with red-wine sauce served with horseradish mashed potatoes; and the veal scaloppini with lemon-caper sauce over Florentine spinach and Parmesan risotto.

OTHER RECOMMENDATIONS Got wine? You'll get it here. The wine list is so long that it has a table of contents, all in a bound leather volume heavy enough to make a fine door stop. Pages 6 through 10 are Italian whites, and 11 through 28 are Italian reds. And that's only about half the book. It's a little overwhelming, so feel free to ask for help. The by-the-glass list is more maneuverable at only one page. And don't forget dessert, particularly the restaurant's namesake tiramisu—creamy, boozy, fluffy, and certainly uplifting, especially with a good cup of coffee. Other rich finds are the warm chocolate cake with hazelnut sauce, peach tart with vanilla ice cream, or the cherry, mandarin, and lemon trio of crème brûlée.

SUMMARY AND COMMENTS The cafe truly offers three dining experiences in one, depending on your location. The coveted outside tables are festive, noisy, and fun, barring rain. Heaters fend off the chill. Inside on the first floor, it's still intimate, still pleasantly noisy, but more traditional and very Italy, with fresco murals of Pompeii and other Roman ruins. Downstairs there are tables tucked in the wine cellar, hidden in soft light. Feels like you're getting away with something.

Calzone's ★★

ITALIAN	MODERATE	QUALITY ★★½	VALUE ★★★

430 Columbus Avenue, North Beach; ☎ 415-397-3600; calzonesf.com

Reservations Accepted. **When to go** Anytime. **Entree range** $10–$19. **Payment** D, DC, MC, V. **Service rating** ★★★★. **Friendliness rating** ★★★. **Parking** Street, nearby lots. **Bar** Full service. **Wine selection** Limited, with a $12 corkage fee. **Dress** Informal. **Disabled access** Yes. **Customers** Locals, tourists. **Hours** Daily, 11 a.m.–1 a.m.

SETTING AND ATMOSPHERE Cool, old North Beach 1960s decor: black-tiled walls, lots of brightly colored glass bottles; Italian cheeses, salamis, garlic hanging everywhere; chandeliers. Seating indoors and out, at one of the cute mosaic tables. A bustling little place with a great location in the heart of North Beach supported by a friendly and attentive staff. Small wood-fired brick oven faces the main dining area.

HOUSE SPECIALTIES Naturally there is lasagna, gnocchetti, ravioli, also many pasta dishes, pizza, roasted chicken, seared lamb loin, and filet mignon.

OTHER RECOMMENDATIONS Italian pot stickers filled with sausage, mushrooms, garlic, and ginger; excellent table bread and desserts.

SUMMARY AND COMMENTS You'll love the wide windows where you can watch the whole world parade by. The food is served on unusually shaped, long oblong platters, and that makes it a little difficult to balance everything on a small round table. Portions are more than ample, but the quality is uneven. Better to stick with the delicious appetizers and then splurge on the chocolate truffle mousse cake. And watch the action on Columbus.

Campton Place Restaurant ★★★★★

COUNTRY FRENCH	EXPENSIVE	QUALITY ★★★★★	VALUE ★★★★★

340 Stockton Street, First Floor, Union Square; ☎ 415-781-5555; camptonplacesf.com

Reservations Recommended. **When to go** Anytime. **Entree range** Breakfast $9–$24; 3-course brunch, $46; lunch, $19–$40; 5-course table d'hote, $85 (additional $55 for wine pairings); 9-course degustation menu, $125 (additional $75 for wine pairings; reservations required). **Payment** All major credit cards. **Service rating** ★★★★★. **Friendliness rating** ★★★★. **Parking** Valet, $6.50 per hour; street parking free on Sundays. **Bar** Full service. **Wine selection** Excellent. **Dress** Wear a tie; dressy. **Disabled access** Yes. **Customers** Businesspeople, tourists, the demanding. **Hours** Monday–Thursday, 7–10:30 a.m., 11:30 a.m.–2 p.m., and 6–9 p.m.; Friday, 7–10:30 a.m., 11:30 a.m.–2 p.m., and 6–9:30 p.m.; Saturday, 8–11 a.m., noon–2 p.m., and 6–9:30 p.m.; Sunday, 8–11 a.m., noon–2 p.m. (brunch), and 6–9 p.m.

SETTING AND ATMOSPHERE In the top-end Campton Place hotel, this room is formal but not fussy. Tieless men won't be turned away, but they'll wish they'd worn a tie. Decor is modern, clean, and spare compared with most luxurious establishments. It's a study in serenity, full of flowers and soothing artwork. An elegant setting for a breakfast of corned beef hash and poached eggs.

HOUSE SPECIALTIES Breakfast is famous here, with all of the traditional favorites, including corn muffins that are light as a cloud. The lunch and dinner menus change with the seasons, but you might encounter slow-roasted pork tenderloin, roasted Atlantic cod with spinach and sweet ginger relish, or creative dishes such as seared foie gras with persimmons and mushrooms. And presentations are as artful as origami.

OTHER RECOMMENDATIONS Rely on the sommelier to match wines from the extensive list. For dessert, try goat-cheese cake with blueberry compote and graham cracker foam. Or turn to the cheese platter, which is admired by every cheese lover in town.

SUMMARY AND COMMENTS In the hotel of the same name. This is a temple to the muse of American cooking in a city famous for its foreign culinary establishments. Excellent American fare prepared to the most rigorous European standards without the emphasis on fancy sauces. It's expensive, right down to the drinks in the bar, but nothing's overpriced. Quality is king, and you get what you pay for.

Chapeau! ★★★

| FRENCH | EXPENSIVE | QUALITY ★★★½ | VALUE ★★★ |

126 Clement Street (between Second and Third avenues), Inner Richmond District; ☎ 415-750-9787; chapeausf.com

Reservations Accepted. **When to go** Anytime. **Entree range** $19–$25. **Payment** AE, D, DC, MC, V. **Service rating** ★★★. **Friendliness Rating** ★★★. **Parking** Street. **Bar** Full service. **Wine selection** Mostly French. **Dress** Casual chic. **Disabled access** Good. **Customers** Neighborhood dwellers, French expatriates. **Hours** Sunday–Thursday, 5–10 p.m.; Friday and Saturday, 5–10:30 p.m.

SETTING AND ATMOSPHERE Chapeau is an intimate neighborhood spot. The dining room looks as if it were imported from a little French town. Oil paintings and copper pans hang on peach walls. Mirrors and soft lighting create a spacious yet cozy effect. Even when the restaurant gets busy, you feel a sense of privacy.

HOUSE SPECIALTIES The menu continues the authentic French approach and changes often. Appetizers might include mussels soup, fried tiger prawns with a tomato-and-onion marmalade, and escargots. *Salade Landaise* with duck confit is delicious. Main dishes, such as filet mignon with potatoes and mushrooms, are well executed. Also recommended are cassoulet de Toulouse (a stew with lamb, duck, sausage, and beans) and bacon-wrapped pork tenderloin.

OTHER RECOMMENDATIONS This is one of the few places in town where you can find traditional French desserts. They offer profiteroles and a trio of sorbets. The chocolate cake served with rum and banana ice cream is heavenly. You may also finish your meal with a cheese plate. The predominantly French wine list is not long, but reflects interesting selections. The restaurant's wine buyer favors lesser-known wines as a way of getting higher quality at a lower cost.

SUMMARY AND COMMENTS Chapeau is a small neighborhood restaurant with food the caliber of a downtown hot spot and "comme il faut" though seating can be cramped. Service is attentive and the overall experience pleasant. This is a good place to keep in mind for smaller parties who like to talk and enjoy a leisurely meal.

Chez Papa Resto ★★★

FRENCH/PROVENCAL	MODERATE	QUALITY ★★★	VALUE ★★★½

4 Mint Plaza at Fifth Street, SoMa; ☎ 415-546-4134; chezpapasf.com

Reservations Accepted. **When to go** Anytime. **Entree range** Lunch, $12–$17, sides $6; prix fixe lunch, $18–23; dinner, $19–$34, sides $7; prix fixe dinner, $35 (Monday–Wednesday only). **Payment** AE, MC, V. **Service rating** ★★★. **Friendliness rating** ★★★½. **Parking** Public garage at Fourth Street and Mission. **Bar** Full service; margaritas, martinis, and Champagne cocktails. **Wine selection** Extensive; many high-end French labels. **Dress** Business casual, cocktail dresses. **Disabled access** Good. **Customers** Business, young professionals, tourists. **Hours** Monday–Thursday, 11:30 a.m.–2:30 p.m. and 5:30 p.m.–10 p.m.; Friday, 11:30 a.m.–2:30 p.m. and 5:30 p.m.–11 p.m.; Saturday, 11:30 a.m.–3 p.m. and 5:30 p.m.–11 p.m.; closed Sunday.

SETTING AND ATMOSPHERE Need a buzzy business rendezvous or elegant pretheater meal in romantic, restful surroundings? Nestling within a pedestrian enclave next to the Old Mint (newly polished up), this has continental pizzazz and is near shopping spots, too. Big picture windows overlook sidewalk tables from a discreet palace of black chandeliers, orange banquettes, and a well-staffed bar.

HOUSE SPECIALTIES Yes, you can get frogs legs or duck breast. But if you want to channel Paris, try the croque monsieur—melting Gruyère and tangy ham on brioche-crisp toast. Chef David Bazirgan's very Provencal menu hits western ingredients hard—Snake River Kobe beef tartare with Dijon mustard, capers, shallots, garlic, and toast points is almost pâté-like. The prix-fixe lunch offers soupe à l'oignon or smoked trout platter, then steak frites, tuna *pan bagnat*, eggplant tartine, or Provencal fish stew for the main course. For an extra $5 you get cherry clafoutis, tart tatin, or profiteroles, all faultless. A good deal and a great find!

OTHER RECOMMENDATIONS Wild mushroom tart comes with local goat cheese and pistou. Warm pear and endive salad rounds off appetizers. Alaskan cod with mushrooms, leeks, and a truffle emulsion is handled with care.

Clement Street Bar and Grill ★★★

NEW AMERICAN   MODERATE   QUALITY ★★★½   VALUE ★★★

708 Clement Street, Richmond; ☎ 415-386-2200

Reservations Recommended. When to go Anytime. Entree range Brunch and lunch, $8–$14; dinner, $12–$20. Payment All major credit cards. Service rating ★★★. Friendliness rating ★★★½. Parking Street, metered during the day. Bar Full service. Wine selection Fair. Dress Casual. Disabled access Good. Customers Locals, businesspeople. Hours Tuesday–Thursday, 4:30 p.m.– 9:30 p.m.; Friday and Saturday, 4:30 p.m.–10 p.m.; Sunday, 10:30 a.m.–3 p.m. (brunch) and 4:30 p.m.–9 p.m.; closed Monday.

SETTING AND ATMOSPHERE From the entrance, Clement Street Bar and Grill seems dim, narrow, and dominated by the bar, but there's a roomy rear dining area with an impressive brick fireplace and a ship's cabin atmosphere. It's simply furnished with dark carpet, varnished plywood benches, and captain's chairs, but the cut-glass candleholders and white tablecloths add a touch of ceremony; coat hooks at the entry lend a genial neighborhood mood.

HOUSE SPECIALTIES They do brunch in wholehearted fashion here with mighty omelets, and daily specials may include roasted garlic with crostini; roasted red pepper filled with three cheeses, herbs, and pine nuts over spinach salad; wild mushroom tortellini; grilled fish specials; veal scaloppine with wild mushrooms. Vegetarian offerings include grilled portobello mushroom with warm spinach and hazelnuts; grilled and roasted vegetables; wild mushroom tortellini with Roma tomatoes, garlic, herbs, and white wine.

OTHER RECOMMENDATIONS Salads, sandwiches, and burgers.

SUMMARY AND COMMENTS Step in and enter the 1930s. Talk discreetly with private eyes, mysterious ladies, and intriguing gentlemen, while the trio plays Gershwin. Indulge your fantasies. This place is rich; better if you are, too, or willing to act and feel like it.

The Cosmopolitan Restaurant ★★★

NEW AMERICAN   MODERATE/EXPENSIVE   QUALITY ★★★   VALUE ★★★★

121 Spear Street, SoMa; ☎ 415-543-4001; thecosmopolitancafe.com

Reservations Recommended. When to go Anytime. Entree range Lunch, $17– $33; dinner, $18–$32. Payment AE, DC, MC, V. Service rating ★★½. Friendliness

rating ★★★. **Parking** Valet at dinner, lot, metered street. **Bar** Full service. **Wine selection** Good. **Dress** Business casual. **Disabled access** Good. **Customers** Businesspeople, tourists. **Hours** Tuesday–Friday, 11:30 a.m.–1:30 p.m. (lunch); Monday–Friday, 5:30 p.m.–9:15 p.m.; Saturday, 6–9:15 p.m. (dinner); closed Sunday.

SETTING AND ATMOSPHERE   The Cosmopolitan Restaurant has two large bars, one upstairs with a television for watching sports and a separate menu of appetizers, and one below in the main dining room. Lots of darkwood paneling, trendy light fixtures, patterned carpet, and a huge portrait of a couple's embrace give the restaurant a young, if somewhat generic, feel. Booths and oversized chairs keep diners comfortable.

HOUSE SPECIALTIES   Chef Steven Levine creates "inspiration trios," appetizers and dessert plates in which he uses one ingredient in three different ways. These allow ingredients in season to shine and make beautiful presentations. Look out for crisp calamari and artichokes, and creative soups on the appetizer menu. High-quality meats such as sautéed sea scallops and Niman Ranch pork confit form the basis for large entrees. Seafood is paired with vegetables in season. Similarly, desserts show off seasonal fruit. The baked-to-order dishes are especially charming.

OTHER RECOMMENDATIONS   A diversity of ingredients come together here to make California and New American dishes. Chiles, soybeans, and "moon-dried" tomato pesto give standard preparations a new twist. The breadth of the menu here is surprisingly wide. It is easy to overload your palate with too many flavors, so order carefully. Look out for some quality California wine choices.

SUMMARY AND COMMENTS   Part sports bar and after-work hangout for young professionals, part California comfort food spot with a complex menu, The Cosmopolitan Restaurant is doing a lot all at once. A fine place to keep in mind for good food in a casual setting.

Digs Bistro   ★★★½

CALIFORNIAN	MODERATE	QUALITY ★★★	VALUE ★★★★

1453 Dwight Way, Berkeley; ☎ 510-548-2322; digsbistro.com

Reservations Necessary. **When to go** Anytime. **Entree range** $19–$23. **Payment** AE, D, MC, V. **Service rating** ★★★. **Friendliness rating** ★★★★. **Parking** Street. **Bar** Beer and wine. **Wine selection** Short but well thought-out. **Dress** Casual. **Disabled access** Good. **Customers** Locals. **Hours** Thursday–Monday, 5:30–9 p.m.; closed Tuesday and Wednesday.

SETTING AND ATMOSPHERE   This snug little restaurant is located far from the madding crowd of the Berkeley-Oakland gourmet ghetto. Diners are cosseted in an earth-tone yellow color scheme, with a charming rounded brick fireplace adding to the coziness. Varied-shaped windows look out onto the quiet neighborhood, and a four-stool bar accommodates waiting guests. Images from local photographers adorn the walls.

HOUSE SPECIALTIES The Digs Bistro menu, like the wine list, is short but well thought-out. It includes such appetizers as stuffed *piquillo* peppers with Dungeness crab and parsley pesto, and a charcuterie plate that is tasty but surprisingly low in sodium. Interesting entrees include Riverdog Farms eggplant Parmesan, braised pork shoulder, and Alaskan halibut and clams. Kudos to the bittersweet chocolate torte on the dessert menu.

SUMMARY AND COMMENTS Digs Bistro is the successor to a popular underground (unofficial) restaurant in Oakland run by Justin Sconce, Heidi DiPippo, and Jesse Kupers. This restaurant showcases, with great success, seasonal New American cuisine with Californian and Mediterranean influences. All dishes are prepared mostly with locally sourced, sustainably produced, and/or organic ingredients. The staff is friendly and most helpful. The 32-seat Digs provides the diner with a welcome quiet and intimate dining experience. Ask for the table by the fireplace.

Dusit ★★½

THAI	INEXPENSIVE	QUALITY ★★★½	VALUE ★★★★

3221 Mission Street, Bernal Heights; ☎ 415-826-4639

Reservations Accepted. When to go Anytime. Entree range $8–$14. Payment All major credit cards. Service rating ★★½. Friendliness rating ★★. Parking Street. Bar Beer, wine. Wine selection House. Dress Casual. Disabled access Limited. Customers Locals. Hours Monday, Wednesday–Friday, 11:30 a.m.–2:30 p.m. and 5 p.m.–10 p.m.; Saturday and Sunday, 5 p.m.–10 p.m.; closed Tuesday.

SETTING AND ATMOSPHERE A small place in an ordinary neighborhood. Nothing remarkable to look at, but it's clean and well lit, and it has just a touch of class. This is a temple of Thai cuisine, and the votaries of this muse are happily at work pleasing anyone who walks in.

HOUSE SPECIALTIES Most of the items you would expect on a Thai menu, but better than usual, especially considering the price. Orchid duck boned and sautéed with ginger, tomatoes, and pineapple; garlic prawns with black pepper and veggies; stir-fried squid with chiles and basil; fried chicken sautéed with Thai-style sweet-and-sour sauce.

OTHER RECOMMENDATIONS Good fried noodles. Vegetarian dinners.

SUMMARY AND COMMENTS Lunchtime prices are somewhat lower, although the food is just as good and plentiful. But even at dinner it's downright cheap. For quality and quantity, this place is at the top of the list. It's worth a trip across town to dine well at low prices in a pleasant, undemanding environment.

E & O Trading Company ★★★

SOUTHEAST ASIAN	EXPENSIVE	QUALITY ★★★★	VALUE ★★★★

314 Sutter Street, near Union Square; ☎ 415-693-0303; eotrading.com

Reservations Highly recommended. When to go Weeknights. Entree range $13–$25. Payment All major credit cards. Service rating ★★★. Friendliness rating ★★. **Parking** Valet after 6 p.m. or Sutter Stockton Garage next door. **Bar** Full service. **Wine selection** Good. **Dress** Casual to business. **Disabled access** Yes. **Customers** After-work crowd, tourists. **Hours** Monday–Thursday, 11:30 a.m.–10 p.m.; Friday and Saturday, 11:30 a.m.–11 p.m.; Sunday, 5 p.m.–9:30 p.m.

SETTING AND ATMOSPHERE Bustling energy comes in from Union Square like the trade winds, halting right at the foot of the 35-foot dragon bar. Following an age-old love story of Theodore Bailey and his escapades, the three-story craft brewery and pan-Asian grill was designed for the downstairs to give the feel of a trading post and the mezzanine to be the meetinghouse of refined merchants. And that it does, with its framed botanical pictures on ivory walls with palm-leaf fans.

HOUSE SPECIALTIES Signature satay (meat skewers) from the wood-fired grill; oven-roasted black cod with matcha green-tea rice; Indonesian corn fritters with chile-soy dipping sauce; ginger mushroom tower with marinated portobello mushrooms with ginger and sweet-soy dipping sauce; Thai-style fried jasmine rice with peas, egg, green onion, and chiles.

OTHER RECOMMENDATIONS Peanut chicken satay marinated in sweet soy, garlic, and spices; hardwood-grilled ahi marinated in Indonesian chilies and sweet soy; smoked pork with crispy taro strips, scallions, lettuce, hoisin and *sriracha* sauces. Choosing whether to have beer or wine with dinner might be a toughie. The beers are excellent and crafted in-house with seasonal selections. The wines are also good, and the waitstaff is exceptionally knowledgeable and adept at making suggestions that complement your meal.

SUMMARY AND COMMENTS The menu is a combination of Asian cuisines inspired by Indonesia, Vietnam, Thailand, Malaysia, and East India. To make the most of the experience, have fun ordering a table full of small plates, salads, and satays. Whether upstairs or downstairs, this is a great place to people-watch and let yourself get sucked into the decor, feeling transported overseas. The plate presentations are equally as imaginative and impressive as the interior designed by Paul Ma.

Enrico's ★★★

CALIFORNIAN	MODERATE	QUALITY ★★★★	VALUE ★★★★

504 Broadway, North Beach; ☎ 415-982-6223; enricossf.com

Reservations Accepted. **When to go** Anytime. **Entree range** $18–$23. **Payment** AE, MC, V. **Service rating** ★★★. **Friendliness rating** ★★★ **Parking** Lot; valet, $10 (valet begins at 5:30 p.m.). **Bar** Full service. **Wine selection** Very good. **Dress** Casual, business. **Disabled access** Yes. **Customers** Eclectic. **Hours** Monday–Friday, 5 p.m.–10 p.m.; Saturday and Sunday, 5 p.m.–11 p.m.

SETTING AND ATMOSPHERE A social gathering place as much as an eatery. Booths line the walls; woodwork and plants throughout. This is one of the more popular bars in North Beach. Topped with polished black granite, the bar is one of the best places in town for a mojito or martini.

between the entry and the sidewalk is an outdoor dining and lounge area. Excellent for people-watching.

HOUSE SPECIALTIES Wood oven-roasted chicken breast with mushrooms; charred pork tenderloin with roasted vegetables and balsamic rum; grilled rib-eye steak with herb butter and fries; saffron risotto with bay scallops and black tiger prawns.

OTHER RECOMMENDATIONS Wood-fired oven pizzas and such delicious side dishes as sautéed spinach with mushrooms and onions, grilled asparagus, and truffle fries with Parmesan cheese.

ENTERTAINMENT AND AMENITIES Live music every night. The music is most often soft jazz trios and quartets. Sometimes it's a small swing ensemble such as Lavay Smith and the Red Hot Skillet Lickers, and on occasion even classic piano. Check the Web site for the schedule.

SUMMARY AND COMMENTS A San Francisco landmark and tradition. Many local writers have used it as a writing studio or general hangout. The young man or woman studiously scribbling away while quaffing black coffee may be someone whose work you'll be reading soon. Enrico's devotees will argue to the death that Irish coffee was invented here. Every night, patrons ensconce themselves in the outdoor lounge and fend off the San Francisco fog with this warm and cheering draught. Who cares where it was invented? This is the place to drink it.

Farallon ★★★★★

MEDITERRANEAN/SEAFOOD EXPENSIVE QUALITY ★★★★★ VALUE ★★★★★

450 Post Street off Union Square; ☎ 415-956-6969; farallonrestaurant.com

Reservations As far in advance as possible. **When to go** Dinner. **Entree range** $35–$47. **Payment** All major credit cards. **Service rating** ★★★★. **Friendliness rating** ★★★★. **Parking** Street or various lots close by. **Bar** Full service. **Wine selection** Excellent. **Dress** Business, dressy. **Disabled access** Yes. **Customers** Locals, tourists, businesspeople. **Hours** Monday–Thursday, 5:30 p.m.–9:30 p.m.; Friday and Saturday, 5:30 p.m.–10 p.m.; Sunday, 5 p.m.–9:30 p.m.

SETTING AND ATMOSPHERE A total sensory experience. Farallon's decor is an imaginative seascape done with fine art and whimsy. The entrance and bar area are a kelp-and-seaweed forest of stylized bronze plants wrapped around glowing light columns that rise to the ceiling. Multicolored blown-glass jellyfish lamps hang at various levels, quietly lighting the sand-colored walls. A bronze seaweed staircase curves up to an intimate balcony overlooking the entrance area. The restaurant swirls like the tide out toward the main dining area, passing a recessed bar overhung with suggestions of fossilized whalebones, flowing by a scooped-out section of rounded booths and whorled columns. The mosaic floor continues to rise gently to the central dining room, a place reminiscent of some ancient sea cave. It's dominated by a curved mosaic ceiling and the huge, fantastical sea anemone lamps hanging from it. Diners are seated in deep, comfortable booths or rounded tables all dressed in snowy napery and elegant table settings. Dinner here needs to be long and slow!

HOUSE SPECIALTIES Seafood superbly cooked and imaginatively presented. Try roasted Maryland striped bass with celery root puree, blue lake beans, and *gribiche* sauce; seared New Zealand tai snapper with crisp leeks, edamame, and coconut-curry broth; roasted garlic stuffed Sonoma rabbit loin with endive gratin, pancetta, and pomegranate *gastrique;* grilled Creekstone Farms filet of beef with Robuchon potatoes, chanterelle mushrooms, and cabernet *gastrique;* grilled Hawaiian ahi tuna with roasted French fingerling potatoes, gypsy pepper pipérade, and niçoise olive tapenade.

OTHER RECOMMENDATIONS The Dungeness crab salad with apple cider gelée, hearts of palm, and petite celery salad; and cornmeal-fried local squid with heirloom squash, pine nuts, and saffron jus. Every dessert, especially the bittersweet chocolate malt gateau with vanilla bean semifreddo, milk chocolate malt crunch, and espresso crème anglaise. And check out the artisan cheeses. Recession-busting interlude: Happy hour is 4:30 p.m.–7 p.m. every evening with small plates such as oysters, crab cakes, gnocchi, and cocktails for $6 a pop.

SUMMARY AND COMMENTS Farallon is a very popular place. Come early, before the appreciative crowds sweep in to savor the incredible decor, fine food, and superb service.

First Crush ★★★

CALIFORNIAN	MODERATE	QUALITY ★★★½	VALUE ★★★★

101 Cyril Magnin Street, Union Square; ☎ 415-982-7874; firstcrush.com

Reservations Accepted. **When to go** Anytime. **Entree range** $14–$29. **Payment** All major credit cards. **Service rating** ★★★. **Friendliness rating** ★★★. **Parking** Street. **Bar** Full service. **Wine selection** Huge. **Dress** Business casual. **Disabled access** Yes. **Customers** 20–30-something locals. **Hours** Sunday–Wednesday, 5 p.m.–10:45 p.m.; Thursday–Saturday, 5 p.m.–11:30 p.m.

SETTING AND ATMOSPHERE Situated on a corner with lots of picture windows, this place offers a splendid view of San Francisco walking by. The L-shaped dining room has what appear to be church pews (cushioned) running along the walls, and comfy booths in the corners. Despite the windows, it maintains a cozy cavelike atmosphere.

HOUSE SPECIALTIES Reflecting the tapas trend, First Crush offers about 11 "small dishes" that are super for sharing as appetizers, or for constructing a complete dinner of six to eight courses; for example, garlic-Parmesan wild mushroom–crusted sea scallops with truffle potato puree, asparagus coulis, and mushroom emulsion; Sonoma duck leg confit; Maine lobster mac and cheese.

OTHER RECOMMENDATIONS There are also about ten full-size entrees available every night. Current selections include organic creamy polenta with ratatouille, eggplant caponata, smoked mozzarella and balsamic reduction; Pittman Farms natural half chicken with rice pilaf, broccoli *di ciccio*, sauce romesco, and Marcona almonds; Madras curry-spiced grilled New Zealand rack of lamb; Angus braised short ribs.

SUMMARY AND COMMENTS So many selections from the menu, and 325(!) from the wine list make it almost a daunting task to dine here. But come in, sit down, close your eyes, and just point to places on the menu. You can't go wrong. And it's one of the best of the few places downtown for a late-night nosh.

Five ★★★★

AMERICAN	MODERATE	QUALITY ★★★★	VALUE ★★★★½

2086 Allston Way at Hotel Shattuck Plaza, Berkeley; ☎ 510-225-6055; five-berkeley.com

Reservations Accepted. **When to go** Anytime. **Entree range** Breakfast, $5–$14; lunch, $8–$18; dinner, $14–$22. **Payment** AE, MC, V. **Service rating** ★★★★★. **Friendliness rating** ★★★★★. **Parking** Public garage across street. **Bar** Full service; huge selection. **Wine selection** Extensive, very Californian. **Dress** Business casual and party attire. **Disabled access** Good. **Customers** Locals celebrating, business, young professionals. **Hours** Monday–Thursday, 11:30 a.m.–1:30 p.m. and 5:30 p.m.–9:30 p.m.; Friday, 11:30 a.m.–1:30 p.m. and 5:30 p.m.–10 p.m.; Saturday, 7 a.m.–11 a.m., noon–2 p.m., and 5:30 p.m.–10 p.m.; Sunday, 7 a.m.–11 a.m., noon–2 p.m., and 5:30 p.m.–9:30 p.m.

SETTING AND ATMOSPHERE Walking into this renovated neoclassical 1910 landmark hotel-restaurant takes your breath away. The new owners have managed to keep the Art Deco vibe in the hotel, but added a terrific restaurant, where the mission of the house is to reinvent familiar favorites.

HOUSE SPECIALTIES It's comfort food *de luxe,* from appetizers such as roasted Tomales Bay oysters, squash blossoms stuffed with goat cheese, apple-walnut salad, and orzo mac and cheese to entrees such as skirt steak with summer succotash and crispy onion rings or short rib pot roast with horseradish-mashed Yukon potatoes, turnips, and carrots. Don't miss the vanilla bean butterscotch pudding.

OTHER RECOMMENDATIONS Five incorporates all five senses both in ambience and food and celebrates the familiar while adding complexity of flavor and texture. Close to Berkeley's theater district, it's perfect for pre- or post-show dinners.

Fleur de Lys   ★★★★

| FRENCH | EXPENSIVE | QUALITY ★★★★★ | VALUE ★★★★ |

777 Sutter Street, Union Square; ☎ 415-673-7779; fleurdelyssf.com

Reservations Accepted. **When to go** Anytime. **Entree range** 3-, 4-, or 5-course dinner, $72–$95; an additional $50–$70 for wine pairings. **Payment** All major credit cards. **Service rating** ★★★★. **Friendliness rating** ★★★★. **Parking** Valet, $10. **Bar** Full service. **Wine selection** Excellent. **Dress** Dressy. **Disabled access** Yes. **Customers** Locals, tourists. **Hours** Tuesday–Thursday, 6 p.m.–9:30 p.m.; Friday–Saturday, 5:30 p.m.–10:30 p.m.; closed Sunday and Monday.

SETTING AND ATMOSPHERE   The interior, designed to resemble the inside of a silken tent, recalls a movie set for the story of a sheik or a medieval joust. Lots of mirrors and cubbyholes; a very busy decor that can entertain the eye throughout the meal. But it's never too much. It's exotic, colorful, entertaining, yet not distracting. All the soft surfaces help to maintain a low noise level, but this is also a place where thoughtful patrons come to dine in a serene atmosphere. While many places in the city have terrifically high noise levels, you can actually have a quiet conversation here.

HOUSE SPECIALTIES   Many seafood selections: sea scallops with hazelnut crust; pistachio-crusted salmon; sea bass with black trumpet mushroom crust; and prawns on fennel confit. Going from surf to turf, try pan-seared buffalo strip steak with lemongrass and ginger; stuffed boneless quail; veal tenderloin and shank with juniper and orange sauce.

OTHER RECOMMENDATIONS   This is a good choice for the vegetarian. Entrees include vegetable ragout with poached egg and truffles and cream of chestnut soup.

SUMMARY AND COMMENTS   One of the best, funnest restaurants in town. The service is attentive and formal, yet, like the decor, it's never too much. The food presentations are always pleasing, showcasing the natural colors and textures of the food; nothing is too sculpted or contrived. It's easy to spend three hours at dinner here, and that's exactly what you should do. It's very splurge worthy.

Fog City Diner   ★★★

| AMERICAN | MODERATE | QUALITY ★★★★ | VALUE ★★★★ |

1300 Battery Street, North Beach; ☎ 415-982-2000; fogcitydiner.com

Reservations Recommended. **When to go** Off hours if possible. **Entree range** lunch, $10–$20; dinner, $12–$28. **Payment** All major credit cards. **Service rating** ★★★. **Friendliness rating** ★★★. **Parking** Street. **Bar** Full service. **Wine selection** Good. **Dress** Casual. **Disabled access** Yes. **Customers** Locals, tourists. **Hours** Monday–Thursday, 11:30 a.m.–10 p.m.; Friday, 11:30 a.m.–11 p.m.; Saturday, 10:30 a.m.–11 p.m.; Sunday, 10:30 a.m.–10 p.m.; Saturday and Sunday brunch, 10:30 a.m.–3 p.m.

SETTING AND ATMOSPHERE The Fog City experience starts from a block away. The streamliner-styled cafe, ablaze with neon, shimmers through the fog like the ghost of a lost dining car. An Art Deco interior, dark wood paneling, comfy leather booths with etched-glass dividers, and low lighting provide the relaxed atmosphere necessary for comfort-food dining. About the booths and tables are brass name plaques of regulars past and present who have graced Fog City over its history.

HOUSE SPECIALTIES There's never been a diner quite like this one. Yes, you can find your shakes, burgers, and fries, but the hungry diner just in from wandering The City can also choose from the Large Plates: Dungeness crab cioppino with prawns and local fish; angel hair pasta with garden vegetables, goat cheese, pine nuts, and tomato basil sauce. If portion size is important, look to the Small Plates: macaroni and gouda cheese with Black Forest ham and sweet peas; ahi tuna tartare with jalapeño, mint, and cilantro. A specialty of the house is the combination bread plate: jalapeño corn bread, sourdough loaf with leek and basil butter, and cheddar biscuits. Coupled with a glass of wine, it's a hardy snack, indeed.

OTHER RECOMMENDATIONS The banana bread pudding and "tortoise" sundae.

SUMMARY AND COMMENTS The generous booth size offers diners a chance to get together with friends or family for the pleasure of great comfort food. It's a popular place, so make reservations or come during off-hours. Singles and couples can enjoy dining at the convivial bar.

Fringale ★★★★

FRENCH BASQUE   **MODERATE**   **QUALITY ★★★★½**   **VALUE ★★★★★**

570 Fourth Street, SoMa; ☎ 415-543-0573; fringalesf.com

Reservations Recommended. **When to go** Lunch and dinner. **Entree range** $17–$25. **Payment** AE, MC, V. **Service rating ★★★★**. **Friendliness rating ★★★★**. **Parking** Street. **Bar** Full service. **Wine selection** Limited but good. **Dress** Business casual. **Disabled access** Yes. **Customers** Locals, businesspeople, tourists. **Hours** Tuesday–Friday, 11:30 a.m.–2:30 p.m.; Sunday–Thursday, 5:30 p.m.–10 p.m.; Friday and Saturday, 5:30 p.m.–11 p.m.

SETTING AND ATMOSPHERE In the fast-growing district of SoMa, Fringale is a warm, southern French bistro that provides a relief from the frenetic energy of Fourth Street. Chef Tripp Mauldin and a superb staff provide a convivial, relaxed atmosphere that has succeeded in building up a cadre of regulars, one of whom often shares his wine with fellow diners.

HOUSE SPECIALTIES Modern interpretations drawn from the rich culinary history of French Basque fare: duck leg confit with green lentils; bacon-wrapped pork tenderloin, served with cabbage, onion, and apple marmalade; seafood Basquaise with red pepper and tomato coulis.

OTHER RECOMMENDATIONS Starters are good enough to make a meal. Try foie gras terrine or Dungeness crab Napoleon; sautéed prawns with shallots and chives; frisée salad with warm bacon dressing, poached egg, and toasted *levain*; spicy Monterey calamari, with jalapeños and chorizo.

SUMMARY AND COMMENTS Embraced by the friendliest of staffs, surrounded by decor both casual and elegant, and comfortably seated, the diner gradually relaxes into the bistro mood. Chefs Hirigoyen and Legendre have created a taste of the south of France here in the south of Market.

The Garden Court ★★★★

NEW AMERICAN	EXPENSIVE	QUALITY ★★★★½	VALUE ★★★★

2 New Montgomery Street, SoMa; ☎ 415-546-5089; gardencourt-restaurant.com

Reservations Recommended. **When to go** Anytime. **Entree range** $21–$27. **Payment** All major credit cards. **Service rating** ★★★½. **Friendliness rating** ★★½. **Parking** Hotel garage. **Bar** Full service. **Wine selection** Excellent. **Dress** Informal, dressy. **Disabled access** Good. **Customers** Tourists, businesspeople, locals. **Hours** Monday–Friday, 6:30 a.m.–10:30 a.m. and 11:30 a.m.–2 p.m.; Saturday, 6:30 a.m.–11 a.m. and 11:30 a.m.–2 p.m. (afternoon tea 1 p.m.–2:30 p.m.); Sunday, 7 a.m.–10 a.m. and 10:30 a.m.–1:30 p.m.

SETTING AND ATMOSPHERE The Sheraton Garden Court may be the most gorgeously rococo room in San Francisco, with its 40-foot atrium ceiling and copious lead-crystal chandeliers dwarfing the baby grand. The room is softly carpeted, with plush sofas in the lounge. This is as grand as it gets.

HOUSE SPECIALTIES Breakfast or Sunday brunch buffet; Japanese breakfast; pan-seared black cod with roasted fingerling potatoes; Thai shrimp salad.

OTHER RECOMMENDATIONS Afternoon tea is not just a cuppa; it's an event.

SUMMARY AND COMMENTS Opulent, plush, hushed, and halcyon; if you've recently won the lottery, the Garden Court's grandeur will no doubt satisfy your need to pamper yourself. You're definitely paying for the atmosphere and deferential service; the food, while meticulously prepared and admirably presented, is among the highest priced in the city and can be equaled in quality elsewhere for considerably less. But it isn't just about the food; it's the total experience. At the least, stop in for a drink on the way to somewhere else. The afternoon teas, topping off with a Champagne tea for $32–$98, are a luxurious treat. There's a Prince and Princess Tea for children ages 5–12 for $32 sandwiches—and a crown and scepter!

Grand Café ★★★½

MEDITERRANEAN	EXPENSIVE	QUALITY ★★★★½	VALUE ★★★★

501 Geary Street, Union Square; ☎ 415-292-0101; grandcafe-sf.com

Reservations Accepted. **When to go** Anytime. **Entree range** Lunch $12–$29; dinner $18–$35. **Payment** All major credit cards. **Service rating** ★★★★. **Friendliness rating** ★★★. **Parking** Street, nearby lots. **Bar** Full service. **Wine selection** Extensive. **Dress** Evening casual. **Disabled access** Yes. **Customers** Locals, tourists. **Hours** Monday–Thursday, 7 a.m.–10:30 a.m., 11:30 a.m.–2:30 p.m., and 5 p.m.–10 p.m.; Friday, 7 a.m.–10:30 a.m., 11:30 a.m.–2:30 p.m., and 5 p.m.–11 p.m.; Saturday, 8 a.m.–2:30 p.m. (brunch) and 5 p.m.–11 p.m.; Sunday, 8 a.m.–2:30 p.m. (brunch) and 5:30 p.m.–10 p.m.

SETTING AND ATMOSPHERE Originally a hotel ballroom, and a very elegant one. Everything is marble, brass work, and wood. Huge columns support the high chandelier ceiling. There is always a lot of hubbub and goings-on here. Tourists gawk at the splendor, regulars table-hop, and everybody eats and drinks well.

HOUSE SPECIALTIES It's a Mediterranean-inspired menu with a good balance of meat, fish, and fowl. For lunch, start with a salad of hearts of romaine and move on to salmon with eggplant, squash, and zucchini, or try the croque monsieur on *leavin* bread. For dinner, consider a starter of Mediterranean mussels steamed in white wine before choosing Sonoma duck breast, roasted fingerling potatoes, heirloom mustard greens, with orange duck jus; boeuf bourguignon; pork tenderloin in a pinot noir sauce; grilled ten-ounce New York steak with sauce Lyonnaise; or chicken fricassee with forest mushrooms and rice pilaf.

OTHER RECOMMENDATIONS Side dishes can make a meal. Roasted fingerling potatoes that are good enough to have for dessert, butter bean and bacon ragout, and sautéed spinach.

SUMMARY AND COMMENTS This is an appropriate place to dress up. It's fancy without being snooty. It opens with a large and comfy cocktail lounge, which is a popular watering hole, so sometimes it's simply impossible to find space there. Have a drink at your table. Being a block from the Geary Theater, this is a good place before or after a show.

Greens ★★★★

VEGETARIAN　　　MODERATE　　　QUALITY ★★★★　　　VALUE ★★★★

Building A, Fort Mason Center (Marina Boulevard and Buchanan), Marina District; ☎ 415-771-6222; greensrestaurant.com

Reservations Required. **When to go** Lunch. **Entree range** $16–$23. **Payment** AE, MC, V. **Service rating** ★★★. **Friendliness rating** ★★★. **Parking** Lot. **Bar** Beer, wine. **Wine selection** Very good. **Dress** Casual. **Disabled access** Yes. **Customers** All walks of life. **Hours** Tuesday–Saturday, 11:45 a.m.–2:30 p.m. and 5:30 p.m.–9 p.m.; Monday, 5:30 p.m.–9 p.m. (Saturday, prix fixe only, $48); Sunday brunch, 10:30 a.m.–2 p.m.

SETTING AND ATMOSPHERE Full view of the Golden Gate Bridge bordered by the southern promontories of Marin County. Large and airy; the restaurant was formerly an enclosed pier. Polished wood floors, lovely paintings on the walls, and comfortable lounging area. Serene atmosphere.

HOUSE SPECIALTIES The menu changes seasonally, but you might be treated to mesquite-grilled winter vegetables; salad of watercress and escarole;

pea ravioli with saffron butter; or masa harina pastry filled with butternut squash, potatoes, tomatoes, grilled onions, and cheddar cheese.

OTHER RECOMMENDATIONS   Chocolate hazelnut mousse cake.

SUMMARY AND COMMENTS   No health food, no hippie food, no orange-and-parsley garnish, but the finest in vegetarian cuisine. This is not a PC restaurant; no one is on a crusade here. Its reason for being is the best of dining without meat. When it opened 30 years ago, this was the only restaurant of its kind. Some people are saying that it's not keeping up with the new competition. It's still good, though not quite great. And it still has what is arguably the best Sunday brunch in town.

Harris' Steakhouse   ★★★★½

| STEAK HOUSE | EXPENSIVE | QUALITY ★★★★★ | VALUE ★★★★½ |

2100 Van Ness Avenue, Civic Center; ☎ **415-673-1888; harrisrestaurant.com**

Reservations Recommended. **When to go** Anytime. **Entree range** $22–$46. **Payment** All major credit cards. **Service rating** ★★★★★. **Friendliness rating** ★★★★. **Parking** Valet ($7). **Bar** Full service. **Wine selection** Excellent. **Dress** Casually elegant. **Disabled access** Yes. **Customers** Locals, tourists, regulars. **Hours** Monday–Friday, 10 a.m.–10 p.m.; Saturday and Sunday, 2 p.m.–11 p.m.

SETTING AND ATMOSPHERE   Elegant old San Francisco charm with dark wood paneling the color of rich chocolate, 17-foot beamed ceilings, and large brass chandeliers. It opened in 1984, but never feels stodgy or outdated thanks to a lively, stylish menu and an energetic staff. Pastoral murals of cows grazing along the banks of Kings River in central California, painted by local artist Barnaby Conrad, grace the walls. The bar is dark and alluring, with a fine jazz trio Thursday through Saturday nights. In the dining room, conversation hums nicely, not noisily. It's a generally older and affluent crowd of diners.

HOUSE SPECIALTIES   Beef. In all shapes and one size—big. Here, they believe in bounty. There are chicken and seafood dishes too, but really the beef is the thing. And if it is possible to fall in love with a steak, this is where it will happen. Harris' uses a 21-day dry-aging process for its midwestern corn-fed beef, which produces tender and succulent cuts of meat. Check out the slabs hanging in the famous display window out front as you're waiting for your table. Then start with the famous house-smoked salmon appetizer, fresh oysters on the half shell with three dipping sauces, or the traditional onion soup. Get some classic side dishes of sautéed mushrooms or creamed spinach. Then prepare for the best beef ever—the filet mignon Rossini, with grilled Sonoma foie gras and black truffle and cabernet sauce. As thick as it is wide—practically round—the filet has a texture that is like slicing through velvet. Or have the porterhouse and exclaim, "Now that's a steak!"

OTHER RECOMMENDATIONS This is the time, the place, and the mood for a classic martini. Try the King Eider Martini: Duckhorn Winery's King Eider dry vermouth with Grey Goose vodka and a swirl of lemon in Harris' traditional barrel presentation—basically a double martini, but in a single glass, so the remainder is kept frosty in a little bottle in a mini wooden barrel of ice. The wine list is long and diverse, both in geography and style, with an emphasis on Napa and Sonoma. And while steak houses are not usually known for their desserts, Harris' is the exception. The peach-blueberry crisp (available seasonally) is so good that you'll be scraping every last crumb of crisp off the edges of the ramekin.

SUMMARY AND COMMENTS This old-style but upscale spot is a refreshing change from so many too-mod, too-trendy scenes. It's elegant yet comfy. The highly professional staff is very familiar with the restaurant's offerings. Many have been there for years, so trust them for recommendations. You will be leaving with a doggie bag.

Helmand Palace ★★★

AFGHAN	INEXPENSIVE	QUALITY ★★★★	VALUE ★★★★★

**2424 Van Ness Avenue at Green Street; ☎ 415-362-0641;
helmandpalace.com**

Reservations Accepted. **When to go** Anytime. **Entree range** $13–$23. **Payment** AE, MC, V. **Service rating** ★★★★. **Friendliness rating** ★★★. **Parking** 468 Broadway; valet $6 on weekdays and $10 on weekends. **Bar** Full service. **Wine selection** Fair. **Dress** Casual. **Disabled access** Yes. **Customers** Locals, businesspeople, tourists. **Hours** Sunday–Thursday, 5:30 p.m.–10 p.m.; Friday and Saturday, 5:30 p.m.–11 p.m.

SETTING AND ATMOSPHERE Helmand is named for a province and river in Afghanistan. Rooms are decorated in classical Persian simplicity, and the tables are set with western, though not stuffy, formality. Beautiful Persian rugs are everywhere; walls are hung with Afghan portraits. Afghan strings and flutes play softly in the background.

HOUSE SPECIALTIES Afghani food is heavily influenced by neighbors India and Iran. It's based on flatbreads like *bolani* and rice, fresh vegetables, and lamb and chicken cooked in mild spice mixtures. Tomatoes or yogurt are common bases for sauces. Dishes include rack of lamb with Persian spices; chicken sautéed with yellow split peas; potatoes and garbanzo beans in vinaigrette with cilantro; meat pies flavored with onion; leek-filled ravioli.

OTHER RECOMMENDATIONS A good number of meatless dishes and salads. The baked fresh pumpkin with yogurt sauce is music in your mouth.

SUMMARY AND COMMENTS This is a good family restaurant, and as such it's a great standby for occasion dining, birthdays and such. This new location between Cow Hollow and Russian Hill is more sedate than the stripper-bar block of North Beach where they raised the tone for so long. The low prices and the generous portions make this one of the best restaurant deals in town. And it's the only Afghan restaurant in town—it's crowded on weekends.

House of Prime Rib ★★★½

AMERICAN	EXPENSIVE	QUALITY ★★★★	VALUE ★★★★

1906 Van Ness Avenue, Civic Center; ☎ 415-885-4605; houseofprimerib.net

Reservations Strongly advised. **When to go** Dinner only. **Entree range** $28–$35. **Payment** AE, MC, V. **Service rating** ★★★. **Friendliness rating** ★★★½. **Parking** Valet, $9. **Bar** Full service. **Wine selection** Good. **Dress** Business, dressy. **Disabled access** Yes. **Customers** Locals, businesspeople, tourists. **Hours** Monday–Thursday, 5:30 p.m.–10 p.m.; Friday, 5 p.m.–10 p.m.; Saturday, 4:30 p.m.–10 p.m.; Sunday, 4 p.m.–10 p.m.

SETTING AND ATMOSPHERE Plush. Large, comfortable rooms with booths and alcoves; tables set with heavy napery. A mirrored bar with hardwood floors. Wall adorned with murals and heavy draperies. Sit by the lounge's fireplace in cooler weather and sip a well-made martini.

HOUSE SPECIALTIES Prime rib, of course. You can have it thick cut or English cut—several thinner slices that some people say brings out more flavor. The jury is out on this, but either taste is accommodated here. Baked or mashed potatoes; creamed spinach; generous tossed salad.

OTHER RECOMMENDATIONS Fresh catch of the day for the occasional patron who prefers not to have red meat. A good children's menu for $9.45.

SUMMARY AND COMMENTS One of the older restaurants in town and a temple to red meat. It would be hard to find more civilized surroundings for indulging in that most primitive of appetites. The meat is wheeled to your table on a silver steam cart, and the great haunch is displayed to you in all its glory. "Thick cut, madam? English cut, sir?" It can make you proud to be a carnivore.

Il Fornaio ★★★½

ITALIAN	MODERATE	QUALITY ★★½	VALUE ★★★★

1265 Battery Street, Financial District; ☎ 415-986-0100; ilfornaio.com

Reservations Recommended. **When to go** Anytime. **Entree range** Lunch, $10–$18; dinner, $18–$38. **Payment** AE, MC, V. **Service rating** ★★★★. **Friendliness rating** ★★★★. **Parking** Valet, metered street. **Bar** Full service. **Wine selection** Good. **Dress** Business casual. **Disabled access** Good. **Customers** Local, tourists. **Hours** Monday–Friday, 11:30 a.m.–10 p.m.; Saturday and Sunday, 9 a.m.–10 p.m.

SETTING AND ATMOSPHERE Il Fornaio is set in a corner of Levi Plaza adjacent to one of the most beautiful fountains in San Francisco. Diners can enjoy the cascading waters from the sheltered outdoor patio or from the spacious, high-ceilinged dining room accented in dark wood and white marble. Large mural-like paintings cover the walls, bringing to mind a Venetian villa. A convivial atmosphere reigns among the patrons—lively but not loud. Those wishing to sit in the inner dining room can observe the chefs and bakers at work in the open kitchen. If you arrive early, have a drink at the long, curving, black-and-white marble bar—a sensuous experience in itself.

HOUSE SPECIALTIES The antipasto dishes are simple but large enough to share: try beef carpaccio with capers, and *calamaretti fritti* or baby squid lightly floured and deep fried, served with spicy tomato-basil, Prosecco vinegar, and parsley sauces. A large variety of house-made pastas are available, as well as Italian specialties from the wood-fired rotisserie and mesquite grill: pollo Toscano with Petaluma chicken; *tagliata* Chianina with beef tenderloin; and scaloppine con Marsala e funghi with local veal. All entrees served with a variety of potatoes and vegetables.

OTHER RECOMMENDATIONS A special menu featuring dishes from various regions of Italy is offered monthly. Also try the thin-crust pizzas with house-made marinara sauce and real mozzarella baked in the wood-fired oven. And the full-service deli and delicious bakery are great for building picnic lunches in the nearby park.

SUMMARY AND COMMENTS Il Fornaio meets its goal of providing the diner with authentic Italian food made with the freshest and best products available. The waitstaff is friendly and knowledgeable and rounds off a fine dining experience.

Izzy's Steak and Chop House ★★★

STEAK HOUSE   **MODERATE**   **QUALITY ★★★★**   **VALUE ★★★★★**

3345 Steiner Street, Marina District; ☎ 415-563-0487; izzyssteaks.com

Reservations Accepted. **When to go** Anytime. **Entree range** $15–$35. **Payment** All major credit cards. **Service rating ★★★. Friendliness rating ★★★. Parking** Street; lot. **Bar** Full service. **Wine selection** Good. **Dress** Casual. **Disabled access** Yes. **Customers** Locals, businesspeople, tourists. **Hours** Sunday–Thursday, 5 p.m.–10 p.m.; Friday and Saturday, 5:30 p.m.–10:30 p.m.

SETTING AND ATMOSPHERE A modernized version of an old-time steak house. Sometimes fills to overflowing with locals who come for beef, booze, and merriment. You'll see a lot of back-slapping, glad-handing, laughing, and carrying on here. In the bar, where patrons are in no particular hurry, the generations mix as the big drinks flow.

HOUSE SPECIALTIES Aged Black Angus beef served in he-man portions: New York steak; pepper steak; Cajun-style blackened steak; untampered with, unalloyed steak.

OTHER RECOMMENDATIONS Creamed spinach. Huge and tasty desserts.

SUMMARY AND COMMENTS Many of the patrons are regulars who live in the neighborhood and know each other. When they meet here, it's party time. Don't come for quiet, and don't come overdressed. Come hungry and happy. On Fridays and Saturdays they can't accommodate parties of more than eight.

Jardinière ★★★★★

CALIFORNIAN	EXPENSIVE	QUALITY ★★★★★	VALUE ★★★★½

300 Grove Street, Civic Center; ☎ 415-861-5555; jardiniere.com

Reservations Recommended. **When to go** Anytime. **Entree range** $26–$45; 6-course tasting menu, $125. **Payment** All major credit cards. **Service rating** ★★★★. **Friendliness rating** ★★★. **Parking** Street. **Bar** Full service. **Wine selection** Short but good. **Dress** Casual. **Disabled access** Yes. **Customers** Locals, tourists. **Hours** Sunday–Wednesday, 5 p.m.–10:30 p.m.; Thursday–Saturday, 5 p.m.–11:30 p.m.

SETTING AND ATMOSPHERE If decor were food you could get fat in this place. In a city full of gorgeous restaurants, this is one of the most gorgeous. Designed by Pat Kuleto, California's most famous restaurant designer, this is over-the-top elegance. But it's in that uniquely San Francisco style that doesn't intimidate. Its sense of frontier egalitarianism says "come one, come all." On the ground floor, the circular bar is the first thing you see, and above it the bar-sized opening in the floor of the second level, and above that the enormous ceiling light. All is plush, with deep carpet and heavy draperies, dark chocolaty woodwork, and heavy furniture.

HOUSE SPECIALTIES The innovative California-style menu changes daily. You'll find Coho salmon or Wolfe Ranch quail and seared Sonoma foie gras, house-made brioche; duck confit salad with Brussels sprouts. Try the Alaskan sablefish with escarole, smoked bacon, gala apples, and fingerling potatoes; or warm bread salad with baby artichokes and marinated Crescenza cheese.

OTHER RECOMMENDATIONS Lamb dishes are especially good here, and you may be offered a plate of lamb in two or three ways, such as roast or sausage. Desserts—like chocolate meringue tart with fromage blanc semifreddo and sea salt caramel, or raspberry crème with Sebastopol Farm raspberries, angel food cake, and lemon streusel—take a backseat to none.

SUMMARY AND COMMENTS About a five-minute walk from the opera house, symphony hall, and Herbst Theater, Jardinière is a great choice for dinner and a show. But it's also the perfect restaurant for lingering. The atmosphere is seductive, and the pampering is divine. Upstairs, a live jazz duo plays at just the right volume and tempo. This is one of the most civilized and civilizing places you could hope to find. Definitely worth a splurge.

John's Grill ★★★

| STEAK HOUSE | MODERATE | QUALITY ★★★½ | VALUE ★★★★★ |

63 Ellis Street, Union Square; ☎ 415-986-3274; johnsgrill.com

Reservations Accepted. **When to go** Anytime. **Entree range** Lunch, $13–28; dinner, $20–$32. **Payment** AE, D, DC, MC, V. **Service rating** ★★★. **Friendliness rating** ★★★. **Parking** Street, lot. **Bar** Full service. **Wine selection** Good. **Dress** Casual, business. **Disabled access** No. **Customers** Locals, businesspeople, tourists. **Hours** Monday–Saturday, 11 a.m.–10 p.m.; Sunday, noon–10 p.m.

SETTING AND ATMOSPHERE Dark wood and brass trim; the 1930s at their best. You're transported to another (many would say better) San Francisco. Sepia photographs of celebs and local potentates cover the west wall. Deep and narrow with booths and small tables; the general feeling is one of cozy intimacy.

HOUSE SPECIALTIES Steaks, chops, and seafood. Dungeness crab (a must at any historic place in the city) in the form of crab cakes and crab legs supreme; fried oysters; Sam Spade's lamb chops; broiled swordfish with a Dijon mushroom sauce; a giant porterhouse steak; broiled calf livers; shrimp aplenty.

OTHER RECOMMENDATIONS Variety of salads; clam chowder; oysters Wellington.

SUMMARY AND COMMENTS "Spade went to John's Grill, asked the waiter to hurry his order of chops, baked potato, sliced tomatoes . . . and was smoking a cigarette with his coffee when . . . " Open since 1908, this landmark restaurant was the setting for Dashiell Hammett's novel *The Maltese Falcon*. To dine or drink martinis here is to imbibe the history and literature of the city.

Kokkari Estiatorio ★★★½

| GREEK | EXPENSIVE | QUALITY ★★★★½ | VALUE ★★★★ |

200 Jackson Street (at Front), Financial District;
☎ 415-981-0983; kokkari.com

Reservations Recommended. **When to go** Anytime. **Entree range** Lunch, $15–$26; dinner, $19–$35. **Payment** AE, D, DC, MC, V. **Service rating** ★★★. **Friendliness rating** ★★★. **Parking** Valet at dinner $8, metered street, lots. **Bar** Full service. **Wine selection** Extensive. **Dress** Fashionable, business, or semiformal attire. **Disabled access** Reasonable (elevator to restrooms). **Customers** Well-heeled crowd of locals and tourists. **Hours** Monday–Thursday, 11:30 a.m.–2:30 p.m. and 5:30 p.m.–10 p.m.; Friday, 11:30 a.m.–2:30 p.m. and 5:30 p.m.–11 p.m.; Saturday, 5 p.m.–11 p.m.; bar menu, daily, 2:30 p.m.–5:30 p.m.

SETTING AND ATMOSPHERE Kokkari has a dramatic setting with a number of unique details, such as huge wood-shuttered windows and an enormous fireplace. Everything, from the chairs to the water glasses, is oversized. The dark and elegant space envelops and transports you to a far-off place more elegant than Athens.

HOUSE SPECIALTIES Traditional Greek dishes are put in their best light through thoughtful preparation and fine ingredients. Lamb shanks and chops brought in from a Texas ranch have diners raving. Seafood offerings such as grilled octopus and calamari are simply but beautifully prepared. Pacific halibut steak pan-roasted with sweet corn, Greek peppers, tomatoes, and olive sauce leaves nothing to be desired. A plateful of Greek spreads makes a mouthwatering appetizer with tzatziki so rich that it is hard to believe it was made with yogurt alone; and don't forget the hot grilled pita bread.

OTHER RECOMMENDATIONS You can't go wrong when ordering at this restaurant, so don't be afraid to try something different. The chefs have respect for tradition but also know how to innovate. Desserts such as yogurt sorbet and walnut and honey baklava lift up the palate at the end of a long meal. There's a $20 corkage fee, waived with the purchase of a 750 ml bottle, as well as wonderful after-dinner drinks and great single malts.

SUMMARY AND COMMENTS Kokkari has a grand and lavish feel befitting a special occasion. Two separate rooms are available for private events, and the main dining rooms, while not packed, feel somehow communal. It's the perfect setting for a family celebration. The food here is fit for kings but retains its connection to the earth. A truly outstanding experience.

Kuleto's ★★★½

CALIFORNIAN/ITALIAN	MODERATE	QUALITY ★★★★	VALUE ★★★★

221 Powell Street, Union Square; ☎ 415-397-7720; kuletos.com

Reservations Recommended. **When to go** Anytime. **Entree range** $22–$38. **Payment** All major credit cards. **Service rating** ★★★. **Friendliness rating** ★★★★. **Parking** Street. **Bar** Full service. **Wine selection** Good. **Dress** Smart casual. **Disabled access** Yes. **Customers** Tourists and local regulars. **Hours** Monday–Thursday, 7 a.m.–10:30 a.m. and 11:30 a.m.–10:30 p.m.; Friday, 7 a.m.–10:30 a.m. and 11:30 a.m.–11 p.m.; Saturday 8 a.m.–10:30 a.m. and 11:30 a..m.–11 p.m.; Sunday, 11:30 a.m.–10:30 p.m.

SETTING AND ATMOSPHERE Here in a corner of the Villa Florence hotel, ask for the advice of the bar staff on how to begin your wine-and-dine experience. After a glass of something sparkling, amble over to the main restaurant. High vaulted ceilings, Italian marble floors, wrought iron and copper railings backed by dark wood, and warm lighting provide a gleeful combination of old San Francisco elegance and Italian verve and vitality.

HOUSE SPECIALTIES Contemporary Italian with a concentration on fresh Californian ingredients. Excellent house-made pastas, traditional Italian salads with balsamic vinegar, mesquite-grilled fish, and flavorful meats. All baked goods, pastries, and desserts are prepared daily in-house.

OTHER RECOMMENDATIONS Side dishes are outstanding, and can make a meal. Try *polentina bianca,* a creamy white polenta; *melanzane alla griglia*, grilled eggplant with aïoli; *patate alla griglia*, grilled fingerling potatoes; *spinaci saltati*, sautéed spinach and pancetta; and *indiva piccante,* sautéed spicy escarole. Or there's a Niman Ranch pork tenderloin dish with crispy lentil risotto cake, and rhubarb agro dolce.

SUMMARY AND COMMENTS This is a warm and festive place, always full of happy, convivial people looking for a good meal and a good time. Tourists and locals alike find their way here, and they usually find their way back.

La Toque ★★★★½

FRENCH/CALIFORNIAN   EXPENSIVE   QUALITY ★★★★★   VALUE ★★★★½

1314 McKinstry Street, Napa; ☎ 707-257-5157; latoque.com

Reservations Required. **When to go** Dinner. **Entree range** A fixed-price tasting menu averages $100 per person. **Payment** All major credit cards. **Service rating** ★★★★★. **Friendliness rating** ★★★★. **Parking** Lot. **Bar** Wine only. **Wine selection** Excellent. **Dress** Business or business casual. **Disabled access** Yes. **Customers** Locals and tourists in the know. **Hours** Daily, 5:30 p.m. until close.

SETTING AND ATMOSPHERE Walk into rustic Wine Country elegance. The room has the feel of a small, country-style cathedral with its high, airy spaces and oculus window at the fore. But it's stripped down to the bare essentials of light, shadow, quiet color, and the soft, easy tone of conversation. Background music is surprisingly hip for such a temple to gastronomy, ranging from soft jazz to 1960s rock, yet it's at such low volume it never screams for your attention.

HOUSE SPECIALTIES The menu changes weekly and sometimes with the chef's whim or inspiration. Smooth soups are a frequent item, and the chef makes especially good use of oils and herbs. Entrees include dishes such as Wolfe Farm quail and West Texas nilgai antelope with leek and black trumpet potato terrine and roasted root vegetable red wine reduction. It's always a fixed-price menu, offering two courses for $49, three for $68, and four for $88.

OTHER RECOMMENDATIONS The sommelier is a master of the extensive wine list, and you should rely on him for advice in choosing your wines. With each night's menu, he composes a suggested pairing for each course and this accompanies your menu. At about $62 per person, this is the "cheap" way to go.

SUMMARY AND COMMENTS The locals are loyal and regular customers. You should reserve a table as far in advance as you can.

Le Cheval ★★★★

VIETNAMESE   MODERATE   QUALITY ★★★★   VALUE ★★★★

1007 Clay Street, Oakland; ☎ 510-763-8495; lecheval.com

Reservations Recommended. **When to go** Anytime. **Entree range** Tapas, $4–$9; entrees, $9–$16. **Payment** All major credit cards. **Service rating** ★★★. **Friendliness rating** ★★½. **Parking** Street. **Bar** Full service. **Wine selection** Good. **Dress** Casual. **Disabled access** Good. **Customers** Locals and politicians of all stripes. **Hours** Monday–Saturday, 11 a.m.–9:30 p.m.; Sunday, 5 p.m.–9:30 p.m.

SETTING AND ATMOSPHERE Elegant without being overwhelming. It's a large venue with three contiguous, different-size spaces, including the bar. The decor might be called Colonial; it might be called classical Vietnamese. There is a lot of polished wood and big, round tables for family-style meals. Vietnamese hangings and artwork dot the rather generous landscape. And the place is always crowded and festive and full of hubbub and buzz.

HOUSE SPECIALTIES All the usual suspects of any good Vietnamese restaurant, plus a few rarely seen outside Vietnam. Appetizers include the standard deep-fried imperial rolls, as well as the fresh spring rolls filled with shrimp and rice vermicelli. A dish of three roasted quail seems straight out of the last emperor's kitchens. Firepot soups are bubbling cauldrons brought to the table into which diners add their own meat, fish, and fowl and enjoy together. Bo 7 Mon is a Vietnamese party favorite, being seven small dishes of beef, each prepared in a different way.

OTHER RECOMMENDATIONS Vegetarians are easily satisfied with a range of tofu dishes, as well as piles of fresh vegetables cooked to perfection. Try the pea sprouts with garlic. Clay pot dishes, both meat and vegetable, are especially rich and savory. They've been long simmered in traditional sauces and are served in the pot.

ENTERTAINMENT AND AMENITIES Spotting local politicos, including former Oakland mayor, former California governor, and now state Attorney General Jerry Brown. And check out the large painting on the north wall. It's of a European ship landing in the Americas about the time of Columbus. You might find that incongruous in a Vietnamese restaurant, until you know that the owners of this place are "boat people" too.

SUMMARY AND COMMENTS Le Cheval was an instant hit when it opened in 1985, and it has never flagged or lost its popularity. It might just be one of the best reasons to come to downtown Oakland at night. It's even worth a trip across the bay. And there are now branches at 2600-A Bancroft Way, Berkeley, CA 94704 ☎ 510-704-8018; and at 1375 North Broadway, Walnut Creek, CA 94596; ☎ 925-938-2288.

Le Colonial ★★★½

FRENCH/VIETNAMESE   EXPENSIVE   QUALITY ★★★★   VALUE ★★★

20 Cosmo Place (between Taylor and Jones, Sutter and Post), Union Square; ☎ 415-931-3600; lecolonialsf.com

Reservations Recommended. **When to go** Anytime. **Entree range** $25–$40. **Payment** All major credit cards. **Service rating** ★★★★. **Friendliness rating** ★★★★. **Parking** Valet, $6 for first hour, $2 each 30 additional minutes. **Bar** Full service. **Wine selection** Very good. **Dress** Casually elegant, no athletic wear. **Disabled access** Yes. **Customers** Trendy locals in the know. **Hours** Sunday– Wednesday, 5:30 p.m.–10 p.m.; Thursday–Saturday, 5:30 p.m.–11 p.m.

SETTING AND ATMOSPHERE Rattan couches and chairs, wooden shutters, ceiling fans, and palm fronds transport you to a bygone time of colonial enterprise. This 1920s-themed two-tiered French-Vietnamese restaurant does more than serve fine food; between the tropical decor and savory tastes, you might forget you're in San Francisco. Downstairs is the more formal dining area. Upstairs, hipsters enjoy the trendy watering hole where jazz can be heard on Friday and Saturday nights starting at 10 p.m.

HOUSE SPECIALTIES Most dishes, particularly the appetizers, are for sharing. The crispy spring rolls with shrimp, pork, and chili fish sauce come highly recommended. Many enjoy the seared pot stickers, filled with scallops, ginger, and herbs with a citrus sauce. Steamed sea bass wrapped in a banana leaf with shiitake mushrooms, ginger, and scallions is a favorite.

OTHER RECOMMENDATIONS There's a fine selection of Scotch and lots of tropical concoctions.

SUMMARY AND COMMENTS Le Colonial is a good place to relax and take in the social scene of San Francisco. There is plenty to contemplate: Asian-inspired dishes prepared with local ingredients; an urban and cosmopolitan crowd; the sounds of many languages; and the teasing aroma of a varied cuisine. Period photographs from Vietnam grace the walls. The Orient, Europe, and California meet here for a gracious time.

Lefty O'Doul's ★★

HOFBRAU	INEXPENSIVE	QUALITY ★★½	VALUE ★★★★

333 Geary Street, Union Square; ☎ 415-982-8900; leftyodouls.biz

Reservations Not accepted. **When to go** Anytime. **Entree range** $6–$10. **Payment** MC, V. **Service rating** ★★. **Friendliness rating** ★★★. **Parking** Street. **Bar** Full service. **Wine selection** House. **Dress** Casual. **Disabled access** Limited. **Customers** Locals, businesspeople. **Hours** Daily, 7 a.m.–2 a.m.; breakfast served daily, 7 a.m.–11 a.m.; lunch and dinner, 11 a.m.–midnight; bar open until 2 a.m.

SETTING AND ATMOSPHERE A rather gritty sports bar with a steam table and a baby grand piano for lusty singalongs. Directly across the street from the elegant Michael Mina in the Saint Francis Hotel, Lefty's seems to have been put there deliberately to add counterpoint to the high-toned hostelry and its expensive watering hole.

HOUSE SPECIALTIES All the usual roasts: beef, turkey, ham. Dinner plates, hot open-faced sandwiches. Polish sausage, corned beef and cabbage, soup, salad, and daily specials. Omelets and pancakes for breakfast.

SUMMARY AND COMMENTS Named for the baseball player, this is a neighborhood institution full of regulars and hungry shoppers. It's big and cavernous, yet it maintains an air of cozy familiarity. It's also considered neutral ground by warring factions. When the San Francisco 49ers won their first Super Bowl, there was pandemonium in the streets and a huge police presence. The celebrations went on long into the night, exhausting cops, revelers, and paddy-wagon drivers. Between skirmishes, both sides could be seen recuperating at adjacent tables in Lefty's.

Lulu ★★★½

RUSTIC FRENCH/PROVENÇAL   MODERATE   QUALITY ★★★★   VALUE ★★★★

816 Folsom Street, SoMa; ☎ 415-495-5775; restaurantlulu.com

Reservations Recommended. **When to go** Anytime. **Entree range** $15–$30. **Payment** AE, DC, MC, V. **Service rating** ★★★. **Friendliness rating** ★★★. **Parking** Valet, $10. **Bar** Full service. **Wine selection** Extensive. **Dress** Fashionably casual. **Disabled access** Good. **Customers** Locals, businesspeople, some tourists. **Hours** Daily, 11:30 a.m. until close.

SETTING AND ATMOSPHERE Towering ceilings, skylights, and statuesque floral arrangements each add to the wide-open feeling of space here. The muted wall tones are offset by a vibrant mural, which complements the bustling and festive ambience of this place. Family-style dining: massive portions served on gorgeous blue and yellow crockery perfect for sharing.

HOUSE SPECIALTIES Changing seasonal menu, nightly rotisserie specials. Predominantly Mediterranean-influenced dishes: delicious fritto misto with aïoli and Parmesan; squab with roasted apples; a very dramatic serving of iron skillet–roasted mussels; wild Coho salmon; grilled quail; and *merguez* sausage. The vegetable side dishes are not to be missed. The olive oil–mashed potatoes and Tuscan kale are particular standouts.

OTHER RECOMMENDATIONS The restaurant pours more than 70 different wines by the glass and offers ample choices for dessert. But the bar itself is also worth note, serving a martini prepared perfectly to instructions as well as an interesting liqueur-laced macchiatto.

SUMMARY AND COMMENTS It's great to see that service has improved radically since previous visits. The noise level is a bit daunting at first, but the knowledgeable and helpful staff put one almost immediately at ease. Lulu is a class act from start to finish.

Luna Park Kitchen and Cocktails ★★

AMERICAN   MODERATE   QUALITY ★★★½   VALUE ★★★★

694 Valencia Street, Mission District; ☎ 415-553-8584; lunaparksf.com

Reservations Recommended. **When to go** Lunch and dinner. **Entree range** Lunch, $13–$17; dinner, $11–$29. **Payment** AE, DC, MC, V. **Service rating** ★★★. **Friendliness rating** ★★★. **Bar** Full service. **Wine selection** Good. **Dress** Very casual. **Disabled access** Good. **Customers** Locals. **Hours** Monday–Thursday, 11:30 a.m.–2:30 p.m. and 5:30–10:30 p.m.; Friday, 11:30 a.m.–2:30 p.m. and 5:30–11:30 p.m.; Saturday, 11 a.m.–11:30 p.m.; Sunday, 11 a.m.–10 p.m.

SETTING AND ATMOSPHERE The Mission District has long been known for down-to-earth restaurants with reasonable prices, and Luna carries on the tradition. A small storefront entrance opens onto an airy rectangular space made cool and inviting by its dark maroon walls. Deep booths line the walls and surround a small central dining area, while colorful crystal chandeliers run the length of the room. The open kitchen bustles with activity and emanates warmth and good smells. A bar extends along one side, providing the neighborhood with a pleasant gathering place.

HOUSE SPECIALTIES Comfort food with patrician taste is what Luna is all about: marinated Hawaiian tuna "poke" with fried wonton chips; pork cutlet stuffed with mushrooms and Swiss cheese combined with mashed potatoes, string beans, and bourbon apple sauce; grilled chicken with butternut squash and creamy jalapeño cheddar grits.

OTHER RECOMMENDATIONS Award-winning mojitos and Manhattans. Desserts made to cure the blues, especially: bananas Foster with banana ice cream and s'mores you make at the table—molten marshmallow and bittersweet chocolate served with house graham cookies. Take advantage of the $10–$12 Blue Plate specials Monday–Thursday.

SUMMARY AND COMMENTS Since Luna is a popular spot, noise can be a big problem. Come early to avoid it or be ready to jump into the bedlam. Management is presently looking into sound abatement devices, but as of this writing, it's still pretty loud.

Masa's ★★★★★

FRENCH	EXPENSIVE	QUALITY ★★★★★	VALUE ★★★★★

648 Bush Street, Union Square; ☎ 415-989-7154; masasrestaurant.com

Reservations Required. **When to go** Anytime. **Entree range** Prix fixe, $79–$120. **Payment** All major credit cards. **Service rating** ★★★★★. **Friendliness rating** ★★★★. **Parking** Valet, $12. **Bar** Full service. **Wine selection** Excellent. **Dress** Formal. **Disabled access** Yes. **Customers** Locals, tourists. **Hours** Tuesday–Saturday, 5:30 p.m.–9:30 p.m.; closed Sunday and Monday.

SETTING AND ATMOSPHERE It isn't cheap, but it's never intimidating. How a place can be so grand and yet not be stuffy, pretentious, or snobby is hard to fathom, but there you have it. The staff is not concerned with impressing or looking down on their patrons, but with seeing that they get the superb gastronomic experience they pay so dearly for.

HOUSE SPECIALTIES A unique blend of French and California turned out in an elegant fashion that no other restaurant could imitate even if it tried. It's the result of the Japanese founder's 30 years in French kitchens, honing his style and making his mark. The rather short menu may include chilled Maine crab with tomato gazpacho, cucumber *gelé,* cilantro oil, and brioche croutons; rib eye of natural Angus beef with German butterball potatoes, roasted bone marrow, sweet white corn, and truffle custard; or Tai snapper with fork-mashed ruby crescent potatoes, tomato marmalade, and fiddlehead ferns.

OTHER RECOMMENDATIONS Handpicked artisan cheeses from Cowgirl Creamery. Guests may choose between three tasting menus, priced at

$105 for the five-course menu or $175 for the chef's nine-course menu. Coffee and dessert are included.

SUMMARY AND COMMENTS This is often said to be a New York restaurant located in San Francisco. That might be saying a little too much for New York. It is without a doubt one of the best restaurants in the city and, indeed, in the state. It could also be the most expensive, especially if you have wine with your meal. And the corkage fee is $30! But if you're swimming in money or content to eat humble fare for a week or two after, it's worth a blow-out splurge.

Max's Opera Café   ★½

DELI/BARBECUE	MODERATE	QUALITY ★★★	VALUE ★★★★

601 Van Ness Avenue, Civic Center; ☎ 415-771-7300; maxsworld.com

Reservations Not accepted. **When to go** Before or after the show. **Entree range** $12–$25. **Payment** All major credit cards. **Service rating** ★★. **Friendliness rating** ★★★. **Parking** Street. **Bar** Full service. **Wine selection** Limited but good. **Dress** Casual to dressy. **Disabled access** Yes. **Customers** Theatergoers, tourists, locals. **Hours** Monday–Thursday, 11 a.m.–10 p.m.; Friday, 11 a.m.–11 p.m.; Saturday, 10 a.m.–11 p.m.; Sunday, 10 a.m.–10 p.m.

SETTING AND ATMOSPHERE New York deli cum piano bar and cocktail lounge with barbecue on the side. Spacious and well lit, with high ceilings and a large window looking out on the streets and city hall. Though it's a broad space, it has lots of nooks, booths, and intimate corners.

HOUSE SPECIALTIES "This is a bad place for a diet." Big deli sandwiches; barbecue with unique sauces, some with subtle hints of Asian spices; pasta with wild mushrooms; pastrami and corned beef (ask for it easy on the lean).

OTHER RECOMMENDATIONS Desserts and salads.

ENTERTAINMENT AND AMENITIES Many of the waiters are aspiring opera singers. Pianists are usually on hand to accompany them as they audition for you. Count yourself lucky if you are there on a night when the tall and elegant Joan is making love to the piano. The music just seems sweeter.

SUMMARY AND COMMENTS Located near the War Memorial Opera House, Herbst Theater, and Davies Symphony Hall, this is an ideal spot for a pre-theater dinner. Service is generally quick and efficient with no fluff or folderol; they know you've got tickets to the show.

McCormick & Kuleto's   ★★★

SEAFOOD	MODERATE	QUALITY ★★★	VALUE ★★★

900 North Point Street (in Ghirardelli Square), Marina District; ☎415-929-1730; mccormickandschmicks.com

Reservations Recommended. **When to go** Anytime. **Entree range** $18–$26. **Payment** All major credit cards. **Service rating** ★★★. **Friendliness rating**

★★★. **Parking** Validated at Ghirardelli garage. **Bar** Full service. **Wine selection** Extensive. **Dress** Casual to dressy. **Disabled access** Yes. **Customers** Tourists and businesspeople. **Hours** Sunday–Thursday, 11:30 a.m.–10 p.m.; Friday and Saturday, 11:30 a.m.–11 p.m.

SETTING AND ATMOSPHERE Great views of the Bay through big plate-glass windows make you feel small. Tables and booths, tiered and facing the waterfront, take full advantage of sunsets flaming over Mount Tamalpais, turning the bay to diamonds, or the traditional puffs of fog curling past the Golden Gate. With the water just outside lapping against the shores of Aquatic Park and historic tall ships bobbing at neighboring Hyde Street Pier, it's easy to pretend you're on board a ship. Dark mahogany beams and brass accents add to this mood, as if in an elegant stateroom. Unusual bathtub-sized-and-shaped stained-glass light fixtures cast a romantic glow when the exterior light fades, and the sparkles of ferry boats, Tiburon, Alcatraz, and the East Bay emerge outside.

HOUSE SPECIALTIES A fresh seafood menu that just won't quit. Literally. It's in perpetual motion, reprinted twice daily to keep up with the latest delivery of fresh fish and shellfish from local waters and all over the globe—Atlantic salmon from New Brunswick, Canada; Dungeness crab from Bodega Bay; halibut from Sitka, Alaska; ahi tuna from Hawaii. At the top of the menu is the list of the day's offerings, often 30 or more. You can have them simply grilled with lemon or try one of the specialty preparations. Either way, plan to spend many minutes in the decision-making process.

OTHER RECOMMENDATIONS Perhaps skip the ubiquitous chowder, which can be a little salty, and opt for one of the creative appetizers. Moving to entrees, there's stuffed monkfish; Alaskan halibut wrapped in *feuille de brick* pastry; stuffed Atlantic salmon with crab, bay shrimp, dill, and brie; oysters Florentine; and white clam linguine. Some yummy desserts include the banana toffee cream pie; it's not just your run-of-the-bakery banana-cream pie. This one comes with fresh-sliced banana chunks as a thick, sweet blanket on top, all draped in a delicious caramel sauce. The truffle cake is so dense, no light could possibly escape its surface. It's almost chewy, in a good way. A cross between cake and fudge.

SUMMARY AND COMMENTS Abundance is the theme here, with wide selections on every front. The wine list is extensive too, emphasizing California chardonnays. The bar menu rivals it in length, with 14 tequilas, 21 vodkas, 23 single-malt scotches, and much more. Try the restaurant's signature drink, the Kuleto Coffee: Kahlua, Cointreau, and coffee served in a caramelized Bacardi 151 and sugar-rimmed glass. There is also an abundance of diners at this busy place. The crowd is a combo of fleece-and-jeans tourists and business diners. Some cluster in the bar, decorated with fishing lures and giant lobster claws. The bar, that is, not the crowd.

Millennium   ★★★½

| VEGETARIAN/VEGAN | MODERATE | QUALITY ★★★★½ | VALUE ★★★★ |

580 Geary Street, Civic Center; ☎ 415-345-3900;
millenniumrestaurant.com

Reservations Recommended. **When to go** Dinner. **Entree range** $21–$24.
Payment AE, MC, V. **Service rating** ★★★. **Friendliness rating** ★★★½.
Parking Valet parking, $11 for 3 hours; street and nearby parking garages. **Bar**
Full service. **Wine selection** Well chosen. **Dress** Casual. **Disabled access** Yes.
Customers Locals. **Hours** Sunday–Thursday, 5:30 p.m.–9:30 p.m.; Friday and
Saturday, 5:30 p.m.–10 p.m.

SETTING AND ATMOSPHERE In the ground floor of the Hotel California and just
off the lobby. Hung with gauzy drapes and low lit, with a popular bar
where singles, couples, and tourists alike gather, this is a place where
you might find love with a perfect stranger.

HOUSE SPECIALTIES Some of the best vegan dining to be had anywhere. The
dedicated carnivore can feast sumptuously at Millennium and not even
realize that he's just had a meatless, dairyless meal. The vegan diet would
be a lot more popular if all the cooks came from here. The signature dish
is black bean mole torte. No words do it justice. It's not too sweet or
spicy, and it doesn't taste Mexican despite the tortillas. If you eat nothing
else in San Francisco besides the famous sourdough bread, eat this.

OTHER RECOMMENDATIONS Black pepper and rosemary–glazed tempeh;
English pea and Israeli couscous cakes; spring vegetable cilantro coconut
curry; mocha crème brûlée; and a chocolate dessert with almond cashew
crust, mocha chocolate filling, raspberry sauce, and white chocolate
mousse that will make you weep for those who will never taste it.

SUMMARY AND COMMENTS An eclectic menu informed by classic cooking techniques makes Millennium one of San Francisco's treasures. The kitchen
makes no compromise in the pursuit of the gourmet dining experience.
Check out its special Aphrodisiac Nights ($45 prix fixe) on Sundays clos-
est to the full moon, its Frugal Foodie menus ($39) Sunday–Wednesday,
and its Convert a Carnivore discounts every second Wednesday.

Momi Toby's Revolution Café   ★★

| ECLECTIC | INEXPENSIVE | QUALITY ★★★½ | VALUE ★★★ |

528 Laguna Street, Civic Center; ☎ 415-626-1508

Reservations Not accepted. **When to go** Anytime. **Entree range** $5–$8.
Payment Cash. **Service rating** ★★. **Friendliness rating** ★★★. **Parking** Street.
Bar Beer, wine. **Wine selection** House. **Dress** Casual. **Disabled access** No.
Customers Neighborhood. **Hours** Monday–Friday, 7:30 a.m.–10 p.m.; Saturday
and Sunday, 8 a.m.–10 p.m.

SETTING AND ATMOSPHERE This renovation of a 100-year-old bakery is
reminiscent of a Berlin cafe, right down to the lamps and the bar.

Dark-paneled walls and hardwood floors create a comfortable atmosphere for long conversations over coffee, lunch, or dinner.

HOUSE SPECIALTIES Along with the usual coffee-shop fare, try enchilada pie, meatless pesto lasagna, taqueria-style burritos, or Caesar salad. It seems at first glance that this is a menu that can't make up its mind, but it all hangs together nicely.

SUMMARY AND COMMENTS This is not just a restaurant, it's a local hangout. The regulars are very regular, and people come often just to relax, linger over coffee, meet friends, and feel at home.

Oliveto Restaurant ★★★★

ITALIAN	EXPENSIVE	QUALITY ★★★★	VALUE ★★★★

5655 College Avenue, Oakland; ☎ 510-547-5356; oliveto.com

Reservations Recommended. **When to go** Anytime. **Entree range** $14–$29. **Payment** All major credit cards. **Service rating** ★★★. **Friendliness rating** ★★★. **Parking** Street. **Bar** Full service. **Wine selection** Extensive. **Dress** Casual. **Disabled access** Yes. **Customers** Locals, frequent visitors. **Hours** Monday–Thursday, 11:30 a.m.–2 p.m. and 5:30–9 p.m.; Friday, 11:30 a.m.–2 p.m. and 5:30 p.m.–9:30 p.m.; Saturday, 5:30 p.m.–10 p.m.; Sunday, 5 p.m.–9 p.m.

SETTING AND ATMOSPHERE The Tuscan villa comes alive with hand-rubbed walls and a limestone bar, elegant but simple, never showy. A fine contrast to the richness and variety of the cuisine. Oliveto is built on two levels, with the main dining room upstairs, where sits the limestone countertop, good for dining or enjoying a glass of wine. Downstairs is the smaller "cafe" with its wood-burning pizza oven and full bar. Also, there is sidewalk dining during the day in fine weather. And this is all situated next to the famous Market Hall, where some of the best fresh food and produce in the state are sold.

HOUSE SPECIALTIES Come here for the rustic cookery of northern Italy. No spaghetti and meatballs here. And if there is ravioli, it's likely two will make a meal and will be stuffed with something like butternut squash. The menu changes often, but you may encounter Tuscan bread soup; chicken cooked under a brick; pan-roasted halibut with artichokes; some kind of squab preparation, even a pigeon salad.

OTHER RECOMMENDATIONS Bold chefs are tired of the tyranny of politically correct nutritionists who rail against the use of fat in the diet. We need some fat, after all. So when you see pork belly featured here, go for it. You won't regret it.

SUMMARY AND COMMENTS The upstairs kitchen is open to view from the limestone counter and the staff are an inspiration to watch as you dine there. The staff are especially well informed about the menu items, and can tell in intimate detail how dishes are made and how they taste. Rely on them. You would also do well to rely on them for suggestions for pairing food to wine, as well as their good selection of craft beer.

Oola   ★★★½

| CALIFORNIAN | MODERATE | QUALITY ★★★ | VALUE ★★★★ |

860 Folsom Street, SoMa; ☎ 415-995-2061; oola-sf.com

Reservations Recommended. **When to go** Dinner. **Entree range** $10–$32. **Payment** Major credit cards except D. **Service rating** ★★★★. **Friendliness rating** ★★★★. **Parking** Valet, $10, and street. **Bar** Full service. **Wine selection** Comprehensive. **Dress** Business casual. **Disabled access** Yes. **Customers** Local tourists. **Hours** Sunday–Monday, 6 p.m.–midnight; Tuesday–Saturday, 6 p.m.–1 a.m.

SETTING AND ATMOSPHERE Popular SoMa dining spot, especially with the late-dinner crowd. Oola reflects the industrial neighborhood, with its sleek minimal design. Large light fixtures are hung in different lengths from the beamed ceiling, and exposed brick walls are softened by warm wood and beige stone accents. An intimate atmosphere is achieved by the low lighting, comfortable booths, and gauzy drapery fluttering above. A mezzanine, set apart by a blue glass partition, seems ideal for a romantic late-night rendezvous.

HOUSE SPECIALTIES The menu ranges from the basics, such as an all-natural Creek Stone Farms hamburger and baby back ribs, to upscale items like foie gras; slow-cooked confit of duck with a grilled peach, Bing cherry, arugula, frisee salad, and a thyme vinaigrette; or Black Mission fig tart with onion jam, aged balsamic, goat cheese, and fresh thyme.

OTHER RECOMMENDATIONS Side dishes are superb, including: goat-cheddar mac and cheese; fried potatoes with Parmesan and truffle oil; fried potatoes; and sautéed Swiss chard with crisp bacon.

SUMMARY AND COMMENTS Oola's total design works to relax diners and prepare them for a tasty meal, and the well-trained and friendly staff add their part. A refuge from the "hard streets" of South of Market!

Palio d'Asti   ★★★★

| ITALIAN | EXPENSIVE | QUALITY ★★★★★ | VALUE ★★★★★ |

640 Sacramento Street, Chinatown; ☎ 415-395-9800; paliodasti.com

Reservations Recommended. **When to go** Lunch, dinner. **Entree range** $16–$33; tasting menu, $70; 2-course prix fixe, $29; 3-course prix fixe, $37; 4-course prix fixe, $45. **Payment** AE, D, MC, V. **Service rating** ★★★★. **Friendliness rating** ★★★★. **Parking** Street. **Bar** Wine bar and full bar. **Wine selection** Excellent and extensive. **Dress** Casual, business. **Disabled access** Yes. **Customers** Locals, businesspeople. **Hours** Monday–Friday, 11:30 a.m.–2:30 p.m. (last seating) and 4 p.m.–9 p.m.; Saturday, 6:30 p.m.–10 p.m.; Enoteca della Douja (wine bar), 5 p.m. until close.

SETTING AND ATMOSPHERE Rough concrete pillars, set at odd angles in the dining room of this 1905 building, disappear into the lofty ceiling, leaving the impression that one has entered the streets of medieval Italy.

Brilliant banners in the colorful designs of the Palio, the ancient bare-back horse race celebrating the harvest in Italy, are suspended overhead. Vast gray reaches of wall are softened by sound-absorbing cloth panels and a dropped ceiling and are warmed by the extensive use of dark woods and glowing brass fixtures. Comfortable banquettes and strategically placed tables round off this pleasant ambience. The glass-enclosed kitchen provides patrons with an intriguing view of kitchen activities.

HOUSE SPECIALTIES Italian, specializing in the Piedmont and Tuscany regions of Italy. The menu changes often but offers such delicacies as grilled Hawaiian swordfish with fried capers, heirloom tomatoes, red onion, red-wine vinaigrette, and toasted breadcrumbs; grilled wild boar chops with a Tuscan-style three-bean ragout of borlotti; thinly sliced, hand-pounded raw ahi tuna and the traditional Sicilian sweet-and-sour eggplant relish studded with pine nuts, raisins, olives, and capers.

OTHER RECOMMENDATIONS The wine bar at the front of the restaurant, Enoteca della Douja, named after the famous wine competition that takes place in Asti each September. Here, 30 wines, mostly Italian, are available by the glass or by the 2.5-ounce taste.

SUMMARY AND COMMENTS A true ristorante Piemontese, known for its pastas, risotto, and freshest and most authentic Italian products. Its wine bar, Enoteca della Douja, is one of the city's foremost gathering places for savvy foodies and society folks. Its location in the Financial District gives it the advantage of relatively easy street parking after hours.

Paragon ★★

NEW AMERICAN	MODERATE	QUALITY ★★★½	VALUE ★★★

701 Second Street (at Townsend), SoMa; ☎ 415-537-9020; paragonrestaurant.com

Reservations Recommended (especially for pre-game meals). **When to go** Anytime. **Entree range** $17–$22. **Payment** AE, D, MC, V. **Service rating** ★★½. **Friendliness rating** ★★★. **Parking** Complimentary with validation at lunch; street. **Bar** Full service. **Wine selection** Small, California focus. **Dress** Casual. **Disabled access** Good. **Customers** Game-goers headed to AT&T Park, young business types. **Hours** Monday–Friday, 11:30 a.m.–2:30 p.m. and 5:30 p.m. until close; Saturday, 5:30 p.m. until close. If there's a crowd, they keep the kitchen running all night.

SETTING AND ATMOSPHERE Located just a block away from AT&T Park, Paragon is a lively young spot. High ceilings, chrome, and mirrors create an industrial chic ambience. A large cherrywood bar is the heart of this large restaurant. A partially open kitchen and a private room can be found toward the back of the house. Jazz plays over the din of conversation that the acoustics of the space encourage.

HOUSE SPECIALTIES French brasserie meets American pub in this restaurant where duck confit with lentils might share the table with a gourmet cheeseburger. Dishes often include seasonal and Mediterranean accents as well. Try the halibut with pea tendrils, pearl onion vinaigrette, and pea puree; grilled hangar steak with asparagus; or braised pot roast with garlic mashed potatoes. There's mac and cheese, or big entrees like grilled double-cut pork chop and roasted chicken are sure to tide you over through every inning of the baseball game.

OTHER RECOMMENDATIONS   Paragon could be described as a drinker's restaurant with a food lover's taste. The bar boasts more than 50 varieties of vodka, 18 wines (mostly California vintages), classic American cocktails, and a menu of house specialty drinks that pair nicely with rich appetizers such as wild mushroom tart and buttery mussels.

SUMMARY AND COMMENTS   Paragon's proximity to AT&T Park makes its pace unique. On game nights, huge crowds have come and gone from the restaurant by 7 p.m. The atmosphere transforms from clamorous to calm and you find yourself enjoying a quiet dinner spot.

Piperade's ★★★

WEST COAST BASQUE   MODERATE   QUALITY ★★★★   VALUE ★★★★

1015 Battery Street, North Beach; ☎ 415-391-2555; piperade.com

Reservations Recommended. **When to go** Lunch, dinner. **Entree range** $18–$30. **Payment** All major credit cards. **Service rating ★★★. Friendliness rating ★★★. Parking** Street. **Bar** Full service. **Wine selection** Extensive, excellent. **Dress** Casual, business. **Disabled access** Yes. **Customers** Locals, businesspeople. **Hours** Monday–Friday, 11:30 a.m.–3 p.m. and 5:30 p.m.–10:30 p.m.; Saturday, 5:30 p.m.–10:30 p.m.; closed Sunday.

SETTING AND ATMOSPHERE   Entering Piperade's from the brick and steel of the Battery Street warehouse area is a comforting experience. Reminiscent of the Basque men's dining clubs of San Sebastian, it surrounds you with warm wood paneling; a low, exposed beamed ceiling; soft lighting; and a sense of conviviality. The bar runs the length of the main dining area, its mirrored back wall adding depth to this small bistro. The bar gives those waiting a chance to observe and lust after the hardy and innovative Basque cuisine on its way to table.

HOUSE SPECIALTIES   Basque, in essence, means comfort food deluxe. The menu is divided into small plates, big plates, and Basque classics. Start with garlic soup, or piquillo peppers stuffed with goat cheese. Follow that with something like braised seafood and shellfish stew in red-pepper sauce, or the lamb Basqualse chop with *gigante* beans.

OTHER RECOMMENDATIONS   Whatever you do, order the Gascon fries, and for dessert choose the *turron* mousse cake with roasted almonds.

SUMMARY AND COMMENTS   Basque food is hearty and savory and needs time to be enjoyed thoroughly. Piperade brings you this experience but not quite at peak hours. It is a San Francisco favorite and can be very crowded. To take advantage of the friendly and knowledgeable staff and fully enjoy the delicious food, go early or at off hours.

Plouf ★★

FRENCH   **MODERATE**   **QUALITY** ★★★   **VALUE** ★★★

**40 Belden Place (between Bush and Pine), Financial District;
☎ 415-986-6491; ploufsf.com**

Reservations Accepted. **When to go** Anytime. **Entree range** $14–$24. **Payment**
AE, MC, V. **Service rating** ★★. **Friendliness rating** ★★. **Parking** Metered street,
neighborhood lots. **Bar** Full service. **Wine selection** Extensive; $17 corkage fee.
Dress Casual. **Disabled access** Good. **Customers** Young clientele, businesspeople.
Hours Monday–Thursday, 11:30 a.m.–3 p.m. and 5:30 p.m.–10 p.m.; Friday,
11:30 a.m.–3 p.m. and 5:30–11 p.m.; Saturday, 5:30–11 p.m.; closed Sunday.

SETTING AND ATMOSPHERE Plouf has an oceanic theme. Huge trophy fish hang
from the walls, and the old-fashioned white-tile floor and high pressed-
tin ceiling with skylights give the restaurant a spacious feel. Cafe-style
tables are somewhat close together, but the folding chairs are more
comfortable than they appear. The mood here is bustling and young, as
friendly staff maneuver hot crocks of mussels amid the crowd. A func-
tional fireplace adds a cozy touch on cold nights, and when it is warm
enough, the outdoor patio fills up like a Parisian cafe.

HOUSE SPECIALTIES Mussels, mussels, and more mussels. Any diner who has
traveled in France will appreciate the authenticity of the menu. Moules
Provençal, Pastis, and Poulette recall the offerings of every French mus-
sel bistro. The seafood doesn't stop with the mussels, though. Plouf
features several fish entrees daily and also has oysters on the half shell,
calamari, ahi tuna, and sardines on the appetizer menu. If anyone in your
party is averse to seafood, there's an asparagus and yellow chanterelle
risotto with prosciutto and fresh Parmesan, and grilled lamb chops. The
prix-fixe lunch is a good deal at $19 for lunch and $25 for dinner.

OTHER RECOMMENDATIONS The offerings from the bar are impressive. In
addition to the large wine list, aperitifs, Champagne, and after-dinner
liqueurs bring the European drinking sensibility to the American table.

SUMMARY AND COMMENTS Plouf is a good spot to know about if you are
working or shopping downtown and need a place to eat or have a drink.
The weekday lunch is a good value. The French staff is upbeat and hard-
working, and the Belden Place location, adjacent to Café Bastille and a
few other casual but trendy eateries that also occupy sidewalk space,
gives Plouf a distinctly European feel.

Ponzu ★★★★½

CONTEMPORARY ASIAN MODERATE/EXPENSIVE QUALITY ★★★★ **VALUE** ★★★★

**401 Taylor Street, Union Square; ☎ 415-775-7979;
ponzurestaurant.com**

Reservations Recommended. **When to go** Anytime. **Entree range** $18–$32.
Payment All major credit cards. **Service rating** ★★★★. **Friendliness rating**

★★★★. **Parking** Validated parking. **Bar** Full service. **Wine selection** Very good. **Dress** Casually elegant, no athletic wear. **Disabled access** Yes. **Customers** Locals in the know. **Hours** Breakfast: Monday–Friday, 6:30 a.m.–10 a.m.; Saturday and Sunday, 7 a.m.–11 a.m.; dinner: Sunday–Thursday, 5 p.m.–10 p.m.; Friday–Saturday, 5 p.m.–11 p.m.; bar: open daily at 4:30 p.m.

SETTING AND ATMOSPHERE Hip and edgy decor softened with a wonderful touch of feng shui: low, undulated walls, artful light fixtures, a circular ceiling pattern repeated on the floor, lots of curves, and soft velvet-covered seats. Festive and youthful atmosphere, particularly after the middle of the week. Lots of space and plenty of romantic nooks for an evening with someone special.

HOUSE SPECIALTIES Blending traditional Asian techniques and cooking styles with local ingredients in a way that cannot be done better, the menu consists of meticulously crafted Thai, Malaysian, Japanese, Chinese, Korean, and Vietnamese dishes. Nothing is muddled together. For starters, try the seven pepper and salt calamari with yuzu aïoli; Korean pork spare ribs with cilantro-lime kimch'i salad; and pork spring roll with chili-plum sauce. Among the entrees are crispy Peking half duck; wok-fried udon noodles with crispy tofu and napa cabbage; and pork chop with butter beans, spicy Asian collard greens, and persimmon chutney.

OTHER RECOMMENDATIONS Ponzu has happy hours twice nightly 5 p.m.–7 p.m. and again 10 p.m.–midnight. Lots of theatergoing folks can be found here, and the actors hang out during the second happy hour. Lots of wonderful finger food to share. Try the specialty cocktails. They're served with swizzle sticks, umbrellas, and other playful garnishes and are as exotic as their names suggest: Spicy Thai Margarita or Bonzai Mojito.

SUMMARY AND COMMENTS One of the best deals in town. The mood shifts to darker and sexier as the evening wears on. Best to valet park; the neighborhood is still a little raw. The restrooms may be the coolest in the city.

Red's Java House ★

DIVE	INEXPENSIVE	QUALITY ★★★	VALUE ★★★★★

Pier 30, SoMa; ☎ 415-777-5626

Reservations No way. **When to go** Daytime. **Entree range** $4–$7. **Payment** Cash. **Service rating** ★. **Friendliness rating** ★. **Parking** Street. **Bar** Beer. **Wine selection** None. **Dress** Work clothes. **Disabled access** No. **Customers** Locals, workers. **Hours** Monday and Tuesday, 8 a.m.–4 p.m.; Wednesday–Friday, 6 a.m.–8 p.m.; Saturday, 9 a.m.–8 p.m.; Sunday, 9 a.m.–3 p.m.

SETTING AND ATMOSPHERE It's little more than a shack on the waterfront, a place where dockworkers once took a hearty breakfast and lunch. The city's waterfront glory days have long passed, but Red's just won't go away. The chief attraction here is the view. In front you can see the East Bay and the Bay Bridge. Behind you is the bulk of the city. Red's history is documented in scores of black-and-white photos of people and patrons from the waterfront. All else is tacky and tattered—that's just how the patrons like it.

HOUSE SPECIALTIES Double burgers; double hot dogs; deviled-egg sandwiches.

OTHER RECOMMENDATIONS What many will argue is a great cup of coffee.

SUMMARY AND COMMENTS A generous burger and a long-neck beer in a place that also serves up huge plates of nostalgia, and for only five bucks. Who could complain? Down to your last dollar? Eat here.

Ruth's Chris Steak House ★★½

STEAK HOUSE	EXPENSIVE	QUALITY ★★★½	VALUE ★★★★

1601 Van Ness Avenue, Civic Center; ☎ 415-673-0557; ruthschris.com

Reservations Strongly advised. **When to go** Anytime. **Entree range** $17–$37 (à la carte). **Payment** All major credit cards. **Service rating** ★★★. **Friendliness rating** ★★★. **Parking** Street; valet, $8. **Bar** Full service. **Wine selection** Good. **Dress** Casual. **Disabled access** Yes. **Customers** Locals, tourists. **Hours** Monday–Thursday, 5 p.m.–10 p.m.; Friday–Saturday, 5 p.m.–10:30 p.m.; Sunday, 4:30 p.m.–9:30 p.m.

SETTING AND ATMOSPHERE A proper-looking steak house in the best tradition. The dark wood suggests a cattle ranch, and the well-set, clean tables tell you you're in a place of serious eating. Any doubts are dispelled by the black-and-white-clad waiters, who look like real pros.

HOUSE SPECIALTIES Serious steak. It's all from the Midwest, where beef is something more than mere food. Corn-fed, aged USDA prime is what you'll get here. It makes up the top 2 percent of market beef; you'll taste the difference.

OTHER RECOMMENDATIONS Barbecued shrimp; lamb chops; seared ahi tuna; chicken; shellfish. Creamed spinach; potatoes au gratin.

SUMMARY AND COMMENTS The menu defines what rare means—as well as the other grades of doneness—and the cooks are good about it. You'll get what you order. Portions are big and may look daunting, but they're so good that they seem to disappear.

Scala's Bistro ★★★½

ITALIAN/FRENCH	EXPENSIVE	QUALITY ★★★★	VALUE ★★★★

432 Powell Street, on cable car line, Union Square; ☎ 415-395-8555; scalasbistro.com

Reservations Accepted. **When to go** Anytime. **Entree range** $14–$30. **Payment** All major credit cards. **Service rating** ★★★★. **Friendliness rating** ★★★. **Parking** Street, nearby lots; valet $11. **Bar** Full service. **Wine selection** Extensive. **Dress** Evening casual. **Disabled access** Yes. **Customers** Locals, tourists. **Hours** Monday–Friday, 7–10:30 a.m., 11 a.m.–4 p.m., and 5:15 p.m.–midnight; Saturday and Sunday, 8–10:30 a.m., 11 a.m.–4 p.m., and 5:15 p.m.–midnight.

SETTING AND ATMOSPHERE Located in the historic Sir Francis Drake hotel. Walking into this place feels like walking into an older, more colorful and vibrant San Francisco. It's very much alive. Rows of wood and leather booths sit beneath mural-painted walls, and large windows give a sweeping view of the street and all its pageant flowing by.

HOUSE SPECIALTIES A mix of regional Italian, Country French, and California. The menu changes often, but steak frites is a signature dish and can be counted on, as is salmon filet with buttermilk mashed potatoes. For pasta, the best is linguine with clams or pesto ravioli—and there's risotto with scallops. The wild salmon is always good, as is the halibut with artichokes.

OTHER RECOMMENDATIONS There is a superb cheese board for dessert. Or if you're a real cheese head, make it your main course. For something sweet, we recommend the Bostini cream pie.

SUMMARY AND COMMENTS It's not often that we can recommend a hotel restaurant, but it's not often that a place like Scala's comes along. While this is one of the best places in town for meats and seafood, the chef is very adept at putting together a vegetarian meal. You just have to ask.

Shanghai 1930 ★★★

CHINESE	MODERATE	QUALITY	★★★	VALUE	★★★★

133 Steuart Street, SoMa; ☎ 415-896-5600; shanghai1930.com

Reservations Accepted. **When to go** Anytime. **Entree range** $11–$38. **Payment** All major credit cards. **Service rating** ★★★. **Friendliness rating** ★★★. **Parking** Valet, $10; street. **Bar** Full service. **Wine selection** Varied; many California wines. **Dress** Business. **Disabled access** No. **Customers** Locals, tourists. **Hours** Monday–Thursday, 11:30 a.m.–2:30 p.m. and 5:30 p.m.–10 p.m.; Friday, 11:30 a.m.–2:30 p.m. and 5:30 p.m.–11 p.m.; Saturday, 5:30 p.m.–11 p.m.; closed Sunday.

SETTING AND ATMOSPHERE Another theme restaurant from SF restaurateur George Chin, this one evoking the glamorous, indulgent, and romantic Shanghai of the 1930s. The gorgeous blue Art Deco–style bar evokes the feel of an elegant opium den and has been used as a set for the television series *Nash Bridges*. Comfortable booths line both sides of the main room, and a large room at the rear is available for groups.

HOUSE SPECIALTIES The seasonal menu is divided into familiar categories but with unusual combinations and flavorings. Signature selections cover the popular mainstays that are unlikely to threaten yet still include a creative twist, such as fish on a vine, a fillet of whole fish shaped to resemble a cluster of grapes; minced duck in lettuce petals; or braised five-spice pork shank with pea shoots. On the more exotic side, try beggar's chicken (24-hour notice needed) or glazed pork belly in red wine lees. The Jin Jiang dish notes it's the "the duck that won over President Reagan."

OTHER RECOMMENDATIONS Go for contrasts and the unusual. Try the tea-smoked squab served with a sour plum sauce and lotus buns.

SUMMARY AND COMMENTS Out-of-town guests searching for a taste of the elegance they've seen in Zhiang Ximou movies will feel as though they have arrived on the set as they descend the stairs into this subterranean restaurant. The atmosphere could only be improved if everyone wore white dinner jackets or slinky satin dresses. There is live jazz nightly.

South Park Café ★★★

FRENCH	MODERATE	QUALITY ★★★★	VALUE ★★★★★

108 South Park Street, SoMa; ☎ 415-495-7275; southparkcafesf.com

Reservations Recommended. **When to go** Anytime. **Entree range** Lunch, $10–$17; dinner, $18–$24; 3-course prix fixe, $34. **Payment** All major credit cards. **Service rating** ★★★½. **Friendliness rating** ★★★½. **Parking** Street. **Bar** Full service. **Wine selection** Limited but good. **Dress** Casual, informal. **Disabled access** Good. **Customers** Locals, businesspeople, tourists. **Hours** Monday–Friday, 8 a.m.–11:30 a.m. (pastries and coffee); Tuesday–Saturday, 11:30 a.m.–2:30 p.m., and 5:30 p.m.–10 p.m.; closed Sunday.

SETTING AND ATMOSPHERE South Park Café's enchanting location creates a pared-down neighborhood bistro ambience: affable clamor with relatively bright lighting. It's a very romantic street but not a romantic restaurant.

HOUSE SPECIALTIES Dinners include grilled hangar steak with a red wine sauce; slow-roasted lamb; Himalayan red rice and lentil salad with red peppers and eggplant.

OTHER RECOMMENDATIONS Nightly specials, including desserts: apple cake with geranium ice cream and Calvados crème anglaise.

SUMMARY AND COMMENTS South Park's minimalist approach arrived as a forerunner antidote to the more flamboyant and expensive dinner houses of the 1980s. Heralding the gentrification of quaint South Park, the original affluent section of old San Francisco then down at the heels, South Park Café offered a small, well-executed bistro menu served in a simple setting for shockingly low prices.

Spenger's Fresh Fish Grotto ★★★

SEAFOOD	MODERATE/EXPENSIVE	QUALITY ★★★	VALUE ★★★★

1919 Fourth Street, Berkeley; ☎ 510-845-7771; spengers.com

Reservations Accepted. **When to go** Lunch or dinner is popular on weekends. **Entree range** Lunch, $8–$20; dinner, $10–$30. **Payment** All major credit cards. **Service rating** ★★★★★. **Friendliness rating** ★★★★★. **Parking** Parking lot across road. **Bar** Full service. **Wine selection** Extensive. **Dress** Business casual. **Disabled access** Yes. **Customers** Regular locals and seniors, families, business folks at weekday lunches. **Hours** Sunday–Thursday, 11:30 a.m.–10 p.m.; Friday and Saturday, 11:30 a.m.–11 p.m.

SETTING AND ATMOSPHERE They don't come more old-timey than this sprawling 1890 East Bay landmark, where several dining rooms of cozy booths and round tables operate around a fresh fish deli, two banqueting halls, cozy bars with happy hour menus, and even a captain's table.

HOUSE SPECIALTIES Local oysters, East Coast clams, and stuffed salmon are primo choices, and newer items like Finnan Haddie (smoked haddock), maple-smoked duck confit, and tuna tartare still take a back seat to reliable petrale sole, crisped to golden bliss with capers and lemon, plus a handful of nostalgic salads. Desserts are chocoliciously over-rich, but passion fruit mousse in chocolate cups has a nice tang.

OTHER RECOMMENDATIONS The rejigged menu matches the decor; since McCormick & Schmick took over, you'll find local standbys such as crab Louis and Shrimp Scatter joined by new appetizers such as prosciutto-rolled figs and well-balanced crab bisque.

SUMMARY AND COMMENTS Fascinating memorabilia—from ancient family photos of the Spenger family to maps and stuffed marlins—fill dark-paneled walls. The decor features ship timbers and portholes; let's call it Captain's Poop meets Phineas Fogg.

SPQR ★★★★

ITALIAN	MODERATE	QUALITY ★★★★	VALUE ★★★★

1911 Fillmore Street, Fillmore District; ☎ 415-771-7779; spqrsf.com

Reservations Accepted for small groups only. **When to go** Early or late; gets crowded. **Entree range** $10–$30. **Payment** All major credit cards. **Service rating** ★★★. **Friendliness rating** ★★★★. **Parking** Street. **Bar** Full service. **Wine selection** Excellent, with many hard-to-find selections. **Dress** Business casual. **Disabled access** Yes. **Customers** Locals and tourists in the know. **Hours** Monday–Friday, 5:30 p.m.–10:30 p.m.; Saturday, 11 a.m.–2:30 p.m. and 5:30 p.m.–11 p.m.; Sunday, 11 a.m.–2:30 p.m. and 5:30–10 p.m.

SETTING AND ATMOSPHERE Recently remodeled, SPQR (The Senate and the Roman People) is a charming Roman osteria in the middle of the Fillmore District serving the food of Italy's Campania region. Flickering candles in glass sconces and warm wood accents soften the long, narrow space and plain decor. The restaurant is popular and busy, which can translate into noisy and chaotic. The owners, also of the acclaimed A-16 in San Francisco, have solved this problem by installing a foam ceiling that addresses the noise issue quite successfully.

HOUSE SPECIALTIES Antipasti compose the largest part of the lunch and dinner menus and are divided into cold, hot, and fried. Offerings change with the seasons, but you might find Spanish mackerel with raisins, grapes, pine nuts, and mint; Wagyu beef tartare; or smoked hen egg, caviar, and vegetable crisps. House-made pasta dishes are varied and include spaghetti with *cacio e pepe*, Pecorino Romano, black pepper, and zucchini blossoms, and carbonara *cuanciale*, eggs, black pepper, and Pecorino. If you still have room, try the cuttlefish with oregano and capers or the quail with dates and pancetta.

OTHER RECOMMENDATIONS Ask about the secret dish of the day!

SUMMARY AND COMMENTS Table seating can be at pretty close quarters, so sitting at the chef's bar will put you in the middle of the action but with elbow room. The staff is very knowledgeable about the food and wine; you can count on their advice.

The Stinking Rose ★★

ITALIAN	MODERATE	QUALITY ★★½	VALUE ★★★

**325 Columbus Avenue, North Beach; ☎ 415-781-7673;
thestinkingrose.com**

Reservations Recommended. **When to go** Anytime. **Entree range** $18–$40.
Payment All major credit cards. **Service rating** ★★★. **Friendliness rating** ★★.
Parking Street. **Bar** Full service. **Wine selection** Short but good. **Dress** Casual.
Disabled access Yes. **Customers** Locals, tourists. **Hours** Daily, 11:30 a.m.–10 p.m.

SETTING AND ATMOSPHERE The main room is a mix of murals, a Rube Goldberg garlic factory, and toy trains. Garlic braids hang from the ceiling, photos of celebrities smile from the walls, and understatement is nowhere in sight. A second room is strewn with plain wooden tables and festooned with straw-wrapped Chianti *fiasci*. All is exuberant without being overpowering, rather like the aroma of cooked garlic.

HOUSE SPECIALTIES "Garlic seasoned with food." The mostly Italian menu is comprised of well-made pastas and seafood laden with garlic. The garlic is usually cooked long and slow to mellow it, so you won't step out of here a bane to vampires, but people will know where you've been. Weekly specials include meat loaf with garlic mashed potatoes and garlic-encrusted baby back ribs.

OTHER RECOMMENDATIONS Forty-clove chicken, pork chops with sweet garlic relish and apples, braised rabbit, vegetarian dishes. Specially marked items can be made without the pungent lily on request.

SUMMARY AND COMMENTS One-and-a-half tons of garlic and 12,000 mints a month! This is a fun place, one that takes itself not too seriously but not too lightly either. It's dedicated to gustatory enjoyment. The bar is a popular place to meet. At AT&T Park, you can buy the Stinking Rose's 40-clove chicken sandwich.

Straits Restaurant ★★★★

SINGAPOREAN	MODERATE	QUALITY ★★★★½	VALUE ★★★★★

**845 Market Street, Fourth Floor, Westfield Centre, SoMa; ☎ 415-668-
1783; straitsrestaurants.com**

Reservations Accepted. **When to go** Anytime. **Entree range** $10–$25. **Payment**
All major credit cards. **Service rating** ★★★★. **Friendliness rating** ★★★★.
Parking Mission Street garage at Fourth Street. **Bar** Full service. **Wine selection**
Limited. **Dress** Casual. **Disabled access** Yes. **Customers** Trendy locals. **Hours**
Sunday–Wednesday, 11 a.m.–10 p.m.; Thursday–Saturday, 11 a.m.–midnight.

SETTING AND ATMOSPHERE Chris Yeo, the owner/chef, has worked magic in the most bustling of locations. The playful decor evokes a darkly romantic nightclub, with banquettes and lighting that is very kind and subtle. Busy with people of every ethnicity.

HOUSE SPECIALTIES Singaporean cookery blends the best of Indonesian, Chinese, Malayan, Indian, and Nonya cuisines (the latter a result of the marriages between Chinese men and Malayan women generations ago). Dishes are designed to be shared. Start with the roti paratha, a grilled Indian bread served with a subtle curry dipping sauce. Another house specialty is the seafood curry with mussels, shrimp, and fish in a jalapeño-coconut curry; and the salmon covered with puréed chili, lemongrass, garlic, and onion wrapped in a banana leaf and grilled.

OTHER RECOMMENDATIONS The bartender specializes in a long list of tropical concoctions and a variety of infused drinks: pineapple, mango, ginger, and apple. The recommended Navarro white wine admirably complements many of the dishes on the menu.

SUMMARY AND COMMENTS A great place for superbly tasty, beautifully presented food in an intimate setting with more than a frosting of glamour.

Swan Oyster Depot ★★

SEAFOOD	INEXPENSIVE	QUALITY ★★★½	VALUE ★★★★★

1517 Polk Street, Civic Center; ☎ 415-673-1101

Reservations Not accepted. When to go Lunch. Entree range $15–$25. Payment Cash. Service rating ★★★. Friendliness rating ★★★. Parking Street. Bar Beer, wine. Wine selection House. Dress Casual. Disabled access No. Customers Locals. Hours Monday–Saturday, 8 a.m.–5:30 p.m.; closed Sunday.

SETTING AND ATMOSPHERE Really a fishmonger's, this little gem boasts a long marble bar where you sit on ancient stools feasting on the freshest seafood in town. It's an old-time San Francisco neighborhood joint.

HOUSE SPECIALTIES Raw oysters; shellfish cocktails; seafood salads.

OTHER RECOMMENDATIONS New England clam chowder and sourdough bread.

SUMMARY AND COMMENTS Friendly family members of this Polk Street business entertain you with continuous conversation while they shuck, peel, and crack your order of shellfish. One of the few places in town that still serves old-fashioned oyster crackers.

Tadich Grill ★★★

AMERICAN	MODERATE	QUALITY ★★★★	VALUE ★★★★★

240 California Street, Financial District; ☎ 415-391-1849; tadichgrill.com

Reservations Not accepted. When to go Anytime. Entree range $15–$30. Payment MC, V. Service rating ★★★. Friendliness rating ★★½. Parking Street. Bar Full service. Wine selection Good. Dress Casual, business. Disabled access Yes. Customers Locals, businesspeople, tourists, day-trippers. Hours Monday–Friday, 11 a.m.–9:30 p.m.; Saturday, 11:30 a.m.–9:30 p.m.

SETTING AND ATMOSPHERE The oldest restaurant in the city; founded in 1849 and still operated by the same family. It's brightly lit, but the heavily draped tables and curtained booths give a warm ambience (if you're lucky enough to get a table or booth). Otherwise, a seat at the long marble counter affords delightful glimpses into the open kitchen.

HOUSE SPECIALTIES Seafood. Or anything else you want grilled. Tadich is a place for plain cooking, no fancy sauces or tarted-up presentations—just straightforward and honest Yankee fare. This is one of the few places that still serves the gold-rush specialty Hangtown Fry, basically a frittata of oysters and bacon, as well as the local favorite fish, petrale sole.

OTHER RECOMMENDATIONS Good bar to help with the long wait for seating.

SUMMARY AND COMMENTS A culinary, cultural treasure. Quite possibly built over sunken ships of the gold rush. Partake of the city's rich gastronomic history here. It's best to come early or late, as the place is jammed most of the time. And order conservatively; portions are heavy.

Thanh Long ★★★

VIETNAMESE   INEXPENSIVE/MODERATE   QUALITY ★★★★   VALUE ★★★★

4101 Judah Street at 46th Avenue, Sunset; ☎ 415-665-1146; anfamily.com

Reservations Recommended on weekends. **When to go** Weeknights. **Entree range** $10–$30. **Payment** All major credit cards. **Service rating** ★★★. **Friendliness rating** ★★★★. **Parking** Street, valet. **Bar** Beer, wine. **Wine selection** House. **Dress** Casual, informal. **Disabled access** Good. **Customers** Locals, businesspeople, tourists. **Hours** Tuesday–Thursday and Sunday, 5 p.m.–9:30 p.m.; Friday and Saturday, 5–10 p.m.; closed Monday.

SETTING AND ATMOSPHERE Operated by the An family for more than 40 years, Thanh Long's dining room is done in shades of faded green, with one room wallpapered with tropical flowers. Simple but pleasant. Not that anyone really notices; crabs and buttery garlic noodles are the stars here. Thanh Long is close to the beach and a neighborhood favorite, so it can get crowded on warm-weather weekends. The soft, green ambience provides a cool backdrop for the vibrant, flame-colored platters of crabs emerging from the kitchen.

HOUSE SPECIALTIES Whole roasted crab with garlic and lemon butter or sweet-and-sour sauce and those secret-family-recipe noodles are the house's signature dishes, and people come from all over town for them; soft rice-paper shrimp rolls; crab cheese puffs; chicken and prawn egg noodles; red snapper in a dill-turmeric essence and red onions; squid stuffed with pork and mushrooms; lemongrass chicken; steamed sea bass; and a sizzling clay pot with the catch of the day.

SUMMARY AND COMMENTS Crab is the main event here, and everyone orders it in one form or another; some say it's the best to be had in a town famous for its crab purveyors. The shrimp rolls are also excellent, as is the grilled pork, beef, and squid. Thanh Long is a good dinner stop after a day at the beach, but make reservations in advance to avoid a wait. If you're staying downtown, come by car or taxi; it's a long bus ride However, it's on the Muni N Judah line.

Thirsty Bear Brewing Company   ★★★

| SPANISH | MODERATE | QUALITY ★★★½ | VALUE   ★★★★ |

661 Howard Street, SoMa; ☎ 415-974-0905; thirstybear.com

Reservations Recommended. **When to go** Anytime. **Entree range** Tapas, $5–$10; entrees, $13–$20. **Payment** All major credit cards. **Service rating** ★★★★. **Friendliness rating** ★★★. **Parking** Self-parking at the Moscone Parking Garage on Third. **Bar** Full service but specializes in house-brewed beers. **Wine selection** Good. **Dress** Casual. **Disabled access** Good. **Customers** Businesspeople and late-20- to 30-somethings. **Hours** Monday–Thursday, 11:30 a.m–10 p.m.; Friday, 11:30 a.m–11 p.m.; Saturday, noon–11 p.m.; Sunday, 5 p.m.–10 p.m.

SETTING AND ATMOSPHERE High energy bounces off the walls and lofty timber-beamed ceilings in this brewpub with Spanish cookery. The modern wall art and stainless steel brewery equipment is balanced by the weathered brick walls. If the noise level in the front bar make it hard to hear conversations, venture upstairs, where there are pool tables and often banquets. Let the desserts, not the crowd, overwhelm you.

HOUSE SPECIALTIES A long list of both hot and cold tapas (small plates) that can be snack, appetizer, or—by ordering a few—a whole meal. Cold tapas include the staples of the Spanish bar, such as *boquerones; patates; empanadas; gambas al ajillo.* For a red-meat fix, try the bite-size pieces of grilled flank steak. Follow it all with classic desserts such as spiced chocolate torte, *crema catalana*, puff pastry cones with almond cream, or white chocolate rice pudding.

OTHER RECOMMENDATIONS It's easy to fill up on a mixture of cold and hot tapas, but leave room for the amazing entrees. The braised short ribs are a huge favorite with regulars. Duck leg with duck sausage is richly flavored and satisfying. Try the paella Valenciana, prepared in a *cazuela* with clams, shrimp, and mussels. Do not miss the *patatas bravas,* deep-fried cubes of potato served with spicy *brava* sauce and lemon aïoli.

This is one of the best microbreweries in the city, so do try the seasonal beers in addition to the favorite standbys such as the IPA.

ENTERTAINMENT AND AMENITIES Frequent live music from klezmer to jazz. Upstairs available for banquets and parties.

SUMMARY AND COMMENTS More than just an after-work hangout for good beer and gossip, Thirsty Bear is a fantastic place to bring out-of-town visitors for dinner.

Ti Couz ★★

| CRÊPERIE | INEXPENSIVE | QUALITY ★★ | VALUE ★★★ |

3108 16th Street, Mission District; ☎ 415-252-7373

Reservations Not accepted. **When to go** Before or after a movie. **Entree range** $6–$14. **Payment** MC, V. **Service rating** ★★. **Friendliness rating** ★★★. **Parking** Street. **Bar** Full bar. **Wine selection** Adequate. **Dress** Casual. **Disabled access** Yes. **Customers** Locals, moviegoers. **Hours** Monday and Friday, 11 a.m.– 11 p.m.; Tuesday–Thursday, 5 p.m.–11 p.m.; Saturday 10 a.m.–11 p.m.; Sunday, 10 a.m.–10 p.m.

SETTING AND ATMOSPHERE Clean, bright, polished blue and white. Simple decor befitting the simple yet good fare. Located across from the Roxie Theater, it's often peopled by a boisterous and friendly mob of film fans and bookstore denizens.

HOUSE SPECIALTIES Sweet crêpes, savory crêpes, plain and fancy crêpes. Fillings include seasonal fruits and butter or chocolate; mushrooms with sauce; seafood with sauce; cheese and crème fraîche.

OTHER RECOMMENDATIONS A pretty good selection of beers.

SUMMARY AND COMMENTS It's quick and good, and the surroundings are undemanding of the discriminating diner. And that's meant in the nicest way.

Tommy's Joynt ★★

| AMERICAN | INEXPENSIVE | QUALITY ★★★½ | VALUE ★★★★★ |

1101 Geary Boulevard, Civic Center; ☎ 415-775-4216; tommysjoynt.com

Reservations Not accepted. **When to go** Anytime. **Entree range** $5–$8. **Payment** Cash. **Service rating** ★★. **Friendliness rating** ★★. **Parking** Lot. **Bar** Full service. **Wine selection** Fair. **Dress** Casual. **Disabled access** Poor. **Customers** Everybody. **Hours** Daily, 11 a.m.–1:45 a.m.

SETTING AND ATMOSPHERE Crowded, noisy, crazy place with everything conceivable on the walls and ceiling. If you've ever lost anything, you might well find it here.

HOUSE SPECIALTIES Hofbrau and deli; you can also find what roams on the range: genuine buffalo stew and buffalo sandwich. Also famous for their pastrami and corned beef. The Irish come here on St. Patrick's Day.

OTHER RECOMMENDATIONS Cheesecake and one of the best collections of imported beers in the city.

ENTERTAINMENT AND AMENITIES The decor.

SUMMARY AND COMMENTS This is one of the older places in the city to survive the earthquake of 1906. Don't come here to relax—come for the beer, buffalo, and fun.

Tommy Toy's ★★★½

CHINESE	MODERATE	QUALITY ★★★★	VALUE ★★★★½

655 Montgomery Street, Financial District; ☎ 415-397-4888; tommytoys.com

Reservations Recommended. **When to go** Anytime. **Entree range** $11–$30; prix fixe, $48. **Payment** All major credit cards. **Service rating** ★★★★. **Friendliness rating** ★★★. **Parking** Street; valet, $5 (dinner only). **Bar** Full service. **Wine selection** Good. **Dress** Business; jacket and tie required for dinner. **Disabled access** Yes. **Customers** Locals, tourists. **Hours** Wednesday–Friday, 11:30 a.m.– 2 p.m.; daily, 5:30 p.m.–9:30 p.m.

SETTING AND ATMOSPHERE The pedestrian entrance to Tommy's belies the magnificent setting that awaits the patron inside. The decor was fashioned after the 19th-century sitting room of the Empress Dowager and is a tapestry of etched-glass panels, carved wooden archways, silvered mirrors, silk draperies, and ancient Chinese artifacts.

HOUSE SPECIALTIES According to Toy, there are only two great cuisines: Chinese and French. The chef prepares "Chinese with a soupçon of French." Try the minced squab imperial served in lettuce cups, seafood bisque baked in coconut and crowned with puff pastry, and lobster over angel hair-crystal noodles.

OTHER RECOMMENDATIONS Reading the menu is its own special delight. It presents unusual but delicious combinations: seafood casserole with lobster, prawns, scallops, calamari, and sole; Mongolian lamb with leeks flavored with hoisin sauce; and eggplant and mushrooms with minced shrimp and chicken, sautéed with sweet basil in a spicy garlic sauce.

SUMMARY AND COMMENTS Prix-fixe lunches are offered. Check the Web site to see selections. It's best to put yourself in the very capable hands of the gracious and knowledgeable staff for your evening of culinary delights. Do start the evening at Tommy's intimate and cozy bar. Just sitting in its tranquil atmosphere melts the day's tensions away.

Town's End Restaurant and Bakery ★★★

NEW AMERICAN	MODERATE	QUALITY ★★★★	VALUE ★★★★

2 Townsend Street, Building 4, SoMa; ☎ 415-512-0749; townsendrb.com

Reservations Recommended. **When to go** Anytime. **Entree range** Breakfast or brunch, $6–$10; lunch, $10–$14; dinner, $12–$16; prix fixe, $23. **Payment** AE, MC, V. **Service rating** ★★★. **Friendliness rating** ★★★½. **Parking** Street, metered during day. **Bar** Beer, wine. **Wine selection** Limited but good. **Dress** Casual, informal. **Disabled access** Good. **Customers** Locals, businesspeople, tourists. **Hours** Tuesday–Thursday, 7:30 a.m.–2 p.m., and 5:30 p.m.–9 p.m.; Friday, 7:30 a.m.–2 p.m., and 5:30 p.m.–9:30 p.m.; Saturday, 8 a.m.–2:30 p.m. and 5:30 p.m.–9:30 p.m.; Sunday brunch, 8 a.m.–2:30 p.m.

SETTING AND ATMOSPHERE Located at the breezy vanguard of the tony South Beach Marina Apartments on the Embarcadero south of the Bay Bridge, Town's End doesn't exactly command a view, but it feels as if it does, with its azure trompe l'oeil mural, glass walls, and the bridge twinkling in the distance to the north. The long, narrow dining area has an airy feel, an open kitchen, and a Zen approach to flower arrangement.

HOUSE SPECIALTIES Baskets of house-baked breads; homemade pastas; and house-smoked red trout and salmon. Also recommended are the Peking duck breast, grilled and served with an orange-gewurztraminer sauce with grilled organic potato-carrot pancakes, and organic vegetables; Rocky the Range chicken pot pie with all-organic carrots, onions, celery, red garnet yams, thyme, and rosemary, and topped with a traditional pie crust; lamb stew, braised with smoked paprika, celery, onions, and carrots with red wine, and garnished with sour cream served over basmati rice pilaf; or choice natural rib-eye steak, grilled and finished with a Port-balsamic reduction, served with organic Yukon Gold garlic mashed potatoes and organic vegetables.

OTHER RECOMMENDATIONS At brunch, all manner of egg dishes, pancakes, and waffles are available.

SUMMARY AND COMMENTS Town's End is another SoMa venue with moderate prices and a tasty, freshly prepared menu. The fresh breads, pastries, and pastas are outstanding, but the sauces frequently do not equal the expertise of the pastas. Still, the unusual waterfront location, with neighboring gardens and parks, offers an idyll within the boundaries of city life.

IRISH BARS GO FOODIE

This is a city of terrific Irish bars, of course. But here, they've added gourmet food to their roll call of draft beer, live music, and trivia quizzes, turning bars into gastro pubs and more. Irish nouvelle cuisine can be found at **O'Reilly's** (622 Green Street; ☎ 415-989-6222; **oreillysirish.com**) in North Beach, where Myles O'Reilly's menu and evenings of music and James Joyce lend a touch of class to nightly rollicking.

Then Eugene Power, who had worked at O'Reilly's, went off to open **The Liberties** at 998 Guerrero Street (☎ 415-282-6789; **theliberties.com**) and **Phoenix Irish Pub** at 811 Valencia Street (☎ 415-695-1811; **phoenixirish bar.com**), both in the Mission. Try the brunch-time boxty hash with smoked salmon—you'll order twice.

Meanwhile **Johnny Foley's Irish House** (243 O'Farrell Street; ☎ 415-954-0777; **johnnyfoleys.com**) near Union Square fought back with Larry Doyle's top-notch cottage pie, champ, soda bread and butter pudding, double-dipped garlic fries, and even live music. Doyle has now published a cookbook and opened **Parkside Tavern** (1940 Taraval Street; ☎ 415-731-8900; **parkside tavernsf.com**) in the Sunset with righteous happy hours.

Trattoria Pinocchio ★★★½

ITALIAN	MODERATE	QUALITY ★★★★½	VALUE ★★★★★

401 Columbus Avenue, North Beach; ☎ 415-392-1472; trattoriapinocchio.com

Reservations Accepted. **When to go** Anytime. **Entree range** $16–$26. **Payment** All major credit cards. **Service rating** ★★★★. **Friendliness rating** ★★★★. **Parking** Street. **Bar** Full service. **Wine selection** Limited but good. **Dress** Casual. **Disabled access** Yes. **Customers** Tourists, locals. **Hours** Sunday–Thursday, 11:30 a.m.–11 p.m.; Friday and Saturday, 11:30 a.m.–midnight.

SETTING AND ATMOSPHERE Traditionally a trattoria is a notch below a ristorante in decor. Not so here. A sleek marble bar runs nearly the length of the restaurant. And a marble counter wraps around the open kitchen, affording views of the skilled staff. But there's still the *la famiglia* feel to the place, as if everyone knows everyone. Almost all the staff is Italian, very professional, and friendly.

HOUSE SPECIALTIES "Tomatoes, basil, and garlic, that's Italian, it's very simple," explains Elena Fabbri, the Tuscan-born chef of Pinocchio. The portobello is her signature dish. The cioppino—mussels, clams, calamari, fresh fish, and prawns in a tomato-garlic sauce—is also a favorite, as is the carpaccio prepared the traditional way: hand-cut and pounded into paper-thin slices. Recommended entrees: scaloppine piccata or veal topped with prosciutto, mozzarella, and sage leaves, and perhaps the only dish with a sauce, the delicious grilled filet mignon with whole peppercorns and a demi-glace sauce served with grilled asparagus and ciabatta bread. The bread absorbs the tasty flavors and the dish goes very well with a wonderful red wine: Montepulciano d'Abruzzo.

OTHER RECOMMENDATIONS Pizza—you can create your own. Desserts are always changing, but you might be offered crème brûlée, poached pear with chocolate, or tiramisu.

SUMMARY AND COMMENTS If you're on a walkabout, this is a great place for a respite. The windows stretch from floor to ceiling and provide a great opportunity to sit and soak up the ambience of North Beach. There are also plenty of outdoor tables, all heated for the inevitable chilly evening.

West Bay Café ★★★

CALIFORNIAN	MODERATE	QUALITY ★★★★	VALUE ★★★★

1177 Airport Boulevard, Burlingame, San Francisco International Airport; ☎ 650-373-7038; sfocp.com

Reservations Accepted. **When to go** Anytime. **Entree range** $8–$20. **Payment** All major credit cards. **Service rating** ★★★. **Friendliness rating** ★★★. **Parking** Hotel lot. **Bar** Full service. **Wine selection** Short but good. **Dress** Casual.

Disabled access Yes. **Customers** Locals, frequent fliers. **Hours** Daily, 6 a.m.–2 p.m. and 5:30 p.m.–9:30 p.m.

SETTING AND ATMOSPHERE A roomy open space with soft lighting welcomes the weary traveler. Earth tones and pecan-colored woodwork form a backdrop for large pictures of grapevines overlooking cozy booths. This is a place to decompress when you have battled the traffic to the airport, or to have that farewell dinner before boarding your flight home next morning (if you're staying in the adjoining hotel).

HOUSE SPECIALTIES It's basically a California cuisine kitchen. Soups are superb, with clam chowder and tomato bisque among the best. Herbed lamb chops are the chef's signature dish, but we love the seafood-and-sausage stew enough to make a special trip for it. Pan-roasted basil chicken is moist and tender and herby, and there is always a vegan or vegetarian plate available, which changes daily.

OTHER RECOMMENDATIONS Crab cakes are superior, served with avocado salad. Desserts are made fresh daily in-house. Try the chocolate molten cake drenched with grappa, sprinkled with cranberries, and topped with butter-pecan ice cream.

SUMMARY AND COMMENTS It's a rare thing when we recommend a hotel restaurant. Such places tend to rely on their "captive audience" and so fall short of the mark. We are always happy to report exceptions to the rule. Only two miles south of SFO, it's an oasis in an otherwise gastronomic desert.

Yank Sing ★★★

| CHINESE | INEXPENSIVE | QUALITY ★★★½ | VALUE ★★★★ |

101 Spear Street (located at One Rincon Center), Financial District;
☎ **415-957-9300; 49 Stevenson Street;** ☎ **415-541-4949; yanksing.com**

Reservations Accepted. **When to go** Lunch. **Entree range** $7–$12 (à la carte). **Payment** All major credit cards. **Service rating** ★★½. **Friendliness rating** ★★½. **Parking** Street. **Bar** Beer, wine. **Wine selection** House. **Dress** Casual. **Disabled access** Yes. **Customers** Locals, businesspeople. **Hours** Monday–Friday, 11 a.m.–3 p.m.; Saturday and Sunday, 10 a.m.–4 p.m.

SETTING AND ATMOSPHERE A modernly furnished restaurant; white tablecloths and impeccable service make it a step above the usual dim sum house. A class act for simple fare.

HOUSE SPECIALTIES Dim sum and yet more dim sum constantly issuing forth fresh from the kitchen. Choose barbecued pork buns; shrimp moons; and silver-wrapped chicken wheeled out on trolleys.

OTHER RECOMMENDATIONS Small portions of Peking duck. A wide variety of vegetarian dim sum, including pea leaves; sautéed eggplant and mustard greens; chrysanthemum blossom tea.

SUMMARY AND COMMENTS Selections are cooked with less fat than usual so one can stuff oneself without having to spend any extra time at the gym.

Yuet Lee ★★½

| CHINESE | INEXPENSIVE/MODERATE | QUALITY ★★★½ | VALUE ★★★★★ |

1300 Stockton Street, Chinatown; ☎ 415-982-6020

Reservations Not accepted. **When to go** Anytime. **Entree range** $7–$15. **Payment** Cash only. **Service rating** ★★★. **Friendliness rating** ★★★. **Parking** Street, public pay lots. **Bar** Beer, wine. **Wine selection** House. **Dress** Casual. **Disabled access** Good. **Customers** Locals, businesspeople, tourists. **Hours** Wednesday–Monday, 11 a.m.–3 a.m.; closed Tuesday.

SETTING AND ATMOSPHERE Nondescript, clangorous, Formica-tabled seafood and noodle shop on a busy corner in north Chinatown; fresh seafood tanks, chartreuse-framed windows, and an open kitchen with flying cleavers. Famously, Gerard Depardieu and French Minister of Culture Jack Lang once hung out here and even joined the kitchen staff from time to time. Best of all, it stays open till at least 3 a.m.

HOUSE SPECIALTIES Fresh seafood specialties: seasonal lobster; pepper-and-salt prawns; crab with ginger and onion; fresh boiled geoduck or razor clams; sturgeon with greens; sautéed fresh and dried squid. Clay pots: salted fish with diced chicken and bean cake; roast pork, bean cake, and shrimp sauce; oyster and roast pork with ginger and onion. Roast squab; braised chicken with abalone; fresh New Zealand mussels with black-bean sauce; steamed live rock cod with ham and shredded black mushrooms. Also, a vast assortment of noodles and noodle soups: wontons and dumplings; braised noodles with beef stew; Amoy- or Singapore-style rice sticks.

OTHER RECOMMENDATIONS Rice soups or plates; roast duck.

SUMMARY AND COMMENTS There are basically two kinds of people in the world: those who believe salvation can be found in a bowl of Chinese noodles and those who do not. If you are among the former, you will not care about Yuet Lee's fluorescent lighting, linoleum floors, and slam-bang service. You will forsake soft music and cloth napkins and candlelight. You will know that each vessel of glistening dumplings swimming in broth perfumed by star anise and ginger and scattered with emerald scallions contains all the mysteries of the universe. You will want to taste every item on the menu; stay until closing time at 3 a.m. just to watch the fragrant platters come steaming from the kitchen, yea, verily, to become one with the noodles and the fish.

Zarzuela ★★★

| SPANISH | MODERATE | QUALITY ★★★★ | VALUE ★★★★★ |

2000 Hyde Street, Marina District; ☎ 415-346-0800

Reservations Not accepted. **When to go** Anytime. **Entree range** Tapas, $4–$9; entrees, $12–$17. **Payment** MC, V. **Service rating** ★★★★. **Friendliness rating** ★★★★. **Parking** Street. **Bar** Beer, wine. **Wine selection** Limited but good. **Dress**

Casual. **Disabled access** Good. **Customers** Locals, tourists. **Hours** Tuesday–Thursday, 5:30 p.m.–10 p.m.; Friday and Saturday, 5:30 p.m.–10:30 p.m.

SETTING AND ATMOSPHERE Disarming warmth beckons as piquant aromas of garlic and seafood waft over the sidewalk. Modest appointments are inside; tawny walls and tile floors, beamed ceilings and arched windows, hand-painted dishes on the walls, and the music of soft guitars. The nuances of Spanish culture and charm softly beguile.

HOUSE SPECIALTIES Thirty-eight types of tapas. Mussels or clams with white wine and garlic; paella; grilled shrimp; poached octopus with potatoes and paprika; snails baked on croutons; grilled scallops and chard with red-pepper sauce; Spanish sausage with wine; cold roast veal with olives; grilled vegetables; rolled eggplant with goat cheese. Entrees include Zarzuela, a Catalan seafood stew; pork tenderloin in raisin-and-pine-nut sauce; paella; lamb chops in garlic, parsley, and sherry vinegar.

OTHER RECOMMENDATIONS Sangria; gazpacho; romaine salad with roasted garlic; caramel flan; Alicante Muscatel dessert wine.

SUMMARY AND COMMENTS Oranges and olives, garlic and olives, red wine and sherries; Spanish cuisine presents a provocative departure from French and Italian in its colorful little tapas plates and the substantial offerings issuing forth from Zarzuela's kitchen. Dishes are as refined as they are close to the earth. Prices are as soothing as the ambience, and a small group of diners can sample a wide assortment of dishes without having to run to the ATM. Darkly sweet and spicy sangria is poured into large goblets. Zarzuela is a quintessential neighborhood restaurant: low-key, low-priced, and welcoming.

Zuni Café and Grill ★★★★

ITALIAN	MODERATE	QUALITY ★★★★	VALUE ★★★★

1658 Market Street, Mission District; ☎ 415-552-2522; zunicafe.com

Reservations Accepted. **When to go** Anytime. **Entree range** $17–$24. **Payment** AE, MC, V. **Service rating** ★★★. **Friendliness rating** ★★★. **Parking** Street. **Bar** Full service. **Wine selection** Superior. **Dress** Casual, business. **Disabled access** Yes. **Customers** Locals, businesspeople, tourists. **Hours** Tuesday–Thursday, 11:30 a.m.–11 p.m.; Friday and Saturday, 11:30 a.m.–midnight; Sunday, 11 a.m.–11 p.m.

SETTING AND ATMOSPHERE Lots of bustle. A happy and exuberant place full of people coming and going, eating and enjoying, at all hours of the day and into the night. There's a long copper bar just right for bellying up and holding forth to all who will listen, and an excellent view of busy Market Street.

HOUSE SPECIALTIES The menu changes daily, and only the best stuff is purchased for Zuni. Rib-eye steak; roast chicken; grilled tuna; braised cod; pasta dishes; any soup; vegetable fritters.

OTHER RECOMMENDATIONS Regulars say the roast chicken for two and warm bread salad is matchless—but it's so popular that they warn you not to order it if rushing to an opera, since it can take up to an hour.

SUMMARY AND COMMENTS This place concentrates on perfecting the simple. The kitchen team will mine a single ingredient or recipe for the most it can give while still retaining its essential character. An example is the use of Meyer lemons. They are grown almost exclusively in the backyards of East Bay homes and are sweeter and more aromatic than other lemons. The Meyer is to lemons what the truffle is to mushrooms.

PART EIGHT

ENTERTAINMENT *and* NIGHTLIFE

▌■ PERFORMING ARTS

SAN FRANCISCO IS ONE OF THE FEW CITIES on the West Coast to boast its own professional symphony, ballet, and opera companies. They benefit from the thriving support of the city's upper crust, who wine and dine their way through glittering fund-raisers. Other hallmarks of the San Francisco cultural milieu include free summer music concerts and a burgeoning theater scene.

CLASSICAL MUSIC

Louise M. Davies Symphony Hall (201 Van Ness Avenue at Grove Street; ☎ 415-864-6000) is the permanent home of the world-class **San Francisco Symphony.** Musical Director Michael Tilson Thomas and the world's best-known soloists and guest conductors offer a year-round season of classical music, as well as occasional performances by offbeat musical and touring groups. The cheapest seats are generally around $30. Call about the availability of standby tickets on the day of a concert; they sometimes cost less than $30; visit **sfsymphony.org.**

A night at the opera in San Francisco is no small affair. The **War Memorial Opera House** in the Civic Center District is an opulent venue for the **San Francisco Opera Association,** which has received rave reviews since the building opened in 1932. The San Francisco Opera consistently wins critical acclaim for operatic warhorses and stunning ring cycle of Wagnerian heroism and starry casts.

With its considerable international weight, the San Francisco Opera pulls in heavy hitters such as Placido Domingo and Anna Netrebko, and it offers movie theater replays as well as free open-air simulcasts. The three-month main season starts at the beginning of September, and opening night is one of the main social events on the West Coast. Tickets start at $15, but standing room is even less. For ticket and schedule information, call ☎ 415-864-3330; or visit **sfopera.com.**

BALLET

THE **San Francisco Ballet** also calls the War Memorial Opera House home. The oldest, and third-largest, ballet company in the United States has a five-month season from January to May. The San Francisco Ballet was the first company in the country to perform *The Nutcracker* as a Christmas event (and still does each December) and offers consistently excellent productions of full-length classic and contemporary ballets. Tickets range from $20 to $199. For ticket and schedule information, call ☎ 415-865-2000; or visit **sfballet.org.**

SUMMER CLASSICAL MUSIC FESTIVALS

THE **Stern Grove Festival** is one of the nation's oldest (since 1938) free summer music festivals. The festival presents ten outdoor concerts on Sunday afternoons from June through August at the sylvan **Sigmund Stern Grove** in San Francisco. Performances include the San Francisco Ballet, Symphony, and Opera, as well as a diverse mix of blues, jazz, popular, and world music. Come early with a blanket to this magnificent, eucalyptus-lined grove. For schedule information, call ☎ 415-252-6252; or visit **sterngrove.org.**

Midsummer Mozart presents a summer season of the works of Mozart in many venues around the Bay Area. The **Festival Orchestra** is conducted by George Cleve and features well-known soloists. Tickets range from $25 to $60. For schedule and ticket information, call ☎ 415-627-9141; or visit **midsummermozart.org.**

THEATER

THE MAJORITY OF SAN FRANCISCO'S THEATERS congregate downtown around the Theater District, just west of Union Square. The **American Conservatory Theater** (ACT) is the Bay Area's leading theater group, offering celebrated classics and new works on the stage of the **American Conservatory Theater** (formerly the Geary) (450 Geary Boulevard at Mason Street). Celebrated thespians appearing in ACT productions have included Olympia Dukakis, John Turturro, and Lily Tomlin. The season runs from September through July, and tickets range from $15 to $100. For more information, call the box office at ☎ 415-749-2228; or visit **act-sfbay.org.**

Three downtown theaters concentrate on Broadway productions; call ☎ 415-551-2000 for schedule and ticket information; or visit **shnsf.com.** The **Curran Theatre** (445 Geary Street at Taylor Street) sometimes tackles the bigger shows, such as Andrew Lloyd Webber's *The Phantom of the Opera* under the direction of its original London production team; the show ran for five years. The **Golden Gate Theatre** (1 Taylor Street at Market Street), built in 1922, is often described as an Art Deco palace. The ornate **Orpheum Theatre** (1192 Market at Eighth Street), a city historical monument, presents a variety of traveling musical productions.

After the ACT, **Magic Theatre** in Fort Mason is one of the city's busiest companies—and consistently rated the most exciting. The company specializes in the works of contemporary playwrights and emerging talent; Sam Shepard traditionally premiered his new plays here. For schedule and ticket information, call ☎ 415-441-8822; or visit **magictheatre.org**.

In the heart of San Francisco, the **Yerba Buena Center for the Arts** presents art and art education in a lovely location. Attractions include award-winning theater groups, film and video presentations, and museum and gallery exhibitions. The center is located at 701 Mission Street across from the Moscone Convention Center in SoMa. For ticket information, call ☎ 415-978-2700; or visit **ybca.org**. The **Marines Memorial Theater** (609 Sutter Street; ☎ 415-771-6900; **marinesmemorialtheatre.com**) is well known for mounting Broadway musicals and comedies. Across the bay, the **Berkeley Repertory Theater** (2025 Addison Street; ☎ 510-647-2949; **berkeleyrep.org**) presents classic and contemporary plays in a beautiful modern setting. **Downtown Restaurant** (2102 Shattuck Avenue; ☎ 510-649-3810; **downtownrestaurant.com**) is across the street and the pair make the trip over the bridge worthwhile.

Live performance is not limited to traditional theater. Folks here love to laugh, sometimes while they eat, so the musical comedy at **Teatro ZinZanni** (Pier 29; ☎ 415-438-2668; **love.zinzanni.org**) takes place around the tables of an excellent dinner. Catch the stand-up comics at places like **Cobb's Comedy Club** (915 Columbus Street; ☎ 415-928-4320) and the **Punch Line** (444 Battery Street; ☎ 415-397-7573; **punchlinecomedyclub.com**).

As San Francisco is arguably the literary capital of the United States (it even names streets after writers and poets), it's no surprise that the locals love a good reading. The **3300 Club** (3300 Mission Street; ☎ 415-826-6886; **3300club.com**) has open mic the last Tuesday of every month. Across the bay the **Starry Plough** (3101 Shattuck Avenue, Berkeley; ☎ 510-841-2082; **starryploughpub.com**) hosts "the West Coast's most exciting literary boxing match" every Wednesday. For a comprehensive listing of spoken-word events visit: **sfstation.com/literary-arts/calendar**.

TICKET AGENCIES

Mr. Ticket (2065 Van Ness Avenue) is the Bay Area's largest ticket agency, offering premium seating for sports, concerts, and theater productions at market prices. Major credit cards are accepted, and delivery is available. For more information, call ☎ 415-775-3031 from San Francisco or ☎ 800-424-7328 outside the area; or visit **mrticket.com**.

Tickets.com offers tickets for theater, sports, concerts, and other Bay Area events through their Web site. A service charge is added to the ticket price.

TIX Bay Area sells half-price, day-of-performance tickets for selected theater, dance, and music events (cash only), as well as full-price, advance-sale tickets for local performing events (by credit card). They also sell half-price advance tickets online. A service charge is added to ticket prices. TIX is located on the western side of Union Square on Powell Street. Call ☎ 415-433-7827 for information; or visit **tixbayarea.com.**

SAN FRANCISCO NIGHTLIFE

YOU'VE JUST LANDED IN ONE OF THE BEST NIGHTLIFE CITIES in the Western world. Do you want to dance—free-form, rumba, tango, or swing? Dressed in formal, leather, or naked (well, almost)? Do you want to drink microbrews with local Bohemians, shoot darts with the Irish, sing off-key with tourists, or prowl a singles meat market where hormones are as thick as San Francisco fog? Do you want fancy, not so fancy, or downright dirty? Straight, gay, bi, all of the above, or just confused? San Francisco opens its Golden Gate to you.

Here in the artistic capital of the western United States a lot of high-tone tippling can be done in art galleries. At **Fly Bar** (762 Divisadero Street; ☎ 415-931-4359; **flybarandrestaurant.com**) you can ensconce yourself amid the jazzy portraits and murals of real people in the music world (all for sale) while enjoying a cocktail or the house's famous sangria and a pizza. The **111 Minna Gallery** (111 Minna Street; ☎ 415-974-1719; **111minnagallery.com**) doubles as a nightclub and draws a very cool crowd from around SoMa. The **Canvas Gallery** (1200 Ninth Street; ☎ 415-504-0060; **thecanvasgallery.com**) is a wine and sake bar, as well as a spoken-word and music venue. Wine and cheese are always on hand at the **Hotel Biron's** gallery (45 Rose Street; 415-703-0403; **hotelbiron.com**).

Everyone knows that San Francisco sits at the edge of the wine country. But the city has also been a major brewing center since gold-rush days. Its signature brew is Anchor Steam, and the brewery is open daily for tours (1705 Mariposa Street; ☎ 415-863-8350; **anchorsteambeer.com**). But for a nighttime pint there are any number of brewpubs throughout the city, crafting their own beers and ales, lagers and porters and stouts, and many have live music nightly. Thirsty Bear Brewing Company (see Dining) offers one of the widest ranges of craft beers, and they are always experimenting with new methods and tastes. **San Francisco Brewing Company** (155 Columbus

Avenue; ☎ 415-434-3344), occupying the site of a former Barbary Coast saloon, is the oldest brewpub in the city. At the edge of North Beach, it's a good place to start or end an evening. **Magnolia Pub Brewery** (1398 Haight Street; ☎ 415-864-7468) is the only such operation in the Haight and offers great beer and fine food. **Beach Chalet** (see Dining) is a perfect marriage of beer and romance. **21st Amendment** (563 Second Street; ☎ 415-369-0900) is close to the ballpark and a perfect place to relive the night game over a pint or two.

The city is also one of the most important musical centers of the nation. All kinds of jazz, rock, punk, acid, and even orchestral music have been incubated here. The only thing you won't find here is country/western music. You'll have to head south to San Jose for line dancing and cowboy hats. Virtually every neighborhood in the city has a variety of music venues, so common and plentiful that they're taken for granted.

Some practical considerations: Most of the clubs listed here are located in a contiguous swath running from North Beach (quaint, excellent views, less fog) through the Union Square area (uptown, elegant) to the SoMa and Mission Districts (leading edge, alternative). And since San Francisco is a small city, clubs are not far apart. If you don't find one to be your cup of tea, just check out its neighbors. In North Beach, all you have to do is walk along Broadway, peering down the side streets as you go. At Union Square, just stand on a corner and point yourself in any direction. In SoMa the greatest concentration of clubs is on Folsom Street, between 7th and 11th streets. In the Mission they are on Mission and Valencia streets between 16th and 24th.

> **unofficial TIP**
> Go to the clubs by foot or taxi. The cops will frequently set up drunk-driver checks on the main streets.

A good way to go club-hopping without having to drive is to travel with **3 Babes & a Bus.** Every Saturday and sometimes on Friday, for $39, the two women and one male of the species will load you and yours onto a party bus with a highly mixed and totally unpredictable crowd of revelers and take you on a nocturnal tour of the city, stopping at three or four of the more popular clubs. You won't have to pay cover charges, you get priority admittance, and you leave the driving and often impossible parking to them. This is also a good way to meet other revelers. Gentlemen should be advised that bachelorette parties are frequent patrons of the 3 Babes. In fact, women usually make up the majority of patrons. You must be at least 21 years old with a valid ID; jeans and tennis shoes are a no no. Pickup is at Ruby Skye (see page 344) at 8:30 p.m., with drop-off around 1:30 a.m. (☎ 800-414-0158; **threebabes.com**).

> **unofficial TIP**
> **The best rooftop bars in town:**
>
> Sky Terrace
> *(Medjool Restaurant)*
>
> The Starlight Room
> *(Sir Francis Drake Hotel)*
>
> Top of the Mark
> *(Mark Hopkins Hotel)*
>
> The View *(Marriott Hotel)*

The babes, as well as this book, will guide you to the best modern dance venues in town. But if you're strictly ballroom, then head to the Metronome Dance Center (1830 17th Street; ☎ 415-252-9000; **metronomedancecenter.com**). Classes are held daily and dances nightly.

Up-to-the-minute club information is listed in the *San Francisco Bay Guardian* (**sfbg.com**) and *San Francisco Weekly* (**sfweekly.com**), free weekly newspapers available at any newsstand. It is illegal to smoke in any restaurant in the state, and in any bar not owner-operated. Most Californians are nonsmokers and support the law. A few clubs have special smoking rooms or patios, but if you have to step outside for an occasional nicotine fix, please don't crush your cigarette out on the sidewalk. Try dropping it down a storm drain.

Ever since the gold rush of 1849, San Francisco has been a city of revels. Many locals live for it. Some make it an art form. People from Los Angeles and Seattle fly in for it. And now you're in the middle of it. Tip a dollar per round, pace yourself, and don't forget your trench coat.

NIGHTCLUB PROFILES

Bimbo's 365 Club

CLASSIC BIG-BAND NIGHTCLUB

1025 Columbus Avenue, North Beach; ☎ 415-474-0365; bimbos365club.com

Cover Varies according to show. **Minimum** 2 drinks. **Mixed drinks** $4.50 and up. **Wine** $4–$8. **Beer** $3–$4. **Dress** Varies. **Food available** Burgers, pasta, and pizza. **Hours** Shows usually begin at 8 p.m., with doors open 1 hour before.

WHO GOES THERE Very mixed crowd.

WHAT GOES ON A wide range of musical entertainment from lounge to jazz to rock and soul. The big draws these days are retro nights, when guys and dolls wear zoot suits, circle skirts, tuxedos, and full-length gowns. The Preservation Hall Jazz Orchestra or Mr. Rick's Martini Band might play after Work That Skirt gives free dance lessons. Tap and bubble dancers often round out the program.

SETTING AND ATMOSPHERE Beautifully restored, 1940s-style nightclub with a large stage and dance floor, roving photographer and cigarette girl, and the famous Dolphina, the nude lady in a giant fishbowl. Put on your black and white and step into another, better time.

IF YOU GO Call for information and reservations. A few short blocks down Columbus Avenue, Kennedy's Irish Pub & Indian Curry House (1040 Columbus Avenue; ☎ 415-441-8855) serves Indian food and Irish beers, and they even have a game room.

Biscuits & Blues

BLUES SUPPER CLUB

401 Mason Street, Theater District near Union Square; ☎ 415-292-2583; biscuitsandblues.com

Cover $5–$30 (varies by artist). **Minimum** None. **Mixed drinks** $3.50–$8. **Wine** Bottles, $14–$28; $6–$8 by the glass. **Beer** $3.50–$4.75. **Dress** Casual. **Food available** Full menu. **Hours** Tuesday–Saturday, 7 p.m.–1 a.m. (depending on length of show); Sunday and Monday, 7 p.m.–midnight (depending on length of show).

WHO GOES THERE Eclectic crowd of blues lovers.

WHAT GOES ON Dedication to the preservation of the blues. Eat Southern country cooking and listen raptly and politely to some great and some not-so-great practitioners of this uniquely American musical form. In recent months, other musical forms have been featured as well: rockabilly, funk, and swing are among the more popular. Call for current acts.

SETTING AND ATMOSPHERE The club is located in the type of basement venue that was first a necessity, then a statement, and now the norm for jazz, blues, and other non-mainstream types of music clubs. It's close, cramped, and intimate, with some splashes of modern art, and candles on tables arranged in a horseshoe shape around the stage and small dance floor. Movie actor Danny Glover is part owner and his culinary background is reflected in a menu featuring fried chicken and biscuits (quite good), hush puppies (not quite so good), deep-fried dill pickles (you be the judge), and black-eyed peas. Some good beers, a short wine list, and a fine collection of single-malt scotch.

IF YOU GO The kitchen can be glacially slow until food service stops about 10 p.m. People start dancing at about the same time. For a quicker, simpler meal, dash across Geary Street to the old Pinecrest Diner. Open 24/7.

Bourbon & Branch

SPEAKEASY-STYLE SECRET COCKTAIL BAR

501 Jones Street, Union Square; bourbonandbranch.com

Cover None. **Minimum** None. **Mixed drinks** $11 and up. **Wine** $11 and up. **Beer** $11 and up. **Dress** Fashionably outrageous is not uncommon. **Food available** None. **Hours** Wednesday–Saturday, 6 p.m.–2 a.m.

WHO GOES THERE The youngish visitor, the very cool local, and the questing night bird in search of adventure.

WHAT GOES ON A wide range of cocktail classes and libations. Specializing in exciting new cocktails, bartenders create fresh ingredients taken from that morning's market. They run a Beverage Academy teaching others how to sling awesome cocktails and have a cocktail bar at the back.

continued on page 332

San Francisco After Dark

1. Bimbo's 365 Club
2. Biscuits & Blues
3. Bourbon & Branch
4. Bubble Lounge
5. The Café
6. Café du Nord
7. CC's Pierce Street Manor
8. Club Deluxe
9. The Elbo Room
10. Fillmore
11. Gold Dust Lounge
12. Great American Music Hall
13. Harry Denton's Starlight Room
14. Harvey's
15. Impala
16. Li Po
17. Make-Out Room
18. Martuni's
19. Noc Noc
20. Pier 23
21. Plough and Stars
22. The Rrazz Room
23. Ruby Skye
24. Tonga Room
25. Top of the Mark
26. Tosca Cafe
27. Trad'r Sam's
28. Yoshi's San Francisco
29. Zam Zam

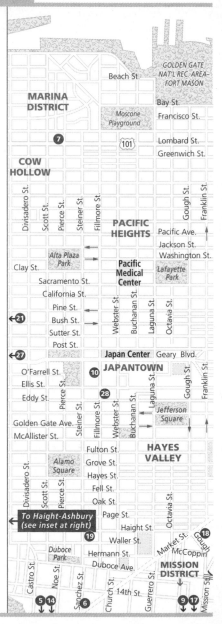

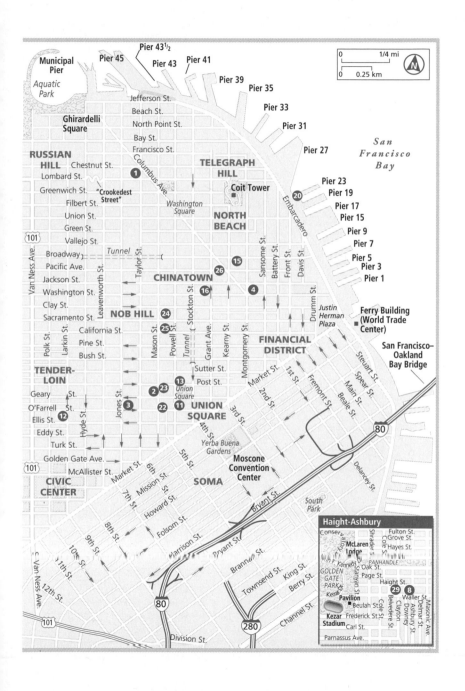

San Francisco Nightclubs by Neighborhood

NAME	DESCRIPTION
CHINATOWN	
Li Po	Dimly lit dive
Tonga Room	Tropical island bar with tropical downpour
Top of the Mark	Rooftop lounge and dance floor
CIVIC CENTER	
The Fillmore	Rock-and-roll ballroom
Great American Music Hall	Rock concert hall
Noc Noc	Cave bar
Yoshi's San Francisco	World-class jazz club with bar menu and sushi restaurant
UNION SQUARE	
Biscuits & Blues	Blues supper club
Bourbon & Branch	Speakeasy-style secret cocktail bar
Gold Dust Lounge	Barbary Coast saloon
Harry Denton's Starlight Room	Rooftop dance club
The Rrazz Room	Cabaret and cocktail lounge
Ruby Skye	Swank nightclub
MARINA DISTRICT	
CC's Pierce Street Manor	Neighborhood bar in a wealthy neighborhood

continued from page 329

SETTING AND ATMOSPHERE Lovingly renovated bar inside a library haunt with a cocktail corner tucked into the rear and an indefinable air of enticing naughtiness. The Tenderloin's back-alley bathtub gin joints of the 1920s and 1930s never looked as swanky as this new-age speakeasy on the site of a former actual Prohibition-era speakeasy. A bar has operated here since 1867. From 1921 to 1933 this place was JJ Russell's Cigar Shop, which imported illegal beverages from Vancouver, and got away with it.

IF YOU GO Put on your game face—and knock it back! The password is *books* for the library, but the main bar requires a reservation. Bourbons include real hand-numbered Noah's Mill, Buffalo Trace, and Rittenhouse 21 Year; Canadian whisky is the rare Crown XR. Scotches include the Monkey Shoulder, Glenmorangie Margaux Finish (only 1,200 bottles in the country!), and Balvenie 1971. Rums and tequilas are Ron Zacapa Centenario 23 Year and Tapatio XA (normally only found in Mexico).

NAME	DESCRIPTION
FINANCIAL DISTRICT	
Bubble Lounge	Champagne bar
NORTH BEACH	
Bimbo's 365 Club	Classic big-band nightclub
Impala	Restaurant and nightclub
Pier 23	Jazz bar and restaurant
Tosca Cafe	Iconic bar, celebs, White Nuns, opera jukebox
SOMA/MISSION DISTRICT	
The Café	Gay and lesbian club
Café du Nord	Dance club
The Elbo Room	Neighborhood pub cum dance club
Harvey's	Famous gay bar
Make-Out Room	Neo-Bohemian hipster bar
Martuni's	Cocktail piano lounge with singers
RICHMOND/SUNSET DISTRICT	
Club Deluxe	Retro hot spot
The Plough and the Stars	Irish pub with live music
Trad'r Sam's	Last of the tiki bars
Zam Zam	1940s cocktail bar

Bubble Lounge

CHAMPAGNE BAR

714 Montgomery Street, Financial District; ☎ 415-434-4204; bubblelounge.com

Cover None. **Minimum** None. **Mixed drinks** $4 and up. **Wine** $6 and up. **Beer** $4–$6. **Dress** Casually elegant. **Food available** Appetizers, oyster bar. **Hours** Tuesday and Wednesday, 5:30 p.m.–1 a.m.; Thursday, 5:30 p.m.–2 a.m.; Friday, 5 p.m.–2 a.m.; Saturday, 6:30 p.m.–2 a.m.

WHO GOES THERE Locals who love sparkling wines and sparkling conversation. WHAT GOES ON No staid wine bar this is. It's more like a mirthful cocktail party, as sparkling as the wines it specializes in. People come here to escape loud music, the press of crowds, and the frenetic experience that city nightlife can become. Yet they don't want to be bored. It's popular as an after-work tipple place, then picks up again in mid-evening, and goes on all night with Champagne corks popping every few minutes.

SETTING AND ATMOSPHERE An elegant (but not pretentious) salon, with settees and couches as well as easy chairs and coffee tables placed strategically about, plus draperies hanging from the walls. Plenty of standing room remains for clustering and table-hopping. The staff go to great lengths to maintain the civilized atmosphere, and a dress code is strictly enforced. "A neat overall appearance is sought, and the following clothing items will not be accepted: sneakers, gym or workout garments, sandals, baseball caps, military or combat fatigues, and swimwear." And gentlemen are required to remove their hats upon entering.

IF YOU GO Go early if you want to sit at the bar.

The Café

GAY AND LESBIAN CLUB

2369 Market Street at Castro Street, Castro District;
☎ **415-834-5840**

Cover None. **Minimum** None. **Mixed drinks** $3.50. **Wine** $2.50–$4.75. **Beer** $1.25–$3. **Dress** Everything from jeans to drag. **Food available** None. **Hours** Monday–Friday, 5 p.m.–2 a.m.; Saturday and Sunday, 4 p.m.–2 a.m.

WHO GOES THERE Women seeking women, men seeking men.

WHAT GOES ON The question is, what doesn't go on? Originally set up by women to be one of the premier lesbian social centers, The Café has become wildly popular among gay male fun-seekers. Mostly a dance house for high-energy techno music, but there's a pool table for variety.

SETTING AND ATMOSPHERE A dark, neon-lit, coed dance club that overlooks the Castro. It's hot and hopping in here, but there's an outdoor balcony where you can take a breather. Don't bother coming if you don't want to be checked out; this is definitely a spot where you'll be hit on, unless you're obviously straight. The drinks are cheap, and the staff is friendly.

IF YOU GO You'd better not care about second-hand smoke, or PDA (public displays of affection) for that matter. On weekends it's nearly impossible to get in, so start early. And don't worry about taking the time to go to the bank; there's an ATM in the back by the bar. For a nearby, bang-up seafood dinner before or after the party, catch Catch Restaurant (2362 Market Street; ☎ 415-431-5000).

Café Du Nord

DANCE CLUB

2170 Market Street, SoMa/Mission District;
☎ **415-861-5016; cafedunord.com**

Cover Varies. **Minimum** None. **Mixed drinks** $4–$9. **Wine** $3.50–$6.50. **Beer** $3.75–$4.50. **Dress** Dress to impress. **Food available** American Continental with European flair; Thursday–Saturday, 7 p.m.–11 p.m., entrees, $13.50–$16. **Hours** Daily; doors open 1 hour before show, usually between 6 p.m.–8:30 p.m., close at 2 a.m.

WHO GOES THERE 20- to 30-something hipsters.

WHAT GOES ON A mix of music and dance. Some nights have DJs instead of live bands and are aimed at the Gen-Xers, with the crowd leaning to the gothic younger side. Check out the club's Web site for updated show schedules. Spoken-word performances are also popular here. Not so much with poets these days, but with urban storytellers.

SETTING AND ATMOSPHERE If you get past the weekend line, you'll walk downstairs to this basement cabaret that used to be a 1920s speakeasy. There are oil paintings alongside black-and-white photos dimly lit by converted gas lamps. Experienced swing and salsa dancers inspire you to take lessons. If the scene is too fast for you, escape back past the bar to cuddle up with a love interest on an antique couch. The polished hardwood floors and trim complement the well-dressed hipsters and specialty liquors. If you're not here on a date, it's quite possible you could leave with one.

IF YOU GO The place doesn't start jumpin' until around 10 p.m., so if you're not into loud rock bands or scary 1980s DJ music, come early for a pint or a whiskey and snuggle on a couch with your honey at one of the most seductive lounges in town.

CC's Pierce Street Manor

NEIGHBORHOOD BAR IN A WEALTHY NEIGHBORHOOD

3243 Pierce Street, Marina District; ☎ 415-346-3523

Cover None. **Minimum** None. **Mixed drinks** $5 and up. **Wine** $6 and up. **Beer** $5 and up. **Dress** Casual to semi-dressy. **Specials** The faux antique jukebox. **Food available** None, though patrons often bring their own. **Hours** 4 p.m.–2 a.m.

WHO GOES THERE Mostly local regulars and the odd lost tourist.

WHAT GOES ON A lot of neighborly hanging out. This is the general living room for local folks. Anyone is welcome, though, and it's easy to chat someone up. You'll also find it's easy to spend an entire evening here.

SETTING AND ATMOSPHERE Imagine somebody's 1950s basement rumpus room, strewn with cushions, mismatched furniture and lamps, footstools, and an old pool table. Now add a full-service bar. It's warm and cozy in cold weather, and the backyard patio is cool and refreshing in summer.

IF YOU GO Check your attitude at the door. For a dinner break, Izzy's Steak and Chop House is around the corner (see Dining).

Club Deluxe

RETRO HOT SPOT

1511 Haight Street, Richmond/Sunset District; ☎ 415-552-6949; liveatdeluxe.com

Cover $3–$5. **Minimum** None. **Mixed drinks** $3.50–$8. **Wine** $3–$5. **Beer** $3–$5. **Dress** Vintage. **Food available** None. **Hours** Monday–Friday, 6 p.m.–2 a.m.; Saturday, 2 p.m.–2 a.m.; Sunday, 2 p.m.–2 a.m.

WHO GOES THERE Gen-X retro hipsters, Haight Street locals.

WHAT GOES ON Sipping cocktails, lounging like a lizard, and looking cool.

SETTING AND ATMOSPHERE A step back from the 1960s world of Haight-Ashbury to the hip, Art Deco 1940s. Smooth leather booths and slick Formica tables accessorize the suspenders, skirts, suits, and 'dos of the impressively retro room and ultimate retro crowd. Often known as the Church of Sinatra. Quality local jazz and swing bands play and DJs spin. ATM inside.

IF YOU GO Known among locals to have the best Bloody Mary in town. And there are many excellent places for cheap eats at the other (east) end of Haight. Parking, like everything else, can sometimes be crazy on Haight Street. Try a few blocks up from the strip or take the 6, 7, 33, or 43 Muni bus.

The Elbo Room

NEIGHBORHOOD PUB CUM DANCE CLUB

647 Valencia Street, SoMa/Mission District; ☎ 415-552-7788; elbo.com

Cover $5–$15. **Minimum** None. **Mixed drinks** $5. **Wine** $4–$8. **Beer** $3.50 and up. **Dress** Casual. **Specials** Drink specials nightly. **Food available** None. **Hours** Daily, 5 p.m.–2 a.m.

WHO GOES THERE Local Bohemians, accomplished dancers, and tourists in the know.

WHAT GOES ON In the large bar downstairs, neighborhood regulars drink beer, shoot pool, and schmooze. One expects to see Archie Bunker in his younger days. Upstairs, soul funk and Latin musicians play for a very discriminating crowd of music aficionados and polished dancers (beginners are welcome, too). On nights with no live music, talented DJs work the sounds.

SETTING AND ATMOSPHERE Look at it with one eye and you'd call it "working class." Look at it with the other eye and you might call it "Bohemian." Either way it's unpretentious, and unventilated as well. People here don't mind sweating.

IF YOU GO $2 drink specials on Mondays. Don't go tired or hungry. Ramblas Spanish restaurant is one block away (557 Valencia; ☎ 415-565-0207).

The Fillmore

ROCK-AND-ROLL BALLROOM

1805 Geary Boulevard (at Fillmore Street), Civic Center;
☎ **415-346-6000; thefillmore.com**

Cover $9 and up. **Minimum** None. **Mixed drinks** $4.75–$7.75. **Wine** $4.75–$7.25. **Beer** $3.50–$5.75. **Dress** Varies. **Food available** American cuisine upstairs amid a selection of infamous vintage psychedelic concert posters. **Hours** Doors usually open at 7 p.m. or 8 p.m.; show starts an hour later.

WHO GOES THERE Those looking to see a great band or needing a nostalgia fix.

WHAT GOES ON "Return to the 1960s" parties, big-name and on-the-rise rock concerts, formal sit-down dinners. This rock-and-roll landmark continues to put out the San Francisco sound that made it famous in the 1960s.

SETTING AND ATMOSPHERE Distinct San Francisco soul still lives and breathes direct from the Fillmore. The place that birthed the Grateful Dead, Janis Joplin, and Santana still gives the leg up to climbing, young, high-quality bands. This hall features the largest collection of historic concert posters on view in the world. A few tables and chairs are in the balconies off to the sides.

IF YOU GO You can always find a listing of upcoming events in the Sunday "pink pages." Tickets are on sale at **tickets.com** (subject to a service charge) and on show nights 7:30 to 10 p.m. Advance tickets are on sale at the Fillmore box office Sunday, 10 a.m. to 4 p.m. only, with a limit of six tickets per person. The hall is available to rent for parties or events and holds 1,200. For dinner before or after the show, SPQR is just up the street serving outstanding Roman fare (see Dining).

Gold Dust Lounge

BARBARY COAST SALOON

247 Powell Street, Union Square; ☎ **415-397-1695**

Cover None. **Minimum** None. **Mixed drinks** $3.75. **Wine** $3.75–$5. **Beer** $3.75–$5. **Dress** Anything goes. **Specials** None. **Food available** None. **Hours** Daily, 6 p.m.–2 a.m.

WHO GOES THERE Mixed crowd of tourists and local regulars.

WHAT GOES ON A variety of musical acts in a bawdy and gaudy San Francisco classic saloon established in 1933. As the place is centrally located and the sound of its rollicking good times spills onto the street, tourists from all over the world and the United States find themselves in here. There's no room to dance, but people do it anyway.

SETTING AND ATMOSPHERE It's deep and narrow and often tightly packed so it's hard not to get friendly with the people next to you. A lot of rich wood, brass and gilt, and paintings of early 20th-century nymphs and satyrs cavorting in what were once considered risqué postures. This is the San Francisco of old-movies fame.

IF YOU GO   Brush up on your foreign-language skills; you may have a chance to use them. And be prepared to sing along with the band. On the same block find a great dinner at Kuleto's (see Dining).

Great American Music Hall

ROCK CONCERT HALL

859 O'Farrell Street (at Polk and Larkin), Civic Center;
☎ **415-885-0750; gamh.com**

Cover Varies. **Minimum** None. **Mixed drinks** $3–$4. **Wine** $3–$5. **Beer** $2.75–$3.50. **Dress** Casual to impressive. **Food available** Assorted appetizers, finger food. Dinner tickets available. **Hours** Vary.

WHO GOES THERE   Music enthusiasts of all types.

WHAT GOES ON   A variety of nationally or internationally recognized music shows ranging from local bands on their way up, to Latin ensembles, folk, country, and even jazz.

SETTING AND ATMOSPHERE   The fact that this turn-of-the-20th-century bordello theater has been preserved is one of the things that makes San Francisco so special. The gold rococo balcony, wood floors, high fresco ceiling, and marble columns make it a timeless classic. For your favorite bands, come early and scream away Beatlemania-style up front by the stage.

IF YOU GO   The hall is available to rent for events and parties of up to 600. Be on the lookout for a touch of the dangerous and the lewd; next door is the famous Mitchell Brothers' O'Farrell Theatre, described by Hunter S. Thompson as "the Carnegie Hall of public sex in America." Check out the huge mural of whales on its western outer wall.

Harry Denton's Starlight Room

ROOFTOP DANCE CLUB

450 Powell Street, Union Square; ☎ **415-395-8595; harrydenton.com**

Cover $5–$10. **Minimum** None. **Mixed drinks** $7 and up. **Wine** $7–$20. **Beer** $4–$5. **Dress** Dressy. **Specials** "Sunday's a Drag" brunch at noon and 2:30 p.m. **Food available** Hors d'oeuvres, raw bar. **Hours** Tuesday–Saturday, 6 p.m.–2 a.m.

WHO GOES THERE   A well-dressed mixed crowd.

WHAT GOES ON   Party, party, party! Dance to a wide variety of music, heavy on rock and retro. Cocktail culture asserts itself in style. Socialites, yuppies, tourists, other club owners, the odd Bohemian stuffed into a jacket and tie, and Harry Denton himself (no dancing on the bar unless accompanied by Harry) are drawn to the Starlight Room like moths to a flame; they all party and dance to the collection of local bands' repertoires, which runs the gamut from the 1940s to the 1990s.

SETTING AND ATMOSPHERE Exuberantly elegant decor and staff on the top floor of the Sir Francis Drake hotel. At the bar, the sound of the cocktail shaker never stops. Through the big picture windows the stars twinkle, and overhead, yes, that's you looking into the mirrored ceiling. The atmosphere is thick and heady, the crowd is at capacity, and there is so much energy that it will be a long time before you sleep again.

IF YOU GO Reservations are highly recommended. Go early or late, unless you're a party animal. Make sure you have a supply of one- and five-dollar bills for tipping the waiters and bartenders and the coat-check girl. Call for information on entertainment and private parties. In the same building on the ground floor find a superb dinner at Scala's Bistro (see Dining).

Harvey's

FAMOUS GAY BAR

500 Castro Street, SoMa/Mission District; ☎ 415-431-4278; harveyssf.com

Cover None. **Minimum** None. **Mixed drinks** $5 and up. **Wine** $5–$6. **Beer** $4–$7. **Dress** Casual. **Food available** Appetizers, burgers, salads, chicken dishes. **Hours** Monday–Friday, 11 a.m.–11 p.m.; Saturday and Sunday, 9 p.m.–2 a.m.

WHO GOES THERE Locals, gay pilgrims, and straight looky-loos.

WHAT GOES ON A hard core of locals use it as their neighborhood pub, and tourists of any persuasion come to pay homage or gawk. Named after Harvey Milk, the assassinated gay city supervisor, this was once a place where members of the local gay community came to relax and take pride. Everybody gets along.

SETTING AND ATMOSPHERE Like a Hard Rock Cafe with a gay theme. Lots of media and sports memorabilia tacked to the walls. It's just a neighborhood good-time bar. A gay Cheers. Some people find it disappointingly "normal."

IF YOU GO Be cool.

Impala

RESTAURANT AND NIGHTCLUB

501 Broadway, North Beach; ☎ 415-982-5299; impalasf.com

Cover $0–$20. **Minimum** None. **Mixed drinks** $5.50 and up. Tequila $8 and up. (Tequila sampler: 4–6 tastes for $60). **Wine** $8–$10. **Dress** Trendy casual. **Food available** Full restaurant; kitchen closes at 10 p.m. **Specials** Wasted Wednesday, $2 cocktails, beer, tacos, burritos, and such. **Hours** Wednesday–Saturday, 6 p.m.–2 a.m.

WHO GOES THERE Trendy 20-somethings, 30-somethings.

WHAT GOES ON Hot nightclub scene in the North Beach strip-club area, a location that at first blush sounds a bit dubious but is really the utmost of trendy and the current place to be. Impala offers two bars—one on street level, one below—with pounding techno-salsa DJ music and dancing for a 20-to-30-something ultrahip crowd, some young professionals just off work, some out for a night on the town. There's not only nightlife but a fine Latin fusion restaurant to boot, serving up creative takes on traditional dishes, such as roasted vegetable and goat-cheese empanadas, or exploring new ground with a smoky ahi tuna dressed in salsa verde and pumpkin seeds—all on a menu designed by Chef Kerry Simon. The premium tequila selection is extensive, with at least 64 options listed alphabetically, from Amate to Tres Generaciones.

SETTING AND ATMOSPHERE Upstairs, it's dark and glamorous, with a rustic edge. Rough-hewn wooden tables dot the dining area; heavy wooden beams crisscross the ceiling with the glitz of mirrors in between. Gauzy fabric in reds and purples drape from columns. The upper bar is separated from the dining tables only by some ceiling-to-floor wrought-iron bars, so it can get a little loud. But by then it's time to head downstairs to the basement lounge and do some serious, sophisticated partying. A line can develop quickly after 10 p.m., so if you're in, you're in like Flynn. Here, reds rule, with plush and modern red velvet chairs and glass-top tables with red feathers inside. Even the restrooms are swanky, with black tile, dramatic lighting, and baskets of hairspray and lotions for the ladies.

IF YOU GO To dine easily, go early. To party, go late; that's when the scene heats up. In the restaurant, note that the waitstaff is possibly hired more on looks than service, but that's not necessarily a bad thing. Make a reservation for bottle service in the lower-level lounge, and ask about private parties. If you just go to party, you might like to have cheap eats at Ristorante Tommaso, a cozy Italian pizza and pasta joint across the street (1042 Kearny Street; ☎ 415-398-9696; **tommasos.com**).

Li Po

DIMLY LIT DIVE

916 Grant Avenue, Chinatown; ☎ **415-982-0072**

Cover None. **Minimum** None. **Mixed drinks** $3.50. **Wine** $4 and up. **Beer** $3. **Dress** Casual. **Specials** Li Po Special Snifter, $6. **Food available** None. **Hours** Daily, 2 p.m.–2 a.m.

WHO GOES THERE Locals in the know and accidental tourists.

WHAT GOES ON Drinking in the dark. Pinball on a "Creature of the Black Lagoon" machine. Low conversations in the nooks and crannies of an

The Prohibition era must have been at its wettest in Chinatown. Li Po and Buddha Lounge are two funky spots that manage to combine shrines to both the Buddha and to booze. Best of all, they're open late. You can drop by after midnight in this not-especially-late-night slice of tourist town and stay until at least 2 a.m. Li Po has a shrine to the Buddha and karaoke, large lanterns, a very funky jukebox featuring Chinese love songs as well as standards, and some of the stiffest mai tais around. On the opposite corner nearby is the Buddha Lounge, an even funkier dive bar with very strong cocktails at very low prices.

ancient labyrinthine structure. A few Chinese-speaking Chinese and a lot of hip folks from North Beach speaking English.

SETTING AND ATMOSPHERE Dark and cavernous. Like a subterranean Chinese shrine to money and Miller Genuine Draft. The main room is dominated by a Chinese deity and currency from around the world tacked to the wall. Chinese lanterns and brewing-company neon leap out at you. If you've ever been a sailor in old Hong Kong, you'll feel nostalgic. If you've seen the movie *Suzy Wong*, you'll feel like you just stepped onto the set. It's a cliché with drinks.

IF YOU GO It's so garish and in such bad taste that it will charm you from the moment you enter. If it's too crowded or noisy, try the Buddha Lounge across the street on the southwest corner. If you're feeling James Bondish, check out the L'amour Nightclub (600 Jackson Street; ☎ 415-781-5224). Do NOT agree to buy a lady a drink.

Make-Out Room

NEO-BOHEMIAN HIPSTER BAR

3225 22nd Street (near Mission Street), SoMa/Mission District; ☎ 415-647-2888; makeoutroom.com

Cover $0–$15. **Minimum** None. **Mixed drinks** $4.50 and up. **Wine** $3.50–$8. **Beer** $3.75 and up. **Dress** Casual. **Food available** None, but you can bring it in. **Hours** Daily, 6 p.m.–2 a.m.

WHO GOES THERE Gen-Xers looking for alternatives.

WHAT GOES ON Nightly entertainment. The main attraction is escaping from the usual shoulder-to-shoulder, ear-shattering trauma that is the delight of so many club-hoppers. You can shoot pool and you won't get a cue in the gut when you turn around. You can enjoy a microbrew or a cocktail at the bar or a booth or table and feel that you're in a happening place, but it won't overwhelm.

SETTING AND ATMOSPHERE This place is cavernous. It looks almost like a high-school gym decorated for a dance. The big space, high ceiling, and darkness sprinkled with colored lights feel outdoorsy, especially when the doors are open and the fog rolls in.

IF YOU GO   Be cool. Relax. Enjoy. Pssst: people don't really make out here. For something a little edgier in the same neighborhood, drop in at Este Noche (3079 16th Street; ☎ 415-861-5757) for the "best Latin drag show in town."

Martuni's

COCKTAIL PIANO LOUNGE WITH SINGERS

4 Valencia Street, SoMa/Mission District; ☎ 415-241-0205

Cover None. **Minimum** None. **Mixed drinks** $6. **Wine** $5–$8. **Beer** $3.50–$4.75. **Dress** Evening casual. **Food available** None. **Hours** Daily, 2 p.m.–2 a.m.

WHO GOES THERE   Mixed crowd of gay and straight.

WHAT GOES ON   A variety of cool jazz and other lounge music accompanied by the cheerful clinking of cocktail glasses. Music might be a trio or a solo at the varnished mahogany piano bar. Classic cocktails and new inventions are served up large, with a smile. If you sit at the piano, you might be asked to sing.

SETTING AND ATMOSPHERE   It's dark in here. And the heavy drapes, thick carpet, and indirect lighting make it more so. Even when you come in at night, you have to let your eyes adjust. But it gives you the sense of being far away in some cozy, friendly getaway where all the strangers are just friends you haven't met.

IF YOU GO   Don't go on an empty stomach. The drinks are huge, and you'll be bombed before you know it. You'll need to go about four blocks down Valencia Street to find plenty of dining choices.

Noc Noc

CAVE BAR

557 Haight Street (at Fillmore and Steiner streets), Civic Center; ☎ 415-861-5811; nocnocs.com

Cover None. **Minimum** None. **Mixed drinks** None. **Wine** $3.25 and up. **Beer** $3.25–$4.75. **Specials** Sake: $3, small; $5, large. **Dress** Casual. **Special comments** Alternative happy hour, Monday–Thursday, 5 p.m.–7 p.m.; Friday–Sunday, 3 p.m.-7 p.m. **Food available** Bar snacks. **Hours** Daily, 5 p.m.–2 a.m.

WHO GOES THERE   Gen-Xers, 30-something locals.

WHAT GOES ON   Gen-Xers come here to be mellow and avoid those who care to see and be seen. Perfect post-date spot for the tragically hip and alternative.

SETTING AND ATMOSPHERE   The Stone Age meets Road Warrior. A small cave den littered with hieroglyphics, metal levers, bombs, and airplane wings.

Scattered large throw pillows and pit booths are great for intimate chatting. A cozy escape from the harried lower Haight scene.

IF YOU GO Great locations for a crawl. The Toronado, known by beer connoisseurs for its wide selection of draft and bottled, is just a few doors down. Also a stone's throw away are the British hangout Mad Dog in the Fog and Nickie's BBQ. These bars specialize in beer; you'll have to go elsewhere if you want a decent cocktail. The ATM inside is an added bonus.

Pier 23

JAZZ BAR AND RESTAURANT

Pier 23, between Green Street and Battery Street, North Beach; ☎ 415-362-5125; pier23cafe.com

Cover $0–$10. **Minimum** None. **Mixed drinks** $4.50. **Wine** $3.50–$8. **Beer** $3.50–$4.75. **Dress** Casual. **Food available** Meat and potatoes, seafood. **Hours** Monday–Friday, 11:30 a.m.–10 p.m.; Saturday, 10 a.m.–10 p.m.; Sunday, 10 a.m.–9 p.m.

WHO GOES THERE Locals, sailors, and jazz aficionados.

WHAT GOES ON In the afternoons you can sit at the beaten copper bar, drink, and watch the parade of watercraft on the bay. In the evenings, dine and listen to popular local jazz bands of all kinds.

SETTING AND ATMOSPHERE An airy waterfront version of a smoky, late-night jazz basement. It's an old-time dockside cafe with a concrete floor; the pier in the back serves as a patio and a place for the fireboats to tie up. A cheery place with lots of regulars.

IF YOU GO The bands play inside, where there's limited seating for dinner, so many dine outside on the pier and listen to the music being piped out. If you do this, remember the highly changeable San Francisco weather and bring a coat. Bartenders can be surly, so bring your patience, too. If the restaurant is crowded, try the nearby Fog City Diner (see Dining).

The Plough and the Stars

IRISH PUB WITH LIVE MUSIC

116 Clement Street, between Second and Third, Richmond/Sunset District; ☎ 415-751-1122; theploughandstars.com

Cover Varies; on Friday and Saturday nights. **Minimum** None. **Mixed drinks** $3.75 and up. **Wine** $3.50–$5. **Beer** $3.50–$4. **Dress** Casual. **Specials** Happy hour all day Monday. **Food available** None. **Hours** Monday–Thursday, 3 p.m.–2 a.m.; Friday–Sunday, 2 p.m.–2 a.m.

WHO GOES THERE Irish gents and lasses, Richmond-area locals.

WHAT GOES ON Home of traditional Irish music in the Bay Area; good local bands play nightly after 9:30 p.m. Pool, darts, and chewing the fat with the regulars.

SETTING AND ATMOSPHERE Accents are thick, and so is the Guinness. No one comes here just once, so make yourself comfortable at the long wooden tables or pull up a stool and chat with the regulars at the bar. It's easy to forget that you're in San Francisco, and not in Ireland, amid the acoustic ballads beneath the Irish Republic flag. It's sometimes hard to have an intimate conversation when everyone is clapping their hands to the music.

IF YOU GO Feel free to do the Irish crawl. Though Plough and Stars is known among locals to have the best Guinness in town, there's a plethora of Irish hangouts just a jig away, including the Bitter End, Ireland 32s, Pat O'Shea's, and the Front Room.

The Rrazz Room

CABARET AND COCKTAIL LOUNGE

222 Mason Street in Hotel Nikko, Union Square; ☎ 866-468-3399; therrazzroom.com

Cover $20–$60, for shows. **Minimum** 2 drinks. **Mixed drinks** $10–$13. **Wine** $8–$14. **Beer** $5–$7. **Dress** Gussied-up, rhinestones and silk; upscale casual. **Specials** Changing jazz and cabaret performances. **Food available** Appetizers. **Hours** Sunday–Thursday, 2 p.m.–midnight; Friday–Saturday, 2 p.m.–2 a.m.

WHO GOES THERE Older gay men, out-of-towners, locals on a tear.

WHAT GOES ON Lounge acts. Sultry cabaret singers and jazz music. Old-time talents include evergreen entertainment stars Tyne Daly, Rita Moreno, and Paula West—even Sandra Bernhard killed here!

SETTING AND ATMOSPHERE A San Francisco nightlife tradition lives on in Nikko's near Union Square, in a small but intimate space with no bad seat in the house and a tirelessly active MC.

IF YOU GO Love a cabaret. If you appreciate the timeless talents and glamour of yesteryear, this is the spot for you. To mix it up, have dinner at Scala's Bistro (432 Powell Street; ☎ 415-395-8555; **scalasbistro.com**).

Ruby Skye

SWANK NIGHTCLUB

420 Mason Street, Union Square; ☎ 415-693-0777; rubyskye.com

Cover $15. **Minimum** None. **Mixed drinks** $5 and up. **Wine** $6 and up. **Beer** $5. **Dress** Impressive. **Food available** Catering for private parties. **Hours** Thursday–Saturday, 9 p.m.–3 a.m.

WHO GOES THERE Well-dressed locals, informed tourists.

WHAT GOES ON Dancing to world-class DJs and live acts by people who are "grown up, make money, and dress nice," according to the owner. A lot of flirting, a lot of quiet conversations in private booths or VIP rooms, and a lot of very good times.

SETTING AND ATMOSPHERE Originally a theater built in the 19th century and said to have served as a house of discreet assignations. The designers have made the most of the original decor while bringing it up to date with the latest in sound and lighting. Four large main rooms give the place a spacious feel even when the dance floors are jammed.

IF YOU GO Dress to the nines. Afterward, decompress at the Gold Dust Lounge (see page 337).

Tonga Room

TROPICAL ISLAND BAR WITH TROPICAL DOWNPOUR

950 Mason Street in the Fairmont Hotel, Chinatown; ☎ 415-772-5278; tongaroom.com

Cover $5–$7. **Minimum** 1 drink. **Mixed drinks** Tropical cocktail specials. $10–$25. **Wine** $8 and up. **Beer** $5 and up. **Dress** Casual to dressy. **Specials** Live music; happy hour, weekdays 5–7 p.m. **Food available** Yes. **Hours** Sunday, Wednesday, Thursday, 5 p.m.–11:45 p.m.; Friday and Saturday, 5 p.m.–12:45 a.m.

WHO GOES THERE Nob Hill locals, tourists, and happy hour crowd.

WHAT GOES ON A wide mix of people come to drink the island cocktails and swoon to their sweetheart beneath straw huts and palm trees, but most just wait for the periodic man-made thunderstorms.

SETTING AND ATMOSPHERE A tropical island oasis in the Fairmont Hotel atop Nob Hill, currently the Tonga Room is fighting for its life and facing doom at the hands of condo developers. But all San Francisco wants it to survive; there's a FaceBook campaign you can join, and in the meantime, come to see it while you still can because it's anyone's guess who'll win. Meanwhile, watch a live band on a moated island while sipping an umbrella-clad drink from a coconut. The South Seas decor is more of an upscale tiki lounge than a seaman's dive.

IF YOU GO Don't miss the all-you-can-eat weekday buffet from 5 p.m. to 7 p.m. (with a one-drink minimum). It's easy to make a meal out of pot stickers, barbecue spareribs, teriyaki drumsticks, veggies and dip, a cheese plate, egg rolls, and more. Watch out for the Scorpion. It's the most expensive drink on the menu for a reason. Close out your evening by gazing at the city with a nightcap at Top of the Mark (see page 346).

Top of the Mark

ROOFTOP LOUNGE AND DANCE FLOOR

999 California Street, 19th floor, Chinatown; ☎ 415-616-6916; topofthemark.com

Cover $5–$10. **Minimum** None. **Mixed drinks** $7 and up. **Wine** $6 and up. **Beer** $5 and up. **Dress** Smart casual to dressy. **Specials** The view at sunset. **Food available** Finger foods, elegant hors d'oeuvres, 3-course prix fixe on Thursday, Friday, and Saturday, $39. **Hours** Opens daily at 3 p.m.

WHO GOES THERE Well-dressed late thirtysomethings plus tourists, and regulars.

WHAT GOES ON Dancing, romancing, schmoozing, and boozing. Musical offerings include in-house pianists, cool jazz combos, and retro groups. People come here for swing and ballroom dancing, sunset cocktails, business talks, romantic assignations, and conspiracies.

SETTING AND ATMOSPHERE Understated elegance on the most romantic rooftop in town, on top of the Mark Hopkins hotel, on top of Nob Hill. The elevated dance floor is in the center of the room and surrounded by plush seating along the huge windows that give a near 360-degree view of the city. Despite the price and the sophistication, it's never intimidating, always welcoming, almost homey.

IF YOU GO Valet parking is $25. Take a taxi or the California line cable car and get off right at the Mark. No minors are allowed after 8:30 p.m. You can dine well on finger foods, but you can enjoy an elegant meal just down the hill a bit at the Big Four Restaurant in the Huntington Hotel (1075 California Street; ☎ 415-474-5400; **huntingtonhotel.com**).

Tosca Cafe

ICONIC BAR, CELEBS, WHITE NUNS, OPERA JUKEBOX

242 Columbus Avenue, North Beach; ☎ 415-986-9651; toscacafesf.com

Cover None. **Minimum** None. **Mixed drinks** $3.50–$3.75. **Wine** $4–$6. **Beer** $2.50–$3.50. **Dress** Come as you are. **Specials** Irish coffee, house cappuccino. **Food available** None. **Hours** Tuesday–Sunday, 5 p.m. until close.

WHO GOES THERE Mostly locals, 30-something and up.

WHAT GOES ON Conversation and playing the jukebox. It's the only jukebox in town with selections from the world of opera. A lot of locals, including a few celebs, camp out here. In the back is an invitation-only poolroom said to be a fave of Sam Shepard and Francis Ford Coppola.

SETTING AND ATMOSPHERE A big place for a bar. All wood with red upholstered booths and a long bar on which sit dozens of Irish coffee glasses already charged with White Nuns with steamed milk, brandy, and Kahlua, or "house cappuccino" of chocolate mocha with steamed milk and brandy. There's also the plain Irish coffee with whiskey, sugar, and cream.

IF YOU GO   Go on a cold or foggy evening. You'll enjoy the warm arias and the spiked coffee drinks all the more.

Trad'r Sam's

LAST OF THE TIKI BARS

6150 Geary Boulevard, Richmond/Sunset District; ☎ 415-221-0773

Cover None. **Minimum** None. **Mixed drinks** $5 and up. **Wine** $6 and up. **Beer** $5 and up. **Dress** Casual to semidressy. **Specials** The rum cocktails. **Food available** None. **Hours** 11 a.m.–2 a.m.

WHO GOES THERE   Locals who long for the bygone days of Trader Vic's and all the other tiki bars that were so popular among the "greatest genera-tion." San Francisco is a city of time warps, and this is another one. Far out on western Geary, among the avenues, few outsiders find their way here. For those who do, a bar bathed in red light, a battered beach chair, and a well-made froufrou drink await. The bar also has a convivial, I-don't-take-myself-too-seriously atmosphere with patrons who just want to have some unpretentious fun.

SETTING AND ATMOSPHERE   Kitsch elevated to nostalgia. Like the Polynesian-themed tiki bars of old, it's littered with palm leaves, thatch, pagan idols, and drinks with paper umbrellas. And they don't even apologize for it! They revel in it.

IF YOU GO   Go early or late. Lines form to get in at peak times. Be careful of the live flame torches. Wear your best Hawaiian shirt. Panama hats optional.

Yoshi's San Francisco

WORLD-CLASS JAZZ CLUB WITH BAR MENU AND SUSHI RESTAURANT

1330 Fillmore Street, Japantown; ☎ 415-655-5600; yoshis.com/sanfrancisco

Cover $15–$30; varies according to show. **Minimum** None. **Mixed drinks** $8 and up. **Wine** $9 and up. **Beer** $5–$8. **Dress** Neither casual nor cocktail are out of place. **Food available** Full menu; sushi, modern Japanese cuisine. **Hours** Dinner: Monday–Wednesday, 5:30 p.m.–9 p.m.; Thursday, 5:30 p.m.–10 p.m.; Friday–Saturday, 5:30 p.m.–10:30 p.m.; Sunday, 5 p.m.–9 p.m. Shows often begin at 8 p.m. Some 10 p.m. and midnight shows.

WHO GOES THERE   Both older and younger hipster locals, tourists.

WHAT GOES ON   Some of the best (and best-priced) jazz you'll ever hear, along with some of the best Japanese food in what is rapidly becoming a storied part of Japantown again. A custom-designed new hangout with swishy dining area and acoustically fine jazz hall.

SETTING AND ATMOSPHERE   Musical fare is everything from Irma Thomas of New Orleans soul to Marcia Ball or Maria Muldaur, or any of the jazz greats from regular jazz festivals (heavily Cuban or Latino oriented).

IF YOU GO Check out the nearby Sundance Kabuki complex with Robert Redford's high-concept movie experience, next door to hot tubs and baths, Japanese noodle and sushi joints and supermarkets, plus Hello Kitty stores. Then, farther up Fillmore, you can window shop the swankiest of clothing boutiques and nibble at luxury patisseries! Really, it's a perfect rainy day combination.

Zam Zam

1940S COCKTAIL BAR

1633 Haight Street, Richmond/Sunset District; ☎ 415-861-2545

Cover None. **Minimum** None. **Mixed drinks** $5–$8. **Wine** $6–$9. **Beer** $4.50–$5.50. **Dress** Business casual. **Specials** Martinis and other classic cocktails. **Food available** None. **Hours** 3 p.m.–2 a.m.

WHO GOES THERE Mostly locals in the know.

WHAT GOES ON A lot of quiet good times. People stop in for a drink on the home or to dinner, or after dinner. Or they just come to hang out. This could be thought of as an upscale Cheers bar. After opening in the 1940s, its original owner, Bruno Mooshei, was well-known for 86ing anybody he didn't like the looks of. Some people went there hoping to be allowed to stay. Others went hoping to be ejected, just for the glory. Nowadays the new ownership welcomes all who are neatly dressed.

SETTING AND ATMOSPHERE This is a 1940s view of something exotically Persian. You could almost call it psychedelic. There is much red light and brocade, Art Deco wall mirrors, Persianesque lamps, bentwood chairs, and a relatively hushed tone. All is dominated by the horseshoe-shaped bar. Outside on Haight Street memories of the Doors and the Dead are still alive and on the jukebox in here the old crooners like Bing and Bob and Frank still croon.

IF YOU GO Dress up a bit. Get into the feel. Then have dinner at Eos (901 Cole at Carl) or Catch in the Castro, or try mixing it up with small plates at Alembic down the road.

PART NINE

SHOPPING

IN THE GOLD-RUSH DAYS OF MINERS, soldiers, sailors, and scoundrels, folks used to come into the city of San Francisco to shop. Well, it's still a frontier town, although today the frontiers are different; multimedia and technology, global commerce, and artistic innovation are some of the new territories.

There's always a new gold rush, of course: Computers, multimedia, and e-commerce have made San Francisco and nearby Silicon Valley one of the most expensive places to live—and shop—in the country. But shopping here is about more than getting the goods; it's about the neighborhood. And shopping in these distinct neighborhoods (they even have their own "microclimates") is a good way to glimpse the city's kaleidoscope of cultures.

San Francisco neighborhoods are notorious for banning chains from their enclaves and supporting mom-and-pop operations (even if the mom and pop in question are a pair of 20-something, mom-and-mom entrepreneurs).

Here's a look at San Francisco shopping, with an eye on the specialties (and peculiarities) of the Bay Area—its fixations on food, wine, recycled and earth-friendly merchandise, and, of course, sex, drugs, and rock and roll. This is the birthplace of such stylish hometown enterprises as Levi Strauss, Gap, Banana Republic, Old Navy, Esprit, Williams-Sonoma, and Bebe. It's also the hothouse of trends; the continuing craze for tattooing and piercing was born here.

unofficial **TIP**
For unusual items, catch annual spring and summer street fairs thrown by the city's major neighborhoods. The biggies are the Union Street Festival (June) and the Haight-Ashbury (June), Castro (October), and Folsom Street fairs (September), or the vast once-a-year flea market in tiny Niles on the last Sunday in August.

If you want some shopping guidance, check online at **CitySearch San Francisco** (**citysearch7.com**) and the more hip **sfstation.com**—both of which are continually updated with up-to-the-minute info on new shops or new tours. Other good sources (for high-end goods) are *San Francisco magazine* and *7x7* magazine. For the quirky and unusual spots, check the free weeklies.

TOP SHOPPING NEIGHBORHOODS

UNION SQUARE

WHILE THE WORD *EPICENTER* should not be thrown around too casually in this town, Union Square—the closest the city comes to a downtown—is indeed the epicenter of shopping. There's an enormous underground public parking lot beneath the 2.6-acre green park at the center of the square; the park is peopled with chess players, street artists and musicians, street characters, and bustling shoppers from around the world.

Framing this colorful square are the main shopping streets (Stockton Street, Powell Street, Geary Boulevard, and Post Street) and the city's densest concentration of major department stores, tony boutiques, restaurants and cafes, big hotels, and corner flower stands.

Moving clockwise from the Saint Francis Hotel on Powell Street, you'll find the following: **Borders Books and Music** (400 Post Street; ☎ 415-399-1633), **Saks Fifth Avenue** (384 Post Street; ☎ 415-986-4300), **Tiffany & Co.** (350 Post Street at Union Square; ☎ 415-781-7000), and **Neiman Marcus** (150 Stockton Street at Geary Boulevard; ☎ 415-362-3900), which each year sends the city's most spectacular Christmas tree soaring to the top of its stained-glass dome. A megalithic **Macy's** (170 O'Farrell Street at Stockton Street; ☎ 415-397-3333) includes **Wolfgang Puck Express,** where you can nosh on made-to-order pastas, salads, entrees, and sushi; **Boudin Bakery,** where you can get clam chowder in a sourdough bread bowl; and for dessert there's **The Cheesecake Factory** on the top floor, sweets with a view.

During the computer boom, the Union Square district saw a burst of new growth, including the state-of-the-art **Apple Store** (1 Stockton Street at Ellis Street; ☎ 415-392-0202), a sleek, high-style, high-tech Mecca complete with Genius Bar and iPod boutique, which landed on downtown like the Apple mother ship.

Like elsewhere in the country, chain stores are moving into San Francisco, robbing the Union Square shopping zone of some of its legendary exclusivity. The square has been colonized by theme park–like megastores, the shopping equivalents of Planet Hollywood and Hard Rock Cafe. **Levi's Superstore** (300 Post Street at Stockton Street; ☎ 415-501-0100) is a four-story retail entertainment hybrid that features clothing-customization services such as 3D body scanning, laser etching, hand painting, and fabric ornamentation and embroidery.

Another Union Square superstore is **Niketown** (278 Post Street; ☎ 415-392-6453). The newest twist on the megastore is the in-store DJ—everyone's got one now—including **Levi's** and **Diesel** (101 Post Street at Kearny Street; ☎ 415-982-7077), where you can shop the four-story oasis of uncasually priced casual gear and denim while grinding your teeth and snapping your fingers to the tweakiest techno in town. The dozens of tony boutiques on the side streets offer shopping with an international feel and "if you have to ask . . ." prices: **Gucci** (200 Stockton Street; ☎ 415-392-2808), **Hermès** (125 Grant Avenue; ☎ 415-391-7200), **Louis Vuitton** (233 Geary Street; ☎ 415-391-6200), and **Cartier** (231 Post Street between Grant and Stockton streets; ☎ 415-397-3180). **Burberry** (225 Post Street; ☎ 415-392-2200) is the inventor of the trench coat, designed in 1914 for wear by British army officers in the trenches. Nowadays Burberry produces an extensive range of apparel and accessories for both men and women.

Tangential to the square is Maiden Lane, a narrow, car-free alley that once housed ladies of the evening, and is thought to be the birthplace of Crab Louis, a San Francisco signature dish. Now the quaint street features pricey designer boutiques, including a three-floor **Chanel** (155 Maiden Lane between Grant and Stockton streets; ☎ 415-981-1550), the Paris-based **Christofle Silversmiths,** purveyors of fine silverware (140 Grant Avenue at Post Street; ☎ 415-399-1931), and an outpost of Seattle's **Sur La Table** (77 Maiden Lane between Grant and Kearny streets; ☎ 415-732-7900), a gourmet kitchenware boutique.

Also in the Union Square area are a handful of San Francisco–based stores, including 150-year-old **Shreve & Co. Jewelers** (200 Post Street at Grant Street; ☎ 415-421-2600) and the equally venerable **Gump's** (135 Post Street between Kearny and Grant streets; ☎ 415-982-1616), one of the world's most beautiful and unusual department stores. Gump's features china, crystal, Asian art treasures, antiques, and one-of-a-kind objects and furniture.

These old-timers are balanced out by fresh-faced young merchandisers near Union Square, such as fun and funky **Urban Outfitters** (80 Powell Street; ☎ 415-989-1515), the **Williams-Sonoma** flagship store (340 Post Street; ☎ 415-362-9450), **Crate & Barrel** (55 Stockton Street at O'Farrell; ☎ 415-986-4000), and the vast khaki-and-cream expanses of the **Banana Republic** flagship store (256 Grant Avenue at Sutter Street; ☎ 415-788-3087) with a great sales section.

San Francisco–based **Gap** boasts a sleek, stark, three-story flagship store at Union Square, which also houses siblings **Gap Kids** and **Baby Gap** (890 Market Street at Powell Street; ☎ 415-788-5909) next to the tourist-choked cable-car turnaround on Market Street. Across the street is the three-story flagship store of Gap's kid-sister store **Old Navy** (801 Market Street at Fourth Street; ☎ 415-344-0375). Across Market Street from the cable-car turnaround is the **San Francisco Shopping Centre** (865 Market Street at Fifth; ☎ 415-495-5656;

westfield.com/sanfrancisco), a multilevel enclosed urban mall anchored by **Nordstrom** (☎ 415-243-8500) with its five-floor spiral escalator, and a "mall-esque" array of shops including **Abercrombie & Fitch** for sporting attire (☎ 415-284-9276) and a great branch of **H&M** for fashionistas (☎ 415-543-1430).

PACIFIC HEIGHTS/COW HOLLOW/MARINA

THE CITY'S SECOND-LARGEST UPSCALE SHOPPING ZONE covers three linked neighborhoods: the five blocks of Fillmore Street between Geary Boulevard and Jackson Street, the six-block stretch of Union Street from Gough to Steiner streets (also known as Cow Hollow because it evolved from grazing pasture to browsing nirvana), and the seven blocks of Chestnut Street known as the Marina District. The beautifully preserved Victorian and Edwardian homes of Union Street, many of which survived the 1906 earthquake, now house hip, upscale, yuppie boutiques and cafes and offer some of the city's best window-shopping. Check out **Tate & Kennedy** for a wide range of personal luxuries and great gifts (2042 Union Street; ☎ 415-474-8283). At **UKO** (2070 Union Street; ☎ 415-563-0330) you'll find women's and men's apparel that is best described as casually elegant.

Fillmore has evolved from a run-down area into a gauntlet of chic boutiques and restaurants. **Gallery of Jewels** (2115 Fillmore Street; ☎ 877-566-9725) offers beautiful handcrafted adornments. And **Plumpjack Wines** (3201 Fillmore Street; ☎ 415-346-9870) is *the* place for both California and foreign wines.

CHINATOWN

A VISIT TO THIS FAMOUS, FASCINATING DISTRICT—home to more than 200,000 Chinese Americans (the Chinese community is second in size only to New York's Chinatown)—begins at the large, ornate gateway at the intersection of Grant and Bush streets, just above Union Square. You'll encounter otherworldly vegetables, live animals, exotic spices, herbs, ivory, jade, and pearls amid the Oriental kitsch. Shops such as **Dragon House** (455 Grant Avenue; ☎ 415-421-3693) and the **China Trade Center** (838 Grant Street between Clay and Washington streets; ☎ 415-837-1509), which is

unofficial **TIP**
Don't even think of driving in Chinatown. You'd miss all the sights, sounds, tastes, and smells of the bustling streets. And for a real Chinese shopping experience, prowl the alleys and side streets.

a three-floor mini-mall, typify the tourist trinket markets of Chinatown and minimize the jostling. A delightful local secret is the **Clarion Music Center** (816 Sacramento Street; ☎ 415-391-1317). Musical instruments from around the world include African drums, Asian strings, Western winds, and lots of gongs and bells. If you want to take home some superior tea, visit **Ten Ren Tea Company** (949 Grant Street; ☎ 415-362-0656). And to really go native, stroll along the food markets on Stockton Street, one block west of Grant.

 Bordering Chinatown is the formerly Italian neighborhood known as North Beach, the main stomping grounds of the Beat poets and artists who made **City Lights Bookstore** (261 Columbus Avenue at Broadway; ☎ 415-362-8193) and **Caffe Trieste** (609 Vallejo Street; ☎ 415-982-2605) their home. You'll find hours of browsing potential on the streets bordering Washington Square Park, especially on Grant Street where specialty shops and restaurants abound.

JAPANTOWN

SUNDAY IS THE BUSIEST SHOPPING DAY IN JAPANTOWN, and the five-acre enclosed mall **Japan Center** (1737 Post Street; ☎ 415-922-6776) is its heart. The shops and boutiques contain everything from antique kimonos and scrolls to ultramodern furniture and electronics. Favorite shops for westerners are **Kinokuniya Stationery and Gifts** (1581 Webster Street at Post Street; ☎ 415-567-8901), with its fascinating array of intricate note cards and writing implements, and **Kinokinuya Book Store** (1581 Webster Street at Post Street; ☎ 415-567-7625), which has a vast assortment of books and magazines in Japanese and English. For a bit of pampering, try **Kabuki Springs and Spa** (1750 Geary Boulevard; ☎ 415-922-6002), a Japanese spa where you can steam, soak, and sigh away a hard day's shop. Or for an afternoon coffee and cake, the **Tan Tan Café** (1826 Post Street; ☎ 415-346-6260) is the best (and only) Viennese coffeehouse in Japantown.

HAYES VALLEY

COLONEL THOMAS HAYES PROBABLY wouldn't recognize the urban "valley" that bears his name. It's more like the Valley of the Interior Decorators: Distressed-furniture boutiques, Art Deco specialty shops, and other retro-contemporary brokers line this relatively small shopping district between the Castro and Civic Center, along with dozens of tiny boutiques that look like settings for photo shoots for *Wallpaper* magazine. Good bets include **Azalea Boutique** (411 Hayes Street; ☎ 415-861-9888), offering an eclectic mix of apparel and accessories for both men and women, stuff that bucks the mass-production lockstep, and a nail bar for a bit of pampering; **Oui, Three Queens** (☎ 415-378-3959; **ouithreequeens.com**), providing custom-blended cosmetics; and **True Sake** (560 Hayes Street; ☎ 415-355-9555; **truesake.com**) for high-end Japanese rice wine.

THE HAIGHT

 HIP AND HIPPIE—that's the essence of the Haight today. To many visitors and residents, the time warp known as Haight Street is still synonymous with hippies. Even though the

famous corner of Haight and Ashbury streets is now bounded by a
Ben & Jerry's and a **Gap,** and even though music and fashion have
passed through punk and techno, the Haight has managed to hang
onto its 1960s reputation. A mishmash of head shops, secondhand
stores, record and bookshops, and the city's most alternative shopping experiences line Haight Street from Masonic to Stanyan streets.

Although the novelty of flower power has faded, today's progressive subcultures add a changing style to the Haight. You'll still find
clusters of head shops, packs of grungy panhandling teens, and other
historical artifacts such as the Red Vic Theater, Haight-Ashbury Free
Clinic, and **Bound Together Anarchist Bookstore** (1369 Haight Street
between Central and Masonic streets; ☎ 415-431-8355), but now the
Haight offers a fusion of old and new.

Some of the street's colorful landmarks include **Positively Haight
Street** (1400 Haight Street; ☎ 415-252-8747), which has all things
hippie and Summer of Lovey—T-shirts, tie-dyes, baggy pants, everything you need for a retro trip back to the 1960s. **Planet Weavers**
(1573 Haight Street at Clayton Street; ☎ 415-864-4415) is a Toys R
Us for fans of new age, world music, and multiculturalism in general,
filled with candles, drums, and fountains, and **Mickey's Monkey** (214
Pierce Street; ☎ 415-864-0693) is an old curiosity shop selling "stuff
for your place."

SOUTH OF MARKET

OTHERWISE KNOWN AS SOMA, the sprawling, industrial South of
Market area, with clusters of outlet and discount stores, is a focal
point for bargain hunters. Check out **Yerba Buena Square,** an urban
outlet mall (899 Howard Street at Fifth) anchored by a handy **Burling-
ton Coat Factory Warehouse** (you forgot Mark Twain's warning about
summer?) and pedestrian **Shoe Pavilion** (only sensible shoes last long in
this town). Not so far away is the **Six Sixty Factory Outlet Center** (660
Third Street at Townsend Street) with bargains on many name brands.
The **REI** outlet (840 Brannan Street; ☎ 415-934-1938) has monthly
sales of used gear for members on first Saturdays and Sundays, and
there's a couple more cool outlets next door. Because the nightclub
scene also thrives in SoMa, there's a host of leather and fetish stores
and other purveyors of "underground" attire and accessories, including **Stormy Leather** (1158 Howard Street; ☎ 415-626-1672).

THE CASTRO

IN THE SUNNY, PREDOMINANTLY GAY and lesbian neighborhood
known as the Castro, you never know what you'll see. A controversy
once erupted over a bookstore's window display, which featured an
anatomically correct porn star; many other gift stores, including the

aptly-named and in-your-face erotic art shop Erotic Art, continue to make window-shopping in the Castro an eye-popping, NC-17, at-your-own-risk experience.

But you'll also find the best-stocked knitting shop in town—**ImagiKnit** (3897 18th Street; ☎ 415-621-6642; **imagiknit.com**). Check their sales wall in the back. Later, amble across the street to the very best Russian tearoom for $10–$15 lunches at **Samovar** (498 Sanchez Street; ☎ 415-626-4700; **samovarlife.com**). Here you can recover from shopping with smoked salmon and gourmet teas. The **Tartine Bakery** (600 Guerrero Street at 18th; ☎ 415-487-2600; **tartinebakery.com**) is within striking distance too, if you're yearning to bring home delicious pastries.

A self-sufficient village, the Castro has its schlocky swag side with funky teddy gift boutiques (a bondage bear in leather chaps, anyone?) and suspect touristy side, along with some honest places that peddle what they say they do and have been there as long as **The Sausage Factory** pizzeria (517 Castro Street; ☎ 415-626-1250; **castrosausagefactory.com**), 30 years and counting. The **Anchor Oyster Bar** (597 Castro Street; ☎ 415-431-3990; **anchoroysterbar.com**) is the spot to buy just that: oysters, washed down with Prosecco. **Twin Peaks** (410 Castro Street; ☎ 415-864-9470) is also known as the Glass Coffin, owing to the seniority of its clientele and also the habit-forming ways of its cocktails. Oh well, the ladies have **The Café** (2369 Market Street; ☎ 415-834-5840; **cafesf.com**). Don't-miss shops include the neoclassic **Cliff's Variety** hardware store (479 Castro at 18th Street; ☎ 415-431-5365; **cliffsvariety.com**), a sort of Mayberry R.F.D. circa 2021, and **Under One Roof** (549 Castro Street at 19th Street; ☎ 415-503-2300; **underoneroof.org**), a lovely, imaginative, upscale gift boutique staffed entirely by volunteers—all profits are divided among more than 35 AIDS organizations in the area.

BERKELEY AND OAKLAND

IN THE PEOPLE'S REPUBLIC OF BERKELEY there is one street that maintains a pretty good balance between indie and mainstream. **Fourth Street** manages to appeal to the newfound yuppiness of the surrounding neighborhood while keeping in tune with the hippie vibe that has marked Berkeley as the brainchild of creative innovation. Whether you are looking for a gift for someone else or looking to indulge yourself, you can find almost anything here. It's niche shopping at its best. You can walk away with hard-to-find CDs or books from **Hear Music** (1809 Fourth Street; ☎ 510-204-9595) or **Moe's Books** (2476 Telegraph Avenue; ☎ 510-849-2087). **Scrapbook Territory** (1717 Fourth Street; ☎ 510-559-9929) is the place for arts-and-crafts supplies. Go to **Stone House** (1717 Fourth Street;

☎ 510-524-1400) for designer olive oils, and **Sur La Table** (1806 Fourth Street; ☎ 510-849-2252) for all things kitchen except the sink. At 708 Addison (at the corner of Fourth Street) is the **Takara Sake** brewery, the only such enterprise in the Bay area (☎ 510-540-8250). Tours and tastings are given daily. And for the truly unexpected, the **East Bay Vivarium** (1827-C Fifth Street; ☎ 510-841-1400) has the largest commercially available collection of reptiles in the United States—and all the crickets and such to keep them fat and happy. And to keep yourself fat and happy, you might have a tamale at **Tacubaya** (1788 Fourth Street; ☎ 510-525-5160; **tacubaya.net**) or just a cold one at **Spenger's** (1919 Fourth Street; ☎ 510-845-7771; **spengers.com**). Berkeley is also where you will find one of the most beautiful grocery stores ever. **Berkeley Bowl** (2020 Oregon Street; ☎ 510-843-6929) boasts the largest produce (mostly organic) section in all of northern California. Come to select food or come to take pictures! Its international section is a one-stop shop for everything—wasabi, pickled ginger, and seaweed paper. Visit the deli and get yourself a picnic to enjoy on the median green across the street. Berkeley isn't the whole of the East Bay. Oakland is no slouch in the shopping world and is surprisingly good for vintage clothing. **Rockridge Rags** (5711 College Avenue; ☎ 510-655-2287) is one of the best places on the bay for bygone elegance, and the nearby **Fortune Cookie Vintage Clothing** (310 Hudson Street; ☎ 510-601-5822) specializes in the exotic and hard-to-find. Being so close to the wine country, it should be no surprise (though it surely is) that there are wineries and tasting rooms here in the East Bay. Hire a limo or call a taxi or two and visit:

Dashe Cellars and **JC Cellars** (55 Fourth Street, Oakland; ☎ 510-452-1800)

Periscope Cellars (1410 62nd Street, Emeryville; ☎ 510-655-7827)

Rosenblum Cellars (2900 Main Street, Suite 1100, Alameda; ☎ 510-865-7007)

The **MALLS**

DESPITE WHAT YOU MAY HAVE SEEN IN MOVIES like *Clueless* and *Valley Girl,* malls no longer define the California shopping experience (and anyway, that was Southern California). The Bay Area is almost actively anti-mall (as well as anti-Wal-Mart), and neighborhood shopping is de rigueur. But if you must mall it, there are several not unattractive options.

kids The cornerstone is the retail and entertainment megaplex called **Metreon** (101 Fourth Street at Mission Street; ☎ 415-369-6000; **metreon.com**), which architects and shoppers once hailed as the wave of the future until it fell into the trap of showing only boy movies. The Metreon features 15 state-of-the-art movie theaters and an eight-story IMAX auditorium, plus a high-tech arcade and restaurants that go way beyond the term *food court*. It's starting to rival the food stalls in the Westfield Centre basement, **Beard Papa** cream puffs and all. As well as the ever-tempting **Just Desserts,** the Metreon includes **Chronicle Books.**

Built in 1988 to house Nordstrom, the downtown **San Francisco Shopping Centre** (865 Market Street at Fifth Street; ☎ 415-495-5656; **sanfranciscocentre.com**) boasts more than 100 different merchants, including **Kenneth Cole, J. Crew, Ann Taylor, Abercrombie & Fitch,** and **Victoria's Secret.** Shoppers wind their way up curved escalators designed by Mitsubishi through four floors of shops; connection to the Powell Street BART and Muni terminal makes getting there easy.

Too fancy to be called a mall, the seriously stylin' **Crocker Galleria** (50 Post Street at Kearny Street; ☎ 415-393-1505; **shopatgalleria.com**) in the heart of the downtown Financial District was fashioned after the Galleria Vittorio Emanuele in Milan. The galleria offers 50 shops, restaurants, and services, including **Versace** and **Ralph Lauren** boutiques and a charming rooftop park. Parking is free on Saturday with a $10 purchase (which, in a place that sells $50 undershirts, should take about ten seconds).

By the waterfront is the monumental **Embarcadero Center** (Clay Street between Battery Street and Justin Herman Plaza; ☎ 415-772-0500; **embarcaderocenter.com**), a complex of four office towers housing two levels of restaurants, movie theaters, and shops, including **Ann Taylor, Banana Republic, Gap, Crabtree and Evelyn,** and **Pottery Barn,** plus a few interesting local boutiques such as **L'Occitane,** an aromatherapy bath and skin-care shop, and **Kidi Niki,** which offers children's clothing.

SPECIALTY SHOPS

ALTERNATIVE SHOPPING

SAN FRANCISCO SPECIALIZES IN ECCENTRICS and subcultures (this is, after all, a city with a church—Saint John Coltrane African Orthodox Church—devoted to jazz music; **coltranechurch.org**). Body modification through tattooing and body piercing is one souvenir that keeps on giving. If you decide to get a new perforation while you're here, get something cool to put in it. For body jewelry and other accessories, visit **Anubis Warpus** (1525 Haight Street at Ashbury; ☎ 415-431-2218). **Cold Steel Piercing & Tattoo** (1783 Haight Street; ☎ 415-933-7233) is perhaps the most upscale place of its kind. The artful displays and furnishings give it a museumlike feel.

The Beats go on, and so do the hippies, at least in the memories and imaginations of most visitors. For Beat memorabilia, **City Lights**

Bookstore (261 Columbus Avenue at Broadway; ☎ 415-362-8193) in North Beach is un-Beat-able; a window-shopping stroll through the Haight District will turn up all sorts of flashbacks, from head shops to vintage rock-concert poster peddlers.

kids Kids love the **Chinatown Kite Shop** (717 Grant Street; ☎ 415-989-5182), the place for your inner child. Find kites in the shapes of airplanes, butterflies, birds, even cars and army tanks. Get one or two and take them out to Crissy Field on a blustery day. You'll thank yourself for it.

Botanica Yoruba (998 Valencia Street; ☎ 415-826-4967) offers candles, potions, herbs, and incantations for every need or desire—sort of a Pagans R Us. One of the most unusual and off-the-beaten-path shops in town, **Paxton Gate** (824 Valencia Street; ☎ 415-824-1872), may be the world's most bizarre gardening store, with displays of eerie air plants, mounted bugs and butterflies, and stuffed and costumed mice.

Extreme Sports

San Francisco has hosted the X-games, and that's no coincidence. The city is full of adrenaline-inducing jumps, trails, surf, rock, and slopes. No place is proper gear more mandatory than this playground of a city.

Despite appearances, it ain't cheap being a skate punk. What with the skater duds, shoes, customized boards, wheels, and magazines, you gotta keep up. At **DLX** (1831 Market Street at Octavia Street; ☎ 415-626-5588) they've got it all. Same goes for snowboarding, another accessory-intensive sport: **SFO** (618 Shrader Street at Haight Street; ☎ 415-386-1666) is the sweet spot for boots, boards, and bundle-up wear. Gear-head heaven for any sport is located in either **Sports Basement** (in the Presidio at 610 Mason Street; ☎ 415-437-0100; or Bryant Street at 15th Street; 415-575-3000; **sportsbasement. com**) or **Lombardi Sports** (1600 Jackson Street; ☎ 415-771-0600). Both places offer helpful and knowledgeable service, and floors are divided by activity. For rock climbing you can visit either of the multipurpose stores mentioned above or head to **Mission Cliffs** (2295 Harrison Street at 19th Street; ☎ 415-550-0515). They have all the necessary gear, including helmets, harnesses, climbing shoes, ropes, biners, and such.

ANTIQUES

SAN FRANCISCANS ARE IN LOVE WITH HISTORY, and the antiques stores are stocked with everything from ultrapricey traditional pieces and 1950s kitsch ware to last month's fads.

In the area once known as the Barbary Coast, Jackson Square, San Francisco's first designated historic district (it was the only group of downtown buildings to survive the 1906 earthquake and fire) has fittingly become the city's official antiques district. Bounded by Jackson, Washington, Montgomery, and Sansome streets, the square, which showcases its pieces like small museums, houses about two dozen dealers, such as **Argentum—The Leopard's Head** (72 Jackson Street near Sansome Street; ☎ 415-296-7757) with 16th- through 19th-century silver and **Daniel Stein Antiques** for traditional English and Continental furniture (458 Jackson Street near Montgomery Street; ☎ 415-956-5620; **danielsteinantiques.com**).

Grand Central Station Antiques (333 Ninth Street at Folsom; ☎ 415-252-8155) is like a classic jumble sale, with two floors of fun finds.

Perhaps the most pleasurable antiques shopping is on Russian Hill at **Russian Hill Antiques** (2200 Polk Street at Vallejo Street; ☎ 415-441-5561). If early American seems a bit too drab for your taste, head to **Retrospect Custom Furniture** (1649 Market Street; ☎ 415-863-7414). It's all about retro here—from the 1940s, 1950s, and 1960s.

BARGAINS AND THRIFT STORES

BEEN TO A GOOD FLEA MARKET LATELY? On Sundays the **Alemany Farmers' Market** gives way to a market full of tables, chairs, pictures, glassware, and even baseball team jackets—you name it—sheltering under the spaghetti-like intersection of Interstate 280 and Highway 101 (until 3 p.m.). You can also zoom way upmarket, of course. At very chic **Cris** (near Broadway at 2056 Polk; ☎ 415-474-1191), you get all the swanky labels you want for less, and it's conveniently open on Sunday afternoons, too.

Although shopping in San Francisco may not be the way of life or contact sport it is in Los Angeles or New York, the locals are nevertheless competitive about what they get. And how they get it. If you compliment a San Franciscan about his new computer bag or her little black dress, be prepared to hear the tale of how cheap it was at a thrift store (or at a sidewalk sale). The more obscure the source and the lower the price, the better. Never underestimate the talent it takes to emerge from **Community Thrift** with something cheap that you'll actually use or wear! In San Francisco, people try on and toss off new personas the way other folks change underwear. Previously owned and recycled everything—from clothes to records to kitchenware—is big business. Nostalgia cycles seem to speed up in this town, and Bohemian, artist-friendly neighborhoods such as the Haight and the upper Mission have particularly high concentrations of vintage and thrift stores, but you can go on a bargain bender even in snooty Pacific Heights.

American Rag (1305 Van Ness Avenue at Sutter Street; ☎ 415-441-0537) has the largest and trendiest selection of retro rags in town, but

unofficial **TIP**
Near the holidays, in early November, and in May before Mother's Day, the merchants of the **Gift Center** (888 Brannan Street at Eighth; ☎ 415-861-7733) offer their samples and overstock on six levels of the building. It's like the world's biggest garage sale. And you can have a nice lunch or a drink at the Pavilion Café and Deli, which also houses the popular **Peet's Coffee** (☎ 415-552-8555).

the eye-popping prices don't really qualify as thrift. (They also offer new designer goods.) Gargoyles guard the carnival-like exterior of the Haight's **Wasteland** (1660 Haight Street at Clayton Street; ☎ 415-863-3150), and if you can bear the famously loud and obnoxious music, you'll be rewarded with great finds. **Community Thrift** is a veritable secondhand department store (623 Valencia Street; ☎ 415-861-4910), where you can specify which of more than 200 charities you want your purchase to benefit. Other old faithfuls include **Crossroads Trading Co.** (1901 Fillmore Street; ☎ 415-775-8885; or 2123 Market Street near Church Street; ☎ 415-626-8989) and **Buffalo Exchange** (1555 Haight Street between Clayton and Ashbury streets; ☎ 415-431-7733). The enormous **Goodwill** store (1580 Mission Street at South Van Ness Avenue; ☎ 415-575-2240) is as brightly lit as any grocery store, and it's always chock-full of new and old trash and treasure.

For a highbrow rummage-sale experience, try the Pacific Heights version. Rich folks unload their castoffs at the **Next-to-New Shop** (2226 Fillmore Street between Sacramento and Clay streets; ☎ 415-567-1628), which gets its goods from the Junior League of San Francisco, and at **Repeat Performance Thrift Shop** (2436 Fillmore Street between Jackson and Washington streets; ☎ 415-563-3123), which benefits the San Francisco Symphony.

Secondhand shopping isn't confined to clothing. The trend for recycled merchandise extends to books, CDs, records, and even cookware. **Cookin'** (339 Divisadero Street near Haight Street; ☎ 415-861-1854) is like your grandmother's attic, filled with used classic kitchen gadgets, dishware, cookbooks, and anything else the gourmet in you might desire.

BOOKS AND MAGAZINES

SINCE MANY COME TO SAN FRANCISCO to be writers, artists, and musicians (or just to be near them), the city has an unusually well-read population and plenty of well-stocked and personable bookstores. The big guys are here, of course, including **Borders Books & Music** (400 Post Street at Powell Street; ☎ 415-399-0522) and **Barnes and Noble** (2550 Taylor Street; ☎ 415-292-6762).

A Different Light is a remarkably well-stocked gay and lesbian bookstore that functions as a de facto community center (489 Castro Street at 18th; ☎ 415-431-0891). Beat headquarters and the publishing home and hangout of Jack Kerouac and Allen Ginsberg, **City Lights Booksellers & Publishers** (261 Columbus Avenue between Pacific Street and Broadway; ☎ 415-362-8193) is probably San Francisco's best-known bookstore. You still may find founder-poet Lawrence Ferlinghetti hanging around.

Magazine lovers should check in at **Harold's International Newsstand** (454 Geary Boulevard between Mason and Taylor streets; ☎ 415-441-2665). **Naked Eye News and Video** (607 Haight Street;

☎ 415-864-2985) specializes in culture rags and 'zines—the more obscure, the better. **The Magazine** (920 Larkin Street; ☎ 415-441-7737) is one of many strangely wonderful shops in town; it's where all those old magazines you threw away wind up, and its obsessively catalogued gay and straight porn section is a miracle of modern library science. Or something.

For the best used bookstore, it's a tie between Russian Hill's **Acorn Books** (1436 Polk Street at California Street; ☎ 415-563-1736), Richmond's bewildering, mazelike **Green Apple Books** (506 Clement Street at Sixth; ☎ 415-387-2272), and the minichain of stellar **Red Hill Books** (401 Cortland Avenue in Bernal Heights; ☎ 415-648-5331), **Dog Eared Books** (900 Valencia Street at 20th Street; ☎ 415-282-1901), and **Phoenix Books** (3957 24th Street; ☎415-821-3477; **dogearedbooks. com**), all founded by Kate Rosenberger Waters and George Kirby Desha, full of tasty Moleskine agendas and calendars too. Bookstores cater to almost every specialized taste. Find books from an African-American perspective at **Marcus Books** (1712 Fillmore Street; ☎ 415-346-4222). **William Stout Architectural Books** (804 Montgomery Street at Jackson Street; ☎ 415-391-6757) is one of the best of its kind in the country. **Fields Book Store** (1419 Polk Street between Pine and California streets; ☎ 415-673-2027) seriously specializes in spiritual and new age books. **The Limelight** (1803 Market Street; ☎ 415-864-2265) is stocked with books on film, TV, acting, and its main attraction, unbound sometimes-yet-to-be-published screenplays. Travelers can map out their lives at **Get Lost Travel Books, Maps & Gear** (1825 Market Street at Pearl Street; ☎ 415-437-0529). For a similar shop downtown, see the **Rand McNally** store (595 Market Street; ☎ 415-777-3131).

CLOTHING

SAN FRANCISCANS TAKE PRIDE in defining themselves by what they are not—as in, not L.A. and not N.Y. A (sometimes ostentatious) lack of ostentation defines northern California style. Sure, San Francisco may be less image conscious and clothes crazy than, say, Los Angeles, but as low-key and (sophisticatedly, sensibly) dressed-down as San Franciscans are, they like to look good. Fortunately, there are plenty of places to dress up (or down).

For women, Union Street is the hot spot for shopping, offering all the famous fashion names in boutiques and department stores. Union Street, in its ten-block shopping area, has more than 40 clothing boutiques, from trendy to traditional, including San Francisco–based **Bebe** (2095 Union Street; ☎ 415-563-2323), which has classic-to-trashy suiting for the chic and slim contemporary woman, and **Girlfriends** (1824 Union Street; ☎ 415-673-9544), whose distinctive logo items have become coveted souvenirs. For the unpredictable San Francisco weather, layering is essential. Stop at **Three Bags Full** (2181 Union

Street at Fillmore; ☎ 415-567-5753) for hand-knit sweaters and sportswear. At **Carol Doda's Champagne and Lace** (1850 Union Street; ☎ 415-776-6900) in a picturesque Union Street alley, San Francisco's famous former stripper sells lingerie and bodywear for women of every size. **Canyon Beachwear** (1728 Union Street; ☎ 415-885-5070) is San Francisco's only women's specialty swimwear shop.

Behind the Post Office (1510 Haight Street; ☎ 415-861-2507) is known for its shabby-chic style made by top local designers. You won't have the problem of duplicates at a party if you shop at this store. Sizes run small so you gotta like them tight-fitted. If you want to sport true 1940s patterns with today's chic infused in the fabric, check out **Manifesto** (514 Octavia Street; ☎ 415-431-4778). Combining the appeal of those sit-and-gossip hair salons, the owner of **Brown Eyed Girl** (2999 Washington Street; ☎ 415-409-0214) opened her boutique in a quaint Victorian home to welcome women inside not just for shopping but for an intimate getaway. You can find evening dresses to just the right everyday purse here. Europe meets Asia for a trendy funk infusion at **Ab Fits** (1519 Grant Avenue; ☎ 415-982-5726). Service is excellent here, especially when it comes to finding the proper fit in jeans, which is the lure for many jeans seekers. Whether you are going to trendy nightspots or looking for a chic outfit to teach the third grade, a city favorite amongst females is **Ambiance,** with two locations: one on 1458 Haight Street (☎ 415-552-5095) and the other at 1864 Union Street (☎ 415-923-9797; **ambiancesf.com**). The store on Union Street is said to be the friendliest around.

Look sharp, men. San Francisco's snazzy former mayor Willie Brown is friendly with the equally dandyish proprietor of **Wilkes Bashford** (375 Sutter Street between Grant and Stockton streets; ☎ 415-986-4380), who keeps Brown in fedoras and tailored suits in an opulent atmosphere; Don Johnson shops here, too. For more traditional men's clothing, **Cable Car Clothiers** (200 Bush Street at Sansome; ☎ 415-397-4740) is a good bet for the jacket-and-tie set. On the other side of the couture coin, **Saks Fifth Avenue Men's Store** (384 Powell and Post streets; ☎ 415-986-4300) stocks gear by Versace, Gaultier, and Dolce & Gabbana. For nightlifers, **Daljeets** (1773 Haight Street at Cole; ☎ 415-752-5610) has off-the-wall clothes for street and club wear, and the clothing and underwear shop **Rolo** (2351 Market Street near Castro Street; ☎ 415-431-4545) is so up-to-date that it's futuristic.

Quaint shoe stores such as **Smash Shoes** (2030 Chestnut Street; ☎ 415-673-4736) redefine that little black shoe. The selection at Haight favorite **Shoe Biz** (1446 Haight Street; ☎ 415-864-0990) will please club kids and even conservative classic dressers with a bit of a funky edge.

Retro Clothing

San Francisco is a nexus of the retro-swing craze, and what with Lindy-hoppin' hot spots such as Club Deluxe and others, some people here make living in the past a full-fledged way of life. Vintage clothing is big business, and while these shops are no bargain, you can find the real deal. **Held Over** (1543 Haight Street; ☎ 415-864-0818) has one of the best collections of formalwear, leather jackets, and trousers in crazy patterns. **La Rosa Vintage** (1711 Haight Street; ☎ 415-668-3744) has enough vintage shoes to satisfy even the shoe-addicted Carrie Bradshaw of *Sex and the City*. (Maybe she should've left New York for San Francisco.) This is a high-class operation, and you'll never feel like you're in a secondhand store.

CREATIVITY AND THE DECORATIVE ARTS

SAN FRANCISCO IS KNOWN FOR ITS CREATIVITY and free spirit. Start beautifying your life with a stop at **FLAX** (1699 Market Street at Valencia Street; ☎ 415-552-2355), a distinctive arts-supply superstore with paints and paper, furniture, lighting, framing, wrapping paper, and unusual jewelry and toys.

You can actually rent a painting (with an option to buy) from the **San Francisco Museum of Modern Artists Gallery** (Building A, Fort Mason Center at Buchanan Street and Marina Boulevard; ☎ 415-441-4777). The gallery's goal is to give exposure to new artists, and if you decide the work looks good over your couch, half of the rental fee goes toward the purchase price. To buy a piece of artwork at a good price, check out **Gallery 444** (444 Post Street; ☎ 415-434-4477). In sight of Union Square this gallery has beautiful works as well as a very friendly staff. No snooty people allowed.

FLOWERS AND PLANTS

THE BAY AREA IS ONE OF THE NATION'S premier flower-growing areas, and the city is abloom with talented florists like the Castro's avant-garde **Ixia** (2331 Market Street between Noe and Castro streets; ☎ 415-431-3134), creating wildly abstract, attention-grabbing bouquets. You can make your own arrangements after a visit to the **San Francisco Flower Mart** (640 Brannan Street at Sixth Street; ☎ 415-392-7944), which fills an entire city block with blooms and branches. And for flowers on the fly just walk around Union Square. You'll see small florists on every other corner. If you want an arrangement to last longer, **Coast Wholesale Florist** (149 Morris Street in the Flower Market; ☎ 415-781-8533) is a warehouse with dried versions of nearly every plant on earth.

*un*official **TIP**
One of the best flower deals in the city is the small metal-and-glass stand that is Rincon Flowers (corner of Spear and Mission streets). Every Friday they run a half-off special.

FOOD

PERHAPS BECAUSE SAN FRANCISCO IS THE HOME of California cuisine, restaurant dining has become one of the city's most popular participatory sports, and locals watch the trades and power plays of big-name chefs the way they watch their quarterbacks and stock options. Many of the city's foodies, known for their sophisticated tastes and obsession with fresh local ingredients, will tell you they live here because it's so near the source of wonderful produce. And with Napa Valley and Sonoma wine country so close, almost everyone knows something about wine.

A few food specialty stores, including an outpost of Seattle's **Sur La Table** (77 Maiden Lane; ☎ 415-732-7900), can be found in Union Square. In North Beach, you can't go wrong at many of the Italian bakeries and delis; start at the century-old deli **Molinari's** for first courses (373 Columbus Avenue at Vallejo Street; ☎ 415-421-2337). In Chinatown, **The Wok Shop** (718 Grant Street between Sacramento and Clay streets; ☎ 415-989-3797) specializes in everything you need for cooking Chinese cuisine, including cookbooks. And for the perfect end to the meal, **Golden Gate Fortune Cookie Company** (56 Ross Alley off Jackson Street; ☎ 415-781-3956) makes traditional fortunes, as well as those with customized messages to order. **Joseph Schmidt Confections** (3489 16th Street; ☎ 415-861-8682) is the city's premier (and quite imaginative) chocolatier, especially famed for its chocolate sculptures. Bring back your souvenirs in chocolate.

Even something as mundane as grocery shopping can provide a California experience at places like **Real Food Company** (2140 Polk Street between Vallejo Street and Broadway; ☎ 415-673-7420); **Whole Foods** (1765 California Street; ☎ 415-674-0500), a gourmet megastore where museum-quality carrots, tomatoes, and peppers are displayed; and **Rainbow Grocery Cooperative** (1745 Folsom at Division Street; ☎ 415-863-0621), a crunchier, co-op version of Whole Foods, with pierced, tattooed staffers ringing up your bulk food items. **Trader Joe's** (555 Ninth Street at Bryant Street; ☎ 415-863-1292) has become a favorite for its discount gourmet snacks, health foods, and fresh juices, and a great selection of wines and beers.

Coffee is still the craze in hyper-caffeinated San Francisco, and you can find a cafe selling java and whole beans on almost every corner. **Blue Bottle Coffee** (☎ 510-653-3394; **bluebottlecoffee.net**) from Oakland is the latest gourmet taste, and you'll find its first cafe at 66 Mint Alley at Jessie Alley off Fifth Street, and a wee kiosk in trendy Hayes Valley. They have interesting roasting techniques; ask them.

Originally from Berkeley, **Peet's Coffee and Tea** (2139 Polk Street; ☎ 415-474-1871) was the inspiration for the creators of Starbucks. The aroma of fresh-roasted coffee in the blocks around **Graffeo** (735 Columbus near Filbert Street; ☎ 415-986-2420), a beloved hometown roastery and wholesale distributor in North Beach, is one of the signature scents (and tastes) of San Francisco. To steep yourself in Chinese culture and gastronomica, take a walking/shopping/eating tour of Chinatown with the city's most renowned tour guide, Shirley Fong-Torres. She'll take you to the best places for Chinese kitchen equipment, as well as foods, spices, and medicinal herbs. You'll see fortune cookies being made, perhaps a cooking demonstration, and best of all you'll have lunch with Shirley. Her operation is known as **Wok Wiz** and offers both tours and classes (☎ 415-981-8989; **wokwiz. com**). Make a stop at **Mitchell's Ice Cream** (688 San Jose Avenue; ☎ 415-648-2300), arguably the best ice cream in the city—proven by the lines of tongue-lapping customers with their numbers in hand, anxiously waiting. You'll find the traditional flavors, but it's the unusual flavors that put Mitchell's on the map. Try mango, *langka* (a tart melon), macapuno (meaty coconut), or—our favorite—cinnamon snap. You can pick up pints and enjoy it all week.

Another distinctive San Francisco shopping experience is an early morning visit to one of the weekly farmers' markets. On Wednesday and Sunday at **United Nations Plaza** (Market Street between Grove and Fulton streets, near the Civic Center), the **Heart of the City Farmers' Market** (1182 Market Street at Eighth Street; ☎ 415-558-9455) replaces the panhandlers with dozens of booths featuring fresh-from-the-farm fruits, vegetables, and flowers. Bernal Heights' **Alemany Farmers' Market** on Saturdays (100 Alemany Boulevard; ☎ 415-647-2043) has a row of ethnic food stalls for brunching on the side. Saturday mornings used to be the day for the outdoor market across the Embarcadero from the Ferry Building. But no more. Now it's also on Tuesdays and Thursdays. Not only is this a grand place to come for fresh produce, but also bakery goods and ready-to-eat foods, as well as restaurants and coffee- and teahouses. To find other farmers markets in the city check: **sfgate.com/food/farmersmarkets.** Chinatown's open produce markets, which have the feel of exotic farmers' markets, are open every day. Look for them on Stockton Street running the length of Chinatown.

PlumpJack Wines (3201 Fillmore Street at Greenwich Avenue; ☎ 415-346-9870) in the Marina is a companion store to Plumpjack Café, and it's one of the best places in San Francisco to find impressive and obscure labels. Free delivery is available anywhere in the city. The name says it all—the **Napa Valley Winery Exchange** (415 Taylor Street between Geary Boulevard and O'Farrell Street; ☎ 415-771-2887; **nvwe.com**) is a wine boutique specializing in hard-to-find vintages and labels from nearby Napa. They ship. Other good spots for California wines are **D&M Liquors** in Pacific Heights (2200 Fillmore Street at Sacramento Street; ☎ 415-346-1325) and **Wine Club** (953 Harrison Street; ☎ 800-966-7835), which sells wine from jug to connoisseur at just above wholesale prices. The Wine Club boasts the largest selection of Burgundy and Bordeaux wines west of the

We've Got What You Need: The Bests

THE BEST GAPS Market and Dolores; Polk and California streets

BEST SHOPPING STREETS Chestnut Street in the Marina or Union Street in Cow Hollow; upper and lower Fillmore; The Haight

BEST TRINKET SHOP Golden Gate Bridge Shop (☎ 415-923-2331)

BEST PLACE TO BUY A GIFT "FROM SAN FRANCISCO" Mark Reuben Gallery (900 North Point; ☎ 415-543-5433)

BEST SHOPS FOR THE NIECES AND NEPHEWS Exploratorium (at Marina Boulevard and Lyon Street; ☎ 415-561-0390); Gamescape (333 Divisadero Street; ☎ 415-621-4263)

BEST DRESSING ROOM Saks Fifth Avenue (384 Post Street; ☎ 415-986- 4300)

BEST USED-BOOK STORE Green Apple Books (506 Clement Street; ☎ 415-387-2272)

Mississippi. For spirits of another sort, head to the Financial District for a visit to **John Walker & Co. Wine and Spirits** (175 Sutter Street between Montgomery and Kearny streets; ☎ 415-986-2707), the city's oldest specialty and import liquor merchant.

INSIDER SHOPS

Cliff's Variety (479 Castro Street between 18th and Market streets; ☎ 415-431-5365)—with its friendly, small-town feeling, everything-but-the-kitchen-sink stock, and outlandish seasonal window displays—has become a Castro institution. **See's Candies** is an old-fashioned candy shop—the kind where people behind the counter give you a free sample if you buy something and sometimes even if you don't. Stores are located throughout the city (☎ 800-347-7337).

And if you need something at any hour, there's a good chance you'll find it (or something that will do until the shops open) at one of the city's all-purpose 24-hour stores, including **Safeway** (2020 Market Street at Church Street; ☎ 415-861-7660) and **Walgreen's** (498 Castro Street at 18th; ☎ 415-861-6276).

KIDS

KIDS WILL GET A KICK OUT OF A visit to the **Basic Brown Bear Factory** (2801 Leavenworth Street, second floor; ☎ 415-409-2806), where they can watch a bear-making demonstration and pick out their own cuddly pal. Pacific Heights and the Marina are the spots for the stroller set; **Dottie Doolittle** (3680 Sacramento Street between Locust and Spruce streets; ☎ 415-563-3244), **Jonathan-Kaye by Country**

Living (3548 Sacramento Street between Laurel and Locust streets; ☎ 415-563-0773), and **Mudpie** (1694 Union Street; ☎ 415-771-9262) are just a few of the upscale kidswear boutiques for label-savvy tots.

As a major metropolis, San Francisco has its **Toys R Us** (2675 Geary Boulevard; ☎ 415-931-8896), of course, but the hometown toy box of choice is **Jeffrey's Toys** downtown (685 Market Street at Third Street; ☎ 415-243-8697), with a great comic book collection and a center for all things *Star Wars*.

MUSEUM SHOPS

SAN FRANCISCO IS RICH WITH MUSEUMS, and the gift shops are full of take-home treasures. Consider the shops your own team of personal shoppers. The **California Historical Society** (678 Mission Street at Fourth; ☎ 415-357-1848) has beautiful graphics of California's parks. There are three museums in Golden Gate Park, each with its own unique shop. The **Legion of Honor** (Golden Gate Park; ☎ 415-750-3642) sells books and objects related to recent shows. The internationally famous **Exploratorium** (3601 Lyon Street next to the Palace of Fine Arts; ☎ 415-561-0390) is an interactive science museum, and its gift shop is full of intriguing science kits and games for children of all ages. The **San Francisco Museum of Modern Art** (151 Third Street; ☎ 415-357-4035) is a San Francisco landmark, and its innovative museum store has racked up high sales.

MUSIC

THE BIRTHPLACE OF ACID ROCK, a hotbed of jazz, and a historically culture-craving town full of classical music buffs and operaholics, San Francisco is rich in record stores.

The used-records scene is a way of life. The biggest used-records game in town is **Amoeba** (1855 Haight Street; ☎ 415-831-1200), which operates a superstore in a former Haight Street bowling alley. Other places to search for that Holy Grail–like CD or record: **Streetlight** (3979 24th Street between Sanchez and Noe streets; ☎ 415-282-3550) and **Recycled Records** (1377 Haight Street at Masonic Street; ☎ 415-626-4075). Vinyl lives on at **Grooves** (1797 Market Street at Elgin Park; ☎ 415-436-9933) and **Rooky's Records** (448 Haight Street; ☎ 415-864-7526), where they boast the largest collection of 45 rpm singles. Albums are also available.

Then there's the new and the next. San Francisco has a thriving dance culture and techno scene, and the hippest kids shop where the local DJs get their discs: **Spundae Reckords + CDs** (678 Haight Street; ☎ 415-575-1580) is where the DJs shop, and you'll likely see a few foraging. It's a great place for the latest house mixes on 12-inch singles, and some CDs are available, too.

PLEASURE CHEST: SEXY SHOPPING

WITH ITS (WELL-DESERVED) ANYTHING-GOES REPUTATION, San Francisco is synonymous with sex. Here's where to get your sensual supplies. **Good Vibrations** (603 Valencia Street between 23rd and 24th; ☎ 415-522-5640) is a friendly, nonfurtive store that's been women-owned and operated for 20 years; it sells sex supplies, books, and videos. Check out the vibrator museum. Often voted "best place to buy drag" in local alternative weeklies, **Piedmont Boutique** (1452 Haight Street; ☎ 415-864-8075) is a glitzy showgirl shop, but most of the showgirls are guys. Piedmont has been dressing strippers and drag queens for 33 years. **Foxy Lady Boutique** (2644 Mission Street between 22nd and 23rd; ☎ 415-285-4980) has wigs, gowns, lingerie, accessories, and shoes and boots up to size 16.

Stormy Leather (1158 Howard Street between Seventh and Eighth; ☎ 415-626-1672) specializes in leather and vinyl fetish wear for women. **Leather Etc.** (1201 Folsom Street; ☎ 415-864-7558; **leatheretc.com**) features PVC lingerie, a wide selection of goth clothing, and acres of leather. You're gonna look good when you leave here. **Madame S. Fetish Boutique** (385 Eighth Street; ☎ 415-863-9447) maintains a safe, secure environment where nobody gets whipped without permission. Come here for corsets, literature, latex, and leather.

TOURISTIANA

IF YOU ABSOLUTELY MUST GO HOME with an Alcatraz shot glass, miniature cable car, or "fog dome," all this tourist merchandise and more (mind-bogglingly more) is conveniently concentrated in the boardwalk-like waterfront area known as **Fisherman's Wharf.** Shopping for nonessentials and unnecessary items is plentiful at the wharf's street vendors, as well as at Pier 39. **Ghirardelli Square** (900 North Point; ☎ 415-775-5500) has clusters of 70 specialty shops surrounding the delightfully old-fashioned **Ghirardelli Chocolate Manufactory and Soda Fountain** (☎ 415-781-2601), and the **Cannery** (2801 Leavenworth Street near Hyde Street; ☎ 415-771-3112) is where you can take a breather from shopping with the live entertainment in the courtyard. One place that stands out is **Golden Gate Bridge Shop** (at the bridge toll plaza on the San Francisco side of the bridge; ☎ 415-923-2331), where you can purchase authentic pieces of cable and rivets from the Golden Gate Bridge.

PART TEN

EXERCISE *and* RECREATION

IN SAN FRANCISCO, simply going from your hotel to your car or out to brunch can be more exercise than most people get in a week. The city is a giant playground equipped with natural jungle gyms—paved hills, zigzagging steps, and green spaces expansive enough to fly a kite or, heck, even paraglide. Those who live here opt to foot it, bike it, climb it, pedal it, and public-transport it, which can require a whole new level of flexibility and balance during those sardined rides. So as the *Unofficial Guide* sets out to do, we want to empower you with the insider scoop—to do as the locals do but with a newcomer perspective!

The GREAT INDOORS

FITNESS CENTERS AND AEROBICS

THE GYMS IN SAN FRANCISCO UNDERSTAND the conditioning demanded by the city's fitness freaks. Whether they are training for foot or bike marathons, or the popular Escape from Alcatraz swim, the gyms provide equipment and classes that can get any glute, tri, bi, quad, or calf pumped up. Hours for most gyms are similar—from 5:30 to 6 a.m. to about 9 p.m. A popular place for biker-shorts clad, fitness-sophisticate Marina types is the heart-thumping, music-blaring **Gorilla Sports** (2324 Chestnut Street, ☎ 415-292-8470; 2450 Sutter Street, ☎ 415-474-2699, 2330 Polk Street, ☎ 415-292-5444, **gorillasports.com**). The gym's three locations offer a free three-day trial pass. Their classes are pretty extensive, incorporating yoga, Pilates, kickboxing, and traditional aerobics.

Club One, clubone.com, has seven locations with free weights, Nautilus, aerobic equipment, Jacuzzis, steam rooms, aerobics classes, and certified fitness trainers. Locations are Citicorp Center (1 Sansome Street; ☎ 415-399-1010), Yerba Buena (350 Third Street; ☎ 415-512-1010), Embarcadero Center (2 Embarcadero Center;

☎ 415-788-1010), Civic Center (450 Golden Gate Avenue; ☎ 415-876-1010), Fillmore Center (17550 O'Ferrell Street; ☎ 415-749-1010), Nob Hill (Fairmont Hotel, 950 California Street; ☎ 415-834-1010), and Jackson Square (30 Hotaling Place; ☎ 415-837-1010). The daily rate is $15 with a member; $20 without.

24-Hour Fitness, 24hourfitness.com, is a locals' favorite. Their color-coded machines, depending on which part of the body you want to work, are a convenient way to a self-guided workout. Although some feel that the gyms are too bare-bones and a bit grungy, the locations are convenient—seven in all, including 100 California Street (☎ 415-434-5080) and 1200 Van Ness Avenue (☎ 415-776-2200). The daily rate for each facility is $15.

Why not the Y? The **YMCAs, ymcasf.org,** in San Francisco are not bleach-smelling, family-infested, cinder-blocked gyms. They are clean and surprisingly effective facilities. The YMCA at the Embarcadero (169 Steuart Street; ☎ 415-957-9622) is a favorite for its five-meter, 25-lane swimming pool; excellent views; and low-key clientele. Cardio equipment, located in two adjoining rooms, includes 18 treadmills and 14 Netpulse Internet-equipped stationary bikes. Keep track of your workouts electronically with the FitLinxx system. The deck on the fifth floor is a hot spot for sun worshippers and runners, also. Daily rate is $15.

At two of the four locations of **Pinnacle Fitness, pinnaclefitness. com,** guests can swim at indoor pools after working out on Cybex weight-training gear or free weights; all locations have steam rooms. The club with a pool is at 1 Post Street (☎ 415-781-6400). Other locations are 345 Spear Street in the Hills Plaza on the Embarcadero (☎ 415-495-1939) and 61 Montgomery Street across from the Sheraton Palace hotel (☎ 415-543-1110). The daily fee is $15.

HOTELS FOR HEAVY SWEATERS

ARE YOU ARE THE TYPE WHO LUGS AROUND a portable ab roller purchased off some infomercial featuring Suzanne Somers? Many of the larger downtown hotels have excellent fitness centers on the premises, including the **Ritz-Carlton,** the **St. Francis,** and the **Nikko.** The Nikko comes with quite an extensive gym and swimming pool, which are free if you purchase certain hotel packages. If not, there is a per-day use fee of $6.

The **Grand Hyatt, Sheraton Palace, Beresford, Diva, Donatello, Juliana, Cartwright,** and the **Hilton Hotels** struck a deal with Pinnacle Fitness Centers allowing guests to work out at any Pinnacle facility for only $10. The **Nob Hill Lambourne** on Pine Street is for the most exercise-obsessed. A stationary bike, treadmill, and rowing machine come in each room, and the hotel offers private in-room yoga sessions. Call ☎ 415-433-2287; **nobhilllambourne.com.**

Spas

Whether you are looking for a back massage, acupuncture, manicures and pedicures, tanning, facials, or even communal baths, San Francisco has plenty of offerings. **Kabuki Springs and Spa** (Japan Center, 1750 Geary Boulevard at Fillmore; ☎ 415-922-6000; **kabukisprings.com**) offers traditional Japanese communal baths. You can take a cold plunge and then soak in hot baths while you polish your skin with sea salts. Your skin will feel cleansed and buffed. No hanky panky goes on here—although bathing suits are optional, except on Tuesday, when they are enforced. The baths are open for women only on Sunday, Wednesday, and Friday, and to men only on Monday, Thursday, and Saturday. Tuesday is open to all. If bathing isn't your forte, the spa also offers 18 different spa treatment rooms, including acupuncture. Appointments are necessary.

CLIMBING

IF YOU'VE EVER DREAMED OF CLINGING TO A WALL or ceiling like Spiderman, **Mission Cliffs** (2295 Harrison Street at 19th Street; ☎ 415-550-0515; **touchstoneclimbing.com**), the Bay Area's premier indoor climbing haven, has more than 14,000 square feet of climbing terrain, and walls exceeding 50 feet in height. It is the best preparation if you plan to take advantage of real rock in nearby climbing haven Yosemite or other national parks. The gym also has a complete weight room, locker rooms, showers, and sauna. It's open seven days a week until 10 p.m. You will have to pass a belay test, which will cost you $20, and once certified you can come and climb until your fingers cramp in. For nonmembers, the weekday price after 3 p.m. and on weekends is $18; before 3 p.m. and for kids ages 6 to 17, it's $8. You can rent all the necessary gear for $5.

TRAPEZE

IT'S ALL AT **Circus Center Trapeze** (577 Frederick Street; ☎ 415-759-8123; **circuscenter.org**). Yes, you can be the man (or woman) on the flying trapeze. Of course, you'll have a safety net as well as a flying harness that prevents you from unexpected abrupt contact with the floor. Climb the ladder, grab the bar, and hurl yourself through the air. Maybe you'll throw a triple somersault. And it's all under careful supervision of the elders of trapeze. You can do the same thing in the East Bay at **Trapeze Arts** (1822 Ninth Street; ☎ 510-419-0700; **trapezearts.com**).

DANCING

Metronome Ballroom (1830 17th Street; ☎ 415-252-9000) is the city's premier venue for ballroom and swing dance. Open daily. Lessons for groups, couples, and singles are offered throughout the day and into the early evening. **Emeryville's Allegro Ballroom** (5855 Christie Avenue, Emeryville; ☎ 510-655-2888; **allegroballroom.com**) hosts salsa on Sunday, taught by one charismatic Garry Johnson and Isabelle Rodriguez. There are two afternoon classes, and a party in the evening is included in your $10 fee. If either salsa or Sunday isn't your speed, try Argentinean tango on Tuesday.

ICE SKATING AND BOWLING

THE **Yerba Buena Ice Skating and Bowling Center** provides public skating and bowling, as well as lessons. The center is located at 750 Folsom Street (☎ 415-777-3727; **skatebowl.com**).

OUTDOORS, NATURALLY!

WALKING: FUN CITY RAMBLES

IMAGINE THIS. An old Dutch windmill to the right, and as you pass, the trees clear with the lightest of ocean breezes revealing Ocean Beach. Whether you prefer simple rambles or full-blown hikes, there are tons of opportunities in San Francisco. It would be a sin to leave the walking shoes at home.

San Francisco's premier rambling destination is the **Golden Gate Promenade**, a three-and-a-half-mile paved footpath that starts in Fort Mason (just west of Fisherman's Wharf) and ends at the famous bridge of the same name. As the trail follows the shoreline along San Francisco Bay, it passes through Marina Green, the Yacht Harbor, Crissy Field, and the Presidio; it ends at Fort Point (a Civil War–era fortress). To lengthen the walk, hike the **Coastal Trail** along the Pacific Coast to Cliff House. Temperatures can change rapidly along the shoreline, and wind is often strong; bring a jacket or sweater.

Visitors can begin a stroll in **South Beach Harbor** on the east side of the city facing Oakland. Start at Pier 40 and walk north along the promenade past the new marina, new apartment complexes, and South Beach Park, where artists sometimes set up their easels on the lawn beneath the colossal red-and-silver Mark di Suvero sculpture *Sea Change*. It's a place where picnickers and dog-walkers gather to watch the boats. As you walk north, the Bay Bridge soon arches above; curving along the sidewalk for nearly half a mile is a ribbon of glass blocks lit with fiber-optic cable and set in concrete; some of it is raised for use as benches or tables. This public art is a nice place to relax and watch the bay and the parade of joggers, skaters, and strollers.

In the northwest corner of the city, the 1,480-acre **Presidio** has 11 miles of trails in a variety of landscapes, including coastal bluffs, forested hills, and historic architectural settings (such as the old Army buildings on the main post). You can pick up a trail map at the visitors center, open from 9 a.m. to 5 p.m. daily. Golden Gate Park features miles of walking, multipurpose bicycle, and bridle paths.

Probably the best place for walkers is **San Francisco Botanical Garden** near the Japanese Tea Garden. The beauty and tranquility of the many gardens inside the 70-acre arboretum and its manicured lawns are unsurpassed.

Only about 30 minutes outside of the city, another not-to-be-missed walk is through the towering redwoods of **Muir Woods** (☎ 415-388-2596). Paved trails wander through the forest of giant trees, and information signs guide your experience. Located on the south side of Mount Tam, 12 miles north of San Francisco, the park is open daily from 8 a.m. to sunset. It can get crowded on weekends. Admission is $3. (For more information, see Part Six.)

HIKING

THE MARIN HEADLANDS Hiking paradise exists just over the Golden Gate Bridge in the **Marin Headlands,** close in distance and time but many moods apart. Within 15 minutes of leaving the city, you are in total solitude, with hiking trails of varying difficulty intersecting all around you. A lovely stretch of the **California Coastal Trail,** a 1,200-mile trail that stretches the entire length of the California Coast (and hugging the Pacific the entire way), travels through the Headlands. You can meet up with it for day hikes, or pack along the tent and sleeping bag and find shelter for a weekend hike. It's also called the Bay Area Ridge Trail, so don't get confused. The trail is used by hikers, bikers, and horseback riders. The approach is different for each user, but all meet up at the trail at a junction called Five Corners. The trailhead for hikers starts shortly after the Golden Gate Bridge.

MUIR WOODS may be full of tourist buses, but just past the concession store and restrooms is the **Ocean View Trail,** that leaves them all far behind and affords views of the ocean just beyond the steep climb past the giant redwoods; it's not a loop.

MOUNT TAMALPAIS is another favorite. Best of all is a hike to the West Point Inn via the **Rock Springs Trail,** around the Mountain Theater, preferably for an overnight stay in this century-year-old inn with its self-catering club room and kitchen and stunning views (**westpointinn.com**; $35–$50 overnight for nonmembers; reservations required). You will be staying in what used to be a restaurant and stop along the route of the crookedest railroad in the West, back in the heyday of hiking. Atop the East Peak, another 15 minutes higher up, you'll find the museum commemorating the Gravity Car (open Saturday–Sunday, noon–4 p.m.) that pulled excursionists the last bit of the way.

Although hikes here are paralleled by the world-class fat-tire trails, there are still top-notch hiking trails for all levels with views and gorgeous scenery. Check the Mt. Tamalpais Interpretive Association's Web site (**mttam.net**) for upcoming guided specials, such as the astronomy, spring flowers, or birding hikes. Or if mountains and altitude have you panting for breath already, try hikes along **Dipsea Trail** or **Steep Ravine** from the Pantoll parking lot on Panoramic Highway down to Stinson Beach. **Olema Valley** is for the more advanced hiker, as the trails are long and steep, ascending to ridge tops for breathtaking ocean views. **Point Reyes National Seashore,** more than 70,000 acres of pristine coastland, has more than 147 miles of trails and four designated backcountry camping areas. This is a preferred hiking destination because of the diversity of trail levels, well-maintained campsites, and the almost certain chance of seeing northern fur seals, sea lions, and herds of tule elk. You can moonlight on the Point during summer months. What's better than hiking under a full moon? You can get a naturalist guide for your nocturnal hike by calling **Abbotts Lagoon** at ☎ 415-663-1200. Muir Woods also hosts evening hikes every full moon. There is nothing more special than to look up at the towering trees illuminated by the moon. No planning necessary. Just come with a flashlight and meet at the Muir Woods Visitors Center at 7 p.m. sharp. For information, call ☎ 415-388-2596.

    Golden Gate National Recreation Area is the largest urban national park in the world, a whopping 76,500 acres of land and water that includes 28 miles of wild coastline. You can get information by calling ☎ 415-556-0560 or browsing **nps.gov/goga.**

    Fog and winds are usually at their fiercest closer to the bridge. Bring a fleece and water, and wear wool socks for ventilation. Depending on the length of your hike, boots or Teva sandals are sufficient.

ONLY IN SAN FRANCISCO
Step Right Up

In no other city will you find more stairs outside, and in the most innovative and creative city in the country, you shouldn't be surprised to find them used as stairways to buns of steel. Here is a breakdown of some of our favorite urban climbs.

The Greenwich Steps (East)

WHERE Bottom, on Sansome and Greenwich streets; Top, Telegraph Hill Place at Greenwich Street

COUNTDOWN TO HEAVEN OR HELL 387 steps

Perched along the precariously steep slopes of Telegraph Hill and set among what seems to resemble gardens in Tuscany, this stairway is chock-full of camera-toting tourists gawking at the view. Sights along the climb include the Art Deco apartment house at 1360 Montgomery Street, the facade used in the Humphrey Bogart and Lauren Bacall flick *Dark Passage*; the doggie park on Montgomery Street; and the quaint restaurant Julius' Castle.

Lyon Steps

WHERE Bottom, Green Street at Lyon; Top, Broadway at Lyon Street
COUNTDOWN TO HEAVEN OR HELL 291 steps; for the best views, the top 166

A meat market of sorts—and a fashion show. Bring your best workout duds and don't forget the makeup. Business cards a necessity.

Pemberton Steps

WHERE Bottom, Clayton Street at Pemberton Place (look for a hidden sign on the right); Top, Pemberton Place and Crown Terrace
COUNTDOWN TO HEAVEN OR HELL 204 seemingly endless stairs up Twin Peaks

A low-key relaxed and shaded atmosphere with daisies and rhododendrons and a view of Mount Diablo in the distance.

Bench Warming

It may not be the most effective for calorie burning or physical recreation, but for many, sitting on a good bench and people-watching is recreation enough. San Francisco has some darn good benches. Consider it a mental exercise to feel the burn of a city and its people in motion. Along the **Marina Green** off of Marina Boulevard, near Crissy Field, offers the best benches for watching the city's yuppie set jog, walk Fido, or in-line skate. There are kite fliers, groups of friends playing volleyball, and the obvious perk of views of Alcatraz, the bay, the Headlands, and the Golden Gate Bridge. Nearby, the **Palace of Fine Arts** is also home to some fine benches. At sunset the Palace lights up and is almost as dramatic as Rockefeller's Christmas tree. Across the bridge in **Tiburon,** while you wait for the ferry to Angel Island or for the return trip back to San Francisco, the benches that line the waterfront are great for watching walkers, dogs, boats, rolling fog, and the cityscape on the horizon.

ISLANDS IN THE BAY

AT 4:30 P.M. THE LAST FERRY floats out from **Angel Island State Park** smack dab in the middle of San Francisco Bay. Why do you need to know this? Because if you are looking for your own private heaven, Angel Island is just that. There are nine campsites complete with picnic areas, food lockers, pit toilet, and grills. Reservations are required and cost $14 per night, plus $6.75 reservation fee. The only way to and from the island is by ferry from Pier 43 in San Francisco ($12) or Tiburon ($5). The price includes the state park entrance fee. The boat drops you at Perimeter Trailhead, which takes you around the island on clearly marked and well-maintained trails. Along the trail are opportunities for bike rentals ($12 to $25 per day depending on style of bike), tram tours ($5 per person), kayak rentals ($20 for two hours), and eating at the Cove Café. For recorded information, call ☎ 415-435-1915, or look at **angelisland.org**.

Prisoners once dreamed of "walking." And now the place that barred them from freedom, **Alcatraz Island,** is an evolving ecological preserve—and a great walking destination. The absence of four-footed predators has made the island a haven for birds, as well as thriving populations of crabs, starfish, and other marine animals living in tide pools. Visitors can see this on the **Agave Trail,** which follows the island's shoreline. For cruises to Alcatraz, visit **alcatrazcruises. com**, or call ☎ 415-981-7625 ($26 to $33 for adults).

RUNNING

THERE ARE ENOUGH RUNNING OPPORTUNITIES in San Francisco to satisfy the Forrest Gump in all of us. You'll see plenty of runners on the sidewalks downtown. But for visitors who would rather avoid traffic, large crowds, and stoplights, there are plenty of other options. Flat but usually windy, the 3.5-mile **Golden Gate Promenade** offers runners a paved and scenic route for a workout, not to mention a friendly camaraderie among other runners; the round-trip from Fort Mason to the Golden Gate Bridge is seven miles. Not that you have to stop at the landmark span; you can run across the bridge on its pedestrian walkway to the challenging **Marin Headlands** or continue along the Pacific Coast on the Coastal Trail. The Coastal Trail is a scenic 9.2-mile run that will lead you through the posh neighborhood of SeaCliff, China Beach, Lands End, and the Cliff House near Ocean Beach. If you want a fun side excursion, run up Sea Cliff Avenue past the mauve house flying the flag with the blue wolf on it—that's where Robin Williams lives.

Usually less windy, Golden Gate Park has plenty of paved roads and miles of pedestrian, bike, and bridle paths on rolling terrain; the main drag, Kennedy Drive, is closed to traffic on Sundays. On the east side of the city in South Beach, a promenade heads north along the shoreline toward the Bay Bridge; it's a favorite destination for joggers and runners.

Although most folks drive or take a tour bus, a more exhilarating way to get to the summit of **Twin Peaks** and its stupendous view is to run or walk. Routes include the back roads from the University of California Medical Center or either of the two main roads that lead to the top. The best time is early morning when the city is quiet and the air is crisp; just make sure you pick a morning that's not fog-bound.

ROAD BICYCLING AND IN-LINE SKATING

IN DOWNTOWN SAN FRANCISCO, most visitors will want to leave bicycling and in-line skating to bike messengers and street-savvy natives. Yet skinny-tire cyclists and skaters don't need to go far to find some excellent places to spin the cranks or skate the black ice. The **Golden Gate Promenade** starts in Fort Mason (just west of Fisherman's Wharf) and follows the bay shore for three and a half miles to the bridge of the same name (which has a pedestrian and bike lane). The scenery from the bridge is spectacular, but winds are usually strong enough to push you over. Across the bridge in **Marin County** at the end of the Vista Point parking lot is a bike lane that parallels US 101 and then turns off to Alexander Avenue through Sausalito. The hills on the Marin side of the bridge run are killer—affectionately called the Rambo run by those who frequent it! Be prepared. Temperatures also increase on this side as well, so hydration is important.

For a more recreational bike run than those in the Headlands and closer to home, **The Presidio** has 14 miles of paved roads, open to cyclists and in-line skaters, that weave through groves of trees and wind past military housing. Because most of the old military post's roads were laid out in horse-and-buggy days, all grades are easy to moderate. **Golden Gate Park** has seven and a half miles of designated paved trails for bikes that extend from the tip of the Panhandle through Golden Gate Park to Lake Merced. In addition, some roads (such as Kennedy Drive, the main drag) are closed to car traffic on Satrudays April–September and year-round on Sundays; it's heaven for San Francisco in-line skaters.

With its three bicycle lanes, the flat, three-mile sidewalk along **Ocean Beach** (Great Highway) provides a great workout and can be incorporated into a longer tour of the Sunset District. Ride south on the Great Highway for two miles past the San Francisco Zoo to Sloat Boulevard and turn right onto Lake Merced Boulevard; then ride for five miles around the lake and nearby golf course.

For another variation along the Pacific shoreline, ride north along the Great Highway from Lake Merced toward Cliff House. Just before you get there, gear down for a 200-foot ascent. Then veer right onto Point Lobos Avenue and turn right onto 43rd Avenue. Then it's all downhill to Golden Gate Park; enter at Chain of Lakes Drive East, which takes you back to Kennedy Drive. Turn right and continue west to the Great Highway, which takes you back to Lake Merced.

A San Francisco classic for the thin-tire set is a 19-mile loop ride across the Golden Gate Bridge to Sausalito and Tiburon that returns you to San Francisco on a ferry. The ride can start at the parking lot at the south end of the bridge or at Fisherman's Wharf; after the one-and-a-half-mile bridge crossing, descend into Sausalito on Alexander Avenue, ride into Tiburon, and catch the ferry to Fisherman's Wharf. Check with a local bike shop for turn-by-turn directions and a map; it's also a good idea to check the ferry schedule by calling the Red and White Fleet at ☎ 800-229-2784.

Biking Wine Country

One way to avoid drinking and driving but still feel a buzz is to bike it! Napa is way too street-crowded for such an excursion, so instead head to the nice, flat, wide Dry Creek Valley. Healdsburg is the starting point. Leave your car here—a convenient place to return to and eat, or hang in the park. Dry Creek Road starts at Healdsburg Avenue, and you can stay on it until you are too tired or too hammered. Wineries line the road and along the turn off at Lambert Bridge Road, which loops you around to West Dry Creek Road for a total trip distance of 14 miles. Check out Spoke Folk Cyclery for rentals (**spokefolk.com**). Then there is Mount Saint Helena, just north of Calistoga in the Napa Valley. The trails on the mountain are excellent, providing the biker with 4,000 feet of pure gravity. Try a rental at Calistoga Bike Shop (**calistogabikeshop.com**).

For Extreme Eyes Only!

This guide wouldn't be called *Unofficial* if it didn't include the Everest of in-line skating ops. **6 Parnassus Ski Lift,** as it is called, that runs down the Ninth and Tenth Avenue "slopes," was first made famous by intrepid and lunatic skateboarders who first discovered the great hill. The procedure: Take the bus at Ninth Avenue and Judah, and don't forget that transfer ticket, because it is what gets you up and down the hill over and over for the next two hours. The hill is long, steep, and will have you close to breaking the sound barrier in no time! You don't want to forget the helmet, kneepads, and wrist guards for this run. If you prefer fancy footwork, try **Hubba Hideout** at Maritime Plaza at Battery Street. Stairs and handrails and hills, oh my!

Renting Bikes and In-Line Skates

Bike and skate rentals are widely available throughout San Francisco; some shops also provide guided tours. **Bay City Bike** at the Cannery in Fisherman's Wharf (☎ 415-346-2453) rents 21-speed hybrid (city) bikes starting at $35; helmet, rear rack and bag, lock, maps, tour info, and water bottles are included. They also offer a guided tour for four or more people across the Golden Gate Bridge to Sausalito and a return to San Francisco by ferry for $40.

Blazing Saddles rents computer-equipped bikes for self-guided tours of San Francisco, the Marin Headlands, Muir Woods, and Mount Tamalpais. Mountain bike rentals start at $7 an hour or $28 a day, and they offer even lower rates for multiday rentals. Also available for rent are road bikes, city bikes, tandems, kids' bikes, and car racks. The shop is located at 1095 Columbus Avenue (at Francisco); call ☎ 415-202-8888, or visit **blazingsaddles.com**. There is also a satellite store at Fisherman's Wharf, which makes it convenient to rent and then hop over to Angel Island or Tiburon.

In Golden Gate Park, **Surrey Bikes & Blades** rents in-line skates starting at $7 an hour and bikes at $8 an hour; the shop, located at Stow Lake (closed Wednesdays and rainy days) also rents tandem bikes, electric bikes, and pedal-powered surreys. For more information, call ☎ 415-668-6699.

Skates on Haight, half a block from Golden Gate Park in Haight-Ashbury, rents in-line skates for $8 an hour and $25 a day; the price includes head, knee, and wrist protection. The shop is open daily; call ☎ 415-752-8375.

At Angel Island State Park in San Francisco Bay, **Angel Island Company** rents 21-speed mountain bikes for exploring traffic-free roads and paths on the island. Basic rentals start at $10 an hour or $30 a day and include a helmet. Open daily May through October, and weekends only in November and March; closed December through February. Call ☎ 415-897-0715 for more information on rentals, or visit **angelisland.com**; call ☎ 800-229-2784 for ferry schedules from Pier 43 in Fisherman's Wharf.

MOUNTAIN BIKING

WHILE FAT-TIRE MOUNTAIN BIKES are fine for riding on San Francisco's streets and paved trails, off-road aficionados who prefer the feel of dirt between their knobbies should look farther afield, but not too far. Across the Golden Gate Bridge lies Marin County, where popular myth says mountain biking was invented 20 years ago.

The cradle of mountain-biking civilization is reputed to be Mount Tamalpais. It's so popular a destination among fat-tire fanatics that the sport has been banned from single-track trails, and cops with radar guns give out tickets to cyclists who exceed 15 miles an hour on the fire roads. The most popular route is technically easy but aerobically demanding. Take the Old Railroad Grade to historic West Point Inn (where, incidentally, you can stop over for a stack of pancakes) and the East Peak. There are lots of scenic spots along the way, and the reward is a breathtaking (not that you'll have much breath left) 360-degree view of San Francisco Bay. And, as they say, it's all downhill from here. Once you reach the top, you'll find a snack bar with hot dogs and bagels and cream cheese. (Not advertised, reserved for those in the know, are the frozen fruit bars. Ask for them.) You could even make a weekend out of it and stay at the West Point Inn.

To reach the Old Railroad Grade (an unpaved fire road), load your bike onto your car and take US 101 north across the Bay Bridge to the Tiburon Boulevard/East Blithedale Avenue exit. Then turn left, heading under US 101 and west onto East Blithedale Avenue. Take East Blithedale as it turns into West Blithedale Avenue and go past an intersection with Eldridge Road. About a mile later, Old Railroad Grade branches off to the right over a wooden bridge. Park as close to this bridge as you can. Unload your bike and ride across the bridge.

If you are new to the sport and want to earn bragging rights for having survived fat-tire trails in California, try Crystal Springs Reservoir in the South Bay. The heart barely pumps and the adrenaline stays at a minimum on the flat, wooded path that starts at the gate just off the Highway 92 West exit. The path circles the reservoir, eventually depositing you at the dam where another trail heading to Skyline Boulevard intersects. Your only obstacles are joggers and trees.

The all-inclusive combo recreational-sightseeing haven is, of course, Angel Island. Again, take the ferry from Fisherman's Wharf or Tiburon to get there; bikes are permitted on the ferry for free except from Tiburon, where they charge you $1. You can also rent one on the island (see above), but rentals are cheaper on the mainland. There are about eight miles of easy, unpaved fire roads to explore, and the scenery is terrific, especially from the upper fire road. Alas, mountain bikes are not permitted on trails on the island, and ferry service is limited to weekends in the winter.

BEACHES

FOR ALL YOU *Bay Watch* wannabes, the bad news is that it's usually too chilly to put on those teeny-weenie bikinis and lather up on the beach. The Pacific is frigid—just dip your toes in and see—and the unpredictable fog causes lines at most area tanning salons. But just because the Bay Area beaches aren't perfect for sunbathing or swimming doesn't eliminate them altogether. Most are Hollywood-perfect, with cliffs breathing down over quiet coves, and each beach creates a unique vibe appreciated by natives and remembered by visitors. To highlight these unique uses and features, we've compiled a rather unofficial survey of what's on offer at the beaches by the bay.

BEST CONTEMPLATIVE CURRENTS Muir Beach in Marin County off Highway 1 (west of US 101; take the Stinson Beach/Mill Valley exit) with its pristine sand and quaint cove surrounded by towering cliffs, is the best beach to bring a copy of *Conversations with God*, or your journal. It's quiet and just an all-around good beach.

BIGGEST WAVES Ocean Beach is the best place to watch surfers who come for the picture-perfect pipes. The Great Highway, which runs parallel to Ocean Beach's four miles (the longest beach in the Bay Area), is sometimes closed due to the too-close-for-car-comfort crashing waves. The water is treacherous even when it looks calm, so use extreme caution if wading or swimming.

MOST ROMANTIC BEACH Drake's Beach along Point Reyes National Seashore off Highway 1, with its sheltered beach and towering white cliffs breathing down upon the fine sand, is one of the most romantic. The drive to get there is all part of the seduction.

BEST BEACH TO RE-CREATE SCENES FROM BEACH BLANKET BINGO Even the road getting there—along Highway 1 off of 101—is good for a party. Put the top down on the car and wind over narrow cliff-clinging roads down to the lively, friend-gathering **Stinson Beach.**

BEST BIRTHDAY SUIT BEACH North Baker Beach is the most popular naked spot in the city. The sand is clean and the parking lot safe.

Temps are chilly though . . . so beware. Also, nudity is not permitted at the south end of the beach. The beach is located at Lincoln Boulevard and Bowley Street, near 25th Avenue. Honorable mentions include: **Fort Funston,** off of Great Highway north of Skyline Boulevard and **Lands End** on the western edge of the city (popular with gay men), just above Cliff House on the Great Highway.

BEST BEACH FOR THE LITTLE ONES The stretch of **China Beach** is small enough to keep an eye on them, and all facilities, including picnic tables and restrooms, are spotless.

BEST BEACH FOR FIDO If you couldn't stomach leaving the dog at the kennel, the beach along Crissy Field at the end of the Marina Green is small, but it is one huge frolicking playground for the pups. Let 'em loose and sit back and enjoy the wind and kite surfers circling the pillars of the Golden Gate Bridge. (Don't forget the plastic gloves to de-poop the beach of your doggy's droppings.)

A Note on Nudity

Many beaches around San Francisco allow nudity, with the interesting caveats that you don't touch anybody and nobody complains. (If you equate nudity with sex, keep in mind that in the Golden Gate National Recreation Area, where many of the nude beaches are located, public sex is a federal offense.) Other negatives to lounging in the buff at San Francisco beaches include cool temperatures, fog, wind, rocky beaches with little or no sand, and gawkers. In addition, many of the beaches are difficult to reach, requiring long walks on narrow, steep paths lined with poison oak.

SEA KAYAKING

THE CURRENTS IN THE BAY ARE QUITE TOUGH to maneuver, but despite this, kayakers come from all over to slide their sleek craft into the waters off San Francisco. **Sea Trek Ocean Kayaking Center** offers tours for novices around Angel Island, Sausalito, and Point Reyes. A novice can glide out from Sausalito's Schoonmaker Point Marina and join seals, pelicans, and even the occasional whale in Richardson Bay. Rentals for single kayaks: $20 an hour; double kayaks are $35 an hour. Wetsuits, paddle jackets, spray skirts, paddles, pumps, and paddle floats are included with rentals. Call ☎ 415-488-1000 for more information or visit **seatrekkayak.com.** To check on tide conditions, look up **tidesonline.nos.noaa.gov** before heading out.

Blue Waters Kayaking in Marin County offers instruction, rentals, and tours in Point Reyes and Tomales Bay; no experience is necessary for some tour packages. They offer a half-day morning tour from 10 a.m.–1 p.m. for $59; $85 for the Day on the Bay tour. An all-day introductory kayaking course is $89. Sea kayak rentals start at $45 for two hours and $55 for four hours. Double kayaks start at $65 for two hours and $85 for four hours. For reservations and more information, call ☎ 415-669-2600, or visit **bwkayak.com.**

ROCK CLIMBING

IF YOU HAVE ALREADY TRIED THE PLASTIC HOLDS of an indoor climbing gym and want to test your skill on real granite, there is no better destination than the Bay Area. **Yosemite** is *the* climbing destination, and it is only about a three-hour drive away! Closer still is **Red Rock Beach,** south of Stinson Beach off of Highway 1 at milepost 11.43. Mickey's, as locals call it, is a demanding rock with a dazzling ocean view. Its face rises and falls with 55 feet of cracks and crevices. You just may want to look down here—nudists populate the beach below. Because the Pacific pounds below, access to most of its face depends on tides. Safety check: The rock isn't appropriate for beginners, and tides control access to most of its face (so check **tidesonline. nos.noaa.gov** before heading up). Skilled climbers only.

Climbers of all levels can head to a more-controlled environment at **Mission Cliffs,** the Bay Area's indoor climbing gym (see page 371).

HANG GLIDING

WITH ITS PERSISTENT COASTAL WINDS, San Francisco is an excellent place to go hang gliding. The **San Francisco Hang Gliding Center** specializes in tandem hang-gliding flights where you can see some of northern California's most beautiful terrain (☎ 510-528-2300; **sfhanggliding.com**). The basic tandem flight is $349. Simply call to arrange a meeting spot at the launch—usually Mount Tamalpais. From there you glide to the north end of Stinson Beach. If you'd rather just watch, head for Fort Funston south of Ocean Beach, where hang gliders launch off 200-foot cliffs and soar on coastal breezes. Benches atop the cliff are perfect for observing. Be careful not to enter the launch and landing zone. Pilots are pretty adamant about it.

SAILING

SAN FRANCISCO BAY, one of the largest and most beautiful harbors in the world, is also a major yachting center—although sailing on the bay is challenging even for the most experienced sailor. Certified skippers can charter anything from day sailors to luxury yachts and sail past all the famous landmarks. Don't know a spinnaker from a jib? You can also learn to sail while you're on vacation in San Francisco.

Cass' Marina charters day sailors that accommodate up to six people, starting at $181 a day on weekdays; each boat is equipped with toilet facilities and life vests. Cruising boats for large daytime outings or overnight charters start at $243 a day; weekend, five-day, and weekly rates are also available. Cass' offers a full complement of instructional courses for beginners to advanced sailors. A basic keelboat certification course with 29 hours of instruction is $775; completion qualifies you to bareboat (no crew) charter a cruising sailboat. Private instruction is available for about $284 for three hours on weekdays (for one or two people), and $315 on weekends. Cass' Marina is located at 1702 Bridgeway at Napa Street in Sausalito (across the bay from San Francisco); call ☎ 415-332-6789, or visit **cassmarina.com**.

Also in Sausalito is **Atlantis Yacht Charters,** where you can charter 30-foot and longer yachts. Bareboat charters start at $295 a day for an Ericson 30 that sleeps four; a Nordic 44 goes for $600 a day midweek and sleeps seven adults. Skippered charters start at $575 for four hours midweek; the price includes captain, yacht, and fuel. For more information, call ☎ 800-65-YACHT, or visit **yachtcharter.com**.

WINDSURFING AND KITE SURFING

GOOD COASTAL WINDS MAKE SAN FRANCISCO one of the top spots in the country for windsurfing, and the increasingly popular kite surfing, where riders are lifted out of the water by—yep, you guessed it—one big kite. The premier location in the city is Crissy Field, where experienced board sailors frolic on wind and waves.

GOLF

San Francisco has two municipal golf courses that are open to the public. **Golden Gate Park Course** (47th Avenue and Fulton Street; ☎ 415-751-8987) is a small nine-hole course covering 1,357 yards. It is open every day, 6:30 a.m. until sunset. Green fees are $14 during the week and $19 on weekends. **Lincoln Park Golf Course** (34th Avenue and Clement Street; ☎ 415-750-4653) offers 18 holes and covers 5,081 yards. The oldest course in the city, it offers beautiful views and fairways—just stop and check out what's in front of you at the 13th hole! It is open every day, 6:30 a.m. until sunset. Green fees are $23 during the week and $27 on weekends and holidays. In Berkeley, the **Tilden Park Golf Course** (Grizzly Peak Boulevard and Shasta Road; ☎ 510-848-7373; **americangolf.com/ca/berkeley-tilden-park-golf-course**) offers the best deals in town. With a $24 twilight rate, it's easy and cheap to get in 18 holes before dark. If you consider yourself more of a morning golfer, how does $18 sound to you?

TENNIS

THE SAN FRANCISCO RECREATION AND PARKS DEPARTMENT operates more than 140 tennis courts throughout the city. All are available free on a first-come, first-served basis, with the exception of 21 courts in **Golden Gate Park,** where a fee is charged and advance reservations are required for weekend play. The courts are off Kennedy Drive opposite the Conservatory; lessons are available.

To make weekend reservations at a court in Golden Gate Park, call ☎ 415-753-7101 on the preceding Wednesday evening between 4 and 6 p.m., the preceding Thursday between 9:15 a.m. and 5 p.m., or the preceding Friday between 9:15 and 11:30 a.m. (Call Wednesday evening to avoid disappointment.) The nonresident court fee is $8 for a 90-minute play period. For more information and the locations of other courts around San Francisco, call the parks department at ☎ 415-753-7100, or visit **parks.sfgov.org**.

FISHING

DEEP-SEA FISHING CHARTER BOATS leave Fisherman's Wharf daily, depending on weather and season. Catches in the Pacific waters beyond the Golden Gate include salmon, sea bass, halibut, striped bass, bonito, shark, tuna, and albacore. Licenses (required), rods, and tackle are available on board; plan for wind and some rough seas, and bring motion-sickness preventatives and warm clothing. *Miss Farallones,* a 50-foot charter boat, sets out on sport-fishing expeditions from Fisherman's Wharf most days and can carry up to 38 passengers. For rates and more information, call ☎ 510-352-5708, or visit **sfsportfishing.com**.

Freshwater fishing is available at **Lake Merced,** south of downtown where Skyline Boulevard meets the Great Highway at the coast. Large trout, catfish, and bass are stocked in the 360-acre lake, open year-round. Anglers must purchase a $9.70 one-day fishing license and pay a $5 access fee. Rowboats are available for rent for $12 an hour. Paddleboats, which can hold up to four people, rent for $15 an hour. You can also fish from the bank of the lake, which stocks trophy trout of two pounds and more. For more information, call ☎ 415-752-7869.

NATURE VIEWING
Whale-Watching

Each year gray whales embark on one of the longest migrations of any mammal, and the coast near San Francisco is one of the best places to observe these giants during their 6,000-mile journey between their arctic feeding grounds and Baja, California. The nonprofit **Oceanic Society** offers naturalist-led expeditions year-round to observe the whales and nature cruises to the Farallon Islands' stark granite cliffs 27 miles from the Golden Gate that teem with marine life.

Gray whale cruises depart from San Francisco at 9:30 a.m. on selected dates from December to May and last six hours, returning to the dock at 4 p.m. Rates for adults start at $50; bring your own lunch and beverages. The expedition transports guests under the Golden Gate Bridge and north along the Marin coast to search for gray whales off the Bolinas and Point Reyes areas.

Farallon Islands nature cruises depart at 8:30 a.m. on selected dates from June through November and last eight hours. Rates for adults start at $60; bring your own lunch and beverages. The cruise sails under the Golden Gate Bridge and goes west to the Farallon

OUTDOORS, NATURALLY! **385**

Islands, where a quarter-million seabirds nest and visible marine mammals include California sea lions, Steller's sea lions, northern elephant seals, harbor seals, and possibly humpback and blue whales. A not-so-visible resident is the great white—this is the largest breeding ground in the world for them, after all!

All cruises are aboard the *New Superfish,* a 63-foot Coast Guard–certified, fully insured motor vessel with an open observation deck, indoor salon, and a passenger capacity of 49. Off-street parking is available at the harbor at Fort Mason. Youths age 15 and under must be accompanied by an adult, and children age 10 and under aren't permitted on the boat. Reservations are required; call ☎ 800-326-7491 or ☎ 415-474-3385 for a schedule, and make reservations at least two weeks in advance (although it's possible to get aboard at the last minute if there are cancellations). Look up **oceanic-society.org** for more information.

Bring raingear and warm clothing. Don't forget binoculars, a camera, sunscreen, and motion-sickness medicine (take before you depart).

California Sea Lions and Seals

OK, it may not be the most pristine of scenes, but the California sea lions that bark, clap, and flop over the floating piers at Pier 39 near Fisherman's Wharf are certainly worth a trip. Otherwise, you can usually spot them popping up for air at any point along the bay. **The Marine Mammal Center** in Fort Cronkite near Rodeo Lagoon in the Marin Headlands, ☎ 415-289-7325, is where you can go to see marine biologists nurse ailing and orphaned California sea lions and seals back to health. You can watch pups being bottle-fed, and ask questions about them as well as the whales found in these waters. A great place for the family.

Zebras?

Yes, zebras as well as giraffes, lemurs, several cats, and other exotic game can be found at **Safari West Wildlife Preserve and Tent Camp** (3115 Porter Creek Road, Santa Rosa; ☎ 707-579-2551; **safariwest. com**). The sanctuary is one of a few in North America that sets out to protect these endangered species through breeding, education, and research. It is home to more than 400 mammals and birds. In fact, two species of birds—the white-naped crane and the Indian hornbill—are currently registered with the international Species Survival Program.

To go on "safari," you will need to make a reservation. Tours run at 9 a.m., noon, and 3 p.m. in the summer season, or 10 a.m. and 2 p.m. the remainder of the year. The tours, consisting of both driving and walking portions, last two-and-a-half hours and are guided by a naturalist. Prices for adults are $58, and for children age 14 and under, $28. The adventurous can rent one of the tents for $240 per night per couple, two-night minimum. If the thought of a wild cat creeping up on you in the middle of the night makes the hairs on your arms stand up, you can stay in a cottage for $300 per night. The price includes four adults and a two-night minimum.

Bird-Watching

Point Reyes National Seashore is probably the premier place to bring the binoculars and spot birds such as California quail, Anna's and Allen's hummingbirds, Nuttall's woodpecker, Pacific-slope flycatcher, Hutton's vireo, chestnut-backed chickadee, oak titmouse, pygmy nuthatch, wrenit, and California towhee. Seabirds such as red-throated and Pacific loons and brown pelicans are also primary residents of this bird haven. Take a self-guided tour if you're an experienced bird peeper, or for tour information, call ☎ 415-454-5100. The park service offers a Beginning Birding tour once a month on Sundays, as well as guided tours to the lighthouse on Saturdays, Sundays, and Mondays at 12:30 p.m. Alcatraz Island is also becoming quite a bird sanctuary. Black-crowned night heron are one of many bird species that nest on Alcatraz. For guided tours, call ☎ 415-705-5555.

SPECTATOR SPORTS

BY AND LARGE, BAY AREA FANS' dedication to their professional sports teams can verge on the obsessive. How much so? Enough that the San Francisco Giants got a new multimillion-dollar stadium, and the 49ers are demanding choice treatment too. The professional sports scene in the Bay Area includes football, baseball, basketball, and horse racing.

PRO TEAMS
Baseball

The National League **San Francisco Giants** play home games at AT&T Park, located at 24 Willie Mays Plaza in the China Basin area, south of Market Street. The season starts in April and goes through October. Tickets are usually available up until game time, but the seats can be regrettably far from the on-field action. Tickets are available through **tickets.com.**

The American League **Oakland Athletics,** the 1989 world champs, play at the sunnier Oakland-Alameda County Coliseum across the bay (take the Hegenberger Road exit off I-880). The stadium seats 50,000 fans and is served by BART's Coliseum station. Tickets to home games are available from the coliseum box office or from **tickets.com.**

Football

The **San Francisco 49ers,** five-time Super Bowl champs, play home games at AT&T Park on Sundays August–December. Good luck getting tickets, though. The games sell out early in the season, but sometimes select tickets are available; call the box office at ☎ 415-468-2249. If you're willing to pay an inflated price, tickets may be available from ticket agents before game days and from scalpers at the gate; expect to pay up to $100 for a seat. Talk to your hotel concierge or stop by **City Box Office** (14 Kearny Street; ☎ 415-392-4400). MUNI operates special express buses to the park, located about eight miles south of downtown, from Market Street on game days; call ☎ 415-673-6864 for more information.

Across the bay is the 49ers' archenemy, the **Oakland Raiders,** who returned to Oakland in 1995 after abandoning the city for Los Angeles 13 years before. Known as blue-collar heroes, the team charges country-club prices; expect to pay at least $60 for a ticket. Home games are played at the Oakland-Alameda County Coliseum off I-880. For ticket information, call ☎ 800-949-2626.

Basketball

The Bay Area's NBA team is the **Golden State Warriors,** who play in the Oakland-Alameda County Coliseum across the bay. The season runs from November through April; most games start at 7:30 p.m. The arena is located at the Hegenberger Road exit off I-880, south of downtown Oakland. For tickets, go to **tickets.com** or **gs-warriors.com.**

If you aren't so interested in spending half your vacation money on courtside tickets, consider heading to the **San Francisco Bay Area Pro Am Summer Basketball League.** It's free, but the talent is top notch. Top pro and former collegiate players gather in Kezar Pavilion from mid-June through mid-August to stay on top of their game. You can get your hoop thrills at 755 Stanyan Street (**sanfranciscoproam.com**).

HORSE RACING

THE BAY AREA IS HOME TO TWO HORSERACING TRACKS. **Scenic Golden Gate Fields,** located in the East Bay off Gilman Street (off I-80 in Albany, ten miles northeast of San Francisco), features thoroughbred racing from November through January and March through June. For post times and more information, call ☎ 510-559-7300, or visit **ggfields.com.**

AMATEUR SPORTS

LOCAL COLLEGE GRIDIRON ACTION is provided by the **University of California Golden Bears,** who play at Memorial Stadium across the bay in Berkeley. For game times and ticket information, call

12 Very Cool Free Things to Do in San Francisco

1. High-speed elevators at The Westin St. Francis hotel on Union Square at 335 Powell Street whisk you up to the 31st floor for spectacular views of the Transamerica Pyramid, Coit Tower, the Financial District, the bridges across the bay, and downtown at your feet below.

2. Hyde Street Pier and Maritime National Historical Park (☎ 415-447-5000; **nps.gov/safr**). While taking in Aquatic Park just west of the tourist traps of Fisherman's Wharf, visit these old tall ships and clamber on board the *Balclutha*.

3. The Wave Organ (**exploratorium.edu/visit/wave_organ.html**) is a chance to really hear the music of the ocean and watch the sails bobbing around the bay. Invented in 1981 and completed in 1986, this acoustical art installation is best experienced at high tide. Twenty-five concrete and PVC pipes planted in the water transmit sounds to a jetty at Yacht Road across from Marina Green, just down from Marina Boulevard at Lyon Street.

4. Connect and feel the spirit move you in an authentic way at Sunday service at Glide Memorial United Methodist Church. The Rev. Cecil Williams is a force for good on a down-at-hell corner of town, where a soup kitchen vies with the strung-out victims of skid row and where the homeless mingle with the well-heeled and even the occasional star, with a message of optimism and brotherhood. No matter your own religion, the righteous Glide Choir will have you on your feet and singing at weekly Sunday celebrations at 9 and 11 a.m. (330 Ellis Street at Taylor; ☎ 415-674-6000; **glide.org**).

5. Slides adorn several hillsides around the city, but the smoothly curved cement slides at the Seward Street Mini-Park in Eureka Valley are the curviest. The side-by-side slides are best experienced on a piece of cardboard. Some folks use sacking or even cafeteria trays here on Seward Street, near Douglass Street. (Adults must be accompanied by a child.)

6. Farmers' markets have popped up everywhere on weekdays too, but the Alemany Farmers' Market (**sfgsa.org/index.aspx?page=1058**) on Saturday is up and running before 7 a.m. and lasts until 3 p.m. Nowadays it has everything from oysters to orchids and a delectable row of ethnic food stalls too, selling everything from Malaysian lace crepes to Afghani potato, onion, or spinach bolanis near the junction of I-280 and US 101 at 100 Alemany Boulevard in Bernal Heights. The high-end version of this teeming scene is the Ferry Plaza Farmers Market

(☎ 415-291-3276; **cuesa.org**) at the end of Market Street outside the Ferry Building, where you'll find pumpkins and fruits of organic gorgeousness Saturday, 8 a.m.–2 p.m., and Tuesday, 10 a.m.–2 p.m.

7. Ocean Beach (☎ 415-388-2595; **nps.gov/goga**) campfire parties are officially teetotal and monitored, but these spontaneous blazes out of crackling driftwood make for weekend birthday bashes with sing-alongs piercing foggy nights and s'mores or baked yams on skewers. The National Park Service says all visitors should be out by the end of day-use hours, and fires should be kept within the fire rings.

8. At 8 a.m. on the first Sunday of every month, a bird-watching walk starts from the main gates of the San Francisco Botanical Garden in Golden Gate Park. With luck you'll see more than the usual geese, marlins, juncos, and blackbirds. Call ☎ 415-661-1316, ext. 400, for more information.

9. Lindy in the Park (**lindyinthepark.com**) is an outdoor dancing session on Sundays at 11 a.m. off John F. Kennedy Drive around Eighth Avenue. The Golden Gate Park is closed to through-traffic on Sundays, when its entire length is given over to recreation.

10. City Guide walking tours include neighborhoods all over town. Volunteer-run, they tackle everywhere and anything. The tours occasionally change, but the Prostitution in the Tenderloin walk is popular! The Inner Richmond walk reveals an unexpectedly rough-and-bawdy past chapter starring Wyatt Earp and his missus, whose house survives. The Mission Murals tour is an especial crowd-pleaser (☎ 415-557-4266; **sfcityguides.org**).

11. Real estate window-shopping is ever popular. Every weekend, dozens of homes show their innermost secrets and treasures to buyers and the fascinated neighbors. Check the *San Francisco Chronicle* on Sundays or real estate Web sites for listings, or watch out for open-house signs.

12. And one more: Summertime is free music, opera, and dance perfor-mance season. Free concerts and other shows fill Mission Dolores Park sporadically, while Stern Grove (**sterngrove.org**) runs every kind of show from ballet to Latino jazz on Sunday afternoons—read the listing pages of the *San Francisco Chronicle* on Sundays to get an idea of what and where, and be sure to show up early with a picnic. The AT&T Park at China Basin shows free opera simulcasts as well; reserve tickets online first (**sfopera.com**).

☎ 800-GO-BEARS; or visit **calbears.com;** tickets are usually available on game day. From November to March the Bears men's basketball squad plays at the $40 million Haas pavilion, which opened on campus in 1999.

The **University of San Francisco Dons** men's basketball team provides on-the-court excitement from November to March at the War Memorial Gymnasium on campus (5300 Golden Gate Avenue). Games start at 7 p.m.; for tickets and schedules, call ☎ 415-422-6USF or visit **tickets.com.**

EVENTS FOR THE OUTDOOR ENTHUSIAST

CONTACT THE VISITORS AND CONVENTIONS BUREAU (☎ 415-391-2000; **onlyinsanfrancisco.com**) for up-to-date information regarding these events and possible participation.

ESCAPE FROM ALCATRAZ TRIATHLON Amateur and professional athletes make the 1.5-mile swim from Alcatraz Island in the treacherous waters of the bay. The race continues with an 18-mile bike ride out to the Great Highway, through the Golden Gate Park, and concludes with an 8-mile run through the Golden Gate National Recreation Area. The finish is at the Marina Green for the Fitness Festival.

SAN FRANCISCO GRAND PRIX This 125-mile biking race starts and finishes on the Embarcadero at the end of Market Street. From the start/finish lines, the course winds through North Beach, along Fisherman's Wharf and the Marina. Halfway through the ten-mile circuit, the flatlands along the scenic bay give way to the intense climb up Fillmore Street. The event is for professionals only, and many from the Tour de France attend. For information, check out the Web site at **sfgrandprix.com**.

BAY TO BREAKERS FOOT RACE Not quite for the competitive at heart, although serious runners do compete. Most come dressed in costume or not (clothes optional) and bring everything including the kitchen sink and kegs of beer. Anyone can participate in this annual spring ritual, usually held in May. For more information, see **baytobreakers.com**.

SAN FRANCISCO MARATHON For the big guns who can handle the 26.2-mile course, and even for those who want to participate in half of that in the Split the Distance Marathon, Half Marathon, or 5K Fun Run—all on the same day, usually in July each year. The course takes in the "best of San Francisco," offering a scenic loop. For more information, including how to register, check out the Web site at **runsfm.com**, or call ☎ 800-698-8699.

ACCOMMODATIONS INDEX

RESTAURANT INDEX

SUBJECT INDEX

Unofficial Guide Reader Survey

If you would like to express your opinion in writing about San Francisco or this guidebook, complete the following survey and mail it to:

> *Unofficial Guide* Reader Survey
> P.O. Box 43673
> Birmingham, AL 35243

Inclusive dates of your visit: _____

Members of your party:

	Person 1	Person 2	Person 3	Person 4	Person 5
Gender:	M F	M F	M F	M F	M F
Age:					

How many times have you been to San Francisco? _____

On your most recent trip, where did you stay? _____

Concerning your accommodations, on a scale of 100 as best and 0 as worst, how would you rate:

The quality of your room?_____ The value of your room? _____
The quietness of your room? _____ Check-in/check-out efficiency? ____
Shuttle service to the airport? ____ Swimming pool facilities? _____

Did you rent a car? _____ From whom? _____

Concerning your rental car, on a scale of 100 as best and 0 as worst, how would you rate:

Pick-up processing efficiency? _____ Return processing efficiency?_____
Condition of the car? _____ Cleanliness of the car? _____
Airport shuttle efficiency?_____

Concerning your dining experiences:

Estimate your meals in restaurants per day? _____

Approximately how much did your party spend on meals per day?

_____

Favorite restaurants in San Francisco:_____

_____

_____

Did you buy this guide before leaving?   while on your trip?

How did you hear about this guide? (check all that apply)

Loaned or recommended by a friend ☐ Radio or TV ☐
Newspaper or magazine ☐   Bookstore salesperson ☐
Just picked it out on my own ☐   Library ☐
Internet ☐

What other guidebooks did you use on this trip?_____

_____

_____

_____

On a scale of 100 as best and 0 as worst, how would you rate them?

_____

_____

_____

Using the same scale, how would you rate the *Unofficial Guide*(s)?

_____

Are Unofficial Guides readily available at bookstores in your area?_____

Have you used other *Unofficial Guides*? _____

Which one(s)? _____

_____

_____

Comments about your San Francisco trip or the *Unofficial Guide*(s):

_____

_____

_____

_____

_____

_____

_____

_____

_____

_____

_____

_____

_____

_____

_____

_____

_____

_____

_____

_____